— THE ESSENTIALS —

GATEWAYS TO DEMOCRACY

AN INTRODUCTION TO AMERICAN GOVERNMENT

SECOND EDITION

JOHN G.
GEER
Vanderbilt
University

WENDY J.
SCHILLER
Brown
University

JEFFREY A.
SEGAL
Stony Brook
University

DANA K.
GLENCROSS
Oklahoma Community
College

WADSWORTH
CENGAGE Learning

Australia • Brazil • Japan • Korea • Mexico • Singapore • Spain • United Kingdom • United States

WADSWORTH
CENGAGE Learning·

Gateways to Democracy, An Introduction to American Government, Essentials, Second Edition
John G. Geer, Wendy J. Schiller, Jeffrey A. Segal, Dana K. Glencross

Senior Publisher: Suzanne Jeans

Executive Editor: Carolyn Merrill

Acquisitions Editor: Anita Devine

Development Editor: Ann Grogg

Assistant Editor: Patrick Roach

Media Editor: Laura Hildebrand

Brand Manager: Lydia LeStar

Market Development Manager:
   Kyle Zimmerman

Art Director: Linda May

Manufacturing Planner: Fola Orekoya

Senior Rights Acquisition Specialist:
   Jennifer Meyer Dare

Production Service: MPS Limited

Text Designer: Red Hangar Design

Cover Designer: Jenny Willingham

Cover Image: ©DRD Photos

Compositor: MPS Limited

Design Element Credits: Gateways image: ©Kletr/Shutterstock.com; Pathways image: ©SVLuma/Shutterstock.com

For product information and technology assistance, contact us at **Cengage Learning Customer & Sales Support, 1-800-354-9706**
For permission to use material from this text or product, submit all requests online at **www.cengage.com/permissions**. Further permissions questions can be emailed to **permissionrequest@cengage.com**.

Library of Congress Control Number: 2012939451

Student Edition:

ISBN-13: 978-1-133-60780-9

ISBN-10: 1-133-60780-2

Wadsworth
20 Channel Center Street
Boston, MA 02210
USA

Cengage Learning is a leading provider of customized learning solutions with office locations around the globe, including Singapore, the United Kingdom, Australia, Mexico, Brazil and Japan. Locate your local office at **international.cengage.com/region**

Cengage Learning products are represented in Canada by Nelson Education, Ltd.

For your course and learning solutions, visit **www.cengage.com**.

Purchase any of our products at your local college store or at our preferred online store **www.cengagebrain.com**.

Instructors: Please visit **login.cengage.com** and log in to access instructor-specific resources.

Printed in the United States of America
1 2 3 4 5 6 7 16 15 14 13 12

Brief Contents

Features

Chapter	Policy Topic	Supreme Court Case	Global Gateways
1. Gateways to American Democracy	The Policy-Making Process		Social Welfare, Public Debt, and Free Enterprise
2. The Constitution	The Death Penalty	*Marbury v. Madison* (1803)	
3. Federalism	Education	*McCulloch v. Maryland* (1819)	Federal Political Systems
4. Civil Liberties	Occupy Wall Street Protests	*Snyder v. Phelps* (2011)	
5. Civil Rights	Workplace Equality	*Brown v. Board of Education* (1954)	
6. Public Opinion	Military Action and Antiterrorism	*Bowers v. Hardwick* (1986) and *Lawrence v. Texas* (2003)	
7. The News Media and the Internet	Censorship	*New York Times v. Sullivan* (1964)	
8. Interest Groups	Energy Policy, Environmental Policy, and Jobs	*Citizens United v. Federal Election Commission* (2010)	
9. Political Parties	Immigration		Proportional Representation Electoral Systems
10. Elections, Campaigns, and Voting	Voting Laws and Regulations	*Bush v. Gore* (2000)	
11. Congress	Health Care	*National Federation of Independent Business et al. v. Sebelius* (2012)	
12. The Presidency	Taxing and Spending		The World Trade Organization and Global Trade
13. The Bureaucracy	The Regulatory Process and Oversight of the Financial Sector		The United Nations Bureaucracy
14. The Judiciary	Affirmative Action and Judicial Activism and Restraint		Judicial Review

Contents

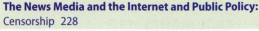

12 THE PRESIDENCY 397

Stephanie Cutter and Work
in the White House

Focus Questions 398

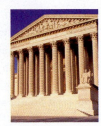
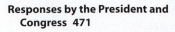

Olga Bogatryenko/Shutterstock.com

Preface

Our book begins with a simple question: How does one individual exert political influence in a country of more than 314 million people? We know that students in American government classrooms across the country are grappling with this question as they develop an appreciation of their role in American public life. In our own classrooms, students ask us: What is my responsibility? Can I make a difference? Does my participation matter? How can I get my opinions represented? These *gateway* questions probe the opportunities and limits on citizen involvement in a democracy.

Although the size and complexity of the American constitutional system is daunting, it is imperative to prepare students for the demands of democratic citizenship. As teachers and scholars of American government, we have come together to write a textbook that explains the theoretical and structural foundations of American democracy and the resulting political process that demands an active and informed citizenry. To help students understand American democracy and see how they can be involved in their government, we peel back the layers of the political system to expose its inner workings and to examine how competing interests can both facilitate and block the will of the people. In doing so, we use the conceptual framework of gateways. We contend that there are gates—formal and informal—that present obstacles to participation and empowerment. But there are also gateways that give students a chance to influence the process and to overcome the obstacles.

The gateways framework helps students conceptualize participation and civic engagement—even democracy itself—with reference to access. Our book is both realistic and optimistic, contending that the American system can be open to the influence

FRONTPAGE/SHUTTERSTOCK.COM

of students and responsive to their hopes and dreams—if they have information about how the system works. But we avoid cheerleading by also pointing out the many gates that undermine the workings of government.

We use the gateways theme to encourage students to develop critical thinking skills. We employ concrete examples of political activism and engagement, from a teenager to the president of the United States, inviting students to enter a conversation about the workings of American democracy. This textbook digs below the surface of standard descriptions of democracy by asking students to consider how democratic we are as a nation. We pose questions: Does equality require an equal process, or does it require equal outcomes? How responsive and accountable is American government? And we challenge students to figure out their own standards for the society in which they want to live in the twenty-first century. Questions like these encourage students to think about the meaning of self-government; these questions constitute a sustained analytical component of this textbook.

Organization of the Textbook

We begin and end with student engagement. Chapter 1 describes the demands of democratic citizenship and asks students to judge American democracy. In the next three parts, we examine the foundations of the American constitutional system, the means of citizen access and influence in a democratic society, and the institutions of American government.

CATWALKER/SHUTTERSTOCK.COM

Chapter 1, Gateways to American Democracy,

provides the rationale and road map for the engagement of citizens in self-government. We describe the Constitution as a gatekeeper, protecting liberty and order but also facilitating representation. The dimensions of representation are set forth as ideological, economic, and partisan. The chapter's overall goal is to establish the nature of democracy, the need for an informed citizenry, and the framework we employ on this intellectual journey.

We include in this chapter a special section that describes the policy-making process as a foundation for policy coverage throughout the book. We view policy as central to understanding American democracy. As a result, we do not isolate the discussion of policy in chapters at the end of the book. Instead, we integrate policy into each of the substantive chapters, situating it as a central part of understanding American politics. By so doing, we underscore the importance of the topic and give students a better understanding of American government.

Part I, Building a System of Government

, includes chapters on the Constitution, federalism, civil liberties, and civil rights that discuss the major issues the Framers confronted when they created a representative government. This section examines why the Framers made particular choices and what the intended and unintended consequences of their decisions have been over time. Students will understand that the ideals expressed in the Declaration of Independence have only slowly been realized and are still evolving. This section of the textbook provides basic information about the operation of American government—the separation of powers, checks and balances, unitary president, lifetime appointments for judges, staggered elections, divided legislature, state and local government, and geographic apportionment—and helps students assess whether the foundations of American government ensure responsiveness and equality.

Part II, Citizen Gateways in a Democracy

, includes chapters on public opinion, the news media and the Internet; interest groups; political parties; and elections, campaigns, and voting. Together these chapters address the question of how a single individual's opinions are formed, expressed, and included in the policy-making process at all levels of government. These matters are essential to our approach. If students are to be part of the political process, they need to understand how to make the best use of the avenues for representation that exist in the American political system. We begin with basic data about how much people know about American government, where they get their information, to whom they listen, and to what extent their opinions change over time. By starting with individual opinion, we help students assess their own opinions about politics and analyze the sources of those opinions.

We continue with the nature of communication among citizens by addressing the impact of the news media and the Internet on American politics. The news media are important sources of information for the public, politicians, and policy elites. They do more than just report the news; they frequently construct the news. We talk about the role of the news media not only historically but also in the context of the rise of cable news networks, the growth of the

Internet, the decline of newspapers, and the potential of social networking. Does the immediacy of the modern media environment have an empowering or a detrimental effect on our democratic system? Does the intense and sometimes intrusive media scrutiny enhance or restrict government's responsiveness to the needs of its citizenry? These are the kinds of questions we address to get students thinking about the political environment in which twenty-first-century government has to function.

We then turn to interest groups as a means by which individual opinions are aggregated and given voice in a democracy, but in markedly different ways and to varying degrees of success. Community or grassroots efforts, from environmental movements to religious organizations to public interest groups, are often a satisfying and empowering form of civic participation. The conventional wisdom is that powerful "special interests" can trounce small citizens' groups when competing for government benefits, but we counter that the increasing number of interest groups means that more people are represented in the formulation of public policy and that improved communication has given small citizens' groups a new gateway for influence.

We next examine how political parties evolved and their crucial and controversial roles in the functioning of government. From the first debates over the ratification of the Constitution to the recent Tea Party movement, this chapter delves into the reasons why the United States remains a predominantly two-party political system. We also address the nature of partisan identification, realignment, modern party organizations, and the nature of party accountability in government. A fundamental theme of the chapter is whether parties have the potential to serve as instruments for engaging and channeling citizens' efforts to elicit responsiveness from government.

The last chapter in this part looks directly at the most basic form of participation in a democracy—elections, campaigns, and voting. When politicians seek elective office, they strive to appear as responsive as possible. Can voters make informed decisions and hold their elected officials accountable? We grapple with the difficult question of whether or how much campaigns as political institutions shape our government. Campaigns tend to be associated with "dirty politics"

and candidates who are willing to say anything to get elected. But such perceptions miss the fact that campaigns are also gateways connecting the public and politicians. We argue that political campaigns provide voters with the information they need to make good choices and to hold public officials accountable. We also provide comprehensive analyses of the accuracy and type of information presented in campaigns, the financing of campaigns, the strategic framing of campaign issues, and the factors that ultimately determine the outcomes of elections.

This chapter also looks at voting, the most straightforward and least costly form of participation in American democracy. It is also the simplest way for individuals to influence their elected officials. But students are often skeptical about the power of the vote. Given the size of the country, how can votes even matter? We discuss why and how individual votes matter, paying close attention to the workings of campaigns and the power of civic participation. We discuss other types of civic participation such as membership in religious and community-based organizations, not-for-profit organizations, and Internet blogging. We use this chapter in part to illustrate how the gateways to involvement in twenty-first-century American life are wider and more direct than they have been in the past.

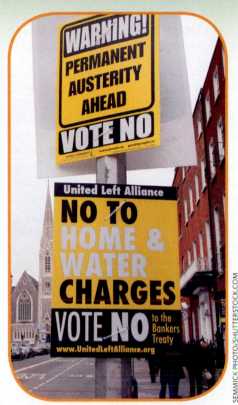

Part III, The Institutions of American Government, provides

an in-depth description and explanation of Congress, the presidency, the bureaucracy, and the judiciary. In these chapters, we describe the fundamental components of Congress, the presidency, and the judiciary as well as the ways each interacts with the other two. We ask students to examine the behavior and outputs of government by responsiveness and equality. For example, does having term limits weaken the president relative to Congress, which does not have term limits? Does the bicameral structure of Congress give the legislative branch an advantage when dealing with the executive branch? We also focus students' attention on how party politics creates a governing dynamic that changes depending on the balance of control of these branches. For the judicial branch, we contend that the courts provide an important gateway for influencing the process and also for advancing the cause of equality. Yet courts are not electorally accountable to citizens, and federal judges hold life tenure. Do the courts mete out equal justice to all citizens, regardless of

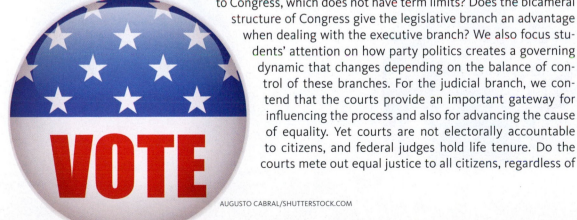

race and income? If they do not, are there means beyond elections by which Congress and the president can help hold courts accountable?

In the chapter on the bureaucracy, our aim is to show students how policy making and the bureaucracy affect day-to-day life. We examine the layers of bureaucratic decision making to demonstrate that the decisions made at each level of an agency or cabinet department can have a profound impact on how laws affect individuals. We discuss decision making in the areas of economic policy, budget policy, entitlement spending for the elderly and the disadvantaged, health care policy, education policy, and environmental policy, all in the context of the dynamics of policy implementation within agencies and the departments that oversee them. In these discussions, we highlight the areas of public policy that students may experience firsthand.

AMYBBB/SHUTTERSTOCK.COM

Throughout the text, we emphasize the importance of the U.S. role in global affairs by integrating key tenets of American politics, such as civil liberties, freedom of the press, executive power, and bureaucracy, and illustrate how they influence U.S. foreign and economic policy, as well as how they operate in other countries.

BRUCE C. MURRAY/SHUTTERSTOCK.COM

VILMOS VARGA/SHUTTERSTOCK.COM

Special Features

Special instructional features facilitate a comprehensive introduction to American government that also takes the demands of citizenship seriously.

PARTICIPATION. A goal of the book is to encourage participation in public life by helping students recognize their own self-interest and a broader civic interest. The book makes the case that democracies demand citizen participation and that citizenship is a serious responsibility.

CRITICAL THINKING. We also want to facilitate critical thinking by asking students to evaluate American democracy through the measures of government responsiveness and citizen equality. This emphasis sharpens students' analytical skills and gives them greater competence and additional confidence to become involved in public life. We devote special sections in each chapter to fundamental types of information that we believe students need to navigate the political process. We also add pedagogical tools to help both instructors and students identify key concepts and terms.

ATTILA JANDI/SHUTTERSTOCK.COM

CONSTITUTIONAL AND LEGAL SETTING. For instructors, the book provides strong support for the institutional foundations of American government. The first section of every chapter is an overview of the constitutional and legal setting of the chapter's subject. This essential basic information helps ensure that students are equipped with what they need to know to understand the process, limits, and safeguards of democracy.

PUBLIC POLICY. We believe public policy is much too important to be relegated to separate chapters at the back of the book. Students cannot take their place as active citizens in American democracy unless they understand how the policy process works. We bring policy applications into our consideration of every aspect of American government by incorporating the policy process and specific policy examples in a dedicated section in every chapter. Attention to a series of specific issues in a variety of contexts helps students understand the political process. And, indeed, specific policies are often the best incentives for getting them engaged.

STUDENT ENGAGEMENT. In the opening of every chapter we focus on people who were young when they got their start in political and civic life, to encourage students and show them reasons and ways to become involved.

GLOBAL CONTEXT FEATURE. A box in several chapters examines a particular topic by looking at the political, social, or economic context in other countries and how that shapes global politics in the twenty-first century.

SUPREME COURT FEATURE. To buttress the book's attention to the legal and constitutional context in which American government operates, most chapters feature a relevant Supreme Court case, stating the facts and the decision, with an analysis of its impact.

New to the Second Edition
Pedagogical Tools for Conceptual Reinforcement

An array of pedagogical tools supports the textbook's purpose and aids in student learning.

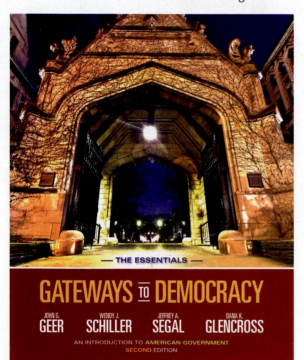

— THE ESSENTIALS —

GATEWAYS TO DEMOCRACY

JOHN G. GEER   WENDY J. SCHILLER   JEFFREY A. SEGAL   DANA K. GLENCROSS

AN INTRODUCTION TO AMERICAN GOVERNMENT
SECOND EDITION

LEARNING OUTCOMES. Each chapter opens with a set of "Need to Know" learning objectives—an answer to the perennial student question: What do I need to know? Each objective is restated at the beginning of the relevant section of the chapter and complemented by a set of Checkpoints at the end of the section that transposes a general objective into specific content. Both objectives and Checkpoints are revisited in a Learning Outcomes chart at the end of the chapter that reinforces what students have learned through an application to participation.

APLIA AND LEARNING OUTCOMES. Aplia is the student online course tool that reinforces student learning with critical thinking questions that correlate directly with the learning outcomes in the text. Students will master core concepts.

FOCUS QUESTIONS. Focus questions at the beginning of each chapter encourage students to think about the chapter topic in terms of government's responsiveness, the people's equality, and the gates and gateways to access. These questions are revisited in the chapter's final section, where we offer interpretive responses to advance students' understanding of how democracy works.

MARGIN QUESTIONS. Brief questions in the margins—called Connections—provoke students to think about the Focus Questions and keep big issues in mind even as they are reading about the details of American government. These questions in the margins keep students thinking critically about the information they are absorbing, serve as prompts for class discussions, and aid in chapter review.

KEY CONCEPTS. Concepts important for an understanding of American government are bold-faced in the text and defined on the page for ease of understanding and review. They are also collated in a glossary at the back of the book.

CONSTRUCT YOUR OWN POLICY. An interactive exercise in each chapter's section on policy challenges students to grasp the complexities of policy making in a democracy.

GATEWAYS TO LEARNING. A special "Gateways to Learning" section at the end of each chapter includes a ten-point list of main ideas for review and learning, a critical thinking question for each key concept to test understanding, and a Learning Outcomes chart that revisits the Need to Know learning objectives, connects objectives with specific content highlighted in Checkpoints, and demonstrates applications for participation in American democracy.

Content

CHAPTER 1

Gateways to American Democracy

- A new emphasis on federal deficits and public debt and how these impact students directly in terms of the costs of education, the opportunity for jobs after they graduate, and the framework of public discourse concerning America's future. This new emphasis gives a sharper focus to the authors' contention that "Your generation has the power to shape the future in which you will live."

- An amplified "Gateways to Learning" section that introduces the book's expanded learning aids and shows students how to use them

CHAPTER 2

The Constitution

- A new table listing deficiencies in the Articles of Confederation and remedies implemented in the Constitution

CHAPTER 3

Federalism

- A new vignette, "Bryan Maughan and the Complexities of Federalism," that foregrounds the complexities of federalism

- A full consideration of the implications of the health care decision for federalism

- An updated discussion of same-sex marriage

Ints Vikmanis/Shutterstock.com

disability rights, racial and religious profiling, and illegal immigrants

- The impact of the Lilly Ledbetter Act and male-female pay differences

Anita Patterson Peppers/Shutterstock.com

Brandon Bourdages/Shutterstock.com

Supplements

Aplia for *Gateways to Democracy, 2e*

Printed Access Card ISBN-13: 9781285058054
Instant Access Code ISBN-13: 9781285058061

- Easy to use, affordable, and effective, Aplia helps students learn and saves you time. It's like a virtual teaching assistant! Aplia helps you have more productive classes by providing assignments that get students thinking critically, reading assigned material, and reinforcing basic concepts—all before coming to class. The interactive questions also help students better understand the relevance of what they're learning and how to apply those concepts to the world around them.

- Visually engaging videos, graphs, and political cartoons help capture students' attention and imagination, and an automatically included eBook provides convenient access. Aplia is instantly accessible via CengageBrain, **http://www.cengagebrain.com**, or through the bookstore via printed access code. Please contact your local Cengage sales representative for more information, and go to **http://www.aplia.com/politicalscience** to view a demo.

CourseReader: American Government 0-30 Selections

Printed Access Card ISBN-13: 9781111479954
Instant Access Code ISBN-13: 9781111479978

CourseReader: American Government allows you to create your reader, your way, in just minutes. This affordable, fully customizable online reader provides access to thousands of permissions-cleared readings, articles, primary sources, and audio and video selections from the regularly updated Gale research library database. This easy-to-use solution allows you to search for and select just the material you want for your courses.

Each selection opens with a descriptive introduction to provide context and concludes with critical-thinking and multiple-choice questions to reinforce key points. CourseReader is loaded with convenient tools like highlighting, printing, note-taking, and downloadable MP3 audio files for each reading.

CourseReader is the perfect complement to any Political Science course. It can be bundled with your current textbook, sold alone, or integrated into your learning management system. CourseReader 0-30 allows access to up to thirty selections in the reader.

Please contact your Cengage sales representative for details, or for a demo please visit us at **http://www.cengage.com/coursereader**. To access CourseReader go to **http://www.cengage.com/sso**, click on "Create a New Faculty Account," and fill out the registration page. Once you are in your new SSO account, search for "CourseReader" from your dashboard and select "CourseReader: American Government" Then click "CourseReader 0-30: American Government Instant Access Code" and click "Add to my bookshelf." To access the live CourseReader, click on "CourseReader 0-30: American Government" under "Additional resources" on the right side of your dashboard.

Free Companion Website for *Gateways to Democracy*, 2e

The Free Companion Website for *Gateways to Democracy*, accessible through www.cengagebrain.com, offers access to chapter-specific interactive learning tools, including flashcards, quizzes, learning objectives, and more.

Custom Enrichment Module: Latino-American Politics Supplement

ISBN-13: 9781285184296

This revised and updated thirty-two-page supplement uses real examples to detail politics related to Latino Americans and can be added to your text via our custom publishing solutions.

Election 2012: An American Government Supplement

Printed Access Card ISBN-13: 9781285090931
Instant Access Code ISBN-13: 9781285420080

Written by John Clark and Brian Schaffner, this booklet addresses the 2012 congressional and presidential races, with real-time analysis and references.

Instructor Companion Website for *Gateways to Democracy*, 2e

ISBN-13: 9781285057989

This password-protected website for instructors features all of the free student assets plus an instructor's manual, book-specific PowerPoint® presentations, JoinIn™ "clicker" questions, Resource Integration Guide, and a test bank. Access your resources by logging into your account at **http://www .cengage.com/login**.

Political Science CourseMate for
Gateways to Democracy, 2e

Printed Access Card ISBN-13: 9781285057972
Instant Access Code ISBN-13: 9781285057965

Cengage Learning's Political Science CourseMate brings course concepts to life with interactive learning, study tools, and exam preparation tools that support the printed textbook. Use **Engagement Tracker** to assess student preparation and engagement in the course, and watch student comprehension soar as your class works with the textbook-specific website. **An interactive eBook** allows students to take notes, highlight, search, and interact with embedded media. Other resources include video activities, animated learning modules, simulations, case studies, interactive quizzes, and timelines.

The American Government News Watch is a real-time news and information resource, updated daily, that includes interactive maps, videos, podcasts, and hundreds of articles from leading journals, magazines, and newspapers from the United States and the world. Also included is the **KnowNow! American Government Blog**, which highlights three current events stories per week and consists of a succinct analysis of the story, multimedia, and discussion-starter questions. Access your course via http://www.cengage .com/login.

The Wadsworth News DVD for American Government 2014

ISBN: 9781285053455

This collection of two- to five-minute video clips on relevant political issues serves as a great lecture or discussion launcher.

To access additional course materials and companion resources, please visit **http://www.cengagebrain.com/shop/ISBN/1133607802** or visit **http://www.cengagebrain.com** and search on the ISBN of this book.

PowerLecture DVD with ExamView® and JoinIn® for *Gateways to Democracy*, 2e

ISBN-13: 9781285057941

An all-in-one multimedia resource for class preparation, presentation, and testing, this DVD includes Microsoft® PowerPoint® slides, a Test Bank in both Microsoft® Word and ExamView® formats, online polling and JoinIn™ "clicker" questions, an Instructor Manual, and a Resource Integration Guide.

- The book-specific **PowerPoint® slides** of lecture outlines, as well as photos, figures, and tables from the text, make it easy for you to assemble lectures for your course, while the **media-enhanced** slides help bring your lecture to life with audio and video clips, animated learning modules illustrating key concepts, tables, statistical charts, graphs, and photos from the book as well as outside sources.

- The **test bank**, revised by James Goss of Tarrant County College, offered in Microsoft Word® and ExamView® formats, includes more than sixty multiple-choice questions with answers and page references along with ten essay questions for each chapter. ExamView® features a user-friendly testing environment that allows you to not only publish traditional paper and computer-based tests, but also web-deliverable exams. **JoinIn™** offers "clicker" questions covering key concepts, enabling you to incorporate student response systems into your classroom lectures.

- **The Instructor's Manual**, revised by Sharon Manna of North Lake College, includes learning objectives, chapter outlines, summaries, discussion questions, class activity and project suggestions, tips on integrating media into your class, and suggested readings and web resources. **JoinIn™** offers "clicker" questions covering key concepts, enabling you to incorporate student response systems into your classroom lectures. A **Resource Integration Guide** provides a chapter-by-chapter outline of all available resources to supplement and optimize learning. Contact your Cengage representative to receive a copy upon adoption.

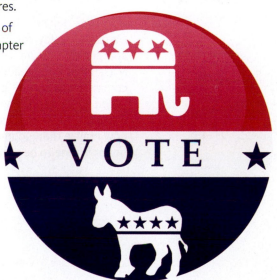

Acknowledgments

Writing the second edition of an introductory textbook requires a dedicated and professional publishing team, and we were extremely fortunate to work with a number of excellent people at Wadsworth Publishing/Cengage Learning. Our development editor, Ann Hofstra Grogg, has been outstanding; she was an essential part of translating our ideas about encouraging students to participate in American politics into an organized and comprehensive textbook. We appreciate the way that our acquiring sponsoring editor, Anita Devine, has brought energy and enthusiasm to the second edition of this book. Bobbie Dempsey has also kept a watchful eye as a top-notch copyeditor for this book. We want to extend a special note of thanks to Carolyn Merrill and Suzanne Jeans, who have been so supportive of this project, and to Joshua Allen and Stacey Dong, who provided key support on format, photos, and production of this book. We also thank Lydia LeStar and the entire sales force at Wadsworth Publishing for their tireless efforts to promote the book.

By definition, an American politics textbook is a sweeping endeavor, and it was not possible to succeed without our reviewers. They provided truly constructive input throughout the writing process. We list their names below, and we are grateful to them for their contributions to the development of this textbook.

Each of us would also like to thank the individuals who supported us throughout the project.

JOHN G. GEER: I wish to thank Corey Bike, Sydney Jones, Meri Long, and Mason Moseley for able research assistance. I also want to express deep appreciation to my daughter, Megan Geer, and my cousin, William Geer Masalehdan, for reading early drafts of my chapters and providing helpful comments. A special note of thanks goes to my coauthors, Wendy and Jeff. When I pulled this team together, I knew that Jeff and Wendy were good people and gifted scholars. Having worked with them over the last few years, I now realize that judgment underestimated their many talents. It has been an honor for me to be part of this collaboration.

WENDY J. SCHILLER: I would also like to express my appreciation for the opportunity to work with John and Jeff—two excellent scholars and terrific colleagues. For their support, past and present, I would like to thank Mary Jane April, Ilene Berman, Linda Cook, Matthew Corritore, Lucy Drotning, Helen Guler, Curtis Kelley, Fiona McGillivray, Molly Phee, Marsha Pripstein Posusney, Jessica Breese Schiller, Jordana Schwartz, Kaitlin Sidorsky, Alastair Smith, Tiffany Trigg, Miriam Wugmeister, and Alan Zuckerman. A special thanks goes to Roger Cobb, with whom I taught Introduction to American Politics at Brown, for all his help. Last, I would like to thank my husband, Robert Kalunian, who provides an endless supply of patience, support, and perspective.

JEFFREY A. SEGAL: I worked on the second edition of this book at the Center for the Study of Democratic Politics, Princeton University, while on sabbatical leave from Stony Brook University. I thank both institutions for their support. I too have special gratitude for my coauthors, who made working on the book as pleasant as possible. I also thank several people for research assistance, including Justine D'Elia, Nasser Javaid, Roland Kappe, Ellen Key, Magen Knuth, Maxwell Mak, Andrew O'Geen, Christopher Parker, and Shannon Stagman.

DANA K. GLENCROSS: I am grateful to many people for supporting me on this second edition project. First, I wish to thank these authors for inviting me to be a co-author on Essentials. Next, thanks to my students, with whom I share a love of learning, especially Annalyn Gill, for your great questions and student perspective. For your tremendous support, thank you to my husband Carl and my parents, Betty and Franklin Delano, and Reagan, the basset hound, who patiently passed many computer hours by my side. Thank you also to my first government teacher, Phyllis Davis, for providing my initial civics education. Finally, to all who capture this book's passion to make government more responsive to those in need, thank you for understanding that the democratic lesson endures through its freedom keepers.

Reviewers and Contributors

We would like to thank the following faculty for leading us through the many gateways we encountered in creating this new edition. Some participated in focus groups, other answered surveys and still others provided valuable feedback on the drafts of the manuscript.

Steve Anthony,
Georgia State University

Wayne Ault,
Southwestern Illinois College

Lynn Brink,
North Lake College

Jane Bryant,
John A. Logan College

Jared Burkholder,
Grace College

Niambi Carter,
Purdue University

Jeffrey Christiansen,
Seminole State College

David Dulio,
Oakland University

Joshua Dyck,
University at Buffalo, SUNY

Matthew Eshbaugh-Soha,
University of North Texas

Jeff Fine,
Clemson University

Charles Finocchiaro,
University of South Carolina

James Goss,
Tarrant County College-Trinity River

Rhonda Gunter,
Mayland Community College

Laurie Han,
Chapman University

Richard Herrera,
Arizona State University

Amy Jasperson,
University of Texas San Antonio

Mark Jendrysik,
University of North Dakota

Whitt Kilburn,
Grand Valley State University

Aaron Knight,
Houston Community College

Lynn Maurer,
Southern Illinois University, Edwardsville

Heather Mbaye,
University of West Georgia

James McCann,
Purdue University

John Mercurio,
San Diego State University

Freidig Monte,
Santa Rosa Jr. College

Michael Moore,
University of Texas at Arlington

Jonathan Morris,
East Carolina University

James Newman,
Idaho State University

Mark Peplowski,
College of Southern Nevada

David Price,
Santa Fe College

Narges Rabii,
Saddleback College

Tim Reynolds,
Alvin Community College

David Ross,
Stark State College

Margaret Scranton,
University of Arkansas at Little Rock

John Shively,
Longview Community College

Alec Thomson,
Schoolcraft College

Nate Vanden Brook,
Oklahoma City Community College

Noreen Warwick,
Richland College

David Woodard,
Clemson University

About the Authors

JOHN G. GEER (PhD, Princeton University) is the Gertrude Conaway Vanderbilt Professor of Political Science at Vanderbilt University. He has been a Visiting Scholar at the Center for the Study of Democratic Politics at Princeton University and a Research Fellow at the Shorenstein Center at Harvard University. Professor Geer is the former editor of the *Journal of Politic*s. He has published numerous articles and several books, including *In Defense of Negativity* (2006), which won the Goldsmith Book Prize from Harvard University in 2008. He has provided extensive commentary in the news media on politics, including live nationwide interviews for FOX, CNN, NBC, CBS, MSNBC, ABC, PBS, and NPR. He has also written op-ed pieces for *Politico*, the *Washington Post*, the *Los Angeles Times, USA Today*, and the *Chicago Tribune*. He teaches a range of undergraduate classes, including Introduction to American Government. In 2005, he received Vanderbilt's College of Arts and Sciences Jeffrey Nordhaus Award for Excellence in Undergraduate Teaching, and in 2009, Vanderbilt's Ellen Gregg Ingalls Award for Excellence in Classroom Teaching.

JEFFREY A. SEGAL (PhD, Michigan State University) is Political Science Department Chair and SUNY Distinguished Professor at Stony Brook University. He has recently been Senior Visiting Research Scholar at Princeton University and a Guggenheim Foundation Fellow. He has also been Global Research Fellow at New York University's Hauser Global Law School Program and Fellow of the Law and Social Sciences Program at Northwestern University. He has worked with the U.S. Department of Labor, the Department of Housing and Urban Development, and the New York State Assembly. Professor Segal has published eight books, including *Senate Elections* (1992, with Alan Abramowitz) and *Advice and Consent: The Politics of Judicial Appointments* (2005, with Lee Epstein). He teaches undergraduate courses on American Government, Constitutional Law, Civil Liberties, and Supreme Court Decision Making. He has received several awards, including Green Bag's award for Exemplary Legal Writing (2008) and an award sponsored by the American Bar Association for innovative teaching and instructional methods (2008). In 2012, Professor Segal was elected as a member of the American Academy of Arts and Sciences.

WENDY J. SCHILLER (PhD, University of Rochester) is Associate Professor of Political Science and Public Policy at Brown University. She was Legislative Assistant for Senator Daniel P. Moynihan and a federal lobbyist for Governor Mario M. Cuomo, and she has been a Guest Scholar and PhD Fellow at the Brookings Institution. Professor Schiller has published *The Contemporary Congress* (2004, 2006, with Burdett Loomis) and *Partners and Rivals: Representation in the U.S. Senate* (2000). Her current research focuses on the indirect and direct election of U.S. senators. She teaches courses on a wide range of American politics topics, including Introduction to the American Political Process, The American Presidency, Congress and Public Policy, The Philosophy of the Founding, and Parties and Interest Groups. Professor Schiller is also a political analyst for local and national news media outlets including CNN.com, MSNBC, Bloomberg Radio, and NPR.

DANA K. GLENCROSS (MA, Oklahoma State University) is Professor of Political Science at Oklahoma City Community College (OCCC), where she has served as Chair of the Department for History, Political Science, Geography, and Medical Terminology, and as Chair of the Faculty Association. Professor Glencross was a governor's appointee to the Oklahoma Commission for Teacher Preparation and a member of the Faculty Advisory Council to the Oklahoma State Regents for Higher Education. She was elected by her peers as the national chairwoman of the Association of Chapter Advisors to the Phi Theta Kappa Honor Society. She co-authors a chapter on "Public Policy" in *Oklahoma Government and Politics: An Introduction*, 4th ed. (2007), and 5th ed. (2012). She teaches such courses as American Federal Government, Introduction to State and Local Government, Introduction to Comparative Politics, and Law. She is a frequently invited guest on local radio and television broadcasts, discussing elections and current political events. Her awards include the OCCC President's Award for Excellence in Teaching and the Oklahoma Political Science Association's Two-Year College Teacher of the Year Award.

Aplia Quick Start Guide

1. To get started, navigate to: **login.cengagebrain.com**

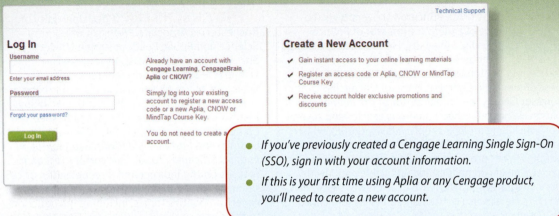

- If you've previously created a Cengage Learning Single Sign-On (SSO), sign in with your account information.
- If this is your first time using Aplia or any Cengage product, you'll need to create a new account.

2. Now you'll need to enter your Aplia Course Key, which is provided by your instructor.

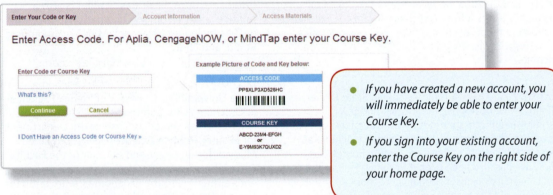

- If you have created a new account, you will immediately be able to enter your Course Key.
- If you sign into your existing account, enter the Course Key on the right side of your home page.

3. Confirm your course information, and click "Continue" to continue to your registration.

4. You can now access your Aplia course by clicking on the "Open" button next to the course. To pay for your Aplia course, click on the "See Payment Options" link under your course.

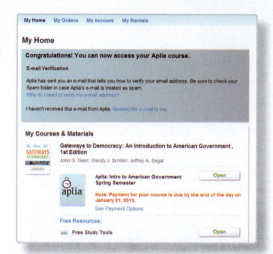

5. After clicking on the "Open" button, you will be directed to your Aplia course as shown below.

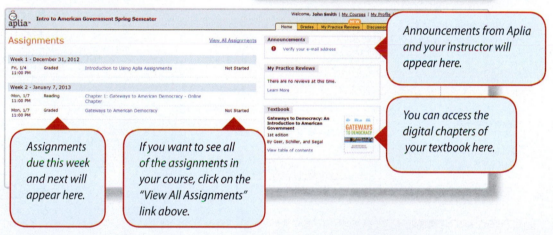

Announcements from Aplia and your instructor will appear here.

You can access the digital chapters of your textbook here.

Assignments due this week and next will appear here.

If you want to see all of the assignments in your course, click on the "View All Assignments" link above.

Need Help?

With your Aplia course?

- Click on the Support link in your Aplia course, and submit a case. Once your case is submitted, you can engage in a live chat to address your support issue.

With your CengageBrain account?

- Check the FAQs in the Support area of your CengageBrain home.
- Login to support.cengage.com using your CengageBrain account to get connected to an expert.
- Call 866-994-2427 Monday through Friday from 8 AM to 6 PM EST.

> *Being there is half the battle. What can happen from there is because you are involved in the process.*

S. R. Sidarth,
University of Virginia,
Charlottesville

1

Gateways To American Democracy

A few years back on a hot summer day, a 20-year-old college student from the University of Virginia was simply doing his job. Volunteering for the Senate campaign of Democrat Jim Webb, S. R. ("Sid") Sidarth was videotaping Webb's Republican opponent, Senator George Allen. Allen, who had solid conservative credentials, had been a popular governor of Virginia. In his first Senate race he had beaten longtime Virginia Senator Chuck Robb. Some observers were comparing Allen to former President Ronald Reagan, and he seemed to be on his way not only to winning his second Senate race but even to being a serious candidate for president.

Sidarth, a computer engineering and American government major at the University of Virginia, had long been interested in politics—a family tradition. He had been an intern on Capitol Hill and a volunteer in John Kerry's presidential campaign in 2004 and in the Virginia governor's race. In 2006, the summer before his senior year in college, he volunteered for Webb. At first he worked behind the scenes at Webb's campaign headquarters in Arlington, helping set up field offices around the state and doing odd jobs. Then,

on August 7 the campaign gave him a digital camcorder and asked him to follow Allen on his "Listening Tour" of Virginia, taping the candidate's appearances in a routine campaign practice known as tracking. Sidarth drove off alone. The work was mostly solitary. At campaign stops he chatted with Allen's aides, and once the senator had walked up to him, shook his hand, and asked his name. "I'm following you around," said Sidarth, and he knew Allen understood what that meant.

On August 11 the Allen campaign held a meet-and-greet picnic at Breaks Interstate Park in far southwest Virginia. Allen picked up his microphone and Sidarth picked up his camcorder.

aplia — Need to Know

- **How the constitutional system balances liberty and order**
- **What the responsibilities of democratic citizenship are**
- **What your best gateway is for participation in American democracy**

During the speech, however, Allen paused and pointed: "This fellow here, over here with the yellow shirt, macaca, or whatever his name is. He's with my opponent. He's following us everywhere." As his supporters began to laugh, Allen continued, "Let's give a welcome to macaca, here. Welcome to America and the real world of Virginia."

Sidarth recorded it all. The episode, posted on YouTube, led to a furor. Within a week, more than two hundred thousand people had watched the clip, and major newspapers across the country were picking up the story. Allen's campaign was in trouble. He had poked fun at Sidarth by using a pejorative term with strong racial overtones. "The kid has a name," said Webb communications director Kristian Denny Todd. "This is trying to demean him, to minimize him as a person." The irony was that Allen, born and raised in California, had first come to Virginia as a college student, and Sidarth had been a Virginian all his life. It was Allen who appeared out of touch with the increasing diversity of the state he was representing.

Allen's lead disappeared, and on election day, out of more than 2.3 million ballots cast in Virginia, he lost by just over seven thousand votes. When asked about his role in this dramatic turn of events, Sidarth chose his words carefully. "I was just doing my job, and I got sort of pulled into this," he said. "I was the only person of color there, and it was useful for him [Allen] in inciting his audience. I was annoyed that he would use my race in a political context." Later, after the election, Sidarth wrote in the *Washington Post*, "I am proud to be a second-generation Indian American and a practicing Hindu," but "I would not wish the scrutiny on anyone." Still, he reflected, "Webb's victory last week gives me hope that Virginia will not tolerate playing the race card. . . . The politics of division just don't work anymore. Nothing made me happier on election night than finding

out the results from Dickenson County, where Allen and I had our encounter. Webb won there, in what I can only hope was a vote to deal the race card out of American politics once and for all."[1]

Webb's victory did not, of course, signal an end for the issue of race in American politics. Nor did it signal the end of Allen's career, as he ran for the Senate again in 2012 but lost. That a summer volunteer could alter the career path of prominent politicians and reshape the composition of the U.S. Senate points to the power of the individual in a democracy. In a democracy, citizens have the right, and the responsibility, to be involved in the public sphere and to take part in governing themselves. In this case, the impact of Sidarth's story was magnified by the Internet, but the ability of citizens to influence the political process does not depend on new technologies. Since the nation's beginnings more than two centuries ago, the actions of citizens have shaped the country's development. We open each chapter of this textbook with the story of one of those citizens. Some of them are ordinary, some are extraordinary; most are college students. Each used one of the many gateways to participation in government that American democracy provides, because American government is about individuals and self-governance. These individuals have worked to get out the vote and have run for office themselves. They have joined with others to promote causes they care about on campus, in state legislatures, and in the halls of Congress. They have challenged laws they thought were wrong through peaceful protests and through lawsuits that went all the way to the Supreme Court. They have worked with political parties and served in government agencies and in the military. Any one of them could be you.

Even though the size of American government is daunting, individuals can make real changes. What often appear to be small and localized efforts can have big impacts. Citizens can hold government accountable by voting legislators and presidents in and out of office. They can make their opinions known more directly because the right to speak out and to join with others in promoting causes is protected by the Constitution. A free press and the Internet allow information and opinion to be widely spread and shared. Courts hear cases brought by citizens, and citizen juries determine the outcome. Elections, protest marches, blogs, the courts, and the constitutional amendment process are all gateways of influence.

Amherst College freshmen hoe a field for a farm run by a local food bank in Amherst, Massachusetts, as part of a school community service project. Four out of five young people do volunteer work in high school and college, and, according to the Harvard University Institute of Politics, 94 percent believe that volunteer service is an effective way to deal with challenges in their local communities.

This textbook, *Gateways to Democracy*, explains how citizen involvement has expanded American democracy and how each of you, too, can influence the political system. We call the avenues of influence "gateways." This book serves as a handbook for democratic citizenship by peeling back the layers of American government to reveal the ways you can get involved and to explain the reasons you should do so. As the term *gateways* implies, there are also gates—obstacles to influence, institutional controls that limit access, powerful interests that seem to block the people's will. We describe these as well, because to be a productive and influential member of American society, you need to understand how American government and politics work.

Through citizen involvement, American democracy has achieved many successes:

- The nation and its institutions are amazingly stable. The United States has the oldest written constitution in the world.

- The government has weathered severe economic crises, a civil war, and two world wars; yet it still maintains peaceful transitions of power from one set of leaders to the next.

- American society has attracted millions of immigrants, giving many of them a gateway to citizenship.

- Americans exhibit more commitment to civic duty than do citizens in nearly all other major democracies.[2]

- Americans show more tolerance of different political views than do citizens in other major democracies.[3]

These successes do not mean that there are not problems:

- Even with the election of President Barack Obama in 2008, racial tensions continue to haunt the country.

Social scientists have been measuring the gap between the rich and the poor since the 1930s, and in the past few decades that gap has grown. Reports in 2012 indicated that the top 1 percent of households took home 93 percent of all income gains in 2010. That same 1 percent earned 20 percent of all income in the country in 2010. During 2010, cities reported an average of a 2 percent increase in homelessness. In February 2012, homeless people camped under an interstate bridge in Portland, Oregon.

- The gap between the rich and the poor continues to grow, with increasing numbers of people living in poverty.[4]
- The public's trust in the institutions of government has never been so low.[5]
- The rate of turnout in elections is among the lowest of the major democracies.
- Efforts to reform immigration policy continue to fail, as the country grapples with conflicting traditions of welcoming and restricting newcomers.
- Political polarization continues to increase, as recently reflected in staggering partisan differences in the public's judgment of President Obama.[6]
- The U.S. national debt is more than $15 trillion and growing every day.[7]

To solve these and other problems, the nation's citizens must be vigilant and engaged. We have framed our book with the goal of demonstrating the demands and rewards of democratic citizenship. As we explore the American political system, we place special emphasis on the multiple and varied connections among citizenship, participation, institutions, and public policy. Our focus is on the following gateway questions:

- How can you get yourself and your opinions represented in government?
- How can you make government more responsive, and responsible, to citizens?
- How can you make American democracy better?

Democracy and the American Constitutional System

> ❯ How the constitutional system balances liberty and order

Today democracy is the kind of government to which the people of many nations aspire. But it has not always been so. Only in the last two centuries—partly through the example of the United States—has democracy gained favor. Let us sketch some of the fundamental aspects of American democracy.

Liberty and Order

Democracy is rule by the people, or self-government. In a democracy, the citizens hold political authority, and they develop the means to govern themselves. In practice, that means rule by the majority, and in the years before American independence, **majority rule** had little appeal. In 1644 John Cotton, a leading clergyman of the colonial period, declared democracy "the meanest and worst of all forms of government."[8] Even after American independence, Edmund Burke, a British political philosopher and politician, wrote that a "perfect democracy is . . . the most shameless thing in the world."[9] At the time democracy was associated with mob rule, and mobs were large, passionate, ignorant, and dangerous. If the mob ruled, the people would suffer. There would be no liberty or safety; there would be no **order**.

John Adams, a signer of the Declaration of Independence and later the nation's second president (1797–1801), was not a champion of this kind of democracy. "Democracy," he wrote, "while it lasts is more bloody than either aristocracy or monarchy. Remember, democracy never lasts long. It soon wastes, exhausts, and murders itself. There is never a democracy that did not commit suicide."[10] Adams knew about mobs and their effects firsthand. As a young lawyer before the Revolution, he agreed to defend British soldiers who had been charged with murder for firing on protesters in the streets of Boston. The soldiers' cause was unpopular, for the people of Boston detested the British military presence. But Adams believed that, following British law, the soldiers had a right to counsel (a lawyer to defend them) and to a fair trial. In later years, he considered his defense of these British soldiers "one of the best pieces of service I ever rendered my country."[11]

Why? In defending the soldiers, Adams was standing up for the **rule of law**, the principle that could prevent mob rule and keep a political or popular majority under control so it could not trample on **minority rights**. An ancient British

Connections:
Key concepts appear in boldface and for this chapter are defined in the "Gateways to Learning" section at the end of the chapter.

THE GRANGER COLLECTION, NEW YORK

Paul Revere printed this famous engraving of the Boston Massacre in 1770. Emphasizing the shedding of innocent blood—five colonists died—it rallied Bostonians to resist British tyranny. Evidence at the trial of the soldiers indicated that they were provoked by the mob with taunts, clubs, and stones. Lawyer John Adams argued for the defense.

legal principle, the rule of law holds that all people are equal before the law, all are subject to the law, and no one is above it. Adams and the others who wrote America's founding documents believed in a constitutional system in which the people set up and agree on the basic rules and procedures that will govern them. Without a constitution and rule of law, an unchecked majority could act to promote the welfare of some over the welfare of others, and society would be torn apart.

The American constitutional system, therefore, serves to protect both liberty and order. The Constitution sets up a governmental structure with built-in constraints on power (gates) and multiple points of access to power (gateways). It also has a built-in means for altering the basic rules and procedures of governance through amendments. As you might expect, the procedure for passing amendments comes with its own set of gates and gateways.

The Constitution as Gatekeeper

"If men were angels," wrote James Madison, a leading author of the Constitution and later the nation's fourth president (1809–17), "no government would be necessary. . . . In framing a government which is to be administered by men over men," he continued, "the great difficulty lies in this: You must first enable the government to control the governed; and in the next place oblige it to control itself" (see *Federalist* 51 in the Appendix). Madison and the other **Framers** of the Constitution recognized that the government they were designing had to be strong enough to rule but not strong enough to take away the people's rights. In other words, the Constitution had to serve as a gatekeeper, allowing and limiting access to power simultaneously.

James Madison, Thomas Jefferson, John Adams, and the other **Founders** had read many of the great political theorists. They drew, for example, on the ideas of the British political philosophers Thomas Hobbes and John Locke in perceiving the relationship between government and the governed as a **social contract**. If people lived in what these philosophers called a state of nature, without the rule of law, conflict would be unending and the strong would destroy the weak. To secure order and safety, individuals come together to form a government and agree to live by its rules. In return, the government agrees to protect life, liberty, and property. The right to life, liberty, and property, said Locke, are **natural** or **unalienable rights**, rights so fundamental that government cannot take them away.

But these ideas about government as a social contract were untested theories when Madison and others began to write the Constitution. There were no working examples in other nations. The only model for self-government was ancient Athens, where the people had governed themselves in a **direct**

democracy. In Athens, citizens had met together to debate and to vote. That was possible because only property-owning males were citizens, and they were few in number and had similar interests and concerns.[12]

The new United States was nothing like the old city-state of Athens. It was an alliance of thirteen states—former colonies—with nearly 4 million people spread across some 360,000 square miles. Direct democracy was impractical for such a large and diverse country, so those who wrote the Constitution created a **representative democracy** in which the people elect representatives who govern in their name. Some observers, including the Framers, call this arrangement a **republic**, a form of government in which power derives from the citizens but their representatives make policy and govern according to existing law.

Could a republic work? No one knew, certainly not the Framers. The government they instituted was something of an experiment, and they developed their own theories about how it would work. Madison, for example, rejected the conventional view that a democracy had to be small and homogeneous so as to minimize conflict. He argued that size and diversity were assets because competing interests in a large county would balance and control—or check—one another and prevent abuse of power. Madison called these competing interests **factions**, and he believed that the most enduring source of faction was "the various and unequal distribution of property" (see *Federalist* 10 in the Appendix).

In a pure democracy, where the people ruled directly, Madison expected that passions would outweigh judgments about the common good. Each individual would look out for himself, for his self-interest, and not necessarily for the interests of society as a whole, what we might call civic interest. In a republic, however, the people's representatives would of necessity have a broader view. Moreover, they would, Madison assumed, come from the better educated, a natural elite. The larger the republic, the larger the districts from which the representatives would be chosen, and thus the more likely that they would be civic-minded leaders of the highest quality. More important, in a large republic it would be less likely that any one faction could form a majority. Interests would balance each other out, and selfish interests would actually be checked by majority rule.

Balance, control, order—these values were as important to the Framers as liberty. So while the Constitution vested political authority in the people, it also set up a governing system designed to prevent any set of individuals, any political majority, or even the government itself from becoming too powerful. The Framers purposely set up barriers and gates that blocked the excesses associated with mob rule.

Consequently, although the ultimate power lies with the people, the Constitution divides power both vertically and horizontally. Within the

Legislative Branch	Executive Branch	Judicial Branch

Makes the laws

Executes the laws

Interprets the laws

© CENGAGE LEARNING

FIGURE 1.1 The Three Branches of Government.

Within the federal government, power is divided into three separate branches.

federal government, power is channeled into three different branches—the legislature (Congress), which makes the laws; the executive (the president and the government departments, or bureaucracy), which executes the laws; and the judiciary (the Supreme Court and the federal courts), which interprets the laws (see Figure 1.1). This vertical division of power is referred to as the **separation of powers**. To minimize the chance that one branch will become so strong that it can abuse its power and harm the citizenry, each branch has some power over the other two in a system known as **checks and balances**. The Constitution also divides power horizontally, into layers, between the national government and state governments an arrangement known as **federalism**.

The American constitutional system thus simultaneously provides gateways for access and gates that limit access. The people govern themselves, but they do so indirectly and through a system that disperses power among many competing interests. This textbook explores both the gateways and the gates that channel and block the influence of citizens.

American Political Culture

As an experiment, the American republic has been open to change in the course of the nation's history. Madison was right about the enduring influence of factions. The people quickly divided themselves into competing interests and shortly into competing political parties, groups organized to win elections. The process by which competing interests determine who gets what, when, and how is what we call **politics**.[13]

Madison was right, too, about the sources of division, which are often centered in the unequal distribution of property and competing ideas about how far government should go to reduce inequality. Public opinion about such matters is sometimes described as falling on a scale that ranges from left to right, and when people have a fairly consistent set of views over a range of policy choices, they are said to have a **political ideology**, that is, a coherent way of thinking about government, a philosophy so to speak. In contrast, **party identification**, or partisanship, is a psychological attachment to a particular party.

A person's ideology can be a strong clue as to what he or she thinks about politics. On the left end of the scale are **liberals** who favor government efforts to increase equality, including higher rates of taxes on the wealthy than on the poor and greater provision of social benefits, such as health care, unemployment insurance, and welfare payments to support those in need. **Conservatives**, on the right, believe that lower taxes will prompt greater economic growth that will ultimately benefit everyone, including the poor. Thus, liberals support a large and active government that will regulate the economy, while conservatives fear that such a government will suppress individual liberty and create a dependency that actually harms those it aims to help.

The left–right division is not just about economics, however. For social issues, liberals generally favor less government interference, while conservatives favor rules that will uphold traditional moral values (see Figure 1.2). Conservatives are, therefore, more likely to support laws that ban abortion and same-sex marriage, while liberals are more likely to favor a woman's right to make decisions over private matters as well as the right of same-sex couples to wed.

Although terms such as *conservative* and *liberal* are often used to label American political attitudes, most Americans are not very ideological in their orientation to politics. They are likely to take independent positions on various issues, leaning left on some and right on others. In fact, most Americans are **moderates**, not seeing themselves on one end of the scale or the other. A sizable number of Americans also describe themselves as **libertarians**, believing that government should not interfere in either economic matters or social matters. Others take a **populist** perspective, opposing concentrated wealth and adhering to traditional moral values.

Despite its many perspectives, American **political culture** as a whole generally favors individualism over communal approaches to property and poverty, especially in comparison to the industrialized democracies of Europe and elsewhere in the world (see Global Gateways: Social Welfare, Public Debt, and Free Enterprise). The United States spends less on government programs to help the less-well-off than many other countries, and it has historically refrained from assuming control of business enterprises, such as railroads and banks, except in times of crisis. The United States tends to favor **capitalism**, an economic system in which business enterprises and key industries are privately owned, as opposed to **socialism**, in which they are owned by government. Yet, to prevent the worst abuses of capitalism, which can arise as businesses pursue profit to the detriment of citizens, Congress has passed laws that regulate privately owned businesses and industries. For example, government monitors banks and financial markets, ensures airline safety, and protects workers from injury on the job.

FIGURE 1.2 American Political Ideology.

Political ideology has been described in many ways. In one version, political thought is plotted on a continuum between left (liberal) and right (conservative). The terms *left* and *right* derive from the seating arrangements for political parties in the Assembly during the French Revolution.

LEFT (LIBERAL):
Greater faith in a large and active government to promote equality.

RIGHT (CONSERVATIVE):
Greater preference for a small and limited government to encourage economic growth.

But this version is somewhat simplistic. A more fully developed version plots a graph that shows where liberals and conservatives stand on both economic and social issues. Liberals favor government regulation of the economy; conservatives do not. Conservatives favor government regulation of traditional moral values; liberals do not.

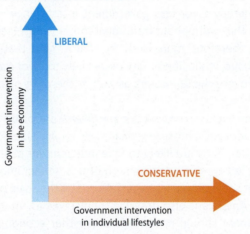

In a third version, the ideological spectrum is further complicated by the inclusion of libertarians, who favor no government intervention in either the economy or society, and populists, who favor government intervention in both the economy and society.

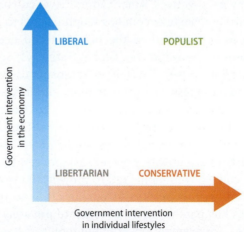

The truth is, however, that Americans are not really very ideological. Most Americans describe themselves as moderates or as independent thinkers who might lean left on some issues and right on others. Americans generally look to government to be active in some areas of life, but they differ on which areas.

globalgateways

Social Welfare, Public Debt, and Free Enterprise

Throughout this book we look at American democracy from a global perspective, comparing aspects of the U.S. government and civic life to those elsewhere in the world. We begin with three related items: the extent to which the United States and other countries provide social welfare benefits, the relative size of government debt, and the extent to which the economies of the United States and other countries are controlled by the government, shown as an economic freedom score.

The first column in the table shows that the United States allocates a smaller percentage of its budget to social welfare programs than do the industrial democracies of western Europe—which have higher tax rates to pay for these benefits. The second column shows government debt as a percentage of its gross domestic product. The United States has a debt ratio that is higher than that of France or Germany but much lower than that of Japan or Greece. The third column presents the amount of control a nation exerts over its economy. Here the United States is pretty typical, while North Korea and Cuba, both nondemocratic, exercise much greater government control. There are no examples of nations that have exercised complete or nearly complete control over economic matters that have not simultaneously exercised complete or nearly complete control over political matters. Also note that nations with extensive social welfare systems can be both politically democratic and free market oriented. There is, in short, no easy formula for determining the economic health and social welfare of a country.

- **Why do countries that have free market economies also tend to be democratic?**

- **On what dimension does the United States stand out in comparison to other countries?**

Social Welfare Spending, Government Debt, and Economic Freedom: Thirteen Nations Compared

Nation	Social Welfare Spending (as a % of GDP), 2007	Debt (as a % of GDP), 2010	Economic Freedom Score, 2012 (lowest [0.0] to highest [100.0])
Cuba	NA	NA	28.3
Denmark	26.1	43.6	76.2
France	28.4	81.7	63.2
Germany	25.2	83.2	71.0
Greece	21.3	142.8	55.4
Ireland	15.5	96.2	76.9
Japan	18.7	220.3	71.6
Mexico	7.2	42.7	65.3
New Zealand	18.4	31.6	82.1
North Korea	7.5	NA	1.0
Spain	21.6	60.1	69.1
Turkey	10.5	41.7	62.5
United States	16.2	93.2	76.3

NA = not available

Sources: Organization for Economic Co-Operation and Development, "Society at a Glance 2011 – OECD Social Indicators," http://www.oecd.org/els/social/indicators/SAG; "Government Debt to GDP, List by Country," *Trading Economics*, 2012, http://www.tradingeconomics.com/government-debt-to-gdp-list-by-country; The Heritage Foundation, "2012 Index of Economic Freedom," http://www.heritage.org/index/ranking, all accessed April 10, 2012.

These regulations tend to moderate vast inequalities in wealth as well. Though prizing individualism, American political culture also has a long-standing **egalitarian** tradition. Americans rejected British inheritance laws, which gave virtually all property to the eldest male. With estates divided more equally, and with a vast frontier that allowed land ownership to spread broadly, property in the United States was never as concentrated in the hands of a few as it had been in Europe. This greater equality, in turn, produced a political culture that values each individual's ability to achieve wealth and social status through hard work, not inheritance, and supports a free enterprise economic system, within limits.

Public Policy under a Constitutional System

The laws that regulate the American economy, as well as the tax rates, exemptions, and subsidies that help direct it, are examples of **public policy**—the intentional action by government to achieve a goal. It is in the arena of public policy—in determining who gets what, when, and how, and with what result—that we can see whether the constitutional system created by Madison and the Framers really works. Can the people pursue policies that advance their own interests? Can the people's representatives, while pursuing policies that advance their constituents' interests, produce a nation that looks out for the civic interest generally, for the common good, and for the welfare of all the people?

With a government deliberately designed to constrain power and the popular will, and a citizenry divided into factions and prizing individualism, the development of public policy has never been easy. In some ways, it has tended to cycle. One argument gains favor, driving policy in one direction. But new problems arise, calling for a redirection of policy. For example, a policy of providing tax benefits to homeowners to spur home ownership sounds like a good thing. It would help homeowners, support the home construction industry, and create jobs, building more stable communities. But what sounds simple rarely is that simple, because there are usually unintended consequences. A policy of tax benefits for homeowners can also encourage sprawl that turns agricultural land into suburbs, thus decreasing crop yields and altering food production, while leaving cities with vacant housing and declining tax bases. Subsequently, government responds to these new problems by developing additional policies to revitalize both agriculture and urban infrastructure.

With so many competing interests and the high potential for unintended negative consequences, government seeks to pursue policy making that maximizes benefits and minimizes costs. Political scientists—scholars who study politics and the processes of government—have categorized the steps in policy making to make the process more understandable.

The first step is **identification** of the problem. For example, constituents might complain to members of Congress that the cost of college is too high. The second step is for the issue of the cost of higher education to make it to the agenda of policy makers.[14] Of all the problems that government might be able to solve, only a small fraction can receive attention at any one time. Those that get on the **policy agenda** get the attention of Congress, the president, the executive branch agency that deals with the issue, the courts, political parties, interest groups, and interested citizens. These **stakeholders** attempt to **formulate** a policy that will solve the problem (see Figure 1.3). In the example of the high cost of college, which has been on the policy agenda since 2009, the stakeholder network considered three proposals: direct federal loans to college students; promoting private loans by paying banks the interest on student loans while the student is in college; and guaranteeing the loans if students are unable to repay them. In a fourth step, **policy enactment**, the legislative branch passes a law that enacts one or more of those proposals, as Congress did with student loans in 2010. Following passage, the legislature grants an executive branch department the authority to **implement** the program. In this case, the Department of Education was given the authority to direct the student loan program. After a few years, Congress may reevaluate the program. Following this **policy evaluation**, the cycle of policy making might begin again, with new legislation to adjust the program to make it work better (see Figure 1.4).

In a republic, policy making should reflect the will of the people expressed through their elected representatives and interest groups. Madison envisioned that the people's representatives managing the policy-making process would be an elite—well-educated people of "merit." But if the people divided into different classes, as Madison also envisioned, there is a danger to democracy if the people's representatives are an elite who represent only their own interests and not civic-minded leaders who consider the common good. In the 1950s the sociologist C. Wright Mills in fact wrote about a narrow **power elite** made up of leaders from corporations, government, and the military that controlled the gates and gateways to power. But in the 1960s the political scientist Robert Dahl took issue with Mills and argued that policy making has a more **pluralist** basis, with authority held by different groups in different areas. Elected representatives seek to balance these various interests even as they seek to do what is best for their constituents.

Although presidents and members of Congress formally appear to be in command of the policy-making process, they have to navigate a maze of gates imposed by competing centers of power. Congress has failed to enact immigration reform despite the fact that a large percentage of Americans think the

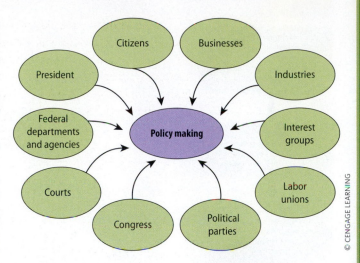

© CENGAGE LEARNING

FIGURE 1.3
Stakeholders in the Policy-Making Process.

One reason policy making is difficult and complex in the United States is that so many citizens, businesses, industries, labor unions, and interest groups as well as the political parties, Congress, the president, federal agencies, the courts, and others have a stake in policy outcomes. For emphasis, we repeat this figure in discussions of policy making throughout this textbook, with the various stakeholders identified.

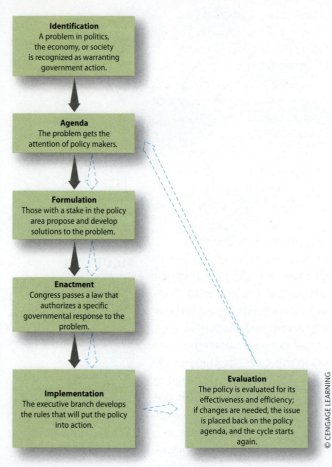

Identification
A problem in politics, the economy, or society is recognized as warranting government action.

Agenda
The problem gets the attention of policy makers.

Formulation
Those with a stake in the policy area propose and develop solutions to the problem.

Enactment
Congress passes a law that authorizes a specific governmental response to the problem.

Implementation
The executive branch develops the rules that will put the policy into action.

Evaluation
The policy is evaluated for its effectiveness and efficiency; if changes are needed, the issue is placed back on the policy agenda, and the cycle starts again.

© CENGAGE LEARNING

FIGURE 1.4 The Policy-Making Process.

immigration system is not working well. Immigration reform has been on the policy agenda for more than a decade, but the divisiveness of the issue has yielded a gate preventing reform. Some Americans favor citizenship for illegal aliens; others want to secure the borders to prevent more immigrants from illegally entering. In the spring and summer of 2010, immigration reform was back on the national policy agenda, following passage of a controversial Arizona law regarding illegal aliens. In 2011 Alabama passed a similar law, and both states became involved in suits brought by the Justice Department, which held that these laws overstepped state authority and intruded on federal responsibility. The Supreme Court ruled in 2012 that some, but not all of the Arizona law was unconstitutional (see Chapter 8).

Responsiveness and Equality: Does American Democracy Work?

Does American democracy work? That is a question we will be asking in every chapter of this book, and we invite you to start working on an answer.

To guide your thinking, we focus on two basic themes, responsiveness and equality. Is government responsive to the needs of its citizens? Do all citizens have an equal chance to make their voices heard? We ask you to keep these themes in mind as you learn about the U.S. political system. To give you a basis for making a judgment, we inform you of the findings of political scientists who have been asking and answering these questions for decades. Throughout this textbook, we present the latest data that speak to these broad issues. It is important to remember that we are not offering our opinions about government; instead, we are putting forward the most important evidence and theories, from a variety of perspectives, over the last fifty or so years. It is up to you to consider them and form your own conclusions.

One way to begin to evaluate American democracy, and to appreciate it, is to look briefly at alternative models of government. In **monarchy**, **autocracy**, and **oligarchy**, a single person or a small elite rules society. Such systems are by definition undemocratic. Rulers in these systems have little need to be responsive to the people. They hold most of the power and are not generally accountable to those they rule. They may try to satisfy the people with programs that meet basic needs for food and safety, but they do so to ensure submission. These rulers have a low regard for the people and do not want them to be engaged in public life. In these systems, the rulers are excessively wealthy, and the people are likely to be impoverished. To maintain order, the rulers typically rely on a strong army or a secret police force to keep the people in line through fear and intimidation. Rulers in such systems are overthrown when dissatisfaction rises to a level at which citizens are willing to risk their lives in open revolt, as they did in Egypt and Libya in 2011, or when the army or police conspire to replace one ruler with another. In contrast, a democracy asks its citizens to be actively engaged in their own governance, for the benefit of all.

The government often has a stake in pursuing what economists call **public goods**: goods from which everyone benefits. The core idea is that no one can be excluded. We all get the benefits of clean air, even if we have been driving cars and not taking buses. **Private goods**, by contrast, can be extended to some individuals and denied to others. When a government awards a contract to build a new library, the firm that wins the contract gets private goods (that is, money) from the government. The firms that lost the bid are denied that chance.

Who determines what goods, whether private or public, the government should provide, at what levels, and how to pay for them? These are core public policy problems. There are competing interests at every point in determining who gets what, when, and how. Politics is the process by which the people determine how government will respond. And it is in evaluating the basic fairness of government's response, and the basic equality of the people's general welfare that is thus secured, that we see whether American democracy is working.

Representative democracy succeeds when there is constant interaction between the people and the government. Government must be responsive to the needs and opinions of the people, and the public must find ways to hold government accountable. Government officials who are unresponsive to the people need to be removed from office.

For a government to respond fairly to citizens, all citizens must have an equal opportunity to participate in it. Each citizen must have a chance to have his or her voice heard, either by voting or by participating in the political process and public life. These ideas form the basis of **political equality**. If citizens are not treated equally, with the same degree of fairness, then the foundation of democratic government is weakened. One way to evaluate American democracy is to evaluate the degree to which political equality has been achieved.

There are other aspects of equality. **Equality of opportunity** is one aspect—the expectation that citizens will be treated equally before the law and have an equal opportunity to participate in government. Does equality of opportunity also mean that citizens have an equal opportunity to participate in the economy (to get a job, to get rich) and in social life (to join a club, to eat at a restaurant)? And what about **equality of outcome**, the expectation that incomes will level out or that standards of living will be roughly the same for all citizens? In the United States, equality of outcome, or results, might entail the proportional representation of groups that have experienced discrimination in the past; that is, for full equality of outcome in Congress or on corporate boards, the number of African Americans would have to be equal to their proportion in the overall population, about 13 percent. What can, or should, government do to ensure equality of opportunity, or equality of outcome? These questions are hotly contested, especially efforts to forge equality of outcome. We return to these issues in the final section of this introductory chapter.

Regardless of one's partisan leanings, the election of Barack Obama as president in 2008 was a significant achievement for American equality. Many observers thought it would be decades before the country elected an African American president.[15] That view reflected the long history of discrimination in this country. But Obama's swearing in as president sent an undeniable signal about equality in America.

"I stand here today humbled by the task before us," said President Obama as he began his inaugural address in January 2009, "grateful for the trust you have bestowed, mindful of the sacrifices borne by our ancestors."[16] Those ancestors include the millions of Americans who over more than two centuries have worked to make American democracy more responsive and to make America more equal. We challenge you to join them. This textbook will give you the information you need to understand the way American government works, to recognize the gates and the gateways. We also invite you to think critically about American democracy, to engage in a class-wide and nationwide conversation about how well it is working, to offer ideas for making it work better, to influence the decision makers who make public policy, and even to become one of them.

 Checkpoint

Can you:

- ☐ Make a connection between minority rights and democratic rule
- ☐ Define social contract
- ☐ Explain the importance of political ideology
- ☐ Name the key players in the policy-making process
- ☐ Explain the differences between equality of opportunity and equality of outcome

The Demands of Democratic Citizenship

> **What the responsibilities of democratic citizenship are**

If you were born in the United States or have been naturalized, you are a citizen, and it is important for you to know what that entails. Politics shapes your life on a day-to-day basis. Citizenship, as a result, carries with it both rights and responsibilities. While the specific reasons to be involved in public life may vary, the need to participate does not.

Self-Interest and Civic Interest

The first reason to be involved is self-interest. You want government to serve your needs. Those needs, of course, range widely, depending on your stage of life, personal circumstances, and values. Some citizens prefer that the government stay out of people's lives as much as possible, and others prefer governmental assistance for the causes they hold dear. As a student, you may want the government to invest more in higher education and job creation; as a parent, you may want more aid for child care and school construction; as a working person, you may view job security as the most important government responsibility. Whatever way you define your self-interest, by getting involved you send signals to elected officials, and if enough people agree with you, the government will likely act.

The second reason, what we call **civic interest**, is more complex. The idea is that citizens get involved in the process because they want to be part of the voluntary organizations that make up the civil society that enables communities to flourish. They want to help others, improve their neighborhoods, and create an even better country. Groups of interested people can accomplish things that individuals acting alone cannot. By working together, people can encourage greater responsiveness from government. In so doing, they become better citizens and are better able to communicate their needs to a government that, in turn, becomes more responsive.

As gains in civic interest lead to broader public involvement, they also advance equality. In a democracy, the power of individual acts can be amplified, as Sidarth's actions demonstrate. Sometimes this amplification takes place through the courts; lawsuits arising from an alleged injustice experienced by one person can result in broad rulings that affect a great many.

Participation in the public sphere serves the larger civic interest. Voting is the most obvious political act, but there are also ways you can also express your views to those in power, who need to know those views so they can respond. With all the new technologies, the interface between people and politicians is now easier than ever.

Politics and the Public Sphere

Your generation has the power to shape the future in which you will live. Will America continue to be a land of opportunity? The following three issues represent some of the important concerns that you and the nation face. Working on these problems is reason enough to take part in the nation's civic life.

Educational Opportunity.   Because you are in college, education policy affects you every day and is important to your future. Education has long

FIGURE 1.5 College Costs, 1980–2011.

Source: Pew Research Center, "Is College Worth It?" May 16, 2011, p. 26, www.pewsocialtrends.org/2011/05/15/is-college-worth-it/. Copyright © 2011 by PEW Research Center. Reproduced by permission.

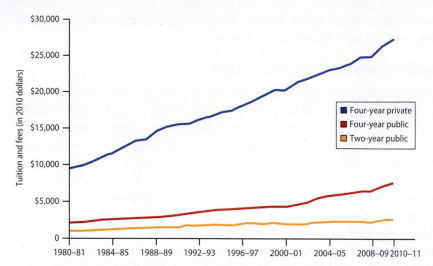

Note: The amounts shown are the list or published tuition and fees, not what students actually pay. Most undergraduates receive grant aid. The amounts shown are "sticker price" and do not account for grant aid. The College Board estimates them by weighting published tuition and fees by full-time undergraduate enrollment. They are deflated using the Consumer Price Index.

been considered both a fundamental component of citizenship in a democratic society and a stepping-stone to economic advancement. But what does it take to get a college degree, and who should bear the burden?

These are important questions, because the cost of a college education continues to rise. Private colleges are increasingly expensive, and during times of economic decline, as states and local governments have faced budget cuts, public institutions of higher learning have also raised tuition (see Figure 1.5). The consequence of these increases is a greater financial burden on younger citizens like you—burdens that correspond to times when you may also be having children and thinking about buying a house (see Figure 1.6).

If an educated citizenry is necessary to democracy, and if the entire nation benefits from the contributions of college-educated citizens, does the federal government have an obligation to promote educational opportunity? Congress has decided it does and authorizes the Department of Education to spend some $33.6 billion annually to fund financial aid for higher education, including Pell Grants, work-study programs, and supplemental education opportunity grants. The federal government

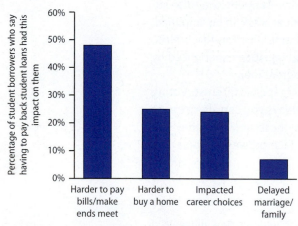

Note: Based on those who took out loans for postsecondary education and are not currently enrolled in school, n=332.

FIGURE 1.6 How Student Debt Impacts Borrowers.

Source: Pew Research Center, "Is College Worth It?" May 16, 2011, p. 26, www.pewsocialtrends.org/2011/05/15/is-college-worth-it/. Copyright © 2011 by PEW Research Center. Reproduced by permission.

spends an additional $136 billion acting as the primary lender of student loans to college students. Student loans used to be administered by banks, but in March 2010 Congress passed the Student Aid and Fiscal Responsibility Act (SAFRA), which ended this arrangement. Students applying for federal loans now deal directly with the federal government, saving an estimated $68 billion in subsidies to banks over the next decade.[17] SAFRA also increased spending for Pell Grants, community colleges, and historically black colleges. In 2012, however, deficit concerns led Congress to reduce Pell Grants back to 2008 levels.[18]

College affordability is a concern of all college students and deserves to be a concern for the nation generally. Yet Americans do not hear much discussion about education in the news media. A 2009 study by the Brookings Institution indicates that only 1.4 percent of coverage by television, websites, and radio deals with issues in education.[19] Does the lack of media attention pose a barrier to getting educational opportunity on the policy agenda? What can you do to make government responsive to concerns about education? Education policy is examined in more detail in Chapter 3, Federalism.

Economic Opportunity. Educational opportunity is linked to economic opportunity because the more education you have, the more you are likely to earn (see Figure 1.7). But will you be able to find a good job after graduation? In recent years college graduates did not fare as well as you are likely to do once the economy improves.

An educated citizenry with jobs that pay well and make a contribution to society is surely good for the entire nation. But does the government have an obligation to create economic opportunity? Should it intervene in business and the marketplace to equalize opportunity, or to preserve competition, or should government allow the economy to be shaped by market forces? Throughout this book, we examine the role of government in the economy by taking a hard look at its obligations as well as at federal and state budgets, deficit spending, the national debt, and tax policy. These concerns are currently at the top of the policy agenda because in recent years the federal government has run historically high deficits (has spent more than it takes in in revenue) that have produced a huge jump in the national debt (see Figure 1.8). In 2012, the national debt was more than $15 trillion.[20] To put this figure in context, consider that the United States has the seventh highest national debt, as a proportion of GDP, in the world (see Global Gateways on page 13).

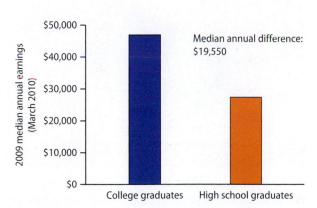

FIGURE 1.7 The Annual College Payoff.

Source: U.S. Census Bureau, Current Population Survey, Pew Research Center, p. 6.

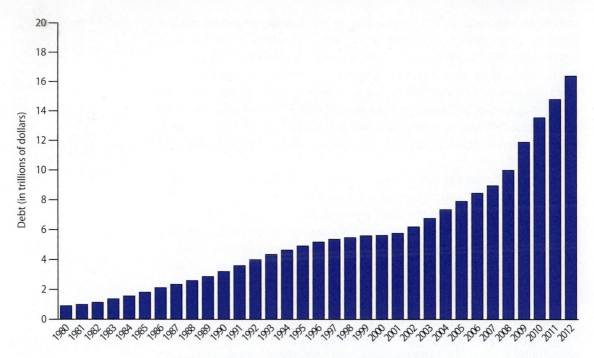

FIGURE 1.8 U.S. National Debt, 1980–2012.

Source: The White House, Office of Management and Budget, Table 7.1, Federal Debt at the End of Year: 1940–2017, U.S. Budget for FY 2013, http://www.whitehouse.gov/omb/budget/Historicals/.

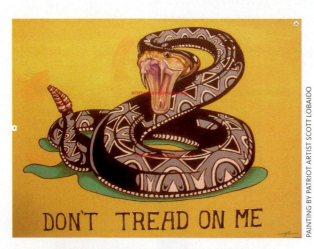

The "Don't Tread on Me" slogan adopted by the Tea Party movement has a long association with resistance and protest. The movement adopted its central symbol, the snake, to represent the colonies in the era of the American Revolution (see the image on page 67).

PAINTING BY PATRIOT ARTIST SCOTT LOBAIDO

Federal deficits and the national debt are also discussed in detail in Chapter 11, Congress, and in Chapter 12, The Presidency.

Paying off this debt will take generations; your great-grandchildren might very well still be paying for it when they reach adulthood. For you, now, the size of this debt means that the federal government has less funding and limited flexibility for investing in programs that might create economic opportunity, such as education, job training, and infrastructure projects. How the government pays off this debt affects you, too, especially changes in the tax system that may alter your future income and job prospects. Thus the federal budget and its ability to expand economic opportunity will directly affect your quality of life and standard of living in both the short run and the long run.

Participation Opportunity. How can you make your voice heard on education policy and economic policy issues that matter to you? During the years 2010–12, two seemingly opposite groups, the Tea Party and Occupy Wall Street, emerged to express opinions that their government was not responsive to their interests. The Tea Party movement grew out of localized groups of citizens who gathered to protest that the federal government has become too big, too expensive, and too intrusive. Tea Party members generally describe themselves as conservative. They aligned with Republican Party candidates in 2010 and 2012 and are now viewed as a crucial voting bloc in the Republican Party.

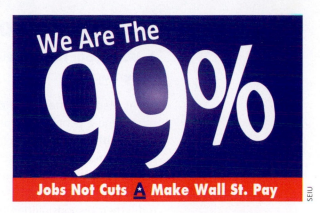

The slogan "We Are the 99%," adopted by Occupy Wall Street protests, calls attention to the concentration of income and wealth among the top 1 percent of earners, while everyone else—the 99 percent—struggles, losing jobs and even homes during economic downturns. Protesters demand jobs—not tax cuts for the wealthy—and social equality and economic justice more generally.

The Occupy movement grew out of a demonstration on New York City's Wall Street—the home of the New York Stock Exchange and symbolic capital of American finance—to protest the salaries and bonuses awarded to executives at money management firms. These protests arose at a time when employees were being laid off and unemployment doubled, shooting up from 5 to 10 percent in what has been called the Great Recession. The idea spread quickly, and organizers in cities throughout the country remained committed to "occupying" public spaces for as long as it took to draw attention to their concerns. They emphasized especially the large and growing gap between the rich and the poor. The Occupy protesters are not as explicitly political as their Tea Party counterparts, although it appears that most participants identify themselves as liberals.[21]

The connection between the Tea Party movement and the Occupy movement is that both exemplify the value of participation and the value the free expression of opinion in American democracy. The Tea Party movement claims credit for electing enough Republicans in 2010 to take control of the House of Representatives and subsequently the movement has maintained pressure on those members to try to reduce federal spending. Members of the Occupy movement have raised awareness of income inequality and have put pressure on Democrats to reform the nation's tax structure to bring more opportunity into the economic playing field. Each group has also been criticized for tactics and language that have been described as inflammatory. As a result, these movements also raise the question of whether and how it is appropriate to limit the free speech rights of citizens.

The point for college students is that participating—whether through exercising your right of expression, engaging in public discourse, or just voting—is a gateway to shaping your future.

Checkpoint

Can you:
- ☐ Compare self-interest to civic interest
- ☐ Describe public policies that encourage you to participate in American democracy

A Gateway to American Democracy

> **What your best gateway is for participation in American democracy**

James Madison offers one final thought: "Knowledge will forever govern igno-rance; and a people who mean to be their own governors, must arm them-selves with the power which knowledge gives."[22] To govern yourself, you will need to understand your government, to be informed about issues you care about, to participate in politics, and to be engaged in the nation's civic life. If the people do not meet the demands of democratic citizenship, if they do not fulfill their responsibilities, they will lose the freedoms they cherish.

We have written this book to give you the information you need to und-erstand your government—its gates and gateways. We hope it will also push you to evaluate whether government is working for you and for all the nation's citizens. How democratic are we? How can we be better? One thing is certain: We will not be better unless you are involved. The only way to make American democracy more responsive and more equal is by participating.

We, therefore, invite you—actually, we urge you—to enter the gateways to democracy. These gateways are open to you as an American. They empower you, as a citizen, to play an important role in American civic life, and they enable you to experience the amazing arena of American politics. We look forward to shar-ing the journey with you.

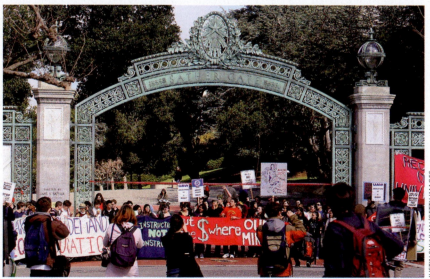

JUSTIN SULLIVAN/GETTY IMAGES

What you need to know about your text and online study tools to study efficiently and master the material

Each chapter of *Gateways to Democracy* is built to maximize efficient studying and help you get the most out of your course in American government. You'll find a "Gateways to Learning" section, like this one, at the end of every chapter. But these study materials are just part of the guidance for learning that *Gateways to Democracy* provides. Study aids start on the first page of every chapter, with a "Need to Know" list of learning objectives. Each objective is keyed to a major section of the chapter, and at the end of that section you'll find a "Checkpoint"—a list of questions that will allow you to test yourself to see if you've mastered specific content before moving on to the next section. Then in "Gateways to Learning" at the end of the chapter, you'll find

Need to Know

- What drove the colonists to seek independence
- What the major compromises at the Constitutional Convention were
- How the structure of the Constitution protects liberty
- Why the Antifederalists opposed the Constitution
- How the Constitution has stayed responsive to changing needs

Before the Constitution

> **What drove the colonists to seek independence**

From the beginning, Great Britain accorded the American colon subjects, a certain amount of self-rule. When the colonists perce liament and the king were blocking their participation in gov moved toward independen

Learning Outcomes

WHAT YOU NEED...

To Know	To Test Yourself
What drove the colonists to seek independence	• Define a constitution • State the colonists' grievances against Great Bri • Explain the key concepts in the Declaration of Independence • Describe the problems with the Articles of Confederation
What the major compromises of the	• Characterize the delegates to the Constitutional Con

Checkpoint

Can you:

- ☐ Define a constitution
- ☐ State the colonists' grievances against Great Britain
- ☐ Explain the key concepts in the Declaration of Independence
- ☐ Describe the problems with the Articles of Confederation

the "Need to Know" objectives and the "Checkpoint" questions repeated with an application for participating in American democracy. Use this Learning Outcomes chart as a chapter review.

Other review tools in "Gateways to Learning" are a ten-point summary and a list of key concepts. "Top Ten to Take Away" presents ten main ideas with cross-references to chapter pages where you'll find the substantive discussion

Key Concepts

amendment (p. 47). Why did the Framers make amending the Constitution so difficult?

Antifederalists (p. 50). What were the Antifederalist arguments against the proposed Constitution?

Articles of Confederation (p. 36). What were the

Electoral College (p. 42). Why does t provide for an Electoral College?

enumerated powers (p. 40). Why are enumerated?

federalism (p. 48). What does a federa

Federalists (p. 50). Who were the fede

general welfare clause (p. 52). What welfare clause do?

implied powers (p. 52). Does the con

Top Ten to Take Away

1. The colonists declared independence from Britain because they believed that the British Parliament and king were denying their rights as British subjects. (pp. 33–35)
2. Congress's powers under the Articles of Confederation were limited, and the structure the Articles established made governing difficult. (pp. 36–37)
3. In 1787 delegates from twelve states met in Philadelphia to amend the Articles; instead, they wrote a new Constitution. (pp. 37–42)
4. To secure the assent of all states represented at the Constitutional Convention, the delegates reached compromises between large and small states over representation, between northern and southern states over issues related to slavery, and between those who favored a strong national government and those who favored strong state governments in the balance of power between the two. (pp. 38–42)
5. This newly proposed Constitution was then sent to

6. The Constitution lays out the structure of democratic government and the means by which the Constitution can be amended. It reflects the Framers' attempt to establish a government powerful enough to ensure public order yet restrained enough to guarantee individual liberty. (pp. 44–50)
7. Debates over the ratification of the Constitution centered on a fear of consolidated federal authority over the states, the scope of executive and legislative power, and the lack of a bill of rights. (pp. 50–53)
8. To achieve ratification, the Federalists gave in to Antifederalist demands for a bill of rights, passing one as the first ten amendments to the Constitution. (pp. 52–54)
9. Subsequent amendments ended slavery, protected the rights of African Americans, and generally extended public participation in government while also

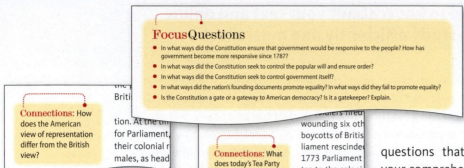

FocusQuestions

- In what ways did the Constitution ensure that government would be responsive to the people? How has government become more responsive since 1787?
- In what ways did the Constitution seek to control the popular will and ensure order?
- In what ways did the Constitution seek to control government itself?
- In what ways did the nation's founding documents promote equality? In what ways did they fail to promote equality?
- Is the Constitution a gate or a gateway to American democracy? Is it a gatekeeper? Explain.

Connections: How does the American view of representation differ from the British view?

Connections: What does today's Tea Party have in common with the Boston Tea Party?

of these topics. "Key Concepts" are boldfaced in the chapter text, defined on page, and amplified in "Gateways to Learning" with questions that will let you test your comprehension. In Chapter 1, however, definitions are consolidated in "Gateways to Learning" to serve as essential vocabulary that you can refer to throughout the course.

Understanding the workings of American government and your role as a citizen involves more than mastering content. Being a citizen means engaging in civic discourse about the issues that concern you. Starting with Chapter 2, "Focus Questions" at the end of the opening story set the framework for your evaluation of American democracy around the measures of government responsiveness and citizen equality; these questions are revisited in interpretive chapter conclusions that reflect on the gates and gateways in the democratic process. Throughout the chapter, margin questions—called Connections—ask you to think for yourself about the role and responsiveness of government, the meaning of citizen equality, and the gates and gateways in American democracy.

Gateways to Democracy also offers an online learning package called Aplia that can be your virtual tutor. Through interactive assignments, including videos, graphs, and political cartoons mapped to the "Need to Know" learning objectives, you can master the essential concepts of American government and understand how they apply to real life. Check out the "Construct Your Own Policy" activity in the following chapters of *Gateways to Democracy*. It's an example of how Aplia assignments strengthen your critical thinking skills. With Aplia,

aplia Construct Your Own Policy

1. Draft a constitutional amendment that would eliminate the death penalty in all fifty states and include an alternative sentence for crimes that might otherwise qualify for the death penalty.
2. Draft a set of five requirements for the imposition of the death penalty that would apply in all fifty states.

For more on the policy-making process, see Chapter 1.

you learn more, are better prepared to participate in class, and improve your grade. Aplia also includes an eBook. Get instant access via CengageBrain (http://www.cengagebrain.com) or via a printed access card in your bookstore.

gatewaystolearning

Top Ten to Take Away

1. American democracy offers many gateways to participation because, at its core, American government is about individuals and self-governance. (pp. 4–6)

2. There are also gates against public participation—obstacles to influence, institutional controls that limit access, and powerful interests that seem to block the people's will. (pp. 5–6)

3. To be an engaged and productive citizen, you need to take advantage of the gateways but also know how to navigate around the gates. (pp. 5–6, 19)

4. Democracy is self-government. In the American constitutional system, the people set up and agree on the basic rules and procedures that will govern them. (pp. 7–8)

5. The American constitutional system works to protect both liberty and order. The Constitution sets up a governmental structure with built-in constraints on power (gates) and multiple points of access to power (gateways). (pp. 8–10)

6. Power in American government is divided among three branches (executive, legislative, and judicial) and between the national government and the states. (p. 10)

7. American political culture favors individualism, and the U.S. economic system favors capitalism. (pp. 10–14)

8. American citizens may lean conservative or liberal, but most are moderates. (pp. 11–12)

9. With a government designed to constrain power and the popular will, and a citizenry divided into different perspectives and prizing individualism, the development of public policy is difficult and complex. (pp. 14–23)

10. One way to evaluate whether public policy is serving the people of the United States and to judge whether American democracy is working is to measure government responsiveness and citizen equality. (pp. 16–18)

Your Virtual Tutor
Master What You Need to Know and Test Yourself.

Learning Outcomes

WHAT YOU NEED...

To Know	To Test Yourself	To Participate
How the constitutional system balances liberty and order	• Make a connection between minority rights and democratic rule • Define social contract • Assess importance of political ideology • Name the key players in the policy-making process • Explain the differences between equality of opportunity and equality of outcome	• Understand the tension that surrounds issues related to government responsiveness and citizen equality
What the responsibilities of democratic citizenship are	• Compare self-interest to civic interest • Describe public policies that encourage you to participate in American democracy	• Recognize all the options for participation and their importance
What your best gateway is for participation in American democracy		• Decide how you will fulfill your citizenship responsibilities

Key Concepts for Understanding American Democracy

Use the list of key concepts for this chapter as a glossary for this course. Each entry below includes the page numbers on which a particular concept is introduced, as well as later chapters in which the concept is discussed. There is also a full glossary of key concepts at the back of the book.

autocracy: System of government in which the power to govern is concentrated in the hands of an individual ruler. (p. 16)

capitalism: Economic system in which businesses and key industries are privately owned and in which individuals, acting on their own or with others, are free to create businesses. (p. 11)

checks and balances: Government structure that authorizes each branch of government (executive, legislative, and judicial) to share powers with the other branches, thereby holding some scrutiny of and control over the other branches. (p. 10, Chapter 2)

civic interest: Concern for the well-being of society and the nation as a whole. (p. 19)

conservatives: Individuals who distrust government, believing that free markets offer better ways than government involvement to improve people's livelihood. In the social sphere, conservatives have more faith in government's ability to enforce traditional values. (p. 11, Chapter 6, 9)

democracy: System of government in which the supreme power is vested in the people and exercised by them either directly or indirectly through elected representatives. (p. 7)

direct democracy: Form of democracy in which political power is exercised directly by citizens. (p. 8, Chapter 3)

egalitarianism: Belief in human equality that disdains inherited titles of nobility and inherited wealth. (p. 14)

equality of opportunity: Expectation that citizens may not be discriminated against on account of race, gender, or national background and that every citizen should have an equal chance to succeed in life. (p. 17, Chapters 5, 14)

equality of outcome: Expectation that equality is achieved if results are comparable for all citizens regardless of race, gender, or national background or that such groups are proportionally represented in measures of success in life. (p. 18, Chapters 5, 14)

faction: Defined by Madison as any group that places its own interests above the aggregate interests of society. (p. 9, Chapters 8, 9)

federalism: System of government in which sovereignty is constitutionally divided between national and state governments. (p. 10, Chapters 2, 3)

Founders: The people who were involved in establishing the United States, whether at the time of the Declaration of Independence or the writing of the Constitution. (p. 8, Chapter 2)

Framers: The people who were involved in writing the Constitution. (p. 8, Chapter 2)

liberals: Individuals who have faith in government to improve people's lives, believing that private efforts are insufficient. In the social sphere, liberals usually support diverse lifestyles and tend to oppose any government action that seeks to shape personal choices. (p. 11, Chapter 6)

libertarians: Those who generally believe that government should refrain from acting to regulate either the economy or moral values. (p. 11)

majority rule: Idea that a numerical majority of a group should hold the power to make decisions binding on the whole group; a simple majority. (p. 7)

minority rights: Idea that majority should not be able to take certain fundamental rights away from those in the minority. (p. 7)

moderates: Individuals who are in the middle of the ideological spectrum and do not hold consistently strong views about whether government should be involved in people's lives. (p. 11, Chapter 6)

monarchy: System of government that assigns power to a single person who inherits that position and rules until death. (p. 16)

natural (unalienable) rights: Rights that every individual has and that government cannot legitimately take away. (p. 8, Chapter 4)

oligarchy: System of government in which the power to govern is concentrated in the hands of a powerful few, usually wealthy individuals. (p. 16)

order: Political value in which the rule of law is followed and does not permit actions that infringe on the well-being of others. (p. 7)

party identification: Psychological attachment to a political party; partisanship. (p. 10, Chapters 6, 9)

pluralism: Political system in which competing interests battle over the direction and content of important policy making. (p. 15, Chapter 8)

policy agenda: The second step in the policy-making process, in which a problem that has been identified gets the attention of policy makers. (p. 15)

policy enactment: The fourth step in the policy-making process, in which Congress passes a law that authorizes a specific governmental response to the problem. (p. 15)

policy evaluation: The final step in the policy-making process, in which the policy is evaluated for its effectiveness and efficiency; if changes are needed, the issue is placed back on the policy agenda, and the cycle starts again. (p. 15)

policy formulation: The third step in the policy-making process, in which those with a stake in the policy area propose and develop solutions to the problem. (p. 15)

policy implementation: The fifth step in the policy-making process, in which the executive branch develops the rules that will put the policy into action. (p. 15, Chapter 13)

political culture: A shared way of thinking about community and government and the relationship between them. (p. 11)

political equality: The idea that people should have equal amounts of influence in the political system. (p. 17)

political ideology: Set of coherent political beliefs that offers a philosophy for thinking about the scope of government. (p. 10, Chapters 6, 9)

politics: Process by which people make decisions about who gets what, when, and how. (p. 10)

populists: Those who oppose concentrated wealth and adhere to traditional moral values. (p. 11)

power elite: Small handful of decision makers who hold authority over a large set of issues. (p. 15, Chapter 10)

private goods: Goods or benefits provided by government in which most of the benefit falls to the individuals, families, or companies receiving them. (p. 17)

problem identification: The first step in the policy-making process, in which a problem in politics, the economy, or society is recognized as warranting government action. (p. 14)

public goods: Goods or benefits provided by government from which everyone benefits and from which no one can be excluded. (p. 17, Chapter 8)

public policy: Intentional actions of government designed to achieve a goal. (p. 14)

representative democracy: Form of democracy in which citizens elect public officials to make political decisions and formulate laws on their behalf. (p. 9, Chapter 2)

republic: Form of government in which power derives from citizens, but public officials make policy and govern according to existing law. (p. 9)

rule of law: Legal system with known rules that are enforced equally against all people. (p. 7)

separation of powers: Government structure in which authority is divided among branches (executive, legislative, and judicial), with each holding separate and independent powers and areas of responsibility. (p. 10, Chapter 2)

social contract: Theory that government has only the authority accorded it by the consent of the governed. (p. 8)

socialism: Economic system in which the government owns major industries. (p. 11)

stakeholders: Participants in the policy-making system who seek to influence the content and direction of legislation. (p. 15, every chapter)

> "An active and engaged citizen must have the ability to pressure politicians for a long period of time and have plenty of resources available."

**Gregory Watson,
University of Texas
at Austin**

2

The Constitution

Gregory Watson, a sophomore economics major at the University of Texas at Austin, had a term paper to write for a government class. It was 1982, the year in which the proposed Equal Rights Amendment to the U.S. Constitution, which would have prevented any state or the United States from denying equality of rights on account of sex, would expire unless three more states ratified it. Congress had proposed the amendment in 1972, setting a seven-year time frame for ratification by the states, following the two-step course established in the Constitution for the passage of amendments. The proposed amendment got off to a quick start, with twenty-two of the thirty-eight states necessary to pass the amendment approving it. Momentum slowed, however, as opposition to the amendment mobilized, and although Congress extended the deadline for three more years, no more states ratified the amendment. It was the legality of this extension—an "odd process," Watson called it, that fascinated him, and he decided to investigate the failure of the amendment.

While researching that issue, Watson discovered another unratified amendment, one that dated back to 1789. This amendment, proposed by James Madison, would prohibit any congressional pay raise from taking effect until after an ensuing election. In essence, it prevented members of Congress from awarding themselves pay raises within sessions; if they did vote an increase, they would have to stand for election before it went into effect. Six states ratified this amendment between 1789 and 1791, but no other state approved it until Ohio did so in 1873. Then, in 1978, Wyoming approved

aplia

Need to Know

- **What drove the colonists to seek independence**
- **What the major compromises at the Constitutional Convention were**
- **How the structure of the Constitution protects liberty**
- **Why the Antifederalists opposed the Constitution**
- **How the Constitution has stayed responsive to changing needs**

it. By that time, it would have needed the approval of thirty-eight states to go into effect, but it seems there was no deadline. Watson switched the topic of his paper to argue that the Constitution does not put time limits on ratification, that the congressional pay raise amendment was still pending, and that it should be passed, for it would help protect members of Congress against charges of corruption.

Watson got a C on the paper. "The professor told me this amendment could not pass. I was disgusted," he later told *USA Today*, and he set out to prove her wrong. Using $6,000 of his own money and voter anger over congressional pay raises, he launched a letter-writing campaign to targeted states. In 1983 Maine ratified the amendment, and other states followed. In 1992 Alabama became the thirty-eighth state to approve the amendment, and on May 14 of that year the archivist of the United States declared it the Twenty-Seventh Amendment. It states: "No law, varying the compensation for the services of the senators and representatives, shall take effect, until an election of representatives shall have intervened."

Watson's professor never changed his grade, but Watson pursued his interest in politics as an aide in the Texas legislature and continued to research the status of other amendments. When he discovered that Mississippi had never ratified the Thirteenth Amendment, abolishing slavery, he launched another letter-writing campaign that also brought success. In 1995 Mississippi officially approved the amendment.[1]

The amendment process that so interested Watson is the means by which the U.S. Constitution, the fundamental law undergirding the structure of American government, can be formally changed over time. Although the basic foundations of government remain essentially as they were established in the 1787 Constitution, amendments to the Constitution have provided guarantees of essential rights and liberties. They have outlawed slavery and guaranteed equality under the law. They have removed gates that limited voting. No constitution can remain impermeable to change if it is to regulate a society that continues to change. Gregory Watson used the gateway of citizen lobbying, in this case a letter-writing campaign, to bring about a change to the nation's fundamental law that had been two hundred years in the making.

In this chapter, we examine the governing documents prior to the Constitution, particularly the Articles of Confederation and its deficiencies. We also track the debates at the Constitutional Convention and afterward, as the people of the United States decided whether to ratify the new Constitution. They did ratify it, but almost immediately they amended it. After we examine the structure and philosophy behind the new Constitution, we consider its responsiveness, through both amendment and less formal procedures, to changing times.

FocusQuestions

- In what ways did the Constitution ensure that government would be responsive to the people? How has government become more responsive since 1787?
- In what ways did the Constitution seek to control the popular will and ensure order?
- In what ways did the Constitution seek to control government itself?
- In what ways did the nation's founding documents promote equality? In what ways did they fail to promote equality?
- Is the Constitution a gate or a gateway to American democracy? Is it a gatekeeper? Explain.

Before the Constitution

> **What drove the colonists to seek independence**

From the beginning, Great Britain accorded the American colonists, as British subjects, a certain amount of self-rule. When the colonists perceived that Parliament and the king were blocking their participation in government, they moved toward independence from Britain. They established a new national government under documents that included state constitutions and a national Articles of Confederation. In this section, we trace that process.

What Is a Constitution?

A **constitution** is the fundamental law undergirding the structure of government. In a modern democracy, a constitution sets forth the basic rules and procedures for how the people shall be governed, including the powers and structure of the government, as well as the rights retained by the people. The British constitution is not a single document but rather a series of documents, beginning with the Magna Carta in 1215, that define the rights of the people and limit the powers of the king, as well as a series of customs and precedents. Following the so-called Glorious Revolution of 1688–89, Parliament asserted its supremacy over the monarch. Thereafter, the monarch was forbidden to suspend the law, to levy taxes, and to maintain a standing army. These powers passed to Parliament, the legislature representing the people, and King William III acknowledged that he ruled not by divine right but by right of contract with his subjects. By the eighteenth century, British subjects believed that the British constitution guaranteed them certain rights, including the right not to be taxed without their consent and the right to be tried by a jury of their peers.

constitution: *Document or set of documents that establish the basic rules and procedures for how a society shall be governed.*

Toward Independence

The American colonists believed they had all the rights of British subjects. Thus they objected when, following the French and Indian War (1754–63), Great Britain tried to recoup some of the costs of defending the colonies by imposing regulations and taxes on them. The Sugar Act of 1764 set forth a long list of items that could be exported only to Great Britain, limiting competition for the colonists' goods. The Stamp Act of 1765 established a tax on virtually all forms of paper used by the colonists. Although Britain had previously levied import and export taxes on the colonies, this was the first direct tax by Britain on the colonists for products made and sold in America.

The colonists reacted angrily, forming trade associations to boycott, or refuse to buy, British goods. They also published pamphlets denouncing the loss of liberty. Led by Patrick Henry, they challenged not just the taxes

Connections: What rights do you think you have as an American? When did you last think about those rights?

themselves, but Parliament's authority to pass such measures. "Give me liberty," proclaimed Henry before the Virginia House of Burgesses, "or give me death." Soon enough, riots broke out against Stamp Act collectors, making enforcement impossible.

Britain repealed the Stamp Act in 1766, replacing it with the Townshend Acts, which imposed taxes on various imports. Having successfully fought off the direct internal taxes on paper, colonists mobilized against the new external (importation) taxes. Led by Samuel Adams, the Massachusetts legislature issued a letter declaring the Townshend Acts unconstitutional because they violated the principle of "no taxation without representation." The colonists thus began to insist that they had the right to participate in the political decisions that affected them, a right they believed they held as British subjects.

The British had a more limited view of both participation and representation. At the time, only about one in six British adult males had the right to vote for Parliament, whereas two-thirds of free American adult males could vote for their colonial representatives.[2] Women and children could not vote anywhere; males, as heads of the family, were assumed to be able to represent them.

Aggrieved by taxation without representation, the colonists continued to resist the Townshend Acts. Britain responded by dissolving the Massachusetts legislature and seizing a ship belonging to John Hancock, one of the leaders of the resistance. Britain also sent troops to quell the resistance, but the presence of soldiers during peacetime aggravated tensions. British soldiers fired on a threatening crowd in 1770, killing five colonists and wounding six others in what became known as the Boston Massacre. With boycotts of British goods costing Britain far more than the taxes raised, Parliament rescinded all of the Townshend Act taxes except the one on tea. In 1773 Parliament granted the East India Company the exclusive right to sell tea to the colonies, and the company then granted local monopolies in the colonies. Angered by both the tax and the monopoly, colonists once again took action. Disguised as Indians, they dumped a shipload of tea in Boston Harbor. In 1774 Britain responded to the Boston Tea Party with the Coercive Acts, which, among other things, gave the royal governor the right to select the upper house of the Massachusetts legislature. The Coercive Acts also denied Massachusetts the right to try British officials charged with capital offenses. These acts convinced many colonists that their liberty was at stake and that rebellion and independence were the only alternatives to British tyranny.[3]

In an attempt to present a more united front about colonial grievances, Benjamin Franklin proposed a congress. The First Continental Congress, with delegates chosen by the colonial legislatures, met in Philadelphia in 1774. It rejected a reconciliation plan with England and instead sent King George III a list of grievances. It also adopted a very successful compact

Connections: How does the American view of representation differ from the British view?

Connections: What does today's Tea Party have in common with the Boston Tea Party?

among the colonies not to import any English goods. Finally, it agreed to meet again as the Second Continental Congress in May 1775. This Second Continental Congress acted as the common government of the states between 1775 and 1781.

In April 1775, following skirmishes with British troops in Lexington and Concord, outside of Boston, the Second Continental Congress named George Washington commander of a new Continental Army. In 1776, with hostilities under way, Thomas Paine penned his influential pamphlet *Common Sense*, which called for independence from Britain. "There is something very absurd, in supposing a continent to be perpetually governed by an island," he argued.[4] *Common Sense* was the most widely distributed pamphlet of its time, and it helped convince many Americans that independence was the only way they could secure their right to self-government.

The Declaration of Independence

In June 1776 the Continental Congress debated an independence resolution but postponed a vote until July. Meanwhile, it instructed Thomas Jefferson and others to draft a **Declaration of Independence**. Congress approved the Declaration of Independence on July 4. Jefferson's Declaration relied in part on the writings of John Locke in asserting that people had certain natural (or unalienable) rights that government could not take away, including the right to life and liberty.

The Declaration that Jefferson penned was a radical document. It declared the right of the people to alter or abolish governments that do not meet the needs of the people; it declared the colonies independent from Britain; it contained a stirring call for equality, human rights, and public participation in government that, though not at the time legally enforceable, has inspired generations of Americans seeking to make these ideas a reality.

> We hold these truths to be self-evident: That all men are created equal; that they are endowed by their Creator with certain unalienable rights; that among these are life, liberty, and the pursuit of happiness; that, to secure these rights, governments are instituted among men, deriving their just powers from the consent of the governed; that whenever any form of government becomes destructive of these ends, it is the right of the people to alter or to abolish it, and to institute new government, laying its foundation on such principles, and organizing its powers in such form, as to them shall seem most likely to effect their safety and happiness.

The Declaration went on to list grievances against King George III, including suspending popularly elected colonial legislatures, imposing taxes without representation, and conducting trials without juries. It then declared the united colonies to be thirteen "free and independent states." (The full text of the Declaration of Independence is in the Appendix.)

Connections: Was the American Revolution really about taxation, or was it about something else?

Declaration of Independence: *1776 document declaring American independence from Great Britain and calling for equality, human rights, and citizen participation.*

Connections: What has the Declaration of Independence's statement on equality meant to Americans? How are Americans equal, and not equal, today?

Members of the Second Continental Congress voted to approve the Declaration of Independence on July 4, 1776, though only John Hancock, president of the Congress, signed it that day.

 Articles of Confederation: *Initial governing authority of the United States, 1781–88.*

Even before the Declaration, the Continental Congress advised the colonies to adopt new constitutions "under the authority of the people." Reacting against the limitation on rights imposed by the British monarch and by royal governors in the colonies, these new state constitutions severely limited executive power but set few limits on legislative authority. At the same time, Americans made little effort to establish a national political authority, as most Americans considered themselves primarily citizens of the states in which they lived. Nevertheless, the Continental Congress needed legal authority for its actions, and in 1777 its members proposed a governing document called the **Articles of Confederation**.

© FRANCIS G. MAYER/CORBIS

The Articles of Confederation

The Articles required unanimous consent of the states for adoption, which did not occur until 1781, just a few months before American victory in the Revolutionary War. They formally established "the United States of America," in contrast to the Declaration, which was a pronouncement of "Thirteen United States of America." According to the Declaration, each of the thirteen independent states had the authority to do all "acts and things which independent states may of right do," such as waging war, establishing alliances, and concluding peace. Thus the states retained all powers not expressly granted to Congress under the Articles.

Moreover, those expressly granted powers were extremely limited. Congress had full authority over foreign, military, and Indian affairs. It could decide boundary and other disputes between the states, coin money, and establish post offices. But Congress did not have the authority to regulate commerce or, indeed, any authority to operate directly over citizens of the United States. For example, Congress could not tax citizens or products (such as imports) directly; it could only request (but not command) revenues from the states.

In addition to limiting powers, the Articles made governing difficult. Each state had one vote in Congress, with the consent of nine of the thirteen required for most important matters, including borrowing and spending money. Amending the Articles required the unanimous consent of the states. The Articles established no judicial branch, with the minor exception that Congress could establish judicial panels on an ad hoc basis to hear appeals involving disputes between states and to hear cases involving crimes on the high seas. There was no separate executive branch, but Congress had the authority to establish an executive committee along with a rotating president who would manage the general affairs of the United States when Congress was not in session.[5]

Connections: Why didn't the Articles of Confederation work as a governing document?

These deficiencies led to predictable problems. With insufficient funds, the nation's debts went unpaid, hampering its credit. Without a centralized authority to regulate commerce, states taxed imports from other states, stunting economic growth. Lack of military power allowed Spain to block commercial access to the Mississippi River. Barbary pirates off the shores of Tripoli captured American ships and held their crews for ransom.

While the government of the United States suffered from too little authority, James Madison, Thomas Jefferson, and others came to believe that the governments of the states possessed too much authority. Popularly elected legislatures with virtually no checks on their authority passed laws rescinding private debts and creating trade barriers against other states. They also began taking over both judicial and executive functions. With the United States in desperate financial straits, James Madison proposed a convention of states to consider granting the national government the power to tax and to regulate trade. Only five states showed up at this 1786 Annapolis Convention, preventing it from accomplishing much.

As the Annapolis Convention took place, word spread of a revolt in western Massachusetts that made the weakness of the national government all too clear. Revolutionary War hero Daniel Shays and several thousand distressed farmers forced courts to close and threatened federal arsenals. Not until February 1787 did Massachusetts put down Shays's Rebellion. The revolt helped convince the states that, on top of the Articles' other problems, there was too much freedom and not enough order, which neither the federal nor the state governments could ensure. The Annapolis Convention thus issued an invitation to all thirteen states to meet in Philadelphia in May 1787 to consider revising the Articles of Confederation. Only Rhode Island declined the invitation.

© BETTMANN/CORBIS

Daniel Shays led a protest movement of debt-ridden farmers facing foreclosures on their homes and farms. Demanding lower taxes and the issuance of paper money, they engaged in mob violence to force the Massachusetts courts to close.

Checkpoint

Can you:

☐ Define a constitution

☐ State the colonists' grievances against Great Britain

☐ Explain the key concepts in the Declaration of Independence

☐ Describe the problems with the Articles of Confederation

The Constitutional Convention

> **What the major compromises at the Constitutional Convention were**

The delegates who met in Philadelphia were charged with amending the Articles of Confederation so that the national government could work more effectively. Almost immediately, however, they moved beyond that charge and began debating a brand new constitution. To complete that newly proposed constitution, the delegates needed to reach compromises between large and small states over representation, between northern and southern states over issues related to slavery, and between those who favored a strong national government and those who favored strong state governments in the balance of power between the two. The document they created, which was then sent to the states for ratification, is, with subsequent amendments, the same Constitution Americans live by today. (The full text of the Constitution of the United States is in the Appendix.)

The Delegates

The fifty-five delegates to the **Constitutional Convention** of 1787 represented large (Virginia) and small (Delaware) states. They represented states in the south with large slave populations (South Carolina, 43 percent of total population), states in the north with small slave populations (Connecticut, 1 percent of population), but only one state (Massachusetts) with no slaves.[6] Not all the delegates were rich, but none were poor. All were white, and all were male. Most were in their thirties or forties, and a majority had legal training.[7] Not surprisingly, the delegates' behavior at the Convention substantially reflected their interests and the statewide interests they represented.[8] The delegates included James Madison, who would draft much of the Constitution; George Washington, the former commander of the Continental Army who presided over the Convention; and Benjamin Franklin, the scientist, inventor, diplomat, and revered elder statesman (see Figure 2.1).

The Convention's rules granted each state one vote, regardless of the size of the state or the number of delegates it sent. To secure the assent of all states represented at the Convention, compromises had to be reached that would satisfy the various interests represented there. To keep the gateways to compromise open, the delegates voted to keep their deliberations secret until they completed their work. This decision also created a gate that limited popular influence.

Large versus Small States

Upon the opening of the Philadelphia Convention in May 1787, Edmund Randolph of Virginia presented the delegates with James Madison's radical proposal for a new government. Known as the Virginia Plan, Madison's proposal included a strong central government that could operate directly on the citizens of the United States without the states acting as intermediaries. The legislative branch would consist of two chambers: a lower chamber elected by the people and an upper chamber elected by the lower chamber. Each chamber would have representation proportional to the populations of the states: the larger the population, the more representatives a state would have. The

John Jay (1745–1829)	John Adams (1735–1826)	Thomas Jefferson (1743–1826)	Benjamin Franklin (1706–90)	James Madison (1751–1836)	George Washington (1732–99)	Alexander Hamilton (1755–1804)
of New York was a delegate to the First Continental Congress and president of the Second, though he was not present when the Declaration of Independence was signed. He was U.S. minister to Spain from 1780 to 1782 and a negotiator of the peace treaty with Britain in 1783. He was an author of the *Federalist Papers* and the first chief justice of the Supreme Court. *The Granger Collection, New York*	of Massachusetts was a delegate to the First and Second Continental Congresses and, with his cousin Samuel, a Signer of the Declaration of Independence. He was a diplomat to France in 1778–79, a negotiator of the peace treaty with Britain in 1783, and U.S. minister to Britain in 1785–88. He was vice president under George Washington and president from 1797 to 1801. *Réunion des Musées Nationaux / Art Resource, NY*	of Virginia, was a delegate to the Second Continental Congress and drafted the Declaration of Independence. He was U.S. minister to France in 1785–89, vice president under John Adams, and president from 1801 to 1809. *© Corbis*	was born in Boston but moved to Philadelphia. He was a delegate to the Second Continental Congress and helped draft the Declaration of Independence. He was a diplomat to France in 1776–85 and a negotiator of the peace treaty with Britain in 1783. He was a member of the Constitutional Convention. *National Portrait Gallery, Smithsonian Institution / Art Resource, NY*	of Virginia was a delegate to the Second Continental Congress. He was an influential member of the Constitutional Convention and an author of the *Federalist Papers,* and he was instrumental in drafting the Bill of Rights. He was president from 1809 to 1817. *The White House Historical Association (White House Collection)*	of Virginia was a delegate to the First and Second Continental Congresses and was commander of the Continental Army. He presided over the Constitutional Convention and was president from 1789 to 1797. *© Bequest of Mrs. Benjamin Ogle Tayloe; Collection of The Corcoran Gallery of Art*	who was born in the West Indies but attended college in New York, served on General Washington's staff during the Revolution. At the Constitutional Convention, he advocated a strong central government. He was an author of the *Federalist Papers* and the first secretary of the treasury. *The Granger Collection, New York.*

FIGURE 2.1 Founders and Framers.

The Founders were the leaders of the American Revolution and the new United States. The Framers were those who wrote the Constitution. All Framers were Founders, but not all Founders were Framers. Only some of the Founders were Signers, the people who signed the Declaration of Independence.

© CENGAGE LEARNING

legislature would have general authority to pass laws that would "promote the harmony" of the United States and could veto laws passed by the states. The Virginia Plan proposed a national executive and a national judiciary, both chosen by the legislature. A council of revision, composed of the executive and judicial members, would have final approval over all legislative acts.

Madison's proposals astonished many of the delegates from the smaller states and some from the larger states as well. To counter them, on June 15 William Patterson of New Jersey presented the Convention with the so-called New Jersey Plan, which strengthened the Articles by providing Congress with the authority to regulate commerce and to directly tax imports and paper items. It also proposed a national executive chosen by the legislature and a national judiciary chosen by the executive.[9] Each state would retain equal representation in Congress.

The convention debated these measures, with the question of proportional or equal representation generating enormous controversy. Madison insisted that proportional representation for both chambers was the only fair system, and the small states insisted that they would walk out if they lost their equal vote. Roger Sherman of Connecticut proposed what became known as the **Connecticut Compromise**. The makeup of the lower chamber, the House of Representatives, would be proportional to population, but the upper chamber, the Senate, would represent each state equally.

Nation versus State

While the question of representation threatened the Convention, there was substantial agreement over the nationalist platform that Madison supported. The delegates rejected the New Jersey Plan, which would have continued government under the Articles.

The delegates did not approve the Virginia Plan in full, but the plan substantially influenced the proposed Constitution. Under the new Constitution, the government had the authority to operate directly on the citizens of the United States. Congress was not granted general legislative power, but rather **enumerated powers**, that is, a list of powers it could employ. Among its enumerated powers were the authority to tax to provide for the general welfare; to regulate commerce among the states and with foreign nations; to borrow money; to declare war, raise armies, and maintain a navy; and to make all laws "necessary and proper for carrying into Execution the foregoing Powers." The tax and commerce powers were among those missing from the Articles.

Congress did not receive the authority to veto state laws, but the Constitution declared that national law would be supreme over state law, bound state judges to that decision, and created a national judiciary that would help ensure such rulings. Moreover, the Convention set explicit limits on state authority, prohibiting the states from carrying on foreign relations, coining money, and impairing certain rights. Finally, the Convention approved a national executive (that is, the president) who could serve as a unifying force throughout the land. Table 2.1 presents the components of the Virginia Plan, the New Jersey Plan, and the proposed Constitution.

North versus South

Resolving the question of nation versus state proved less difficult than resolving the question of representation. More difficult still were questions related to slavery. Although slavery existed in every state except Massachusetts, the overwhelming majority of slaves, nearly 95 percent, were in the southern states.[10] As Madison put it, "The States were divided into different interests not by their difference of size, but principally from their having or not having slaves."[11] Not all northern delegates at the Convention opposed slavery, but those who were abolitionists wanted an immediate ban on importing slaves from Africa, prohibitions against the expansion of slavery into the western

Connecticut Compromise: *Compromise on legislative representation whereby the lower chamber is based on population and the upper chamber provides equal representation to the states.*

Connections: What compromises made the Constitution possible? Is compromise, as a political strategy, good or bad for democracy? Why is it out of favor today?

enumerated powers: *Powers expressly granted to Congress by the Constitution.*

Connections: Were the delegates right or wrong to compromise on slavery?

TABLE 2.1 The Virginia and New Jersey Plans Compared to the Constitution

Issue	Virginia Plan	New Jersey Plan	Constitution
Operation	Directly on people	Through the states	Directly on people
Legislative structure	Bicameral and proportional	Unicameral and equal	Bicameral, with lower chamber proportional and upper chamber equal
Legislative authority	General: power to promote the harmony of the United States	Strict enumerated powers of the Articles of Confederation, plus power to regulate commerce and limited power to tax	Broad enumerated powers
Check on legislative authority	Council of revision	None	Presidential veto, with possibility of a two-thirds override
Executive	Unitary national executive chosen by legislature	Plural national executive chosen by legislature	Unitary national executive chosen by Electoral College
Judiciary	National judiciary chosen by legislature	National judiciary chosen by executive	National judiciary chosen by president with advice and consent of Senate

territories, and the adoption of a plan for the gradual freeing of slaves. Delegates from Georgia and South Carolina, whose states would never accept the Constitution on these terms, wanted guaranteed protections for slavery and the slave trade and no restrictions on slavery in the territories. To secure a Constitution, compromises were necessary.

Many supporters of slavery recognized the horrors of the foreign slave trade, and by 1779 all states except North Carolina, South Carolina, and Georgia had banned it. Leaving the authority to regulate the foreign slave trade to Congress would inevitably have resulted in its being banned everywhere and probably would have kept those three states from joining the union. Thus, a slave trade compromise prohibited Congress from stopping the slave trade until 1808. This compromise also resulted in a ban on taxing exports, a substantial benefit to the export-driven economies of the southern states.

A second compromise involved how slaves should be counted when calculating population for purposes of representation. Madison's Virginia Plan based representation on the number of free inhabitants of each state, whereas the southernmost slave states wanted slaves to be fully counted for purposes of representation. Delegates from the northern states, on the other hand, argued that slave states, which by definition denied the humanity of slaves, should not benefit by receiving extra representation based on the number of slaves that they had. Under the Articles, taxes requested of the states were based on the population of each state, with five slaves counting as three people. The Convention agreed to use this **three-fifths** formula not

 **three-fifths compromise:**
Compromise over slavery at the Constitutional Convention that granted states extra representation in the House of Representatives based on their number of slaves at the ratio of three-fifths.

just for representation, but also for whatever direct or population taxes the national government might choose to levy.

A third compromise involved slavery in the western territories, and it came not from the Convention but from the government under the Articles, which passed the Northwest Ordinance in July 1787. This ordinance, which established the means for governing the western lands north of the Ohio River (eventually the states of Ohio, Indiana, Illinois, Michigan, and Wisconsin, and parts of Minnesota), prohibited slavery in this territory but also provided that fugitive slaves who escaped to the territory would be returned to their owners. The Constitution repeated these provisions.

With the precedent of prohibiting slavery in the Northwest Territory established in the Northwest Ordinance, the Convention gave Congress the right to regulate the territories of the United States without mentioning whether slavery could be allowed or prohibited. Silences such as this often allow compromises to be reached in instances where explicit statements would force one side or the other to object.

Gates against Popular Influence

Compared to the British constitutional system, the 1787 Constitution provided direct and indirect gateways for popular involvement (see Figure 2.2). Nevertheless, the Framers did not trust the people to have complete control over choosing the government. In two important ways—the election of the president and the election of the Senate—the Constitution limited popular control. One of these gates against the people's participation—the election of the president through the **Electoral College**—remains in effect today. (See Chapter 10, Elections, Campaigns, and Voting, for a full discussion of the Electoral College and its consequences for presidential elections and campaigns.) State legislatures also selected U.S. senators. The Framers feared that a Congress elected directly by the people would be too responsive to the popular will. The indirect election of senators was thus intended to serve as a check on the popular will. In 1913 the Seventeenth Amendment granted the people the right to elect senators directly.

The Ratification Process

With agreements reached on representation in Congress, federal or national power, and slavery, the delegates made a few final decisions. First,

Electoral College: *The presidential electors, selected to represent the votes of their respective states, who meet every four years to cast the electoral votes for president and vice president.*

Connections: Why did the delegates set up gates against citizen participation? Whose participation did they not consider at all?

Bill of Rights: *First ten amendments to the Constitution, which provide basic political rights.*

FIGURE 2.2 Relative Balance of Freedom and Order.
© CENGAGE LEARNING

TABLE 2.2 Deficiencies of the Articles of Confederation and Constitutional Remedies

Deficiency in the Articles of Confederation	Remedy in the Constitution
Legislative branch could not regulate commerce	Congress can regulate commerce "among the states"
Legislative branch could only request taxes from states	Congress can directly raise taxes from individuals
Approval of nine of thirteen states needed for passage of major legislation	Approval of a majority of both legislative chambers needed for passage of all legislation; a two-thirds majority needed to override presidential vetoes
No permanent executive branch	A "President of the United States"
No permanent judicial branch	A Supreme Court plus other inferior courts that Congress can establish
Unanimity for constitutional amendments	Approval of two-thirds of each chamber plus three-fourths of the states
Few limits on state authority, mostly over foreign affairs	States limited in foreign affairs, plus could not suppress certain rights through bills of attainder, *ex post facto* laws, etc.

despite the urging of George Mason of Virginia, the delegates chose not to include a **Bill of Rights**—a listing of rights retained by the people that Congress did not have the authority to take away, such as freedom of speech and freedom of religion. Because Congress had enumerated powers only, and because the authority to regulate speech, religion, and other freedoms was not among the powers granted to Congress, delegates believed there was no need to prohibit Congress from abridging such rights.

Second, the delegates needed a method for ratifying, or granting final approval of, the Constitution. The delegates at the Constitutional Convention chose to send the proposed Constitution to the states for approval via special ratifying conventions to be chosen by the people. The Constitution would take effect among those states approving it when ratified by nine of the thirteen states. In September 1787, with these final steps taken, delegates to the Constitutional Convention believed they had produced a constitution that remedied the deficiencies of the Articles (see Table 2.2), and they voted on the final document. Some of the delegates had left by September, but thirty-nine signed the document, with only three refusing to do so. Crucially, given Convention rules, a majority of the delegates from each of the states voted yes.

Connections: Do the people today retain the right to institute new government?

Checkpoint

Can you:

☐ Characterize the delegates to the Constitutional Convention

☐ Explain how the interests of large and small states differed

☐ State why the Convention rejected the Virginia Plan

☐ Explain how the interests of the North and the South differed

☐ Describe how the 1787 Constitution protected against too much popular influence

☐ Recall who would ratify the new constitution

Government under the Constitution

> ## How the structure of the Constitution protects liberty

The final document sent to the states for ratification laid out a structure of democratic government and proposed mechanisms whereby the Constitution could be amended. It also reflected the Framers' attempt to establish a government powerful enough to ensure public order yet containing enough gateways to guarantee individual liberty.

The Structure of Government

The Constitution established three branches of government: the legislative, the executive, and the judicial.

Connections: Why did the delegates establish three branches of government?

The Legislative Branch. The legislative branch makes the laws. The Constitution established a bicameral Congress, consisting of two chambers. The lower chamber, the House of Representatives, is proportioned by population (until the Thirteenth Amendment, the slave population was added to the free population according to the three-fifths formula described above). Members of the House are elected for two-year terms directly by the people, with voting eligibility determined by each state.

The upper chamber, the Senate, consists of two senators from each state, regardless of size. Designed to serve as a check on the popular will, which would be expressed in the House of Representatives, state legislatures chose senators until in 1913 the Seventeenth Amendment granted the people of each state the exclusive right to do so.

Bills to levy taxes have to originate in the House, but other bills may originate in either chamber. To become law, a bill has to pass each chamber in identical form. It is then presented to the president for his signature. If the president signs the bill, it becomes law, but if he disapproves, he can **veto** the bill. Congress can then override the veto by a two-thirds majority in each chamber.

veto: *Authority of the president to block legislation passed by Congress. Congress can override a veto by a two-thirds majority in each chamber.*

Article I, Section 8 of the Constitution limits Congress's authority to an eighteen-paragraph list, or enumeration, of certain powers. The first paragraph grants Congress the authority "to Collect Taxes . . . to pay the Debts and provide for the common Defence and general Welfare of the United States." Paragraphs 2 through 17 grant additional powers such as borrowing and coining money, regulating commerce, and raising an army. Then paragraph 18 grants Congress the authority to pass all laws "necessary and proper for carrying into Execution the foregoing Powers."

Additionally, the Constitution gives the House the authority to impeach—to bring charges against—the president and other federal officials. The Senate has the sole authority to try cases of impeachment, with a two-thirds vote required for removal from office. The Senate also has the sole authority to ratify treaties, which also require a two-thirds vote, and to confirm executive and judicial branch appointments by majority vote.

The Executive Branch.

The executive branch of government consists of a unitary president, chosen for a four-year term by an Electoral College. The Electoral College itself is chosen in a manner set by the legislature of each state. Eventually, every state gave the people the power to vote for its electors. Each state receives the number of electors equal to its number of representatives plus senators. If no person receives a majority of the Electoral College vote, the election goes to the House of Representatives, where each state gets one vote. The Electoral College also chooses a vice president who presides over the Senate, casting votes in case of a tie. The vice president becomes president following the death, resignation, removal, or disability of the president.

Because the Framers believed that the legislative branch would naturally be stronger than the executive branch, they did not feel the need to enumerate the executive powers as they did the legislative powers. Recall that Congress does not have a general legislative authority, but only those legislative powers granted under the Constitution. In contrast, the Constitution provides the president with a general grant of "the executive Power" and certain specific powers, including the right to veto legislation and grant pardons. The president also is commander in chief of the armed forces. With the advice and consent of the Senate, the president makes treaties and appoints ambassadors, judges, and other public officials. The president leads the executive branch of government, being charged with taking care that the laws are faithfully executed.

The Judicial Branch.

The Constitution vests the judicial authority of the United States in one Supreme Court and other inferior courts that Congress might choose to establish. The president appoints judges with the advice and consent of the Senate. They serve "during good Behaviour," which, short of impeachment, means a life term.

The Constitution extends the authority of the federal courts to hear cases involving certain classes of parties to a suit—cases involving the United States, ambassadors, and other public ministers; suits between two or more states or citizens from different states—and certain classes of cases, most notably cases arising under the Constitution, laws, and treaties of the United States. In the historic case *Marbury v. Madison* (1803), the Supreme Court took this authority to hear cases arising under the Constitution of the United States to establish the power of **judicial review**, the authority of the Court to strike down any law passed by Congress when the Court believes the law violates the Constitution (see Supreme Court Cases: *Marbury v. Madison*).[12]

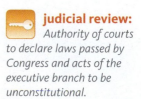

judicial review: *Authority of courts to declare laws passed by Congress and acts of the executive branch to be unconstitutional.*

supremecourtcases

Marbury v. Madison (1803)

QUESTION: Does Congress have the authority to expand the Supreme Court's original jurisdiction beyond that granted by the Constitution?

ORAL ARGUMENT: February 10, 1803

DECISION: February 23, 1803 (read at http://www.findlaw.com/casecode/supreme.html)

OUTCOME: No, thus establishing the power of judicial review (4–0)

It is hard to imagine a more momentous decision resulting from what the historian John A. Garraty called this "trivial squabble over a few petty political plums."* In the closing days of President John Adams's administration, the Federalist Adams nominated William Marbury to the position of justice of the peace for the District of Columbia, and the Federalist Senate confirmed the nomination. But in the hectic final hours of Adams's administration, Secretary of State John Marshall neglected to deliver the commission. When Democratic-Republican Thomas Jefferson became president, his new secretary of state, James Madison, refused to deliver the commission, thus keeping Marbury from assuming his office.

Marbury filed suit at the Supreme Court, believing that the Judiciary Act of 1789 expanded the Court's original jurisdiction to give the Court the authority to hear cases involving writs of *mandamus* (orders to government officials to undertake specific

* John A. Garraty, *"Marbury v. Madison:* The Case of the 'Missing' Commissions," in *Quarrels That Have Shaped the Constitution,* ed. John A. Garraty (New York: Harper and Row, 1964), 13.

acts) as an original matter, that is, as a trial, and not just as an appeal. The Supreme Court declared that, because the Constitution precisely specified which types of cases the Supreme Court could hear as an original matter, the section of the Judiciary Act that expanded the Court's original jurisdiction conflicted with the Constitution. Moreover, if a law conflicts with the Constitution, either the law is supreme over the Constitution, or the Constitution is supreme over the law. The Court ruled that it must be the case that the Constitution is supreme over the law. Finally, the Court declared that the judiciary would decide such issues. "It is emphatically the province and duty of the judicial department to say what the law is," wrote Marshall, who in the closing days of the Adams administration had been nominated and confirmed as chief justice of the United States. The Supreme Court would not order Madison to deliver the commission to Marbury. The Court in *Marbury* granted itself the momentous authority of judicial review, the power to strike down laws passed by Congress on the grounds that those laws violate the Constitution.

- **How does judicial review provide a gateway to participation in the political system?**
- **Why is it the judiciary's job to determine whether a law is unconstitutional?**

The Amendment Process

The Constitution provides two paths for changing the Constitution, or **amendment**. The first path requires a two-thirds vote in each chamber of Congress, followed by the approval of three-fourths of the states. That state-wide approval can be attained either through the state legislatures or through state ratifying conventions, as directed by Congress. The second path allows two-thirds of the states to request a national constitutional convention that could propose amendments that would go into effect when approved by three-fourths of the states (see Figure 2.3). Again, this approval could be obtained through state legislatures or through state ratifying conventions. Additionally, the Constitution prohibits amendments that would deny any state an equal vote in the Senate or any amendment that would have allowed a banning of the foreign slave trade before 1808.

Both paths for amending the Constitution are complex and difficult, and that has kept the Constitution from being modified over popular but short-lived issues. Recently, these have included proposed amendments that would require a balanced federal budget, allow the federal or state governments to prosecute those who burn the American flag, and prohibit states from recognizing same-sex marriages. The Equal Rights Amendment that interested Gregory Watson did not pass, nor did a proposed 1978 amendment granting the District of Columbia representation in Congress, but the Twenty-Seventh Amendment, which Watson revived, did.

The Partition of Power

In attempting to explain and justify the constitutional structure, James Madison wrote of "the necessary partition of power among the several departments as laid down in the constitution" (see *Federalist* 51 in the Appendix). He acknowledged that "a dependence on the people is no doubt the primary control on the government," and thus

amendment:
Formal process of changing the Constitution.

> **Connections:** Why did the delegates make it hard to amend the Constitution?

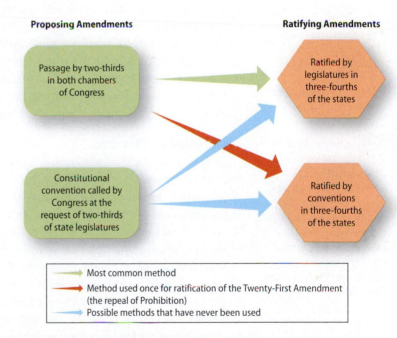

FIGURE 2.3 **Amending the Constitution.**

An amendment can be proposed by two-thirds of each chamber of Congress or by a constitutional convention called by two-thirds of state legislatures. Either way, ratification requires three-quarters of the states to approve the amendment. Why do you think the methods indicated by the blue arrows have never been used?

© CENGAGE LEARNING

federalism:
System of government in which sovereignty is constitutionally divided between national and state governments.

separation of powers:
Government structure in which authority is divided among branches (executive, legislative, and judicial), with each holding separate and independent powers and areas of responsibility.

Connections: Has the division of power between the national government and the states hindered or advanced democracy?

checks and balances:
Government structure that authorizes each branch of government (executive, legislative, and judicial) to share powers with the other branches, thereby holding some scrutiny of and control over the other branches.

elections serve as the primary means of ensuring that the government is responsive to the wishes of the people. If it is not, the people can vote for a new government. Under the Constitution, the people have direct authority to elect the House of Representatives. But to prevent the majority from imposing oppressive laws on the minority, the rest of the government was chosen indirectly: the Senate by the state legislatures, the president by the Electoral College, and judges by the president, with the advice and consent of the Senate.

Lest the people not be sufficient to keep government under control, however, the Constitution had built in "auxiliary precautions," as Madison called them, to make sure government could not concentrate power. Thus, **federalism** splits power between nation and state, **separation of powers** divides the powers that remained with the national government among the three branches of government, and **checks and balances** give each branch some authority over the powers of the other branches. Even after all this, the Constitution places additional limits on both federal and state powers.

Federalism.   The first means of preventing a concentration of power was to divide authority between the national and state governments. Rather than provide Congress with a general power to legislate in the national interest, the Constitution granted Congress enumerated powers. All powers not granted to Congress remained with the states. This division of power is made explicit in the Tenth Amendment to the Constitution: "The powers not delegated to the United States by the Constitution, nor prohibited by it to the States, are reserved to the States respectively, or to the people."

Separation of Powers.   After dividing power between the national and state governments, the Constitution separates those powers that it grants to the national government among the three branches. Under the Constitution, all legislative powers granted belong to Congress, the executive power vests in the president of the United States, and the judicial authority resides in a Supreme Court, plus any lower courts Congress might choose to establish. Moreover, because the "legislative authority . . . necessarily, predominates" in a republican government (*Federalist* 51), legislative power was further separated into two distinct chambers—a House and a Senate—each with different manners of election and terms of office. This separation of powers followed the recommendations of the eighteenth-century French philosopher Charles, Baron de Montesquieu, who believed that a government in which powers were separated and balanced was the best guarantee of freedom of the individual.

Checks and Balances.   Under the Constitution, balance among the branches was achieved by giving each one some authority to counteract, or check, the authority of the other two (see Figure 2.4). Thus the president has

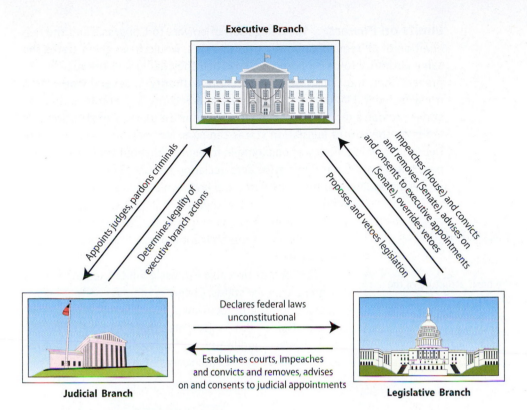

Executive Branch

Appoints judges, pardons criminals

Determines legality of executive branch actions

Impeaches (House) and convicts and removes (Senate), advises on and consents to executive appointments (Senate), overrides vetoes

Proposes and vetoes legislation

Declares federal laws unconstitutional

Establishes courts, impeaches and convicts and removes, advises on and consents to judicial appointments

Judicial Branch

Legislative Branch

FIGURE 2.4 Checks and Balances.

© CENGAGE LEARNING

the authority to propose legislation to Congress and to veto bills passed by Congress; Congress can override that veto by a two-thirds majority of each chamber. The president also nominates federal judges, subject to the advice and consent of the Senate. The Senate also advises and consents to high-ranking executive branch appointments, such as ambassadors and cabinet officials. The House can impeach executive and judicial appointees, and the Senate can convict and remove impeached officials from office by a two-thirds majority. Congress, subject to presidential veto, has the authority to establish lower courts and set their jurisdiction (decide what cases they can hear). It also has the authority to set the Supreme Court's appellate jurisdiction. The appellate jurisdiction is the Supreme Court's authority to hear cases on appeal from lower courts and is the heart of the Supreme Court's judicial power. Congress has this authority over the courts; the courts, on the other hand, can decide the constitutionality of laws passed by Congress. While the Constitution does not explicitly grant this power of judicial review to courts, judicial review has been largely unchallenged since announced by the Supreme Court in *Marbury v. Madison*. The courts also have the authority to review the legality of actions taken by executive branch officials.

Connections:
What is the purpose of checks and balances?

Limits on Powers. The delegation of powers to Congress, and the reservation of all remaining powers to the states, would have given states the same authority to pass oppressive laws that they had under the Articles. To prevent that, the Constitution limits state authority in several ways. First, it makes federal law supreme over state law. Second, it guarantees that the states provide a republican form of government. Third, the Constitution sets limits on the sort of legislation states can pass. Not only are states prohibited from coining money or engaging in foreign affairs, but they also cannot pass bills of attainder (legislative acts declaring people guilty of crimes) or prosecute individuals under *ex post facto* laws, which make behavior illegal after individuals have engaged in it. The Constitution also prohibits states from passing laws that would allow individuals to disregard the obligation of contracts, such as laws negating debts.

The Constitution also expressly limits the authority of Congress. Like the states, Congress can pass neither bills of attainder nor *ex post facto* laws. It also cannot suspend the writ of *habeas corpus*—a guarantee that incarcerated people can go before a judge to have the legality of their confinement determined—except in cases of invasion or rebellion.

Checkpoint

Can you:

☐ Describe the basic structure of the U.S. Constitution

☐ Explain how amendments get proposed and ratified

☐ Evaluate why power is partitioned

The Ratification Debates

> **Why the Antifederalists opposed the Constitution**

With the proposed Constitution to be accepted or rejected by the people of the various states, the state ratification debates largely ignored the issue of slavery and the question of representation that led to the Connecticut Compromise Instead, most of the debate concerned the extent of national power under the Constitution, including a feared consolidation of federal authority over the states, the scope of executive and legislative power, and the lack of a bill of rights.

Federalists and Antifederalists

By the time the state ratifying conventions started meeting, two distinct camps had formed. Those who supported the Constitution cleverly named themselves **Federalists**, even though they were really more nationalist than federalist. ("Federal," according to Madison, meant "a Confederacy of sovereign states,"[13] which better described the Articles of Confederation, or even the New Jersey Plan, than the new Constitution.) Those who opposed the Constitution, whose leaders included the outspoken Revolutionary leader Patrick Henry of Virginia, became known as the **Antifederalists**.

Federalists: *Initially, those who supported the Constitution during the ratification period; later, the name of the political party established by supporters of Alexander Hamilton.*

Antifederalists: *Those who opposed the new proposed Constitution during the ratification period.*

Madison, along with John Jay, who later became the first chief justice of the United States, and Alexander Hamilton, who later founded the Federalist Party and served as the first secretary of the treasury, wrote eighty-five essays, today known as the *Federalist Papers*, that attempted to convince the citizens of New York to ratify the Constitution. They wrote anonymously under the pen name "Publius," taken from an early leader in the ancient Roman Republic. Two of the most famous essays, numbers 10 and 51, are in this book's Appendix. The Antifederalists published their attacks under anonymous pen names as well, most notably "Brutus"—another leader of the ancient Roman Republic—and "Old Whig," named after the English political party that opposed the monarchy.

Consolidation of Federal Authority

The Antifederalists found much to disapprove of in the proposed Constitution. They argued that the Constitutional Convention had violated the Articles by moving beyond mere amendment and proposing a new government, one that did not require the unanimous consent of the states. They worried that because sovereignty, the ultimate lawmaking authority, could not be split, and because national law was supreme over state law, a national government under the Constitution would inevitably consolidate its authority over the state governments.

The Federalists answered both of these charges by claiming that sovereignty rested not in the legislature, as had typically been believed, but in the people, as the preamble to the Constitution suggested. Therefore the people could propose any new form of government they wished. And if the people were sovereign, they could split their grant of lawmaking authority between the national and state governments as they saw fit.

Connections: Were the Antifederalists more concerned about liberty or about order?

The Scope of Executive Authority

Other concerns centered on the scope of executive authority. With no term limits on the executive in the original Constitution, the Antifederalists feared that the president would turn into a monarch. Alexander Hamilton responded in *Federalist* 69 with an explanation of the limits on the executive: elections, whereby the president could be voted out of office; impeachment, whereby the president could be removed from office for "high crimes and misdemeanors"; and the limited veto power, which could be overridden. The president of the United States, Hamilton concluded, was much closer in power to the governor of New York than to the king of England.

Connections: Why were the Antifederalists opposed to a strong executive?

The Scope of Legislative Authority

Two provisions in Article I, Section 8 of the Constitution, which specified the powers of Congress, particularly alarmed the Antifederalists: the

**general
welfare clause:**
*Gives Congress the power
to tax to provide for the
general welfare (Article I,
Section 8).*

**necessary and
proper clause:**
*Gives Congress the power
to pass all laws necessary
and proper to the powers
enumerated in Section 8
(Article I, Section 8).*

Connections:
What elements of
the Antifederalist
argument do you
detect in political
arguments today?

**implied
powers:** *Powers
not expressly granted to
Congress but added
through the necessary and
proper clause.*

general welfare clause and the **necessary and proper clause**. This section of the Constitution begins by stating that "Congress shall have Power To lay and Collect Taxes . . . to . . . provide for the . . . general Welfare of the United States." It concludes by stating that Congress has the power "to make all Laws which shall be necessary and proper for carrying into Execution the foregoing Powers." Antifederalist Brutus contended that "the legislature under this constitution may pass any law which they may think proper."[14] Brutus further wrote that the necessary and proper clause, labeled "the sweeping clause" by the Antifederalists, granted the government "absolute and uncontroulable power, legislative, executive and judicial."[15] James Monroe, who would later serve as the fifth president (1817–25), told the Virginia ratifying convention that the sweeping clause gave Congress "a general power . . . to make all laws that will enable them to carry their powers into effect. There are no limits pointed out. They are not restrained or controlled from making any law, however oppressive in its operation, which they may think necessary to carry their powers into effect."[16]

Madison responded in *Federalist* 41 that the power to tax "to provide for the general Welfare" was not a general grant of power to tax for any purpose whatsoever but, rather, a power to tax for the enumerated powers that followed. "Nothing is more natural nor common than first to use a general phrase, and then to explain and qualify it by a recital of particulars."[17] To Madison, when Article I, Section 8 granted the right to tax to provide for the general welfare, and then listed various other powers, those other powers defined the scope of the general welfare clause. Similarly, the Federalists argued that the necessary and proper clause was not a general grant of authority to pass all laws that were necessary and proper, but rather, as the clause explicitly stated, the authority to pass all laws that were "necessary and proper for carrying into Execution the foregoing [that is, previously listed] Powers."

Nevertheless, to clarify that the Constitution did not provide general powers to Congress, the Federalists agreed to an amendment to the Constitution that declared that "The powers not delegated to the United States by the Constitution, nor prohibited by it to the States, are reserved to the States respectively, or to the people." Interestingly, the amendment parallels a similar provision from the Articles that declared that the states retained all powers not "expressly delegated" to the national government. By limiting congressional authority to those powers delegated to it, rather than the stricter standard of those powers expressly delegated to it, the Constitution creates a somewhat greater authority for **implied powers**.

The Lack of a Bill of Rights

The most serious charge against the Constitution was that it did not contain a bill of rights. The Federalists argued that a bill of rights was not necessary because Congress had only those powers granted by the Constitution. The Federalists went further to claim that a bill of rights could be dangerous because listing some rights but not others could imply that the rights not listed could be abridged.

Consider two documents. The first one states that Congress has the right to regulate commerce between the states, to tax to provide for the general welfare, and to raise armies. Under this document, does Congress have the right to abridge the right to assemble? The Federalist answer was no, because Congress has enumerated powers only, and the right to limit freedom of assembly is not one of them. The Antifederalist answer was yes, because the power was not prohibited.

Now consider a second document that states that Congress has the right to regulate commerce between the states, to tax to provide for the general welfare, and to raise armies. In addition, it states that Congress may not abridge freedom of the press. May Congress abridge the right to assemble? The Federalists argued that the potential for Congress to regulate the right to assemble is greater in the second document than in the first. That is, in the second case, Congress could say "we are prohibited from abridging freedom of the press, but we are not prohibited from abridging the right to assemble, so we are allowed to do that." By listing certain rights, the Constitution could be interpreted as allowing Congress to limit those freedoms not listed.

It is hard to imagine people concluding from the Federalist argument that rights would be safer without a bill of rights. Not only is this a complicated argument, but combining the necessary and proper clause with the broad powers granted Congress under the Constitution—such as regulating interstate commerce and taxing to provide for the general welfare—probably means that Congress could have found ways to pass laws abridging freedom of assembly, freedom of speech, and other freedoms. The Federalists eventually gave in to the Antifederalist argument, agreeing that amending the Constitution to provide a bill of rights would be among the first items of business under a newly ratified Constitution. To prevent the listing of certain rights to create an assumption that Congress could abridge other rights not listed, the Bill of Rights included the Ninth Amendment: "The enumeration in the Constitution, of certain rights, shall not be construed to deny or disparage others retained by the people."

Despite the Antifederalist arguments about excessive national power, the lack of a bill of rights, and a too-powerful executive, states began ratifying the new Constitution. Government under the Articles was simply not an acceptable alternative. Just two months after the Convention sent the proposed Constitution to the states, Delaware became the first state to ratify. By June 1788 ten states had ratified, one more than needed to establish the new Constitution.

Connections: Was the Bill of Rights necessary in 1787? Is it necessary today?

Connections: What would have happened if the Constitution had not been ratified?

 Checkpoint

Can you:

☐ Characterize the Federalists and Antifederalists

☐ Compare competing arguments over who was sovereign under the Constitution

☐ Explain why the Antifederalists believed the president had too much power

☐ Explain why the Antifederalists believed Congress had too much power

☐ Recall which problem in the proposed Constitution the Federalists agreed to correct

The Responsive Constitution

› How the Constitution has stayed responsive to changing needs

Connections:
The Articles of Confederation, once ratified, did not last a decade. Why has the Constitution lasted for more than two centuries?

The government the Framers devised has lasted more than two hundred years. As in 1787, it still has three branches of government, Congress still consists of two chambers, and the Electoral College still chooses the president. But other parts of the U.S. constitutional system have changed substantially, some to fix flaws and some to respond to new circumstances and developing ideas about the nature of equality. Some of these changes, such as the Bill of Rights, came through the formal amendment process. Others were the result of changing interpretation by the Supreme Court about what the Constitution means. Still others are what some call "extraconstitutional." That is, they affect the way the constitutional system operates even though the Constitution itself has not been amended to reflect them. Most prominent is the development of political parties (see Chapter 9, Political Parties).

The Bill of Rights

As part of the fight over ratification, the Federalists agreed that they would propose a Bill of Rights once the new Constitution was ratified, and some state ratifying conventions forwarded proposals for specific amendments. Madison, elected as a member of Congress from Virginia, quickly selected twelve proposed amendments, among them the congressional pay raise amendment that Gregory Watson revived nearly two hundred years later. The states then ratified ten of the amendments in 1791 as a Bill of Rights that became part of the Constitution.

The First Amendment guarantees major political rights, including freedom of speech, press, and assembly and the free exercise of religion. It also prohibits establishing a national religion or, more precisely, any law "respecting an establishment of religion." The Second Amendment protects the right to bear arms; the Third Amendment prohibits the quartering of soldiers in one's home in times of peace. The Fourth, Fifth, Sixth, and Eighth Amendments protect rights relating to criminal procedure, including the right at trial to the assistance of an attorney and the right to a trial by jury (Sixth). (The Seventh Amendment protects the right to a trial by jury in civil cases over $20.) The criminal procedure amendments also prohibit unreasonable searches and seizures (Fourth), compulsory self-incrimination (Fifth), double jeopardy, or being tried a second time for a crime after one is found not guilty (Fifth), and cruel or unusual punishments (Eighth). The Fifth Amendment also prohibits deprivations of life, liberty, or property without due process of law, and it prohibits the government from seizing private property for a public use without fair or "just" compensation. We examine the meanings of these amendments in Chapter 4, Civil Liberties.

The Civil War Amendments

Following the Civil War, Congress proposed and the states ratified three amendments. The Thirteenth Amendment (1865) prohibits slavery. The Fourteenth Amendment (1868), aimed at protecting the newly emancipated slaves, makes all people born in the United States citizens of the United States. It also prohibits states from denying anyone due process of law, the equal protection of the law, and the privileges or immunities of citizens of the United States. The Fifteenth Amendment (1870) prohibits states from denying anyone the right to vote on account of race or prior status as slaves. All three amendments give Congress the authority to enforce the measures by appropriate legislation, thus adding to Congress's enumerated powers. These amendments radically changed the structure of the federal government by giving the national government authority over internal matters of the states. We deal with these civil rights more extensively in Chapter 5, Civil Rights.

> **Connections:** How has the Constitution changed, and why?

Amendments That Expand Public Participation

Other amendments have further extended the gateways to public participation in government by giving the people the right to vote for their senators directly (Seventeenth, 1913), guaranteeing women the right to vote (Nineteenth, 1920), allowing residents of the District of Columbia to vote in presidential elections (Twenty-Third, 1961), prohibiting states from setting poll taxes as a requirement of voting in federal elections (Twenty-Fourth, 1964), and guaranteeing the right to vote for those age 18 or older (Twenty-Sixth, 1971). For a summary of all the amendments, see Figure 2.5.

Constitutional Interpretation

The Constitution has also changed through interpretation by the Supreme Court. Following the explicit establishment of judicial review in *Marbury v. Madison,* the Court has exercised the authority to determine what the Constitution means. Under that authority, the powers of Congress have grown enormously. During the Great Depression of the 1930s, the Court began to interpret Congress's power to tax to provide for the general welfare as extending beyond the enumerated powers. Rather, in line with the interpretation of the general welfare clause that the Antifederalists feared, the Court now holds that Congress can tax and spend for virtually any purpose that is not expressly prohibited.

> **Connections:** What is the significance of judicial review?

Additionally, Congress's authority to regulate commerce between the states is now so grand that it covers virtually all commercial activity, including wheat grown by a farmer for consumption by livestock on that farmer's land because of the effect that all similarly situated wheat could have on national

FIGURE 2.5 The Amendments to the Constitution.

Following the specific protections of the first eight amendments to the Constitution, many subsequent amendments have corrected structural problems in the operation of government. Others have expanded participation and equality.

Color Code: Criminal procedure   Participation   Equality   Structure   Miscellaneous

First	1791	Prohibits abridging freedoms of religion, speech, press, assembly, and petition
Second	1791	Prohibits abridging the right to bear arms
Third	1791	Prohibits involuntary quartering of soldiers in one's home during peacetime
Fourth	1791	Prohibits unreasonable searches and seizures
Fifth	1791	Affirms the right to indictment by a grand jury and the right to due process; protects against double jeopardy, self-incrimination, and taking of property without just compensation
Sixth	1791	Affirms rights to speedy and public trial, to confront witnesses, and to counsel
Seventh	1791	Affirms right to jury trials in civil suits over $20
Eighth	1791	Prohibits excessive bail, excessive fines, and cruel and unusual punishments
Ninth	1791	Declares that the enumeration of certain rights does not limit other rights retained by the people
Tenth	1791	Reserves the powers not granted to the national government to the states or to the people
Eleventh	1798	Prevents citizens from one state from suing another state in federal court
Twelfth	1804	Requires that electors cast separate votes for president and vice president and specifies requirements for vice presidential candidates
Thirteenth	1865	Prohibits slavery in the United States
Fourteenth	1868	Makes all persons born in the United States citizens of the United States and prohibits states from denying persons within its jurisdiction privileges or immunities of citizens, the due process of law, and equal protection of the laws; apportionment by whole persons
Fifteenth	1870	Prohibits states from denying the right to vote on account of race
Sixteenth	1913	Grants Congress the power to tax income derived from any source
Seventeenth	1913	Gives the people instead of state legislatures) the right to choose U.S. senators directly
Eighteenth	1919	Prohibits the manufacture, sale, or transportation of intoxicating liquors
Nineteenth	1920	Guarantees women the right to vote
Twentieth	1933	Declares that the presidential term begins on January 20 (instead of March 4)
Twenty-First	1933	Repeals the Eighteenth Amendment
Twenty-Second	1951	Limits presidents to two terms
Twenty-Third	1961	Grants Electoral College votes to residents of the District of Columbia
Twenty-Fourth	1964	Prohibits poll taxes
Twenty-Fifth	1967	Specifies replacement of the vice president and establishes the position of acting president during a president's disability
Twenty-Sixth	1971	Guarantees 18-year-olds the right to vote
Twenty-Seventh	1992	Sets limits on congressional pay raises

© CENGAGE LEARNING

grain markets.[18] But in 2012, the Supreme Court held that the commerce clause did not give Congress the right to mandate that individuals purchase health insurance, upholding that requirement under the taxing part of the general welfare clause.[19]

This growth of national authority confirms that the Antifederalists were correct to insist on a Bill of Rights. Although Congress has not been granted the explicit right to abridge freedom of speech or freedom of the press, it would have the authority to do so under current readings of the commerce, taxing, and various other clauses, were it not for the Bill of Rights.

Future Amendments

A perennial suggestion for future constitutional change is the replacement of the Electoral College with some form of popular vote. Calls for this reform by Democrats revived after George W. Bush became president in 2000 despite losing the popular vote. Bush was not the first to win the electoral vote without winning a popular majority. John Quincy Adams in 1824, Rutherford B. Hayes in 1876, and Benjamin Harrison in 1888 won the presidency without popular majorities, and the election of 1960 was so close that John F. Kennedy, too, might have become president despite losing the popular vote.[20] Nevertheless, expanding participation through the direct election of the president remains unlikely given the difficulties of amending the Constitution and the influence of small states.

Connections: What new amendments to the Constitution would you like to see passed?

Checkpoint

Can you:

☐ List the major rights protected by the Bill of Rights

☐ List the major rights protected by the Civil War Amendments

☐ Explain how amendments have expanded the gateways to public participation

☐ Describe how the meaning of the Constitution can change without formal amendments

☐ Discuss a potential future change to the Constitution

Policy Making in a Constitutional System: The Death Penalty

The decisions the Framers made in constructing the constitutional system have profound implications for public policy making. The U.S. constitutional system imposes separation of powers, but that separation is limited by a system of checks and balances that adds complexity to the policy-making process. Additionally, the federalism component adds a level of inconsistency by allowing each state, within the bounds of the Constitution, to pursue its own policies. This inconsistency generates an inequality in the application of the death penalty, which we examine as an example.

Checks and Balances

Although the separation of powers established under the Constitution means that it is generally true that the legislature makes laws, the executive enforces laws, and the judiciary interprets laws, the checks and balances established in the Constitution complicate the process, granting all three branches a say in policy making. The president can set the legislative agenda and veto legislation. If the legislation passes, implementing the law is up to the executive branch, and because laws cannot cover every circumstance, the executive branch usually uses discretion in carrying them out. For example, if state or federal law allows for the death penalty in certain types of cases, state or federal prosecutors in their respective executive branches must decide whether to seek the death penalty in an appropriate case. When the executive branch has little discretion in carrying out a law, such as deciding the amount paid to Social Security recipients, it does little policy making. But where discretion is substantial, such as regarding the death penalty, the executive branch becomes a key player in policy making.

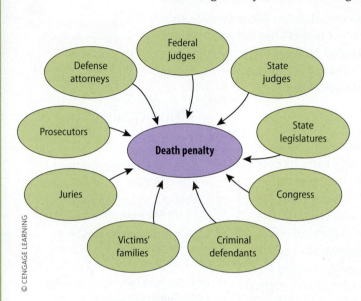

Another notable feature of checks and balances is that the judiciary can strike laws passed by the legislative branch if it believes that those laws violate the Constitution. The judiciary can also strike actions the executive branch takes if those actions violate constitutional provisions. Thus, under the U.S. constitutional system, all three branches of government can have a say in policy making.

Federalism

The fact that each state has its own separate government and set of laws further complicates the policy-making process. The Constitution, particularly as interpreted by the Supreme Court, leaves some policies in exclusive federal control, some under exclusive state control and many others under both state and federal control. States, for example, may generally establish their own criminal justice systems, but those systems must abide by guarantees found in the Constitution.

Connections: Does the federal system make government more or less responsive? Does it make citizens more or less equal?

The Death Penalty

This balancing act among the branches of the federal government and between the nation and the states affects a wide range of policy issues, including the imposition of the death penalty, also known as capital punishment. The Constitution contains some degree of ambiguity about the death penalty. In several places, it seems to allow capital punishment. The Fourteenth Amendment's due process clause says that states may not deprive people of life, liberty, or property without due process of law, thus suggesting that life, liberty, and property may be taken so long as the states follow due process. Similarly, the Fifth Amendment's declarations that no person shall be held for a capital crime without indictment by a grand jury similarly suggests that a person can be held for a capital crime when indicted by a grand jury.

Alternatively, the Eighth Amendment prohibits "cruel and unusual" punishments. The Supreme Court interprets that clause to mean that the constitutionality of punishment is to be subject to evolving standards of justice and that the death penalty might violate those standards.

Before 1972, most states allowed capital punishment and did so by declaring crimes for which capital punishment could be imposed (usually murder, but sometimes also rape) and then leaving it up to the jury to decide whether capital punishment should be inflicted in a specific case. In 1972 the Supreme Court put a temporary halt to capital punishment, declaring that the process of complete jury discretion was cruel and unusual in that it led to an arbitrary and unequal imposition of the death penalty.[21] According to one justice in this sharply divided case, who received the death penalty and who did not was as arbitrary as who gets hit by lightning. (Figure 2.6 shows the fluctuations in the number of executions per year.)

Various states responded to this decision by requiring juries to follow certain guidelines before imposing the death penalty. In 1976 the Supreme Court ruled 7–2 that the death penalty with such guidelines did not constitute cruel and unusual punishment under the Constitution.[22] Currently, thirty-three states permit capital punishment.[23] Given strong public approval for the death penalty, Congress allows it for certain federal crimes, including terrorist acts that result in death, murder for hire, kidnappings that result in murder, and murder related to the smuggling of aliens.[24] The

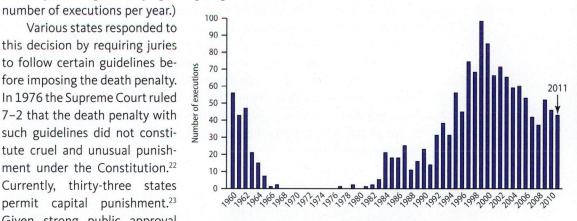

FIGURE 2.6 **Annual Executions, 1960–2011.**

Annual executions dropped significantly in the years before the Supreme Court's temporary halt of capital punishment in 1972, but public support for capital punishment remained high. After the Court reinstituted capital punishment in 1976, the number of executions rose. The number later dipped, as DNA evidence revealing that some death row inmates had been wrongly convicted made the public wary about the death penalty.

Source: Annual Executions, 1960–2011. Death Penalty Information Center, 2011. © 2012 Death Penalty Information Center. Reproduced by permission.

federal death penalty can be imposed throughout the country, even in states that do not allow the death penalty for violations of state law.

Though the Supreme Court has attempted to limit the unequal application of the death penalty, one clear finding from studies is the effect of the race of the victim: Juries are far more likely to impose the death penalty when the victim is white than when the victim is black.[25] The Supreme Court has ruled that, even if this were the case overall, someone challenging a death sentence based on such statistics would have to prove that the jury intentionally discriminated in the particular case.[26]

The Supreme Court has put limits on who can be sentenced to death. Offenders who were under the age of 18 when their crimes were committed and those convicted of rape, even the rape of a child, cannot receive the death penalty.[27]

Connections:
Do you think the death penalty is constitutional?

Some states have begun to limit their own use of this punishment. The Innocence Project, a group dedicated to reversing convictions of people who were innocent, reports 218 death penalty cases in which DNA testing demonstrated that the wrong person was convicted of the crime.[28] This finding has led many states to reduce the number of death penalty sentences. It has also led many, but not all, states to allow convicted criminals access to DNA evidence, though the Supreme Court does not require them to do so.[29] Illinois was the first state to suspend the use of the death penalty because the evidence in several death penalty cases was shown to be insufficient in establishing guilt and the newest scientific methods using DNA exonerated several death row inmates. The Illinois legislature removed the death penalty from the criminal statutes in 2010.

In considering how well policy making works in the constitutional system, it is worth noting the inconsistent use of the death penalty across states. If two individuals commit the same crime in different states, one criminal might be put to death, and the other might be allowed to live. Should states have their own policies on capital punishment, or should the federal government impose a uniform policy on them? The inconsistent use of the death penalty raises questions about equality under the constitutional system and serves as one of the most important examples of the unintended consequences of constitutional design.

 Construct Your Own Policy

1. Draft a constitutional amendment that would eliminate the death penalty in all fifty states and include an alternative sentence for crimes that might otherwise qualify for the death penalty.

2. Draft a set of five requirements for the imposition of the death penalty that would apply in all fifty states.

For more on the policy-making process, see Chapter 1.

The Constitution and Democracy

Government under the 1787 Constitution would today be considered severely lacking in both democracy and equality. The government allowed some of the people, mostly white males with property, to choose one chamber of the legislative branch of their government but did not grant the people a direct vote for the other chamber of the legislature or for the chief executive. And a government that allowed slavery would today be a pariah, an outcast, among the nations of the world.

Moreover, in 1787 states regulated the right to vote. Slaves were not allowed to vote, but states differed as to whether free blacks, women, and men without property could vote. In 1790 Georgia, South Carolina, and Virginia prohibited free blacks from voting. South Carolina required voters to believe in God, heaven, and hell. Only New Jersey granted women the right to vote, a right that lasted only until 1807. Every state except Vermont required some form of tax payment for voter eligibility.[30]

Yet, compared to the despots and monarchs who had long ruled other countries, the government of 1787 allowed for a remarkable degree of participation by the common person. By giving voters a direct say in their state legislatures and at least indirect influence in all branches of the national government, the 1787 Constitution was a striking break with the past, even if it did not live up to the Declaration's statement that "all men are created equal."

Today participation is much more widespread than in 1787. Although the Electoral College continues to play its role every four years, each state allows the people to choose their electors.

Although the 1787 Constitution allowed the national government to exercise direct control over the citizenry, the tiny size of the national government left the people with far more control over their daily lives than they have today. But it is also the case that today the people have more control over the government. In addition to new constitutional gateways, opportunities for participation are greater than ever, with the Internet relaying information virtually instantly. It is much easier for representatives to be responsive to their constituents' desires when they can easily learn what their constituents believe, and constituents can readily learn what their representatives have done.

Focus Questions Revisited

- In what ways did the Constitution ensure that government would be responsive to the people? How has government become more responsive since 1787?

- In what ways did the Constitution seek to control the popular will and ensure order?

- In what ways did the Constitution seek to control government itself?

- In what ways did the nation's founding documents promote equality? In what ways did they fail to promote equality?

- Is the Constitution a gate or a gateway to American democracy? Is it a gatekeeper? Explain.

gateways to learning

1. The colonists declared independence from Britain because they believed that the British Parliament and king were denying their rights as British subjects. (pp. 33–35)

2. Congress's powers under the Articles of Confederation were limited, and the structure the Articles established made governing difficult. (pp. 36–37)

3. In 1787 delegates from twelve states met in Philadelphia to amend the Articles; instead, they wrote a new Constitution. (pp. 37–42)

4. To secure the assent of all states represented at the Constitutional Convention, the delegates reached compromises between large and small states over representation, between northern and southern states over issues related to slavery, and between those who favored a strong national government and those who favored strong state governments in the balance of power between the two. (pp. 38–42)

5. This newly proposed Constitution was then sent to the states for ratification, and it is, with subsequent amendments, the same Constitution Americans live by today. (pp. 42–43)

6. The Constitution lays out the structure of democratic government and the means by which the Constitution can be amended. It reflects the Framers' attempt to establish a government powerful enough to ensure public order yet restrained enough to guarantee individual liberty. (pp. 44–50)

7. Debates over the ratification of the Constitution centered on a fear of consolidated federal authority over the states, the scope of executive and legislative power, and the lack of a bill of rights. (pp. 50–53)

8. To achieve ratification, the Federalists gave in to Antifederalist demands for a bill of rights, passing one as the first ten amendments to the Constitution. (pp. 52–54)

9. Subsequent amendments ended slavery, protected the rights of African Americans, and generally extended public participation in government while also expanding federal authority over the states. (pp. 55, 57)

10. The constitutional system established in 1787 has also been changed by constitutional interpretation and its operation altered by the development of political parties. (pp. 55–57)

Key Concepts

amendment (p. 47). Why did the Framers make amending the Constitution so difficult?

Antifederalists (p. 50). What were the Antifederalist arguments against the proposed Constitution?

Articles of Confederation (p. 36). What were the deficiencies of the Articles of Confederation?

Bill of Rights (p. 43). What are the basic protections in the Bill of Rights?

checks and balances (p. 48). Why does government need checks and balances?

Connecticut Compromise (p. 40). What did the Connecticut Compromise accomplish?

constitution (p. 33). Why is a constitution needed instead of ordinary laws that can say the same things?

Constitutional Convention (p. 38). What were the major compromises reached at the Constitutional Convention?

Declaration of Independence (p. 35). What are the basic principles of the Declaration of Independence?

Electoral College (p. 42). Why does the Constitution provide for an Electoral College?

enumerated powers (p. 40). Why are Congress's powers enumerated?

federalism (p. 48). What does a federal system try to do?

Federalists (p. 50). Who were the federalists?

general welfare clause (p. 52). What does the general welfare clause do?

implied powers (p. 52). Does the constitution grant implied powers?

judicial review (p. 45). What is judicial review?

necessary and proper clause (p. 52). What does the necessary and proper clause do?

separation of powers (p. 48). Why do governments chosen by the people still need a separation of powers?

three-fifths compromise (p. 41). What were the problems of the three-fifths compromise?

veto (p. 44). Why is the president given veto power?

Learning Outcomes

WHAT YOU NEED...

To Know	To Test Yourself	To Participate
What drove the colonists to seek independence	• Define a constitution • State the colonists' grievances against Great Britain • Explain the key concepts in the Declaration of Independence • Describe the problems with the Articles of Confederation	• Appreciate American political culture • Formulate grievances you might have about the government today • Evaluate the impact of governing documents
What the major compromises at the Constitutional Convention were	• Characterize the delegates to the Constitutional Convention • Explain how the interests of the large and small states differed • State why the convention rejected the Virginia Plan • Explain how the interests of the North and the South differed • Describe how the 1787 Constitution protected against too much popular influence • Recall who would ratify the new constitution	• Characterize the people who hold power today • Justify (or critique) equal representation in the Senate • Evaluate compromise as a tool for governing
How the structure of the Constitution protects liberty	• Describe the basic structure of the U.S. Constitution • Explain how amendments get proposed and ratified • Evaluate why power is partitioned	• Evaluate whether the Constitution provides gateways for, or gates against, public participation • Determine whether the amendment process is too difficult • Evaluate the dangers of unified power
Why the Antifederalists opposed the Constitution	• Characterize the Federalists and Antifederalists • Compare competing arguments over who was sovereign under the Constitution • Explain why the Antifederalists believed the president had too much power • Explain why the Antifederalists believed Congress had too much power • Recall which problem in the proposed Constitution the Federalists agreed to correct	• Identify these positions in politics today • Argue whether the national government or the people are sovereign today • Evaluate the extent of presidential power • Evaluate the extent of congressional power
How the Constitution has stayed responsive to changing needs	• List the major rights protected by the Bill of Rights • List the major rights protected by the Civil War Amendments • Explain how amendments have expanded the gateways to public participation • Describe how the meaning of the Constitution can change without formal amendments • Discuss potential future changes to the Constitution	• Propose new rights that you would like to see constitutionally protected • Contrast the gateways to public participation that exist today and those that existed in 1787 • Examine the evolution of constitutional meaning and judge whether it is valid

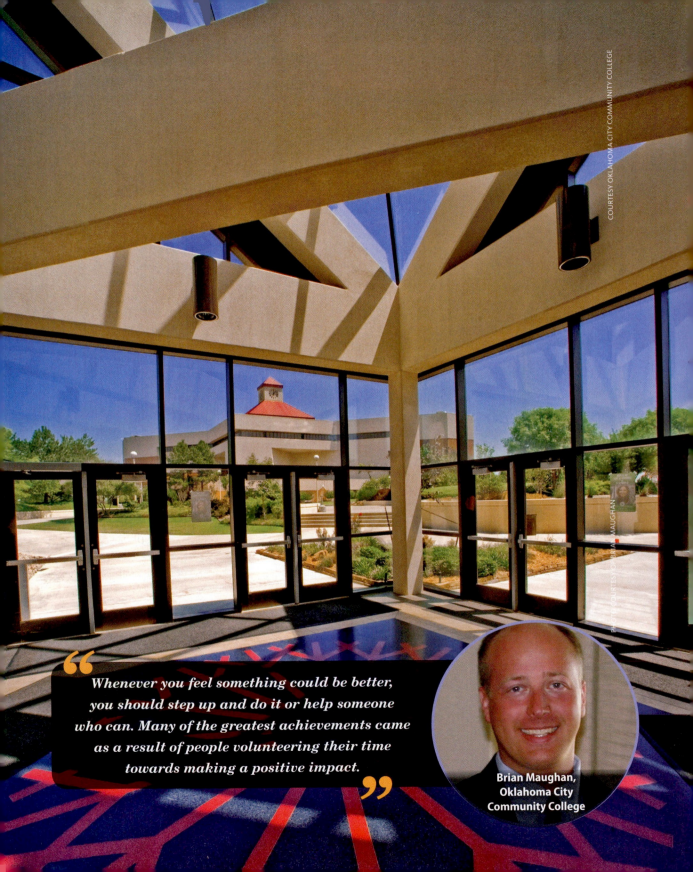

Whenever you feel something could be better, you should step up and do it or help someone who can. Many of the greatest achievements came as a result of people volunteering their time towards making a positive impact.

Brian Maughan, Oklahoma City Community College

3

Federalism

The impacts of federal, state, and local government decisions are not just theory to Brian Maughan. They first got his attention when he was a student at Oklahoma City Community College (OCCC), and now, in his job as county commissioner, they are daily fare.

Maughan grew up in the community he now serves. His commitment to it developed in high school, when his principal used community service to instill self-worth in at-risk students. For college, Maughan remained close by, where he could stay in touch with Ben, his best friend, who was a quadriplegic as the result of a car accident and who faced a difficult situation. The state program that supplemented federal funding for his in-home health care was being defunded, and it looked like he would be removed from his home and placed in a state care facility. The federal program—Social Security Disability Insurance (SSDI)—would not pay for a family member to provide in-home health care at the advanced level Ben's condition required. If state funding could be restored, however, Ben could remain at home, and the family member who cared for

him would receive compensation. Obviously, this arrangement was preferred. Maughan took on Ben's cause as his own. While keeping up with his classes and holding down a job to pay his tuition, Maughan researched funding options and learned that the Oklahoma Developmental Disability Council could provide the aid Ben needed. For two years, he actively sought the governor's support. Because of his commitment, the governor appointed Maughan to the council, and shortly after Maughan's graduation, funding for Ben's situation was restored. Ben was able to remain at home where his family cared for him until his

aplia — Need to Know

- Why the Framers chose a federal system
- How the Constitution reflects the federal system
- How U.S. federalism has changed over time
- How state governments differ from the national government

death, a short time later. Maughan's success on behalf of his friend demonstrates the gateways for influence at the state and local levels that are often easier to access than the federal level.

Recognizing that active citizenship can change policies with negative effects, Maughan decided to make government and community service his career. As director of economic development for the county district he now represents, he helped businesses maneuver among the delays in inspections for business improvements and the unfunded mandates that present obstacles in a federal system with multiple layers of government and overlapping authorities. As a county commissioner, he faces these obstacles daily. In 2010, an accidental fire, propelled by raging winds and severe drought conditions, consumed many homes in his district. Then a tornado caused more property loss and raised public safety concerns. Maughan's job was to oversee federal disaster assistance in the removal of debris so that homeowners could begin to clean up and rebuild. But federal and county disaster aid funded only the removal of trees and natural materials; the removal of other debris was the responsibility of the homeowner and the insurance company. Frustrated homeowners leveled criticism at Maughan. He found an innovative solution: he mobilized more than a thousand volunteers, who donated more than ten thousand hours assisting homeowners.

Maughan does not ask more of others than he asks of himself. In a 2009 snowstorm, when snow removal resources were limited, he helped plow, sand, and salt the 177 lane miles in his district. To clean up blight, he enlists college students and offenders sentenced to community service in a program called SHINE (Start Helping Impacted Neighborhoods Everywhere), which he founded. He likes to tell volunteers the "broken window" story that the political scientist James Q. Wilson made famous—how one unattended broken window can invite trash, graffiti, and an opportunity for more serious crimes. Volunteer labor helps Maughan stretch tight budgets and inspires civic engagement that improves the community as a whole.[1]

In federal political systems where national, state, and local governments wield power, the interplay of responsibilities is often complex and overlapping or may leave areas unfunded, as Maughan's experiences reveal. But they also offer multiple gateways to participation, policy change, and government office. In this chapter, we examine the federal system of government, including the authority of national, state, and local governments, how that authority has shifted over time, and how federalism can both enhance and impede American democracy.

FocusQuestions

- How does federalism affect government's responsiveness? To what and to whom are federal systems accountable?
- What does it mean for citizen equality when different states are allowed to have different laws on certain subjects?
- How does a federal system make it easier for citizens to have an influence in government?
- What has been the relationship between federalism and the push for equality in the United States?
- Is federalism a gate or a gateway to democracy? Explain.

Why Federalism?

› Why the Framers chose a federal system

The delegates to the 1787 constitutional convention in Philadelphia recognized that the system of government established by the Articles of Confederation was failing. Congress did not have the authority to regulate commerce or to raise money by taxing citizens or imports; it could only request revenues from the states. Thus, the nation's debts went unpaid, and its credit was sinking. Moreover, trade barriers erected by states against other states impeded commerce. If the delegates were not able to fix the problems caused by the Articles, James Madison and others feared, the union could disintegrate.[2]

Why Unify?

The original colonies took their first step toward union when they sent delegates to meet as the First Continental Congress in 1774. The Second Continental Congress approved the Declaration of Independence, which declared the colonies to be united. The Articles of Confederation further declared that the union "shall be perpetual." Finally, the Constitution established itself in the name of "We the People of the United States." In these actions, the colonies—now states—chose to unify. They need not have taken this path. Federalism presupposes some form of union, so the answer to the question "why federalism?" first requires an answer to the question "why unify?"

The primary answer is that some form of union allows smaller political entities to pool their resources to fight a common enemy. Benjamin Franklin published his famous "Join or Die" cartoon to represent the need for the colonists to stick together in military battles in the French and Indian War (1754–63).[3] By the late 1760s, however, the cartoon had come to symbolize the need for united action against British rule. After the Revolution, common threats remained from England, France, and various Indian tribes.

A nation is said to exist when people in a country have a sense of common identity due to a common origin, history, or ancestry, all of which the colonists shared. This sense of common identity made some form of

THE GRANGER COLLECTION, NEW YORK

Benjamin Franklin published this political cartoon in his *Pennsylvania Gazette* on May 9, 1754, shortly after hostilities began in the French and Indian War. The earliest depiction of the need for union among Britain's American colonies, it shows New England as one segment and leaves out Delaware and Georgia altogether. Later, during the Revolution, it was a powerful symbol of American unity.

Connections:
Today the people of the United States no longer share a common origin, history, or ancestry. Does it matter?

JIM MCISAAC/GETTY IMAGES

Although bitter rivalries exist between some state universities, fans of both teams consider themselves Americans first. Before the 2007 NCAA women's basketball championship game, the Tennessee Lady Volunteers and the Rutgers Scarlet Knights stand at attention during the singing of the national anthem.

union not only a military necessity but also a political advantage. The American people, however, also had strong loyalties to their states, an attachment that would have made eliminating states politically impossible. How strong the national government would be was the subject of heated debate at the Constitutional Convention.

Confederal, Unitary, and Federal Systems

Because splitting up was an unattractive option, one of the forms of union available to the colonists was to continue, but strengthen, the **confederal system** that existed under the Articles of Confederation. In a confederal system, independent states grant powers to a national government to rule for the common good in certain limited areas such as defense. The independent states that make up the confederation usually have an equal vote, and the confederation might require unanimous consent or other supermajorities (for example, two-thirds or three-quarters) to pass legislation. The confederal organization usually acts through the states that constitute it rather than acting directly on the citizens of those states.

But the Framers who met in Philadelphia in 1787 were not inclined to continue the confederal system. A majority of the delegates believed that the New Jersey Plan, which would have strengthened the Articles but still granted each state one vote and still required a supermajority to pass most important issues, did not go far enough. They knew that the United States needed a stronger national government.

If a confederal system gives hardly any power to the national government, a **unitary system** of government gives it virtually every power. State or regional governments might still exist under a unitary system, but their powers and, in fact, their very existence are entirely up to the national government. The authority of a state or regional government in a pure unitary system is similar to the relationship between a state government today and the cities and counties that exist under the state's jurisdiction. Counties can make local decisions, but they exist only because their state established them, and a county has only the authority the state grants to it. Madison's original Virginia Plan did not propose a pure unitary system—Congress could

Confederal system: *System of government in which ultimate authority rests with the regional (for example, state) governments.*

unitary system: *System of government in which ultimate authority rests with the national government.*

not eliminate the states—but by giving Congress a complete veto over laws passed by the states and by granting Congress the general authority to pass laws that would promote "the harmony" of the United States,[4] it would have moved the United States in that direction.

A confederal system was too weak for the United States, and an overly strong central government would pose its own set of problems. The Framers particularly feared that too much power in any government could lead to tyranny. Freedom would be better guaranteed by dividing governmental powers, rather than by concentrating them in a central government.

The Framers thus established a new system of government, **federalism**. A federal system, like the United States, mixes features of confederal and unitary governments. The Constitution created one legislative chamber chosen by the people and based on population and another chosen by the states and based on equal representation. Within the states' areas of authority—those areas not granted to the national government—their decisions are final and cannot be overturned by the national government. Moreover, the existence of states in a federal system does not depend on the national government; rather, the states derive their authority directly from the people. Nevertheless, within areas of authority granted to the national government, or areas of authority shared by the states and the national government, the national government reigns supreme. The political scientist William Riker defines federalism as a system of government in which there exists "a government of the federation [that is, a national government] and a set of governments of the member units [that is, the states] in which both kinds of governments rule over the same territory and people and each kind has the authority to make some decisions independently of the other" (see Figure 3.1).[5]

federalism: *System of government in which sovereignty is constitutionally divided between national and state governments.*

Connections: Which government has the biggest impact on you—the federal government or your state government?

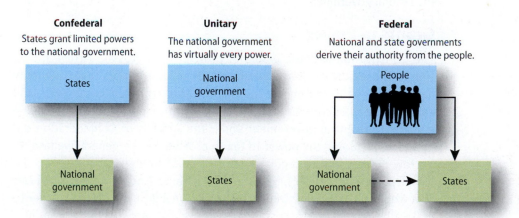

Confederal	Unitary	Federal
States grant limited powers to the national government.	The national government has virtually every power.	National and state governments derive their authority from the people.

FIGURE 3.1 Confederal, Unitary, and Federal Systems of Government.

© CENGAGE LEARNING.

Connections: In addition to federalism, in what other ways was the Constitution of 1787 innovative, even experimental?

A federal system not only reduces the risks of tyranny; it promotes self-government. While any representative democracy involves **self-government**, or government by the people, self-government is enhanced when the decisions that affect the citizens' lives are made by representatives who are local, closer to them, and more similar to them, rather than by representatives who live far away and are dissimilar.

The Framers' choice of a federal system of government was innovative, as virtually all of the world's governments at the time were either unitary or confederal. The American system was an experiment, and its evolution has been shaped by the tensions, even conflicts, inherent in a system in which power is both divided and shared. Since 1787 about two dozen other nations have ordered themselves as federal systems (see Global Gateways: Federal Political Systems).

Checkpoint

Can you:
- ☐ Explain why the Founders chose to unify
- ☐ Compare the alternatives to federalism

self-government: *Rule by the people.*

Constitutional Framework

> **How the Constitution reflects the federal system**

The Constitution lays the framework of the U.S. federal system in a variety of ways. First, the Constitution grants specified powers to the national government, reserving all remaining powers to the states or the people. Second, the Constitution sets limits on both the powers granted to the federal government and the powers reserved to the states. Third, the Constitution lays out the relationships among the several states as well as between the states and the federal government.

Grants of Power

The Constitution lists the grants of power to Congress in Article I, Section 8. These **enumerated powers** include several powers that could only lie in a national government. These are raising armies, declaring war, and establishing rules for citizenship. The enumerated powers also grant powers that the central government under the Articles of Confederation did not have, including the power to tax to provide for the general welfare, to borrow money, and to regulate interstate and foreign commerce. To the list of powers in Article I, Section 8, the Framers added one final power that would substantially strengthen the national government: the power to make all laws that are "necessary and proper" for carrying out the enumerated powers.

Although the Antifederalists who opposed the ratification of the Constitution claimed otherwise, this **necessary and proper clause** does not grant

enumerated powers: *Powers expressly granted to Congress by the Constitution.*

necessary and proper clause: *Gives Congress the power to pass all laws necessary and proper to the powers enumerated in Section 8 (Article I, Section 8).*

globalgateways

Federal Political Systems

Only a small percentage of the world's nations are federalist systems, but the tendency of larger nations to rely on federalism means that they cover a vast majority of the world's landmass. Of the world's largest countries—Russia, Canada, the United States, China, Australia, and Brazil—all but China are federalist. Of the world's most populous countries—China, India, the United States, Indonesia, and Brazil—all but China and Indonesia are federalist. Note that federalism does not necessarily mean democratic (as in Russia), and democratic does not necessarily mean federalist (as in the United Kingdom).

With the recent devolution of power to Scotland, Wales, and Northern Ireland, however, the United Kingdom is not quite as unitary as it once was. India, a multilingual nation, has a federal system with twenty-eight states and seven territories. Its federal system has a stronger national government as compared with the government of the United States, with reserve powers belonging to the national government and the states' powers enumerated. Mexico is a federal system with thirty-one states plus a federal district. The Mexican constitution limits the form of those state governments in ways that the U.S. Constitution does not. In short, within federal political systems, there are many variations, as those governing multilingual and multiethnic nations around the globe perceive a greater need to provide the local autonomy that comes with federalism.

- **Why have certain nations chosen a federal system?**
- **Why have most nations not chosen a federal system?**

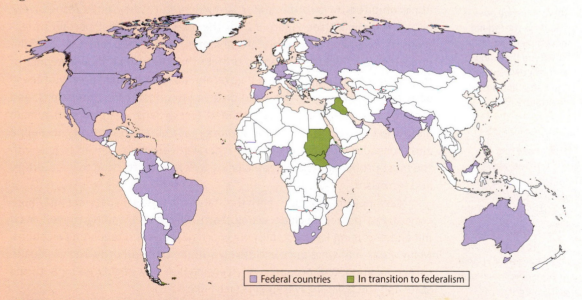

☐ Federal countries   ☐ In transition to federalism

COUNTRIES WITH FEDERAL POLITICAL SYSTEMS.

Source: © Cengage Learning; data from Forum of Federations, "Federalism by Country."

FIGURE 3.2 Constitutional Amendments That Pertain to Federalism.

Color Code:	Criminal procedure	Participation	Equality	Structure	Miscellaneous

Fifth	1791	Affirms the right to indictment by a grand jury and right to due process; protects against double jeopardy, self-incrimination, and taking of property without just compensation
Tenth	1791	Reserves the powers not granted to the national government to the states or to the people
Eleventh	1798	Prevents citizens from one state from suing another state in federal court
Thirteenth	1865	Prohibits slavery in the United States
Fourteenth	1868	Makes all persons born in the United States citizens of the United States and prohibits states from denying persons within its jurisdiction the privileges or immunities of citizens, the due process of law, and equal protection of the laws; apportionment by whole persons
Fifteenth	1870	Prohibits states from denying the right to vote on account of race
Sixteenth	1913	Grants Congress the power to tax income derived from any source
Seventeenth	1913	Gives the people (instead of state legislatures) the right to choose U.S. senators directly

© CENGAGE LEARNING.

Congress the authority to pass any law that it desires. Rather, the clause requires that the law be necessary and proper to one of the listed powers, such as collecting taxes or regulating commerce.

The original Constitution does not list the powers of the state governments, as the states retained all powers that were not prohibited by the Constitution. But to ease the concerns of the Antifederalists who wanted this relationship spelled out in the Constitution, the Tenth Amendment declares that "the powers not delegated to the United States by the Constitution, nor prohibited by it to the States, are reserved to the States respectively, or to the people" (see Figure 3.2 for the amendments that pertain to federalism). The **reserve powers** of the states, sometimes referred to as the police powers, include powers to protect the safety, health, and welfare of their citizens, though the federal government now regulates many of these activities. However, marriage and divorce laws, insurance regulations, and professional licensing (of teachers and electricians, for example) remain almost exclusively within state authority. States have authority to define and prosecute most crimes, but the federal government may do so too, with the most prominent examples including federal laws relating to guns, drugs, and terrorism.

Many powers belong to both the state and national governments. These **concurrent powers** include taxing, borrowing and spending money, making and enforcing laws, establishing court systems, and regulating elections. Many areas that were once exclusively within state authority, such as health care, education, and occupational licensing, are now regulated by both the state and the federal governments (see Figure 3.3).

Connections: Are there any state powers you think the federal government should have? Are there any federal powers you think should belong to the states?

reserve powers: *Powers retained by the states under the Constitution.*

concurrent powers: *Powers held by both the national and state governments in a federal system.*

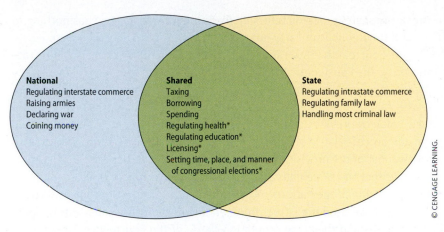

FIGURE 3.3
Examples of National, State, and Shared Powers.

National
Regulating interstate commerce
Raising armies
Declaring war
Coining money

Shared
Taxing
Borrowing
Spending
Regulating health*
Regulating education*
Licensing*
Setting time, place, and manner
  of congressional elections*

State
Regulating intrastate commerce
Regulating family law
Handling most criminal law

© CENGAGE LEARNING.

*These were once reserved powers of the states, but the growth of federal authority means that they are now regulated by both.

Limits on Power

The Constitution grants only specified powers to the national government, but even those powers are limited. The Constitution prohibits Congress from suspending the writ of *habeas corpus*, the right of individuals who have been arrested and jailed to go before a judge who determines whether their imprisonment is legal. Also prohibited are the passage of any law that declares an individual guilty of a crime (a bill of attainder) and any law that makes an act illegal after the fact (an *ex post facto* law).

Following concerns expressed by Antifederalists during the state ratification debates that the proposed Constitution granted the national government too much power, one of the first orders of business for the First Congress was a proposed bill of rights. The first ten amendments to the Constitution created associational freedoms (speech, press, assembly, and religion) that Congress could not abridge; limited the authority of governmental prosecutions against alleged criminals by restricting searches and seizures and guaranteeing the right to counsel and to public trials; and protected certain additional rights, including the right to bear arms and the right to jury trials in civil suits over $20 (see Chapter 4, Civil Liberties, for more details on these rights). The Bill of Rights originally applied only to the national government, not to the states.

The Constitution contains its own set of limits on the state governments. Like the national government, states cannot pass bills of attainder or *ex post facto* laws or create titles of nobility. Moreover, states cannot enter into treaties or alliances with foreign nations. The Constitution also limits the authority of states to tax imports and exports. The guarantee clause of the Constitution (Article IV, Section 4) guarantees that states shall have a "Republican Form of Government," meaning that a state cannot establish a pure **direct democracy** (although New England towns sometimes run along these

direct democracy:
Form of democracy in which political power is exercised directly by citizens.

lines), a monarchy, or a dictatorship (here the term *republican* has nothing to do with the Republican Party but refers to representative democracy).

The Fourteenth (1868) and Fifteenth Amendments (1870) also limit state authority. The Fourteenth Amendment prohibits the states from denying "any person" due process of law and the equal protection of the laws, and the Fifteenth Amendment prohibits states from denying voting rights on account of race, color, or previous condition of servitude. The Supreme Court later used the due process clause of the Fourteenth Amendment to require the states to follow most of the provisions of the Bill of Rights (see Chapter 4). Thus states must protect the same liberties as the federal government does, resulting in a nationalizing of the nation's most basic rights. Both the Supreme Court and Congress have used the Fifteenth Amendment to protect equal voting rights in the states and the equal protection clause of the Fourteenth Amendment to protect other civil rights (see Chapter 5, Civil Rights).

Groundwork for Relationships

In the U.S. federal system, where both the states and the federal governments have the final say over different matters, the Constitution lays out the powers of the national government and restrictions on the powers of both the national and the state governments. In addition, it lays out the groundwork for the relationship between the national government and the state governments and for relationships among the state governments.

Relationships between the Nation and the States.
The Constitution regulates the relationship between the national government and the states through three main clauses: the supremacy clause, the Tenth Amendment, and the sovereign immunity provision of the Eleventh Amendment. The **supremacy clause** (Article VI) makes the Constitution of the United States, plus all laws and treaties made under the Constitution, supreme over state law. Thus, if federal law conflicts with state law, the federal law (assuming it is within the powers of Congress) is supreme. Moreover, because state and federal courts might differ about whether state law and federal law actually conflicts in a particular case, the ultimate decision rests with the U.S. Supreme Court.[6]

The supremacy clause also allows for the preemption of state laws. If Congress and the states both seek to regulate an area of concurrent authority, such as pollution control or the minimum wage, the supremacy clause requires states to meet national standards if national standards are higher than state standards. More recently, in response to illegal immigration into the United States, Arizona and various other states have passed their own laws to deal with the problems, such as the right of local police officers to request documentation of those suspected of being in the United States illegally as well as harsh punishment for employers who hire undocumented workers. In 2012 the Supreme Court declared

supremacy clause: *Makes federal law supreme over state laws (Article VI).*

Connections:
Should the state or the national government set the minimum wage? Should the minimum wage vary with local conditions?

that federal law preempted most of the provisions of the Arizona law, but did allow Arizona to confirm people's immigration status while enforcing other laws.[7]

The Tenth Amendment states that all powers not delegated to the national government under the Constitution are reserved to the states or to the people. The Articles of Confederation had a similar clause, but it included the word *expressly* before the word *delegated*. Because the Tenth Amendment omits the word *expressly*, the implication is that the national government retains the sort of **implied powers** granted by the necessary and proper clause.

If the government illegally harms an individual or seizes the person's property, that person might be inclined to sue the government. The doctrine of sovereign immunity, however, means that a government cannot be sued without its permission. In a federal system with both state and federal courts, a state can prevent suits against itself in its own courts simply by passing a law preventing such suits. It cannot necessarily prevent lawsuits against it in federal court. Thus in 1793 the Supreme Court allowed the lawsuit of a South Carolina man against the state of Georgia.[8] Following this decision, Congress proposed and the states quickly ratified the Eleventh Amendment, which prohibits federal courts from hearing suits against a state by citizens of another state. The Eleventh Amendment is not absolute: Congress can allow suits based on provisions in constitutional amendments passed after the Eleventh, such as the due process and equal protection clauses of the Fourteenth Amendment.

Relationships among the States.

One of the many problems of governance under the Articles of Confederation was that the states could establish trade barriers against one another, thus limiting economic growth. Therefore, in the **commerce clause** (Article I, Section 8) the Constitution established Congress's exclusive authority to regulate commerce among the states. Thus states may not establish trade barriers against goods from other states. A state may tax goods from other states equal to the amount that it taxes goods produced in its own state, but it cannot charge extra taxes on goods that are made out of state. Congress cannot establish trade barriers in interstate commerce either, because Article I, Section 9 prohibits Congress from taxing exports from any state.

The Constitution also requires agreements between two or more states to receive the approval of Congress. States that share rivers, lakes, or other natural resources frequently make agreements over the use of their shared resources so that no one state overuses or overpollutes those resources.[9]

 implied powers: *Powers not expressly granted to Congress but added through the necessary and proper clause.*

 commerce clause: *Gives Congress the power to regulate commerce with foreign nations, with Indian tribes, and among the various states (Article I, Section 8).*

JUSTIN SULLIVAN/GETTY IMAGES

Same-sex marriage is a contentious issue related to federalism. Regulating family law has been a state power, and some states have approved same-sex marriage. The federal Defense of Marriage Act affirms that other states do not have to recognize these marriages. But in 2012 first and second circuit Appeals Courts declared the act unconstitutional in those circuits.

Article IV of the Constitution establishes additional rules that guide relationships among the states. The full faith and credit clause generally requires states to accept court decisions made in other states. What happens in Vegas does not necessarily stay in Vegas, as couples who are married (or divorced) there are married (or divorced) throughout the United States. This seemingly simple constitutional rule is now highly controversial, as some states have recognized same-sex marriages as valid. Under the full faith and credit clause, same-sex marriage performed in Massachusetts would presumably be valid throughout the nation. But the clause allows Congress to create exceptions. Congress passed and President William Jefferson (Bill) Clinton (1993–2001) signed one such exception into law with the Defense of Marriage Act (1996), which relieves states of the obligation of accepting the validity of same-sex marriages performed in other states. President Barack Obama, however, believing the law unconstitutional, in 2011 ordered the Justice Department not to defend it. Another general exception to the full faith and credit clause concerns child custody decisions. Because the best interests of a child may change over time, when a child is moved from one state to another, the courts in the new state need not accept the child custody determinations made by the previous state.

Through its privileges and immunities clause, Article IV also requires states to treat people from other states as equal to their own residents. Thus a state may not limit the right to practice law to residents, nor may it require people to live in the state for a set amount of time to receive welfare benefits. The courts, however, have allowed certain exceptions to this constitutional guarantee, the most notable being the higher tuition that out-of-state residents pay at state universities.

Connections:
Should all states be required to recognize same-sex marriages that are valid in one state?

Connections:
Should out-of-state students pay higher tuition at state universities? Why?

✓ Checkpoint

Can you:

☐ Describe the different types of powers in the Constitution

☐ State the limits on powers established in the Constitution

☐ Explain how the Constitution helps set the relationship between the national and federal governments

The Changing Nature of American Federalism

❯ **How U.S. federalism has changed over time**

The ratification of the Constitution pitted the state-centered Antifederalists against the nation-centered Federalists, and pro-state and pro-nation interests have contested the relative balance between the two ever since. Because a federal system presupposes separate states with guaranteed rights, tension between the layers of government is built in and inevitable.

Nationalization in the Founding Generation

During the administration of the nation's first president, George Washington (1789–1797), divisions over the extent of the authority of the national government split Secretary of the Treasury Alexander Hamilton and his allies from Secretary of State Thomas Jefferson and his allies. Hamilton favored a nation-centered federalism. He sought expansive federal power, and in 1790 he proposed that Congress establish the National Bank of the United States under a broad reading of the necessary and proper clause. Jefferson, who favored a state-centered federalism, unsuccessfully opposed the bank, which Congress created with a twenty-year charter. Jefferson's allies, however, were able to limit Hamilton's plan to promote manufacturing through subsidies to producers and taxes on imports.

In 1798, when the Federalist administration of John Adams (1797–1801) passed the Sedition Act (see Chapter 4), making criticism of the government illegal, Jefferson wrote a resolution adopted by the Kentucky legislature that declared the act void, claiming that states could decide for themselves which national laws to obey. James Madison authored a similar resolution that the Virginia legislature passed. Known as the Virginia and Kentucky Resolutions, these acts argued for **nullification**, the right of states to nullify, or reject, national laws that went beyond the powers granted in the Constitution. Though the Virginia and Kentucky Resolutions met with little approval outside their home states, the doctrine of nullification has reappeared when pro-state forces have questioned national authority.

The debate over national authority to establish a bank resurfaced after the first National Bank charter expired and Congress chartered a Second National Bank. The Supreme Court resolved this issue in **McCulloch v. Maryland** (1819) in an opinion written by Federalist Chief Justice John Marshall.[10] Marshall stated that Congress had the explicit authority to coin money and collect taxes and declared that the creation of a bank helped reach those goals. Thus creating a bank was an implied power that fell within the scope of authority granted by the necessary and proper clause (see Supreme Court Cases: *McCulloch v. Maryland*).

Five years later the Court, in another opinion by Marshall, established a broad construction, or interpretation, of Congress's enumerated power to regulate interstate commerce. In *Gibbons v. Ogden* (1824) the Court ruled that Congress's authority to regulate commerce among the states gave it, rather than the states, the authority to manage the licensing of steamboats traveling between New York and New Jersey. Marshall further declared that the authority of Congress to regulate commerce between the states did not begin or end at state boundaries but necessarily included commercial activities interior to each state.[11] Between the decisions in *McCulloch* and *Gibbons*, the Supreme Court under Marshall supported the Federalist Party position of a strong national government with expansive powers.

The Revolt against National Authority: Nullification, Slavery, and the Civil War

As Marshall's Supreme Court pushed the United States in a national direction, the precedent set by the Virginia and Kentucky Resolutions led various states

nullification:
Right of states to invalidate acts of Congress they believe to be illegal.

McCulloch v. Maryland: *1819 Supreme Court decision upholding the right of Congress to create a bank.*

supremecourtcases

McCulloch v. Maryland (1819)

QUESTION: May the federal government establish a bank? If so, does a state have the right to tax that bank?

ORAL ARGUMENT: February 22, 1819

DECISION: March 6, 1819 (read at http://www.findlaw.com/casecode/supreme.html)

OUTCOME: Yes, the bank is constitutional, and no, Maryland may not tax it (6–0).

Following the decision of Congress to establish the Second National Bank, the state of Maryland imposed a tax on the Maryland branch. The bank manager, James McCulloch, refused to pay the tax, and Maryland brought suit. The Maryland Supreme Court ruled that the bank was unconstitutional because the Constitution does not grant Congress the specific authority to create a bank. McCulloch appealed to the Supreme Court.

Attorney Daniel Webster, who had served in the House and would later serve in the Senate and as secretary of state, represented McCulloch before the Supreme Court. Among the most famed litigators of his day, Webster also represented the nationalist position before the Supreme Court in a District of Columbia lottery case and a New York steamboat case.*

The Supreme Court's decision, written by Chief Justice John Marshall, began by accepting the nation-centered view of the Constitution's founding: Rather than a compact of states, the government established by the Constitution "proceeds directly from the people; is 'ordained and established,' in the name of the people."

Regarding the power to establish a bank, Marshall noted that while the Constitution makes no reference to a bank, it does provide for coining and borrowing money, paying

government debts, and levying taxes. It also allows Congress to pass all laws that are "necessary and proper" to any of the enumerated powers. Declaring that "necessary and proper" does not mean "absolutely necessary," Marshall read the necessary and proper clause to mean "ordinary and appropriate."

In explaining the scope of the necessary and proper clause, Marshall declared, "Let the end be legitimate, let it be within the scope of the constitution, and all means which are appropriate, which are plainly adapted to that end, which are not prohibited, but consist with the letter and spirit of the constitution, are constitutional." Thus, creating a bank was an appropriate means of legitimate ends: regulating money and collecting taxes.

As for state taxation of the bank, Marshall based his response on the supremacy clause, observing that "the power to tax involves the power to destroy." Because states cannot destroy creations of the federal government, neither can they tax them.

The *McCulloch* decision created a broad scope for implied powers under the Constitution, powers that are not explicitly in the Constitution but are related to powers that are. Without this broad set of implied powers, Congress could not establish criminal laws for offenses, investigate executive wrongdoing, provide student loans, establish administrative agencies, or conduct many of the other activities it routinely engages in today.

- **If Congress does not have the express authority to establish a national bank, by what authority may it do so?**
- **What is the harm to federalism if a state can tax a national bank?**

* *Gibbons v. Ogden*, 22 U.S. 1 (1824).

to claim the right to disregard national laws that they believed were unconstitutional or unwise. Vice President John C. Calhoun argued that the union was merely a compact among the states, so dissenting states even had the right to **secede**. However, Senator Daniel Webster insisted that the union was not a compact of states, but a compact among the people of the United States.

It was federal authority to regulate slavery that eventually led to secession. Slavery concessions at the Constitutional Convention included the **fugitive slave clause** of Article IV, requiring states to return runaway slaves. Congress passed a Fugitive Slave Law in 1793 that established procedures for the return of slaves. In 1850, Congress strengthened the national authority over runaways by actually forcing states to aid in their return.[12]

Because nothing in the Constitution suggested that Congress had the power to limit slavery in the states, the most heated contests over congressional authority to regulate slavery involved the territories. In 1857 the Supreme Court sided with the states' rights supporters, declaring in *Dred Scott v. Sandford* that Congress had no authority to regulate slavery in the territories.[13] Southern states seceded when Abraham Lincoln (1861–65), who favored federal efforts to prohibit slavery in the territories, won the 1860 presidential election.

During the Civil War, Lincoln issued the Emancipation Proclamation, which prohibited slavery in states under rebellion, as slave labor was an asset to the Confederate army. However, slaves in the so-called border states of Delaware, Kentucky, Maryland, and Missouri, which allowed slavery but remained in the union, were not emancipated until ratification of the Thirteenth Amendment, which prohibited slavery throughout the nation as of December 18, 1865, after the war ended.

The Congresses that followed the Civil War tried to exert federal power over the states to promote equality between freedmen and whites, but President Andrew Johnson (1865–69) vetoed a civil rights bill that granted former slaves the rights to make contracts, sue, and give evidence and to inherit, purchase, lease, and convey real and personal property. In 1866, Congress passed it over Johnson's veto. But as part of the effort to ensure that all such laws would be constitutional, Congress proposed and the states ratified the Fourteenth Amendment (1868) and the Fifteenth Amendment (1870). These expanded the authority of the national government over the states. The Fourteenth Amendment requires states to provide each person due process of law and the equal protection of the laws. The Fifteenth Amendment prevents states from abridging the right to vote on account of race. Like the Thirteenth Amendment, the Fourteenth and Fifteenth Amendments granted Congress the authority to enforce their provisions by appropriate legislation, thus adding to Congress's enumerated powers. In 1883, however, the Supreme Court decided in the *Civil Rights Cases* to keep Congress's powers within the words of the amendments: Congress could prevent states from denying people equality, but it could not prevent private businesses or

secessio
seceding, or formally withdrawing, from a nation-state.

fugitive slave clause: *Required states to return runaway slaves; negated by the Thirteenth Amendment (Article IV, Section 2).*

individuals from doing so, for example, by refusing to hire former slaves or to serve them at inns or restaurants. The Court thus invalidated Congress's Civil Rights Act of 1875, which had prohibited this type of private discrimination. This era—the period before and after the Civil War—saw the defeat of the most strident (secessionist) state-centered views, but with the Supreme Court's interpretation of the Civil War amendments, state authority remained strong.

Dual Federalism

dual federalism:

Doctrine holding that state governments and the federal government have almost completely separate functions.

Although the supporters of state-centered federalism lost the Civil War, the viewpoint of a national government with limited powers did not disappear. A new viewpoint, **dual federalism**, recognized that, while the national government was supreme in some spheres, the state governments remained supreme in others, with layers of authority separate from one another, an arrangement that political scientists later compared to a "layer cake"[14] (see Figure 3.4). Thus the national government would be supreme over issues such as foreign affairs and interstate commerce, and the states would be supreme in matters concerning intrastate commerce and police powers.

Given that the Constitution does not specifically define the difference between interstate commerce and intrastate commerce, this division worked out well so long as Congress made little effort to regulate any form of commerce. In fact, for more than a decade following its 1875 attempt to prevent discrimination at inns and other places of public accommodation, Congress left the regulation of the economy to the states. With an increase in the industrialization at the end of the nineteenth century, however, came increases in economic inequality, with calls for Congress to help those who were harmed by the increasing concentration of wealth. Congress responded with the Interstate Commerce Act of 1887, which established the first federal regulatory agency, the Interstate Commerce Commission. The act charged the commission with making sure that railroads charged fair rates to farmers and other shippers.

Because concentrations of wealth and power were not limited to the railroads, Congress passed the Sherman Antitrust Act of 1890, an antimonopoly law that prohibits all contracts and combinations in restraint of trade. The United States went to court using the law to break up the Sugar Trust, a monopoly that controlled 98 percent of the nation's sugar refining. In 1895 the Supreme Court conceded in *United States v. E.C. Knight Co.* that the Sugar Trust was a monopoly and recognized that it conducted

Layer cake

Marble cake

FIGURE 3.4 Dual Federalism and Cooperative Federalism.

Dual federalism has been likened to a layer cake (left), and cooperative federalism has been likened to a marble cake (right).

Source: LAITS, University of Texas College of Liberal Arts, © Cengage Learning.

business throughout the United States. The Court nevertheless declared that Congress had no authority to regulate that monopoly because manufacturing was a subject of intrastate commerce only, even when the company in question manufactured its product in several states.[15] Here the Court used the Tenth Amendment as a gate protecting state powers against federal encroachment, declaring that it is up to the states to regulate the harms caused by monopolies. Thus, the Supreme Court limited national authority that Congress had claimed over areas that states' rights supporters thought belonged to the states.

This period of dual federalism left the national government and the states supreme in their respective spheres but granted Congress only a very narrow sphere. Regulations of manufacturing and mining remained under the control of the states, even if the goods later crossed state lines and entered interstate commerce. But a countertrend was emerging. In 1913 Congress passed and the states ratified the Sixteenth Amendment, which granted Congress the power to tax income from whatever source derived, giving the national government access to millions of dollars in revenue. The increase in federal authority over areas once left to the states was aided that same year by the ratification of the Seventeenth Amendment, which required that U.S. senators be directly elected by the people of each state. Before 1914 state legislatures selected senators, hoping they would be responsive to the needs of the states, but with direct elections, senators had to be responsive to the needs of the people.[16]

Cooperative Federalism: The New Deal and Civil Rights

With the onset of the Great Depression following the stock market crash of 1929, the people wanted national action to aid the economy. Nation-centered federalism, signaled by the Sixteenth and Seventeenth Amendments, strengthened considerably. Following Franklin Roosevelt's inauguration in 1933, Congress passed a series of laws designed to lift the ailing economy. As before, Congress asserted its authority under the commerce clause to regulate American industry. As before, the Supreme Court rejected such legislation.[17]

Given that the power to tax for a given purpose also grants the power to spend for that purpose, Congress alternatively attempted to regulate industry through the taxing clause—Congress's power to "lay and Collect Taxes" to "provide . . . for the general Welfare" (Article I, Section 8). Again the Supreme Court said no, declaring in one case that the taxing and spending provisions in a farm bill, whether for the general welfare or not, violated the Tenth Amendment.[18]

Despite vast support from Congress and the American people for his New Deal policies, Roosevelt (1933–45) saw the Supreme Court strike down one law after another. In response, Roosevelt proposed in 1937 to increase the number of justices on the Supreme Court. He would then be able to pack

Court-packing plan: *President Franklin Roosevelt's proposal to add new justices to the Supreme Court so that the Court would uphold his policies.*

Connections:
Should the drinking age be 21 or 18? Who should decide?

the Court with his own appointees. This controversial **Court-packing plan** met with fierce opposition in Congress. The Supreme Court, however, made passage of the plan unnecessary, for shortly after Roosevelt's proposal, the Court reversed itself and started accepting the broad authority of Congress to regulate the economy.

On taxing and spending, the Court accepted the view that virtually any taxing or spending plan that Congress believed supported the general welfare would be acceptable. Today, for example, although Congress has no direct authority to set drinking ages, it effectively does so by denying federal highway funds to states that set the drinking age under 21; for a variety of reasons, including low voting rates by younger Americans, no states do.

On commerce, the Court began by accepting the regulation of a giant steel company with operations throughout the United States as an appropriate regulation of interstate commerce.[19] Congress could also use the commerce clause to regulate employment conditions, said the Court, rejecting the Tenth Amendment as a limit on federal power.[20] The Court's definition of what constituted interstate commerce grew to include anything that affected interstate commerce, whether over several states or confined to one state. With federal intervention in manufacturing, farming, and other areas traditionally governed by the states, Roosevelt's nation-centered federalism was said by political scientists to more closely resemble a "marble cake," with specific powers under both national and state authority, than the layer-cake structure of dual federalism.[21]

Nation-centered federalism continued to dominate dual federalism through World War II and beyond. President Lyndon Baines Johnson's (1963–69) Great Society program expanded national authority even further, with federal aid to public schools and health care coverage to the poor (Medicaid) and elderly (Medicare). The Johnson administration also expanded national power to ensure greater equality, pushing for passage of the Civil Rights Act (1964), which prohibited job discrimination and segregation in public accommodations, and the Voting Rights Act (1965), which regulated voting rules that had largely been left to the states since the adoption of the Constitution.

State-centered federalism gained some traction, though, in opposition to the push toward equality and civil rights. In 1954 in *Brown v. Board of Education*, the Supreme Court struck down school segregation, which had been legally mandated or permitted in twenty states plus the District of Columbia.[22] This Supreme Court decision helped put the federal government at the forefront of the fight for equality.

The New Federalism

In the 1960s voters began to display a degree of wariness about the powers of the national government. Politicians—starting with Richard Nixon, the winner of the 1968 election—responded to these concerns.[23]

Presidents, Congress, and the New Federalism.   The Nixon administration (1969–74) began the trend, labeled New Federalism, of shifting powers back to the states.[24] While the Democratic Johnson administration gave money to the states in categorical grants, that is, money for the states to use on what the national government wanted, the Republican Nixon administration began a general revenue sharing program that gave the states greater leeway about how the funds could be spent. The main idea behind Nixon's federalism was that states could more efficiently spend governmental resources than the enormous federal bureaucracy could.

Republican President Ronald Reagan (1981–89) sought to reduce the power of government in general and, as an avid supporter of the New Federalism, of the federal government in particular. In his first inaugural address, he declared, "Government is not the solution to our problem; government is the problem."[25] He thus cut back on categorical grants, replacing them with fewer, more flexible block grants, which set fewer restrictions on how the money could be spent. He also eliminated general revenue sharing (see Table 3.1). Nevertheless, Reagan did sign the National Minimum Drinking Age Act, which withheld a percentage of federal highway funds from states that did not increase their drinking age to 21.

During the Clinton administration, Congress moved to shift the balance of power toward the states. First, it limited unfunded mandates—legal requirements Congress imposes on the states (for example, to provide clean air, disability access, or health benefits to poor people under Medicaid) without supplying the resources to accomplish those activities. Congress did not eliminate such mandates, but it did make them harder to impose. Second, Clinton and Congress overhauled the federal welfare system, ending the federal guarantee of welfare to poor families with children.

Although Republicans have typically supported state authority over that of the national government since the New Deal, President George W. Bush (2001–2009) oversaw an administration that strengthened national authority, sometimes at the expense of the states.[26] His most prominent actions in this regard included the No Child Left Behind Act (2002), which increased federal involvement in public education, and his prescription drug plan for Medicare.[27] The Bush administration went to court along with the auto industry in an attempt to preempt California's fuel economy and emission standards for cars, which were stricter than national standards (see Chapter 13, The Bureaucracy).[28] Following the terrorist attacks of September 11, 2001, Congress and the Bush administration expanded national power in various ways, including the establishment

> **Connections:** Was Reagan right in stating that "government is the problem"?

TABLE 3.1 Annual Percent Change in Federal Aid to State and Local Governments, in Constant Dollars

President	Percent Change
Lyndon Baines Johnson (1963–69)	11.7%
Richard M. Nixon (1969–74)	9.0%
Gerald R. Ford (1974–77)	8.7%
Jimmy Carter (1977–81)	−1.0%
Ronald Reagan (1981–89)	−1.3%
George H. W. Bush (1989–93)	8.4%
William J. Clinton (1993–2001)	4.2%
George W. Bush (2001–2009)	3.9%
Barack Obama	7.8%*

*2009–2011 only.

Source: Derived by authors from Office of Management and Budget, Historical Tables, Table 12.1, accessed May 2, 2012, http://www.whitehouse.gov/omb/budget/Historicals/.

of national standards for driver's licenses. Although Bush was a Republican and a former governor—two factors that might ordinarily indicate greater support for the states over the federal government—his administration was, conclude two political scientists, "routinely dismissive of federalism concerns."[29]

On the other hand, two early decisions by the Obama administration signaled support for state-centered federalism, at least where the policies support Democratic Party positions: support for permitting states to set higher standards than the federal government on fuel economy and tailpipe emissions and a reversal of the Bush administration's crackdown on state medical marijuana programs.[30] In addition, the stimulus package of 2009 directed more than $100 billion in federal revenue to the states.[31] Some Republican governors, however, refused some of the stimulus funds that were earmarked for unemployment insurance because accepting them would have required expanded unemployment coverage once the federal stimulus funds ran out.

Connections:
Do you tend to support nation-centered federalism or state-centered federalism? Which is more responsive? Which ensures citizen equality?

The Supreme Court and the New Federalism.

President Reagan was supportive of state-centered federalism. By nominating William Rehnquist to be chief justice in 1986, Reagan hoped to move the Court toward greater judicial respect for the states. He was not disappointed. As chief justice (1986–2005), Rehnquist further advanced New Federalism, now aided by a Republican bloc that grew to include seven justices. The Rehnquist Court put together pro-state majorities in two series of decisions: interstate commerce and sovereign immunity.

Concerning interstate commerce, for the first time since 1937 the Court rejected national laws as beyond Congress's authority to regulate under the commerce clause. In one case, the Court struck down congressional legislation banning the possession of guns near schools, declaring that the possession of a gun near a school is not an economic activity.[32] Permitting Congress to regulate noneconomic activity because of the effect it might have on economic activity allows the national government to regulate virtually everything. The Roberts Court (2005–) continued this trend, ruling in the 2012 health care case that not purchasing health insurance was not economic activity either.[33]

Connections:
Should guns be allowed in or near schools and college campuses? Who should decide?

The Rehnquist Court also limited national authority over the states through the doctrine of sovereign immunity. Although the Eleventh Amendment prevents citizens of one state from suing a different state in federal court, the Court ruled that the amendment limits the rights of citizens to sue their own states in federal court. The Court thus prevented citizens from suing their own states for violations of federal labor law,[34] for harm

AP PHOTO/REED SAXON

The La Brea Collective medical marijuana dispensary in Los Angeles displays varieties of marijuana in canning jars. Fourteen states including California have legalized medical marijuana. Elsewhere in the United States, marijuana cannot be sold or used for medical purposes, although cancer patients report that it relieves nausea and vomiting during chemotherapy, and others claim a variety of additional medical benefits.

to businesses by unfair competition and for infringements of patents or copyrights by state universities,[35] and for otherwise illegal discrimination against a breast cancer victim by her employer, the Alabama State University system. According to the Court in the Alabama State University case, "the ultimate guarantee of the Eleventh Amendment is that nonconsenting States may not be sued by private individuals in federal court."[36]

While these decisions stand in contrast to the decidedly pro-national decisions of the Court since the New Deal, most questions of federal authority still are decided in favor of the national government. The Court affirmed that Congress can criminalize home-grown marijuana production and use even if state law allows it for medical purposes.[37] The Obama administration used its discretion not to prosecute such cases when state laws allow such use for medicinal purposes. Indeed, while the Supreme Court routinely continues to uphold Congress's authority to regulate commercial activity, there has been no return to the pre-New Deal distinction between commerce and manufacturing. And while the Roberts Court did not uphold the health care law on commerce grounds, it did uphold the law through the taxing clause.[38]

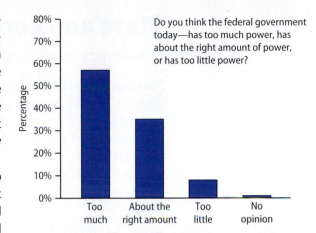

FIGURE 3.5 Public Opinion on the Power of the Federal Government, 2011.

Source: Gallup Poll, September 2011, retrieved April 9, 2012, from the iPOLL Databank, The Roper Center for Public Opinion Research, University of Connecticut Copyright © 2011 Gallup, Inc. All rights reserved. The content is used with permission; however, Gallup retains all right of republication.

> **Connections:** Were the Antifederalists right to fear the power of the national government?

Summing Up: Were the Antifederalists Correct?

The people of the United States ratified the Constitution over the protests of Antifederalists, who claimed that the Constitution gave virtually unlimited powers to the national government. Nevertheless, until the New Deal, either because of congressional inaction or Supreme Court reaction when Congress did act, the powers exercised by the national government were clearly limited. Today, however, between the popular belief in the need to regulate a complex economy and the Supreme Court's interpretation of the Constitution, Congress has vast powers. In 2011 a majority of Americans reported that they thought the federal government had too much power (see Figure 3.5). The 2012 election contest between President Obama and Governor Mitt Romney featured candidates with differing views about the balance of the nation-state relationship. In the U.S. federal system, the voters get to decide on that balance.

 Checkpoint

Can you:

☐ Compare Jefferson's and Hamilton's views on federalism

☐ Describe the role that federalism played in the run-up to the Civil War

☐ Explain the "layer-cake" analogy in dual federalism

☐ Compare dual federalism with cooperative federalism

☐ Explain what led to the New Federalism

☐ Find Antifederalist arguments in today's political debates

State and Local Governments

> ❯ **How state governments differ from the national government**

The Constitution requires that the states maintain a republican form of government, and all have done so by patterning their structure after the national government, with separate legislative, judicial, and executive branches. With the exception of procedures that allow citizens to place proposed laws directly on the ballot, state governments look remarkably similar to the federal government. Local governments, however, use a greater range of organizational options.

State Governments

All fifty states have separate legislative and executive branches, and all fifty states choose the head of the executive branch by direct election. Most states have four-year gubernatorial terms, limit their governors to two consecutive terms, and provide for succession by the lieutenant governor.

The governors of all fifty states have the authority to veto laws subject to override by the state legislatures. Most states further grant their governors a line-item veto, the ability to veto certain parts of a spending bill without vetoing the entire bill. The president does not have this power, so when Congress passes spending bills, it usually does so by combining tens of thousands of separate spending items in an omnibus bill. The president's choice is to sign the entire bill or to veto it; he cannot veto only the appropriations he disfavors. Governors in forty-four states do have that authority, however, giving them a much stronger tool to control spending than the president has.

Of those forty-four states, twenty-six allow governors to veto not just appropriations, but also language in appropriations bills.[39] Wisconsin's veto authority, known as the "Frankenstein" veto, allows the governor to create entirely new language by crossing out words and numbers throughout a bill, leaving behind new language that could radically change the meaning of the law. For example, when the state created a five-person Minority Business Development Board that gave other individuals the authority to appoint three of the five members, the governor vetoed the words of the law that delegated those three appointments to others, thus taking the authority to appoint all five members. A state constitutional amendment approved by the voters in 2008 retained the governor's authority to change the meaning of laws by crossing out particular words or numbers (eliminating "not" from a sentence can have enormous consequences!), but the governor can no longer stitch together new sentences from two or more previous sentences.[40]

Connections: What would happen if the president had a line-item veto?

In addition to the line-item veto, some states grant governors special budgetary authority to limit spending. West Virginia's constitution does not allow the legislature to increase spending on any item over the amount proposed by the governor. New York's governor has sole authority over the language in spending bills. The legislature can increase or decrease the amounts, but it cannot add provisions excluded from the governor's budget, nor can it change formulas for distributing aid contained in spending bills.[41] Every state except Vermont requires a balanced budget. Unlike the federal government, which can borrow money to pay for spending programs, typically popular spending increases in the states have to be matched by typically unpopular tax increases. Even states with balanced budget requirements can accumulate long-term liabilities, either by issuing bonds to finance capital projects such as roads or bridges or by underfunding future pension obligations.

On the legislative side, forty-nine of the fifty states have bicameral (two-chamber) legislative branches; Nebraska has only a single chamber. Nebraska also has nonpartisan elections, meaning that candidates for election are not listed under a party banner. Most states have four-year terms for their upper chambers and two-year terms for their lower chambers. The Twenty-Second Amendment (ratified in 1947) limits the president of the United States to two terms in office. Similarly, thirty-five states limit governors to two terms, Virginia limits governors to one consecutive term, and fourteen states allow unlimited terms.

The greatest differences between the national and the state governments appear at the judicial level. Federal judges are nominated by the president and confirmed by the Senate. States have various procedures for selecting judges: nearly half use an appointment process for judges on their highest court, while the rest use elections. For states that use appointments, most grant the governor the right to make appointments (usually with the consent of the state senate).

Connections: What effects do judicial elections have on judges' decisions? What effects should they have?

While federal judges serve during good behavior, which essentially means life terms, only Rhode Island does that at the state level, with Massachusetts and New Hampshire judges serving until age 70. In the rest of the states, judges have set terms. For example, in the widely copied **Missouri Plan** for selecting judges, also known as the merit plan, a board of experts recommends candidates to the governor, who selects judges from the list. The selected judges are then subject to retention elections: When a judge's term expires, voters get to vote yes or no on retaining the judge. Although judges overwhelmingly win retention elections, being unresponsive to voter preferences on important issues can cost them their seats. Such was the case when, in November 2010, Iowa voters rejected the retention of the three Iowa Supreme Court justices who were part of the unanimous court decision in 2009 blocking the ban on same-sex marriage in Iowa. Because voters

Missouri Plan: *Process for selecting state judges whereby the original nomination is by appointment and subsequent retention is by a retention election.*

are more likely to be upset by judges who are too lenient—rather than too harsh—on criminals, many judges are more likely to approve death sentences or longer prison terms as their elections draw near.[42]

The Supreme Court ruled that the First Amendment's right to freedom of speech protects the right of judicial candidates, including their right to discuss their views on relevant issues.[43] Judicial campaigns also mean campaign contributions, and these are most likely to come from people who might have business before the judges in question. In Texas, for example, where the state supreme court, like the U.S. Supreme Court, chooses whether to hear cases appealed to it, people who contributed to the campaigns of the justices of the supreme court were nine times more likely to have their cases heard than people who did not.[44] This situation arguably violates the common view of how the judiciary should operate.

In West Virginia the president of a coal company appealing a $50 million jury verdict spent $3 million to defeat an incumbent West Virginia Supreme Court justice and elect a challenger who would be friendlier to the company. After the newly elected justice joined a 3–2 majority overturning the award, the U.S. Supreme Court declared that the state court justice could not rightfully participate in the case, given the risk of bias.[45] More of these cases will undoubtedly come before the federal courts. Generally, state courts can conduct their affairs free of federal court interference unless a federal law, a treaty, or the U.S. Constitution is under consideration. The broad terms in the Constitution and the broad scope of congressional lawmaking mean, however, that the Supreme Court often has the ability to review state court decisions.

Connections: What impact does your local government have on you?

Local Governments

Local governments are far more diverse in function and design than state governments. First, there can be several different layers of local governments, with residents regulated by villages, cities, and towns or townships at the most local level and by counties above that. Some local governments run all local services, including police, schools, and sanitation. Many states, however, delegate specialized activities to special jurisdiction governments, such as school boards, water districts, fire districts, library districts, and sewer districts. The United States contains more than 37,000 special jurisdiction governments plus another 13,000 school boards. Overall, there are nearly 90,000 governmental units in the United States[46] providing hundreds

... I WROTE THE GOVERNOR...

WHO SENT ME TO THE LEGISLATURE...

WHO STEERED ME TO MY COUNTY EXECUTIVE...

WHO DIRECTED ME TO THE TOWN SUPERVISOR...

WHO LED ME TO THE VILLAGE LEADERS...

TO ASK THE BEST WAY TO REDUCE GOVERNMENT.

of thousands of citizens a ready gateway for citizen involvement in public affairs, as Brian Maughan's story illustrates.

Second, local governments, unlike state governments, do not necessarily consist of three separate branches. One reason is that criminal and civil trials are usually handled in state courts, leaving little need for a local community to have its own judicial branch. Many local governments have elected leaders of the executive branch—mayors for villages and cities, county executives for counties, and supervisors for townships—but many use a city-manager system in which the legislative branch appoints a professional administrator to run the executive branch.

Recall, initiatives, and referendums are used frequently as gateways of direct democracy (see Figure 3.6). Recall allows citizens who gather enough petition signatures to force a special vote to remove state or local elected officials before their terms expire. Permitted in eighteen states,

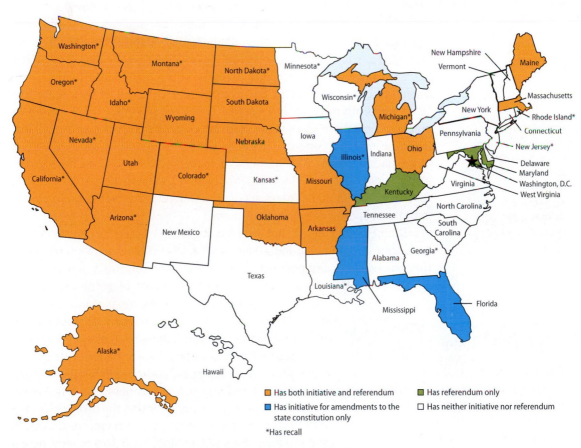

Has both initiative and referendum
Has initiative for amendments to the state constitution only
Has referendum only
Has neither initiative nor referendum
*Has recall

FIGURE 3.6 **States That Allow Recall, Initiative, and Referendum.**

Source: © Cengage Learning; data from Council of State Governments, *The Book of the States*, 2010.

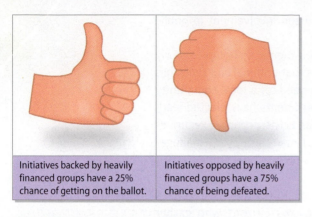

| Initiatives backed by heavily financed groups have a 25% chance of getting on the ballot. | Initiatives opposed by heavily financed groups have a 75% chance of being defeated. |

FIGURE 3.7 Initiative Spending.

Large interest groups with abundant funds powerfully influence initiatives. Most initiatives have no chance of getting on the ballot, but money makes a difference. The influence of money in initiatives calls into question their reputation as direct democracy.

Source: Thomas E. Cronin, *Direct Democracy: The Politics of Initiative, Referendum, and Recall* (Cambridge, Mass.: Harvard University Press, 1989).

Connections:
The last time you voted, were there any initiatives or referenda on the ballot? Did you know enough about them to make an informed choice?

Checkpoint

Can you:

☐ Compare the general features of state governments to their national counterparts

☐ Compare the features of local governments to their national counterparts

recall allowed Wisconsin voters in 2012 to reconsider the tenure of Governor Scott Walker, who had tried to severely curtail the collective bargaining rights of public employees. Walker won. In 2003, California voters recalled Governor Gray Davis and replaced him with Arnold Schwarzenegger in a special election. Initiative is a process that allows citizens who collect the required number of petition signatures to place proposed laws directly on the ballot for the state's citizens to vote on. Referendum allows legislatures to put certain issues on the ballot for citizen approval and requires legislatures to seek citizen approval for certain actions. Depending on the state, these actions could be proposals to borrow money, increase taxes, or approve constitutional amendments. All fifty states require referenda on some issues. Only twenty-four states allow initiatives.[47] Both procedures allow well-organized citizens to bypass the elected representatives in their state. The U.S. Constitution, in setting specific terms for senators, representatives, and presidents, prohibits recall of federal officials, and in granting all legislative powers to Congress, it similarly prohibits initiative and referendum at the national level. The number and importance of initiatives have grown in more recent years. California's Proposition 13 famously slashed property taxes in 1978. In 2010 voters across the United States voted on forty-two initiatives, approving eighteen of them.[48]

Direct democracy is not without its critics. As are other aspects of American government, initiatives are heavily influenced by money. Although socialists and populists originally pushed for direct democracy to expand the influence of ordinary citizens, the cost of gathering enough signatures to get on the ballot means that initiatives are limited largely to those with great financial resources. In 1998, for example, California Indian tribes spent $66 million in support of a successful California proposition that would allow them to expand casino gambling on Indian reservations. Fearful of losing business, Las Vegas casinos spent $26 million in opposition to the proposal. In the 2008 California vote banning gay marriage, contributions totaled more than $72 million, with the money nearly evenly split between the supporters and opponents of the successful ban (see Figure 3.7).

Federalism and Public Policy: Education

The structure of the federal system has a profound effect on public policy. It allows states to copy policies from one another but sometimes forces them into competition with one another. Many state policies involve issues in which the national government does not get involved, whereas in other areas, such as welfare policies, federal mandates and incentives push the states to do what the federal government wants. In this section, we examine education policy as an example.

Federal Aid to the States

Through the supremacy clause, Congress has the final say on many issues, but an intergovernmental lobby, made up of groups such as the National Governors Association (NGA), the National Conference of State Legislatures, and the National League of Cities, pressures Congress to limit mandates and provide funding for state and local needs.

Federal aid to the states is influenced by a large number of factors, including equal representation in the Senate.[49] The fact that small states have the same number of senators as large states do means that small states receive a disproportionate amount of federal aid. For example, in 2010 Wyoming and Alaska received the most aid per capita.[50] These states and eighteen more get more antiterrorism aid per capita than does New York, a frequent terrorist target.[51] As the president is particularly responsive to the people and party who elected him, it is hardly surprising that states that heavily supported the incumbent president in the previous election, and states whose governors are of the same party as the president, get more federal aid than other states.[52]

> **Connections:** Where does your state rank in the amount of federal aid it receives?

Policy Diffusion

In a 1932 opinion Supreme Court Justice Louis Brandeis wrote, "It is one of the happy incidents of the federal system that a single courageous State may, if its citizens choose, serve as a laboratory; and try novel social and economic experiments without risk to the rest of the country."[53] Oregon is currently experimenting with the nation's only physician-assisted suicide law. Perhaps other states will reject physician-assisted suicide, or perhaps states or the federal government will see the benefits of such laws.

The main benefit of states serving as laboratories of change is that other states can learn about successful programs and copy them or learn what not to do if an experimental program fails. This takes place through a process

policy diffusion:

Process by which policy ideas and programs initiated by one state spread to other states.

race to the bottom:

Situation in which states compete with one another to lower protections and services below the level they might otherwise prefer.

known as **policy diffusion**, and it typically starts with states that border one another. Examples are numerous, including the Children's Health Insurance Program,[54] regulation of air pollution,[55] school choice plans (allowing students to choose which school in a district to attend),[56] health care reform,[57] and Indian gambling casinos.[58]

The Race to the Bottom

If diffusion is the good side of policy making in a federal system, the **race to the bottom** can, depending on one's point of view, potentially involve negative consequences. A race to the bottom exists when states compete against each other to reduce taxes, environmental protections, or welfare benefits in order to create incentives for businesses to come to the state or disincentives for poor people to come. For example, lower tax rates draw people to a state, yet to keep people there, the state cannot raise taxes even when the public might desire more spending.[59] When states compete economically with one another, if one state decreases environmental enforcement, a neighboring state may be forced to do so as well.[60] In terms of welfare benefits, individuals seeking benefits move to the most generous states. This situation led states to establish residency requirements for welfare until the Supreme Court prohibited them.[61] Consequently, states that want to increase welfare benefits for their own citizens hesitate to do so unless neighboring states also do so, lest they attract an overload of recipients from those other states.[62] Alternately, the Obama administration established a "Race to the Top" (RTTP) in education, whereby states that implement education reforms, such as increasing the number of charter schools, receive more federal aid. This action coincides with increasing federal involvement in education over the past fifty years.

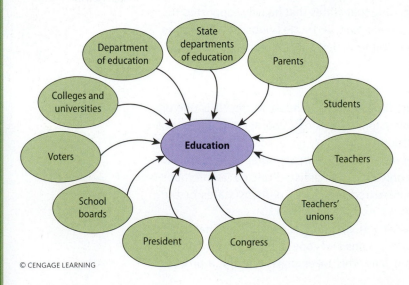

© CENGAGE LEARNING

Education Policy

The Founders considered an educated citizenry essential to the survival of the democracy. John Adams wrote that "Wherever a general knowledge and sensibility have prevailed among the people, arbitrary government and every kind of oppression have lessened and disappeared in proportion."[63] In other words, sound education helps people hold their leaders accountable and be attentive to the overall responsiveness of their government.

Despite the fact that federally elected politicians talk frequently about the importance of education, the federal government itself funds less than 10 percent of all elementary and secondary education spending.[64] The primary reason for this minimal funding is the federal structure. With education among the reserved powers left to the states, state and local governments developed the responsibility for educating the populace. Originally, states set education policy that local communities then implemented through locally elected school boards, or what one book called "ten thousand democracies."[65] Depending on the state, local school boards had differing amounts of power to establish the curriculum, support extracurricular activities, hire and fire teachers, negotiate salaries for school district employees, and set standards for graduation. Over time, funding for elementary and secondary education became based on local property taxes, with some additional assistance from state governments. Just as the overall wealth of local communities and states varies, so does the amount of funding available for education. While many factors beyond money contribute to a high-quality education, the enormous disparity between states—New York spent more than $18,000 per pupil in 2008–2009 while Utah spent only $6,000[66]—undoubtedly adds to disparities in the quality of education provided by elementary and secondary schools across the country.

The Civil Rights Act of 1964 put Congress in the role of regulating education. Title IV of the act grants the attorney general the authority to file suits on behalf of the United States to end school segregation. Title VI prohibits schools that receive federal funds from discriminating on the basis of race. The act left enforcement to the Department of Health, Education, and Welfare (HEW; today there is a separate Department of Education). The importance of the funding provision increased when the Elementary and Secondary Education Act of 1965 vastly increased federal spending on education. This act gave HEW a powerful tool to fight segregation. According to one analysis of school desegregation, "Districts under HEW enforcement were significantly less segregated than court-ordered districts."[67]

AP PHOTO/GREG WAHL-STEPHENS

At a Head Start Program in Hillsboro, Oregon, children work on an art project. The federal Head Start Program, which began in 1965, promotes school readiness for about 1 million children from low-income families each year. Federal grants are awarded to qualified local public and private agencies, which provide a portion of the funding with cash or in-kind services. In 2012 the Obama administration implemented new regulations requiring underperforming programs to compete for federal funding.

Today the federal government has numerous programs to provide equal access to education across income level, race, and level of disability. These programs are under the jurisdiction of a variety of agencies. For example, the Department of Health and Human Services (HHS) oversees the Head Start and Early Head Start programs for low-income children, while the Department of Education has programs for homeless children and remedial education for disadvantaged children, and it also implements programs for children with disabilities under the Individuals with Disabilities Education Act (IDEA, 1975, amended in 2004 and 2011). All of these programs serve those who have historically not had access to high-quality education because of low income or disability.[68]

Despite the stronger federal role, however, education under a federal system still permits inequality by allowing a vast disparity in how much states and local communities choose to spend on it.

 Construct Your Own Policy

1. Draft a federal law that would equalize funding for elementary and secondary education within states and across states. Be sure to state the role of the federal government in implementing this change in education funding.

2. Draft legislation that would design national universities directly funded by the federal government in order to improve access to higher education for more students.

For more on the policy-making process, see Chapter 1.

Federalism and Democracy

A federal system has more gateways to influence than a confederal or unitary system. In confederal systems, citizens can influence their local governments, but there is little value in influencing the national government given its limited scope. Alternatively, in unitary systems, the national level has a lot of authority, but citizens cannot work their way through more localized structures to influence it. Although federal systems create multiple gateways to influence, they also make it less clear who is responsible if policies are not well run. If health care falters, for example, is that the fault of the national government or the state government?

Under a unitary system, there is little doubt about who is responsible if a policy fails. A unitary system also means that diverse state laws would be replaced with one set of laws on issues such as medical marijuana, gay marriage, divorce, and gun control. Given that Americans have different views on these issues, the strength of a federal system is that it allows people in, say, Arizona, to live under laws created by other people in Arizona, rather than by people throughout the United States.

A unitary system also increases so-called conformity costs by increasing the number of people who disagree with the policies of the government. Conformity costs are not financial; they represent the dissatisfaction that people feel when they live under laws they do not like. Consider medical marijuana, for example. Under a unitary system, the nation would have a single set of medical marijuana laws. Either medical marijuana supporters or opponents would not get their way, regardless of local public opinion. With federalism, each state gets to choose for itself whether to allow the use of medical marijuana. Federalism does not eliminate conformity costs, but it does lower them. Overall, federalism allows the people who live in the most conservative states to have local rules that favor conservative values and those who live in the most liberal states to choose local rules that favor liberal values.

Citizens in states with conservative majorities can obtain conservative government by electing conservative representatives, and citizens in states with liberal majorities can elect liberal representatives. These citizens can also obtain results they desire through direct governing procedures such as the initiative and referendum. Although initiative procedures presumably provide for greater democratic responsiveness than does filtering preferences through elected representatives, initiatives may be too responsive to citizen desires. Madison, though not referring to the initiative itself, feared direct democracy, believing that citizens were prone to factions that would put self-interest over the best interests of society. Thus Madison and the Framers preferred a large-scale republic over local democracies, fearful that local majorities would infringe the rights of local minorities (see *Federalist* 10 in the Appendix). One disadvantage of federalism in the United States has been that people opposed to equality for blacks have used arguments about states' rights to limit civil rights. Alternatively, the nation-centric view of federalism has been used to create a more equal society for minorities subject to discrimination.

Overall, though, federalism enhances democracy by enabling more people to live under laws that are made locally, rather than forcing everyone in the nation to live under all of the same rules. State experiments with direct democracy procedures such as the initiative and referendum give citizens a gateway to influence that they do not have with the national government.

Focus Questions Revisited

- How does federalism affect government's responsiveness? To what and to whom are federal systems accountable?

- What does it mean for citizen equality when different states are allowed to have different laws on certain subjects?

- How does a federal system make it easier for citizens to have an influence in government?

- What has been the relationship between federalism and the push for equality in the United States?

- Is federalism a gate or a gateway to democracy? Explain.

gateways**to**learning

Top Ten to **Take Away**

1. The American colonies joined together as a nation to pool their resources in fighting for their independence from Britain, but they also shared a common identity based on origin, history, and ancestry. (pp. 67–68)

2. In writing a new Constitution in 1787, the Framers established a new system of government—federalism—in which state and national governments share power. (pp. 68–70)

3. The Constitution grants specified powers to the national government, reserving all remaining powers to the states and to the people. It also limits both federal and state powers and lays out the relationships among the states and between the states and the federal government. (pp. 70–74)

4. The American system was an experiment, and its evolution has been shaped by the tensions, even conflicts, inherent in a system in which power is both divided and shared. From the beginning, nation- and state-centered interests have been pitted against each other. (pp. 74–76)

5. One recurring substantive theme in the federalism debate has involved slavery, race, and equality, with nation-centered federalism used generally to advance equality for minorities subject to discrimination. (pp. 77–80)

6. Over the years nation-centered federalism has generally expanded through legislation and court interpretation, though there have been eras in which the Court held Congress back and elections in which the people indicated that they thought the national government had too much power. (pp. 76–85)

7. All fifty states have separate legislative, executive, and judicial branches that look remarkably similar to those of the federal government, while local governments use a greater range of organizational options. (pp. 86–90)

8. The structure of the federal system has a profound effect on public policy, allowing states to learn from each other but sometimes forcing them into competition with each other. (pp. 91–92)

9. The federal system also allows for vast disparities among the states, particularly in the quality of elementary and secondary education. (pp. 92–94)

10. Benefits of federalism include multiple gateways to influence, including methods of direct democracy such as the initiative and referendum. Federalism also enhances democracy by enabling more people to live under laws that are made locally, rather than forcing nationwide conformity. (pp. 89–90)

Key **Concepts**

commerce clause (p. 75). How has the Supreme Court's interpretation of the commerce clause changed over time?

concurrent powers (p. 72). Why do concurrent powers exist?

confederal system (p. 68). What are the likely problems of confederal systems?

Court-packing plan (p. 82). How would this plan have impacted the independence of the judiciary?

direct democracy (p. 74). What forms of direct democracy exist in the United States?

dual federalism (p. 80). Can dual federalism work in a modern nation?

enumerated powers (p. 70). Why are Congress's powers enumerated?

federalism (p. 69). What type of nation is more likely to adopt a federal system?

fugitive slave clause (p. 79). Why did fugitive slave laws cause so much friction between North and South?

implied powers (p. 75). What are some examples of implied powers?

McCulloch v. Maryland (p. 77). Does Congress need to establish a national bank?

Missouri Plan (p. 87). What are the advantages of appointing, rather than electing, judges?

necessary and proper clause (p. 70). How has the Supreme Court interpreted "necessary and proper"?

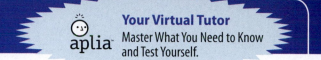

Your Virtual Tutor
aplia™ Master What You Need to Know and Test Yourself.

nullification (p. 77). What happens to a federal system if the subunits retain the right of nullification?

policy diffusion (p. 92). Why is policy diffusion an advantage of federalism?

race to the bottom (p. 92). Why is the race to the bottom a disadvantage of federalism?

reserve powers (p. 72). What does it mean that states have reserve powers?

secession (p. 79). Should there ever be a right to secede from a national government?

self-government (p. 70). If you were to rank personal liberties, where would you rank self-government?

supremacy clause (p. 74). What would happen to the U.S. constitutional system without the supremacy clause?

unitary system (p. 68). What is the effect of unitary systems on gateways to participation?

Learning Outcomes

WHAT YOU NEED...

To Know	To Test Yourself	To Participate
Why the Framers chose a federal system	• Explain why the Founders chose to unify • Compare the alternatives to federalism	• Appreciate why you are a citizen of the nation of and of a state
How the Constitution reflects the federal system	• Describe the different types of powers in the Constitution • State the limits on powers established in the Constitution • Explain how the Constitution helps set the relationship between the national and federal governments	• Propose additional limits that you would like to see on governmental power
How U.S. federalism has changed over time	• Compare Jefferson's and Hamilton's views on federalism • Describe the role that federalism played in the run-up to the Civil War • Explain the "layer-cake" analogy in dual federalism • Compare dual federalism with cooperative federalism • Explain what led to the New Federalism • Find Antifederalist arguments in today's political debates	• Evaluate whether the federal government is too powerful • Detect friction in your community between state and federal powers • Decide whether the Antifederalists were correct
How state governments differ from the national government	• Compare the general features of state governments to their national counterparts • Compare the features of local governments to their national counterparts	• Lobby a state representative on a state issue that is important to you • Lobby a local official on a local issue that is important to you

© SAM LEVITAN PHOTOGRAPHY

COURTESY OF STEPHANIE GOOD

> *My greatest regret is that rather than believing in myself, I allowed someone else's opinion to postpone my dreams.*

**R. Stephanie Good,
Stony Brook University,
Stony Brook,
New York**

4

Civil Liberties

R. Stephanie Good started her college career later in life than many people, waiting until she was in her mid-thirties before enrolling first at Nassau Community College on Long Island in New York and then at nearby Stony Brook University. She graduated from both schools with highest honors, but she was as well known for her political activism as she was for her academic excellence. During her college years, she campaigned for public officials, demonstrated on behalf of environmental issues, and got arrested at Stony Brook as part of a "tent-city" protest over housing for graduate students. Committed to the idea that justice is served only when citizens take action on their own behalf, she went on to law school, earning a JD at Hofstra University and, ten years later, an LLM.

While practicing law, Good started writing. Her first book, *Law School 101,* presents survival techniques for law school and life as an attorney. Her next two books (both coauthored) uncovered corruption in notorious criminal proceedings.

Aruba: The Tragic Untold Story of Natalee Holloway and Corruption in Paradise, a *New York Times* best seller, recounts the disappearance and presumed murder of a high school student on a school graduation trip. *A Rush to Injustice* tells the story of the Duke lacrosse case, in which a reelection-seeking

aplia | Need to Know

- **What civil liberties are**
- **Why civil liberties are limited in times of crisis**
- **What rights of expression the First Amendment protects**
- **What religious freedoms the First Amendment protects**
- **How the "right to bear arms" has been interpreted**
- **What protections the Bill of Rights provides to those accused of crimes**
- **What constitutes the right to privacy**

prosecutor maliciously filed felony sexual assault charges against college students whom he knew were innocent.

Good's commitment to protection of the innocent was also personal. When she was in law school, she learned that one of her sons had been subjected to inappropriate solicitations by an instructor at their local church. After she went public about this violation, other families revealed inappropriate touching by the instructor. Yet the judicial system did not consider the matter to be serious, and the instructor received only a 15-day sentence. Years later, when Good thought the instructor might be seeking out her son again, she decided to go online to try to find boys who also received unwarranted attention from the instructor, creating a 13-year-old-girl with the AOL handle "teen2hot4u." That handle attracted interest from adult men interested in sex with an underage girl. Good then contacted the Federal Bureau of Investigation, which asked her to continue to play out her undercover role. Agents schooled Good on how to avoid violating the rights of the people with whom she communicated, because although they may have been breaking laws regarding the molestation of children, their rights as citizens also had to be protected, including their right to fair legal proceedings and their right to be considered legally innocent until proven guilty. First, she could not initiate conversations with anyone. Second, she could not be the first person to mention sex. And third, she could not be the first person to suggest a meeting. Despite these restrictions, teen2hot4u attracted the attention of hundreds of men, more than twenty of whom tried to arrange a sexual meeting, got arrested, and then, with

Good's testimony, were convicted and sentenced to prison. Good's efforts literally saved hundreds of young children from having their lives ruined. She recounted the story in her fourth book, *Exposed: The Harrowing Story of a Mother's Undercover Work with the FBI to Save Children from Internet Sex Predators*. In 2010, Congressman Tim Bishop (D-N.Y.) awarded Good a certificate of commendation for her work.[1]

In a democracy, criminal investigations must be conducted in a way that protects both the victims and society and those who are accused of crimes. Reprehensible crimes, such as sexual abuse of children, test people's willingness to recognize the rights of the accused. Yet without standard and fair criminal proceedings, citizens would be subjected to arbitrary arrest and possibly punishment, as the Duke lacrosse case shows. The tensions surrounding freedom and fair treatment in a democracy extend beyond criminal procedure. Disagreements about politics, particularly during wartime, also test people's willingness to tolerate differences in opinion. Even outside of wartime, the tension between liberty, the desire to say or do what one wants, and order, the need for rules necessary for society to function, divide society. Americans want their homes to be secure against police intrusions, but they also want the police to be able to find evidence of crimes committed by others. They want freedom to follow their personal religious beliefs, but they do not want illegal practices to be allowed just because one religion might endorse them. In this chapter, we examine the balance and tension between liberty and order, with particular attention to the liberties guaranteed in the U.S. Constitution.

What Are Civil Liberties?

❯ What civil liberties are

In 1787 the most powerful argument of the Antifederalists against the proposed constitution was that it did not protect fundamental liberties. The Antifederalist who wrote under the name Brutus declared that these liberties, including the rights of conscience and the right of accused criminals to hear the charges against them, needed to be explicitly stated.[2] As we saw in Chapter 2, The Constitution, the Federalists eventually agreed and, to secure ratification of the Constitution, promised to amend it immediately.

Civil Liberties and Civil Rights

The **civil liberties** that were then written into the Constitution as the first ten amendments, or **Bill of Rights**, were freedoms that Americans held to be so fundamental that government may not legitimately take them away. This placed into law some of the **natural** or **unalienable rights** that Thomas Jefferson spoke about in the Declaration of Independence. These include, among others, freedom of speech and religious belief. As Supreme Court Justice Robert Jackson wrote in 1943, in a case striking down a state requirement that children salute the flag in school, "If there is any fixed star in our constitutional constellation, it is that no official, high or petty, can prescribe what shall be orthodox in politics, nationalism, religion, or other matters of opinion or force citizens to confess by word or act their faith therein."[3] By this, Jackson meant that the Constitution prohibits the government from interfering in what individuals say or think. Civil liberties are outside government's authority, whereas civil rights are rights that government is obliged to protect. These are based on the expectation of equality

civil liberties: *Those rights, such as freedom of speech and religion, that are so fundamental that they are outside the authority of government to regulate.*

Bill of Rights: *First ten amendments to the Constitution, which provide basic political rights.*

Connections: Why aren't civil liberties subject to majority rule?

natural (unalienable) rights: *Rights that every individual has and that government cannot legitimately take away.*

Civil liberties   Civil rights

FIGURE 4.1 **Distinction between Civil Liberties and Civil Rights.**

Civil liberties provide a gate or barrier that protects people against interference by the government in fundamental liberties, such as freedom of speech or religion. Civil rights often require active involvement of the government in opening gateways to full civic participation by all, regardless of race, gender, or religion.
© CENGAGE LEARNING

under the law and relate to the duties of citizenship and to opportunities for full participation in civic life (see Figure 4.1). They are the subject of the next chapter.

Balancing Liberty and Order

Connections:
What freedoms do you have as an American citizen that government cannot take away?

The protection of civil liberties requires a governmental system designed to do so. James Madison noted in *Federalist* 10 (see the Appendix) that a representative democracy will be able to keep a minority from abridging the rights of others but may not be able to hold back a majority. Yet civil liberties, by their very nature, are so basic that they cannot be taken away. Thus if a majority wishes to abridge rights, it often falls to the judiciary, which is not designed to be responsive to public desires, to protect those rights.

Connections:
Which is more important to you, liberty, order, or equality?

While maximizing individual liberty might seem like a great idea, complete liberty could lead to a breakdown of order. As Supreme Court Justice Oliver Wendell Holmes wrote in a World War I speech case, *Schenck v. United States*, freedom of speech does not mean that an individual has the right to falsely shout "Fire!" in a crowded theater and cause a panic.[4] Nor can liberty completely protect people from police investigations when criminal activity is suspected. Too much freedom can lead to anarchy, a state in which everyone does as he or she chooses without regard to others. Alternatively, too much order can lead to tyranny, a state in which the people are not free to make decisions about the private aspects of their lives. Protecting civil liberties thus requires a balance between individual liberty, public order, and equality.

Society must decide how to strike such balances, and, often, making that decision is difficult.

Constitutional Rights

The main sources of civil liberties are the Constitution and the Bill of Rights. The Constitution protects the right to a **writ of *habeas corpus***, the right of individuals to be brought before a judge to have the legality of their imprisonment determined. It also prohibits *ex post facto* laws, which make an act a crime after the act is committed, and bills of attainder, legislative acts that declare individuals guilty of a crime. The Constitution also guarantees the right to a trial by jury.

The Bill of Rights, ratified in 1791, protects various rights surrounding freedom of expression and criminal procedure, plus a few additional rights (see Figure 4.2). The expression-based freedoms are included in the First Amendment; they are freedom of speech, freedom of the press, freedom of assembly, freedom to petition the government, and the free exercise of religion. The criminal justice provisions of the Bill of Rights protect individuals accused of crimes by directing how the government may investigate crimes (Fourth and Fifth Amendments), conduct trials (Fifth and Sixth Amendments), and punish those convicted (Eighth Amendment). The Fifth

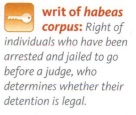 **writ of *habeas corpus*:** *Right of individuals who have been arrested and jailed to go before a judge, who determines whether their detention is legal.*

FIGURE 4.2 Constitutional Amendments That Pertain to Civil Liberties.

Color Code:	Criminal procedure	Participation	Equality	Structure	Miscellaneous		
First	1791	Prohibits abridging freedoms of religion, speech, press, assembly, and petition
Second	1791	Prohibits abridging the right to bear arms
Third	1791	Prohibits the involuntary quartering of soldiers in a person's home during peacetime
Fourth	1791	Prohibits unreasonable searches and seizures
Fifth	1791	Affirms the right to indictment by a grand jury and right to due process; protects against double jeopardy, self-incrimination, and taking of property without just compensation
Sixth	1791	Affirms rights to speedy and public trial, to confront witnesses, and to counsel
Seventh	1791	Affirms right to jury trials in civil suits over $20
Eighth	1791	Prohibits excessive bail, excessive fines, and cruel and unusual punishments
Ninth	1791	Declares that the enumeration of certain rights does not limit other rights retained by the people
Tenth	1791	Reserves the powers not granted to the national government to the states or to the people
Fourteenth	1868	Makes all persons born in the United States citizens of the United States and prohibits states from denying persons within its jurisdiction the privileges or immunities of citizens, the due process of law, and equal protection of the laws; apportionment by whole persons

Amendment also protects certain economic and property rights: individuals cannot be deprived of their property without due process of law, and if the government takes private property for public purposes, such as to build a highway or park, it must provide just compensation. The Second Amendment protects a very particular property right: the right to keep and bear arms. Finally, starting in the 1960s the Supreme Court has interpreted the Ninth Amendment to include a very general right, the right to privacy.

The Bill of Rights and the States

incorporate:
Process of applying provisions of the Bill of Rights to the states.

As originally written, the Bill of Rights limited the activities of the national government, not the state governments. Only at the end of the nineteenth century did the Supreme Court slowly begin to apply, or **incorporate**, the provisions of the Bill of Rights to the states.

The First Amendment is explicit about its application to the national government as it forbids certain actions by Congress. But other amendments are not explicitly tied to the national government. Thus the Fifth Amendment prohibits taking private property without just compensation. Was this a protection of citizens only against actions by the federal government, or against their state governments as well?

Connections:
Which government are citizens more likely to need a gate against—national or state?

The original answer, given by the Supreme Court in *Barron v. Baltimore* (1833), was that the Bill of Rights applied to the national government only. Under the *Barron* decision, state governments could abridge freedom of speech, the press, and religion, could conduct unreasonable searches and seizures, and more without violating the Constitution. State constitutions might protect such rights, but often they did not. During World War I, one citizen of Minnesota was convicted and sentenced to prison for stating that the war was a plot to protect Wall Street investments, another for stating that America needed to be made more democratic.[5]

Connections:
What laws, if any, should protect the American flag?

The potential for the application of the Bill of Rights to the states began with the passage of the Fourteenth Amendment (1868), which adds several restrictions on what the states can do. One section declares, "No State shall make or enforce any law which shall abridge the privileges or immunities of citizens of the United States; nor shall any State deprive any person of life, liberty, or property, without due process of law." Some of those who wrote this amendment stated that one of its purposes was to overturn the *Barron v. Baltimore* decision and make the entire Bill of Rights applicable to the states.[6]

The Supreme Court never agreed with this position, known as total incorporation. But beginning in 1897 it slowly began to use the protection of "life, liberty, or property" in the Fourteenth Amendment's due process clause to incorporate some of the provisions of the Bill of Rights as binding on the states. In the 1897 case the Court used this clause to hold that states could not deprive a railroad of its property without just compensation, a right similarly protected by the Fifth Amendment.[7] In 1925, in *Gitlow v. New York,* the Court assumed that the protection of liberty in the due process clause prevented states from abridging freedom of speech, a right similarly protected by the First Amendment.[8] By 1937 the Court had settled on a process of **selective incorporation**, using the due process clause to bind the states to those provisions of the Bill of Rights that it deems to be fundamental rights.[9] This process helps equalize the protection of rights across the United States.

Today, almost all of the provisions of the First, Second, Fourth, Fifth, Sixth, and Eighth Amendments have been incorporated, with the exception of grand jury indictment and excessive bail (see Table 4.1). Thus, states can indict people, or bring them up on charges, through the decision of judges, though charges in federal courts need the approval of a grand jury, a special jury whose sole duty is to determine whether an individual should be put on trial. The Third Amendment's protection against the quartering of soldiers in one's home during peacetime, a practice that angered the colonists, has not been incorporated but is not likely to be used today. Nor are states required, as the Seventh Amendment commands, to provide jury trials in civil suits over $20.

The fact that a right has been incorporated does not answer how the Court will determine whether that right has been violated. Generally speaking, rather than rule on each case purely on its own, the Court adopts a test to guide its decision and applies the test to the case at hand to determine whether a particular limitation of rights is acceptable. For the political rights in the Bill of Rights, such as freedom of speech, the Court most commonly uses variations of the **compelling interest test**. Under the

selective incorporation: *Doctrine used by the Supreme Court to make those provisions of the Bill of Rights that are fundamental rights binding on the states.*

compelling interest test: *Standard frequently used by the Supreme Court in civil liberties cases to determine whether a state has a compelling interest for infringing on a right and whether the law is narrowly drawn to meet that interest.*

TABLE 4.1 **Incorporated and Not Incorporated Provisions of the First through Eighth Amendments**

Amendment	Incorporated Provisions	Provisions Not Incorporated
First	Religion, speech, press, assembly, petition	
Second	Keep and bear arms	
Third		Quarter soldiers
Fourth	No unreasonable searches and seizures	
Fifth	Double jeopardy, self-incrimination, due process, taking of property without just compensation	Grand jury indictment
Sixth	Speedy and public trial, right to confront witnesses, right to counsel	
Seventh		Jury trials in civil suits over $20
Eighth	Cruel and unusual punishments, excessive fines	Excessive bail

Checkpoint

Can you:

☐ Compare civil liberties to civil rights

☐ Contrast the problems of too much freedom to those of too much order

☐ Compare the importance of the rights in the 1787 Constitution with those in the Bill of Rights

☐ State the extent and the limits of the original Bill of Rights

compelling interest test, the federal government or a state can limit rights only if the Supreme Court decides that (1) the government has a compelling interest in passing the law (for example, the law is necessary for the functioning of government), and (2) the law is narrowly drawn to meet that interest. For example, the government might have a compelling interest in banning speech that might incite religious wars, but such a law would have to be narrowly drawn so as not to prevent religious speech that merely calls for struggle against oppression. The extent of these and other rights have been fought over throughout American history.

Civil Liberties in Times of Crisis

> ❯ **Why civil liberties are limited in times of crisis**

> **Connections:**
> What civil liberties are you willing to give up to ensure more protection against terrorist attacks?

Attempts to limit civil liberties are more frequent in wartime or during other threats, given the government's increased concern for order and citizens' increased concerns about security. Popular support for civil liberties usually rebounds once the crisis ends.

The World Wars

> **Connections:**
> Can you trust the people to decide whether an idea has merit? Do good ideas survive and bad ideas fade away?

During World War I, Congress passed the Espionage Act of 1917, which made it a crime to obstruct military recruiting, and amendments known as the Sedition Act of 1918, which banned "disloyal, profane, scurrilous or abusive language" about the Constitution or the government of the United States, as well as speech that interfered with the war effort. Subsequently, juries convicted antiwar activist Charles Schenck for circulating a flyer to draftees that compared the draft to the involuntary servitude prohibited by the Thirteenth Amendment, and Socialist Party presidential candidate Eugene V. Debs for giving a speech criticizing the war. The Supreme Court upheld both convictions, noting that greater restrictions on speech could be allowed in wartime.[10] After the war, Congress repealed the Sedition Act and President Warren G. Harding (1921–23) pardoned Debs. In no subsequent wars has the government restricted speech as it did with the Sedition Acts of 1798 and 1918.

The War on Terror

After 9/11, Congress passed the USA PATRIOT Act, which allowed greater sharing of intelligence information and enhancement of law enforcement's ability to tap telephone and e-mail communications. It also regulated financial transactions with overseas entities and eased the process of deporting immigrants suspected of terrorist activities. Beyond the act, President George W. Bush (2001–2009) claimed the right, as commander in chief, to indefinitely detain alleged enemy combatants, whether U.S. citizens or foreign nationals. Thus Bush declared Jose Padilla, an American allegedly involved in a plan to detonate a radioactive bomb in the United States, an "enemy combatant" and transferred him from civilian to military authority, where he would have few, if any, procedural rights. The government kept Padilla in complete isolation for more than three and a half years. Unique among those declared enemy combatants, Padilla had not been captured on the field of battle but on American soil, and, having been born in Brooklyn, he was an American citizen.

In June 2004, when the Supreme Court ruled that noncitizens could not be held indefinitely as enemy combatants, it became clear that the government could not hold Padilla either. So, in November 2005, the Justice Department removed Padilla from military custody and charged him under federal criminal law with providing material support to terrorist organizations. The government did not charge him with attempting to detonate a radioactive bomb in the United States or with conspiring to commit terrorist acts in the United States, suggesting that the original claims against him might not have held up in a court of law. The government proved its case, and a jury quickly determined that Padilla was guilty of conspiring to kill people overseas. The judge then sentenced him to seventeen years in prison.

Although fewer rights exist for enemy combatants who are not U.S. citizens,[11] the Supreme Court has ruled that Congress must authorize hearings to determine the legality of the detention of even foreign enemy combatants. Such hearings must be consistent with the 1949 Geneva Conventions, an international treaty that protects the rights of prisoners of war.[12]

Beyond the enemy combatant cases, President Bush ordered warrantless wiretapping of conversations and interception of e-mail between American citizens and suspected foreign terrorists; normally, wiretapping requires a warrant signed by a judge or magistrate backed by probable cause that a crime is being committed. No court decisions exist on the wiretapping, although Congress did endorse aspects of the president's plan after the *New York Times* published stories about the then-secret program. The Obama administration continued the program and in 2009 moved—on national security grounds—to block a lawsuit over the wiretapping.[13] In December 2011, President Obama signed the Defense Authorization Act of 2012, which arguably gives the president the authority to detain U.S. citizens indefinitely and without trial. In Obama's signing statement he wrote, "My Administration will not authorize the indefinite military detention without trial of American citizens,"[14] But in response to an Obama-ordered execution of a U.S. citizen who allegedly had supported al-Qaeda, the group behind the 9/11 attacks, and who had encouraged terrorist acts against the United States, Attorney General Eric Holder laid out the criteria by which the president could order

Connections: Should government have access to your phone calls and e-mail messages?

Connections: Should the United States obey the Geneva Conventions?

the execution, stating that "due process and judicial process are not one and the same particularly when it comes to national security."[15] The executive branch, with the most direct responsibility over national security, is more likely to support restrictions on civil liberties during times of crisis than is either the legislative or judicial branch.

Civil Liberties and American Values

As these examples have demonstrated, in times of crisis Congress and the president limit civil liberties to secure order, often with public support. The courts, however, being less responsive to public pressure, can push back against these efforts. Thus, the courts forced the government to try Padilla in civilian courts, knowing that if the evidence fell short of the "guilty beyond a reasonable doubt" standard required for conviction, an alleged terrorist could have been freed. The courts have also blocked efforts to censor newspapers even when the government has believed that the publication of certain reports would benefit wartime enemies. Nevertheless, in wartime or other times of crisis, concerns about order are at their highest, and protections for civil liberties by national and state governments typically decline. Following the emergency, a political culture that favors freedom means that public support for civil liberties, as well as the government's protections of those liberties, generally rebounds.

The First Amendment and Freedom of Expression

> **What rights of expression the First Amendment protects**

The civil liberties most at risk during times of crisis are those protected by the First Amendment—freedom of speech, freedom of the press, and freedom of association. In this section, we examine each of these freedoms of expression individually. Their scope has expanded over time, despite occasional ratcheting back during wartime.

Freedom of Speech

While the First Amendment declares that "Congress shall make no law . . . abridging the freedom of speech," the Court has never taken the phrase "no law" literally. Today the Court allows limits on advocacy of unlawful activities, the use of fighting words, hate speech, and symbolic speech, and limits imposed by time, place, and manner regulations. It has also consistently ruled that campaign contributions are a form of speech protected by the First Amendment. For a full discussion of campaign finance, see Chapters 8, Interest Groups, and 10, Elections, Campaigns, and Voting.

Advocacy of Unlawful Activities.

When Justice Holmes wrote, in the opinion in the case of Charles Schenck, that free speech does not mean that a person can falsely shout "fire!" in a theater, he went on to explain that words spoken in wartime may have a different impact than they would in peacetime. "The question in every case," he continued, "is whether the words used are used in such circumstances and are of such a nature as to create a clear and present danger that they will bring about the substantive evils that Congress has a right to prevent." From this statement, the Court adopted the **clear and present danger test**. The Court shifted standards in subsequent decades, at one point allowing states to limit speech that merely had a tendency to cause unlawful acts. But in 1969 the Court moved back toward a stricter protection of civil liberties, ruling in *Brandenburg v. Ohio* that speech cannot be banned unless it leads to "imminent lawless action."[16]

Fighting Words and Hate Speech.

Besides speech that imminently incites unlawful activities, the Supreme Court also allows restrictions on the basis of the fighting words doctrine. "Fighting words" are phrases that might lead the individual to whom they are directed to respond with a punch. Today, hateful racial epithets are the leading examples of fighting words.

Related to fighting words is hate speech, which attacks or demeans a group rather than a particular individual. Over the past thirty years more than 350 public colleges and universities have attempted to provide equal, nonhostile educational environments through speech codes that tell students what they are and are not allowed to say.[17] For example, the University of Wisconsin prohibited speech that created "an intimidating, hostile, or demeaning environment for education (or) university-related work."[18] The University of Connecticut's speech code banned "inappropriately directed laughter" and purposefully excluding people from conversations.[19] Tufts University established three separate free speech zones: public areas, where speech could not be prohibited; classrooms and libraries, where derogatory and demeaning speech could be punished; and dorms, where the university placed the strictest restrictions on speech. Whereas students at many universities accepted speech codes, students at Tufts debated the issue, held public forums about freedom of speech, and physically marked off "free speech" from "non–free speech" zones.[20] Under this pressure, Tufts, a private university not legally bound by the Bill of Rights, rescinded the code.

The University of Michigan's speech code prohibited any speech that "stigmatizes or victimizes individuals or groups on the basis of race, ethnicity,

Connections: Given the nature of terrorist attacks, is it possible to establish a "clear and present danger" before prosecuting the advocacy of unlawful activities?

 clear and present danger test: *First Amendment test that requires the state to prove that there is a high likelihood that the speech in question would lead to a danger that Congress has a right to prevent.*

Connections: How can you distinguish between fighting words and hate speech?

religion, sex, sexual orientation, creed, national origin, ancestry, age, marital status, handicap, or Vietnam-era veteran status." A graduate student in psychology was concerned that Michigan's code would prevent class discussions of theories that claimed the existence of biological differences between sexes and races, and he brought suit against the code in federal court. The court struck down the code as violating the First Amendment.[21] Two years later, a federal court struck down the University of Wisconsin's speech code.[22] Thus the courts have made it clear that while state universities may encourage the goal of equality, they cannot do so by limiting First Amendment rights. Note that the First Amendment applies to these schools because they are state universities. The Bill of Rights limits the national government and, through the selective incorporation doctrine, also limits state governments and thus state universities. Private colleges, though subject to certain federal regulations, are not subject to the Bill of Rights.

The Supreme Court has not reviewed any of the college speech codes, but it has heard other cases related to hate speech. In one case it ruled that cross-burning, a terrorist tactic historically used by the white supremacist Ku Klux Klan to intimidate African Americans, to be a form of hate speech that could be banned.[23] On the other hand, the Court did not consider picketers at the funerals of U.S. soldiers to be engaged in hate speech, despite the protesters' association of U.S. soldiers with lenient military policies toward homosexuality, which the protesters hated (see Supreme Court Cases: *Snyder v. Phelps*).

Symbolic Speech.

In the 1960s, the Des Moines school district suspended students Mary Beth Tinker, her brother John, and a third student when they wore black armbands to protest the Vietnam War. The students voiced no opinions while wearing these armbands, and no disruptions in their schools occurred. The Iowa Civil Liberties Union, an interest group that supports civil rights and liberties, brought suit against the school board, claiming that students are equal to other Americans and retain the freedom of speech rights granted by the First Amendment. The Supreme Court agreed.[24] In this instance, the armbands were considered **symbolic speech**, like other nonverbal activities that convey a political message, such as saluting the flag, burning the flag, or burning draft cards. Alternatively, in another case, employees of a local sheriff's office

> **Connections:**
> Does your college have a speech code? Should your college regulate what you can and cannot say?

symbolic speech: *Actions, such as burning the flag, that convey a political message without spoken words.*

Mary Beth and John Tinker were teenagers in 1965 when they wore black armbands to school to protest the Vietnam War, and they were suspended. Arguing that students have free speech rights, the Iowa Civil Liberties Union sued the school district on their behalf and appealed the suspension in a series of cases that were finally appealed to the Supreme Court. In 1969, the Court ruled in the Tinkers' favor, stating: "It can hardly be argued that either students or teachers shed their constitutional rights to freedom of speech or expression at the schoolhouse gate."

supremecourtcases

Snyder v. Phelps (2011)

QUESTION: May anti-military and anti-gay protesters be sued for the distress they caused to the father of a marine killed in action in Iraq when they picketed at the marine's funeral?

ORAL ARGUMENT: October 6, 2010 (listen at http://www.oyez.org/cases/)

DECISION: March 2, 2011 (read at http://www.findlaw.com/casecode/supreme.html)

OUTCOME: The protesters are protected by the First Amendment because they are speaking out on a question of public concern.

For more than twenty years the congregation of the Westboro Baptist Church in Topeka, Kansas, has picketed the funerals of members of the U.S. military. The church does so to show its opposition to homosexuality and the army's toleration thereof since the establishment of the "Don't Ask, Don't Tell" policy during the Clinton administration. Their pickets infamously declare that "God hates f* [pejorative for homosexuals]" and "Thank God for Dead Soldiers." These pickets at the funeral of Matthew Snyder aggravated his father, who sued the church, the minister (Phelps), and several of Phelps's daughters for intentional infliction of emotional distress. A jury awarded Snyder nearly $11 million in damages. When the U.S. Court of Appeals overturned the verdict, Snyder appealed to the Supreme Court.

The Supreme Court ruled 8–1 in favor of the protesters, declaring that the church's views on homosexuality in the military were a matter of public concern, and as such, it did not matter how crudely those concerns were expressed. They compared this intentional infliction of emotional distress to an earlier case upholding a suit dealing with an individual's credit report, which was purely a private matter. Nor did the Court find that the Westboro protests involved "fighting words," which the Court has ruled to be beyond the protections of the First Amendment. Justice Samuel Alito, in dissent, argued that the First Amendment does not give the church the right to brutalize Matthew's father while he is burying his only son. In an earlier speech case, the Court ruled that the function of the First Amendment is to "invite dispute." The boundary between "inviting dispute," which is protected, and "fighting words," which are not, is not always clear.

- Do you believe that the Westboro Church's position on homosexuals and the military is a question of public concern? Explain.

- Do you believe that the Westboro Church's protests at the funeral constituted "fighting words"? Explain.

content-neutral: *Free speech doctrine that allows certain types of regulation of speech, as long as the restriction does not favor one side or another of a controversy.*

Connections:
Should Americans be required to salute the flag? Should they be prevented from burning the flag?

"liked" the Facebook page of the person running for office against the sheriff. The sheriff fired the employees, who argued that their First Amendment rights had been violated. The court has ruled that "liking" a Facebook page is too shallow as an expressive act to count as constitutionally protected speech.[25]

The Court has allowed prohibitions on the burning of draft cards, because Congress has a **content-neutral** justification for requiring draft-eligible citizens to be in possession of their draft cards. That is, draft cards are essential to the smooth running of the draft,[26] and prohibiting their destruction is not intended to suppress the views of those who burn them. States also have a neutral justification for limiting protests near health care facilities, even if most of the protesters are advocating pro-life positions.[27] But the Court has overturned laws that require saluting the flag, as such laws do intend to instill a political viewpoint.[28] Similarly, in *Texas v. Johnson,* the Court has overturned laws prohibiting flag burning, as they are based almost entirely on opposition to the idea being delivered by flag burning.[29] Of course, flag burners can be arrested on charges that would apply to anyone who starts a fire in public. On the other hand, the content-neutral rule, like most constitutional rules, is not absolute. Some messages can be regulated solely because of opposition to the message, as when the Supreme Court upheld a student's suspension for unfurling a banner at a parade that declared "Bong Hits 4 Jesus" because of the banner's promotion of drug use.[30] It is easy for the Court to formulate simple rules, such as a prohibition on content-based regulations, but harder for the Court to apply those rules consistently in the unusual cases that come before it.

CLAY GOOD/ZUMA

In 2002 high school student Joseph Frederick unfurled this banner while his class watched the Olympic Torch relay pass through Juneau, Alaska. When the principal suspended Frederick for the banner's message about drugs, Frederick sued, saying that his free speech rights had been violated. The court of appeals, relying on the *Tinker* case, reversed the suspension, but in 2007 the Supreme Court upheld it, saying a student's free speech rights did not extend to the promotion of illegal drugs.

Time, Place, and Manner Regulations.

The fact that the First Amendment protects freedom of speech does not mean that there is a right to speak wherever one wants, whenever one wants. Regulations of the time, place, and manner of speech, such as when or where protests may take place, are generally valid as long as they are neutral or equal, that is, they do not favor one side or another of a controversy. Thus states can prohibit protests near school grounds that interfere with school activities as there is no indication that such bans favor one side of any controversy over any other side.[31]

Freedom of the Press

Thomas Jefferson, among other Founders, thought freedom of the press crucial to a free society because the press keeps the public informed about the government's activities. When the Bill of Rights was written, "the press" meant newspapers; today the term covers not only the large companies that own television and radio stations but also individually run blogs and Internet sites that anyone can create. While freedom of the press once belonged to those who owned one, today it belongs to everyone.

Like freedom of speech, however, freedom of the press is not absolute. In extraordinarily extreme cases, the government can censor items before they are published. This practice is known as **prior restraint**. In other situations, the government can punish people after the fact for what they publish.

Prior Restraint.
Today, an extraordinary burden of proof of imminent harm is needed before the courts will shut down a newspaper before a story is printed. Even when the *New York Times* began publishing excerpts from a top-secret Pentagon analysis of U.S. involvement in the Vietnam War, the courts refused to stop the presses. The story of this case, *New York Times v. United States* (1971),[32] is told in more detail in Chapter 7, The News Media and the Internet. One case in which the courts said that the government had met the extraordinary burden standard involved the publication of instructions on how to build a hydrogen bomb,[33] but generally, court approval of censorship by prior restraint has been so difficult to achieve that the federal government has not sought it since the 1970s.

First Amendment law protects the Internet and blogs from government censorship in much the same way that it protects newspapers, but the technology of the Internet makes censorship far more difficult. This was the lesson learned in 2008 by a federal judge who tried to censor the Wikileaks website,[34] which publishes confidential documents from government, business, and religious organizations. Though the judge ordered the Wikileaks.org domain name disabled, Wikileaks already had mirror sites set up all over the world. Facing a barrage of criticism from bloggers and mainstream media groups, and given the ineffectiveness of his original decision, the judge reversed himself. But while many people may support the right of Wikileaks to publish allegations of money laundering by a Swiss bank, as in this case, what happens when Wikileaks publishes, as it has, a diagram of the first atomic bomb or secret documents about the war in Afghanistan?[35] Such cases show the difficulty of balancing freedom of the press versus censorship in a dangerous world.

Connections:
Should the American Nazi Party, the Ku Klux Klan, or the Communist Party be allowed to march in public streets?

 **prior restraint:** *Government restrictions on freedom of the press that prevent material from being published.*

Connections:
What information on the web should the government censor?

Subsequent Punishment.   In certain instances, the government can engage in subsequent punishment, fining and/or imprisoning writers and publishers after the fact for what they publish. Examples here include penalties for libel and for publishing obscenity, incitement to acts of violence, and secret military information.

The standards for convicting in a case of libel—the publishing of false and damaging statements about another person—vary according to whether that person is a public figure. The Supreme Court has made it harder for public figures than for ordinary individuals to sue for libel, because public figures have access to the media and can more readily defend themselves without lawsuits. For public figures to sue, the materials must be false and damaging, and the writer or publisher must have acted with actual malice, that is, with knowledge that the material was false or with reckless disregard of whether it was true or false. For private figures to sue for libel, the material must be false and damaging, and there must be some degree of negligence, but the actual malice test does not apply.

Today, the government can seek subsequent punishment against individuals who publish military secrets or obscene materials. Pornographic material is not necessarily obscene, and pornography that falls short of the legal definition of obscenity receives First Amendment protection. Specifically, for materials to be obscene, they must pass all three parts of what has become known as the ***Miller* test**: (1) to the average person, applying contemporary community standards as established by the relevant state, the work, taken as a whole (not just isolated passages), appeals to the prurient (sexual) interest; (2) the work depicts in an offensive way sexual conduct specifically defined by the state law; and (3) the work lacks serious literary, artistic, political, or scientific value.[36]

Under the *Miller* test, only "hard-core" materials could be banned.[37] The government has much greater leeway to prohibit "kiddie porn" that uses actual children[38] but not "virtual child pornography," which uses computer-simulated children.[39] Nor can the government's desire to protect children from indecent materials be used as a justification for prohibiting pornography that does not reach the level of obscenity from the Internet.[40] Similarly, the state may not ban the purchase of violent video games by minors.[41] According to a 2010 decision, *United States v. Stevens*, under the *Miller* test states may not ban fetish videos that, in the case at hand, showed women in high heels crushing the skulls of puppies.[42]

The Right of Association

The First Amendment's protections include the right of the people to peaceably assemble. This right includes the right to hold public protests that meet time, place, and manner regulations, and it was crucial to the success of the civil rights and women's suffrage movements (see Chapter 5, Civil Rights).

In the United States the right of association also includes the right to associate with whom one wants, as well as the right not to associate with those with whom one does not want to associate. But if a private group's expressed beliefs reject association with people of certain groups, such as Boy Scouts rejecting homosexuals and the Ku Klux Klan rejecting blacks and Jews, the group has a right of association that overrides state laws banning discrimination.

If a group discriminates for no apparent purpose, however, state laws can limit the right of association. Thus the Court declared that Minnesota has the right to prevent the Jaycees from discriminating against women because the presence of women does not violate any of the expressive interests of the Jaycees.[43] On the other hand, New Jersey's law prohibiting private groups from discriminating against homosexuals did not override the Boy Scouts' stated belief that homosexuality is inconsistent with the group's values. The Court thus allowed the Scouts to prohibit homosexuals from being members.[44]

Connections:
Which is more important to you, freedom of association or laws banning discrimination?

Checkpoint

Can you:

☐ State the limits on the First Amendment's right to freedom of speech

☐ Compare prior restraint on the press to subsequent punishment

☐ Explain the right of association

Religious Freedom

> **What religious freedoms the First Amendment protects**

The First Amendment sets forth two distinct protections about religion. Congress and now the states generally may not prevent people from practicing their religious beliefs. They also cannot pass laws that establish an official religion or even favor one religion over another.

Free Exercise

Victories for religious freedom, though significant, were rare in the colonial period. In 1786, however, the Virginia General Assembly passed Thomas Jefferson's Statute for Religious Freedom, which declared freedom of religious conscience to be a natural right of mankind that governments could not abridge. Five years later, this right was affirmed in the **free exercise clause** of the Bill of Rights.

Under the First Amendment, the government cannot criminalize an individual's private religious beliefs. Nor can the government ban specific religious activities, including student-run publications, as in *Rosenberger v. University of Virginia*,[45] just because they are based on religious beliefs. For example, the Supreme Court struck down a ban on religious-based animal sacrifices because killing animals for other reasons was not prohibited.[46] But not all religious-based activities are protected, and states are generally free to pass laws that restrict religious practices as long as such laws have

free exercise clause: *First Amendment clause protecting the free exercise of religion.*

Connections:
Should all religions get equal treatment?

WILLIAM F. CAMPBELL//TIME LIFE PICTURES/GETTY IMAGES

Ronald Rosenberger, the plaintiff in *Rosenberger v. University of Virginia*, stands in front of the statue of Thomas Jefferson on the campus of the University of Virginia. Rosenberg sued the university for denying student aid funds to a Christian student magazine called *Wide Awake*. On June 29, 1995, the Supreme Court ruled that the university engaged in viewpoint discrimination when it prohibited student funds from being spent on religious organizations.

a **valid secular** (nonreligious) **purpose**. For example, states can ban polygamy, even though marriage with multiple wives is a central belief in some religions.[47] In the 1960s, however, the Court ruled that states must have a compelling interest before they can abridge people's religious practices, even if the law has a valid secular purpose. Thus even though the government has a valid secular purpose in conducting a military draft, members of religious groups that oppose warfare, such as Quakers, may be exempt.

One case that demonstrates the contest between the branches of government over what constitutes free exercise concerns the use of the hallucinogenic drug peyote in religious rituals. In 1990, when two Native American drug counselors who used peyote were fired from their jobs and denied unemployment compensation, the Supreme Court used the valid secular purpose test to uphold Oregon's decision to deny this compensation.[48] Members of Congress overwhelmingly disapproved, however, and passed legislation stating that the Supreme Court must use the compelling interest test in deciding free exercise cases. The Supreme Court responded by declaring that law unconstitutional, repeating the statement from *Marbury v. Madison* that the province of the judicial branch is "to say what the law is."[49] Congress does have the authority, however, to declare the religious use of peyote to be legal, and it has done so. Generally, states need only have a valid secular purpose to pass laws that also happen to restrict religious practices. On the other hand, the Supreme Court has established a "ministerial exception" that frees religious organizations from having to abide by federal anti-discrimination laws—in this case, the Americans with Disabilities Act—when choosing their ministers. The Court here used the free exercise clause to limit the scope of an otherwise valid act of Congress.[50]

 **valid secular purpose:** *Supreme Court test that allows states to ban activities that infringe on religious practices as long as the state has a nonreligious rationale for prohibiting the behavior.*

 **establishment clause:** *First Amendment clause prohibiting governmental establishment of religion.*

The Establishment of Religion

The **establishment clause** of the First Amendment prevents Congress from recognizing one church as the nation's official church, as Britain had done with the Anglican (Episcopal) Church. Originally, states were free to establish state religions if they chose to, and when the Constitution was adopted nearly half the states had done so.[51] In an 1802 letter to the Baptists of Danbury, Connecticut, Thomas Jefferson (1801–1809) called for a "wall of separation" between church and state. The Supreme Court adopted that phrase in 1947 but declared that using taxpayer funds to provide public transportation to parochial schools did not breach the wall.[52]

The establishment clause literally prohibits not just the establishment of religion but also any law "respecting an establishment of religion." The Supreme Court has taken this phrase to mean that steps by the government that favor one religion over another, or even religion over no religion, cannot be taken, even if those steps fall far short of an official establishment of religion.

The Supreme Court's test for determining whether laws violate the establishment clause is known as the *Lemon* **test**, named after a litigant in a 1971 case.[53] Under this test, a challenged law must be shown to have a secular (nonreligious) legislative purpose and a primary effect that neither advances nor inhibits religion. The law must also avoid an excessive entanglement between church and state, such as a strict monitoring of church activities. Using these standards, the Supreme Court has banned organized school prayers (*Engel v. Vitale*) and devotional Bible readings (*Abington School District v. Schempp*).[54] The Bible can be read as part of a comparative religion course, however, and students can pray silently. The Supreme Court has also used this test to strike down laws that prohibited the teaching of evolution[55] as well as laws granting equal time for creation science—the position that scientific evidence supports the biblical view of creation—if evolution is taught.[56] Whether doctrines are called creation science or intelligent design, courts have ruled that they are religious doctrines that cannot be taught as part of the science curricula in public schools.

It is often difficult to understand why some activities violate the establishment clause and others do not. Separationists believe, with Jefferson, that there should be a strict wall between church and state. Accommodationists, on the other hand, believe that as long as the state does not favor one religion over another, it can generally pass laws that support religion. The Supreme Court's decisions on these grounds have been mixed, with conservative justices typically supporting the accommodationist position and liberal justices typically supporting the separationist view (see Chapter 14, The Judiciary, on ideology and the Supreme Court). The end result has been confusion: The Court allows short religious prayers by clergy at high school graduation ceremonies as long as students are not compelled to participate[57] but not by students at high school football games.[58] States may provide textbooks for secular subjects in parochial schools[59] but not instructional aids like charts and maps.[60]

 *Lemon* **test:** *Test for determining whether aid to religion violates the establishment clause.*

Connections: Should prayers be allowed in school? Under what circumstances? What types of prayers? Is saying a silent prayer the same as wearing an armband?

 ## Checkpoint

Can you:
- ☐ Explain the difference between free exercise of religion and the establishment of religion
- ☐ State the difference between separationists and accommodationists

The Right to Keep and Bear Arms

> ❯ How the "right to bear arms" has been interpreted

Connections:
What are the arguments for and against gun control? What is your position?

While many if not most Americans agree about the fundamental aims of the various First Amendment rights, no such agreement exists about the fundamental aims of the Second Amendment. The amendment declares, "A well regulated Militia, being necessary to the security of a free State, the right of the people to keep and bear Arms, shall not be infringed." Supporters of gun rights view the amendment as providing an individual right to keep and bear arms, while opponents view the "well regulated Militia" clause as limiting this right to those in organized militias.

Not until the 1934 National Firearms Act did the federal government attempt to regulate gun ownership. In 1939 the Supreme Court upheld a conviction under the act for possession of a sawed-off shotgun against a Second Amendment challenge, unanimously ruling that because such weapons had never been used by any militia, they did not receive Second Amendment protection. The Court sidestepped the question about whether there was an individual right to bear arms.

The Supreme Court finally decided the issue in 2008, ruling that there is an individual right to possess a gun, at least for self-defense in one's home.[61] The case involved a law prohibiting the private possession of firearms by the District of Columbia, which is a "federal enclave" and, for constitutional purposes, is considered part of the federal government rather than a state. The conclusion that the Second Amendment protects an individual right to bear arms does not answer the question of whether that amendment is also binding on the states. The Supreme Court answered that question in 2010, declaring that the right is incorporated.[62]

✓ Checkpoint

Can you:

☐ Explain why the Second Amendment is ambiguous about an individual's right to keep and bear arms

Criminal Procedure

> ❯ What protections the Bill of Rights provides to those accused of crimes

Provisions in the Fourth, Fifth, Sixth, and Eighth Amendments contain the heart of the protections afforded people against arbitrary police and law enforcement tactics. They protect the manner in which the police conduct investigations, the procedures used at trial, and the punishments that may be given following conviction.

Investigations

The major limits on investigating crimes involve the authority to search for physical evidence and the warnings that must be given before questioning a suspect. The police also cannot entrap people into committing crimes they would not otherwise commit, which is why Stephanie Good, in her role as "teen2hot4u," could never be the first person to bring up the subject of potential sexual activity.

Searches and Seizures.   The Fourth Amendment prohibits unreasonable searches and seizures. Though the amendment does not specify what makes a search unreasonable, it does specify that warrants must be backed by probable cause.

The Supreme Court has never interpreted the amendment to require warrants for all searches or seizures. If the police see illegal goods in plain view, they may seize them without a warrant. Similarly, if they observe a crime, they do not have to get a warrant before they arrest the individual. The Supreme Court has also established a broad right to search the person and the area within his or her control following an arrest and incident to it. This right now permits the police to conduct strip searches of arrestees entering the general population of a jail, even for the most minor violations, such as driving without a seat belt.[63]

The areas over which individuals have Fourth Amendment protections are those in which there is an **expectation of privacy**. According to the Supreme Court, there are no Fourth Amendment rights in areas over which there is no expectation of privacy, such as discarded garbage, someone else's home, a hotel room once one has checked out, or an international border. The Supreme Court has not ruled on the issue, but several state supreme courts have upheld the right of schools to search lockers used by students, because students have a diminished expectation of privacy over their lockers. While students at public universities do have an expectation of privacy in their college dorm rooms, many schools require them to waive their Fourth Amendment rights when they sign their dorm contracts. More generally, people waive their Fourth Amendment rights whenever they grant permission for the police to search, as long as the police request is not coercive.[64]

expectation of privacy test: *Supreme Court test for whether Fourth Amendment protections apply.*

For areas over which there is an expectation of privacy, the degree of Fourth Amendment protection depends on the level of that expectation, as determined by the Supreme Court. For example, the Court has ruled that individuals have the highest expectation of privacy in their homes, nearly as much in their places of business, but substantially less in their cars.[65] There is no expectation of privacy in what is exposed in plain view, even if, like a marijuana patch on private property, it requires a low-flying plane to view it.[66] There is no expectation of privacy over smells, allowing police to use drug-sniffing dogs to establish probable cause. There is, however, an expectation of privacy over the thermal (heat) signals given off by homes, thus prohibiting the police from using heat monitors to establish probable cause for indoor marijuana growing.[67]

Searches of homes almost always require a warrant (and thus probable cause). Searches of businesses usually do, but the Court allows warrantless searches of businesses that are subject to health, safety, or administrative regulations, such as restaurants, construction sites, and banks. For example, a restaurant kitchen suspected of health violations may be searched without a warrant. The police may establish, without probable cause, roadblocks to stop all cars on a road to check for licenses and registration or for drunk drivers. They may, of course, pull over any car for an observed violation, and they may search the car incident to arrest if they choose to arrest the person for that violation.[68] In 2012 the Court ruled that police require a warrant to physically place a GPS transmitter on a car to trace a person's movements.[69] The Court explicitly left open the constitutionality of relying on cell phone towers to provide the same information, as such information does not involve a physical intrusion by the police. The Court also allows drug testing without probable cause in "special needs" cases, such as student athletes and people applying for jobs at the U.S. Customs Office, but not of politicians seeking elective office.[70]

Connections: If the police are tracking your car's movements, does it matter if they physically touched your car to do so?

If the police conduct a search that is later found to be in violation of the Fourth Amendment, the **exclusionary rule** holds that the evidence cannot be used in trial. Originally established by the Supreme Court in 1914, the doctrine was made binding on state and local governments, where most law enforcement takes place, by means of selective incorporation in *Mapp v. Ohio* (1961).[71] Police will have less incentive to violate the Fourth Amendment if they know that the evidence from illegal searches cannot be used in court. Critics complain that excluding such evidence allows guilty people to go free simply because the police made a mistake.[72] The Supreme Court has backtracked a bit on the rule, establishing a good faith exception, which allows evidence to be used if the police obtain a warrant but the warrant is later found to lack probable cause.

exclusionary rule: *Supreme Court rule declaring that evidence found in violation of the Fourth Amendment cannot be used at trial.*

Interrogations.   The Fifth Amendment protects the right against self-incrimination, being forced to give testimony against oneself during criminal investigations or at criminal trials. The Supreme Court originally interpreted the self-incrimination clause to prohibit coerced confessions because they are inherently unreliable. But in the famous 1966 decision *Miranda v. Arizona*, the Court declared that the right against self-incrimination would be protected regardless of whether there was any evidence of coercion.[73] Rather, before police interrogate subjects who are in custody, the subjects must be told that (1) they have the right to remain silent, (2) anything they say may be used against them, and (3) they have the right to an attorney, free if they cannot afford one. In 2000 the Court upheld the *Miranda* decision, noting that its requirements had become so embedded in routine police practice that they had become part of the national culture.[74]

Connections: Why did the First Congress write so many protections regarding criminal procedure into the Bill of Rights?

Trial Procedures

The trial protections of the Bill of Rights include the right to indictment by a grand jury (Fifth Amendment), the right to counsel and an impartial jury (both Sixth Amendment), and the right against self-incrimination (Fifth Amendment), which, as noted, applies to trials as well as investigations. The Fifth Amendment also contains a general right to due process of law. To prevent the government from bringing people to trial without sufficient cause, the Fifth Amendment requires indictment by a grand jury, which indicts by majority vote.

The Sixth Amendment's right to counsel originally meant that defendants could have an attorney represent them if they could afford one. In *Powell v. Alabama* (1932), a case involving undoubtedly false allegations of rape filed against several black youths, the Supreme Court ruled that, in death penalty cases where the defendants were ignorant, illiterate, or the like, the government must provide an attorney if defendants cannot afford one.[75] In 1963 the Court recognized in the landmark *Gideon v. Wainwright* case how crucial counsel is in even simple felony cases.[76] Today, the rule applies to any case in which a defendant could receive as little as one day of jail time.[77]

Connections:
Is the U.S. criminal justice system too harsh? Or does it let too many criminals get off on "technicalities"?

Checkpoint

Can you:

☐ Describe the limits on police investigations of crimes

☐ Explain the trial rights protected by the Constitution

The Right to Privacy

> **What constitutes the right to privacy**

Although a number of constitutional provisions bear on privacy, such as search and seizure, self-incrimination, and First Amendment freedoms, none explicitly grants a general right to privacy. Nevertheless, the Ninth Amendment demands that the listing of certain rights, such as speech and religion, should not be understood as invalidating rights not listed. Since 1965 the Supreme Court has used the Ninth Amendment, the due process clause of the Fourteenth Amendment, and other privacy-related amendments to establish a general right to privacy. Subsequently the Court has faced decisions about whether to expand this privacy right to include abortion, homosexual behavior, and the right to die.

Birth Control and Abortion

In 1873 Anthony Comstock, a crusader for traditional morality, lobbied Congress to pass a law prohibiting the transportation in interstate commerce of both pornography and birth control. Many states, including Connecticut, passed their own Comstock Laws, which prohibited the use of birth control, even by married couples. In 1961 Estelle Griswold, executive director of the Planned Parenthood League of Connecticut, opened a birth control clinic in order to get arrested or fined so that she could challenge the constitutionality of the law. Her $100 fine, upheld by the Connecticut Supreme Court, allowed her to appeal to the U.S. Supreme Court. In *Griswold v. Connecticut* (1965), the Court voided what one justice called "an uncommonly silly law."[78] The case established a **right to privacy**, and the Court soon expanded this decision to cover the right of unmarried people to use birth control.[79]

Even more controversial than the question of birth control is the question of abortion. Before the middle of the nineteenth century, most states followed the English practice of making abortion illegal only after "quickening," that is, noticeable movement by the fetus, usually around the sixteenth to eighteenth week of pregnancy. By the end of the nineteenth century, most states had eliminated the quickening distinction, making abortion illegal throughout pregnancy. By the 1950s every state but Alabama banned abortion except to save the life of the mother; Alabama's broader exception included preserving the mother's health.

Following a substantial increase in birth defects caused by the sedative thalidomide (1957–61) and a German measles epidemic (1962–65), deaths from illegal abortion, and the resurgence of the women's rights movement, interest groups such as the National Association for the Reform of Abortion Laws (NARAL) organized for the loosening of anti-abortion laws. Between 1967 and 1969 ten states passed laws allowing abortion if there was a "substantial risk" that the child would be born with a "grave physical or mental defect" or that continuing the pregnancy would "gravely impair the physical or mental health of the mother" and in cases of rape or incest.[80] In 1970 three states legalized pre-viability abortions, those performed before the sixth month of pregnancy, when the fetus could not survive on its own.

Then, in 1973 the Supreme Court decided *Roe v. Wade*, which established a national right to abortion.[81] Using the compelling interest test, the Court declared that states had a compelling interest in preventing abortion in the third trimester, when the fetus could live on its own, and a compelling interest in regulating abortion during the second trimester to protect the health of the woman seeking the procedure. The state had no interest in regulating or preventing abortion in the first trimester. The Court's ruling took the issue out of state politics, where it had been located, and situated it in national politics, where it has become a perennial controversy, with presidential candidates regularly vowing to nominate Supreme Court justices who would either uphold or strike down *Roe v. Wade*. Since that time, states have sought to regulate and limit the procedure, and in the past twenty years abortion rates have slowly declined.

Following years of debate about *Roe v. Wade*, the Court reconsidered the decision in 1992.[82] The decision in *Planned Parenthood of Southeastern*

🔑 **right to privacy:**
Constitutional right inferred by the Court that has been used to protect unlisted rights such as sexual privacy and reproductive rights, plus the right to end life-sustaining medical treatment.

🔑 ***Roe v. Wade:***
1973 Supreme Court case extending the right to privacy to abortion.

Connections:
What are the arguments for and against the right of privacy in relation to abortion? What is your opinion? Are you "pro-life" or "pro-choice"?

Pennsylvania upheld the basic right to abortion established in *Roe v. Wade* but replaced the compelling interest/trimester framework, declaring that states could regulate abortion prior to viability as long as those regulations did not constitute an undue burden on a woman's right to terminate her pregnancy. According to the Court, spousal notification constitutes an undue burden, but requiring doctors to provide the woman with information about the risks of abortion and a twenty-four-hour waiting period does not. Parental consent for minors is not an undue burden as long as the minor has an option of seeking a judge's approval if she cannot obtain a parent's consent.

Abortion remains a salient issue in national politics, with the Supreme Court's role front and center. At confirmation hearings for Supreme Court nominees (see Chapter 14), senators ask more questions about *Roe v. Wade* than about any other case.[83]

Connections: When the people disagree with a Supreme Court decision, what can they do about it?

Homosexual Behavior

As of 1961 every state had laws prohibiting sodomy, and these laws were broad enough to cover virtually all sexual conduct between people of the same sex. In the next decades some states decriminalized sodomy, and by 1986 only twenty-four states continued to outlaw sodomy between consenting adults. Georgia, one of the states that continued such laws, authorized twenty-four years of imprisonment for a single act of consensual sexual behavior that fell under its sodomy laws. In a case challenging this law, *Bowers v. Hardwick,* the Supreme Court declared that the right to privacy did not cover homosexual behavior.[84] At the time, more than 80 percent of Americans thought that homosexual behavior was "always" or "almost always" wrong.[85] But by 2003, with the percentage of Americans with this belief down more than 20 percentage points, the Supreme Court reversed itself, declaring in **Lawrence v. Texas** that "the liberty protected by the Constitution allows homosexual persons the right to choose to enter upon relationships in the confines of their homes and their own private lives" (see Supreme Court Cases in Chapter 6, Public Opinion).[86]

Lawrence v. Texas: *2003 Supreme Court case extending the right to privacy to homosexual behavior.*

The Right to Die

As part of the right to privacy, the Supreme Court has held in *Cruzan v. Director, Missouri Department of Health,* that that people who make their wishes clearly known have a constitutional right to terminate life-sustaining care, such as artificial feeding or insertion of breathing tubes.[87] This right does not, however, include the right to assisted suicide, when physicians or family members provide ill people with pills or other means of ending life.[88]

✓ Checkpoint

Can you:

☐ Compare privacy rights in birth control and abortion

☐ Evaluate the role of public opinion on public laws toward homosexuality

☐ Compare the right to refuse life-sustaining medical care to the right to assisted suicide

Civil Liberties and Public Policy: Occupy Wall Street Protests

The Great Recession (2007–2009) caused enormous economic hardship and increased the gap between the rich and the poor in the United States. The government's reaction to the crisis included bailing out banks that signed reckless mortgage loans and then packaged those loans as high-grade debt to mislead investors. While the banks then used the profits from those hazardous securities to pay enormous bonuses to their top executives, the homeowners who could not afford their mortgage payments after the economy tanked originally received no support at all from the government. The sense of frustration with the government's response to the crisis led students and community activists to highlight what they considered to be the economic oligarchy of the upper 1 percent over the remaining 99 percent. The original protest, called "Occupy Wall Street," began with protesters heading to two locations near Wall Street, the financial center of the United States, in lower Manhattan: Chase Plaza, home to megabank JP Morgan Chase & Co. and Bowling Green Park, home to the iconic Wall Street Bull. Both are public spaces, and the police blocked them off before the protesters arrived because the protesters did not have permits. The protesters then moved to Zuccotti Park, which is privately owned by Brookfield Properties, a real estate conglomerate that did not originally object to the occupation of the park.

The protesters pitched tents and stayed in place from September 17 to November 18, 2011. Their form of protest—sleeping outside to call attention to economic inequality—can be considered a form of symbolic speech, an action that conveys a political message without spoken words. The Supreme Court has said states and locales can regulate symbolic speech so long as the regulations are content-neutral. Nevertheless, although the protesters had permission to occupy Zuccotti Park, their prolonged protest caused enormous problems for the local residents and businesses, including noise, nuisance, and unsanitary conditions. The protesters banged drums, for example, and while not permitted to use megaphones by the content-neutral time, place, and manner regulations on free speech that the Supreme Court has also sustained, they created human microphones, a system in which one person spoke and several people up front would shout out what the speaker said so that everyone could hear. Although the Constitution guarantees a basic right to assemble, that does not mean that a person or a group has a right to assemble and speak wherever one wants, whenever one wants. For protesters and local authorities, the protest at Zuccotti Park clearly tested the balance between liberty and order that the Constitution seeks to maintain.

As the Occupy Wall Street protests spread to include Occupy Oakland, Occupy Boston, Occupy D.C., and other movements, courts were used on both sides. Occupy protesters used the courts to try to overcome "gates" that police and local authorities established to prevent protests, claiming the regulations were unconstitutional. Municipal governments used the courts to try to keep the peace. Some of the rulings include the following:

- Oakland, California: The local court denied protesters an injunction against police use of excessive force, stating that there is a low probability of future such behavior.
- Oklahoma City, Oklahoma: Protesters were denied the right to camp overnight as there is plenty of opportunity to protest during the day.
- Columbia, South Carolina: Governor Nikki Haley sought to have protesters removed from the state capitol grounds every evening by 6:00 P.M., but other groups protesting on the grounds were not similarly removed. The local court ruled that sleeping on the grounds was protected symbolic speech under the First Amendment and that the 6:00 P.M. curfew was not content-neutral as it was only enforced against Occupy protesters.

In New York City, because Zuccotti Park is a privately owned public space, First Amendment protections did not necessarily apply. As sanitary and safety conditions worsened at the park, Brookfield Properties established rules prohibiting camping or lying down at the park. The local trial court noted that while it was mindful of the protesters' "rights of freedom of speech and assembly.... even protected speech is not equally permissible in all places and at all times."[89] As the owner's rules were designed to maintain a "clean, safe, publicly accessible

The "Occupy" movement began in Zuccotti Park in lower Manhattan, just one block from Wall Street. Protesters stayed through miserable weather until ordered out by the courts. While the protesters had a variety of different complaints, the young woman pictured here protests having gotten only a rotten job despite a college education.

space,"[90] the restrictions were reasonable and valid. Ultimately the New York City police were authorized to clear the park of protesters, and when some sought to "reoccupy" it, they were arrested. In sum, most court decisions have favored the ability of municipal governments to enforce content-neutral time, place, and manner restrictions on Occupy protesters, tilting toward the value of order over the value of freedom.

 Construct Your Own Policy

1. Create guidelines for the use of force by police in dealing with protesters.
2. Create guidelines for designating protest space in towns and cities across the country. Would you include a time limit on protests?

   For more on the policy-making process, see Chapter 1.

Civil Liberties and Democracy

Focus Questions Revisited

- What is government's role with regard to civil liberties? How responsive can or should it be to the people's will?

- What is the proper balance between liberty and order?

- Under what circumstances should civil liberties be restrained?

- What happens when rights clash? Are restrictions of civil liberties justified if they promote equality?

- In what ways does the guarantee of civil liberties promote democracy? Or does it pose challenges for democratic government that can be considered gates?

At the beginning of the chapter, we quoted Justice Jackson's opinion from the flag salute case that no government official can declare what shall be required in terms of basic beliefs and values. But what if elected officials do so anyway? Jackson responded that it was then the Court's job to protect such rights: "The very purpose of a Bill of Rights was to withdraw certain subjects from . . . political controversy, to place them beyond the reach of majorities and officials and to establish them as legal principles to be applied by the courts. One's . . . fundamental rights may not be submitted to vote; they depend on the outcome of no elections."[91]

Judicial decisions do not exist in a vacuum. Over the long run, if the Court is unresponsive to the people, new presidents will appoint new judges who better represent the people's preferences.[92] And while the Supreme Court is not accountable to the electorate in the same way that Congress and the president are, Congress and the president do have ways to try to hold the Court accountable. In recent years, members of Congress have threatened to impeach justices over Court decisions with which they disagreed.

These attempts failed largely because the Court proved responsive to the threats and backed away from its original positions. This outcome suggests that one way or another, the Court cannot stand alone in protecting civil liberties if popular support is not behind it. One of the difficulties in protecting civil liberties in a democracy is that although it is easy to feel sympathy for teenagers who wear black armbands to protest war, most litigants whose cases set precedents that protect all of the nation's freedoms are not as wholesome, and the causes they espouse may be racist, sexist, or violent.[93]

Unlimited liberties can also harm social order, particularly in times of crisis. Note, however, that in the period following 9/11, Congress made no attempt to criminalize antiwar speech, as it had during World War I; there was little public demand for such restrictions, as tolerance of opposing viewpoints among Americans has increased dramatically over the years. Political tolerance, the willingness of people to put up with ideas with which they disagree, is essential to both the marketplace of ideas and democratic stability.[94] If the people are tolerant, elected politicians will be tolerant also.

Similarly, the appointment process furthers responsiveness. Although critics have attacked the Supreme Court for establishing a right to privacy that is not explicitly in the Constitution, this decision remains highly popular, with 98 percent of Americans considering the right essential or important.[95] But if the public loses its concern over civil liberties, sooner or later, the Supreme Court will as well.

Top Ten to Take Away

1. Civil liberties are freedoms so fundamental that they are outside the authority of government to regulate. It often falls to the judiciary to protect them. (pp. 101–102)
2. They include, among others, rights surrounding freedom of expression and criminal procedure, and they were written into the Constitution in 1791 as the first ten amendments, or Bill of Rights. (pp. 103–104)
3. Although these protections of individual freedoms at first applied only to the federal government, Supreme Court decisions have gradually applied many of them to the states as well. (pp. 104–106)
4. Attempts to limit civil liberties are more frequent in wartime and during other threats, given increased government need for order and increased citizen concern about security. But support for the protection of civil liberties usually rebounds after the crisis ends. (pp. 106–108)
5. The scope of First Amendment freedoms of expression has generally expanded, although during wartime they are likely to be curtailed. (pp. 108–115)
6. Even in wartime, the courts have almost always protected the press from government censorship, but the government can prosecute newspapers for publishing obscenity, secret military information, and articles that incite violence. (pp. 113–114)
7. The First Amendment also protects freedom of religious practice and prevents the government from establishing one religion over all the others. (pp. 115–117)
8. Provisions in the Fourth, Fifth, Sixth, and Eighth Amendments protect individuals accused of crimes in police investigations and regulate trial procedures and types of punishments. (pp. 118–121)
9. Although the Constitution and its amendments do not explicitly grant a general right to privacy, the Supreme Court has used various constitutional provisions to establish this right, creating one of the most contentious areas of constitutional law and interpretation. (pp. 121–123)
10. While in the short run the Supreme Court can protect liberties without public approval, in the long run procedures relating to the presidential appointment and Senate approval of justices keep the Court responsive to the people. (pp. 126–127)

Key Concepts

Bill of Rights (p. 101). Why is the Bill of Rights so important?

civil liberties (p. 101). What is the difference between civil liberties and civil rights?

clear and present danger test (p. 109). How much leeway does the clear and present danger test provide to dangerous speech?

compelling interest test (p. 105). What does the compelling interest test require?

content-neutral (p. 112). Why must time, place, and manner regulations be content-neutral?

establishment clause (p. 116). What were the Framers trying to prohibit with the establishment clause?

exclusionary rule (p. 120). Is the exclusionary rule fair?

expectation of privacy test (p. 119). What problems can you foresee with the expectation of privacy test?

free exercise clause (p. 115). Can the free exercise clause protect behavior, or does it just protect beliefs?

incorporate (p. 104). Why has incorporation been so important to our liberties?

Lawrence v. Texas (p. 123). Are laws that discriminate against gays or lesbians likely to continue to survive?

prior restraint (p. 113). How does prior restraint harm the public's right to know?

Miller test (p. 114). Does the *Miller* test go too far in regulating pornography, or does it not go far enough?

natural (unalienable) rights (p. 101). Which rights do you believe are unalienable?

right to privacy (p. 122). What rights are protected under the right to privacy?

Roe v. Wade (p. 122). What would happen if the Constitution did not protect abortion rights?

selective incorporation (p. 105). How does selective incorporation differ from total incorporation?

symbolic speech (p. 110). How might one protest inequality without speaking any words?

valid secular purpose (p. 116). Why is the valid secular purpose test necessary?

writ of *habeas corpus* (p.103). Why was this one of the few rights originally enshrined in the Constitution?

Your Virtual Tutor
Master What You Need to Know and Test Yourself.

Learning Outcomes

WHAT YOU NEED...

To Know	To Test Yourself	To Participate
What civil liberties are	• Compare civil liberties to civil rights • Contrast the problems of too much freedom to those of too much order • Compare the importance of the rights in the 1787 Constitution with those in the Bill of Rights • State the extent and the limits of the original Bill of Rights	• Know your constitutional rights • Decide if any constitutional rights provide too much freedom • Consider what would happen if civil liberties were subject to majority rule
Why civil liberties are limited in times of crisis	• Identify the major targets of civil liberty restrictions during wartime • Describe the change and continuity in security regulations from President Bush to President Obama • Explain why wartime deprivation of rights ratchet back after the crisis ends	• Consider whether dissent in wartime is unpatriotic • Evaluate the threats to freedom from responses to terrorism
What rights of expression the First Amendment protects	• State the limits on the First Amendment's right to freedom of speech • Compare prior restraint on the press to subsequent punishment • Explain the right of association	• Discuss whether First Amendment rights can be absolute • Evaluate whether the right of association or the right to equal treatment is more important
What religious freedoms the First Amendment protects	• Explain the difference between the free exercise of religion and the establishment of religion • State the difference between separationists and accommodationists	• Consider what would happen if the First Amendment granted a complete exemption from secular laws that violated one's religious beliefs • Debate the "wall of separation" between church and state.
How the "right to bear arms" has been interpreted	• Explain why the Second Amendment is ambiguous about an individual's right to keep and bear arms	• Debate what limits should exist on gun rights and on what grounds
What protections the Bill of Rights provides to those accused of crimes	• Describe the limits on police investigations of crimes • Explain the trial rights protected by the Constitution	• List any additional limits you might like to see on police investigations or trial rights
What constitutes the right to privacy	• Compare privacy rights in birth control and abortion • Evaluate the role of public opinion on public laws toward homosexuality • Compare the right to refuse life-sustaining medical care to the right to assisted suicide	• Debate whether health insurance laws should require coverage for birth control • Consider whether judicial protection of homosexual rights are necessary • Write your own "living will" stating your preferences for medical treatment if at the time you were unable to make them known

> " I think it's really important to realize that each individual shoulders a great deal of responsibility, . . . and that's the way the movement in the sixties was accomplished. "

**Diane Nash,
Fisk University, Nashville,
Tennessee**

5

Civil Rights

In 1956, when Diane Nash went to college, she first chose Howard University in Washington, D.C., where she enrolled as an English major. But she soon transferred to Fisk University in Nashville, Tennessee. Attending school in the segregated South was something of a shock for the Chicago native. "I understood the facts," she later recalled, but "when I went south and saw the signs that said 'white' and 'colored,' and I actually could not drink out of that water fountain or go to that ladies' room, I had a real emotional reaction." Nashville was more of a shock than Washington, and humiliation turned to outrage.

But the ethic of service that Howard and Fisk promoted in African American students was familiar to Nash, who had grown up in a Catholic family and considered becoming a nun. Instead, while at Fisk, she began attending workshops on social change and Christian nonviolence led by John Lawson, a graduate student in theology at nearby Vanderbilt University, and she also attended workshops at the Highlander Folk School, where civil rights leaders such as Rosa Parks and Martin Luther King had received training. When four African American college students in Greensboro, North Carolina, launched a sit-in movement to integrate lunch counters in February 1960, Diane Nash was ready.

Quickly, Nash organized and trained local students to carry out nonviolent protests at downtown lunch counters. When she was arrested, she spoke eloquently of injustice to

aplia Need to Know

- What civil rights are
- How the federal and state governments suppressed civil rights
- How equal protection has expanded
- Which groups have been at the forefront of the civil rights movement
- What the new battles for civil rights are

the judge. Confronting the mayor of Nashville, she turned his plea for praying together into a case for eating together, and the mayor caved in. After the lunch counters were desegregated, Nash organized college students to replace Freedom Riders who had been beaten while testing the enforcement of desegregation orders on buses and in bus stations across the South. A founding member of the Student Nonviolent Coordinating Committee (SNCC), she left Fisk to become a full-time activist, leading civic education and voting rights campaigns in Mississippi and Alabama.

Twenty years later, reflecting on her role in the civil rights movement, Nash was astonished at her own courage. "I remember realizing that with what we were doing, trying to abolish segregation, we were coming up against governors of seven states, judges, politicians, businessmen, and I remember thinking, 'I'm only 22 years old. What do I know? What am I doing?'" But she also felt "the power of an idea whose time had come." "The movement had a way of reaching inside me and bringing out things that I never knew were there," she continued. "Like courage, and love for people." "I think it's really important," she concluded, "that young people today understand that the movement of the sixties was really a people's movement. . . . Young people should realize that it was people just like them, their age, that formulated the goals and strategies, and actually developed the movement. When they look around now, and see things that need to be changed, they should say: 'What can I do? What can my roommate and I do to effect that change?'"[1]

Fifty years after Nash and young people throughout the South risked their lives for the right to drink at a water fountain, to eat at a lunch counter, and to vote and participate in American civic life, Barack Hussein Obama, the child of a white mother and an African father, was elected president of the United States. An African American president could scarcely have been imagined at the time, but the gateways that civil rights activists like Nash forced open changed American law and politics forever. Yet the road from slavery to segregation, and from segregation to Obama, was long, and the continuing struggle for equality was led not only by African Americans but by women, immigrants, and other groups who were blocked from participation in America's civic life. In this chapter, we examine the changing concept of equality from exclusive to inclusive and track the changing responses and responsibilities of government.

FocusQuestions

- What is the meaning of equality? How has its meaning changed since the Constitution was written in 1787?
- What role has government played with regard to equality in the past? What role does it assume today?
- What means have various groups used to secure their civil rights? What means has government used to respond?
- What is the effect on a democracy if some of its people lack civil rights?
- Are civil rights a gate or a gateway to democracy? Explain.

What Are Civil Rights?

› What civil rights are

Although the Declaration of Independence declared that "All men are created equal," the 1787 Constitution had little to say about equality. The Antifederalists insisted on a Bill of Rights that would protect fundamental liberties, but they did not argue for equality. Today equality is a hallowed principle of American political culture, but the notion and the reality evolved slowly over two centuries.

Civil Rights and Civil Liberties

Civil rights are rights related to the duties of citizenship and the opportunities for participation in civic life that the government is obliged to protect. These rights are based on the expectation of equality under the law. The most important is the right to vote. In contrast to civil rights are civil liberties, freedoms so fundamental that government may not legitimately take them away. Civil rights also differ from civil liberties in that while government is the only authority that can suppress liberties—for example, by suppressing freedom of speech—both government and individuals have the capacity to engage in discrimination by treating people unequally: the government through laws that discriminate, and individuals or businesses through actions that discriminate.

The government can take three different roles when it comes to civil rights. It can engage in state-sponsored or **public discrimination** by actively discriminating against people. It can treat people equally but permit **private discrimination** by allowing individuals or businesses to discriminate. Finally, it can try, as the U.S. government has since the 1960s, both to treat people equally and to prevent individuals or businesses from discriminating. Thus it falls to government to protect individuals against unequal treatment and to citizens to ensure that the government itself is not discriminating against individuals or groups. In a democracy, the majority rules, but the gateways for minorities must also be kept open.

The Constitution and Civil Rights

Despite the statement on equality in the Declaration of Independence, the role of the government with regard to ensuring equality was not written into the Constitution, and the United States has a bleak history on civil rights. Though the Constitution does not use the words *slave* and *slavery*, it endorsed the slave system by requiring states to return runaway slaves and by prohibiting a ban on importing slaves from Africa until 1808. The Constitution also gave the states authority over voting, and most states restricted the right to vote to free males with a certain amount of property. Slaves could not vote, and in a few states free African Americans could not either. Neither could women (except in New Jersey) or Native Americans.[2] During the nation's first century

civil rights: *Set of rights centered around the concept of equal treatment that government is obliged to protect.*

Connections: Why would a government discriminate?

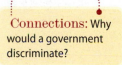

public discrimination: *Discrimination by national, state, or local governments.*

private discrimination: *Discrimination by private individuals or businesses.*

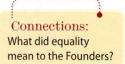

Connections: What did equality mean to the Founders?

equality of opportunity:
Expectation that citizens may not be discriminated against on account of race, gender, or national background and that every citizen should have an equal chance to succeed in life.

equality of outcome:
Expectation that equality is achieved if results are comparable for all citizens regardless of race, gender, or national background or that such groups are proportionally represented in measures of success in life.

Connections:
What is your idea of equality—equality of opportunity or equality of outcome?

Checkpoint

Can you:
- ☐ Compare civil rights to civil liberties
- ☐ Track changes in civil rights from the Constitution as originally ratified to today

and even thereafter, state laws and the national government actively discriminated against people on the basis of race, gender, and ethnic background.

Following the Civil War, the Thirteenth Amendment ended slavery, and the Fourteenth Amendment forbade states to deny any person "the equal protection of the laws." Nevertheless, the equality of African Americans was not thereby guaranteed. Some of the members of Congress who wrote the Fourteenth Amendment believed that equality was limited to "the right to go and come; the right to enforce contracts; the right to convey his property; the right to buy property" and little more.[3] The courts agreed, and the federal government made little effort to ensure equal treatment during the nation's second century.

During these years, however, women won the right to vote (1920) but not the right to full participation in public life. Native Americans became citizens (1924), but not until the civil rights and women's movements of the 1950s and 1960s did legal discrimination against African Americans, women, and ethnic minorities end.

In the last half-century, the meaning of "all men are created equal" has been expanded to include women and all people subject to the jurisdiction of the United States. Americans now look to the government to protect equality and enforce equal treatment under the law. But they still debate the meaning of *equality*. Should, or can, the government ensure **equality of opportunity** for all people? Should, or can, it engineer **equality of outcome**? That is, is it enough for society to provide equality of opportunity by prohibiting discrimination? What if that still leaves members of groups that have historically been discriminated against, such as women and minorities, with fewer advanced degrees and lower incomes? As it has throughout the course of the nation's history, the meaning of equality continues to evolve.

In the next sections, we see how, as the idea of equality expanded, the federal government moved from actively treating different groups unequally under the law, to asserting equality under the law but doing little to protect it, to actively enforcing it. Equality of rights is now a central feature of the Constitution and the Court's interpretation of it.[4]

Legal Restrictions on Civil Rights

› How the federal and state governments suppressed civil rights

Slavery split the United States from the founding of the nation through the Civil War. After the Civil War, the Constitution prohibited slavery. It also prohibited the states from denying equality, but many states continued to discriminate. Both Congress and the Supreme Court had the authority to enforce equality, but neither took action. Women as well as African Americans suffered under unequal laws, with denial of the right to vote and laws that limited their full participation in labor markets, professions, and public life. Discriminatory laws also affected Asians, prohibiting those who were not born in the United States from becoming citizens and later preventing them from immigrating to the United States altogether.

Slavery

Slavery came to the colonies in 1619 when a Virginian purchased Africans from a Dutch shipper. Colonial Africans originally were servants, largely indistinct from indentured servants of other races who bound themselves to service for a limited number of years in return for free passage to Britain's American colonies. But African slavery soon became established in colonial law. In 1664 Maryland passed legislation declaring that all "Negroes or other slaves hereafter imported . . . shall serve for life."[5] The law also made slaves of the children of slaves.

The compromises made at the Constitutional Convention allowed the United States to form, but they also allowed slavery to grow and spread. By 1808, when Congress banned the further importation of slaves from Africa, the slave population had reached 1 million, and it continued growing through natural increase thereafter. With neither slave nor free forces dominant politically, Congress continued to compromise. The Missouri Compromise (1820) banned slavery in the territories north of the southern border of Missouri, thus keeping most of the vast lands of the Louisiana Purchase free. The Compromise of 1850 allowed territories captured in the Mexican War to decide for themselves whether to be free or slave. The Kansas-Nebraska Act (1854) undid the Missouri Compromise by allowing each territory to vote on whether to allow slavery. The Supreme Court further extended the reach of slavery in *Dred Scott v. Sandford* (1857).[6]

Dred Scott, a slave who had moved with his master from the slave state of Missouri to the free Wisconsin Territory and then back to Missouri, sued in federal court for his freedom based on his extended stay in free territory. The Supreme Court's decision in the case, written by Chief Justice Roger Taney, a former slave owner, declared (1) that no black—slave or free—could be an American citizen, and thus that no black could sue in a federal court; (2) that blacks were "beings of an inferior order" who had "no rights which the white man was bound to respect"; (3) that the Declaration of Independence's statement that "all men are created equal" did not include men of African heritage; (4) that Congress's authority to "make all needful Rules and Regulations respecting the Territory . . . [of] the United States" did not include the right to prohibit slavery in those territories; and (5) that slaves were the property

Connections:
Describe the role of compromise in American politics. Is it wise or foolish for politicians to compromise?

Dred Scott v. Sandford: *1857 Supreme Court decision declaring that blacks could not be citizens and Congress could not ban slavery in the territories.*

In 1846 Dred Scott, a black slave pictured here with his family, sued for his freedom, claiming that since his owner had taken him to a free territory, he should be free. The Supreme Court said no, going further to say that Scott, as an African American, had no standing to sue and that Congress could not prohibit slavery in any territory. The 1857 ruling pleased southerners but infuriated northerners.

of their owners, so freeing Scott would violate his owner's Fifth Amendment right not to be deprived of his property without due process of law. With this decision, the regulation of slavery in the territories was removed from the national authority of Congress and placed in the hands of local authorities in the territories.

The 1860 election of Abraham Lincoln (1861–65), who opposed the extension of slavery, prompted southern states to secede from the union. During the ensuing Civil War, Lincoln issued the Emancipation Proclamation, which made slavery illegal in those states in rebellion as of January 1, 1863. The Proclamation did not pertain to border states that retained slavery but remained in the Union. Slavery was finally ended in the United States following Union victory and ratification of the Thirteenth Amendment in 1865 (see Figure 5.1).

Racial Segregation and Discrimination

The end of slavery did not make former slaves equal citizens. Immediately after the war, southern states wrote new constitutions that severely limited the civil and political rights of the freedmen. These so-called black codes prevented them from voting, owning land, and leaving their plantations. Congress responded with the Civil Rights Act of 1866, which guaranteed the right of freedmen to make contracts, sue in court if those contracts were violated, and own property. Congress also established military rule over the former Confederate states, which would end in a state when it passed a new state constitution that guaranteed black suffrage and when it ratified the Fourteenth Amendment. With former Confederates barred from

FIGURE 5.1 Constitutional Amendments That Pertain to Civil Rights.

Color Code:	Criminal procedure	Participation	Equality

Thirteenth	1865	Prohibits slavery in the United States
Fourteenth	1868	Makes all persons born in the United States citizens of the United States and prohibits states from denying persons within its jurisdiction the privileges or immunities of citizens, the due process of law, and equal protection of the laws; apportionment by whole persons
Fifteenth	1870	Prohibits states from denying the right to vote on account of race
Nineteenth	1920	Guarantees women the right to vote
Twenty-Four	1964	Prohibits poll taxes

voting, blacks constituted a majority of the electorate in several states, and more than six hundred freedmen served in state legislatures during **Reconstruction**, as this era was called.

The Fourteenth Amendment (1868), in addition to guaranteeing that no state shall deny any person due process of law (see Chapter 4, Civil Liberties), prohibits states from denying any person the **equal protection** of the law. It also makes all people born in the United States citizens of the United States, overturning the Supreme Court's ruling in the *Dred Scott* case that blacks could not be U.S. citizens. In an attempt to prevent states from rescinding the right of black suffrage, the Fifteenth Amendment (1870) declared that the right to vote could not be abridged on account of race.

Opponents of freedmen rights turned to violence. In 1866 Confederate veterans formed the Ku Klux Klan (KKK), a terrorist organization aimed at restoring white supremacy. In 1873 white supremacists massacred more than a hundred blacks in Colfax, Louisiana, as part of an ongoing election dispute. The federal government brought charges against three of the perpetrators, but the Supreme Court reversed their conviction in *United States v. Cruikshank,* arguing that the Fourteenth Amendment gave Congress the authority to act only against states that violated civil rights (public discrimination), not against individuals who did so (private discrimination).[7]

Reconstruction ended with a deal over the 1876 election. A close and contested race between Republican Rutherford B. Hayes and Democrat Samuel Tilden was resolved when southern Democrats in Congress agreed to allow Hayes to become president in return for the withdrawal of federal troops from the South. Freed from military rule, white supremacist groups such as the Klan embarked on a campaign of lynching and other forms of terrorism against blacks.

State governments were not responsive to the victims because, despite the Fifteenth Amendment, southern politicians established a set of rules that kept blacks from voting. **Poll taxes** limited the voting of poor blacks (as well as of poor whites). The white primary took advantage of the fact that, with the Republican Party negatively associated with Lincoln and the Civil War, the Democratic Party completely dominated southern politics. Therefore, whoever won the local Democratic primary for an office was sure to win in the general election. Excluding blacks from voting in Democratic primaries meant that blacks had no effective vote at all. Even so, states used literacy tests to disqualify voters. These involved reading and interpreting difficult passages. To avoid disqualifying white voters as well, grandfather clauses gave exemptions to men whose grandfathers had been eligible to vote. The men who received these exemptions were, of course, always white (see Chapter 10, Elections, Campaigns, and

Connections:
After ratification of the Fifteenth Amendment, who could not vote?

Reconstruction: *The period from 1865 to 1877 in which the former Confederate states gained readmission to the Union and the federal government passed laws to help the emancipated slaves.*

equal protection clause: *Prevents states from denying any person the equal protection of the laws (Fourteenth Amendment).*

poll taxes: *Tax on voting; prohibited by the Twenty-Fourth Amendment (1964).*

Connections:
If some people are blocked from voting, what is the effect on government?

Connections: Do members of Congress represent all the people in their district or state or only those who voted for them?

Voting, for further discussion of these techniques and an example of a literacy test).

These legal strategies effectively disenfranchised black men. In addition, state and local **Jim Crow laws** enforced segregation of whites and blacks in all public places. When a New Orleans civil rights organization challenged a Louisiana law requiring segregated railway cars by having Homer Plessy, who was one-eighth black, sit in the whites-only car, the Supreme Court upheld the segregation.[8] *Plessy v. Ferguson* (1896) established the **separate-but-equal doctrine**, which held that states could segregate the races without violating the equal protection clause of the Fourteenth Amendment as long as the separate facilities were equal.[9] Southern states segregated schools, libraries, and other public institutions and required the segregation of restaurants, inns, and other places of public accommodation. The facilities were almost never equal. African Americans in northern states often experienced discrimination in hiring, housing, hotels, and restaurants, though segregation was not enforced by law. African Americans could serve in the military but generally in segregated units under white officers. During the late nineteenth and early twentieth centuries, discrimination was state-sponsored in the South; elsewhere in the nation, people engaged in private discrimination without challenge.

Other ethnic groups besides blacks also suffered discrimination. California's 1879 constitution prohibited Chinese from voting and from employment in state and local government. Three years later, Congress passed the Chinese Exclusion Act, which prohibited Chinese immigration. In 1913 California prohibited Japanese immigrants from purchasing farmland.[10] Segregation in the South often placed Hispanics in the same position as African Americans. Segregation also

In segregated school systems, the schools for black children and the schools for white children were almost never equal. These insurance photographs show Liberty Hill Colored School and Summerton Graded School in Clarendon County, South Carolina, in 1948. They were used as evidence in *Briggs v. Elliott,* one of the school segregation cases decided with *Brown v. Board of Education* (1954).

SOUTH CAROLINA DEPT. OF ARCHIVES AND HISTORY

SOUTH CAROLINA DEPT. OF ARCHIVES AND HISTORY

existed in the West. Phoenix, Arizona, ran separate schools for blacks, Indians, and Mexicans.[11] California ran separate schools for Asians as well as Mexicans,[12] while Texas kept Mexican Americans in separate classrooms.[13]

Women's Suffrage

By law and by custom, women were also excluded from public life from the earliest days of the nation. In 1776 Abigail Adams had urged her husband, John Adams, to "remember the ladies" in drafting the nation's founding documents. In language similar to that later used by Jefferson in the Declaration, she warned, "if particular care and attention is not paid to the ladies, we are determined to foment a rebellion, and will not hold ourselves bound by any laws in which we have no voice or representation."[14] Nevertheless, neither the Declaration nor the Constitution made any provision for women's rights. Rather, the states continued the English policy of coverture, which granted married women no rights independent of their husbands. They could not own property, keep their own wages, or sign contracts. As for voting, each state set its own rules. In 1789 only New Jersey allowed women the right to vote (provided the women met the state's property requirements), a right it rescinded in 1807.[15]

In 1848 leaders of the **women's suffrage movement** met in Seneca Falls, New York, to organize for the right to vote. They prepared a "Declaration of Sentiments" that used the language of the Declaration of Independence to assert that "all men and women are created equal," but few results came from this meeting. Then, in 1869 Susan B. Anthony and Elizabeth Cady Stanton formed the National Woman Suffrage Association (NWSA), which lobbied for the right of women to vote and unsuccessfully opposed the Fifteenth Amendment unless it was changed to include women's suffrage. With the NWSA focused on gaining national suffrage through constitutional amendment, an alternative organization, the American Woman Suffrage Association (AWSA), formed to press for state-by-state suffrage rights.

Although women's rights advocates typically opposed protective legislation, they focused their attention on the right to vote. Anthony presented the 1887 Congress with ten thousand petition signatures demanding women's suffrage. In 1894 suffragists presented the New York legislature with six hundred thousand signatures. The suffragist movement, though, was not universally admired; many people opposed voting equality for women because it threatened their notions of appropriate gender roles.

While state control of voting gave southern states the power to disenfranchise blacks, it also gave western states the power to experiment with women's suffrage. The territory of Wyoming granted women's suffrage in 1869 and continued it upon statehood in 1890. Males in Colorado voted for women's suffrage in 1893. Utah granted women the right to vote in

Jim Crow laws: *Southern laws that established strict segregation of the races and gave their name to the segregation era.*

separate-but-equal doctrine: *Supreme Court doctrine that upheld segregation as long as there were equivalent facilities for blacks.*

women's suffrage movement: *Movement to grant women the right to vote.*

Connections: Were Anthony and Stanton right or wrong to lobby against the Fifteenth Amendment?

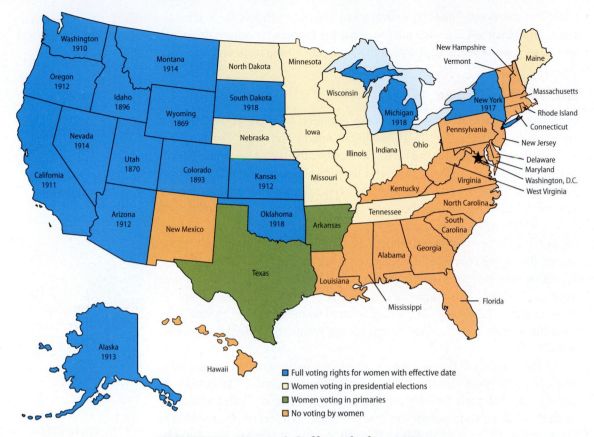

FIGURE 5.2 Women's Suffrage before 1920.

Because states control voting laws, women's suffrage advocates campaigned at the state level, and, before the Nineteenth Amendment was ratified in 1920, women could vote in some elections in most states. The Nineteenth Amendment superseded state law, stating that the right to vote could not be denied or abridged by the United States, or by any state, on account of sex.

Source: © Cengage Learning; data from Mary Beth Norton et al., *A People and a Nation: A History of the United States*, 8th ed. (Boston: Houghton Mifflin, 2008), 608.

1895. In 1913 Illinois granted women the right to vote for president but not for other national offices. In 1916 the people of Montana elected the first woman to serve in the U.S. House of Representatives, Jeannette Rankin (see Figure 5.2).

Suffragist amendments failed numerous times in Congress before receiving the necessary two-thirds vote in both chambers in 1919.[16] By August 1920, with effective lobbying by suffragist groups, three-quarters of the states ratified the Nineteenth Amendment, guaranteeing women the right to vote in the November 1920 presidential election.

Connections:
Should women be protected by an equal rights amendment?

Restrictions on Citizenship

In the case of both African Americans and women, the status of **citizenship** did not guarantee the right to vote or serve on juries. Yet on the basis of ethnic background, some groups were denied even the status of citizenship and the privileges it entailed, such as protection, under the Fourteenth Amendment's privileges or immunities clause, from state laws that curtail rights that other citizens hold.

citizenship: *Full-fledged membership in a nation.*

Citizenship in the Constitution.

The Constitution was not explicit on birthright citizenship, but the clause requiring that presidents be natural-born citizens seemingly implies that people born in the United States are citizens.[17] But the *Dred Scott* ruling, until overturned by the Fourteenth Amendment, belied that assumption, as did the status of Native Americans.

In 1823 the Supreme Court declared that Native Americans were merely inhabitants, "an inferior race of people, without the privileges of citizens."[18] The Fourteenth Amendment's citizenship clause did not remedy this situation: The Court ruled in 1884 that the clause did not provide citizenship to Native Americans born on reservations because reservations are not fully under the jurisdiction of the United States.[19] Not until the Indian Citizenship Act of 1924 did Congress provide natural-born citizenship to Native Americans born on reservations.

Connections: Should all citizens have the right to vote? Are there any citizens who should not have this right?

Naturalization.

The Constitution explicitly allows people not born in the United States to become citizens through naturalization by granting Congress the authority "to establish a uniform rule of naturalization." Congress's first such law, the Naturalization Act of 1790, restricted citizenship to "free white persons" who had lived in the United States for two years, swore allegiance to the United States, and had "good character." Though restrictive on race, the act allowed Catholics, Jews, and other "free white persons" to become naturalized citizens, rights that most European nations did not allow. The act also declared people born overseas to parents who were U.S. citizens to be natural-born citizens.

Connections: Who should be a citizen?

Congress first allowed nonwhites to become naturalized citizens in 1870, when it extended naturalization to "persons of African descent." Asians, however, still could not become naturalized citizens. Indeed, fear of Chinese immigrants led to an 1882 prohibition on the immigration of Chinese to America. That ban was the first significant restriction on immigration to the United States. Congress extended this ban to all Asians in 1921. The ban stayed in effect until 1943, when Congress allowed an annual quota of 105 immigrants from China, a World War II ally. The 1943 act also allowed Chinese to become naturalized citizens but did not allow other Asians to do so. Congress ended this restriction on Asian naturalization in 1952 but kept strict limits on the number of Asian immigrants until 1965.

Connections: What restrictions, if any, should there be on immigration?

The Immigration Act of 1924 established quotas for ethnic groups based on the proportion of Americans from each nationality resident in 1890, thereby severely limiting the number of whites considered to be of "lower race," that is, those from southern and eastern Europe,[20] who constituted a huge proportion of immigrants from the 1890s on. Under the act, the quota for Italy, for example, dropped more than 90 percent[21] from the percentage allowed in the Immigration Act of 1921, which also established quotas but based them on the proportion of each nationality resident in 1910.

In 1952 President Harry S. Truman (1945–53), claiming that such quotas were un-American, vetoed a bill that continued the national quota system, but Congress overrode his veto. With the Immigration and Nationality Act of 1965, Congress rescinded the quota system and the especially severe restrictions on Asian immigration. Today, to apply for citizenship, one must have had legal permanent residence for five years, or three years if married to a U.S. citizen. Applicants also must be of good moral character and must be able to pass a test on questions such as "who elects the president?" (see Table 5.1; Can you pass the test?).

Restraints during Wartime

As noted in Chapter 4, civil liberties suffer during wartime because the balance between freedom and order tilts toward order when survival is at stake. When the wartime enemy is racially or ethnically distinct from the majority of the American people, civil rights are also likely to suffer.

Two months after the Japanese attack on Pearl Harbor, President Franklin Delano Roosevelt (1933–45) issued an executive order for the evacuation of all 110,000 people of Japanese ancestry who resided west of the Rocky Mountains—whether citizen (most of them) or not—and their placement in relocation camps. Congress ratified the president's order, and in 1944 the Supreme Court endorsed it in *Korematsu v. United States*, ruling that the authority for relocation was within the war power of the United States.[22]

After the terrorist attacks of September 11, 2001, which were carried out by Muslim Arabs, other Arabs and Muslims in the United States came under suspicion. The government immediately rounded up and detained more than five thousand immigrants, most from Muslim or Middle Eastern countries. Of these detainees, three were convicted of terrorism-related crimes unrelated to 9/11, and two of those had their convictions overturned.[23] None of the other detainees had terrorism-related charges brought against them.

Connections:
Does military necessity overrule civil rights? If so, under what circumstances?

Checkpoint

Can you:

- ☐ Describe the role of the Supreme Court in the expansion of slavery
- ☐ Enumerate ways that racial discrimination persisted after emancipation
- ☐ Track the steps in the achievement of women's suffrage
- ☐ Identify the groups that have been denied rights to U.S. citizenship
- ☐ Discuss restraints on civil rights during wartime

TABLE 5.1 Questions on the Citizenship Test

The U.S. Citizenship and Immigration Service administers a citizenship test to applicants for naturalization. Following is a sampling of the questions from the American Government section of the test. There are also American History and Integrated Civics sections.

1. What is the supreme law of the land?

2. What does the Constitution do?

3. The idea of self-government is in the first three words of the Constitution. What are these words?

4. What is an amendment?

5. What do we call the first ten amendments to the Constitution?

6. What is <u>one</u> right or freedom from the First Amendment?

7. How many amendments does the Constitution have?

8. What did the Declaration of Independence do?

9. What are two rights in the Declaration of Independence?

10. What is freedom of religion?

11. What is the economic system in the United States?

12. What is the "rule of law"?

13. Name <u>one</u> branch or part of the government.

14. What stops one branch of government from becoming too powerful?

15. Who is in charge of the executive branch?

16. Who makes federal laws?

17. What are the two parts of the U.S. Congress?

18. How many U.S. senators are there?

19. We elect a U.S. senator for how many years?

20. Who is one of your state's U.S. senators?

21. The House of Representatives has how many voting members?

22. We elect a U.S. representative for how many years?

23. Name your U.S. representative.

24. Who does a U.S. senator represent?

25. Why do some states have more representatives than other states?

Source: See http://about.com/usgov.info for the answers, plus more questions.

The Expansion of Equal Protection

> **How equal protection has expanded**

Today the public discrimination documented in the previous section has been ended by acts of Congress, constitutional amendments, and court decisions, and no clause has been as powerful in this effort as the equal protection clause of the Fourteenth Amendment, which prohibits states from denying any person the equal protection of the law. The amendment gives Congress the authority to enforce its provisions by appropriate legislation, adding to Congress's enumerated powers by allowing the passage of laws that prevent states from discriminating. Additionally, the Supreme Court, through the power of judicial review, retains the authority to strike state laws that violate equal protection. Thus the federal government has a crucial role in the push for equality. This section examines equal protection before we continue the account of how the U.S. government shifted from engaging in discrimination to protecting against it.

The Changing Meaning of Equality

Equality had a very different meaning in 1776 than it does today. At the time of the Declaration of Independence, Thomas Jefferson saw nothing inconsistent about owning slaves, on the one hand, and declaring that "all men are created equal" on the other. The Civil War and the Thirteenth Amendment ended slavery, with the Fourteenth Amendment guaranteeing every person equal protection under the law. This constitutional protection did little to stop the massive inequalities imposed on black people by Jim Crow laws that denied them basic political and civil rights. The civil rights movement following World War II pushed to end state-sponsored segregation and private discrimination in businesses and public accommodations. The equality of opportunity goal of that era has been superseded, among some civil rights activists, by the goal of equality of outcome, wherein economic well-being should be roughly equal and employment in various professions should be roughly proportional to each group's proportion of the population.

State Action

Shortly after the passage of the Fourteenth Amendment, Congress tried to ban private discrimination at inns, public conveyances, theaters, and other public places. The Supreme Court rejected congressional authority to do so in the *Civil Rights Cases* (1883), ruling that the Fourteenth Amendment prohibited public discrimination by the states only, not private discrimination by businesses or individuals. From the 1880s until the 1940s, the federal government remained passive with regard to discrimination, allowing states and

Connections: If equality was not explicitly protected in the Constitution as originally ratified, how did it get to be so important today?

Connections: Why is majority rule not always congruent with civil rights?

locales to require segregation of the races and permitting public and private institutions to make their own rules regarding it.

In 1948, however, the Court ruled that private discrimination can be prohibited if it involves significant **state action**. The case involved housing. A group of homeowners signed a contract pledging never to sell their homes to blacks, but one of the homeowners did so. The neighbors sued to prevent the new owners from taking possession of the house, and the state supreme court ruled in favor of the neighbors. The U.S. Supreme Court reversed the state supreme court, ruling that judicial enforcement of the discriminatory private contract constitutes state action and thus is prohibited by the Fourteenth Amendment.[24]

 state action: *Action by a state, as opposed to a private person, that constitutes discrimination and therefore is an equal protection violation.*

Judicial Review

While the state-action doctrine allowed the Supreme Court to prohibit limited types of private discrimination, the equal protection clause of the Fourteenth Amendment is better suited to fighting public discrimination. In the next two decades, the Supreme Court actively applied the equal protection clause of the Fourteenth Amendment to do so. Congress also has the authority to enforce the equal protection clause, but democratically elected legislatures and executives are not necessarily designed to be responsive to minority groups, for they are chosen by a majority of voters. Thus civil rights organizations such as the National Association for the Advancement of Colored People (NAACP) turned to the judiciary, whose members are not elected and so do not directly depend on majority support, for assistance in establishing legal equality. Congress later wrote protections of civil rights into law.

As with civil liberties issues, for which the Court uses the standard of compelling interest (see Chapter 4), in civil rights cases the Court has constructed tests to determine whether laws violate the equal protection clause. Depending upon the group whose right has been violated, the Court sets different standards of how closely it will scrutinize the law alleged to violate equal protection. There are at least three levels. The Court reserves the toughest standard of review, strict scrutiny, for laws alleged to discriminate on account of race, ethnicity, religion, or status as an alien. It uses mid-level, or heightened scrutiny, for laws that discriminate on account of sex and the lowest level of scrutiny, rational basis, for general claims of discrimination (see Table 5.2).

We now turn to an examination of how grassroots racial, ethnic, and gender-based movements pressured the courts to protect civil rights and how Congress enforced court rulings with legislation. As with civil liberties (see Chapter 4), however, finding the right balance of rights for minority groups frequently divides members of society from one another, and democratically responsive legislatures from lifetime-appointed judges.

Connections: Who should ensure citizen equality? State governments? The federal government? The president? Congress? The courts? Citizens?

 Checkpoint

Can you:

☐ Track the changing meaning of equality

☐ Explain why "state action" is so important to the equal-protection clause

☐ Demonstrate that the judicial branch might be a better protector of civil rights than the legislative branch

TABLE 5.2 Supreme Court Scrutiny in Equal Protection Cases

Claim of Discrimination	Standard of Review	Test
Unprotected category	Lowest	Rational basis to achieve a legitimate governmental objective
Sex	Heightened	Exceedingly persuasive justification; use of sex as a governmental category must be substantially related to important governmental objectives
Race, ethnicity, religion, and alien status	Strict	Most rigid scrutiny; use of race as a governmental category must be precisely tailored to meet a compelling governmental interest

© CENGAGE LEARNING

The End of Legal Restrictions on Civil Rights

> **Which groups have been at the forefront of the civil rights movement**

Connections:
What gateways did citizens use to end segregation?

The events that brought about the government's shift from enforcing discrimination to protecting against it did not begin with the government. It began with pressure from groups that were discriminated against that mobilized on their own behalf. This gateway of public pressure generally involves the use of civil liberties such as freedom of speech and of assembly to engage in protests and other activities aside from voting, because minority groups, by definition, do not have the numbers to change policies through the ballot box alone.

The African American soldiers and sailors who fought for freedom in World War II against totalitarian regimes in Nazi Germany, fascist Italy, and imperial Japan often returned uneasily to hometowns, particularly in the South, where segregation remained the law. The three largest legal barriers African Americans faced in the post–World War II era were state-sponsored segregation of supposedly separate-but-equal public facilities, such as schools and buses; the legal right of private businesses to discriminate, that is, the right not to serve customers or hire people on account of race; and effective prohibitions on the right to vote, such as discriminatorily enforced literacy tests. These gates blocking full civic participation existed throughout the United States but were most prevalent in the former slave states. After we trace the African American struggle for equal rights, we turn to the women's movement, which likewise pressured the government to dismantle gender-based discrimination.

Brown v. Board of Education:
1954 Supreme Court decision striking down segregated schools.

Dismantling Public Discrimination Based on Race

Among the most consequential forms of segregation from the Jim Crow era was the mandatory separation of schools for whites and blacks. Beginning in 1935 the NAACP's Legal Defense Fund embarked on a legal campaign—led by Thurgood Marshall, who would later become the first African American to serve on the Supreme Court—to dismantle the system of separate-but-equal schools in southern and border states that were always separate but rarely equal. After a series of cases in which the Supreme Court struck down specific segregated schools because they were not equal,[25] the Court ruled more generally in **Brown v. Board of Education** (1954) that separate schools were inherently unequal, even should facilities be essentially similar (see Supreme Court Cases: *Brown v. Board of Education*). Segregation in schools violated the equal protection clause of the Fourteenth Amendment. The Fourteenth Amendment only requires that states provide equal protection of the laws, but on the same day as the *Brown* decision, the Supreme Court used the due process clause of the Fifth Amendment to prohibit the national government from denying equal protection.[26]

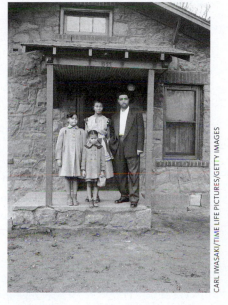

In 1950, when Linda Brown was entering third grade, her father Oliver Brown tried to enroll her in the Sumner School. The 10-year-old had been going to Monroe School, walking between train tracks and along streets without sidewalks to get there. Although it was closer, Sumner was for white students, and when Oliver Brown was told Linda could not attend, he took his case to the NAACP. Here the family stands in front of their home; Linda is on the left.

As historic as the *Brown* decision was, the case by itself did little to desegregate southern schools. Part of the problem was that the Court allowed local circumstances to influence the rate of integration, ambiguously requiring that local districts desegregate "with all deliberate speed."[27] Further, southern segregationists launched a massive resistance to the *Brown* decision. This campaign included "The Southern Manifesto," a document signed by 101 southern members of Congress deploring the *Brown* decision; the denial of state funds to any integrated school; and tuition grants for white students to attend segregated private schools. In addition, unruly segregationist mobs threatened black students seeking to integrate previously white schools. While neither the Supreme Court nor the Dwight D. Eisenhower administration (1953–61) could prevent every school disruption by segregationist mobs, both intervened in Little Rock, Arkansas. Eisenhower federalized the Arkansas National Guard and sent in the 101st Airborne to protect the black students seeking to integrate Central High School, while the Supreme Court, declaring that it had the final say on what the Constitution means, rejected the threat of violence as a justification for delaying integration.[28]

Connections:
Chapter 3 asked: What has been the relationship between federalism and the push for equality in the United States? What was your answer?

supremecourtcases

Brown v. Board of Education (1954)

QUESTION: Can states provide segregated schools for black and white schoolchildren?

ORAL ARGUMENT: December 7–9, 1953

DECISION: May 17, 1954 (read at http://www .findlaw.com/casecode/supreme.html)

OUTCOME: No, separate educational facilities are inherently unequal (9–0).

When Linda Brown was in third grade, her father, with the help of the NAACP, brought a suit against the Topeka school board for refusing to allow her to attend the local school that white children in their neighborhood attended.

In *Plessy v. Ferguson* (1896), the Supreme Court had ruled that the equal protection clause of the Fourteenth Amendment did not prohibit the states from establishing separate-but-equal facilities for whites and blacks. The Court did not really begin to look at whether the facilities were equal or not until 1938, when it held that Missouri's paying for blacks to go to law school out of state was not the same as providing facilities within the state that were equal to its white law school.* A pair of 1950 cases declared, first, that admitting a black to an all-white school but forcing him to sit in a separate row and dine at a separate table was unconstitutional,† and second, that the equality of separate schools had to be compared on both objective factors that could be measured, such as the number of faculty members, and subjective factors that could not be measured, such as the reputation of the faculty.‡

The *Brown* case came to the Supreme Court with similar desegregation cases from South Carolina, Virginia, Delaware, and Washington, D.C. Thurgood Marshall, who was in charge of legal strategy for the NAACP and would later become the first African American to serve on the Supreme Court, argued the *Brown* case. He readily admitted that the schools in Linda Brown's case were roughly equal in objective characteristics but argued that segregation in and of itself denied black students the equal protection of the laws by creating a feeling of inferiority among them.

The Supreme Court's preliminary vote following the arguments showed a majority favoring striking segregation, with two or three dissenters. Chief Justice Earl Warren, however, thought that a decision that was bound to be met with resistance in the South should be unanimous if at all possible. Following several months of bargaining and persuasion, he eventually got every member of the Court to agree that the Court should strike down school segregation.

- **Can separate schools ever be equal?**
- **Why were the courts more likely to be responsive to the problems of segregated schools than the legislature would be?**

---

* *Missouri ex rel. Gaines v. Canada*, 305 U.S. 337 (1938).

† *McLaurin v. Oklahoma*, 339 U.S. 637 (1950).

‡ *Sweatt v. Painter*, 339 U.S. 629 (1950).

Nevertheless, with few blacks able to vote, there was little need for southern politicians or school board officials to be responsive to their concerns, especially given massive opposition to desegregation by those who could vote. Only when the federal government took action did states respond. After Congress cut off federal aid to segregated schools in 1964, many districts began to integrate.[29] The rate of integration increased further in the late 1960s when the Supreme Court ended the "all deliberate speed" era and required an immediate end to segregated schools, thus pushing open the gateways to greater equality.[30]

Outside of schools, civil rights activists fought segregation in public facilities. The first grassroots action to receive nationwide attention was a bus boycott in Montgomery, Alabama. On December 1, 1955, police arrested Rosa Parks, a 42-year-old black seamstress and an active member of the NAACP, for refusing to give her seat to a white person. In response, the black community, led by a 26-year-old Baptist minister, Martin Luther King Jr., launched a boycott of city buses. Blacks walked, bicycled, and shared rides to avoid using the Montgomery bus system. Although the city arrested boycotters and violent segregationist terrorists firebombed King's home, the boycotters held firm for more than a year. The Supreme Court then declared Montgomery's segregated bus system unconstitutional.[31] A new ordinance allowing blacks to sit anywhere on any bus ended the boycott. King became one of the national leaders of the emerging civil rights movement and Rosa Parks its first heroine.

AP PHOTO/MONTGOMERY COUNTY SHERIFF'S OFFICE

Rosa Parks was often described as being too tired to stand up and give her seat to a white man on the day she was arrested. But in fact she was a civil rights activist—secretary of the Montgomery NAACP and participant in a workshop on resisting segregation at the Highlander Folk School in Tennessee.

Connections:
What are terrorists? Were the people who bombed King's house terrorists?

Dismantling Private Discrimination Based on Race

The decisions of businesses about whether to serve customers or hire workers on account of their race (or sex) were largely beyond judicial authority, because the Fourteenth Amendment's equal protection clause only prevents states from discriminating; it does not bar private discrimination. Thus, if a restaurant chose not to serve blacks or an employer chose not to hire them, there was little a court could do unless Congress passed legislation forbidding such actions. The effort to dismantle private discrimination thus took two tracks: protests to pressure businesses into serving blacks, and lobbying to pressure Congress into passing legislation that would make private discrimination in commercial matters illegal.

On April 19, 1960, following a wave of sit-in protests, Diane Nash and three thousand others promoting integration marched to the courthouse square in Nashville. On the way, some of them sang "We Shall Overcome," a gospel song that became the anthem of the civil rights movement. Confronting the mayor on the courthouse steps, the protesters forced him to admit that segregation was morally wrong.

The grassroots protests began when four African American freshmen at North Carolina Agricultural and Technical College in Greensboro sat down at the whites-only counter at Woolworth's, asked for coffee, and refused to leave when not served. Within weeks the sit-ins spread to dozens of other cities, with Diane Nash leading Nashville's protests. Tens of thousands of people participated in the sit-ins, and local police arrested thousands.[32] Nash and other young participants in these protests formed the Student Non-violent Coordinating Committee (SNCC), which along with the Congress of Racial Equality (CORE) served as the more activist "younger brothers" of the NAACP.

In the spring of 1963, Martin Luther King Jr.'s Southern Christian Leadership Conference (SCLC) led demonstrations in Birmingham, Alabama, to bring about the integration of downtown businesses. The police met demonstrators with fire hoses, police dogs, and cattle prods. Police arrested hundreds of protesters, including King. When white clergymen questioned why King, an outsider, had come to Birmingham, King answered in his famous "Letter from Birmingham Jail": "I am in Birmingham because injustice is here."[33] Rejecting violence, King insisted that peaceful civil disobedience was the only gateway to negotiation. The negotiations took place and ended with Birmingham businesses agreeing to integrate lunch counters and hire more blacks. Nevertheless, or perhaps because of this, members of the KKK exploded a bomb at a local black church on a Sunday morning, murdering four young girls.

Earlier that summer, King had led two hundred thousand protesters at the March on Washington. It was there that King delivered his historic "I Have a Dream" speech, in which he declared:

I have a dream that one day this nation will rise up and live out the true meaning of its creed: "We hold these truths to be self-evident: that all men are created equal." I have a dream that one day on the red hills of Georgia the sons of former slaves and the sons of former slave owners will be able to sit down together at the table of brotherhood. I have a dream that one day even the state of Mississippi, a state sweltering with the heat of injustice, sweltering with the heat of oppression, will be transformed into an oasis of

Connections: What is more important, equality or freedom of association?

Connections: If a law is immoral, are you right or wrong to disobey it? What is the remedy?

freedom and justice. I have a dream that my four little children will one day live in a nation where they will not be judged by the color of their skin but by the content of their character.[34]

President Kennedy proposed a civil rights bill that would have banned discrimination in public accommodations, such as restaurants and hotels. Five days after Kennedy's assassination in November 1963, President Lyndon Baines Johnson (1963–69) told Congress that nothing could better honor Kennedy than passage of this bill. The next year, Congress passed the **Civil Rights Act**, which significantly strengthened Kennedy's original bill by also prohibiting employment discrimination on account of "race, color, religion, sex, or national origin."

Because the Fourteenth Amendment's equal protection clause applies only to state-sponsored discrimination, the Supreme Court upheld Congress's authority to ban private discrimination under the interstate commerce clause. Given the Court's broad interpretation of interstate commerce (see Chapter 3, Federalism), the Court ruled that even small inns and restaurants had to abide by the act.[35]

In 1971 the Supreme Court interpreted the Civil Rights Act to limit job qualification requirements that had a disparate impact on whites and blacks.[36] For example, if more whites receive high school diplomas than blacks, requiring a high school diploma for a job would be more harmful to blacks than to whites. A business seeking to establish job requirements that have a disparate impact would have to prove that the requirement is necessary to the job. In the late 1970s and through the 1980s, a more conservative Supreme Court reached a series of decisions that restricted civil rights protections, for example, making disparate impact more difficult to prove and ruling that discrimination against pregnant women was not a form of sex discrimination under the Civil Rights Act.[37] Passing new laws, Congress overturned these Court decisions plus several others, thus demonstrating widespread support for the continued protection of civil rights. The new rules, for example, make it easier to find that job tests have a disparate impact but leave it to the courts to determine whether disparate impact, by taking race into account, conflicts with the equal treatment obligation of the Civil Rights Act.[38]

Connections: Which branch of government has been most powerful in ensuring equality? Why?

Civil Rights Act: *Prohibits discrimination in employment, education, and places of public accommodation (1964).*

AP PHOTO/FILE

On August 28, 1963, more than two hundred thousand people gathered on the Washington Mall in a March for Jobs and Freedom. Among them were seventy-five members of Congress who were working to pass a civil rights bill that had President Kennedy's support. Folk singer Joan Baez led the crowd in singing "We Shall Overcome," but the day belonged to Martin Luther King Jr., whose "I Have a Dream" speech still challenges Americans to work for equality.

Dismantling Voting Barriers Based on Race

As noted previously, the end of Reconstruction left black men in the South with a constitutional right to vote but a hostile social and legal environment that made it extremely difficult for them to do so. The Supreme Court pushed things along, striking down grandfather clauses (1915) and white primaries (1944), the latter in a suit filed by the NAACP.[39] Congress and the states pushed things along further, outlawing poll taxes with the Twenty-Fourth Amendment (1964). Martin Luther King Jr. identified four gates that kept blacks from voting: white terrorist control of local governments and sheriffs' departments; arrests on trumped-up charges of those seeking to vote; the discretion given to registrars, where "the latitude for discrimination is almost endless"; and the arbitrary nature of literacy tests.[40]

During the summer of 1964, voting rights supporters from around the country, many of them college students, moved south to help with voter registration drives. In March 1965 King organized a voting rights march from Selma to Montgomery, Alabama. With national news media on hand, Alabama police, under the authority of Governor George Wallace, beat the marchers with whips, nightsticks, and cattle prods. Selma natives murdered two more voting rights activists.

A week later President Johnson addressed a joint session of Congress, calling for passage of the strictest possible voting rights legislation. He ended the speech by adopting a line from the civil rights movement, telling Congress and the nation, "we shall overcome."[41] Congress responded by passing the **Voting Rights Act** in August 1965. The act banned literacy, interpretation, and other such tests for voting. It required states with low voter registration levels, essentially seven southern states plus Alaska, to receive Justice Department approval for any changes to its voting laws. It also established new criminal penalties for those who sought to keep people from voting on account of race. The law was an enormous success. By 2008 blacks and whites voted at essentially the same rate nationwide[42] and at slightly higher rates in some southern states[43] (see Figure 5.3).

Voting Rights Act: *Gives the federal government the power to prevent discrimination in voting rights (1965).*

Connections: What restrictions, if any, should be placed on voting?

Connections: How has expansion of the right to vote affected citizen participation? How has it affected public policy?

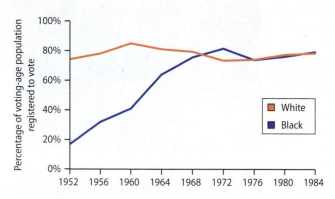

FIGURE 5.3 **White and Black Southern Voter Registration, 1952–1984.**

Dramatic increases in black voter registration preceded passage of the Voting Rights Act in 1965, but substantial equality between whites and blacks did not occur until after its passage.

Source: Data from Harold W. Stanley, *Voter Mobilization and the Politics of Race* (New York: Praeger, 1987), Appendix A.

Dismantling Discrimination Based on Gender

The success of the civil rights movement inspired other groups, most notably women, to put pressure on the political system to obtain equal rights under the law. Women active in the civil rights movement easily shifted the movement's strategies to promoting rights for women, particularly after the publication of Betty Friedan's *The Feminine Mystique* (1963), a book considered by many to have launched the modern American feminist movement. Based on a survey Friedan sent to her Smith College classmates in advance of their fifteenth reunion, the book broadcast the dissatisfaction that many American women felt in their roles as wives and mothers. About the same time, the Kennedy administration's President's Commission on the Status of Women, charged with making recommendations for overcoming sex discrimination, urged passage of the **Equal Pay Act**. Passed by Congress in 1963, the act prohibits employers from paying different wages for the same job on account of sex. Although the act did not prohibit discrimination in the hiring of male and female workers, that prohibition came with the Civil Rights Act of 1964.

Following passage of the Civil Rights Act, Friedan helped found the National Organization for Women (NOW), which advocated for women's rights through education and litigation. NOW protested airline policies that forced stewardesses to retire at marriage or age 32 and help-wanted ads that listed jobs by gender, as well as protective legislation. NOW also supported abortion rights and a proposed Equal Rights Amendment (ERA), which would have prohibited the federal government and the states from discriminating on account of sex.

Passed by Congress and sent to the states for ratification in 1972, the ERA began to falter. An anti-ERA movement led by political activist Phyllis Schlafly reversed the momentum by arguing that the amendment would remove special privileges women enjoyed with regard to protective legislation, Society Security benefits, and exemption from the draft. Ironically, another argument against the ERA was that it was unnecessary because the Supreme Court was striking down most laws that discriminated on account of sex. Despite an extension of the deadline to 1982, the ERA ultimately fell three states short of the three-quarters majority needed to pass an amendment (see Figure 5.4).

By the 1980s the civil rights era was over and the nation had taken a conservative turn. But like African Americans whose officeholding and participation in civic life generally increased after passage of the Voting Rights Act, women were increasingly taking public roles. In 2008 the Democratic presidential primary campaign of New York Senator Hillary Clinton and the Republican nomination of Alaska Governor Sarah Palin for vice president were evidence that the nation was ready.

Connections: Why, in U.S. history, do women's rights movements follow, rather than precede, movements to remove racial barriers?

 Equal Pay Act: *Prohibits different pay for males and females for the same work (1963).*

Connections: Should there be an Equal Rights Amendment to the U.S. Constitution?

 ## Checkpoint

Can you:

☐ Explain why the *Brown* decision by itself had only a minimal effect on school desegregation

☐ Identify the grassroots protests that opened the gateways to ending private discrimination

☐ Describe how Congress and the courts have pushed along voting rights

☐ Draw parallels between the civil rights movement for African Americans and the women's rights movement

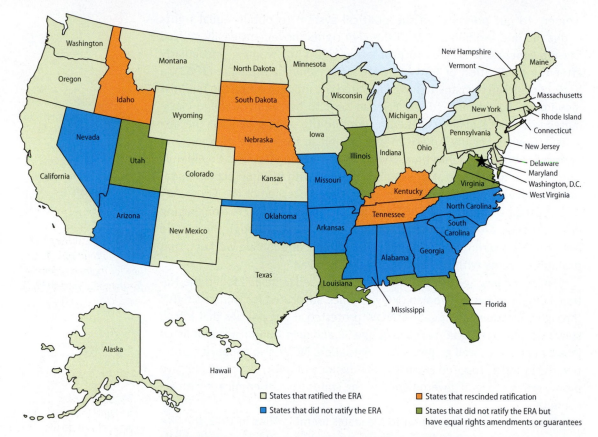

FIGURE 5.4 States Approving the Equal Rights Amendment.

- ☐ States that ratified the ERA
- ☐ States that did not ratify the ERA
- ☐ States that rescinded ratification
- ☐ States that did not ratify the ERA but have equal rights amendments or guarantees

Passed by Congress in 1972 and sent to the states for ratification, the Equal Rights Amendment got a quick start and then faltered as opposition materialized and grew. In 1979 Congress extended the deadline for ratification to 1982, but in 1982 the amendment expired. Thirty-five states (of the thirty-eight needed) had voted to ratify it, and five states had voted to rescind ratification.

Source: © Cengage Learning; data from http://www.equalrightsamendment.org.

Frontiers in Civil Rights

› What the new battles for civil rights are

> **Connections:** Is the era of civil rights over? Have all the battles been fought and won?

Many of the civil rights battles against legal discrimination have been won: Governments cannot discriminate on account of race or sex, and businesses cannot discriminate in hiring employees or serving customers. But the expanded notion of equality promoted by the civil rights and women's rights movements inspired other groups, such as homosexuals and the disabled, to demand full access to equality. At the same time, as the fight over the ERA made clear, the extension of rights for some may involve a loss of privileges for others, and sometimes rights clash. Congress and the courts have sought to define the meaning and limits of rights as new areas of conflict emerge over such issues as racial and religious profiling, the voting rights of felons, and the civil rights of illegal immigrants. Whatever the new issues, however, the trend in the United States has been for a broader meaning of equality and greater support for civil rights.

Sexual Orientation and Same-Sex Marriage

The movement to protect the rights of homosexuals first received widespread public attention in 1969 when a police raid on the Stonewall Inn, a gay bar in New York City, turned into a riot by the bar's patrons and gay rights supporters living in the area. The **Stonewall riots** became the signature event of a growing gay rights movement. Activists soon formed the Gay Liberation Front, which established branch organizations around the world. By the 1990s the movement had expanded into a broader LGBT movement that sought to protect the rights of lesbians, gays, bisexuals, and transgendered persons.

At the time of the Stonewall riots, all states banned sodomy, which would include virtually all sexual activity between same-sex couples.[44] In the following years several states decriminalized homosexual activity, but as noted in Chapter 4 the Supreme Court ruled in 1986 that homosexual activity was not a fundamental right, so states could still keep homosexuality illegal if they so chose. In *Lawrence v. Texas* (2003), the Supreme Court reversed the 1986 decision and declared that states could not prohibit sexual activity between people of the same sex.[45]

Nevertheless, Americans remain split as to whether homosexual relationships between consenting adults is morally wrong,[46] and issues related to homosexual rights have been fraught with conflict. Under President William Jefferson (Bill) Clinton (1993–2001), Congress enacted a "don't ask, don't tell" policy for the military. Prior to the implementation of this policy, simply having homosexual tendencies, without any evidence of homosexual activities, was sufficient grounds for discharge. Under the policy, sexual orientation alone was not a ground for discharge, but lesbians, gays, and bisexuals were discharged for engaging in homosexual relationships or for discussing their sexual orientation. Barack Obama opposed the "don't ask, don't tell" policy and in 2010 signed a bill repealing it.

Thousands of citizens in same-sex partnerships want to be married but are not eligible for that legally recognized status, which brings advantages with regard to the right to make health care decisions for a spouse, inheritance rights, and tax benefits. The issue of same-sex marriage is highly controversial. State laws typically govern family matters, including marriage,

Stonewall riots: *Street protest in 1969 by gay patrons against a police raid of a gay bar in New York; the protest is credited with launching the gay rights movement.*

Connections:
Do court decisions follow public opinion? Do they lead public opinion? What should be the relationship?

divorce, child custody, and wills, and in most states marriage is limited to one man and one woman. While each state can set its own rules, the full faith and credit clause of the Constitution generally requires each state to accept the status granted by other states. Thus, opposite-sex couples who get married in Las Vegas under Nevada law are recognized as married throughout the United States.

When the Hawaii Supreme Court ruled in 1993 that, under the state constitution, Hawaii would have to show a compelling interest in its prohibition of same-sex marriages, opponents feared that same-sex marriages performed in Hawaii would have legal recognition throughout the United States. In 1996 Congress passed and President Clinton signed the Defense of Marriage Act, which defines marriage, for the purpose of federal law, as between a man and a woman and declares that states do not have to recognize same-sex marriages performed in other states. Later that year, the Hawaii Supreme Court ruled that the state did not have a compelling interest in prohibiting same-sex marriages, but voters then approved a state constitutional amendment allowing the state legislature to ban same-sex marriage. Since that time, courts, legislatures, and citizen initiatives have battled over same-sex marriage, with judicial protection sometimes overridden by popular opposition, as in California (2008) and Maine (2009) (see Figure 5.5). In 2012, a federal appeals court ruled that the California initiative banning same-sex marriage violated the equal protection clause.[47] This decision will almost certainly be appealed to the Supreme Court.

National public opinion remains mixed on the matter of same-sex marriage (see Figure 5.6). While a majority of Americans favor some form of legal recognition for same-sex couples,[48] only seven states and the District of Columbia have legally recognized same-sex marriage; another nine recognize civil unions. The major political parties are internally divided on the issue; while Democrats are typically more supportive of same-sex marriage than Republicans are, and Barack Obama, a Democrat, said that he supported federal recognition of same-sex marriage.[49] Because support for same-sex marriage is much greater among younger Americans than among older Americans, the legality of same-sex marriage will almost certainly increase over time.

Connections:
What government (state or federal) or branch of government (executive, legislative, or judicial) should have the power to decide whether same-sex marriage is legal?

Affirmative Action

Almost as controversial as gay rights are remedies for overcoming the effects of centuries-long discrimination. Known as **affirmative action**, these programs grant preferences to African Americans, other minorities, and/or women in employment, education, or contracting. They not only aim to ensure equality of opportunity but also to promote equality of outcome.

President Johnson first stated the rationale for affirmative action: "You do not take a man who for years has been hobbled by chains, liberate him,

affirmative action: *Policies that support greater equality, often by granting racial or gender preferences in hiring, education, or contracting.*

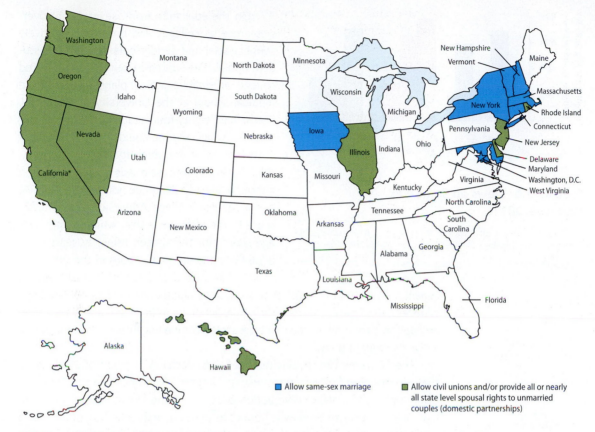

*In 2008, a successful ballot initiative in California amended the California Constitution to state that only a marriage between a man and a woman is valid or recognized, but this amendment was struck down by a U.S. District Court in 2010, which stayed its own decision until all appeals were final. In 2012, the U.S. Court of Appeals upheld the district court and continued the stay. The case is currently pending appeal to the U.S. Supreme Court.

Note: November 2012 referenda in Maine and Washington State legalized same-sex marriage.

FIGURE 5.5 States Approving Same-Sex Marriage, 2012.

Source: © Cengage Learning; data from National Conference of State Legislatures.

bring him to the starting line of a race, saying, 'you are free to compete with all the others,' and still justly believe you have been completely fair."[50] But do the effects of unequal treatment in the past justify potentially unequal treatment in the present? Is fear of causing inequality in the present sufficiently compelling to not correct the inequalities of the past? The Supreme Court has struggled to find the right balance between these positions. Today affirmative action programs by private businesses must comport with the Supreme Court's interpretation of the nondiscrimination clauses of the Civil Rights Act; affirmative action programs by national, state, and local governments also must comport with constitutional requirements of equal protection. The Supreme Court has upheld narrowly tailored, race-based affirmative action plans but will be revisiting those decisions during its 2012–13 term.

Connections: Why are rules and decisions regarding affirmative action murky and contested?

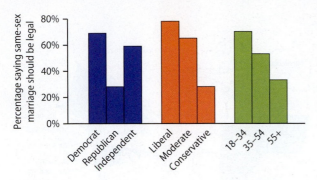

FIGURE 5.6 **Views on Same-Sex Marriage, 2011.**

Source: Gallup Poll, May 20, 2011. Copyright © 2011 Gallup, Inc. All rights reserved. The content is used with permission; however, Gallup retains all right of republication.

On the education front, several controversies arose as colleges and universities actively sought racial and gender balances in their student bodies. The Supreme Court first confronted college affirmative action plans in 1978. The medical school at the University of California, Davis, had eighty-four seats in each entering class for which anyone could apply and sixteen seats set aside for minority candidates only. Allan Bakke, a white male, was denied admission although he had a 3.5 grade point average (GPA) and a Medical College Admission Test (MCAT) score in the 90th percentile, whereas the average scores for the sixteen minority seats were a 2.6 GPA and an MCAT score in the 20th percentile. Bakke sued, and a split Court decreed in *Regents v. Bakke* that this sort of quota system violated the Civil Rights Act. Nevertheless, the Court held that affirmative action plans in which race is a "plus" in an applicant's overall file did meet the state's compelling interest in establishing a diverse student body.[51]

The Supreme Court revisited the *Bakke* decision in a pair of 2003 cases that are discussed more extensively in Chapter 14. In one case the Supreme Court upheld the affirmative action program at the University of Michigan Law School because the law school considered race as one part of an entire file.[52] In the other case the Court struck down the program at the University of Michigan's undergraduate college in which race automatically created a set number of points toward admission without individualized consideration of how particular applicants who were minorities might contribute to the school's diversity.[53]

In the law school case, Justice Sandra Day O'Connor, the first woman to serve on the Court, expressed the belief that the Constitution required affirmative action programs to be temporary solutions only and the hope that by 2028 they would no longer be necessary. Opponents of affirmative action, such as Ward Connerly, chair of the American Civil Rights Institute, hope that such plans will not last that long. Connerly has launched state-level initiatives in Arizona, California, Colorado, Michigan, Nebraska, and Washington to let voters decide whether such programs should be allowed. Voters rejected affirmative action in all those states except Colorado.

Disability Rights

Advocates for the rights of the disabled, encouraged by the civil rights, women's rights, and other movements, successfully lobbied for the Rehabilitation

Act of 1973, which prohibits discrimination against disabled individuals by any federal agency or by any private program or activity that receives federal funds. The landmark Americans with Disabilities Act (ADA) passed in 1990 goes further, requiring public and private employers to make "reasonable accommodations" to known physical and mental limitations of employees with disabilities and, if possible, to modify performance standards to accommodate an employee's disability.

To comply with the act, public transportation authorities have made buses and trains accessible to people in wheelchairs. Public accommodations, such as restaurants, hotels, movie theaters, and doctors' offices, must also meet ADA accessibility standards, within reason, removing barriers from existing structures. Related legislation, the Individuals with Disabilities Education Act (IDEA; 1990, updated 2004) requires states to provide free public education to all children with disabilities in the least restrictive environment appropriate to their particular needs.

Congress does not provide a full list of disabilities covered under the ADA, but rather covers any disability that "substantially limits a major life activity." Thus, a trucking company need not make accommodations for a driver who can see clearly out of only one eye because the disability does not substantially limit a major life activity. On the other hand, the ADA does protect people who have HIV or AIDS. It even protects people with severe drug and alcohol problems, provided the drug use in question is not illegal.[54]

Racial and Religious Profiling

Profiling—the use by police of racial, ethnic, or religious characteristics in determining whom to investigate for particular kinds of crimes—is controversial because it entails unequal treatment under the law. For example, along the I-95 corridor north of Baltimore, a team of observers found that about 17 percent of cars had black drivers and nearly 76 percent had white drivers and that the drivers observed traffic laws in similar proportions. Nevertheless, more than 80 percent of the cars stopped and searched by the Maryland State Police were driven by blacks and Hispanics, while cars driven by whites constituted fewer than 20 percent of the searches.[55] So much more likely were blacks to be pulled over than whites that the phrase "driving while black" came to signify African American drivers' feeling that they risked being treated as criminals on the roads. In 2008 the Maryland State Police agreed to pay more than $400,000 to settle racial profiling suits, and litigation continues in eight other states.[56] State and federal courts have specifically prohibited the use of race as a factor in "drug courier profiles."[57] Many suspect that the 2012 killing of Trayvon Martin in Florida resulted from racial profiling by a neighborhood watch captain.

Connections:
Should profiling be used to protect American citizens against terrorist plots?

Illegal Immigrants

The Fourteenth Amendment's equal protection clause prohibits states from denying to any person—in other words, not just citizens—equal protection under the law. Thus even illegal immigrants receive some degree of legal protection in the United States. The level of that protection is deeply controversial, especially as the number of illegal immigrants, estimated to be about 12 million, has skyrocketed in recent years (see Chapter 9, Political Parties, for further discussion of immigration policy).

Congress has been considering a number of actions, including creating easier paths to citizenship for illegal immigrants or, alternatively, denying natural-born citizenship to U.S.-born children of illegal immigrants. By a 48 percent to 46 percent margin, Americans do not believe such children should automatically become citizens, but the constitutionality of a law that would deny them citizenship, given the Fourteenth Amendment's citizenship clause, remains unclear.[58]

While the Court reviews laws that discriminate against legal immigrants under its strictest level of scrutiny, it reviews laws that discriminate against illegal immigrants under the easier rational-basis standard. Yet, the Court has held that states may not deny public education to illegal immigrants,[59] and federal law requires hospitals to provide emergency care to illegal immigrants through Medicaid, the federal program that supports health care to poor people. The growth of civil rights to cover illegal immigrants is surely one of the most controversial of the frontiers we have examined.

> **Connections:**
> Should children of illegal immigrants who are born on American soil be U.S. citizens?

✓ Checkpoint

Can you:

- ☐ Explain why support for same-sex marriage is likely to increase over time
- ☐ State the rationale for affirmative action and survey the resistance to it
- ☐ Recall why legislatures have been so responsive to people with disabilities
- ☐ Define racial, ethnic, and religious profiling
- ☐ State why the U.S.-born children of illegal immigrants are automatically U.S. citizens

Civil Rights and Public Policy: Workplace Equality

Although national legislation and constitutional amendments define civil rights policy and the Supreme Court interprets such laws—deciding whether they are constitutional and, if so, what they mean—the day-to-day protection of civil rights now falls to two separate executive branch agencies. One is the Civil Rights Division of the Department of Justice, with sections on educational opportunity, employment, housing, voting, and disability rights. The other is the Equal Employment Opportunity Commission, which protects against sexual harassment in the workplace and promotes gender equity.

The Equal Employment Opportunity Commission

The Equal Employment Opportunity Commission (EEOC) is an independent agency with commissioners selected for five-year fixed terms. Unlike the heads of government departments, EEOC commissioners cannot be removed by the president. They are thus thought to be shielded from political pressures, but fixed terms also limit responsiveness to the president, who is the chief executive of the United States.

Congress established the EEOC as part of the Civil Rights Act of 1964. The original EEOC could receive and investigate complaints of discrimination on the basis of race, sex, religion, and national origin (Congress later added age and disability status). As one of the compromises that allowed the act to pass, the EEOC originally had no enforcement power. Rather, it could refer to the Justice Department any case in which there were patterns or practices of discrimination. In 1972 Congress provided the commission with the right to file lawsuits against companies that discriminate.

Sexual Harassment

The problem of discrimination on account of sex can take many forms, and one of the most prevalent in the workplace is sexual harassment. Survey data reveal that 17 percent of women report having been sexually harassed

Connections: Should laws regarding the behavior of women in the workplace be different from laws regarding the behavior of men? Do women need or warrant added protection?

© CENGAGE LEARNING

at work.[60] The EEOC receives more than eleven thousand sexual harassment complaints per year.[61] The commission first set regulations against sexual harassment in 1980, stating that such harassment was a form of sex discrimination prohibited by the Civil Rights Act.

The Supreme Court recognizes two distinct types of sexual harassment. Some harassment takes quid pro quo form in which supervisors link the benefits of employment to sexual favors. But to be harassment, behavior does not have to be linked to benefits or threats. Sexual harassment takes place whenever one or more employees establish, on account of sex, a hostile work environment, one that interferes with a worker's ability to do his or her job.

Gender Equality in the Workplace

From a policy standpoint, the underlying principle of equal pay is that two people who are employed in the same job and do the same quality of work should be paid the same wage. Achieving gender equality in the workplace means that there are no barriers to advancement or hiring based on gender and that gender plays no role in how employees are treated and compensated.

© JASON REED/REUTERS

Lilly Ledbetter's pay discrimination suit went all the way to the Supreme Court. After the Court ruled against her and Congress overturned that decision, she spoke at the 2012 Democratic National Convention. She noted that the Lilly Ledbetter Fair Pay Act was the first bill President Obama signed once in office. She then said, "The president signed the bill for his grandmother, whose dreams hit the glass ceiling, and for his daughters, so that theirs never will. Because of his leadership, women who faced pay discrimination like I did will now get their day in court."

Unfortunately, true pay equity has not been achieved in the American workplace. Though the census statistics below do not control for the type of job worked, data from 2011 show that women earned only 77.4 percent of what men earned in 2011. For African American and Latina women, this percentage was even lower: African American women earned only 67.7 percent and Latinas earned only 58.7 percent of what men made.[62] Alternatively, the gap falls to slightly above 92 percent for women under the age of 35.[63]

Though the Equal Pay Act is supposed to guarantee equal pay for the same work, and the Civil Rights Act aims to protect against any form of employment discrimination on account of sex, the judicial branch has also played a pivotal role. A recent set of Supreme Court decisions has prompted changes in the laws governing discrimination, harassment, and pay equity in the workplace. The Court's 2007 ruling in *Ledbetter v. Goodyear Tire and Rubber Co.* had the greatest impact on public policy.[64] In 1998 Lilly Ledbetter filed a complaint with the EEOC that she had consistently received poor job performance evaluations because of her gender and that over the nineteen years she had worked at the Goodyear Tire plant she had fallen well below her male colleagues who did the same type of job. Her employer countered that, even if that had been true in the past, she did not file her complaint within the 180 days required by the Civil Rights Act. The Court ruled in favor of Goodyear, stating that Ledbetter's claims alleging sex discrimination were time-barred because the discriminatory decisions relating to pay had been made more than 180 days prior to the day she filed the charge with the EEOC. In her dissent, Justice Ruth Bader Ginsburg wrote that the effect of this ruling would allow "any annual pay decision not contested immediately (within 180 days) . . . [to become] grandfathered, a fait accompli beyond the province of Title VII ever to repair."[65] Basically, a company could pay a woman less on the basis of gender, and as long as she did not contest the discriminatory wage within 180 days, the discriminatory wage could not be challenged in federal court.

In 2009 Congress reversed the Court's ruling by passing the Lilly Ledbetter Fair Pay Act, which President Obama signed into law. The act restarts the clock each time an employee receives a paycheck that has been compromised by discriminatory practices.[66] Many equal pay advocates think that this new law will be helpful but not nearly helpful enough to close the salary gap between men and women. Indeed, early reports suggest that some individual women have been able to sue who would not have been able to do so before the act but that these individual suits have done little to close the gender pay gap.[67]

Connections: Why do women still earn less than men do for performing the same job? Do women warrant equality of opportunity or equality of outcome?

 ## Construct Your Own Policy

1. Design a system of evaluation in the private sector workplace to ensure that decisions on pay raises and promotions are not made on the basis of on race, sex, or sexual orientation.

2. Develop a plan for state and local government enforcement of workplace equality, replacing federal government oversight.

   For more on the policy-making process, see Chapter 1.

Civil Rights and Democracy

Focus Questions Revisited

- What is the meaning of equality? How has its meaning changed since the Constitution was written in 1787?

- What role has government played with regard to equality in the past? What role does it assume today?

- What means have various groups used to secure their civil rights? What means has government used to respond?

- What is the effect on a democracy if some of its people lack civil rights?

- Are civil rights a gate or a gateway to democracy? Explain.

The core demand of civil rights is equal opportunity under the law. When laws discriminate or allow discrimination, people are effectively excluded from civic life. The demands for equal opportunity are often made to government, which alone has the authority to prohibit discrimination.

While a democratic system of government works to be responsive to its citizens, responsiveness to minorities is harder to obtain when majorities seek to limit minority rights. As noted in Chapter 2, The Constitution, James Madison saw a large republic with varied interests as a cure for the mischiefs of faction. But when factions form on the basis of majority group versus minority group, such as white versus black, heterosexual versus gay and lesbian, or native-born versus immigrant, responsiveness to minority preferences has been achieved through the gateways of lawsuits, protests, and other forms of civic engagement by the minority group. In response, the government has struck laws that discriminated and passed laws that prevented other people from discriminating.

Out of all the activities by groups seeking equal rights, voting might be key. With the vote, declared Martin Luther King Jr. in 1965, comes accountability. Blacks could "vote out of office public officials who bar the doorway to decent housing, public safety, jobs, and decent integrated education. It is now obvious that the basic elements so vital to Negro advancement can only be achieved by seeking redress from government. . . . To do this, the vote is essential."[68]

While voting rights provide accountability by allowing citizens to "throw the bums out," they also provide responsiveness. A minority group's elected opponents are not as forceful once a group has the right to vote. More generally, the voting patterns of southern House and Senate members on issues related to civil rights have moderated over the past forty years, proving that King was certainly correct about the value of the ballot.[69] While members of Congress representing southern states once voted in lockstep opposition to civil rights issues, their votes on such issues now differ only slightly from those of representatives of other states.[70]

These changes are part of a larger evolution in the idea of equality that has proceeded over the course of the nation's more than two centuries. Americans once believed that slaveholding was not inconsistent with demands for equality; today African Americans, women, and others once discriminated against have achieved full participation in the nation's civic

Forty-three years after the passage of the Voting Rights Act the United States elected its first African American president, Barack Obama. The son of an African American White House staffer asked to touch the president's hair to see if it really was like his own hair. To the boy's delight, it was.

life. But the frontiers of civil rights will continue to evolve. Some Americans believe that equal opportunity is not enough, that the government must take stronger measures to ensure greater equality of outcome. Because there is no constitutional right to equal results, the battle over this meaning of equality will be fought not in the courts, but in democratically elected legislatures.

gatewaystolearning

Top Ten to Take Away

1. Civil rights relate to the duties of citizenship and opportunities for civic participation that the government is obliged to protect. They are based on the expectation of equality under the law. The most important is the right to vote. (pp. 133–134, 137–138, 140, 152–153)

2. With regard to civil rights, the government can engage in state-sponsored or public discrimination; treat people equally but permit private discrimination; or try, as it has since the 1960s, both to treat people equally and to prevent individuals or businesses from discriminating. (p. 133)

3. It falls to government to protect individuals against unequal treatment and to citizens to ensure that government does not discriminate against individuals or groups. (p. 133)

4. During the nation's first century, and even thereafter, state laws and the national government actively discriminated against people on the basis of race, gender, and ethnic background. (pp. 135–136, 139–140)

5. During the nation's second century, discrimination was state-sponsored in the South; elsewhere private discrimination was practiced without challenge. (pp. 136–139)

6. Today public discrimination has been ended by constitutional amendments and the courts, largely through the Fourteenth Amendment's equal protection clause. (pp. 144–145)

7. Beginning in the 1950s, litigation and grassroots protests led the federal government to end segregation and secure voting rights for African Americans and to end limits to women's full participation in public life. (pp. 146–153)

8. The expanded notion of equality promoted by the civil rights and women's rights movements inspired other groups, such as homosexuals and the disabled, to demand full access to equality. (pp. 154–159)

9. The extension of rights for some may involve a loss of privileges for others, and sometimes rights clash. Congress and the courts seek to define the meaning and limits of rights in new areas of contention. (pp. 159–160)

10. The trend has always been for a broader meaning of equality and greater support for civil rights. (pp. 164–165)

Key Concepts

affirmative action (p. 156). How do affirmative action plans increase or decrease equality?

Brown v. Board of Education (p. 147). What was the reasoning behind the *Brown* decision?

citizenship (p. 141). What are the different paths to citizenship?

civil rights (p. 133). What is the government's role with regards to civil rights?

Civil Rights Act (p. 151). What did the Civil Rights Act prohibit?

Dred Scott v. Sandford (p. 135). What seems wrong about the *Dred Scott* decision?

equality of opportunity (p. 134). How would you measure equality of opportunity?

equality of outcome (p. 134). How would you measure equality of outcome?

Equal Pay Act (p. 153). How effective has the Equal Pay Act been?

equal protection clause (p. 137). What does the equal protection clause command?

Jim Crow laws (p. 138). What were Jim Crow laws?

poll taxes (p. 137). What were the various types of poll taxes?

private discrimination (p. 133). What constitutes private discrimination?

public discrimination (p. 133). What constitutes public discrimination?

Reconstruction (p. 137). What happened when Reconstruction ended?

separate-but-equal doctrine (p. 138). Can separate schools ever be equal?

state action (p. 145). What makes state action so important to government efforts to protect civil rights?

Stonewall riot (p. 155). What movement did the Stonewall riots spark?

Voting Rights Act (p. 152). What did the Voting Rights Act prohibit?

women's suffrage movement (p. 139). What gateways did the women's suffrage movement use to gain the right to vote?

Learning Outcomes

WHAT YOU NEED...

To Know	To Test Yourself	To Participate
What civil rights are	• Compare civil rights to civil liberties • Track changes in civil rights from the 1787 Constitution to today	• Know your civil rights • Understand the debt you owe to the actions of citizens for the civil rights you enjoy today
How the federal and state governments suppressed civil rights	• Describe the role of the Supreme Court in the expansion of slavery • Enumerate ways that racial discrimination persisted after emancipation • Track the steps in the achievement of women's suffrage • Identify the groups that have been denied rights to U.S. citizenship • Discuss restraints on civil rights during wartime	• Read excerpts from the *Dred Scott* decision (http://www.academicamerican.com/expansion_antebellum/docs/dredscott.htm) and from the black codes established after the Civil War (http://home.gwu.edu/~jjhawkin/BlackCodes/BlackCodes.htm) and comment on them • Consider how disenfranchisement of women affected U.S. politics before 1920 • Speculate on why the United States limited citizenship • Evaluate what these mean for living in a time of prolonged terrorism
How equal protection has expanded	• Track the changing meaning of equality • Explain why "state action" is so important to the equal-protection clause • Demonstrate that the judicial branch might be a better protector of civil rights than the legislative branch	• Decide whether we are all equal now • Weigh your respect for the legislative branch vs. the judicial branch
Which groups have been at the forefront of the civil rights movement	• Explain why the *Brown* decision by itself had only a minimal effect on school desegregation • Identify the grassroots protests that opened the gateways to ending private discrimination • Describe how Congress and the courts have pushed along voting rights • Draw parallels between the civil rights movement for African Americans and the women's rights movement	• Weigh the impact on social policy of the legislative branch against that of the judicial branch • Appreciate the impact active citizens can have on government • Appreciate the impact law can have on politics and society
What the new battles for civil rights are	• Explain why support for same-sex marriage is likely to increase over time • State the rationale for affirmative action and survey the resistance to it • Recall why legislatures have been so responsive to people with disabilities • Define racial, ethnic, and religious profiling • State why the U.S.-born children of illegal immigrants are automatically U.S. citizens	• Determine whether you think all of the civil rights battles have been won • Understand the basis for affirmative action and assess its value • Find disability rights organizations in your community • Find instances of profiling in the news or in your community • Debate whether the Constitution should be amended with regard to citizenship

Entire states may change hands as a result of motivating the youth vote, particularly in the South . . . and the West . . . where young voters are abundant.

**Nate Silver,
University of Chicago**

6

Public Opinion

At the University of Chicago, Nate Silver was an economics major. He might have studied math or statistics, given his love of numbers. His father recalls that Nate would start counting when they dropped him off at preschool. "When we picked him up two and a half hours later, he was 'Two thousand one hundred and twenty-two, two thousand one hundred and twenty-three....'" By kindergarten Nate was multiplying two-digit numbers in his head, and by age 11 he was using advanced statistics to determine whether there was a relationship between the size of a baseball stadium and attendance. Growing up in Michigan, he was a Detroit Tigers fan, and his love of baseball was almost as great as his love of numbers. He spent his junior year studying abroad at the London School of Economics.

After graduation Silver worked as an economic consultant for an accounting firm in Chicago. But the work was boring. For fun he started a website called the Burrito Bracket, rating Mexican restaurants in Wicker Park. Now adopting the Chicago White Sox and Cubs as his home teams, he began using statistics to predict

player performance. His system generated a huge amount of attention within the baseball world. In 2004 he sold his PECOTA projection system to Baseball Prospectus and joined its staff, writing books and articles forecasting team and player performance.

Three years later Silver turned his forecasting skills to politics. He began by writing a political blog for Daily Kos under the pseudonym "Poblano." Frustrated by sloppy polling and reporting, in March 2008 he established his own

aplia | Need to Know

- **Why public opinion is powerful**
- **How well polls measure public opinion**
- **Who drives public opinion—citizens or elites**
- **How ideology and partisanship shape public opinion**
- **What demographic characteristics influence public opinion**

blog, *FiveThirtyEight* (the total number of electoral votes in a presidential election), which tracked and predicted the outcome of the 2008 presidential primaries so accurately that it got attention from pundits and commentators. Silver sliced and diced the political polls in a way that made them easy for the public to grasp. Sometimes he dismissed the results of a new poll, explaining why he did not trust it. At other times he was able to show important trends in public opinion that warranted close attention. On election night, at 9:46 P.M., he called the election for Barack Obama, whom he had forecast as the winner way back in March.

FiveThirtyEight has now become a daily staple of political junkies and political observers of all stripes. In 2010, Silver's blog moved to the *New York Times*, giving him a very visible platform for sharing his political insights. His rise in 2008 "from obscurity to quotable authority" was compared to Barack Obama's, the candidate he had supported all along. Since the 2008 election, Silver has proven to be an important and durable part of the American political landscape. His predictions and insights carry weight in the political world.[1]

Nate Silver's gateway to participation in the American political system came by doing what he loved—working with numbers—and applying those skills to politics. He speaks with authority because his work has made political polling more useful and understandable to the public. His gateway to influence also highlights the importance of public opinion in a democracy. The expression of the public will is the bedrock of democracy. For politicians, knowing which way the public leans or what citizens think is one of their gateways to power. For citizens, being able to express an opinion and know it is being heard is a gateway for their influence. But reading public opinion correctly is not easy. Polls are a great help, but they can be flawed. Even if well measured, public opinion does not always point toward the best path for the country. Making the right choices requires an informed citizenry. In this chapter, we investigate the contours, sources, and impact of public opinion.

FocusQuestions

- How does public opinion influence public policy?
- In what ways are elected officials responsive to public opinion? How responsive should they be?
- Is every citizen's voice equal, or are some people more influential? Why?
- How well does polling capture public opinion? Should polls direct public policy?
- Does public opinion provide a gateway or a gate to democracy?

The Power of Public Opinion

❯ Why public opinion is powerful

"Our government rests on public opinion," claimed Abraham Lincoln. "Public sentiment is everything. With public sentiment, nothing can fail. Without it, nothing can succeed."[2] Lincoln (1861–65) understood that democratic government must be responsive to the will of the people. The hope in a democracy is that each citizen has an equal voice and that those voices, collectively, will be heard by government officials and will guide their actions. Knowing what the public is thinking and having public support are a powerful combination. Writing more than one hundred years ago, James Bryce, a famous observer of U.S. politics, contended that public opinion is "the greatest source of power" in the United States, more important than the power of presidents, Congress, and political parties.[3]

The Power of Presidential Approval

Perhaps no one appreciates the power of public opinion more keenly than former President George W. Bush (2001–2009). He came to office in 2001, following a contested election in which more than half the electorate had voted against him. However, following the terrorist attacks on September 11 of that year, the country rallied to his side.[4] President Bush then enjoyed the approval of 90 percent of the public. No president had ever scored higher. With this unprecedented level of public support, Bush was able to get Congress to agree to nearly everything he wanted. It passed the Patriot Act, which expanded the powers of the federal government in the area of national security, and it approved his call for a new cabinet-level Department of Homeland Security.

When President Bush launched the Iraq War in March 2003, his **approval rating** was above 70 percent. Then it began to drift downward (see Figure 6.1). In 2004 he won reelection in a tight race, but the increasing unpopularity of the Iraq War undermined his support among the American people and his influence with Congress. Even on the heels of his successful reelection, he could not convince Congress to reform Social Security. Then the inadequate federal response to Hurricane Katrina, which devastated the Gulf Coast, further eroded Bush's standing with the public. By 2007 Bush's public approval rating hovered around

approval rating: *Job performance evaluation for the president, Congress, or other public official or institution that is generated by public opinion polls and is typically reported as a percentage.*

Connections: How did public opinion influence public policy during the George W. Bush administration?

Standing on the rubble of the World Trade Center in New York City, President George W. Bush commends firefighters and police for their response to the terrorist attacks of September 11, 2001. For his own response to the attacks, the president enjoyed near-unanimous public approval.

ERIC DRAPER/WHITE HOUSE/GETTY IMAGES

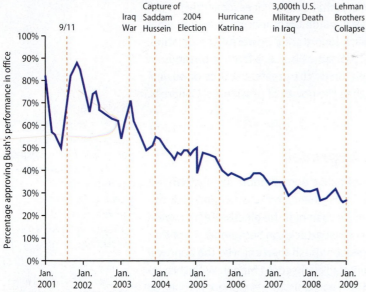

FIGURE 6.1 **Approval Ratings of President George W. Bush, 2001–2009.**

President George W. Bush's approval ratings went from an all-time high to an all-time low. Presidents' approval ratings generally decline during their time in office, but Bush's popularity was hard hit by an increasingly unpopular war in Iraq, an inadequate federal response to Hurricane Katrina, and a severe downturn in the economy.

Source: NBC/Wall Street Journal.

35 percent, and he faced a Democratic Congress—the consequence of the "thumping," as he put it, that the Republicans took in the 2006 midterm elections.

In 2007, when the immigration reform bill he backed was defeated, President Bush visited Congress personally in an effort to revive the legislation, but even this unusual move had little effect. In fact, Bush was rebuked by his own party when Senator Jeff Sessions (R-Ala.) stated that the president "needs to back off."[5] By the time of Barack Obama's election in November 2008, Bush's approval stood in the mid-20s, and one CBS/*New York Times* poll indicated only 20 percent of Americans approved of his job—the lowest rating for any president since the start of scientific polling in the 1930s.[6]

President Bush's political roller coaster reveals the power of the public. The views of average citizens can humble the most experienced statesman and elevate a novice to great influence.

What Is Public Opinion?

Public opinion is recognized for its power, but it is ever changing, hard to measure, harder to predict, and nearly impossible to control. **Public opinion** is the aggregate of individual attitudes or beliefs about certain issues or officials, and it is the foundation of any democracy.

Of course, the electorate expresses its opinion primarily through voting, and elections are the most visible means by which citizens hold elected officials accountable. But a system that claims to be democratic should not rely just on elections to ensure that politicians are doing the people's will. Elections are not held very often. Further, they give signals, but not directions. For example, the electoral success of the Republicans in the 2010 midterm elections was hailed as a sign that the public was unhappy with the Obama administration's handling of the economy. But what should be

---

Connections:
Were President Bush's policies responsive to public opinion?

 **public opinion:**
Aggregate of individual attitudes or beliefs about certain issues or officials.

done? Did the people want big spending cuts? Or did they want additional government efforts to stimulate the economy? Election results do not send clear signals on such specific questions. Voters can indicate only whether they like one candidate more than the other; they cannot convey the reasons for their vote. So legislators and elected executives who want to stay in power expend considerable energy trying to find out what the public wishes and to respond accordingly. Because public opinion plays such an important role in forging responsiveness, it is central to understanding U.S. politics.

Today, public opinion polls are the most reliable indicators of what Americans are thinking, and a whole industry and science have grown up around measuring opinion on everything from presidents to toothpaste. Polls are not the only sources of public opinion. Other sources of public opinion are the size of rallies and protests, the tone of letters sent to elected officials or newspapers, the amount of money given to particular causes or candidates, the content of newspaper editorials, and information gleaned from day-to-day conversations with average Americans. Shifts in public opinion can also be detected in Supreme Court decisions, as cases pertaining to birth control, abortion, and homosexual behavior indicate (see Chapter 4, Civil Liberties, and Supreme Court Cases: *Bowers v. Hardwick* and *Lawrence v. Texas*).

The Public's Support of Government

Just as government must respond to what the people want, so citizens must view the system as legitimate and want to be part of it. If the public withdraws its support, the government collapses. For these reasons, political scientists have sought to measure the public's faith in the political system. Two of the most common efforts involve assessing whether the people trust their government and whether they believe their participation in government matters. Political scientists call the latter **efficacy**—the extent to which people believe their actions affect the course of government. **Political trust** is the extent to which people believe the government acts in their best interests. It has generally declined over the last fifty years, with steeper declines following the beginning of the Iraq War in 2003 and the financial collapse that began in 2008. One estimate in October 2011 suggested that just 10 percent of the public trusted "the government in Washington to do what is right."[7] This is a very low rating by historical standards.[8]

Efficacy has also declined. It stood at more than 70 percent in 1960; by 1994 it had fallen by half. In other words, only one-third of Americans felt that their opinions mattered to government. The figure rebounded to 60 percent by 2002 but then declined again during the Iraq War and financial crisis. It has fallen well below 40 percent in the current environment.[9]

efficacy: *Extent to which people believe their actions can affect public affairs and the actions of government.*

political trust: *Extent to which people believe the government acts in their best interests.*

Connections:
What does a decline in efficacy and public trust mean for American democracy?

supremecourtcases

Bowers v. Hardwick (1986)
Lawrence v. Texas (2003)

QUESTION: May states prosecute consensual sexual activity by members of the same sex?

ORAL ARGUMENT: *Bowers*: March 31, 1986. *Lawrence*: March 26, 2001 (listen at http://www.oyez.org/cases/)

DECISION: *Bowers:* June 30, 1986; *Lawrence:* June 26, 2003 (read at http://www.findlaw.com/casecode/supreme.html)

OUTCOME: *Bowers:* There is no right to homosexual sodomy (5–4). *Lawrence:* The "liberty" in the Fourteenth Amendment prohibits states from criminalizing private sexual behavior (6–3).

When the police came to Michael Hardwick's home looking for him, his roommate let them in. When the police got to Hardwick's room, they observed him engaged in sexual behavior with another male. They arrested him under Georgia's anti-sodomy statute, which prohibits "any sexual contact involving the genitals of one person and the mouth or anus of another." Hardwick argued that the statute violated the right to privacy that the Court established in the *Griswold* birth control case (1965), which the Court later held to protect rights that were "deeply rooted in this Nation's history and tradition."* Noting that prohibitions on sodomy had "ancient roots," the Court voted 5–4 against the claim, calling the argument that homosexual sodomy is among those traditions "facetious." Chief Justice Warren Burger concurred, approvingly citing medieval English sources that declared sodomy as an offense of "deeper malignity" than rape. At the time, only about 20 percent of the American public disagreed with the opinion that homosexual relations were "always wrong" or "almost always wrong."†

Almost twenty years later the Court revisited the decision in *Lawrence v. Texas*. By then, public attitudes about homosexual behavior had softened somewhat, with the percentage of the public disagreeing that sodomy was always or almost always wrong had doubled to 40 percent.‡ With seven new members on the Court, the justices voted 6–3 that the Texas law was unconstitutional, with the majority opinion resting the decision on the liberty protected by the due process clause of the Fourteenth Amendment.

Whether this new result was directly due to the change in public opinion or due to new justices from a different generation who reflected that changed opinion, the Court's decision moved with the change in public opinion.§

- **Should the justices of the Supreme Court be influenced by public opinion?**
- **How should the Court decide which rights, among those not specifically listed in the Constitution, should be protected as fundamental rights?**

† General Social Survey, various years.

‡ Ibid.

§ See Barry Friedman, *The Will of the People: How Public Opinion Has Influenced the Supreme Court and Shaped the Meaning of the Constitution* (New York: Farrar, Straus and Giroux, 2009).

* *Griswold v. Connecticut,* 381 U.S. 479 (1965); *Washington v. Glucksberg*, 521 U.S. 702, 721 (1997).

There is little doubt, as President Obama said in his 2009 inaugural address, that there has been a "sapping of confidence across our land."[10]

Public trust and efficacy react to changes in government and whether the nation is experiencing good or bad times. Yet, through it all, Americans' commitment to the country and its core institutions has remained strong. Patriotism, for example, shows little decline. In 2011 less than 5 percent of Americans viewed themselves as unpatriotic.[11] Almost no one in the country favors overthrowing the government.[12]

Checkpoint

Can you:

☐ State the reasons public opinion has a powerful impact on the presidency

☐ Define public opinion

☐ Track efficacy and public trust in government

Public Opinion Polls

› **How well polls measure public opinion**

Polls make it possible to gauge the public's thinking on a variety of issues or officials, but they have been scientifically conducted only since the 1930s. Even today, a poorly designed or executed poll can produce misleading results. Moreover, there is so much information available from surveys that it is important to know which findings warrant attention and which warrant caution. Poll results can be biased, contradictory, and confusing, which is why Nate Silver's clear assessments of them during the 2008 presidential race were so popular.

Scientific Polling and the Growth of Survey Research

In the 1800s newspapers and other organizations polled the people to assess public opinion, but these polls were of limited help because it was unclear who was being surveyed. So-called straw polls, for example, sought to predict the outcome of elections.

Though straw polls were often inaccurate, newspapers and magazines continued to poll readers' opinions well into the twentieth century. During the 1936 presidential campaign, the *Literary Digest* conducted a poll that predicted Republican Alf Landon would win the election by 57 percent over President Franklin Roosevelt. The reverse happened: Roosevelt won with a landslide 61 percent of the vote.

Although the *Literary Digest* had sent out 10 million ballots, it had sent them to names drawn from automobile registration lists and telephone books and asked recipients to mail the ballots back. The sample, as a result, was biased. First, in 1936 those who owned automobiles and had telephones were wealthier than average Americans and were more likely to be Republicans. Less wealthy Americans, responding favorably to Roosevelt's actions to end the Great Depression, were increasingly aligning themselves with

random sample: *Method of selection that gives everyone who might be selected to participate in a poll an equal chance to be included.*

Connections: Are polls the best way to find out what the public thinks?

the Democrats. Second, the poll asked respondents to mail in their ballots, introducing additional bias. Those who would take the time to do so would likely be better off, further increasing the Republican bias of the sample. Even though 2 million ballots were returned, the poll did not offer a sound basis on which to make a prediction.

George Gallup, who had founded the American Institute of Public Opinion in 1935, correctly predicted the outcome of the 1936 election by using a **random sample** to generate a way to select people to participate in surveys. He made his sample representative of the American public by giving, in effect, every American an equal chance to be part of it. The end product was a sample of five thousand, which was far smaller than the *Literary Digest's* sample but far more representative of average Americans. As a result of his innovative approach, Gallup is often considered the father of modern polling, and the best-known name in polling today remains the Gallup Poll. His scientific polling and survey research techniques have been refined over the years.

The advent of scientific polling made it possible to assess the opinions of the public with some degree of ease and accuracy. Scientific polling also permitted greater equality in assessing public opinions of all Americans.

Types of Polls

In a nation of more than 200 million adults, gathering opinions from everyone is not practical. Even the U.S. census, a count of the population required by the Constitution every ten years, has trouble reaching every adult.[13] So polls draw a sample from a larger population. But first the population must be defined. It might be all adults over age 18, or only voters, or only citizens who contributed to Republican candidates in 2012.

The typical size of a sample survey is one thousand people, though it can vary between five hundred and about fifteen hundred. Size does not matter as much as whether the sample is representative of the population being assessed. Having a representative sample means, in effect, that everyone in that population has an equal chance of being asked to participate in the poll. If a random one thousand people are asked to be part of the survey, they should be representative of the population generally—in, say, wealth, ethnicity, or educational attainment. The key to a representative sample is the randomness. It should be much like drawing numbered balls for a lottery: each ball has the same chance of being chosen.

W. EUGENE SMITH//TIME LIFE PICTURES/GETTY IMAGES

In the 1930s George Gallup developed a scientific approach to polling, greatly increasing its accuracy and authority.

There are various ways to collect the information being sought. For in-person interviews, survey researchers send interviewers into neighborhoods and communities to ask questions in person. This was long the favored method, but it became increasingly expensive. With the near universal presence of telephones by the 1970s, calling people became a more viable and much less expensive option. Telephone polls have dominated survey research over the last thirty years and continue to be used much of the time. The latest platform for polling is the Internet. Internet polls have much potential, but the fact that older and poorer Americans may lack access to computers introduces bias. As with telephones in the past century, however, more and more people are using computers and the web, so in the future Internet polling will likely become the dominant platform for survey research.

Call-in polls or write-in polls are other means of securing a sample. For the former, a telephone number is posted on the television screen, for example, and people are asked to call to register their views. In the latter, a newspaper publishes an appeal for subscribers to write letters offering their opinions. Such approaches can yield a large number of participants, but the size of the sample can be misleading, for those who are willing to call or write are different from those who are not. The samples yielded in these polls are not representative and, thus, are highly suspect.

Presidential elections are awash in polls. In the heat of the fall campaign, nightly polls gauge changes in voters' preferences for the major contenders. These surveys are called **tracking polls**. Another type of survey involving elections is the **exit poll**, conducted as voters leave the polling booth. The goal here is to learn about the reasoning behind the votes citizens just cast but, more important, to predict the outcome of the election before all the ballots are formally counted.

A final kind of election poll is actually a campaign strategy. **Push polls** are conducted by interest groups or candidates who try to affect the opinions of respondents by priming them with biased information. During the 2000 presidential primary in South Carolina, for example, Senator John McCain (R-Ariz.) claimed that George W. Bush ran a push poll against him. Interviewers had called people to ask if they knew that McCain was a "cheat" and a "liar." The question was not designed to get information but to turn people against McCain.[14] Such polls seek to shift public opinion, not to measure it.

Error in Polls

Pollsters do everything they can to ensure that their samples are representative. Even if the sample is drawn properly, however, there is still a chance of error. To capture this uncertainty, all poll numbers come with a **confidence interval** that captures the likely range 95 percent of the time. The poll produces a single estimate of the public's thinking, but the best way to think of

tracking polls: *Polls that seek to gauge changes of opinion of the same sample size over a period of time, common during the closing months of presidential elections.*

exit polls: *Polls that survey a sample of voters immediately after exiting the voting booth to predict the outcome of the election before the ballots are officially counted.*

Connections: Have you ever looked at a poll and questioned its validity? If so, did you do more research on the issue?

push polls: *Polls that are designed to manipulate the opinions of those being polled.*

confidence interval: *Statistical range, with a given probability, that takes random error into account.*

that estimate is as a range of possible estimates. For a sample of six hundred respondents, the sampling error is ±4 percent. That 4 percent generates the confidence interval. Assume, for example, that 65 percent of those sampled support the efforts of Congress to reform the campaign finance laws. With a sampling error of 4 percent, the best way to think of the proportion is that, with 95 percent certainty, the actual amount of public support is somewhere between 61 percent and 69 percent. This range is the confidence interval. Note, however, that there is still a one in twenty chance (5 percent) that the true proportion is above or below that 8-point confidence interval. Hence, caution is always required when interpreting poll data.

In addition to sampling error, the wording of the question can introduce bias. The controversial issue of abortion offers a vivid example. What the public thinks about this issue depends a great deal on the way the question is asked. An NBC News/*Wall Street Journal* poll asked a representative sample of Americans the following question: "Which of the following best represents your views about abortion—the choice on abortion should be left up to the woman and her doctor, abortion should be legal only in cases which pregnancy results from rape or incest or when the life of the woman is at risk, or abortion should be illegal in all circumstances?"

The answers show that 53 percent of the public felt that abortion was a decision best left to the woman and her doctor. Only 15 percent of Americans felt it should be illegal in all circumstances, with 29 percent wanting to have exceptions. In short, a majority of the public appeared to support abortion rights for women. That is an important finding.

But is it true? Consider the following question asked at about the same time by Fox News/Opinion Dynamics: "Once a woman is pregnant, do you believe the unborn baby or fetus should have all the same rights as a newborn baby?" The answers tell a different story. Nearly 60 percent of the public said yes, the unborn fetus should have the same rights as a newborn baby. Only 26 percent said no. According to this poll, a strong majority wants to protect the rights of the unborn and, therefore, to limit abortion rights for women.[15]

So what is American public opinion on abortion? Clearly, the answer depends on the wording of the question, specifically on whether respondents are asked to focus on the rights of women or the rights of the unborn. Although interviewers are trained to be neutral in their questioning, respondents sometimes try to give responses that they think the questioner wants to hear. Another source of error in polls involves what political scientists call **nonattitudes**.[16] When asked, many people feel compelled to answer, even if they do not have opinions or know much about the question. They do not want to seem uninformed, but their responses create error in the survey.

Connections:
Should public officials be influenced by polls?

nonattitudes:
Sources of error in public opinion polls in which individuals feel obliged to give opinions when they are unaware of the issue or have no opinions about it.

The Future of Polls

Despite all the concerns about potential errors in polls, surveys are powerful tools, and pollsters learn from their mistakes. If done correctly, surveys open a valuable window on the public's thinking.

Today polling is in transition. Representative sampling in telephone surveys is increasingly affected by the growing number of cell phones, as many pollsters do not have access to cell phone exchanges and many cell phone users, especially young people, do not have landlines, which are used in telephone polls. At this point, there is not a lot of evidence to suggest that people without landlines vote differently from those with them, but the shift from landlines to cell phones continues.[17] Perhaps more important is the widespread use of caller ID and answering machines. By 2011, 56 percent of the public had answering machines at home,[18] which means that today more and more Americans can screen their calls and refuse to participate in surveys. In fact, there is a general "polling fatigue" among the public. People are asked to participate not only in political polls but also in surveys for insurance companies, health care providers, and an endless array of products. The result is that fewer people are willing to participate in telephone surveys. The declining response rate is lessening the ability of pollsters to capture public opinion accurately. In the 1990s the rate of response was nearly 40 percent, and now it is about 15 percent.[19]

Pollsters are finding ways to adjust, but Internet polls represent the future for measuring public opinion. Through the Internet, polls can be done quickly and cheaply, but respondents may not be representative of the population. Once statisticians develop reliable ways to correct for bias, the web will become an even more powerful tool than it is now to measure the public's thinking. As more people gain access to the web, the amount of bias will decline. Such trends suggest that the future of survey research lies with the Internet.

> **Connections:** Do all Americans have an equal chance of being included in polls?

Checkpoint

Can you:
- ☐ Define scientific polling
- ☐ Identify three types of polls
- ☐ Explain potential errors in polls
- ☐ State why the Internet is important to the future of polling

What Drives Public Opinion?

❯ Who drives public opinion—citizens or elites

Where does public opinion come from? If it is the aggregate of citizen attitudes and beliefs, it starts with individuals. In this section, we examine the major forces that shape political thinking on a personal level, including the social and political environment in which one grows up and the generation and family into which one is born. Self-interest also affects political attitudes, as do the ideas of opinion leaders such as journalists, political observers, policy makers, and experts.

Social and Political Environment

Political attitudes are shaped by environment—the kind of place in which one grows up and lives. Each of us is a product of our family, friends, and community. We call the process by which our attitudes are shaped **socialization**.

The way we live our lives, the kinds of foods we eat, the types of vacations we enjoy, and the houses of worship we attend—all shape how we are socialized. Our political attitudes are no different. The clearest embodiment of political socialization is partisanship, and evidence shows that parents pass their partisan views along to their children. If parents are Democrats, there is a two-thirds chance that their children will identify themselves as Democrats. They might identify as **Independents**, but there is just a 10 percent chance they will be Republicans. The impact of socialization depends, of course, on whether both parents identify with the same party. If the parents are split on partisanship, the chance of the children being Independents rises considerably.[20]

Whether through family socialization or genes, parents have the biggest impact during a child's early life, but, starting in the teenage years, friends also influence attitudes and behavior, as do schools and communities. Communities that are homogeneous, in which most people share many of the same views and opinions, are likely to reinforce the attitudes of parents. Colleges, too, influence attitudes, and college attendance often offers students a chance to break out of the homogeneous settings of their early years. Students meet people from different states or communities, people with different backgrounds and attitudes. College classes and experiences can also shape political leanings. Socialization does not end at college graduation, however. It continues as young people pursue careers and choose where and how they will live.

Generational Effects

Major events can change an entire generation's thinking about politics. The terrorist attacks of 9/11 were a defining event that caused Americans to change their views on national security. Quite suddenly, many were willing to give up some personal freedom to reduce the threat of terrorism (see Figure 6.2). Searing events such as terrorist attacks can have long-term effects on public opinion, especially if the generation that experienced them most acutely reacts as a bloc.

Generational effects need not be limited to life-altering events, however. They can also be affected by the era in which one is young and first active as a citizen. America's **Millennial** generation seems to be more trusting of government than previous generations were. There is also evidence from 2012 that suggests that this group is less patient than previous generations and has "a thirst for instant gratification."[21] Perhaps having a world of information at one's fingertips has altered the expectations held by this new generation of Americans.

Self-Interest and Rationality

Forming political opinion is much more than just a psychological process tied to socialization, however. People also respond to the context in which they find themselves. That is, to a certain extent people are "rational" in that they act in a way that is consistent with their **self-interest**. For example, as income rises, the chance of someone being a Republican increases. Why? The Republicans have pursued tax policies that protect individual wealth, while the Democrats pursue tax policies that tax the wealthy at higher rates to pay for social programs that benefit the less wealthy. In fact, one could argue that although the transmission of partisanship reflects socialization, the reason it sticks is that it is in one's self-interest.

Examples of **rationality** and self-interest abound. Couples with school-age children get interested in education policy. As citizens approach retirement age, they become protective of Social Security and Medicare benefits. Recently, young people, too, have been concerned about these benefits, but in ways that reflect their self-interest. They wonder if the entitlement programs will be bankrupt before they are of age to receive the benefits. Gay Americans are more interested in debates over whether same-sex couples can get married than straight Americans are. Similarly, Latinos show greater concern for reforms in immigration laws than do Americans who are not recent immigrants.[22]

Self-interest clearly shapes political attitudes, but that does not mean that people are selfish. It means that they are trying to advance and protect their own interests, and that in itself is encouraging. Since a democracy rests on the sound judgments of the electorate, it is good to know that there is some evidence that citizens act rationally.

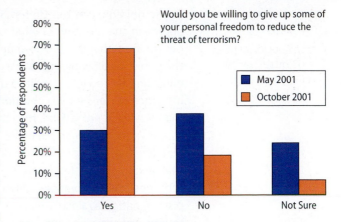

FIGURE 6.2 Shift in Public Opinion following the Terrorist Attacks of September 11, 2001.

The terrorist attacks of September 11, 2001, are likely to have a long-term effect on public opinion. The graph shows before and after responses to the question about being willing to give up personal freedom.

Source: Fox News/Opinion Dynamic Poll, May 2001, October 2001.

self-interest:
Concern for one's own advantage and well-being.

rationality:
Acting in a way that is consistent with one's self-interest.

Connections: What are the sources of public opinion?

Elites

One of the big questions in the field of public opinion is what role elites—leaders of opinion—play in shaping citizens' thinking. A democracy is supposed to be a system in which the average person has a say in government and the people's preferences drive public policy. Yet some people worry that experts, policy makers, political observers, journalists, and others in the news media have an undue influence in shaping public opinion. If elites shape public opinion, can the United States be a democratic nation? One way to approach the question of what political scientists call elite theory is to recognize, first, that it is not so simple a matter as elites offering an opinion and the public swallowing it. That assumption attributes far too much influence to elites and far too little credit to the people. Instead, it appears that elites can influence citizens if two conditions are met: first, citizens must be exposed to the message, and, second, they must be open to it.[23]

Let's assume that scientists find clear evidence that being gay is completely genetic. Such evidence does not exist, but if it did, that would mean that sexual orientation is fixed, just as eye color is fixed. If true, the public's attitudes toward homosexuality would surely change, as it is harder to justify discrimination against homosexuals if sexual orientation is an inborn characteristic. Yet some citizens, when learning this new information, would be resistant to the idea due to their moral beliefs. Social conservatives, for example, would on average be far less likely to accept this information than social liberals would. The prior beliefs of social conservatives would serve as an obstacle to accepting it. By comparison, social liberals would have preexisting views that would fit better with the new information. They would be open to it.

This theory of who changes opinions and who does not has a number of implications. First, massive change in public opinion is not likely because the public is not made up of puppets. There is some degree of stability to opinion, although a major event such as 9/11 will shift the public's thinking on a number of important topics. Second, elites' ability to change public opinion is a product of the intensity and consistency of the message. Disagreement among elites on a new issue will decrease the potential for change. When there is consensus among elites, however, it probably means that the position has merit. Moreover, people respond only to ideas that they find appealing and that fit with their own values and opinions. As a model for how people change opinions in response to events, acting out of both self-interest and rationality, we can look at how Americans are viewed by others.

Connections: Does every citizen have an equal chance to be heard?

Checkpoint

Can you:

- State why socialization is so important to public opinion
- Track the influence of generational effects on political attitudes
- Explain both self-interest and rationality as shapers of political opinion
- Describe the influence of elites on public opinion

The Shape of Public Opinion

› **How ideology and partisanship shape public opinion**

To understand public opinion, it is essential to appreciate the ways it is shaped by partisanship and ideology. These two variables can, to a large extent, explain the opinions of citizens. Although not everyone is partisan or ideological, these forces provide useful frameworks for understanding the public's thinking on issues. With a firm understanding of partisanship and ideology in place, we can address two major questions about public opinion: How informed is the public? And is the public polarized?

Partisanship

Party identification, or partisanship, is central to understanding how people think politically. Party identification represents an individual's allegiance to a political party. This psychological attachment usually forms when an individual is young. The attachment, through what is called the perceptual lens, shapes the way partisans view the political world and process information. The result, for example, is that a Republican would be slower to turn against the Iraq War, initiated by a Republican president, than would a Democrat. Conversely, a Republican would be less sympathetic to Barack Obama's reform of health care than would a Democrat.[24]

By knowing party identification, political scientists can predict—with considerable accuracy—attitudes on a range of issues. Republicans, for example, are less likely than Democrats to support government spending to help the poor and elderly. Republicans are not opposed to helping such people, but they want to do so through private charities and individual initiative. More generally, Republicans are less supportive of an activist federal government, while Democrats are more open to giving government an active role in the lives of citizens.

Although partisanship shapes how an individual thinks about politics, it can subside in times of national crisis. Following the 9/11 terrorist attacks, Americans put aside partisan differences. In late September 2001 more than 98 percent of Republicans and more than 80 percent (up from 25 percent) of Democrats approved of the job President Bush was doing.[25] Partisanship returned the next year, however, with the 2002 midterm elections.

Because party identification is central to understanding public opinion, pollsters have been asking about partisanship since the 1940s. The American National Elections Studies, a premier academic survey organization, has been asking the same question since 1952: "Generally speaking, do you usually think of yourself as a Republican, a Democrat, an Independent, or what?"[26] This question asks respondents how they think about themselves in order to capture political identification and the general tendency, or the perceptual lens, of their thinking. The theoretical underpinnings are psychological. Partisanship can also be likened to loyalty, like the loyalty to sports teams or to friends that lasts through ups and downs. Partisanship can change over a person's life, but it tends to be stable, especially when compared to other political attitudes.

In the last few years, there has been much discussion in the press about Independents, with claims that they are the "largest group in the electorate."[27]

party identification:
Psychological attachment to a political party; partisanship.

Connections: Does party loyalty shape public opinion?

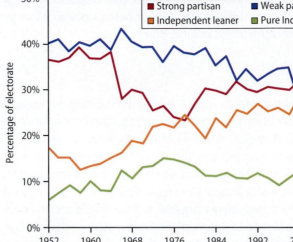

FIGURE 6.3 **Independents in the Electorate, 1952–2008.**

These data show that pure Independents constitute a small part of the American electorate and that their proportion has remained about the same for the last fifty years. Such data are vital in understanding the continuing importance of partisanship in America.

Source: John Sides, George Washington University.

Source: John Sides, George Washington University.

---

political ideology: *Set of coherent political beliefs that offers a philosophy for thinking about the scope of government.*

liberals: *Individuals who have faith in government to improve people's lives, believing that private efforts are insufficient. In the social sphere, liberals usually support diverse lifestyles and tend to oppose any government action that seeks to shape personal choices.*

conservatives: *Individuals who distrust government, believing that private efforts are more likely to improve people's lives. In the social sphere, conservatives usually support traditional lifestyles and tend to believe that government can play a valuable role in shaping personal choices.*

Connections:
How does party identification relate to ideology?

With the rise of the Tea Party movement, their numbers are increasing. The view that Americans are mostly Independents is, however, a myth.[28] It is true that many citizens claim to be Independents, but they actually behave like partisans. That is, most Independents lean toward one party or the other. Figure 6.3 charts changes in the share of "pure Independents" as contrasted with "Independent leaners" since the 1950s. The number of those of the pure variety has been pretty much flat during these six decades. The growth has been in the leaners, and that growth has been substantial. But such individuals vote consistently for one party and are very much partisans, despite self-professed labels. Their behavior is testimony to the strength of partisanship in the United States.

Ideology

Political ideology has a complex relationship with partisanship. **Liberals** tend to be Democrats, and **conservatives** tend to be Republicans, but ideology speaks to both political and social values. Conservatives view a good society as one that allows individuals to pursue their economic interests in an unfettered fashion. Liberals worry that, without some governmental regulation to curb abuse and moderate economic cycles, the rich will get very rich and the poor will get very poor. This concern leads liberals to believe that government can improve people's lives and prevent inequalities that harm society and the economy as a whole. Conservatives are much more leery of government and view it as a problem in and of itself. They contend that less government interference will give the poor the opportunity to improve their lives by themselves. On social issues, the tables are turned. That is, liberals tend to believe that people should be able to make personal choices free from government interference. Conservatives, by contrast, value more traditional lifestyles and want government, at times, to enforce such choices.

Not all citizens think of themselves as liberals or conservatives. Depending on the wording of the question, 37 percent of Americans in March 2012 viewed themselves as ideological **moderates**, 23 percent as liberals, and the remaining 37 percent as conservatives.[29] But there is also a debate among political scientists about whether citizens think ideologically at all. That is, do people have coherent views about politics? One famous effort to measure the ideological foundations, or **levels of conceptualization**, of the public's thinking found little evidence of such organized opinions. Data from the 1950s indicated that only about 12 percent of the public viewed the political parties in ideological terms, whereas more than 40 percent judged the parties by the groups (such as social classes or racial and ethnic groups) they were thought to represent rather than the policies they pursued. About 25 percent evaluated the parties by "the nature of the times": Is the economy doing well? Are we embroiled in a war? The remainder—just over 20 percent—did not think about issues at all when evaluating the parties and candidates; this part of the public showed "no issue content."[30] Over the last fifty years, there have been some changes in the sizes of these four groups, but not major ones.

Nevertheless, it is still worth looking at the public's ideological mood. Is the public, collectively, becoming more liberal or more conservative? Such changes should aid understanding of the general direction of the country. Figure 6.4 maps changes in the public's ideological mood between 1952 and 2011.

Is the Public Informed?

A democracy depends on having an engaged and well-informed electorate. Otherwise, how can the public make good choices? If the power is to rest with the people, the people need to be

moderates: *Individuals who are in the middle of the ideological spectrum and do not hold consistently strong views about whether government should be involved in people's lives.*

Connections: How coherent is public opinion?

levels of conceptualization: *Measure of how ideologically coherent individuals are in their political evaluations.*

Connections: Is the public becoming more liberal or more conservative? How can you tell?

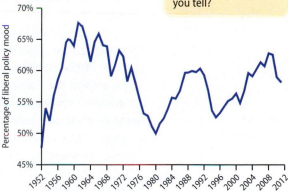

FIGURE 6.4 **Liberal Policy Mood of Americans, 1952–2011.**

The policy mood of Americans is rarely fixed, moving toward liberalism following George W. Bush's election in 2000 and then toward conservatism following Barack Obama's election in 2008.

Source: James Stimson, "Policy Mood," accessed August 16, 2012, http://www.unc .edu/~jstimson/Welcome.html. Copyright © James Stimson. Reproduced by permission.

knowledgeable about the issues of the day and the candidates who compete for public office.

The Framers were definitely concerned about the public's capacity to be informed and make good choices, especially because only 10 percent of Americans at the time were literate.[31] Literacy in 2012 stands at about 99 percent,[32] suggesting that citizens are better able today than in the eighteenth century to meet the demands of being "informed." But are they? When survey research began in the 1940s, it became possible to gather systematic information on the public's knowledge about politics. The early evidence was not encouraging. In a detailed study of the 1940 presidential campaign, scholars from Columbia University assumed that voters were like consumers and would look for the best deal and that the campaign would be an important source of information as they made their choices. But the data told a different tale. Instead, most voters made up their minds before the campaign, and their choices were driven by where they lived and whom they knew.[33] In a subsequent study, the Columbia researchers went so far as to argue that low turnout in elections might actually be a good thing, because the uninformed would not be choosing the nation's leaders.[34] This argument has strong elitist overtones and certainly strays far from the assumptions about government responsiveness and citizen equality on which American democracy rests. Together with previous findings about levels of conceptualization,[35] the argument suggested that the public may not be capable of meeting its democratic responsibilities. What ensued was a debate over the accuracy and interpretation of these core findings.

Political scientists went, in effect, in search of the "informed voter," and they learned that citizens do not know many details about politics. Only 10 percent of the public knows the name of the Speaker of the House. Only about a third can name one U.S. Supreme Court justice. Only about half of Americans know which party controls Congress, and fewer than half know the name of their own congressional representative.[36] These facts suggest that average citizens do not possess the detailed information necessary to hold their government accountable.

Should these data be taken as evidence that the public is not able to meet its democratic responsibilities? Let us consider some findings that give reason for optimism. First, the public, collectively, seems to make reasonable choices. For example, when the economy is doing poorly, the party in power suffers. Voters hold presidents and legislators accountable; failures are punished and successes are rewarded. Further, Americans do not favor costly wars, and they tend to reward candidates who pursue peace.[37]

Second, although individuals do not know all the details about candidates' views on all the issues, they do tend to know candidates' views on the issues that are salient to them. Hunters know candidates' views on gun control; college students know candidates' views on student loans. One study estimates that when an issue is salient to an individual, that individual knows candidates' views on that issue correctly more than 90 percent of the time.[38]

Third, the public can learn quickly if an issue is salient enough to them and receives attention in the news media. The public quickly learned about AIDS when it started to become a public health crisis in the 1980s. Following 9/11, the public understood the need to consider some curtailment of civil liberties to ensure security.

Fourth, public opinion is more stable than is suggested by the shifting answers people give to the same question just a few months apart. The instability reflected in polls does not speak to a fickle or poorly informed public. Instead, it appears that polls themselves may be at fault.[39] That is, survey questions and the normal error associated with these questions make people's attitudes appear more unstable than they really are. Further, most issues are complex and leave many people genuinely conflicted. Being conflicted is not a sign of lack of information, but perhaps a realization that some problems are thorny and not easily answered.

Fifth and finally, personal decision making is not always based on complete information, so why should political decision making be expected to conform to rational models that scholars use? Individuals often rely on cues and instincts to make decisions, rather than on analyses of detailed information. Scholars have termed such thinking low information rationality.[40] In 1992, President George H. W. Bush (1989–93) asked what milk cost in grocery stores. His admission that he did not know suggested that he was out of touch with ordinary Americans, who do their own shopping. His competitor, William Jefferson (Bill) Clinton (1993–2001), knew the price of milk and other items, such as jeans. Simple things like not knowing what groceries cost turned some voters against Bush. These individuals concluded that the candidates were not like them and were not likely to understand their problems. Small bits of information can be informative.

It is easy to make any member of the public—even a president!—look uninformed, and of course it would be better if the public knew more about politics. But individuals do appear to learn about the issues that matter to them. Gaining information is a gateway to influence because, individually, people learn what they need to know to advance their interests, and collectively voters do hold government officials accountable.

Is the Public Polarized?

The engaged and informed citizens of a democracy cannot be expected to agree on everything. They will naturally have different views on issues. When the differences become stark, however, the danger is that **polarization** will

 polarization: *Condition in which differences between parties and/or the public are so stark that disagreement breaks out, fueling attacks and controversy.*

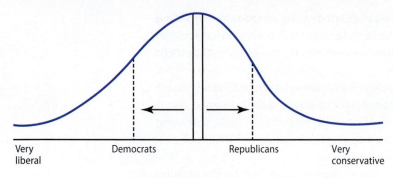

FIGURE 6.5 How Polarization Works.

When the parties are polarized, they move toward the tail of these distributions. When parties are depolarized, they adopt positions near each other. Currently the parties are polarized, but that was not the case in the 1970s.

Source: John G. Geer, © Cengage Learning.

fuel controversy and personal attacks to the point that compromise and consensus become impossible. Congress has clearly become more polarized over the last thirty years. Figure 6.5 tries to capture the idea of polarization on a simple left–right continuum. In the 1970s the parties adopted positions that were closer to the middle; forty years later, their positions are more at the extremes. In fact, Democrats and Republicans disagree on more issues now than at any time since the end of the Civil War.[41]

In the 1970s there were numerous liberal Republicans and conservative Democrats. By 2008 these two groups were nearly extinct. The differences between the parties have continued to grow,[42] evidenced by victories by candidates from the Tea Party movement in the 2010 congressional elections.[43] Figure 6.6 documents the rise in polarization between the parties since the 1990s.

What is less clear is whether the public is also polarized. Some scholars have argued that the public has polarized along with parties, but there is also evidence that the public is more moderate, even though the choices the parties offer them are not.[44] For example, according to a series of surveys conducted by the Pew Research Center between 1987 and 2007, "the average difference between Republican and Democratic identifiers on forty political and social issues increased from 10 to 14 percent, a surprisingly small difference."[45] These data suggest that the public is more moderate than the choices that are laid before them in elections would suggest. But scholars

> **Connections:** Does polarization prevent good policy making?

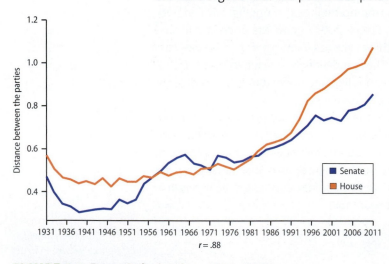

FIGURE 6.6 Party Polarization, 1931–2011.

Since 1975, polarization in the U.S. Congress has been on the increase.

Source: Keith Poole, Polarized America/voteview.com. Copyright © 2012 by Keith Poole. Reproduced by permission.

disagree about the extent of differences among the electorate, with some suggesting that the political center has collapsed.[46] Even some who think that the public is not as polarized as the parties are worry that polarization will yield more personal attacks and greater incivility. Others offer a more optimistic view, arguing that increasing polarization will activate people's interest in elections, which in turn will spur more interest in politics.

Having a clear choice engages people and gives them a stake in an election outcome. If the system became depolarized, as in the 1950s (see Figure 6.6), the public would lack a choice. It would no longer matter whether Democrats or Republicans won, because they would do the same thing once in office. For these reasons, many scholars in the 1950s called for parties that would offer the public a real choice (see Chapter 9, Political Parties). Citizens, under such conditions, can more effectively hold officials accountable for misdeeds and reward successes.

Connections:
Do political parties influence public opinion, or is it the other way around?

Checkpoint

Can you:

☐ Explain how partisanship relates to public opinion

☐ Explain how political ideology relates to public opinion

☐ Assess how well informed the American public is

☐ Describe polarization and its effects

Group Differences

❯ What demographic characteristics influence public opinion

Public opinion is shaped by partisanship and ideology. Social scientists find that demographics also matter—that is, the tendency for certain groups within the American population to hold similar views. These breakdowns by group are the microfoundations of public opinion. In this section, we look at the ways that socioeconomic status, religion, gender, race and ethnicity, and education tend to organize public opinion.

Socioeconomic Status

Socioeconomic status is a combined measure of occupation, education, income, wealth, and relative social standing or lifestyle. It influences where one lives, what kind of work one does, whom one knows, the kinds of schools one attends, and the kind of opportunities one can take advantage of. These matters inevitably mold political attitudes. Working-class people are more likely than wealthier people to favor more government programs to help the poor and provide child care, more funding for public education, and more protection for Social Security. Around 70 percent of Americans earning between $15,000 and $35,000 support increased spending by government on such social services. Among those earning between $75,000 and $105,000, the proportion drops to about 55 percent.[47]

Part of the reason for the strong differences in opinion among different income groups is that political parties have a class bias. Republicans draw far more support from those who come from higher socioeconomic status than do Democrats. Starting in the 1980s, however, Republicans also began to draw support from working-class people who supported a conservative social agenda and a decreased role for government welfare-based programs. These so-called Reagan Democrats were central to Republican success in the ensuing decades.

Age

Age also influences opinions on issues, because the stage of one's life affects how one thinks about issues. Younger people are much more likely to favor making marijuana legal than are older people. Those under 30 also are more supportive of gay marriage than are people over 30 and especially those older than 65 (see Figure 5.6). In general, older citizens are more socially conservative than are younger citizens,[48] and there is evidence that people tend to become more conservative as they age.

Connections: Does being a member of a demographic group shape opinion?

Religion

Religious affiliation is another indicator of opinion. Overall, for example, Protestants are more conservative than Catholics or Jews. Only 12 percent of Jews describe themselves as conservative, compared to 36 percent of Protestants. On some issues, Muslims have been found to be more liberal than the general population and significantly more liberal than Protestants and Catholics. For example, 70 percent of Muslims favor an activist government, whereas just 43 percent of the public as a whole subscribes to that view. On social issues, however, Muslims show a much more conservative tendency.

Recent studies of religion and public opinion have focused on differences within denominations, particularly with the rise of evangelical Christianity among Protestants. Starting in the 1970s, and especially after the *Roe v. Wade* Supreme Court decision made abortion legal under some conditions in 1973, evangelicals became more active in politics. They strongly oppose abortion and gay rights, and they support school prayer. On the issue of same-sex marriage, in 2004 evangelical Protestants were six times more likely to oppose same-sex marriage than are non-evangelical—or "mainline"—Protestants.[49] Table 6.1 explores differences among Protestants, Catholics, and those not affiliated with a religious group on the issue of abortion.

gender gap: *Differences in the political attitudes and behavior of men and women.*

TABLE 6.1 **Differences of Opinion on Abortion among Religious Groups, 2011**

	Legal in all/ most cases %	Illegal in all/ most cases %	Don't Know %
Protestant	47	49	4
White evangelical	34	64	2
White mainline	60	37	3
Catholic	52	45	3
White Catholic	54	44	2
Unaffiliated	71	26	2
Total	54	42	4

Note: Figures may not add to 100% because of rounding.
Source: "Fewer Are Angry at Government, but Discontent Remains High: Republicans, Tea Party Supporters More Mellow," March 3, 2011, The Pew Research Center For the People & the Press. Copyright © 2011 by Pew Research Center. Reproduced by permission.

Gender

Starting in 1980, a **gender gap** emerged in U.S. politics. Before 1980 the differences in political attitudes among men and women were not large and did not draw much attention. However, in elections since Ronald Reagan's 1980 victory over Jimmy Carter (1977–81), women have been generally more supportive of Democrats than of Republicans. In 2008, Barack Obama secured 56 percent of the female vote and just 49 percent of the male vote. In April 2012, among women, Obama held a substantial lead in the polls over then-presumptive Republican nominee Mitt Romney—as much as 20 percentage points.[50] Such differences remind us that if only women were allowed to vote, the Democrats might have won every presidential election since 1980 save for Reagan's landslide against Walter Mondale in 1984.[51]

In general, women are more liberal than men, and gender gaps are also evident on specific issues. Women were less supportive of the Iraq War, believing in larger numbers in 2004 that the war "was not worth fighting." Women favor more spending on social programs than men. In 2000, 67 percent of women favored more spending on child care, whereas 58 percent of men held this view. Men are much more likely to support the death penalty than are women (62 percent versus 38 percent). This gap disappears when it comes to abortion. In 2011, 21 percent of women and 21 percent of men thought abortion should be illegal in all circumstances.[52]

Race and Ethnicity

Another divide in public opinion involves race and ethnicity. For more than a hundred years after the Civil War, Americans remained divided about issues involving race. In 1964 African Americans overwhelmingly endorsed desegregation, whereas white Americans were split on the issue. In 1974 only 23 percent of white Americans felt "government should help blacks," whereas 69 percent of African Americans believed that government should take that role.[53] Similar gaps exist in regard to support for affirmative action policies that grant preferences to people (not only African Americans but also women) who have suffered discrimination in the past in job hiring, school admissions, and contracting. In 2004 only 11 percent of whites favored "preferences for hiring blacks." Four times as many African Americans favored affirmative action.[54]

The term *Latino* is used to describe a broad array of groups that do not necessarily share common experiences, so opinion among Latinos tends to be

Ann Romney, wife of Republican presidential candidate Mitt Romney, speaks at the Connecticut GOP Prescott Bush Awards dinner on April 23, 2012. During the spring primaries, a contentious debate about women's roles erupted when commentator Hilary Rosen claimed that Ann Romney was not a valid source of information about the economic situation of women because she had "never worked a day in her life." Romney fired back that raising five sons was hard work and asked that women's choices to be stay-at-home moms be respected. The debate drew attention, in part, because Democrats have long enjoyed more support among women than men. This so-called gender gap has been evident in American politics since the 1970s.

Connections: Is your political opinion shaped by your social class, age, religion, gender, race and ethnicity, and/or education level?

divided. Some Latino families have lived in the Southwest for centuries, since before the area became part of the United States in 1848. Others came to the United States within the last few years from homelands throughout Central and South America. Cuban immigrants, who left their homeland following the rise of Fidel Castro and the Communists in the late 1950s, tend to be much more conservative than Puerto Ricans and Mexican Americans. According to one study, about 60 percent of Cuban Americans are Republican identifiers, compared to only about 15 percent of Mexican Americans.[55]

Thus, both parties compete for the support of the Latino community. In 2004 Latino support for President George W. Bush helped him defeat John Kerry. In 2008, however, Barack Obama gained two-thirds of the Latino vote, a shift partly owing to actions by Republicans in Congress to block immigration reform. As a group, Latinos support bilingual education and policies that favor immigration more than do Anglos. These differences surely reflect the fact that the issues are more salient to them.[56]

Asian American public opinion has not drawn the same level of attention as that of other groups. Asian Americans are, however, a growing segment of the population and constitute a sizable part of the population of some states, especially California. In general, Asian Americans are a bit more liberal than white Americans. Their disapproval of the Iraq War was stronger than that of white Americans, but not nearly as strong as that of African Americans.[57] Like Latinos, the Asian American population is diverse, including people from Korea, Vietnam, Japan, and China.

Connections:
Think again: does being a member of a demographic group shape opinion?

Education

One important change in the American population is the increasing level of education. Figure 6.7 charts the share of Americans who had attended college for at least a year over the last sixty years. The pattern is striking. In 1948 about one in seven Americans had gone to college for at least one year. By 2008 more than one in two Americans had attended college. There are two key reasons for this upward trend. The first is that more young people have access to a college education. The second is what is called "generational replacement." That is, older,

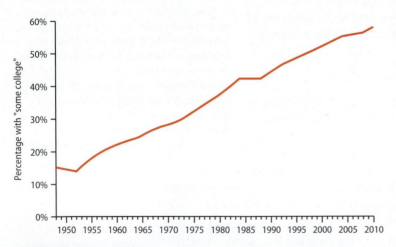

FIGURE 6.7 Percentage with "Some College" Education, 1948–2010.

Since the end of World War II, education levels have steadily increased. Level of education is a factor affecting public opinion on a range of specific issues.

Source: American National Election Studies.

less-educated citizens have passed on, and the average level of education of the American public has thus increased.

It matters that people in the United States are more educated. In broad strokes, there is a long-standing belief that a democracy is best able to endure when its citizens are engaged and informed. With more education, the public should be more aware of politics and better able to find ways to ensure that government responds to them. In the language of this book, a better-educated public should be in better position to travel through the gateways of influence and find ways around the many gates in the American political system.

Education level is also connected to public opinion. Views on the controversial issue of immigration reform offer an instructive example. Among college graduates in April 2009, 75 percent favored making it possible for those here illegally to become citizens (providing they pass background checks, pay relevant fines, and have jobs). Among those with a high school education or less, the proportion falls to 56 percent.[58] The 20-percentage-point gap is significant. Individuals with a higher level of education generally take a more liberal position on a variety of social and economic issues, ranging from government spending to defense policy to gay marriage.[59]

Checkpoint

Can you:

☐ State the relationship between socioeconomic status, on the one hand, and partisanship and ideology on the other

☐ Describe how age affects political thinking

☐ Distinguish differences in political views between evangelical and non-evangelical Protestants

☐ Characterize the impact of the gender gap

☐ Survey the impact of race and ethnicity on political thinking

☐ Track the effect of increasing educational levels on political views

Public Opinion and Public Policy: Military Action and Antiterrorism

To see how public opinion affects the policies pursued by government, we examine foreign policy, focusing on military action and antiterrorism measures. The relationship between public opinion and domestic policy is taken for granted, but with continuing terrorist attacks around the world and a war in Afghanistan, it is important to consider their relationship. Public opinion exerts a different type of influence on each.

Military Action

The president, as commander in chief, has always made the decision to engage in military action. Although Congress has formally declared war only five times,

Connections:
Should public opinion influence foreign or defense policy when military secrets are withheld from the public?

rally-around-the-flag effect:
Surge of public support for the president in times of international crisis.

U.S. troops have been sent into conflicts and potential conflicts about 250 times since the beginning of the nation.[60] Today, in making the decision to engage in military action, the president is heavily influenced by the recommendations of the secretary of defense, the national security adviser, and the director of the Central Intelligence Agency. For military missions that are publicized, not secret, a president usually enjoys widespread support if the mission can be clearly tied to preserving national security. In cases in which the United States is attacked on its own soil, support for a military response is even higher. This so-called **rally-around-the-flag effect** is a surge in patriotic sentiment that translates into presidential popularity.[61] President George W. Bush experienced a spike in popularity after 9/11; his job approval ratings went from 52 percent to 90 percent, and they remained above 70 percent for almost an entire year.[62]

The public's influence on the president's decision to engage in military action is always limited because the amount of information available to the public is purposely restricted, both to ensure the safety of the troops involved and to preserve military advantages in conflict. The fundamental imbalance of information held by the government and what the general public understands poses a major problem for the assumptions of a democracy because the people cannot hold the government fully accountable if they are not fully informed. Nevertheless, when a president decides to send troops, he has to anticipate public reaction and hope that the public maintains its trust and confidence in his decision to take such action.

As the rally-around-the-flag effect fades over time, public support for extended military engagements also declines, as the polls reveal. Americans do not like war, and this core value drives public opinion and U.S. defense policy. The fundamental problem for the American public is that once the United States enters into a military conflict, there are few ways for the public to effectively change military strategy or troop levels. Only when public opinion turns against a war effort is there any real pressure on the president and Congress to take steps to end it.

Antiterrorism Measures

The 9/11 terrorist attacks prompted a huge increase in government's efforts to stop future terrorism against U.S. citizens at home and abroad. In general, public opinion was highly supportive of the steps that President George W. Bush claimed were necessary to fight terrorism. These steps were taken with advice from the same units that handle military policy, with the important addition of the Federal Bureau of Investigation and the Department of Justice. The Bush

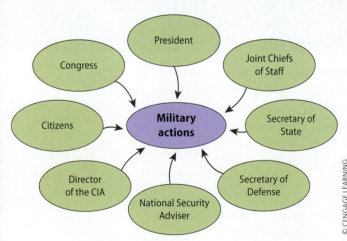

© CENGAGE LEARNING

administration authorized the detention of suspects, whether U.S. citizens or not, without charges or trials, and wiretapping (eavesdropping) without a warrant. With the onset of the war in Iraq, the measures employed in the name of antiterror security increased. Then, in 2004 CBS News and the *New Yorker* magazine broke the story about the Abu Ghraib facility in Iraq, where Iraqi prisoners were subject to activities that violated international norms of treatment and might be considered torture.[63] Subsequently, it was revealed that the U.S. interrogators used waterboarding, a near-drowning technique, as a means of getting information from prisoners about potential terrorist plots. The international community considers waterboarding to be torture, and many Americans also objected. The issue of treatment of detainees became a major issue in the 2008 presidential campaign. After he took office, President Obama declared that the United States would no longer engage in any practice that violated international norms. The president also announced that the Guantánamo Bay facility located in Cuba, where suspected terrorists were being detained and questioned outside of the United States, would be closed. Despite an early consensus in the White House to close this controversial facility, deciding what to do with existing detainees and how best to handle others who may be engaged in terrorism has proven difficult.[64]

Americans remain conflicted about the type of force necessary to preserve national security. In 2009, a Gallup Poll reported that 55 percent of respondents supported the use of harsh interrogation techniques on suspected terrorists, while 36 percent believed these techniques were not justified. The same poll revealed, however, that 51 percent of the respondents favored an investigation into how these techniques were used.[65] Here is the same dilemma the public faces with military action: by their very nature, antiterrorism policies must remain secret to be effective, and the only opportunity the public has to register an opinion about government action is after that action has been taken. If harsh interrogation techniques save American lives by uncovering and then preventing a terrorist attack, the public will support the use of these techniques. Even with the killing of Osama Bin Laden by Navy Seals in May 2011, which could have eased people's fears about terrorism, the public still backs harsh interrogation techniques to secure information from suspected terrorists. In November 2011, more Americans continued to believe that such techniques were justified than were not justified, according to a poll conducted by the CBS News (see Figure 6.8).

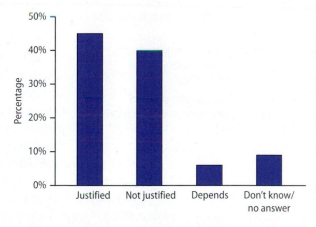

FIGURE 6.8 Support for Harsh Interrogation Techniques, 2011.

A majority of the public supports the use of harsh interrogation techniques on terrorism suspects.

Source: Conducted by CBS News, November 6–November 10, 2011, and based on 1,182 telephone interviews.

Construct Your Own Policy

1. Using modern technology, devise a way of accurately measuring public opinion so that the president and Congress consider it before deciding to enter a foreign conflict.

2. Design a comprehensive antiterrorist policy that can effectively protect the United States from attack and safeguard individual liberty at the same time.

For more on the policy-making process, see Chapter 1.

Public Opinion and Democracy

Focus Questions Revisited

- How does public opinion influence public policy?

- In what ways are elected officials responsive to public opinion? How responsive should they be?

- Is every citizen's voice equal, or are some people more influential? Why?

- How well does polling capture public opinion? Should polls direct public policy?

- Does public opinion provide a gateway or a gate to democracy?

For a country to be considered democratic, the views of the public must affect the course of government. For this reason, the public must be sufficiently well informed to be able to make good decisions and to ensure that politicians act in a way consistent with public preferences. Average Americans do not know a lot of details about politics, but the nation's many successes indicate that the public is equal to the task of self-government. As Key observed nearly fifty years ago, "Voters are not fools."[66]

Elections are one means by which the public expresses its will, but on a year-to-year, even day-to-day, basis, public officials can stay in touch with what the public thinks through public opinion polls. Scientific polling permits researchers to measure people's thinking with considerable accuracy and gives average Americans a chance to speak out on policy and contribute to policy making. Scientific polling not only created greater equality but also provided the gateways through which the public could affect the course of government. Polls are not perfect, but they do open up the democratic process.

Although it is clear that public officials are generally responsive to public opinion,[67] there are legitimate questions about how responsive American government actually is. Some observers suggest that the connection between opinion and policy is weak. Others point out that the public has mixed feelings on many issues and does not have concrete opinions about some of the toughest questions and can thus offer little guidance. Still others argue that politicians use policy to manipulate public opinion. That interaction is troubling and not the way a democratic system in which the government is accountable to the people should work. These concerns are why it is so instructive to look at the general patterns and the nation's general successes.

It is also important to recognize that, in a democracy, politicians know the kinds of issues the public will respond to and rebel against, and so they adopt views that will not arouse the electorate's anger. They are aware, in other words, of what political scientists call latent public opinion,[68] and this awareness makes them responsive and accountable. The ability to anticipate public opinion is an invaluable skill, helping officials avoid quagmires and stress issues that hit a responsive chord with the public. Thus the power of public opinion in a democracy is both direct and indirect. It is also imperfect in that there are both gates and gateways that shape how the public directs the course of government.

gateways**to**learning

Top Ten to **Take Away**

1. Public opinion—the aggregate of citizen attitudes—is essential to the workings of a democracy. (pp. 170–175)
2. Scientific polling enables public officials to gauge public opinion with some degree of confidence, though polls can be in error. (pp. 175–179)
3. Citizens' opinions and attitudes are shaped by environment, political socialization, generational effects, and self-interest. (pp. 179–181)
4. Elites do drive public opinion, but only to the extent that citizens are exposed and open to their message. (pp. 181–182)
5. Party identification can help predict individual attitudes, and liberal or conservative leanings shape views on political and social issues. Generally, the public has been becoming less liberal, although there has been a recent uptick. (pp. 182–185)
6. People generally know what advances their interests and hold government accountable. (pp. 185–187)
7. Although parties have grown more polarized in recent years, the electorate is more moderate than party choices allow. (pp. 187–189)
8. Political opinion also differs among demographic groups. (pp. 189–193)
9. In recent years, efficacy and public trust in government have fallen. (pp. 173–175)
10. In national security issues, the public is often deliberately not informed, and public officials have to work hard to maintain public trust, especially as the American public has a strong preference for peace. (pp. 193–196)

 ## Key **Concepts**

approval rating (p. 171). Why do presidential approval ratings tend to fall?

confidence interval (p. 177). Why do you need to know the confidence interval for any poll?

conservatives (p. 184). What party do conservatives usually support?

efficacy (p. 173). Why is the efficacy of citizens important in a democracy?

exit polls (p. 177). Describe problems with exit polls.

gender gap (p. 191). Which party do women tend to support?

Independents (p. 180). What has happened to Independents over the last thirty years?

levels of conceptualization (p. 185). How sophisticated is the public's ideological thinking?

liberals (p. 184). Why did the ideological direction of public mood move away from liberalism following Barack Obama's inauguration as president in 2008?

Millennials (p. 180). How are the Millennials' political opinions generally different from previous generations?

moderates (p. 185). Are most Americans moderates?

nonattitudes (p. 178). Give an example of a nonattitude that might arise from a poll.

party identification (p. 183). What is the main way people develop a party identification?

polarization (p. 187). Describe trends in party polarization over the last twenty years.

political ideology (p. 184). What is the relationship between ideology and partisanship?

political trust (p. 173). What are the trends in public trust in recent years?

public opinion (p. 172). Why is public opinion so important to a democracy?

push polls (p. 177). Why are push polls less accurate than random telephone surveys?

rally-around-the-flag effect (p. 194). What is a recent example of a rally-around-the-flag effect?

random sample (p. 176). Why is it important to have a random sample?

rationality (p. 181). What is an example of shifts in public opinion that speaks to the rationality of citizens?

self-interest (p. 181). Why can self-interest be a good thing in a democracy?

socialization (p. 180). How does socialization help to shape people's partisan leanings?

tracking polls (p. 177). How do tracking polls work?

Your Virtual Tutor
Master What You Need to Know and Test Yourself.

Learning Outcomes

WHAT YOU NEED...

To Know	To Test Yourself	To Participate
Why public opinion is powerful	• State the reasons public opinion has a powerful impact on the presidency • Define public opinion • Track efficacy and public trust in government	• Express your opinion of the presidency • Grasp the connection between public opinion and democracy • Evaluate why public trust in government is low
How well polls measure public opinion	• Define scientific polling • Identify three types of polls • Explain potential errors in polls • State why the Internet is important to the future of polling	• Evaluate whether polling is more or less accurate • Participate in a political poll • Improve your reading of polls • Evaluate Internet polling
Who drives public opinion— citizens or elites	• State why socialization is so important to public opinion • Track the influence of generational effects on political attitudes • Explain both self-interest and rationality as shapers of public opinion • Describe the influence of elites on public opinion	• Examine the sources of your political socialization • Evaluate how your views differ from those who are older or younger than you • Determine whether your views on issues arise from self-interest or rationality • Evaluate whether elites have the power to dictate public opinion on issues
How ideology and partisanship shape public opinion	• Explain how partisanship relates to public opinion • Explain how political ideology relates to public opinion • Assess how well informed the American public is • Describe polarization and its effects	• Examine your partisanship in the context of public opinion • Examine your political ideology in the context of public opinion • Determine whether the American public is worth listening to • Evaluate the impact of partisanship on democracy
What demographic characteristics influence public opinion	• State the relationship between socioeconomic status, on the one hand, and partisanship and ideology on the other • Describe how age affects political thinking • Distinguish differences in political views between evangelical and non-evangelical Protestants • Characterize the impact of the gender gap • Characterize the impact of race and ethnicity on political thinking • Track the effect of increasing educational levels on political views	• Examine your socioeconomic status in light of your partisanship and political ideology • Speculate whether your position on issues will change as you age • Evaluate the effect of religion on politics • Evaluate the effect of race and ethnicity on politics • Speculate whether your college education and experience will change your political views

> *I didn't have the pedigree to be 'heard,' and the media and political gatekeepers worked to marginalize me and my new allies in the nascent but growing netroots. But it didn't matter. The floodgates were open, and technology allowed us to easily (and gleefully) crash those gates.*

Markos ("Kos") Moulitsas Zúniga, Northern Illinois University, DeKalb

7

The News Media and the Internet

In 1992 Markos ("Kos") Moulitsas Zúniga started taking classes at Northern Illinois University. He approached college a bit differently from many students, for he had just finished a three-year tour with the U.S. Army, where he trained as a 13P, a specialist in the multiple launch rocket system (MLRS). Kos did not experience combat, but he knew something of war from his childhood. Born in Chicago in 1971 to a Salvadoran mother and a Greek father, he had spent his formative years in El Salvador, where he saw firsthand the ravages of the Salvadoran civil war.

Kos was a little older than most college students, and his military training had accustomed him to a demanding schedule. It had also forged his interest in politics. With his background and interests, he sought to earn two bachelor's degrees, majoring in philosophy, journalism, and political science and minoring in German. But Kos did much more than take a demanding set of courses. By his senior year, he was editor of the

university's student newspaper, the *Northern Star*. Following graduation in 1996, Kos went straight to law school at Boston University, but he did not want to be a lawyer. Law school provided training that would further his interest in politics.

Kos had been a Republican when he joined the army. But his time in the army and college shifted his attention to liberal causes. In May 2002 he launched the *Daily Kos*, a blog through which he voiced his opinions, particularly his frustration

aplia Need to Know

- Why the media are important in a democracy
- How the law protects the press
- What trends define the history of the press
- How changes in the mass media have changed the information environment
- How the news media affect public opinion
- How the news media can be evaluated

with the presidency of George W. Bush. Blogging was still relatively new at the time, and Kos had no sense of what would unfold. But his blog coincided with the partisan battles that raged once the shock of the terrorist attacks of September 11, 2001, had subsided. Americans' concerns about terrorism and how to combat it were reshaping political life. Kos's commentary drew a large audience, and his blog became a forum for criticism of Bush and of the Iraq War, which began in 2003. He tapped into the anger surrounding the war, and his support for Howard Dean's presidential run in 2004 made him a powerful player in Democratic Party politics. For Kos, blogging has been a gateway to influence. In 2007 he was named one of the fifty most important people on the web by *PC World*. *Forbes* magazine listed him as the third most influential person on the web in the same year. Today *Daily Kos* remains one of the top five most influential blogs about politics in the country, announcing itself as source for "news, community, and action" and serving as an outlet for liberal opinions.[1]

Kos's gateway to influence involved more than just blogging. The title of one of the books he coauthored—*Crashing the Gate: Netroots, Grassroots, and the Rise of People-Powered Politics*—suggests how the Internet has transformed the way Americans learn and share news about politics. The Internet provides a new platform for distributing the news. Rather than passively learning about events from professional journalists, citizens now take active roles in communicating news and opinion and in shaping political debate about issues that are important to them. Political information flows from the bottom up, not just from the top down. The Internet is a gateway that makes it possible for more Americans to participate in the political process. But these changes in the media have also established some gates, since the poor have less access to the Internet than middle- and upper-income people do.

In this chapter, we examine and assess these changes. We do so with the understanding of the critical role that the news media play in a democracy. As a result, we also analyze the functions and impact of the press, survey its history, and describe and evaluate the new forms of communication in the twenty-first century.

FocusQuestions

- How do the mass media help make government accountable to the people?
- How has the rise of the Internet increased or decreased the ability of the public to hold government accountable?
- How does the bottom-up approach of twenty-first-century mass media affect citizen participation and equality? What are its other effects?
- When, and under what conditions, should government regulate the media?
- In what ways do the mass media offer gateways to American democracy? In what ways do the modern media establish new gates?

The Political News

› **Why the media are important in a democracy**

In a democracy such as the United States, citizens are supposed to be the ultimate source of power. The decisions made by the public shape the course of government. The public, therefore, needs information about politics to make good choices. Most people cannot directly observe political events, so they rely on the mass media for information about politics and government.

What Are the Mass Media?

The **mass media** represent the vast array of sources of information that are available to the public. These sources include newspapers, television, radio, blogs, online sources, cell phones, and social networks like Facebook. The **news media** (also called the press) are a subset of the mass media that have traditionally provided the news of the day, gathered and reported by journalists. But, with all the new technologies of the twenty-first century, the news media are changing; now the average citizen is able to participate in politics through blogs such as *Daily Kos* and websites such as YouTube. These new media have recast journalism by providing a proliferation of news outlets without a monolithic entity that shapes and defines political reporting. In this chapter, we use the term *mass media* to describe the many ways citizens learn about government and politics.

One aspect of the mass media today is speedy communication. What used to take days, weeks, and sometimes months now takes seconds. Most young people today (the Millennials born between 1982 and 2003) grew up with the 24-7 news cycle, an information world that is very different from that of their parents (and their professors). This chapter takes those changes into account.

Access to information is important because an enduring and effective democracy demands a knowledgeable public.[2] For the people to be informed, the press needs to be able to do its job free from government interference, and journalists must feel free to be critical of the government. This **watchdog** role of the press lies at the very heart of a democracy, and the First Amendment to the Constitution protects it.

The Functions of the News

The mass media help ensure government accountability and responsiveness by performing three important tasks: informing, investigating, and interpreting the news.

 mass media: *News sources, including newspapers, television, radio, and the Internet, whose purpose is to provide a large audience with information about the nation and the world.*

Connections: How do you get your news?

news media: *Subset of the mass media that provide the news of the day, gathered and reported by journalists.*

Connections: How often do you pay attention to the news?

watchdog: *Role of the press in monitoring government actions.*

KEN FEIL/THE WASHINGTON POST/GETTY IMAGES

Washington Post reporters Bob Woodward and Carl Bernstein became legends for their work in following up on a news story about what seemed to be a routine break-in. But it was the Democratic campaign headquarters that was broken into on June 17, 1972, and the trail they picked up led to the White House. Certain to be impeached, President Richard M. Nixon resigned on August 9, 1974.

Informing. Journalists, simply put, inform. If there is a crisis in the economy, for example, journalists provide information about the problem, explain the solutions being proposed, and indicate what can be expected in the future. In August 2008—just a month before a financial crisis rocked the nation—about 5 percent of news stories dealt with the economy. In September that proportion soared to nearly 30 percent.[3]

Investigating. The media can also make news by researching and revealing information about events. The Watergate scandal, uncovered by two reporters from the *Washington Post*, revealed questionable activities in the Richard M. Nixon administration (1969–74) (see also Chapter 12, The Presidency). Bob Woodward and Carl Bernstein played the ultimate role of watchdog, creating a news story that gripped the country for more than a year. The episode ended with Nixon's resignation on August 9, 1974, the only time a U.S. president has resigned. This scandal would never have been uncovered without the tireless efforts of the *Post's* investigative reporters.[4] Their work was surely the high point of investigative journalism.

Politicians often court the press, but they want favorable coverage. They want journalists to advertise their accomplishments to voters. Yet journalists and politicians are usually in an adversarial relationship because journalists want to report new stories on topics of interest to the public. So reporters love to unearth scandals—something that politicians want to avoid. The investigative function not only allows the press to fulfill its role as the watchdog of democracy; it makes reporters' jobs exciting and important. Also, scandals sell newspapers, and the profit motive is a central part of the process.

Interpreting. When the media inform, they also interpret the news. Just giving one story front-page coverage and relegating another to an inside page involves interpreting what is more and less important. The role of interpretation has taken on even greater significance in the last few decades. In 1960,

Connections: Does the news inform you about American government and politics?

Connections: Why is the relationship between the press and politicians adversarial?

for example, journalists covered presidential campaigns in a very descriptive fashion. About 90 percent of campaign stories focused on describing what happened in the campaign that day. But in the following decades, journalists started to interpret events more frequently, assessing why something happened. By the 1990s more than 80 percent of campaign stories were interpretive.[5]

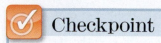

> **Checkpoint**
>
> **Can you:**
> - ☐ Describe the role of the press as watchdog
> - ☐ State the functions of the news media

The Law and the Free Press

❭ How the law protects the press

The First Amendment to the Constitution states that "Congress shall make no law . . . abridging the freedom . . . of the press." This protection is not unlimited. During times of war (or threat of war), national security concerns may require that the press not publish a story. The government, however, is often too eager to stop publication of controversial stories, whereas the press may be too willing to report on controversial stories that will boost sales. This conflict plays out in debates over prior restraint—government's ability to restrict the publication of sensitive material (see Chapter 4, Civil Liberties). When can government invoke prior restraint? At what point does prior restraint become censorship and thus undermine the ability of the press to be a watchdog?

Answers to these difficult questions have been shaped by Supreme Court decisions. In the early 1930s, for example, the state of Minnesota stopped a small newspaper from publishing controversial claims about the mayor of Minneapolis and convicted the publisher, Jay Near, under state libel laws. Near appealed the conviction all the way to the Supreme Court. In *Near v. Minnesota* (1931), the Court ruled that only in exceptionally rare cases could the government stop the printing of a story, overturning Near's conviction and invalidating the Minnesota law that led to his conviction.[6] The Court has reinforced the protections of press freedom in a **libel** case, *New York Times v. Sullivan* (1964), which also set a very high standard—proof of **actual malice**—to convict in a libel suit. Justice William J. Brennan wrote, "We consider this case against the background of a profound national commitment to the principle that debate on public issues should be uninhibited, robust, and wide open, and that it may well include vehement, caustic, and sometimes unpleasantly sharp attacks on government and public officials" (see Supreme Court Cases: *New York Times v. Sullivan*).

The modern landmark case on the freedom of the press was the *Pentagon Papers* case (1971).[7] During the Vietnam War, the *New York Times* secured a copy of a top-secret Department of Defense analysis detailing U.S. involvement in Vietnam and began publishing it, believing that the information,

libel: *Publishing false and damaging statements about another person.*

actual malice: *Supreme Court test for libel of a public figure, in which the plaintiff must prove that the publisher knew the material was false or acted with reckless disregard of whether it was true or false.*

supremecourtcases

New York Times v. Sullivan (1964)

QUESTION: What level of negligence must be found when public officials sue newspapers for libel?

ORAL ARGUMENT: January 6–7, 1964 (listen at http://www.oyez.org/cases/)

DECISION: March 9, 1964 (read at http://www.findlaw.com/casecode/supreme.html)

OUTCOME: Actual malice must be found to convict for libel, thus overturning the libel conviction of the *New York Times* (9–0).

Libel is the publication of false and damaging information about someone. Prior to libel laws, the defamed person often responded to libel by challenging the libeler to a duel, as when Vice President Aaron Burr challenged *Federalist* author and former Treasury Secretary Alexander Hamilton to a duel and killed him. To prevent such acts, various states made libel a criminal act. Today libel is almost exclusively a question for a civil suit, in which one person sues another for damages.

The *Sullivan* case derived from an advertisement placed in the March 29, 1960, *New York Times* by an ad hoc group of civil rights supporters called the Committee to Defend Martin Luther King. The ad condemned the "wave of terror" against nonviolent civil rights activists by unnamed "southern violators." Because some of the actions against King included arresting him, the chief of the Montgomery, Alabama, police department claimed that all of the allegations were about him and that he had been libeled.

Under Alabama law, once damaging statements are found, the only defense is for the publication to prove that all the particulars are true. The ad in this case was not true in all the particulars. For example, it claimed that protesting students sang "My Country 'Tis of Thee" when they actually sang "The Star-Spangled Banner." The jury thus found against the *Times*, awarding the police chief $500,000 in damages.

The Supreme Court reversed the verdict, declaring that a law holding a newspaper liable for criticism of a public official only if the paper could prove that every statement in the article was true would lead to massive self-censorship by the press. Instead, the Court declared that libel against a public official required a finding of actual malice, that is, knowledge that the statement was false or reckless disregard of whether it was true or false. Under this standard, the Court found that the ad was substantially true, but even if it had not been substantially true, there was no evidence that the *Times* acted with malice.

This decision has made it much easier for newspapers to criticize public officials. The Court has expanded the ruling to cover public figures as well. When a supermarket tabloid trashes a popular actor or singer, the individual thus harmed has to prove actual malice to win a suit for libel.

- **What would happen if the media were held legally responsible for any false statement they made?**
- **Should the burden of proof for proving libel of public officials be treated equally to the burden of proof for libel of private people?**

some of which contradicted official statements, was essential to public understanding of government policy. Citing national security, the Nixon administration secured a court injunction forcing the *Times* to cease publication, but the newspaper appealed, and the case quickly went to the Supreme Court. While not denying the possibility that censorship can be warranted, the Court in this instance rejected the government's argument that national security took precedence over the right to publish documents embarrassing to the government. The government, said the Court, had not met the extraordinary burden of proof needed for prior restraint.

In general, the courts have tended to give the edge to the press in the belief that, in the long run, it is better to protect press freedoms so that the press can, in turn, help inform the public, which can then hold elected officials accountable. Consistent with this general predisposition, there are very few laws that constrain the print media, such as newspapers and magazines. The electronic media, however, are more heavily regulated by government. In 1934 Congress created the Federal Communications Commission (FCC), now a powerful agency that regulates all forms of electronic media, including radio, broadcast television, cable television, cell phones, and even wireless networks. Anyone can start a newspaper, but starting a radio station requires a license from the FCC.

The FCC monitors media ownership as well. For a long time, the FCC worked to ensure that ownership of the news media was not concentrated in just a few hands, concerned that a monopoly would undermine the ability of the media to be fair and able to perform its watchdog function. The Telecommunications Act of 1996 eased the rules concerning multiple ownership, and the FCC has started to relax this standard. As a result, there has been a trend toward greater concentration of media ownership in the last decade. Without genuine competition, the press, some fear, will become lapdogs, not watchdogs. But even the changes of the last few years have not eliminated competition. It is true that newspapers are now dominated by seven major chains; Gannett alone controls more than eighty newspapers. But that is still only about a circulation of 7 million (or about 15 percent of newspapers nationally).[8] Of course, newspaper readership is down over the last few decades, making this number even less consequential.[9] With so many outlets for news in the twenty-first century, one person or company will not likely be able to control them all.

Any effort to monopolize the press or curtail its freedom is met by strong protests from people fearing a trend toward authoritarian rule. A government that limits press freedom seeks to insulate itself from criticism, thereby decreasing the chance for the public to hold leaders accountable. It is for all these reasons that an evaluation of how democratic a nation is rests on how much freedom its press enjoys.

Connections: Should the standard for press freedom be the same in cases of terrorism as in wartime?

Connections: What are the newspapers in your city or town? Who owns them?

Checkpoint

Can you:
- ☐ Name the laws, government agencies, and court rulings that regulate press freedom

The History of the Press in America

> ## What trends define the history of the press

The press in America has always been dynamic. Newspapers have developed from occasional pamphlets in the early 1700s, to comprehensive daily publications that aimed for objective reporting of political news, to today's online mix of news and entertainment. By the 1900s journalism emerged as a profession with a commitment to objectivity. In the twentieth century radio and then television changed how Americans received the news and how they reacted to it. Throughout, the press has at times supported government and elected officials and at times assumed an adversarial role as it has given citizens the information they need to make government accountable and responsive.

The Colonial Era, 1620 to 1750

In the early colonial period newspapers were not widely available, and there were few printing presses. Newspaper publication was more of a hobby for publishers than anything else, and the notion that the press had the right to criticize government was not widely accepted. In fact, colonial governments feared that harsh criticism would incite the public and create instability, so publishers who attacked those in power could be thrown into jail and their printing presses confiscated.

In 1734 John Peter Zenger was jailed for criticizing the colonial governor of New York in his *New York Weekly Journal*. When his case came to trial the next year, his lawyer, Andrew Hamilton of Philadelphia, decided on a bold strategy. Zenger would admit guilt—he had published the critical statements—and then argue that the jury should find him not guilty because the statements were true. In other words, the press had a fundamental right to criticize government, and a free press was more important than the law against **seditious libel** that had put Zenger behind bars. Much to the surprise of the governor and his supporters, the jury agreed and freed Zenger. The case is a landmark in advancing the idea of a free press.

In the same decade, in Philadelphia, Benjamin Franklin was laying the groundwork for the press as a viable institution in America with his *Philadelphia Gazette*. The paper would set the standard for American news with its ability to present news accounts in an interesting and enlightening manner. Franklin had a gift for writing and a flair for satire and parody. His accounts of government and stories of personal interest, including crime, sex, violence, and mysteries, became the foundation for modern American news coverage. But Franklin was trying to do much more than simply pique the interest of readers. He also believed that the news was critical to educating the public. His "An Apology for Printers" (1731) defended objectivity in journalism.

Connections: Why was freedom of the press so important to the colonists and members of the Founding generation?

seditious libel: *Conduct or language that incites rebellion against the authority of a state.*

Though it contradicted the prevailing view at the time, it helped set the standard for the future of American journalism.[10]

The Founding Era, 1750 to 1790

As tensions between the colonies and Britain increased, interest in politics grew as well, and the press responded. The circulation of newspapers grew twice as fast as the population did between 1760 and 1776.[11] That year, when Thomas Paine published *Common Sense*, a pamphlet attacking King George, it sold 150,000 copies, far more than the 2,000 copies political documents normally sold.[12] Given that there were only 2.5 million people in the colonies, that is the equivalent of 18 million copies today.

The press helped spread the idea of independence because newspapers served as networks for sharing information. They reached not only subscribers but also many people who could not read, for the papers were read aloud in taverns and town squares. Newspapers were also shared in places of business. Information was a valuable commodity, and people sought it. In this era newspaper editors and writers did not try to be objective; rather, they explicitly supported partisan causes. During the Revolution, some papers backed independence; others supported the British Crown.[13]

Partisanship in the press carried over to the battle for ratification of the Constitution, and newspapers provided a vital forum for debate. The Antifederalists waged a fierce campaign against the Constitution,[14] and those supporting the Constitution responded, most famously in a series of essays published in New York newspapers. These essays, by Alexander Hamilton, James Madison, and John Jay, are today known as the Federalist Papers and are still regarded as a leading source for understanding the Constitution. At the time, the essays helped to lay the groundwork for ratification of the Constitution by the state of New York—a state absolutely critical for making the new government a reality. It is also worth noting that the Antifederalists' criticisms led to the adoption of the Bill of Rights.

The Partisan Era, 1790 to 1900

Following the adoption of the Constitution, most newspapers allied themselves with the Federalists or with the newly emerging Jeffersonian party. In this era of the partisan press, writers made no effort to adjudicate between the claims and ideas of competing parties.

The 1798 Sedition Act made it illegal to print or publish any "false, scandalous, and malicious writing" about the federal government, either house of Congress, or the president.[15] At the time, the United States was engaged in a limited and undeclared war with France over trade issues, and the Federalists believed that attacks on President John Adams (1797–1801) and the government were ripping apart the new nation, which was barely a decade old. The

Articles of Confederation had not even lasted ten years; might not the same fate await the Constitution? But the Jeffersonians were equally adamant that laws suppressing criticism of the government violated the Constitution. Jeffersonian publishers did not cease their attacks, and some went to jail and paid fines. After he and his party won the 1800 presidential election, Thomas Jefferson (1801–1809) pardoned all publishers convicted under the act, and Congress refunded their fines.

While Jefferson had long been a proponent of a free press and had severely criticized the Sedition Act, the attacks he endured were so vicious that he began to question the merits of this partisan press. In 1807 he conceded, "The man who never looks into a newspaper is better informed than he who reads them."[16] This was quite a change for a man who, twenty years earlier, had argued that newspapers were more important than the institutions of republican government itself. Jefferson's dilemma reveals a core issue about the press. The media do inform, playing a vital function. But informing almost always carries some bias, and when informing is deliberately intended to manipulate public opinion, the public responds with distrust.

Newspapers continued to have close alliances with political parties in the next decades of the nineteenth century. They not only served to attack the opposition but also provided a way for presidents and party leaders to express their opinions on the issues of the day. Some presidents, such as James K. Polk (1845–49), even started their own newspapers to get out their message.[17]

During the 1830s and 1840s new steam presses reduced the cost of publishing newspapers. In 1833 Benjamin Day sold his *New York Sun* for a penny an issue, initiating the era of the **penny press**. At the same time literacy throughout the nation was growing, and newspaper owners began to realize that they could make higher profits through circulation and advertising than as arms of political parties.[18] They also saw that partisanship drove away customers who did not share their political views. So to increase circulation, newspapers began to move toward sensationalism, printing news of crimes and scandals and stories about personalities, much as tabloids do today. The circulation of newspapers rose from about 1.4 million in 1870 to more than 8 million within the next thirty years. The quest for market share led to competition over which newspaper could grab the most attention with sensational headlines and stories. Known as **yellow journalism**, this form of news reporting distorted the presentation of events and could mislead the public, all in the interest of boosting sales. Joseph Pulitzer and William Randolph Hearst, the most famous newspaper publishers at the time, used large type, provocative headlines, pictures, and color to attract readers. Hearst introduced comics as a way to sell more papers. The competition became particularly fierce over American relations with Spain, as stories of Spanish atrocities in Cuba inflamed the public. When the USS *Maine* sank in Havana Harbor on February 15, 1898, the newspapers quickly blamed Spain. The U.S. Navy launched a

Connections: In the standoff between Adams and Jefferson over the Sedition Act, who do you think was right?

Connections: What are the advantages and disadvantages of partisan control of the press?

penny press: *Newspapers sold for a penny, initiating an era in which the press began to rely on circulation and advertising for income and not on political parties.*

Connections: What are examples of sensationalized news stories today?

yellow journalism: *Style of journalism in the late nineteenth century characterized by sensationalism intended to capture readers' attention and increase circulation.*

four-week investigation, finding that the *Maine* had been destroyed by an underwater mine but placing no blame. However, the American public, fed by the press, continued to blame Spain, and on April 25, the U.S. Congress declared war on Spain. Many observers credit these sensational newspaper stories with fueling the start of the Spanish-American War.[19]

The Professional Era, 1900 to 1950

The development of mass circulation newspapers also led journalism to develop into a serious profession with an ethic of objective reporting. Pulitzer, despite his role in advancing yellow journalism, was a key figure in this transition, believing that a vibrant independent press was essential for a democracy to endure.

The idea of a public-spirited press was increasingly realized in efforts to investigate wrongdoing in government, business, and industry. Adolph Ochs purchased the *New York Times* in 1896 with the goal of pursuing objective reporting. Such commitments led journalists, with the backing of people like Ochs and Pulitzer, to expose corruption and encourage genuine reform. Although President Theodore Roosevelt (1901–1909) labeled such efforts as **muckraking**—after a character in *Pilgrim's Progress* who rakes "muck," looking for the worst rather than the best—he came to appreciate the service these investigative journalists provided. Perhaps the most famous example was Upton Sinclair's *The Jungle* (1906), a novel that exposed the horrors of the meatpacking industry. Roosevelt, who had read an advance copy of the book, called for government regulation of the food industry.[20] In response, Congress passed the Pure Food and Drug Act and the Meat Inspection Act to help ensure food safety.

Muckraking gave politicians an additional reason to pursue good public policy: to avoid bad press. It is overly simplistic (and optimistic) to claim that muckraking single-handedly led to a fundamental change in politicians' behavior, but investigative journalism has helped hold public officials accountable, even as it has transformed the press into an institution that seeks to advance the public interest.

The rise of professional journalism is also tied to an ethic of objectivity. The goal of being impartial and unbiased in reporting became part of the journalist's creed, especially as taught in new schools of journalism. The American Society of Newspaper Editors adopted a set of principles that declared that

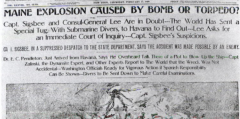

The New York World a day after

who had been Populists and those who became Progressives — clamored for the United States to rescue the Cuban people from the Spanish malefactors.

President William McKinley and the conservative Republican leaders in Congress reluctantly gave way before this pressure. Senator Henry Cabot Lodge warned McKinley, "If the war in Cuba drags on through the summer with nothing done we [the Republican party] shall go down in the greatest defeat ever known."

Already, in November 1897, Spain, at the urging of President McKinley, had granted

William Randolph Hearst's *New York Journal* and Joseph Pulitzer's *New York World* competed for circulation with sensational news and screaming headlines. The frenzy they stirred up over the sinking of the USS *Maine* in Havana Harbor in February 1898 helped lead to war with Spain. It is now generally believed that the explosion on the *Maine* was not caused by a Spanish bomb or torpedo but was accidental, a spontaneous combustion in inadequately vented coal bunkers.

muckraking: *Journalistic practice of investigative reporting that seeks to uncover corruption and wrongdoing.*

Connections: Give other examples of investigative journalism that have made government responsive.

"news reports should be free from opinion or bias of any kind."[21] Reporters were trained to present facts, not personal opinions, and to describe, not judge.

The muckraking impulses faded by about 1916 or so, but the press's role as a watchdog did not. Now a key goal became to write a story that presented the public with new and important information that was well researched and carefully documented. Journalists sought to cultivate politicians for access to news and stories, leading to a different dynamic between politicians and the press. It remained adversarial, but both sides knew they needed each other. As the press and politicians formed closer relationships, the potential for conflicts of interest increased. To retain the relationship, politicians made certain statements "off the record," with the understanding that journalists would not use them in a story except as background, information that could help set the context and provide a broader understanding for the story. As a result, journalists have a strong ethic about not revealing confidential sources. In addition, the press chose not to report on the personal lives of politicians.

Connections:
Should the press expose the personal lives of politicians? Why or why not?

The Television Era, 1950 to 2000

The rise of television recast the news media and the information available to the public. At mid-century the *New York Times* was the most influential newspaper and clearly the leader in American journalism, although the *Los Angeles Times* and the *Washington Post* were gaining in importance. News magazines such as *Time* and *Life* had nationwide circulations, but they were not daily sources of information. Most people got their daily news from local newspapers and radio stations that broadcast news summaries—usually five minutes of news, weather, and sports on the hour. Then television began to nationalize the news. That is, the evening broadcasts from the three major networks—ABC, CBS, and NBC—gave all Americans access to the same news, and by the 1960s they relied on television for political information.[22]

From 1961 to 1981, Walter Cronkite was the anchor of the CBS *Evening News* and one of the most trusted men in America. Usually calm and objective, he broke down when announcing that President John F. Kennedy, shot in Dallas on November 22, 1963, had died. His emotions on the air exemplified the feelings of all Americans.

CBS /LANDOV

TV news was shaped by a handful of "anchormen." Walter Cronkite, anchor of CBS *Evening News,* was an icon. Not only was he famous, but he was also widely admired and trusted. In 1973 Americans rated him "the most trusted man in America."[23] Cronkite represented both the height of what might be called "objective" journalism and the dominance of TV network news. Most Americans assumed that Cronkite provided the facts and did not let partisanship shape his reporting.

Television's visuals also redefined the news and even political events. Politicians now aimed to look good on television because viewers could detect nervousness and judge body language. The 1960 presidential campaign is a well-known example of the new emphasis on the visual side of politics. Most viewers of the televised presidential debates between Senator John Kennedy and Vice President Richard Nixon thought that Kennedy performed better.[24] He looked tanned and rested; in fact, he had spent a few days before the debate resting on a beach. Nixon, by contrast, had continued to campaign and had spent time in the hospital for a very sore leg. He was tired and in pain. He also refused to wear makeup. Nixon was not at his best, while Kennedy looked presidential. People who listened to the debate on the radio, however, thought that Nixon had won, further suggesting the power of visuals. Many commentators attribute Kennedy's razor-thin victory in the election to his performance in the debates.[25]

Connections: Is it better for Americans to have a single source of trusted news or many sources, some of which may be less trustworthy?

Checkpoint

Can you:

- ☐ State the Zenger case's importance
- ☐ Describe the role of the press in the Revolution and the ratification of the Constitution
- ☐ Track the evolution from partisan press to yellow journalism
- ☐ Elaborate on the ethics of professional journalism
- ☐ State the effect of television on news reporting

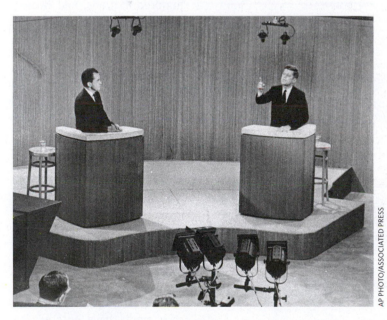

Television proved its importance as a source for political information when the NBC board chair invited the 1960 presidential candidates to debate the issues on television. John F. Kennedy accepted first, saying, "I believe you are performing a notable public service in giving the American people a chance to see the candidates of the two major parties face to face." More than 70 million Americans watched the Kennedy-Nixon debates, and today presidential debates are fixtures of the fall campaign.

AP PHOTO/ASSOCIATED PRESS

The Mass Media in the Twenty-First Century

> **How changes in the mass media have changed the information environment**

The media have always been a dynamic institution, but the speed of changes in the last few decades is truly staggering. The impact of television, for example, changed further with the rise of cable television from the 1970s to the 1990s. It was now possible to bring news to the public any time of day, reshaping the American news environment. Recent advances in technology have opened up additional avenues of communication—nearly all at the same time. The pace and the depth of these changes make the information environment of the twenty-first century different from those that preceded it.

The Changing Media Environment

The options open to Americans for gathering information about politics have constantly expanded. Figure 7.1 displays the changing media environment and suggests two main lessons. First, Americans adopt new media quickly. In the early 1920s there were only five radio stations, and few households owned radios. By 1927 there were seven hundred stations, and ownership was rapidly increasing.[26] By the end of the 1930s almost everyone in the United States had access to a radio. Television caught on even more quickly. Only 10 percent of Americans had TV sets in their homes in the early 1950s; by 1960 the figure was 90 percent. Today, nearly all American households have not one television set but often two or three. Internet access also shows a steep upward trend, from few households in the mid-1990s to about 80 percent of Americans in 2010.[27] The speed by which these new media have entered the

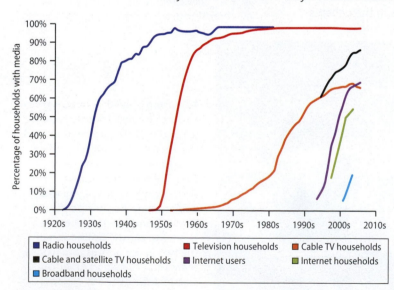

FIGURE 7.1 **The Changing Media Environment, 1920s–2000s.**

Source: Markus Prior, *Post Broadcast Democracy* (New York: Cambridge University Press, 2007).

marketplace itself increases. It took television thirteen years to reach 50 million users. In just three years on the market, more than 50 million iPods were sold, and when the iPad was released in 2010, about 3 million were sold in eighty days. Facebook added 100 million users in just nine months![28]

Second, there are more options for gathering news than ever before. In the 1930s newspapers and radio were the main sources. In the 1950s television was a new option, but there were only three networks, and they broadcast the news only in the evening. Now cable television, satellite TV, and the Internet make news available night and day.

The Decline of Newspapers

Traditional printed newspapers are in decline. The number of daily papers dropped from about 1,600 in 1990 to just under 1,400 in 2011.[29] Newspaper readership is also declining. Figure 7.2 shows the drop in readership in the last decade. This pattern is part of an even longer-term trend. In 1977 about 70 percent of the public read newspapers. In 2011 the figure was below 50 percent, and only about 25 percent of the Millennial generation are newspaper readers.[30]

Connections: What newspapers do you read? Print or online?

The decline of newspapers and newspaper readership raises concerns because newspapers tend to contain more hard news—fact-based stories, as opposed to interpretive narratives—than is reported on TV. In 2009, Alex Jones, one of the leading observers of the press, indicated that 85 percent of hard news comes from newspapers rather than from TV.[31] Will the decline of newspapers deprive Americans of hard news, of the facts they need to hold government accountable?

Some observers counter that readers are simply migrating from printed newspapers to online versions. In January 2004 online newspapers had about 41 million visitors; by 2012 the number had jumped to more than 100 million.[32] Although the move from the printed to online versions may offer some hope about the continued significance of the newspaper industry, it has not solved the industry's financial difficulties. Fewer readers of print newspapers mean fewer advertisers buying space and lower rates

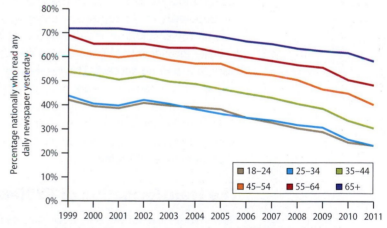

FIGURE 7.2 **Newspaper Readership, 1999–2011.**

Source: Scarborough Research survey data, 1999–2011 Scarborough Report, Release 1, Pew Research Center's Project for Excellence in Journalism, *The State of the News Media 2012.* Copyright © 2011 by Pew Research Center. Reproduced by permission.

Connections: Are the newspapers in your town struggling? How can you tell?

being charged for the space; online advertising has not been able to make up the difference.[33] Commercial ad revenue is not all that has been lost. The number of want ads has shrunk as well, as potential buyers and sellers turn more often to Craigslist and other specialty websites that share information without charge. With revenue plummeting, newspapers survive only by cutting staff. The *Boston Globe* once sent journalists overseas to report on international events. That is no longer true.[34] The *Los Angeles Times* has seen its newsroom decline from 1,200 to 850 reporters.[35] Fewer reporters, editors, and other journalists mean that newspapers have less ability to inform and investigate. If the press cannot perform its watchdog role, the people stand to lose the means by which they hold government accountable.[36]

The Durability of Radio

In many ways, radio is underappreciated as a medium of communication; current debates center on newspapers, television, and the Internet. But radio remains important, especially considering how often Americans listen to the radio in their cars. The percentage of Americans who listen to the radio has remained unchanged in the last decade. In 1998, 95 percent of the American public tuned into an AM or FM station at least once a week; in 2011, 93 percent had listened to the radio in the previous seven days. Radio is expanding its reach by means of satellite radio and streaming audio on desktop and laptop computers. In fact, it is possible that "radio" is becoming "audio," reflecting advances in digital technology.[37]

Political talk radio, a medium dominated largely by conservatives, is increasingly popular.[38] In 2012 around 50 million Americans listened to talk radio,[39] most to conservative programs. No "liberal" shows are even close to the popularity of the top-rated conservative commentators. Rush Limbaugh is by far the best known and the most controversial. Liberals at one time tried to make inroads into talk radio with the now-defunct Air America radio network, but had no success. The reasons for this lack of success are unclear. Perhaps it is because there are more conservatives than liberals in the United States. In addition, conservatives tend to live in the suburbs and rural areas and therefore spend more time driving their cars than do city dwellers. Their greater opportunities for listening may be another reason for the dominance of conservative programming.[40]

The Transformation of TV News

Newspapers are not the only news outlets facing a decline in customers. The audience for the TV network evening news is also shrinking. Nearly 25 percent of Americans watched the evening news in 1980; by 2011 that figure was just 8 percent.[41] The downward trend is likely to continue because older Americans make up the current audience for TV news. Young people, who represent the future audience, are not big consumers of network news. Their habits are not likely to change, painting a bleak picture for the industry in the coming years.

This decline, like that of newspapers, generates concern about how well informed the public is about politics. But these concerns are counterbalanced by the rise of cable news, which has become increasingly available since 1980. Households are now watching two or three hours a week of cable news, a rate of viewership higher than that for network news in the 1980s. Of the cable networks, Fox has the largest audience, more than CNN and MSNBC combined. Bill O'Reilly has become exceptionally popular, though not nearly as popular as Walter Cronkite once was.

Cable news is not like the evening news shows of the 1970s, which were thirty-minute broadcasts around dinnertime. Cable news is available twenty-four hours a day. Events are covered live, transforming the news cycle. No longer do politicians time public appearances to appear on the evening news. News now comes at viewers at a rapid-fire rate, and cable news networks include interpretation in their constant programming. MSNBC's *Hardball with Chris Matthews* and *The Rachel Maddow Show* and Fox's *The Huckabee Show* are examples. Cable news has taken the interpretive function of the news media to a whole new level in response to the demands of 24-7 news programming.

The web offers yet another platform for gathering and distributing the news, one that seems to be on the rise. MSNBC.com, FoxNews.com, and CNN.com have all registered significant gains in the number of visitors in recent years.[42] Their average monthly audiences are in the millions, with CNN in the lead (34.6 million), followed by MSNBC (29.4 million) and Fox (17.8 million).[43] Overall, the number of sources for news has increased. We examine the impact of these developments later in the chapter.

Infotainment

Television viewers also get political news through talk shows, such as *The Ellen DeGeneres Show*, the *Late Show with David Letterman,* and *Jimmy Kimmel Live*. These sources offer what is called "infotainment" or **soft news**, news with fewer hard facts of the kind newspapers generally report and more emphasis on personal stories that engage (or shock) the public and often appeal to the emotions rather than the intellect.

Nearly 2.5 million people, mostly young adults, watch *The Daily Show* hosted by Jon Stewart, which delivers the news with humor and satire four days a week.[44] With Stewart's tough questions and hard-hitting reporting, it would be misleading to suggest that the news the show provides is "soft." The guests who appear on *The Daily Show* cover the full ideological spectrum, and Stewart subjects those in power—regardless of party—to his rapier wit.

Connections: Which cable news station do you watch? Do you think the presentation of the news is fair?

Connections: Would you describe the news you seek as hard or soft?

soft news: News stories focused less on facts and policies than on sensationalizing secondary issues or on less serious subjects of the entertainment world.

Though considered by many to be liberal, he aims for on-air balance.[45] *The Colbert Report,* with host Stephen Colbert, is also an exceptionally popular comedy/news show. In 2012, an episode in which Colbert announced he would run for president after signing over control of his Super PAC to Jon Stewart drew national attention to issues related to the funding of presidential campaigns.[46]

Blogs

Blogs like *Daily Kos* provide a forum for bottom-up commentary, descriptions of events, video postings, and general conversation. Through blogs, average citizens are able to express their opinions to a wider audience, and they offer a gateway for people to influence politics. In fact, blogs have given rise to a new category of journalists—citizen-journalists—who, although not professional journalists, circulate opinions and interpretations that clearly influence political debates. There are all kinds of blogs, with political blogs representing a subset. Of the fifteen most popular blogs in 2012, two are political: the *Huffington Post* (number 1) and the *Daily Beast* (number 11).[47]

In many ways, blogging symbolizes the modern transformation of the mass media. Blogs capture the interest of people of all ages, and some observers hope that they will provide a forum for more participation and deliberation. While there is some evidence that blogs do foster participation, they do not seem to foster deliberation. Liberals read liberal blogs, and conservatives read conservative blogs—in fact, 94 percent of people read blogs that share their ideological viewpoint. These data suggest that blogs reinforce existing preferences and do not provide opportunities to hear the other side.[48] In addition, blogs are usually strong in their ideological leanings. Conservative blogs include those of Matt Drudge and Rush Limbaugh.[49] *Daily Kos* and *Huffington Post* are liberal blogs. During the 2008 presidential campaign, interest in liberal blogs was very high, and although their appeal declined after the election of Barack Obama, they continue to attract a substantial following.

Blogs have the potential to spread false information. Because no one checks the accuracy of a posting, individuals—some call them trolls—can say outrageous things merely to get attention without penalty.[50] In contrast, the traditional press has a well-established set of norms for vetting the accuracy of information; when false statements do get through, the journalists are likely to pay a heavy penalty. Trolls, on the other hand, often gain notoriety for lying.

Nevertheless, the importance of blogs continues to increase. In 2011, bloggers wrote about business and consumer news, including technology such as new cell phones, Apple products, and Google, even as they

Connections: How could you be a citizen-journalist?

Connections: Have you ever written a blog? What inspired you?

commented on the 2012 presidential campaign.[51] News that is not picked up in the mainstream media often gets play in the blogosphere and can force the mainstream media to cover the story. Politicians understand the powerful effects blogs can have on the news.

Social Networking

The Internet has also enabled new social networks for sharing information. Just as personal conversations are important sources of information, social networking websites are increasingly important ways to spread political news.

Facebook is, of course, the leading platform for social networking. It is a worldwide phenomenon with launches in more than fifteen different languages. By 2011, at least 80 percent of college students had Facebook accounts—and about half the parents of college students had accounts.[52]

Politicians are also using social networks; a recent study found that nearly 70 percent of 2008 congressional candidates had a Facebook presence.[53] In 2012, all of the major presidential candidates made use of Facebook.[54] Facebook also teamed up with NBC News and the *Manchester Union Leader* in New Hampshire to sponsor the Republican presidential debates on January 8, 2012. After the debates, users could go to the website and discuss the issues and positions of the candidates.[55]

Facebook has become a valuable means whereby candidates reach out to a younger generation of voters, both to convey their messages and to raise money. Candidates can list biographical details, post advertisements and other Internet feeds, provide links for donations, and create discussion groups. Users are, in turn, able to become candidates' supporters with access to all posted information. Private individuals have also used Facebook to campaign for candidates on their own. It is a new gateway for volunteering that is less costly and may reach more voters.

Another development in social networking is the rise of Twitter. Members of Congress and other politicians, as well as actors, sports figures, and celebrities, use Internet-based messages ("tweets") to share information simultaneously with large numbers of people, and this technology has spread rapidly around the world. Cell phone usage is nearly universal now, and text messaging is so common that most people have "unlimited" texting as part of their payment plan. Politicians and political parties use this medium to communicate with supporters. Supporters can also send messages to various political organizations. Text messaging is yet another gateway, and the increasing popularity of iPhones and other advanced cellular devices promises new means of communicating and sharing information in the future.

Connections: Is Facebook a source of political news or action for you?

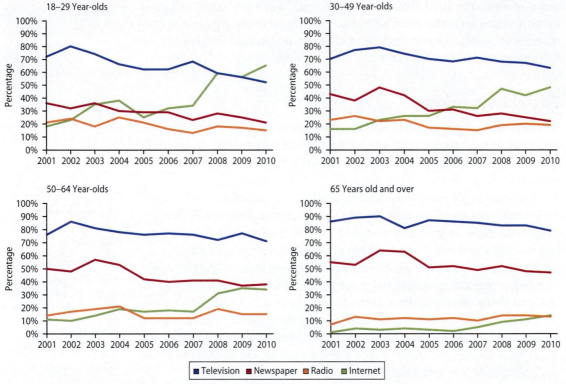

FIGURE 7.3 **Main News Sources, by Age, 2001–2010.**

Source: "Internet Gains on Television as Public's Main News Source: More Young People Cite Internet than TV," Pew Research Center, December 1–5, 2010. The Pew Research Center for The People & The Press, 2011. Copyright © 2011 by Pew Research Center. Reproduced by permission of Pew Research Center For the People & the Press, a project of the Pew Research Center.

The News and the Millennials

The changes in the media environment do not affect all citizens equally, as suggested by Figure 7.3. The Millennial generation, for example, is much more likely to get its news from the Internet than from newspapers. In addition, when younger Americans read a newspaper or listen to a radio program, they do so for a much shorter period of time than do those who are older than 50. The youth seem to do more channel surfing, while older Americans are more likely to sit down and watch an entire news program. These habits may reflect differences in lifestyles between, for example, college students and adults with full-time jobs and families.[56] It may also be that older adults are more cautious about new technology, whereas younger people embrace it.

Conventional wisdom has always said that young people are less interested in politics than older Americans are. But Millennials appear to be

Connections: Which do you trust more—bottom-up or top-down journalism?

Connections: What is the future of political communication?

more interested in politics at this point in their lives than were previous generations. This interest is not gauged by whether they watch the evening news or read newspapers, but by the ways they use new media to share information and learn about and express interest in politics.[57] Young adults tend to reject the top-down approach to learning about politics in which the news is filtered by professional journalists and trusted news anchors such as Cronkite. Instead, they seem much more interested in the bottom-up approach made possible by the wide-open availability of new media for citizen participation.

These changes are going to become more important over time as more Millennials become eligible to vote and older generations pass on. Technological change continues to spread. The United States is in the midst of a major transformation in the media environment, and observers are only beginning to understand the changes in how Americans transmit and consume the news.

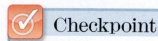

Checkpoint

Can you:

☐ Describe the changing media environment

☐ Survey the impact of the decline of newspapers

☐ Survey the impact of developments in radio

☐ Survey the impact of the transformation of TV news

☐ Survey the impact of the rise of infotainment

☐ Survey the impact of blogs

☐ Survey the impact of social networking

☐ Survey the impact of the changing media environment on young people

The Impact of the News Media on the Public

> **How the news media affect public opinion**

The press provides information, investigation, and interpretation of the news. The news media, both old and new, make decisions about what to cover, what not to cover, and how to cover it. How does the public respond to this information? This section looks at several models ranging between two extremes: that the mass media have no effect on the public and that the mass media dominate the public's thinking.

The Propaganda Model

Few people believe that the media have no influence on citizens. To hold such a view, one must either believe that the public ignores the media or that citizens learn about politics by observing the events themselves. Neither is true. We can confidently label this the "naïve model" and dismiss it.

The polar opposite has been called the **propaganda model**. This approach is exemplified by the Nazi dictatorship in Germany in the 1930s and 1940s. The Nazi Party controlled the content of newspapers and radio. It dictated the information available to citizens, affecting the direction and shape

 propaganda model: *Extreme view of the media's role in society, arguing that the press serves the interest of the government only, driving what the public thinks about important issues.*

of public opinion. Through controlled programming, the German people often heard about the greatness of Adolf Hitler and the dangers of racial impurity. By holding a monopoly on information, the government could easily marshal public support. This is a dangerous model, and it is also inconsistent with how the press works in open societies. In the United States media sources control programming, and they compete for audience share; the government does not control the flow of information. The Constitution guarantees a free press.

The Minimal Effects Model

Toward the end of World War II, having seen the powerful effects of propaganda in Nazi Germany, scholars in the United States began to study public opinion and the influence of the media on it. Paul Lazarsfeld and others examined the media's influence on voting in the 1940 presidential election. The results were surprising: The researchers discovered that people had made up their minds before the campaign, and new information altered only a handful of people's choices.[58] Lazarsfeld's study gave rise to what has been called the **minimal effects model**. Lazarsfeld and his colleagues contended that the news media had only marginal influence on the public's thinking about politics. The public did not have much information about politics, and attitudes were shaped by long-standing forces such as partisanship or the neighborhood in which people lived.

According to this model, in a process described as **selective exposure**, people secured information from sources that agreed with them, leading to the reinforcement of beliefs, not to a change of beliefs. The minimal effects model was also based on a complementary process called **selective perception**—a concept developed in a study of the American voter published by Angus Campbell and three coauthors in 1960.[59] Selective perception describes partisans as interpreting the same information differently. In other words, partisanship involves a perceptual lens (see Chapter 6, Public Opinion) that shapes how outside events are viewed. So, for example, in early 2011, 75 percent of Democrats supported President Obama's health care reform legislation, passed in 2010, whereas only 17 percent of Republicans did.[60]

The Not-So-Minimal Effects Model

The minimal effects model dominated the field of political science for about forty years. Then, starting in the 1970s, scholars began to reassess it.[61] This reassessment took place at two levels. First, rather than looking at whether the news media shifted citizens' opinions about an issue, scholars examined the more subtle effects that might arise from how the press covered politics (more will be said about this later). Second, they started to gather better data that could more effectively test for the impact of the news media. This next generation of research produced the **not-so-minimal effects model**.

 minimal effects model: *View of the media's impact as marginal, since most people seek news reports to reinforce beliefs already held rather than to develop new ones.*

 selective exposure: *Process whereby people secure information from sources that agree with them, thus reinforcing their beliefs.*

 selective perception: *Process whereby partisans interpret the same information differently.*

Connections: What are your sources for the news? Do you select sources that agree with your views or that challenge your views?

 not-so-minimal effects model: *View of the media's impact as substantial, occurring by agenda setting, framing, and priming.*

Connections: Have the news media changed your mind about a political issue or figure?

While not overstating the power of the news media, the model acknowledges that the coverage of politics by the press matters in subtle and important ways. In particular, there are three kinds of media effects: agenda setting, priming, and framing.

Agenda Setting. By stressing certain issues, the media influence what the American public views as the most pressing concerns. This effect is called **agenda setting**. Given that on any particular day there are literally hundreds of stories that could be reported, journalists' decisions about which stories to cover (and which story to lead with, and which to bury inside the paper or at the end of a newscast) matter considerably. Politicians and their advisers make a huge effort to convince the media to cover some stories and ignore others. Should the news lead with a story about casualties in the war in Afghanistan or about growing problems in the nation's public education system? As one scholar explains, the media "may not be successful most of the time telling people what to think, but it is stunningly successful in telling its readers what to think about."[62] The evidence is compelling. If the media talk about crime, the public starts to care about it. If the press starts paying additional attention to the federal budget deficit, the issue becomes more salient to citizens. Since only about 1 percent of news coverage is dedicated to the topic of education, it is not surprising that education policy rarely rises to the top of politicians' agendas.[63]

Priming. An extension of agenda setting is **priming**. Emphasis by the media can alter the criteria that citizens use when evaluating political leaders. Following 9/11, for instance, the news media's coverage of terrorism was the most powerful force shaping President Bush's popularity.[64] The public gave Bush credit for dealing effectively with these tragic events. So when terrorism was the focus of the media, Bush's approval rating was high. But when late in Bush's second term the primary topic covered by the media shifted to the economy, the public was less supportive of the president.

Priming can also affect how people vote. In the 2012 campaign, the Republican candidate Mitt Romney hoped the public would perceive the economy as struggling and vote for him on that basis. The Obama reelection team wanted the public to perceive the economy as better than it was when Obama

© Randy Glasbergen
www.glasbergen.com

"Today in school we learned about the three main branches of government: lobbyists, fund-raisers and media."

© RANDY GLASBERGEN

Connections: What issues are the media putting on the political agenda right now?

agenda setting: *Ability of the media to affect the way people view issues, people, or events by controlling which stories are shown and which are not.*

priming: *Process whereby the media influence the criteria the public uses to make decisions.*

took office in January 2009. Both sides recognized that the way the news media primed the public to think about the economy would have an impact on the election. With Obama's victory, it appears his message was more effective than Romney's.

Framing. Framing is the ability of the media to alter the public's view on an issue by presenting it in a particular way. If the battles waged in Afghanistan are framed as an issue of fighting terrorism, the public thinks about the war in a much more favorable light than if these conflicts are framed by the casualties incurred. Framing can have a very powerful effect, actually changing public opinion on an issue.

Checkpoint

Can you:

- ☐ Define the propaganda model
- ☐ Distinguish selective exposure from selective perception
- ☐ State three ways media coverage of the news affects politics

framing: *Ability of the media to influence public perception of issues by constructing the issue or discussion of a subject in a certain way.*

Connections: Do you trust the news media? What source, if any, gets it right?

Evaluating the News Media

> **How the news media can be evaluated**

Concerns about the modern news media are widespread. Worries about the news media often center on two general concerns. One is that the media are biased and do not present objective information. The second, which is related, focuses on the general quality of information available to the public. The emphasis on soft news, for example, worries observers who do not think the public has enough exposure to more substantive hard news. Without enough hard news, these observers fear, the public will not be well enough informed to hold elected officials accountable.

Whether these concerns are valid or not (we examine them later), it is clear that the public's faith in the press has declined (see Figure 7.4). In 1973, 15 percent of the public had "hardly any" confidence in the press and 23 percent had "a great deal." Thirty-five years later those numbers had flipped. Only 9 percent of the public had "a great deal" of confidence and 45 percent had "hardly any."[65]

Is there reason to worry about the media? Are the mass media of the twenty-first century less able to fulfill their watchdog role? This section looks at media bias, the quality of information, and the implications of the Internet and media choice.

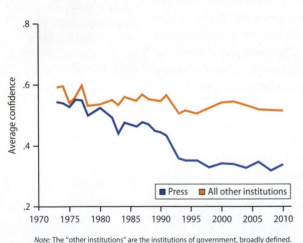

Note: The "other institutions" are the institutions of government, broadly defined.

FIGURE 7.4 **Public Confidence in the Press, 1973–2010.**

Source: Jonathan M. Ladd ; *Why Americans Hate the Media and Why It Matters.* Princeton University Press, 2012. Reprinted by permission of Princeton University Press.

Are the Media Biased?

The press claims to be objective, and professional journalists subscribe to an ethic of neutrality. Yet, given that even the selection of stories covered influences public opinion, bias may be inevitable.

With the rise of the 24-7 news cycle, bias in selecting what to cover becomes even more evident. For example, during the 2008 presidential campaign, three candidates—John McCain, already the Republican nominee, and Barack Obama and Hillary Clinton, still contending for the Democratic nomination—were scheduled to give speeches on the evening of June 2. McCain spoke first, and all of the major cable networks covered his speech. During the middle of the speech, however, Obama secured the few extra delegates that officially gave him the presidential nomination. MSNBC broke away from McCain's speech to announce this important development. Fox News did not. It flashed the information on the lower part of the screen, but continued to cover McCain's speech. Both networks were informing the public, but they were making different choices about what was most newsworthy and what was not. Insofar as MSNBC's choice seemed to support a liberal outlook and Fox's choice a conservative outlook, they might be described as biased.

A broader point is that, for many years, conservative commentators have claimed that the news media are liberal. Accuracy in Media, a conservative watchdog organization, contends that more than 80 percent of mainstream journalists support the Democratic Party. Such partisan loyalties, according to critics, drive the liberal bias.[66] Yet the people who own the most major media outlets—such as Rupert Murdoch, whose media properties include the *Wall Street Journal* and Fox News—are conservative. Should one assume that because most news outlets are owned by conservatives, the media are really conservative? It is far from clear whether the media are liberal or conservative.

The debate over whether the news media are too liberal or too conservative misses the central point about the news today. With so many sources of information, it is easy to find news with a liberal spin and news with a conservative spin. In fact, in the second decade of the twenty-first century, much news reporting is partisan, more like the party-dominated press of the nineteenth century than the objective and neutral press of the twentieth century. Media choice and multiple outlets mean that a Democrat can find a Democratic-leaning source for news and a Republican can find a Republican-leaning source. It is fair to conclude that individual news outlets are biased, but collectively the media provide a full range of ideological viewpoints.

Quality of Information

The idea that people are getting news from Ellen DeGeneres rather than from Walter Cronkite is disconcerting to political observers. The general worry is

Connections: If you think a media source is biased, do you ever listen to or view it? How can you evaluate it?

that people are getting less hard news and instead are relying on what we earlier called soft news—feature stores that are more personal and less policy focused, more sensationalized and less objective, than the political facts of hard news.[67] News about crime or natural disasters can fit the soft news category when the focus is about the drama surrounding the event (such as loss of life or homes) rather than a discussion of public policy that could reduce crime or perhaps provide quicker government response to disasters.[68]

Part of this underlying concern is the emphasis on image as opposed to substance. The assumption here is that visuals (television and Internet news, in contrast to print news) appeal to the emotions more than to the intellect, so visual news formats are in themselves less "hard" and more superficial. It is true that visual images convey impressions that go beyond the facts, but that does not mean that such information is not valuable. There is a great deal to be learned from visual images.

All media of communication shape how information is shared and digested. Radio, for example, puts a premium on the quality of people's voices. Consider politics before the invention of the microphone. Who were the most effective politicians? Perhaps it was individuals with deep voices that could project to a large audience. A soft-spoken politician would have been at a real disadvantage. It is also important to realize that images did not begin with the advent of television. Although it may be easier to engage in "image" politics in an era of video, politicians have always wanted to convey a favorable image and have done so using the media of their time. In the same way, so-called sound bites—very brief snippets of information—did not begin with the advent of television. Many observers fear that by stressing short catchy statements rather than more detailed substantive statements, sound bites undermine the quality of information. Campaigns, however, have always made effective use of simple slogans.

The purpose of this discussion is to urge caution in making hasty judgments about differences in the kinds of information available via the news media over the last two centuries. Soft news may be more informative than hard news because people find it easier to understand and more enjoyable. It is important, therefore, not to let the definition of what counts as news shape judgment of the press. That news reporting is no longer filtered by Walter Cronkite but instead by Bill O'Reilly does not mean the news media are no longer doing their job. They are just doing it differently.

Despite recent changes in the mass media, evidence suggests that Americans have as much information about politics as they did before the arrival of the Internet and the 24-7 news cycle. According to a 2007 survey released by the Pew Research Center for the People & the Press, "the coaxial and digital revolutions and attendant changes in the news audience behaviors have had *little* impact on how much Americans know about national and international affairs."[69]

Implications of the Internet

There is evidence that the arrival of the Internet has not changed the overall amount of information the public possesses, but it is important to acknowledge that the Internet is not equally available to all Americans. In 2009, only about 35 percent of Americans making less than $20,000 a year had access to the Internet; for those making $75,000 or more, the proportion climbed to 85 percent.[70] But these patterns are changing because of Internet access through mobile devices such as cell phones. In 2011, more than 60 percent of Americans had Internet access through their cell phones, so this technological shift is helping to bridge the digital divide.[71] Even with these shifts, older Americans continue to have less access to the Internet than do younger Americans.

These data suggest a further inequality—that those with Internet access may be much better informed than the public generally just twenty years ago, whereas those without access may be even less informed. Variations among groups buried in discussions of the public as a whole are significant. These variations will likely decrease as more people secure access to the Internet. Figure 7.1 on page 214, which shows the many options people have for information, suggests that Americans will move toward universal access. There will always be a gap between the well informed and the poorly informed, but in time the Internet will give older and less wealthy Americans a better chance to become informed about politics than they currently are.

Connections: What kinds of news do you seek? What should the American people seek?

The Era of Media Choice

Perhaps the best word to describe today's media environment is *choice*.[72] The spread of cable television, the Internet, and satellite radio means that people have many possible sources for political information, as well as a huge array of entertainment programming that may lead them to opt out of political news altogether. In the mid-twentieth century, when the network evening news was the source of information, viewers had fewer choices and less opportunity to opt out. The evening news was the only show available during the dinner hour. The lack of choice may have given people more exposure to politics than they wanted.[73]

TV network news standardized the information that many Americans had access to. With the wide array of choices now available, information is more polarized today. Viewers who choose a conservative TV network such as Fox and listen to Rush Limbaugh on the radio will have different information from those who watch MSNBC and tune in to National Public Radio. Those who lack interest in politics can avoid political news altogether. In other words, media choice cuts two ways: polarizing the type of information available, and making it possible to receive no political information at all.

The consequences of media choice are complex and are only beginning to be understood. New technologies in the future could further fragment

Connections: What are the consequences of media choice?

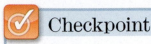

Checkpoint

Can you:

☐ State the concerns over media bias

☐ Track changes in the quality of news and information over time

☐ Survey the implications of the Internet

☐ Connect media choice to polarization

what Americans as a people know. Efforts to make political news more interesting may mean a further "softening" of the news. The main point is that Americans have access to a vast amount of information, but the availability of more information does not necessarily mean that the public as a whole is better informed. Moreover, people follow news outlets that conform to their existing ideological preferences. This self-segregation can fuel further polarization, because many people are not getting information from the other side.

The News Media and the Internet and Public Policy: Censorship

Any effort by government to control the media or to curtail the freedom of the press faces an immediate debate and often strong protest. When the courts decide between national security concerns and press freedoms, they usually support the press. Libel suits rarely result in convictions. Yet the advent of radio and television and the recent proliferation of electronic media have brought new challenges to determining what kinds of content should be restrained and what kinds should be allowed to flow freely. No government agency regulates the print media, but the Federal Communications Commission has the authority to regulate the content and ownership of radio, television, the Internet, and all electronic media. One area of special concern has been what might be considered obscene or offensive material.

Obscene Content in Broadcast Media

The landmark Supreme Court decision in *FCC v. Pacifica Foundation* (1978) established the precedent that the FCC has the legal authority to fine any media outlet that knowingly allows the expression of obscene content, under certain circumstances. The background of the case was that in 1973 a New York radio station aired George Carlin's monologue "Filthy Words," which included seven words that could not be said on the public airwaves. The station had prefaced the monologue with a warning to listeners that it included "sensitive language which might be regarded as offensive to some." A listener who was

Connections:
Should the government censor language on the air?

in the car with his young son when he heard the broadcast filed a complaint with the FCC.

The underlying question in this case was whether the First Amendment inhibits the power of the government to restrict the public broadcast of indecent language under any circumstances. The Supreme Court ruled in a 5–4 decision that the government could invoke limited civil sanctions against the radio broadcast of patently offensive words dealing with sex and excretion without violating the First Amendment. The Court also said that the words did not have to be obscene to warrant sanction and that, in decisions on whether sanctions on media content are fair and justified, other factors such as audience type, the time that the broadcast was aired, and how it was transmitted are relevant.[74]

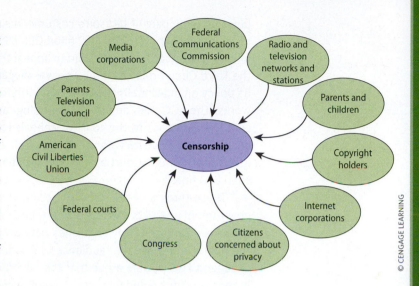

In today's television, music, and video climate, the boundaries for socially acceptable visual and verbal content are constantly evolving. Two recent cases reflect the ongoing policy discussion about acceptable restrictions on media expression. In *FCC v. Fox Television Stations,* Fox Broadcasting Company appealed fines that the FCC imposed for its 2002 and 2003 broadcasts of the Billboard Music Awards, during which participants uttered expletives. Fox claimed that participants on previous broadcasts had used similar language and that the FCC had ruled that the use was "fleeting" and was not seriously harmful, so it objected to a change in FCC enforcement with no warning. In a 5–4 decision, the Supreme Court ruled that the FCC needed to prove only that its new policy was justifiable and reasonable.[75] In response to what has been viewed as a stricter crackdown on language content, network television and radio stations have taken to "bleeping" or "buzzing" over words that might be viewed as harmful by the FCC. In live broadcasts, networks typically use a five-second delay in sending their signals over the airways to make sure they have time to bleep out offensive language. Cable television outlets are not under this same type of restriction because they broadcast to paid subscribers who thus have more control over the content they choose to view.

Using similar reasoning, the Supreme Court also ruled in support of the FCC in *CBS Inc. v. FCC*, which dealt with an incident during the halftime show for the 2004 Super Bowl. During a performance by Justin Timberlake and

Janet Jackson, part of Jackson's costume was ripped off, and her breast was momentarily exposed. The FCC fined CBS $550,000 for allowing the viewing of indecent images, and CBS sued to appeal the fine. The Court of Appeals for the Third Circuit ruled that the fine was illegal because the FCC had changed its policy on indecent images without notifying CBS and other broadcast networks. The FCC then appealed that ruling, and in 2009 the Supreme Court sent the case back to the court of appeals for reconsideration in light of its decision in the *Fox Television* case.[76] In April 2012 the Obama administration asked the Supreme Court again to reconsider the Janet Jackson case and the $550,000 fine.[77]

These three Supreme Court cases exert a significant impact on the way government restricts expression of speech and visual images through the media. Current policy distinguishes between media outlets that are free to the public and those that audiences subscribe to and pay for. Supporters of expanded FCC powers argue that the government has a compelling interest in keeping airways and television "clean" or at least in promoting content that does not contain language or behavior deemed socially undesirable. Opponents of a strong FCC believe that media content should be restricted only when it can be shown to be seriously and deeply damaging to the social fabric of the democracy. Given advances in the technical delivery of media content, such as the delivery of print and video to cell phone converters, further controversies involving FCC restrictions are likely to occur.

Safety, Social Networking, and the Internet

The Internet is not exactly a broadcast medium, but given its wide availability to the general public, Congress has sought to restrict its content. In 1996 Congress passed the Communications Decency Act, which established broadcast-style content regulations for the Internet. The act banned the posting of "indecent" or "patently offensive" materials in a public forum on the Internet, including in newsgroups, chat rooms, web pages, and online discussion lists. The American Civil Liberties Union (ACLU) challenged the law, and in 1997 the Supreme Court ruled unanimously that it was unconstitutional because it imposed sweeping restrictions that violated the free speech protections of the First Amendment.[78]

In 1998 Congress tried for a second time to limit content on the Internet when it passed the Child Online Protection Act (COPA).[79] The act made it a crime for anyone using an Internet site or e-mail over the Internet to make any communication for commercial reasons considered "harmful to minors" unless the person had prohibited access by minors by requiring a credit card number to access the material. In addition, the act imposed fines of up to $50,000 a day. Again, the legislation was ultimately struck down, this time by the Court of Appeals for the Third Circuit. The court ruled that COPA, like the Communications Decency Act before it, violated the First Amendment in that it "effectively suppresses a large amount of speech that adults have a constitutional right to receive and to address one another" and thus was too broad.[80] Further, in 2009 the U.S. Supreme Court refused to hear the government's appeal of this decision.

Congress subsequently responded by passing the Children's Online Privacy Protection Act (COPPA), which requires sites directed to children under the age of 13 to gain parental consent before collecting, maintaining, or using children's information. Parents can review their children's online activity under COPPA. The act also requires such a site to post a privacy policy on its home page and a link to the privacy policy on every page where personal information is collected.[81] In addition, in 2003 Congress passed a law designed to prevent the exploitation of children by prohibiting pornographic websites from showing sexually explicit material involving children on their home pages.[82]

In a related move, the government has acted to shield consumers from receiving unsolicited e-mail. The CAN-SPAM Act (2003) requires all commercial e-mailers to provide Internet users with the opportunity to opt out of getting further messages, restricts them from sending e-mail with false header information, and sets civil penalties for misleading subject lines on commercial e-mail.[83]

Although society has a legitimate interest in censoring explicit sexual and violent images on the Internet, the Supreme Court has repeatedly ruled that using broad or vague language to create blanket restrictions jeopardizes the right to free speech guaranteed by the First Amendment. Now that the Internet has created a global community, balancing the individual right to public expression and upholding community standards of behavior will continue to be a challenge in the twenty-first century.

Connections:
What should the government do about pornography on the Internet? If you think there should be a restriction of freedom of expression or access, what is the justification?

 ## Construct Your Own Policy

1. Establish a set of definitions for what constitutes indecent language or indecent exposure in public communication that is consistent with Supreme Court rulings.

2. Describe how social media companies such as Facebook and Google can take steps to prohibit individuals from using the Internet to commit crimes against children and but also maintain freedom of speech.

   For more information on the policy-making process, see Chapter 1.

The News Media and the Internet and Democracy

Focus Questions Revisited

- How do the mass media help make government accountable to the people?

- How has the rise of the Internet increased or decreased the ability of the public to hold government accountable?

- How does the bottom-up approach of twenty-first-century mass media affect citizen participation and equality? What are its other effects?

- When, and under what conditions, should government regulate the media?

- In what ways do the mass media offer gateways to American democracy? In what ways do the modern media establish new gates?

The news media, as watchdogs, are a central player in democratic politics. In the twenty-first century the mass media are far more open than they were just a few decades ago, providing additional chances to forge accountability, responsiveness, and equality. But these are only chances because the media are in the midst of a transformation the repercussions of which are not yet known.

For example, nearly all public appearances and statements of political figures can now be caught on video or audiotape. As a result, politicians have a tougher time ducking responsibility; they are more easily held accountable for their actions and words. However, the threat of being caught on tape in an embarrassing moment may encourage politicians to stay in "the bubble," sheltered from public scrutiny and shielded from assertive journalists or potentially harmful situations. Politicians build staffs and organizations designed to keep them from making mistakes and from interacting with journalists and citizens. They want to appear at staged events where they can control the message.

The more open and more democratic new media thus have the potential to let citizens know more about the politicians who lead them; they also give people more opportunities to express opinions for politicians to consider as they develop and enact laws. Thus blogs and other new media may help forge responsiveness. But these gateways have potential costs: The opinions may come from people who are not representative of the American mainstream. Information offered as fact in these settings has not been checked and is potentially filled with errors.

The many changes in the news media have also led to a decline in the number of professional journalists who are covering politics. With fewer professional journalists, the press may be less able to investigate stories that might unearth corruption or provide a more complete account of some politicians' backgrounds.

The decline in investigative reporting could, in short, undermine accountability. But there is some reason for optimism. For example, Paul Steiger, former editor of the *Wall Street Journal*, has formed a nonprofit organization called ProPublica that pursues investigations, offering the findings to newspapers and magazines. By taking advantage of funding from private sources, the organization offers a way to compensate for the decline of investigative journalism.[84] In a sense, the rise of the Internet has lessened the need for professional journalists, but the power of the Internet has also provided a way to pool resources and undertake important investigations. It is still too early to know how successful ProPublica will be, but in 2011 it secured its second Pulitzer Prize for investigative reporting.[85] Its presence alone underscores both the innovative uses of the Internet and the dynamic nature of the mass media in the twenty-first century.

Concern about the media's ability to advance democratic government comes mostly from people who favor a top-down approach for providing political information. For those who see the merit and appeal in a bottom-up approach, the changes seem far less worrisome. On average, the Millennial generation will not be so worried; these young people have grown up with the transformed mass media. They see the potential that the Internet and other media have for promoting equality—and for providing more chances to be part of the process. But until access to the Internet becomes universal, these changes offer more hope than reality.

Top Ten to Take Away

1. In a democracy, the people rely on the mass media for the information they need in order to hold government accountable and make it responsive. The press plays the role of watchdog, and the First Amendment protects the freedom of the press. (pp. 203–207)

2. The mass media perform three important tasks: informing, investigating, and interpreting the news. (pp. 204–205)

3. When the government attempts to constrain the press, the Supreme Court generally sides with the press, believing that it is better to protect press freedoms than to permit government censorship. (pp. 205–207)

4. Unlike the press, radio, television, and electronic media are heavily regulated by the Federal Communications Commission. (p. 207)

5. The history of the press in America is dynamic, developing from occasional pamphlets to comprehensive daily publications and online enterprises with a mix of news and entertainment. The profession of journalism has developed over time as well, with a commitment to objectivity. In the 1950s television began to replace newspapers as the source of news. (pp. 208–213)

6. In the twenty-first century technological advances are changing the media environment once again. The rise of cable television, satellite TV, and the Internet make news available day and night. Soft news, with personal stories and emotional content, is replacing hard news. Blogs are evidence of a new bottom-up journalism by citizens. (pp. 214–221)

7. Political scientists describe the impact of the news media on the public as agenda setting, priming, and framing. (pp. 223–224)

8. Although the public has lost faith in the media and generally think the media are too liberal, media choice and multiple outlets ensure a full range of ideological viewpoints. The sources of information are changing, but the public has as much information about politics as ever. (pp. 224–228)

9. The decline of newspapers is a real concern. The decreasing number of journalists means that newspapers have less ability to inform and investigate. If the press cannot perform its watchdog role, the public loses a means by which it holds government accountable. (pp. 215–216, 232–233)

10. Technology has changed the media and the way Americans receive the news since before the nation was founded. Americans quickly adopt new technologies, and they have always sought the news. Increasing Internet access will eventually even out inequalities, giving all Americans a chance to be informed about politics. (pp. 214–215, 233)

Key Concepts

actual malice (p. 205). Why should actual malice be hard to prove in a nation with a free press?

agenda setting (p. 223). How can the news media influence political agendas?

framing (p. 224). Describe the health care debate as an example of framing.

libel (p. 205). Why is libel not protected by the First Amendment's freedom of speech clause?

minimal effects model (p. 222). Why did scholars think the media only had "minimal effects"?

muckraking (p. 211). Why is muckraking protected by the First Amendment's freedom of press clause?

news media (p. 203). What is the role of the news media in a democracy?

not-so-minimal effects model (p. 222). What do scholars mean when they contend the media's effects are "not so minimal"?

penny press (p. 210). What was the effect of the penny press?

priming (p. 223). How do the news media prime the American public to hold certain opinions?

propaganda model (p. 221). Could the propaganda model ever be applicable to the United States?

selective exposure (p. 222). Why does selective exposure lead to reinforcement of beliefs?

selective perception (p. 222). How did selective perception help support the minimal effects model?

yellow journalism (p. 210). How does yellow journalism undermine accountability?

Your Virtual Tutor
aplia
Master What You Need to Know and Test Yourself.

Learning Outcomes

WHAT YOU NEED...

To Know	To Test Yourself	To Participate
Why the media are important in a democracy	• Describe the role of the press as watchdog • State the functions of the news media	• Evaluate whether the media are fulfilling this role today
How the law protects the press	• Name the laws, government agencies, and court rulings that regulate press freedom	• Consider whether the government should protect or regulate the news media
What trends define the history of the press	• State the Zenger case's importance • Describe the role of the press in the Revolution and ratification of the Constitution • Track the evolution from partisan press to yellow journalism • Elaborate on the ethics of professional journalism • State the effect of television on news reporting	• Analyze the importance of a free press to American democracy • Decide if the profit motive for the mass media is a gateway to democracy or a gate • Weigh the value of professional journalists against the value of citizen-journalists • Weigh the value of nationalized news against the value of media choice
How changes in the mass media have changed the information environment	• Describe the changing media environment • Survey the impact of the decline of newspapers • Survey the impact of developments in radio • Survey the impact of the transformation of TV news • Survey the impact of the rise of infotainment • Survey the impact of blogs • Survey the impact of social networking • Survey the impact of the changing media environment on young people	• Assess the twenty-first-century mass media as democratic and in service to democracy • Speculate on how the role of the news media will continue to change as the Millennial generation matures
How the news media affect public opinion	• Define the propaganda model • Distinguish selective exposure from selective perception • State three ways media coverage of the news affects politics	• Understand how your partisanship shapes your understanding of political news • Understand how the mass media can alter your political views
How the news media can be evaluated	• State the concerns over media bias • Track changes in the quality of news and information over time • Survey the implications of the Internet • Connect media choice to polarization	• Assess media bias • Decide which source for news you trust • Debate whether the Internet increases citizen equality or impedes it • Assess the connections between media choice and polarization

> "Citizens are the engineers of their own destiny. They have to be proactive in order to achieve the goals they set for themselves and for the nation as a whole."

Al Baker,
University of Idaho,
Moscow

8

Interest Groups

At the University of Idaho, Al Baker was a mechanical engineering student and a gun rights activist. While in college, he served as Idaho's state director for Students for Concealed Carry on Campus (SCCC) and the organization's Rocky Mountain regional director, where he worked with college students, parents, teachers, and other educators to persuade state legislators and college administrators "to grant concealed handgun license holders the same rights on college campuses that those licensees currently enjoy in most other unsecured locations." This is the group's mission statement. Today the group is known as Students for Concealed Carry (SCC), and Baker continues to serve as Idaho's state director as well as legal liaison while he pursues his graduate studies at the University of Idaho College of Law.

SCC was founded in April 2007, in response to the tragic loss of life in the shooting deaths on the Virginia Tech campus. Chris Brown, a political science major at the University of Texas, organized SCC from his dorm room. Beginning with a website and Facebook, the organization now has more than 350 chapters on college campuses and universities and some

43,000 members. Although the group's core principle is gun rights, it is not officially associated with the National Rifle Association or with any political party.

Baker, a sportsman and a responsible firearms owner, has been a campus leader in SCC since its inception. He wants colleges and universities to allow members of their communities to legally carry licensed concealed weapons because, he points out, students are citizens and they have an actual need for self-defense in light of the crimes common on college campuses, including assault, robbery, and rape. On February 13, 2008, Baker testified before the Idaho state legislature in favor of a bill that

aplia Need to Know

- **How interest groups have developed over time**
- **What types of interest groups have evolved**
- **What activities interest groups engage in**
- **What balances out power among interest groups**
- **What makes an interest group successful**

would prevent localities from banning guns. He made the point that the tragedy at Virginia Tech and other campus shootings have made students afraid of being attacked on campus. Students need to be able to protect themselves, he argued. Challenged that the risk of violence from armed students in the classroom would outweigh any potential protection guns on campus might provide, Baker disagreed. Students are at the mercy of crazed gunmen, he countered: "We sit there as sitting ducks waiting and hoping some madman doesn't come and kill us." For Baker and the members of SCC, it is better to have the opportunity to fight off an attacker with a gun than to be a victim. As an interest group, the SCC serves as a gateway to influence that allows students to make their views about gun rights known throughout the nation.

SCC students lobby state legislators in defense of their position as well as sign petitions, write letters and op-ed pieces, organize e-mail drives, and plan Empty Holster protests, days on which members wear empty holsters on campus to call attention to their cause. In 2009, the group filed a lawsuit against the University of Colorado Board of Regents' ban on legally concealed weapons on campus. Groups that support gun rights, including the National Rifle Association, filed briefs supporting SCC's position; they were opposed by gun control advocates, including the

Brady Center. On March 5, 2012, the Colorado Supreme Court struck down the ban, giving SCC its most significant legal victory in support of its efforts to allow students to carry guns on campus. Whether one agrees or disagrees with SCC's perspective, its grassroots origins and current activities are examples of students engaging in collective action to generate change and using university and political resources to raise awareness and support for a cause.[1]

Small or large, student-run or established national organizations more than a century old, interest groups are a mechanism of representation in a democracy because they help translate individual opinions and interests into outcomes in the political system. Interest groups form for many reasons: to advance economic status, express an ideological viewpoint, influence public policy, or promote activism in international affairs. In a democracy, the most crucial role of interest groups is their attempt to influence public policy. In this chapter we examine the history of interest groups, why they form, what they do, and their impact on democratic processes. We also identify how and why some groups are more influential than others. Throughout the chapter we focus on interest groups as gateways to citizen participation and, at the same time, point out how they can erect gates when they pursue narrow policy interests.

FocusQuestions

- How do interest groups influence economic and social policy?
- How do interest groups help or hinder government responsiveness to all citizens in an equal and fair way?
- Are interest groups themselves democratic organizations? Are their leaders accountable to their members? Explain.
- Do interest groups balance each other out across income levels, regions, and ethnic backgrounds? Explain and give examples.
- Are interest groups gates or gateways to democracy?

Interest Groups and Politics

> **How interest groups have developed over time**

In 1831 the French political theorist Alexis de Tocqueville came to the United States to observe American social and political behavior. He stayed for more than nine months and later published his study as *Democracy in America,* a classic of political literature. He wrote, "The most natural right of man, after that of acting on his own, is that of combining his efforts with those of his fellows and acting together. Therefore the right of association seems to me by nature almost as inalienable as individual liberty."[2] Tocqueville noticed that Americans in particular liked to form groups and join associations as a way of participating in community and political life. To Tocqueville, the formation of group life was an important element of the success of the American democracy.

Connections: Why do you think Americans like to join organizations? How does this tendency relate to American political culture?

What Are Interest Groups?

Tocqueville used the term *association* to describe the groups he observed throughout his travels in America; today we call them interest groups. An **interest group** is a group of citizens who share a common interest, whether a political opinion, religious affiliation, ideological belief, social goal, or economic objective, and try to influence public policy to benefit members. Other types of groups form for purely social or community reasons, but this chapter focuses on the groups that form to exert political influence.

Most interest groups arise from conditions in public life. A proactive group arises when an enterprising individual sees an opening or opportunity to create the group for social, political, or economic purposes. A reactive group forms to protect the interests of members in response to a perceived threat from another group, or to fight a government policy that the members believe will adversely affect them, or to respond to an unexpected external event. Groups whose members share a number of common characteristics are described as homogeneous, whereas groups whose members come from varied backgrounds are described as heterogeneous. All interest groups are based on the idea that members joining together in a group can secure a shared benefit that would not be available to them if they acted alone.

Citizens most often join groups to advance their personal economic well-being, to get their voices heard as part of a larger group's efforts on an issue, or to meet like-minded citizens who share their views. There is no legal restriction on the number of groups that people can join, and citizens are frequently members of a number of organizations. On the large scale, citizens join groups as a way of participating in democratic society.

interest groups: *Groups of citizens who share a common interest—a political opinion, religious or ideological belief, a social goal, or an economic characteristic—and try to influence public policy to benefit themselves.*

right of association:
Right to freely associate with others and form groups, protected by the First Amendment.

Connections: Do you think interest groups are divisive and polarizing? Or do they bring citizens together? Can you give examples to support your opinion?

faction: *Defined by Madison as any group that places its own interests above the aggregate interests of society.*

right of petition: *Right to ask the government for assistance with a problem or to express opposition to a government policy, protected by the First Amendment.*

Connections: Have you ever signed a petition? What was it for?

lobbying: *Act of trying to persuade elected officials to adopt a specific policy change or maintain the status quo.*

The Right to Assemble and to Petition

The First Amendment states that Congress cannot prohibit "the right of the people peaceably to assemble, and to petition the Government for a redress of grievances." This right to assemble is the **right of association**. The Framers understood that human beings naturally seek out others who are similar to them, and the Framers believed that the opportunity to form groups was a fundamental right that government may not legitimately take away. At the same time, however, they were fearful that such groups, which Madison called **factions**, might divide the young nation. In *Federalist* 10 Madison wrote, "By a faction I understand a number of citizens, whether amounting to a majority or minority of the whole, who are united and ac-tuated by some common impulse of passion, or of interest, adverse to the rights of other citizens, or to the permanent and aggregate interests of the community." Although he recognized that such groups could not be sup-pressed without abolishing liberty, he also argued in *Federalist* 51 that, in a large and diverse republic, narrow interests would balance out each other and be checked by majority rule. (See *Federalist* 10 and *Federalist* 51 in the Appendix.) Factions are not exactly the same as political parties, which form explicitly to win elections (and which we examine in Chapter 9, Po-litical Parties), but Madison feared they could have the same divisive or polarizing effect in a democracy. Nevertheless, the Bill of Rights contains protections for the rights of association and petition because these rights are essential for citizens to be able to hold their government accountable, ensure the responsiveness of elected officials, and participate equally in self-government.

The **right of petition** gives individuals with a claim against the govern-ment the right to ask for compensation, and it also includes the right to pe-tition to ask for a policy change or to express opposition to a policy. It was the earliest and most basic gateway for citizens seeking to make government respond to them. In the twenty-first century groups such as change.org use the Internet to make it possible for individuals to directly "ask" Congress for a benefit via e-mail or to sign onto a "virtual" petition that can be presented to Congress. Interest groups also use their high membership numbers as a proxy for the direct expression of support that once came from petitioners' personal visits to lawmakers.

Today the rights of association and petition most often take the form of **lobbying**, or trying to persuade elected officials to adopt or reject a spe-cific policy change. Lobbying is a legitimate form of petitioning, and interest groups of all sizes and purposes engage in it, from Students for Concealed Carry on Campus, to big corporations such as Microsoft and Google, to large-scale grassroots groups such as the Sierra Club. The term *lobbying* was coined more than three hundred years ago when individuals seeking favors from the British government would pace the halls, or lobbies, of the Parliament building, waiting for a chance to speak with members. The practice was immediately adopted in the new United States. Lobbying is well established as a means of political participation in America.

Interest groups lobby the legislative, executive, and even judicial branches of government at the state and federal levels. For example, when groups lobby Congress or state legislatures, they typically meet with members' staff aides to make the case for their policy goals. Lobbyists may also try to influence the executive branch by meeting personally with key bureaucrats and policy makers. Lobbying of the judicial branch takes the form of lawsuits against government policies that interest groups see as fundamentally unconstitutional or that go against the original intent of law. Such lawsuits can be high profile and are initiated by groups of all political ideologies. For example, cases orchestrated by the National Association for the Advancement of Colored People (NAACP) and other liberal interest groups ended school segregation (see Chapter 5, Civil Rights). For other cases, interest groups can also submit *amicus curiae* briefs ("friend of the court") that record their opinions even if they are not the primary legal participants in a case. Interest groups also lobby for and against judicial nominees, especially Supreme Court appointments. Lobbying strategies and tactics differ according to the branch of government at the state and federal levels, but no government entity is outside the scope of lobbyists' efforts.[3]

Checkpoint

Can you:

☐ Describe what an interest group is

☐ Explain why Madison and the Framers feared factions

Types of Interest Groups

> ### What types of interest groups have evolved

Because the universe of interest groups is so large and diverse, it can be helpful to categorize groups by their core organizing purposes and the arenas in which they seek to influence public policy. In this section, we survey three types of interest groups—economic, ideological, and foreign policy–focused—to illustrate and explain differences in interest group policy goals and strategies.

Economic Interest Groups

Economic interest groups form to advance the economic status of their members and are defined by a specific set of financial or business concerns. Their membership bases tend to be exclusive because their purpose is to secure tangible economic benefits for themselves; if they grow too large or too

economic interest group: *Group formed to advance the economic status of its members.*

inclusive, members' benefits are necessarily diluted. However, if the underlying industries represented by these groups disappear or merge with others, the groups have to adapt in order to attract new members.

Trade and Professional Associations.

Trade associations focus on particular businesses or industries and make up a subcategory of economic interest groups. Examples include the National Association of Manufacturers, the Chamber of Commerce, the National Retail Federation, and the Semiconductor Industry Association. Trade associations form because business owners believe that they will have more influence on the policy process collectively than they would individually.

Professional associations are formed by individuals who share similar jobs. Examples include the American Bar Association (lawyers), the American Medical Association (doctors), and the American International Automobile Dealers Association (car dealers). These associations are frequently responsible for setting guidelines for professional conduct—from business practices to personal ethics—and for collectively representing the members in the policy process.

Connections: What are the professional associations in the career field you are thinking of now? Are they worth joining?

Corporations.

Large corporations are a type of economic interest group in that they try to influence policy on their own as well as by joining trade associations comprising businesses with similar goals. Corporations such as Wal-Mart, Comcast, and Boeing have thousands of employees, and that alone encourages politicians to listen to their concerns. Recently, corporations have aggressively contributed to political campaigns to influence policy, as will be discussed in detail later in this chapter. (For more on campaigns, see Chapter 10, Elections, Campaigns, and Voting.)

Unions.

Unions are a type of economic interest group that aims to protect workers through safer working conditions and better wages. They are traditionally organized as local chapters that are part of a national organization representing workers in specific fields and industries. For example, autoworkers might join the United Auto Workers (UAW), truck drivers the International Brotherhood of Teamsters, health care workers the Service Employees International Union, and high school teachers the National Educational Association.

unions: *Interest groups of individuals who share a common type of employment and seek better wages and working conditions through collective bargaining with employers.*

Unions' strength comes from their ability to call or threaten strikes and to bargain collectively with employers over wages and working conditions. In recent years, however, collective bargaining by public sector unions, such as those representing teachers and government employees, has come under attack by advocates for smaller government, including members of the Tea Party movement. In Indiana, Wisconsin, and Ohio, Republican governors and state legislators have severely curtailed the collective bargaining rights of state workers. Unions have fought back, however. In November 2011, Ohio voters repealed a law they viewed as too restrictive on the rights of union workers.[4] And in Wisconsin, Governor Scott Walker faced a recall election in June 2012 that was instigated primarily by supporters of collective bargaining rights, but he defeated the Democratic challenger 53 to 46 percent.[5] The biggest threat to unions, however, is the loss of jobs in the industries they represent. Then union membership shrinks, and the smaller the union, the less power it can exert on both manufacturers and elected officials. Following the Triangle fire, the ILGWU grew very powerful, but as the manufacture of women's clothing shifted overseas, thousands of jobs disappeared. By 1976 the union existed in name only and merged with the Amalgamated Clothing and Textile Workers Union (ACTWU), but even that merger could not save it. By 1996 it was officially extinct.

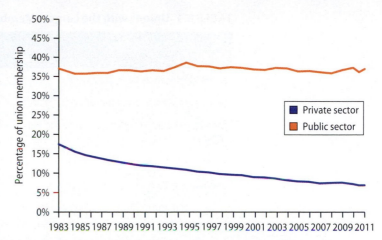

Notes: Data refer to the sole or principal job of full- and part-time workers. All self-employed workers are excluded, regardless of whether or not their businesses are incorporated. Data for 1990–93 have been revised to reflect population controls from the 1990 census. Beginning in 2000 data reflect population controls from census 2000 and new industry and occupational classification systems. Beginning in 2000 private sector data refer to private sector wage and salary workers; private sector data for earlier years refer to private nonagricultural wage and salary workers.

Percentages are based on the percentage employed.

FIGURE 8.1 Percentage of Wage and Salary Workers with Union Membership, 1983–2011.

Private sector union membership has been declining over time, while public union membership has increased.

Source: Bureau of Labor Statistics, http://www.bls.gov/news.release/union2.t03.htm.

Overall, private sector union membership has been declining (see Figure 8.1). Part of the reason for this decline is that government regulations now require the protections that unions long sought in terms of safe working conditions, overtime compensation, and nondiscrimination. In a sense, unions have been victims of their success in pushing for government regulations, and workers do not have to join a union to receive these protections. Thus the incentive for union membership has decreased. Additionally, as of 2012, more than one-third of states have right-to-work laws that allow individuals to choose not to join a union even if their workplace has a designated union in place.[6] Unions have responded to this downturn in membership by seeking to represent workers in a wider range of industries. For example, the UAW now represents cafeteria and janitorial staffs on college campuses all over the nation. Despite the downturn in membership in large industrial and manufacturing unions, unions representing teachers, health service workers, communications workers, and government employees have

Connections: Do you know any union members? Are you a union member, or would you join a union?

TABLE 8.1 Unions with the Largest Membership, 2012

Union	Number of Members (in millions)
National Education Association (NEA)	3.2
Service Employees International Union (SEIU)	2.1
American Federation of State, County and Municipal Employees (AFSCME)	1.6
American Federation of Teachers (AFT)	1.5
International Brotherhood of Teamsters (IBT)	1.4
United Food and Commercial Works International Union (UFCW)	1.3

Sources: National Education Association, http://www.nea.org/home/2580.htm; Service Employees International Union, http://www.seiu.org/a/ourunion/fast-facts.php; American Federation of State, County and Municipal Employees, http://www.afscme.org/union; American Federation of Teachers, http://www.aft.org/about/; International Brotherhood of Teamsters, http://www.opensecrets.org/orgs/summary.php?id=D000000066; United Food and Commercial Workers International Union, http://www.ufcw.org/about_ufcw/.

ideological interest groups: *Groups that form among citizens with the same beliefs about a specific issue.*

citizens' groups: *Groups that form to draw attention to purely public issues that affect all citizens equally.*

single-issue groups: *Groups that form to present one view on a highly salient issue that is intensely important to members, such as gun control or abortion.*

grassroots movement: *Group that forms in response to an economic or political event but does not focus on only one issue.*

all made large gains over the past two decades. Table 8.1 lists the top six unions in the country, which together have more than 11 million members. Today unions represent 11.8 percent of the overall workforce in the United States.[7]

American unions are both economically and politically powerful because they can mobilize their members to vote for candidates they see as favorable on issues such as higher minimum wages, standards for overtime pay, better access to health care insurance, worker safety, and international trade agreements.

Ideological and Issue-oriented Groups

Ideological interest groups form among citizens with the same beliefs about specific issues. We describe these groups as ideological rather than economic because economic benefits are not the primary basis for their existence. This category can include **citizens' groups** (Common Cause, Public Citizen), **single-issue groups** (National Rifle Association, Right to Life), and **grassroots movement** groups (MoveOn.org, National Organization for Women). Citizens' groups, sometimes called public interest groups, are typically formed to draw attention to public issues that affect all citizens equally, such as environmental protection, transparency in government, consumer product safety, ethics reform, and campaign finance reform. Single-issue groups form to present one view about a highly salient issue that is intensely important to its members, such as the right to carry a concealed weapon for members of Students for Concealed Carry. In contrast, broader organizations typically emerge in response to an economic or political event but do not focus solely on one issue. For example, MoveOn.org was founded by two wealthy men who were angry that President William Jefferson (Bill) Clinton (1993–2001) was impeached even though most people opposed the proceedings. MoveOn.org called for an end to the Iraq War during the George W. Bush administration (2001–2009). During the Obama administration, the group called for a fairer taxation system and greater advocacy for women's rights.[8]

Ideological groups provide a way for individual members to express their opinions on issues more forcefully than would be possible for any one person alone. Members of ideological groups benefit from knowing that others share their views and from feeling empowered. In this way, ideological groups can encourage political participation in a democratic society. At the same time, these groups contribute to the polarization of the American public. Because a group of this type gets its power from agreement within its ranks on a highly salient issue, it discourages debate and disagreement within the group and any type of compromise on that issue.

Ideological groups not only balance out each other but may also block the way forward. The intensity with which each side holds its position discourages cross-group dialogue and makes it harder for elected officials to achieve a reasonable and widely acceptable resolution of the issue. Because an interest group seeks a favorable government response on a narrowly defined issue important to it, the group can also create imbalances that verge on inequalities.

> **Connections:** How do ideological interest groups contribute to polarization?

Foreign Policy and International Groups

Some interest groups address cross-border concerns. Foreign policy groups form to generate support for favorable U.S. policies toward one or several foreign countries. International aid groups encourage citizens to provide voluntary assistance to people in need all over the world. International groups concerned with human rights work to call attention to violations in the hopes of ending oppression.

Groups That Influence Foreign Policy.
One of the best-known organizations that seeks to influence foreign policy is the American Israel Public Affairs Committee (AIPAC). This group aims to ensure a strongly pro-Israel American foreign policy and uses public advocacy, member mobilization, and campaign contributions to influence members of Congress to support its goals. AIPAC first formed in the early 1950s, and it claims credit for getting the first aid package to Israel—$65 million to help relocate Holocaust refugees—passed by Congress in 1951.[9] Today, AIPAC has more than one

hundred thousand active members and is widely considered to be one of the most influential groups of its kind in Washington.

Groups That Advocate International Aid and Support for Human Rights.

Religious organizations often encourage members to provide international assistance. For example, Catholic Relief Services sponsors the Global Solidarity Network, which allows college students to communicate with people living in small villages or towns in developing countries. The National Council of the Churches of Christ in the USA provides funding and coordinates religious and humanitarian missions to foreign countries.[10] Since September 11, 2001, Muslim organizations have been hampered by restrictions on fundraising and distribution of funds to Muslims in other nations, especially in the Arab world.[11]

Other interest groups focus attention on human rights violations or starvation in certain areas of the world. Many are **nongovernmental organizations (NGOs)**, which are not affiliated with any government and work hard to preserve their neutrality so that they can operate in as many parts of the world as possible. They illustrate the power of interest groups to draw attention to a situation occurring in a foreign land and to solicit a powerful response from both average citizens and elected officials.

Checkpoint

Can you:

☐ Describe the different types of economic interest groups

☐ Explain how ideological and issue-oriented groups can lead to polarization

☐ Compare and contrast the missions of foreign policy and international interest groups

nongovern-mental organizations (NGOs): *Organizations independent of governments that monitor and improve political, economic, and social conditions throughout the world.*

What Interest Groups Do

> ### What activities interest groups engage in

Interest groups perform a number of functions in the political process. They collect information about the implications of policy changes and convey that information to lawmakers and other policy makers. Their lobbying efforts aim to construct policies in ways that will most benefit their members. This section examines the tactics of lobbying, from providing information, to contributing to campaigns, to orchestrating grassroots movements that increase political participation on an issue. Lobbying is one of the fundamental gateways for expressing views and securing a favorable response from government officials.

Inform

All interest groups provide information to their members, the media, government officials, and the general public. The type of interest group dictates the kind of information it disseminates. Before the Internet, groups provided members with this sort of information through newsletters and sessions at annual conventions. Today they disseminate information on their websites and try to limit access by requiring members to register and sign in to the websites. Social media, such as Facebook and Twitter, also enable groups to keep members informed and to rally them to take action on the group's behalf.

Interest groups do more than merely report on current policy developments; they also provide members with interpretations of how the developments will affect their mission and goals. For example, in January 2012, when President Barack Obama rejected the application for the Keystone XL pipeline due to concerns about its environmental impact, the Sierra Club immediately posted a blog entry informing its members of the president's action and asking them to thank him.[12] Although Sierra Club members might be able to find information about the Keystone project from other sources, it would take them more time and effort to gather a complete picture. Interest groups such as the Sierra Club see it as their responsibility to effectively package information to members in the most efficient and complete way possible. Interest group positions on the Keystone Pipeline project are examined later in the chapter.

Interest groups also work hard to inform government officials about the impact of specific public policies. Most of the time, lobbyists have pro or con positions on a policy proposal, and their goal is to persuade government officials to agree with their perspective. Legislators and government officials are generally knowledgeable in their areas of expertise, but the vast size of the federal and state governments makes it hard to know the impact of policies on every citizen. Economic and ideological groups constantly monitor policies that might affect their members in a positive or negative way and strive to make legislators and government officials aware of the impact of policy proposals.

Groups convey information via e-mail, telephone, and personal meetings with staff, elected officials, and bureaucrats. For example, the National Education Association, a teachers' union, sent a letter to the Obama administration commenting on its proposed rules for implementing the Race to the Top program, which is designed to provide funds to local communities to improve education. In this letter, the NEA supported some of the provisions but was critical of others, in this way conveying the views of its members to bureaucrats.[13] The NEA then posted the letter on its website to inform teachers across the country about the specific ways that the program might impact their schools and school systems.

Lobby

Almost every kind of group with every kind of economic interest or political opinion—including business firms, trade and professional organizations, citizens' groups, labor unions, and universities and colleges—engages in one

Connections: When interest groups gather and disseminate information, are they performing a public service? Or do they do it just to advance their own causes? If so, is there anything wrong with that?

form of lobbying or another.[14] State, county, and city government officials maintain lobbying offices in Washington, D.C., both separately and as part of larger national groups like the National Governors Association or the United States Conference of Mayors. Lobbyists for these government entities frequently visit with the state's congressional delegation to keep the representatives informed about how federal programs are operating back home and to ask for legislation that will benefit their states. Mayors and county executives do the same thing, trying to influence their state legislators and governor by keeping them informed about how policies affect their constituents.

Groups can use their own employees as lobbyists or contract with firms that specialize in lobbying. According to the Center for Responsive Politics, in 2011 there were 12,654 individuals registered as active lobbyists in Washington, D.C. That amounts to nearly 24 lobbyists for each member of the House and Senate.[15] The offices of many of these lobbyists are concentrated in an area of northwest Washington known as the K Street corridor; when people say they work on K Street, it is safe to assume that they are lobbyists.

In 2011 interest groups and lobbying firms spent nearly $3.3 billion on a wide range of expenses associated with lobbying, including salaries for in-house lobbyists, consulting fees charged by lobbying firms, overhead for office space, and travel costs of staff[16] (see Table 8.2). In the past, the costs of lobbying also included paid trips for members of Congress and their staffs

TABLE 8.2 Top Spenders on Lobbying, 2011

Lobbying Client	Issues	Dollars Spent
U.S. Chamber of Commerce	Product liability, finance, copyright, patent and trademark	$66,370,000
General Electric	Defense, taxes, federal budget and appropriations	$26,340,000
National Association of Realtors	Taxes, finance, housing	$22,355,463
American Medical Association	Health issues, Medicare and Medicaid, doctor liability	$21,490,000
Blue Cross/Blue Shield	Health issues, taxes, Medicare and Medicaid	$20,985,802
ConocoPhillips	Taxes, fuel, gas and oil, federal budget & appropriations	$20,557,043
American Hospital Association	Health issues, Medicare and Medicaid, federal budget and appropriations	$20,452,147
AT&T Inc	Telecommunications, labor, antitrust and workplace, radio and TV broadcasting	$20,230,000
Comcast Corporation	Radio and TV broadcasting, telecommunications, copyright, patent and trademark	$19,260,000
Pharmaceutical Research and Manufacturers of America	Health issues, Medicare and Medicaid, copyright, patent and trademark	$18,910,000

Sources: Center for Responsive Politics, "Lobbying: Top Spenders, 2011." Copyright © 2012 by Center for Responsive Politics. Reproduced by permission. www.opensecrets.org.

(known as junkets), as well as expensive meals. Lobbyists justified these expenses as a way of getting to know members of Congress in a smaller and more relaxed setting, which they claimed would enable them to enhance their or their client's influence in the policy process. In 2007 congressional ethics reforms prohibited paid trips and meals for members and staff.[17] Still, lobbyists can use money to maintain their influence in other ways. For example, their salaries typically include allocations to make strategic campaign contributions to members of Congress who preside over issues that are important to their companies or clients.[18]

During a typical day, lobbyists phone, e-mail, or meet with congressional staffers, their clients, and possibly members of the media to gather information about relevant issues for their clients or to promote their clients' policy positions. Lobbyists also attend congressional hearings, executive branch briefings, and even committee markups in which members of Congress write legislation. Interest groups, businesses, and industries do not survive by lobbying only, but lobbying is a natural outgrowth of their purpose, because members expect their leaders to advocate for them when it is necessary to do so.

Campaign Activities

Interest groups also promote their views by engaging in campaign activities, though federal law regulates their participation through the Federal Election Commission. Candidates and their campaign organizations must comply with reporting and disclosure requirements, which are monitored by the FEC. Groups with tax-exempt status are prohibited from engaging in any activity on behalf of a candidate or party in an election campaign. These groups, commonly referred to as **501(c)(3) organizations**, after the section of the Internal Revenue Code that governs their activities, are likely to be charities, religious organizations, public service organizations, employee benefit groups, and fraternal societies, which are exempt from paying federal tax. Although they cannot engage in lobbying in any significant way, they can produce voter education guides or other nonpartisan educational materials that explain issues brought up during a political campaign and keep the public informed.[19]

Groups that fall outside the tax-exempt category are free to engage in lobbying and campaign activities. But to set boundaries between the group's core mission and politics, they generally create parallel organizations that make campaign contributions to legislators. These **political action committees (PACs)** raise funds to support electoral candidates and are subject to campaign finance laws (see Chapter 10). In one sense, PACs serve as gateways for expanding interest groups' political influence through financial involvement in campaigns.

501(c)(3) organizations: *Tax-exempt groups that are prohibited from lobbying or campaigning for a party or candidate.*

political action committees (PACs): *Groups formed to raise and contribute funds to support electoral candidates and that are subject to campaign finance laws.*

Connections:
Should there be
limits on how much
money interest groups
can contribute to
campaigns? Why or
why not?

PACs began growing in number and force after the Supreme Court's landmark decision *Buckley v. Valeo* (1976) upheld limits on donations to congressional campaigns.[20] As the costs of campaign spending rose over time, groups realized that creating or expanding an affiliated PAC to make campaign contributions could increase their influence over elected officials. Unaffiliated PACs, groups that make campaign contributions but are not associated with specific interest groups, also grew in size as a means of coordinating campaign contributions from individual citizens who wanted to express their campaign support as part of a larger group. All PACs make campaign contributions to the candidates whom they believe will be supportive of their policy goals (see Table 8.3). Thus PACs expand the reach of interest groups well beyond lobbying to include active engagement in the electoral arena.

Given the amount of money that PACs spend on campaign support, many observers have expressed concern that PACs exert a disproportionate influence over legislators, which creates an imbalance in government responsiveness toward some groups. However, scholars have had difficulty establishing exactly what PACs are getting for their money. Although campaign contributions can make it easier for groups to get access to legislators, they generally do not buy results. Interest groups tend to lobby and contribute to members of Congress who are leaning in their direction, so it is difficult to prove the impact of a campaign contribution.[21]

More generally, campaign finance laws impose limits on what interest groups can do in terms of issue advocacy, the practice of running advertisements or distributing literature on a policy issue rather than for a specific candidate. In general, the Supreme Court has ruled that campaign spending is a form of speech and that, as with other forms of speech, Congress must show a compelling interest before it can pass laws to regulate it. The McCain-Feingold Bipartisan Campaign Reform Act (2002) restricted corporations and unions from using television and radio ads for "electioneering communications"—commercials that refer to a candidate by name—within thirty days of a primary and sixty days of a general election. Since 2002 many groups have run ads that could be interpreted as issue advocacy or as outright campaigning. In 2007 in *Federal Election Commission v. Wisconsin Right to Life, Inc.*, the Supreme Court ruled that if a campaign advertisement could be reasonably viewed as issue-based, it was protected under the guarantee of free speech and could not be prohibited under the McCain-Feingold Act.[22]

Running issue ads has become a regular feature of interest group activity, even in nonelection years. Before 2010, interest groups could run issue ads on specific issues within a certain time frame prior to an election according to federal election laws; many interest groups used these ads to generate support or opposition to President Obama's health care plan before it became law. Although they served the purposes of interest groups, they also

Connections: Are
issue ads fair or unfair?
Are they informative or
"disinformative"?

TABLE 8.3 Top Twenty PAC Contributors, 2011–2012

PAC Name*	Total Amount	Percentage to Democrats	Percentage to Republicans
Honeywell International	$1,746,428	36%	64%
National Association of Realtors	$1,628,900	45%	54%
National Beer Wholesalers Association	$1,511,500	42%	58%
AT&T Inc.	$1,355,000	37%	64%
International Brotherhood of Electrical Workers	$1,319,150	98%	2%
American Association for Justice	$1,300,500	96%	4%
Lockheed Martin	$1,289,500	41%	59%
Credit Union National Association	$1,184,800	47%	53%
American Bankers Association	$1,146,100	25%	75%
Every Republican Is Crucial PAC	$1,101,000	0%	100%
Boeing Co.	$1,068,500	40%	60%
Carpenters & Joiners Union	$1,037,500	77%	23%
American Crystal Sugar	$1,021,500	54%	46%
New York Life Insurance	$991,500	44%	56%
National Auto Dealers Association	$985,000	28%	72%
Sheet Metal Workers Union	$984,500	92%	6%
Comcast Corporation	$980,000	48%	52%
Teamsters Union	$939,610	96%	3%
United Parcel Service	$917,290	31%	69%
Deloitte & Touche	$905,000	29%	70%

Note: Totals include subsidiaries and affiliated PACs, if any.

*For ease of identification, the names listed here are those of the organizations connected with the PACs, rather than the official PAC names.

Sources: Center for Responsive Politics, http://www.opensecrets.org, based on data released by the Federal Election Commission, March 5, 2012.

encouraged elected officials to be more responsive to constituents' needs because they focused attention on issues of importance to constituents. In 2010, the Supreme Court removed virtually all limits on issue ads, and individuals, corporations, and unions can spend as much money as they want on issue ads. (See this chapter's Supreme Court Cases: *Citizens United v. Federal Election Commission*, as well as the discussion of issue ads in Chapter 10.)

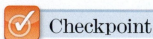 Checkpoint

Can you:

☐ Explain how interest groups keep members informed

☐ Describe how interest groups lobby

☐ Define political action committee

supremecourtcases

Citizens United v. Federal Election Commission (2010)

QUESTION: Can the government limit campaign spending by corporations and unions without violating First Amendment rights?

ORAL ARGUMENT: March 24, 2009, reargued September 9, 2009 (listen at http://www.oyez.org/cases/)

DECISION: January 21, 2010 (read at http://www.findlaw.com/casecode/supreme.html)

OUTCOME: No, governmental restrictions on corporate speech violate First Amendment rights (5–4).

In an attempt to equalize finances in political campaigns, Congress passed the Bipartisan Campaign Reform Act of 2002, also called the McCain-Feingold Act after its two leading sponsors. In 1976 the Supreme Court upheld limits on contributions to congressional campaigns but struck down limits on what independent groups unaffiliated with the campaign could spend. In response, McCain-Feingold restricted corporations and unions from using television or radio ads for "electioneering communications"—commercials that refer to a candidate by name—within thirty days of a primary or sixty days of a general election.

While corporations are often for-profit operations, such as General Motors or Microsoft, nonprofit and political entities such as the NAACP also organize as corporations under the tax code. One such political organization is Citizens United, a conservative interest group "dedicated to restoring our government to citizen control." During the 2008 Democratic primary campaign, it released a documentary called *Hillary: The Movie,* which was severely critical of Senator Clinton (D-N.Y.). Citizens United planned to show the documentary on pay-per-view television and to market it in advertisements on broadcast television. Concerned about violating McCain-Feingold, Citizens United sued the FEC, seeking an injunction prohibiting enforcement of the act as a violation of the First Amendment rights of corporations.

In a break with past decisions, the Supreme Court declared that corporations and unions had the same First Amendment rights as U.S. citizens. Using the compelling interest test (see Chapter 4, Civil Liberties), the Court ruled that Congress cannot disfavor certain subjects or different speakers. While recognizing that corporations may have more money to spend than individual citizens do, the Court ruled that First Amendment protections do not depend on the speaker's "financial ability to engage in public discussion." Such limitations violate the marketplace of ideas that the First Amendment is designed to protect. The ruling left open the question of whether Congress could limit the speech rights of foreign corporations operating within the United States.

The dissenters claimed that money is not equivalent to speech and that the law was a reasonable attempt to level the playing field in campaigns. President Obama attacked the decision in his State of the Union Address in February 2010.

- **Why is campaign spending a form of speech?**
- **Should corporations receive the same free speech protections as ordinary citizens?**

The Impact of Interest Groups on Democratic Processes

› What balances out power among interest groups

"I have often admired the extreme skill," wrote Tocqueville, "with which the inhabitants of the United States succeed in proposing a common object to the exertions of a great many men, and in inducing them voluntarily to pursue it."[23] Both Tocqueville and James Madison assumed that voluntary association or the forming of factions was a natural process of citizens interacting in a free society. Scholars have been interested in the same process, examining why interest groups form and what effects they have in a democratic society. In this section, we survey various perspectives on interest groups that relate to government responsiveness and citizen equality.

Natural Balance or Disproportionate Power

Over the last sixty years scholarly debate has centered on the process of interest group formation and its consequences. In the 1950s David Truman agreed with Tocqueville and Madison, describing interest group formation as natural. He observed that when individuals have interests in common, they naturally gravitate toward each other and form a group. So long as those individuals share a characteristic, opinion, or interest, the group continues to exist, but if the commonality disappears, the group disappears.[24] Writing in the mid-1960s, Mancur Olson argued that merely having something in common with other people was not enough to give a group life and keep it going as an effective organization.[25] Olson focused on the costs of organizing and maintaining a group, noting that costs increase as a group grows in size and reach. The people who pay membership dues expect benefits in return. To Olson, the cost-benefit structure that underlies group formation contradicts Truman's claim that all groups naturally form and sustain themselves.

The debate between Truman and Olson raises the fundamental issue of whether interest groups are natural and can compete on an equal basis or artificial because they distort public policy in favor of some citizens over others. Other scholars have addressed this question in different ways. Robert Dahl argued that in a **pluralist** society, the battles over public policy by the varied interest groups that emerge to represent their members will produce a consensus that serves the public's common interest.[26] As noted in Chapter 1, scholars such as C. Wright Mills worried that a power elite controlled power in the American democracy.[27] His concerns were echoed by Theodore Lowi, who argued that in a democracy some voices are louder than others and that government is more responsive to louder voices and will consistently serve such groups at the expense of those who cannot make their voices heard.

Connections: Do you think interest groups form from the bottom up or from the top down?

pluralist: *View of democratic society in which interest groups compete over policy goals and elected officials are mediators of group conflict.*

Connections: Do interest groups bring people into the democratic process, or do they strengthen some voices at the expense of others?

According to Lowi, this kind of policy making is elitist and fundamentally antidemocratic.[28]

Traditionally, the narrow focus of interest groups has engendered a sense of illegitimacy. Interest groups form and survive by appealing to a particular segment of society (economic, ideological, or social), so they are inherently exclusive. Exclusive groups act only in the best interests of their members, even if nonmembers thereby lose out. E. E. Schattschneider described this aspect of interest groups as an actual threat to democracy. He argued that if interest groups are given legitimacy because they claim to represent citizens' interests, but in fact they seek narrow benefits for their members at the expense of nonmembers, there is an inherent unfairness to them.[29]

There is a middle ground between these contrasting views. Given the approximately seven thousand registered groups in America today, it is clear that group formation is a natural outgrowth of the freedom to associate and of community life in which human beings share social, economic, and political goals. The interest group system provides multiple gateways through which individuals can see their views represented. Theoretically, because there are so many different interest groups, they balance each other, as Madison hoped they would.

But if Olson is right and successful cost-benefit strategies determine whether a group can survive or grow, groups led by individuals with sufficient time and money stand a greater chance of winning a policy fight than do groups without such resources. In this view, interests become **special interests**, a term with negative connotations that is more frequently used during campaign season to suggest that some groups exert a disproportionate amount of power in the American democracy. To the extent that a well-funded interest group can more easily pressure the government to produce policies that are beneficial to its members, government responds unequally across all citizens. In this view, financial advantage creates an artificial imbalance of influence that acts as a gate against equality.

Self-Service or Public Service

In assessing the relative power of interest groups in a democratic political system, it is essential to remember that interest groups do not pass or implement laws; they try to influence state and federal governments to enact their policy goals. To do so, they constantly interact with political parties, members of Congress, executive branch bureaucrats, and even the judicial system. The question of legitimacy of an interest group's activities comes when a victory for one group means a loss for another, or more broadly a loss for the general public.

For example, during most of the 1990s and 2000s, car manufacturers—acting alone and as part of their larger trade association, the American Association of Automobile Manufacturers—successfully lobbied to block efforts by environmental groups to secure an increase in government-mandated fuel

Connections:
What distinguishes a legitimate interest from an illegitimate interest?

Connections:
Do interest groups balance out each other the way that Madison thought they would?

special interests: *Set of groups seeking a particular benefit for themselves in the policy process.*

efficiency standards. These standards, known by the general term *corporate average fuel economy* (CAFE), are designed to ensure that automobiles use as little fuel as possible to run efficiently. The government has an interest in requiring such efficiency in order to promote energy conservation more generally. However, automobile manufacturers argued that increased fuel efficiency is more expensive to produce and that CAFE standards would cut into their profits and might even decrease sales. In other words, the auto manufacturers would pay the price for accomplishing the public goal of promoting energy conservation. On this issue, the self-interest of the auto manufacturers conflicted with that of the general public.

But by 2007, with high increases in fuel prices and a general increased awareness of global warming, President George W. Bush agreed to a modest increase in fuel efficiency standards. When President Obama took office in 2009, he reiterated support for those standards. In 2010 the Environmental Protection Agency issued final regulations putting those tougher standards in place.[30] At the same time, an economic crisis hit the American automobile industry, undermining its financial and organizational ability to fight the increases. As the economic health of the domestic automobile industry improved during 2011, the Obama administration felt freer to speed up the timetable for implementing those standards. The case of CAFE standards is one example of how time and circumstances almost always shift the playing field and the balance of power in the interest group arena.

The frustrating aspect of the role that interest groups play in a democracy is that groups contesting a single issue frequently talk over each other, not with each other. It is often left to members of Congress and the executive branch to balance their own responses to interest group requests and still maintain responsiveness to constituents and the nation at large. Over time, most interest groups experience wins and losses in the policy system; the necessary condition for a democracy is that every group has a chance to make its case.

Open or Closed Routes of Influence

Although interests may ultimately balance each other and changing conditions may ultimately level the playing field, the fact that a tightly knit group of specialists often controls policy areas raises concern about fairness both inside and outside interest group organizations. For example, lobbyists work to build good relationships with legislators and officials in the bureaucracy. Are lobbyists always thinking of their groups' members when they engage in their activities, or are they thinking about their next jobs? Do they constitute an insider group that is ultimately self-serving rather than serving the public?

Scholars have long used the phrase **iron triangle** to describe the relationship among interest groups, members of Congress, and federal agencies. In essence, an iron triangle is a network forged by members in three categories

Connections:
Name two or three interest groups that you think have a lot of power in American politics. Do you agree or disagree with their positions?

iron triangle:
Insular and closed relationship among interest groups, members of Congress, and federal agencies.

Connections:
Is government responsive to interest groups? Are interest groups responsive to the people?

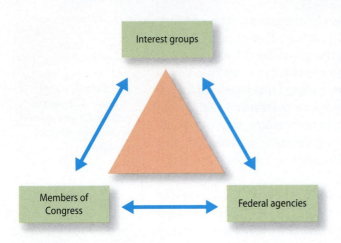

FIGURE 8.2 **Iron Triangle.**

The iron triangle is a policy-making structure that includes congressional committees, federal agencies, and interest groups.

© CENGAGE LEARNING

issue network:
View of the relationship among interest groups, members of Congress, and federal agencies as more fluid, open, and transparent than that described by the term iron triangle.

Connections: How does government prevent corruption among government officials?

revolving door:
Movement of members of Congress, lobbyists, and executive branch employees into paid positions in each other's organizations.

that works to seal off access to public policy making. Lobbyists and interest groups want to maximize their benefits from federal programs; members of Congress want to maximize their power to shape the programs; and federal bureaucrats want to maximize their longevity as administrators of these programs.

Critics of the influence of interest groups in a democracy often describe iron triangles as unbreakable and argue that they contribute to the inefficiency of the federal government because they sustain programs that should be eliminated or enlarge programs beyond what is necessary to meet their intended purposes. The term can be seen as operative in issues related to health care and prescription drugs (see Figure 8.2).

The well-known interest group scholar Hugh Heclo claims that the interconnection of interest groups and the government is more benign, suggesting that the term **issue networks** is better than *iron triangle* to describe the relationship.[31] Heclo argues that interest groups, members of Congress, and bureaucrats all share information constantly, and that their interactions are open and transparent, not closed. Heclo wrote thirty years ago, before the advent of the 24-7 news cycle, Twitter messaging, and other telecommunications innovations, so it stands to reason that it is harder than ever for self-serving interconnections to go unnoticed. In addition, citizens' watchdog groups, such as Common Cause, and policy institutes, such as the Center for Responsive Politics, monitor interest group influence on government activities and policies. When these groups find evidence of wrongdoing in government, they loudly blow a whistle by issuing reports and holding press conferences to inform the media and the general public.

What remains true is that lobbyists, members of Congress and their staffs, and members of the executive branch do pass through what scholars describe as a revolving door of paid positions in one another's organizations, with knowledge and experience on a specific issue the valued commodity. The term **revolving door** has a negative connotation, suggesting that an iron triangle of influence consists of the same set of people moving from one branch of government to another and then to the private sector. The image of a revolving door also suggests that the system does not stop to include outsiders with new perspectives; in other words, it can act as a gate against wider political participation.

Take, for example, Representative Billy Tauzin (R-La.), who as chair of the Energy and Commerce Committee was instrumental in passing the Medicare

Prescription Drug, Improvement, and Modernization Act in 2003. In 2005 Representative Tauzin left the House of Representatives to be named president of the Pharmaceutical Research and Manufacturers of America (PhRMA), a major beneficiary of that Medicare Prescription Drug bill. At the time, government watchdog groups were concerned about Representative Tauzin's behavior because he was in a position to provide disproportionate benefits to PhRMA in the Medicare bill, and PhRMA might have rewarded him for these benefits with a job when he left Congress. In 2009 Representative Tauzin led the negotiations on behalf of PhRMA with Democrats in Congress and President Obama on health care reform, but the deal they worked out was subsequently abandoned. The board of PhRMA was displeased, and Tauzin resigned his position in June 2010. Although it was never proven that Tauzin was "bought" by the pharmaceutical industries, at the very least the revolving door creates the perception that members of Congress and the bureaucracy are improperly influenced by industries seeking preferential treatment in an issue area.

It is also essential to remember that not all relationships among lobbyists, members of Congress, and federal officials are tainted or suspicious. Congress and the federal bureaucracy each have elaborate rules governing their behavior with respect to interest groups and lobbyists, and most members and bureaucrats follow them closely.

In the iron triangle, a member of Congress can serve as chair of a key committee, write legislation, and then leave to head an organization that directly benefits from the legislation. For example, Billy Tauzin (R-La.) chaired a key House committee that wrote legislation for the Medicare Prescription Drug Improvement and Modernization Act and then left Congress to head PhRMA, the interest group that represents drug manufacturers.

 Checkpoint

Can you:

☐ Compare the pluralist and elitist views of democratic society

☐ Explain why interest groups may be detrimental to the general public

☐ Recall the routes of influence that interest groups can use

Characteristics of Successful Interest Groups

› What makes an interest group successful

The measure of a successful interest group is how well it accomplishes its goals. Some groups want to stay in existence forever, but other groups form temporarily for a specific purpose and disband once they accomplish their goal. For the groups that want to establish an enduring voice in a democracy, success can be measured in four ways: leadership accountability, membership outreach, financial stability, and public influence.

Connections:
Identify two interest groups with an enduring voice in American democracy.

Leadership Accountability

As anyone who has tried to get a group of students together to perform a task, lodge a protest, or plan an event knows, coordination can be difficult. It typically takes an individual who acts as an interest group entrepreneur to organize citizens into a formal group that agrees on a united purpose. In return for organizing the group, the interest group entrepreneur typically takes a leadership role in directing the group's activities.

There are benefits that come from being a group leader, ranging from salary as a paid staff member to prestige and influence over the group's goals and strategies. The interest group scholar Robert Salisbury calls the trade-off between the work and the benefits of being a leader the "exchange theory of interest groups," and he argues that no one would rationally expend the energy and time to start a group if he or she could not take a prominent role in directing it.[32] Members are willing to pay their group leaders and give them power in the group in return for accomplishing the group's collective goals.

Transparency about the group's political and financial activities in pursuit of its goals is an important democratic element of an interest group; without it, there is a risk that the leaders could act in ways that do not properly serve the members. When leaders take such actions at the expense of rank-and-file members, the internal governance of the interest group breaks down. Flaws in interest group management can be a major problem for a democracy if citizens join a group with the expectation that the group will accurately represent their opinions and interests, and it does not.

Members must be able to register satisfaction or dissatisfaction with the group's leadership. The simplest way to do that is to leave the group, but in doing so, the individual may lose the benefits that the group provides. Using the group's website, members can convey their opinions to the leadership, but members cannot really control the group's actions, especially if the group is large. Citizens have a right to expect accountability from interest group leaders, and interest groups that want to sustain themselves understand that their membership needs to remain satisfied over time.

Membership Stability

Whether a group is small or large, attracting members and keeping them over time are essential to its survival. People join groups because they share similar interests or political viewpoints or because they want to protect their economic livelihoods. For the leaders of groups, the challenge is to find the right balance between membership size and the organization's purpose. Too many members may create internal disagreements about policy goals, but too few may weaken the group's ability to exert influence in the policy system.

Connections: How do groups perpetuate themselves at the expense of their mission? Can you give an example?

Selective Benefits.   One way to attract and keep members is to provide **selective benefits** exclusive to members.[33] These can include material benefits, such as direct monetary benefits from policies that the group advocates, discounts on travel or prescriptions, and even monthly magazines. Solidary benefits are less tangible. They range from the simple pleasure of being surrounded by people with similar interests and perspectives to the networking benefits of interacting with people who share professional or personal concerns. Expressive benefits are the least tangible in that they consist of having a specific opinion expressed in the larger social or political sphere. When individuals join a group, they know that their viewpoint is being actively represented in the policy system, and that knowledge can be gratifying all by itself.

The Free Rider Problem.   Many of the benefits that large interest groups seek on behalf of their members—clean air by the Sierra Club or gun rights by the National Rifle Association—are **public goods**. That is, they are available to all people, whether they have contributed toward the provision of that good or not. Public goods are typically the spillover effects of public policies that affect all citizens. If a group lobbies for public goods or collective benefits that are so widespread that members and nonmembers alike receive them, incentives to join the group disappear. Olson addressed this collective action dilemma, calling it the **free rider problem**.[34] Why pay to join a group if one can get the benefits for free? Why join if the group is so large that it does not actually need an additional member?

The Problem of Economic and Political Change.   Changes in the economy and the political environment can also have a negative impact on a group's membership stability. From a political standpoint, groups can "succeed" their way out of existence. The NAACP is an example: In the course of its hundred-year history, it successfully fought discrimination and secured civil rights, and today it seems less urgently needed than it was in the past. In recent years, the group experienced leadership turmoil and membership decline, and it has reformulated its core mission to focus on multiracial human rights.[35]

Financial Stability

Together with keeping a membership base, a group must also maintain financial stability. Groups of all types require money to sustain their organizations' staffing, lobbying, and information distribution. The Internet has made fundraising easier because it allows groups to solicit money without incurring costs for printed advertising, mailers, and postage. Most organizations also rely on dues. Grassroots groups that seek to attract as many members

Connections:
Would you join an interest group for its material benefits? Its solidary benefits? Its expressive benefits? What would make you decide to join?

selective benefits: *Benefits offered exclusively to members of an interest group.*

public goods: *Goods or benefits provided by government from which everyone benefits and from which no one can be excluded.*

free rider problem: *Problem faced by interest groups when a collective benefit they provide is so widespread and diffuse that members and nonmembers alike receive it, reducing the incentive for joining the group.*

as possible keep their dues relatively modest. For example, the dues for the National Rifle Association are between $35 and $125 a year.

Interest groups also achieve financial stability by creating not-for-profit businesses within the organization. AARP is a classic example of a large interest group that wears two hats: a politically powerful lobby on policies that affect senior citizens and a multimillion-dollar business that provides health insurance, life insurance, and discounts on movies, travel, and prescriptions to members, who have to be at least 50 years old to join. A basic AARP membership costs only $16 a year, and it provides the opportunity to purchase the other services at discounted rates. In turn, AARP receives payments from businesses that it contracts with to provide services to its members. AARP is among the most successful large-scale interest groups in American history; in 2010 it claimed a membership of 37 million and took in more than $248 million in operating revenue.[36]

The financial challenge for many groups is to keep their operating costs in line with their expected income. For the very largest interest groups, such as AARP, a single year's operating budget can be more than $1 billion.[37] Groups can experience financial difficulty as a result of financial mismanagement by group leaders, or, in some cases, they may simply outlive their usefulness and members cease paying dues. In such cases, they may be forced to scale back their activities and close local chapter offices.

Influence in the Public Sphere

The extent to which an interest group appears to influence public debate is a sign of its success. One indicator of influence is being quoted in the press. For example, in 2011–12, Grover Norquist and the interest group he leads, Americans for Tax Reform (ATR), were heavily featured in the press because they persuaded 236 U.S. House members and 41 U.S. senators in the 112th Congress to sign the Taxpayer Protection Pledge—a promise not to vote for any income tax increases. The mainstream media has portrayed Norquist and ATR as strongly influential in the debate over how to contain the federal deficit and reduce the national debt. ATR has vocally opposed any tax increase whatsoever and has publicized its intention to inform voters in the districts and states of members who break the pledge. Other, less dramatic, indicators of influence include a group's being asked to testify in Congress or being cited by an elected official when discussing a key issue of concern. Each such instance signals to the group's membership, as well as to the public at large, that it has a significant role in policy formation on the issues about which it is most concerned.

Checkpoint

Can you:

☐ Explain the importance of leadership accountability in interest group success

☐ Describe issues in membership stability

☐ Name sources of financial stability

☐ Identify indicators of interest group influence

Interest Groups and Public Policy: Energy Policy, Environmental Policy, and Jobs

Energy and environmental concerns become hot-button issues when increases in oil and gas prices hit the pocketbooks of Americans. Against the backdrop of higher energy costs, projects such as the Keystone XL oil pipeline, a Canadian funded pipeline that would run from Canada to the Texas coast, underscore the growing tension between groups such as unions who see the creation of the pipeline as a source of revenue and jobs, and environmental groups who see it as damaging to some of the nation's most important natural resources. Energy projects such as Keystone can act as a gateway for Americans today in terms of jobs, but it can be a gate against a future that ensures a clean environment in which to live and work.

Connections: Why are environmental issues that concern the creation of jobs difficult to resolve?

The Keystone Pipeline Chain of Events

On September 19, 2008, the energy company TransCanada submitted an application to the State Department to build a 1,700-mile oil pipeline from Alberta, Canada, to Nederland, Texas.[38] Because the project crossed over the border from a foreign nation, it fell under the jurisdiction of

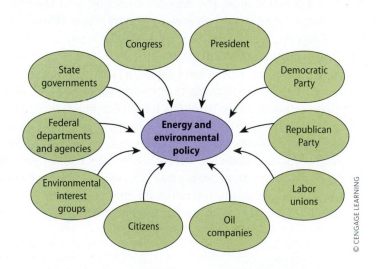

© CENGAGE LEARNING

the U.S. State Department, which required TransCanada to submit an application for a presidential permit.[39] Following submission of the application, the State Department conducted a study for an Environmental Impact Statement (EIS) to see if the pipeline would have any adverse environmental effects on the regions through which the pipeline would run. Although the State Department was designated as the lead agency for the review of the project, President Obama understood that the pipeline decision also fell under the jurisdiction of the Environmental Protection Agency (EPA), which is the federal agency charged with monitoring the environmental impact of federal policies.[40] Consequently, the EPA was also involved and reviewed the environmental impacts of the project.[41]

Almost two years later, on April 16, 2010, the State Department released a draft of its EIS, which stated that the construction and operation of the pipeline would have minimal environmental impacts. The State Department then solicited public comment on the draft. By the time the opportunity for public comment closed, in August, it had received thousands of public comments from interest groups and industry members with a stake in the outcome of the decision. On August 26, 2011, the State Department released its final EIS, concluding that the project was in line with President Obama's environmental policies.[42]

Although the State Department gave the go-ahead for the project, the EPA and numerous environmental interest groups were not persuaded by the State Department's findings. The division over the pipeline could also be seen in Congress, where representatives from both sides of the aisle struggled over the project and its merits. Proponents of the project saw it as key to economic growth in the United States, while opponents had serious concerns about the potential for environmental damage from a pipeline leak. The Republican majority in the House of Representatives wanted to push President Obama into making a final decision on the project, so, as part of a bill to extend the payroll tax cut (see Chapter 12, The Presidency), they attached a provision requiring that the president issue a decision within sixty days. On January 18, 2012, Obama responded by denying TransCanada the permit to build the pipeline, citing inadequate information to gauge its full environmental impact. One major concern was the pipeline's proximity to the Sand Hills region that covers the Ogallala Aquifer, which provides most of the drinking and irrigation water for the Midwest. Protection of the aquifer was also a major concern of the state of Nebraska.[43] In response to this concern, on May 4, 2012, TransCanada reapplied for the presidential permit to build the pipeline, proposing a route that avoided the Sand Hills region in Nebraska.[44]

The Tension between Unions and Environmental Groups on Keystone

Throughout the three-year presidential permit process, numerous interest groups, including labor unions, environmental activists, and energy producers, stated their positions on the Keystone XL Pipeline. In an interesting twist, labor and energy interest groups were allies, as both supported the construction of the pipeline. On September 14, 2010, the International Brotherhood of Teamsters and the International Union of Operating Engineers endorsed the pipeline.[45] A month later, on October 25, the presidents of four major labor unions urged the State Department to approve the pipeline.[46] For the unions, the building and operating of the pipeline would create jobs for their members, many of whom were unemployed.

Environmental groups, which normally find labor unions to be their ideological allies, vigorously voiced their objections against the pipeline.[47] Large and powerful environmental groups such as the National Resources Defense Council, the Sierra Club, and 350.org pooled resources to lobby against the pipeline. They were joined by celebrities and environmental activists such as Al Gore.[48] In addition to the concerns about the aquifer in Nebraska, environmental groups argued that the danger of oil spills, the creation of greenhouse gases,[49] and the overstatement of the number of jobs the project would create made the Keystone Pipeline beneficial to very few people and costly to everyone.[50]

> **Connections:** In the Keystone Pipeline debate, would you side with the labor unions or the environmental interest groups?

The Electoral Impact

The Keystone Pipeline presented a particularly difficult issue for politicians in 2012 because of the November presidential and congressional elections. President Obama attempted to delay a decision on the Keystone Pipeline until after the elections, in part because two key constituencies within his own party were divided over the issue. Environmental groups and labor unions were on opposite sides of the issue, so any decision would have alienated at least one core constituency in the Democratic Party. These divisions were also reflected among Democrats in Congress as well.[51]

As was discussed earlier in this chapter, interest groups donate to campaigns and help activate their members to vote. Two unions with interests in the pipeline—the Sheet Metal Workers Union and the Plumbers/Pipefitters Union—were within the top twenty PAC contributors to Democratic candidates in 2011–12.[52] The Teamsters Union, with well over 1 million members, also provides crucial votes for Democratic candidates in some areas of the nation. Union interest in the issue was a key reason why the Keystone XL Pipeline received heightened attention during the presidential and congressional campaigns.

Construct Your Own Policy

1. Develop policy criteria for deciding whether to grant TransCanada a permit to build the Keystone Pipeline.

2. Evaluate which set of interest groups should weigh more heavily in this decision from a public policy perspective and explain why.

   For more on the policy-making process, see Chapter 1.

Interest Groups and Democracy

Focus Questions Revisited

- How do interest groups influence economic and social policy?

- How do interest groups help or hinder government responsiveness to all citizens in an equal and fair way?

- Are interest groups themselves democratic organizations? Are their leaders accountable to their members? Explain.

- Do interest groups balance each other out across income levels, regions, and ethnic backgrounds? Explain and give examples.

- Are interest groups gates or gateways to democracy?

Interest groups are a powerful instrument of democracy because they crystallize the opinions and interests of average citizens and present those views to elected officials during the policy-making process. It was precisely this power to influence policy that Madison feared so much and why he hoped that in a large republic competition among interest groups would prevent any one of them from gaining too much influence. Interest groups contribute to a democracy by holding the government accountable for its actions, pressuring elected officials to be responsive to their constituents, and serving as a vehicle to equalize the influence of different groups of citizens in the policy process.

A group can channel the power of separate individuals into a single collective voice that is more likely to be heard throughout the policy system. In addition, the very existence of an interest group can keep citizens informed about the direct impact of policy on their lives; with that information, constituents can better hold their elected officials accountable for those policies.

Interest groups engage in several methods to influence economic, social, and foreign policy, including direct lobbying, media campaigns, legal challenges, and grassroots organizing. When interests clash, as in the case of the Keystone Pipeline, elected officials, bureaucrats, and even the judiciary often act as intermediaries. In Congress, political parties adopt positions that are favored or opposed by specific interest groups and thus create alliances between parties and interest groups. Although there are more interest groups today than ever before, political parties serve as a counterweight to the influence of interest groups. As partisanship has grown stronger in the House, the Senate, and even the White House, members who are asked to choose between an interest group and a political party choose the party. However, given that political parties tend to align very closely with supportive interest groups, members do not have to make that choice very often. To the extent that interest groups can influence politicians to address narrow or exclusive interests to the detriment of what is best for all citizens, they can be viewed as a negative aspect of the U.S. democracy.

Yet interest groups also represent a positive aspect of democracy when they serve to express wide-ranging viewpoints, and they continue to be an effective way of giving voice to citizens' needs and concerns. Interest groups continuously win and lose within the American policy-making system, and they reinvent their lobbying strategies in response to changing political and economic conditions. However, sole reliance on interest groups as a means of citizen participation is dangerous, because some groups have more re-sources—time, money, and membership—than others and consequently win more often. In this way, interest groups can be both gateways and gates to citizen equality and the securing of policy benefits. Ultimately, citizens must hold both their interest group leaders and their elected officials accountable for public policy outcomes.

gatewaystolearning

1. Interest groups are groups of citizens who share a common interest—political opinions, religious affiliations, ideological beliefs, social goals, or economic objectives—that try to influence public policy to benefit their members. (p. 239)

2. The constitutional basis for interest groups lies in the First Amendment, which guarantees both the right to assemble and the right to petition the government for redress of grievances. (pp. 240–241)

3. Individuals and interest groups lobby legislators and executive branch officials and attempt to influence judicial appointments and the courts through lawsuits and *amicus curiae* briefs. (pp. 240–241)

4. Interest groups can be categorized as economic, ideological, and foreign policy and international, and each has different policy goals and strategies. (pp. 241–246)

5. Generally, interest groups gather and disseminate information in their issue areas and contribute to political campaigns and advertising to the extent that federal law allows. (pp. 246–251)

6. Scholars who study why interest groups form and their effects in a democratic society debate whether the wealthy have disproportionate power to use interest groups to their advantage, and so to the disadvantage of others. Scholars also debate whether interest groups balance out each other. (pp. 253–255)

7. Lobbyists, federal regulators, and members of Congress form networks that some describe as "iron" and closed to citizen influence and some describe as transparent and open to citizen influence. (pp. 255–257)

8. Issue networks can tend or appear to be self-serving when members of Congress and federal agency employees leave their jobs to become lobbyists in the issue area of their specialty. (pp. 256–257)

9. The success of interest groups can be measured in four ways: leadership accountability, membership stability, financial stability, and public influence. (pp. 257–260)

10. In today's democracy, elected officials, bureaucrats, and even the judiciary often act as intermediaries in interest group conflict. (pp. 264–265)

Key Concepts

citizens' groups (p. 244). How are citizens' groups different from single-interest groups?

economic interest groups (p. 241). What are the concerns of economic interest groups?

faction (p. 240). When is an interest group the same as a faction, and when is it different?

501(c)(3) organizations (p. 249). Why are 501(c)(3) organizations prohibited from lobbying?

free rider problem (p. 259). Why are free riders a problem for interest groups?

grassroots movement (p. 244). How is a grassroots movement different from an interest group?

ideological interest groups (p. 244). How do ideological interest groups differ from economic interest groups?

interest groups (p. 239). How are interest groups a gateway to democracy?

iron triangle (p. 255). Describe the iron triangle as a gate against democracy.

issue network (p. 256). How is an issue network different from an iron triangle?

lobbying (p. 240). How is lobbying a form of an individual's rights of association and petition?

nongovernmental organizations (NGOs) (p. 246). What role do NGOs play in shaping U.S. foreign policy?

pluralist (p. 253). What is the role of interest groups in a pluralist society?

political action committees (PACs) (p. 249). How are PACs gateways for expanding interest groups' political influence?

public goods (p. 259). How should a public good be defined in a democracy?

revolving door (p. 256). What steps should Congress take to dismantle the revolving door?

right of association (p. 240). Why is the right of association a constitutional guarantee?

right of petition (p. 240). Why is the right of petition a constitutional guarantee?

selective benefits (p. 259). How do selective benefits attract and keep interest group members?

single-issue groups (p. 244). What is the impact of single-issue groups on campaigns and elections?

special interests (p. 254). What is a negative aspect to special interests?

unions (p. 242). What techniques do unions use to gain better wages and working conditions?

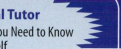

Your Virtual Tutor
Master What You Need to Know and Test Yourself.

Learning Outcomes

WHAT YOU NEED...

To Know	To Test Yourself	To Participate
How interest groups have developed over time	• Describe what an interest group is • Explain why Madison and the Framers feared factions	• Create strategies to get more people involved in interest groups • Debate the negative aspects of lobbying against the positive aspects of maintaining representation
What types of interest groups have evolved	• Describe the different types of economic interest groups • Explain how ideological and issue-oriented groups can lead to polarization • Compare and contrast the missions of foreign policy and international interest groups	• Devise an appropriate limit on the role of economic interest groups in a democracy • Consider whether single-issue groups help preserve constitutional rights • Consider whether foreign governments should be allowed to lobby members of Congress
What activities interest groups engage in	• Explain how interest groups keep members informed • Describe how interest groups lobby • Define political action committee	• Debate whether interest groups are a biased or unbiased source of information • Evaluate the potential impact of limiting the amount of money spent on lobbying • Assess the value of PACs as gates and gateways to democracy
What balances out power among interest groups	• Compare the pluralist and elitist views of democratic society • Explain why interest groups may be detrimental to the general public • Recall the routes of influence that interest groups can use	• Decide whether the United States should be a pluralist or elitist society • Propose ways of balancing power across interest groups • Propose ways to make interest groups help ensure government responsiveness and citizen equality
What makes an interest group successful	• Explain the importance of leadership accountability in interest group success • Describe issues in membership stability • Name sources of financial stability • Identify indicators of interest group influence	• Consider how internally democratic interest groups really are • Evaluate whether the free rider is a problem for democracy • Debate whether an interest group can be too powerful

> *Self-government is not an easy thing to do. It requires a lot from citizens. . . . I believe it is my obligation, not a choice, to be informed about my local, state, and national government.*

Josh McKoon, Furman University, Greenville, South Carolina

COURTESY OF JOSH McKOON

© JONATHAN ANDERSEN·WWW.JONATHANANDERSEN.COM

9

Political Parties

Josh McKoon, elected to the Georgia Senate in 2010, credits his experience at Furman University in Greenville, South Carolina, for launching "his lifetime commitment to conservative politics." As a political science and communications major, he volunteered on Republican Bob Dole's 1996 presidential campaign and worked for both a state representative running for Congress and a U.S. congressman running for the Senate. His wealth of campaign experience was one reason he was elected president of the College Republicans chapter at Furman. McKoon maintains that his time at Furman allowed him to become plugged into the Republican network. "I learned very early," he said in a phone interview, "that it is 90 percent about who you know, and making those contacts with the right individuals."

In 1999 McKoon met George W. Bush, the governor of Texas who was running for president. By making contacts with Bush's campaign team, McKoon landed a job as a director of field operations on Bush's primary campaign in South Carolina. As a field director, he coordinated campaign activities with Bush supporters at Clemson and Furman universities and built volunteer networks that facilitated Bush's get-out-the-vote efforts. After completing law school, McKoon headed back to Columbus, the Georgia city where he was born, reconnected with the Muscogee County Republican Party, and started a Young Republicans chapter, which he eventually chaired.

As party chair, McKoon sought to get more Republicans involved in state and local government using a three-pronged approach. First, he worked to expand grassroots campaign operations throughout Muscogee County to give Republican

aplia · Need to Know

- How political parties evolved in American politics
- Which issues divided the first political parties
- Why two parties dominate the U.S. political system
- How to define partisan affiliation and ideology

challengers the capacity to wage better campaigns. Second, he tried to recruit more viable Republican candidates with the talent and qualifications to challenge incumbent Democrats in the Georgia statehouse. Third, he used his fundraising skills to fill the party coffers to support local races. As it turned out, McKoon became one of the Republican candidates himself, running to represent the 29th district in the state senate. His fundraising skills came in handy; he raised more than $200,000 for his successful state senate campaign. He also generated a lot of volunteer support from college students. One of them, Theresa Garcia, was quoted in a local newspaper as saying that she got involved "because of Josh's concerns about issues folks my age are concerned about. . . . Josh is concerned about jobs—and jobs are on everybody's minds. Will there be jobs when we graduate? . . . We want to see Josh in the state Senate because he is not far removed from us."

McKoon calls the Republican Party his "gateway." "In Columbus as a high school student and as an attorney," he says, "in Tuscaloosa as a law student, and in Greenville as a college student, the Republican Party offered me an access point to candidates, campaigns, and political experiences." Since joining the state senate, McKoon has introduced bills relating to education, elections, ethics, and criminal justice. His political career shows how young people can themselves run for elective office and generate support among young people who want to elect someone who can relate to and respond to their needs.[1]

Political parties offer every citizen in America the opportunity to participate in politics and even to run for elected office. In this chapter, we look at the role of political parties in the American constitutional system by examining what they do, how they formed and evolved over time, and what role they play in shaping electoral choices for candidates and voters alike.

FocusQuestions

- How do political parties shape the choices voters face in local, state, and federal elections?
- In what ways do political parties allow voters to hold their elected officials accountable for the policies they produce?
- How do political parties respond to changes in public opinion on key issues?
- Do political parties enable all citizens to participate equally in self-government, or do they help give more power to some people, and less to others? Explain.
- Are political parties a gate or a gateway to democracy?

The Role of Political Parties in American Democracy

› **How political parties evolved in American politics**

A democratic government must be responsive to its citizens, and for government to be equally responsive, every citizen must have an equal opportunity to influence it. In the United States, political parties fill an essential need by shaping the choices that voters face in elections, which serve as the key mechanism by which voters hold their government accountable. With many public offices to fill, voters need a road map to compare candidates and make the choices that will serve their best interests. The danger of relying on parties to shape these choices is that parties become interested only in winning office, not in serving the interests of the people.

In this section, we look at the role of parties in the American democratic system, specifically at the way they organize the electorate, shape the elections that determine whether their candidates win office, and guide the actions of elected officials.

Connections: In what ways are parties gateways for citizen participation? As you read this chapter, look for evidence.

What Are Political Parties?

A **political party** is a group of individuals who join together to choose candidates for elected office—whether by informal group voting or a formal nominating process. These candidates agree to abide by the **party platform**, a document that lays out the party's core beliefs and policy proposals. Parties operate through national, state, and county committees; members include party activists, citizen volunteers, and elected officials. A party's main purpose is to win elections in order to control governmental power and implement its policies.

At the national level, the party issues its platform during presidential election years. In their 2012 platforms, for example, the Republican Party and the Democratic Party stated their positions on national security, health care, energy policy, the environment, and taxes. These platforms serve as a general guide to the policy positions of all the candidates running under the party label. From time to time, individual candidates may disagree with elements of the party's platform, but in general, candidates who choose to run under a party label are defined by it. Using party labels as a shortcut for the party platform, voters can hold the elected officials accountable for their policy successes and blame them for policy failures.

Citizens tend to vote for one party over the other in somewhat predictable patterns. Classic political scientists, such as V. O. Key, use the term *party in the electorate* to describe the general patterns of voters' party identification and their behavior on election day. A main goal of any political party is to maximize party affiliation among voters so that it translates into a solid majority of the party in the electorate, which can in turn translate to a solid majority of the *party in government*. To accomplish this goal, the *party as an organization* is created, with internal structures that guide how the party functions.[2] The modern American political party is multilevel, with committees at the federal, state, and local levels.

political parties: *Broad coalitions of interests organized to win elections in order to enact a commonly supported set of public policies.*

party platform: *Document that lays out a party's core beliefs and policy proposals for each presidential election.*

What Political Parties Do

In this section, we move from theoretical ideas about political parties to what they actually do in the American political system.

Parties in the Electorate.

Parties offer several layers of opportunity for political participation. Most simply, a person can claim to be a member of a party by stating that he or she identifies with it, for example, by saying "I am a Republican." That statement is an acknowledgment of party identification—an attachment or allegiance to a political party. Voters identify with parties for several reasons. The simplest is the belief that the policies put forth by one party will serve their interests better than the policies proposed by other parties in the political arena. Another reason to join a party stems from family or social environment, in which being a member of a party is similar to other personal characteristics. As Chapter 6, Public Opinion, explains, many young people adopt the party identification of their parents. Although parties ask for contributions, there are no membership fees. For this reason, parties provide the broadest and most open gateway to participation in American politics.

A more formal step of party identification is stating party affiliation when registering to vote. Voter registration rules vary by state, but they typically require a citizen to show proof of identity and address to an official government office. In some places voters can register by mail or when they get their driver's licenses, but in others they must fill out the forms in person at a local board of elections.

At the next level of participation, voters can become active in the party at the town, county, state, and federal level. Parties encourage people to volunteer on campaigns at every level—making phone calls to prospective voters, passing out bumper stickers, or maintaining e-mail contact through the campaign website. Parties also rely on supporters to make financial contributions.

Political parties serve as a gateway to elected office. Josh McKoon, for example, got his start in politics through volunteer work with a local party on a campaign. Parties also actively recruit individuals in their county, district, or state to run for elected office. Candidate recruitment involves party leaders at all levels trying to identify people who will make good candidates for elected office, because they are well known in the community, have personal wealth, or have a professional record that speaks to current issues and would appeal to voters.

Parties in Government.

Parties also serve to organize members of Congress and state legislatures into cohesive groups, known as **party caucuses**, that consistently vote, year after year, for the policies that the parties promise in their platforms. The party in government is made up of the elected officials who share the same party affiliation and work together to accomplish the party's electoral and policy goals. Even the president, whose primary responsibility is to govern, is expected to serve as leader of his political party by setting the agenda according to party policy goals. The president is also increasingly expected to engage in political support for party candidates, from campaign appearances to party fundraisers.

Connections:
Which political party do you identify with?

Connections:
Have you formally affiliated with a political party? What are the advantages and disadvantages of doing so?

party caucus:
Group of party members in a legislature.

Party Organization.   The modern political party is structured as a multilevel organization with units at the federal, state, and local levels. **National committees** are at the top of the party organization, and their members are chosen by each state party organization (see Figure 9.1). A new president can select the national committee chair; in the case of the presidential "out" party, the national committee itself elects the party chair. The national committee is responsible for running the party's presidential nominating convention every four years. Key to that effort is overseeing the states' primary delegate selection process and officially recognizing a state's delegation at the convention.

The main job of the national committee is to do everything possible to elect the party's presidential nominee every four years, and that requires strengthening all party organizations, from the national down to the local levels. The national committee runs training workshops on party-centered activities like candidate recruitment and fundraising. The national party can spend its money on coordinated expenditures, that is, in cooperation with the presidential campaign, and it can make independent expenditures, which

 **national committee:** *Top level of national political parties; coordinates national presidential campaigns.*

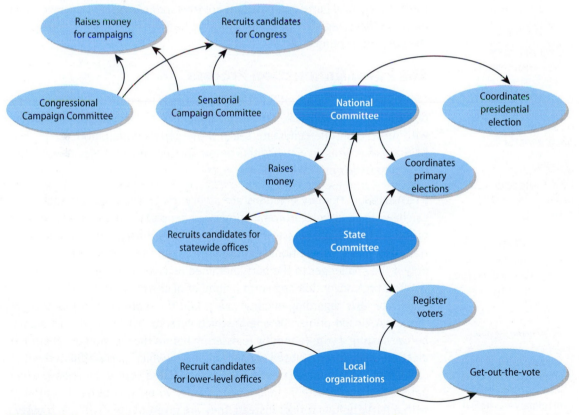

FIGURE 9.1 Party Organization at the National, State, and Local Levels.

© CENGAGE LEARNING

are funds spent separately on general efforts to increase voter turnout for the party's nominee.

Each major political party has a committee dedicated to raising money for incumbent House and Senate members. For the Democrats it is the Democratic Congressional Campaign Committee and the Democratic Senatorial Campaign Committee, and for the Republicans, the National Republican Congressional Committee and the National Republican Senatorial Committee. These congressional party committees are also responsible for recruiting qualified challengers to run for seats held by the opposing party and helping to fund their campaigns.

State political parties are the next level of party organization, and they are regulated by state law, so their responsibilities can vary by state. Typically a political party has a state central committee that tries to elect candidates to statewide office and also works with local organizations to recruit new voters and raise money. Local party organizations exist at the county, town, and precinct or ward levels. The Muscogee County Republican Party, which Josh McKoon chaired, is an example of a local party organization. The essential functions of local party organizations are to recruit candidates for lower-level elected offices, register voters, and, most important, ensure that voters get to the polls on election day.[3]

The Party Nomination Process

One of the most important functions of parties is to nominate candidates for office and then elect them, a process accomplished in two stages. In elections with more than one candidate seeking the party's nomination, states hold **primary elections**, in which voters determine the party's choice to run in the next stage, the **general election**.

Primaries. Primary elections are a very important way that each voter can have an equal voice in nominating his or her party's candidates for elected office. Although most states rely heavily on the primary, some states authorize nominating conventions and primaries, with the primaries taking place only if the challenger to the party nominee receives a certain percentage of votes at the convention or a certain number of citizen petition signatures.[4]

State laws regarding elections vary, and there are several types of primaries. A closed primary is one in which voters must affiliate with a party before casting a vote (either by registering before the election or on primary election day). A semi-closed primary is one in which party-affiliated voters cast votes in their party's primary, and nonaffiliated voters can choose which party's primary to vote in. In an open primary voters do not have to affiliate with a party before voting. Instead, they are given **ballots** with each party's list of candidates, and they can choose which ballot to use but are restricted to voting for only one party's nominees.

primary election: *Election in which voters select the candidates who will run on the party label in the general election; also called direct primary.*

general election: *Election in which voters choose their elected officials.*

ballot: *List of candidates who are running for elected office; used by voters to make their choice.*

Connections: Have you voted in a primary election? What kind of primary was it? Did you have to identify your party affiliation?

In 2011, an organization called Americans Elect launched an effort to nominate an alternative candidate to those selected by the two major parties in 2012. With the slogan "Pick a President, Not a Party," it used the Internet as its key mobilization tool.[5] As of April 2012 the organization had collected more than 2.5 million signatures to get on the presidential ballot in twenty-five states, and it planned to hold an online convention in June 2012 to nominate a candidate to run under its label. Americans Elect is the first major political organization to operate almost entirely via the Internet. But Americans Elect struggled. In May 2012, the organization admitted difficulty in finding a possible nominee. None of the candidates it had hoped would run under its label agreed to do so.[6] Ultimately Americans Elect did not have a major impact on the 2012 elections, but the organizers demonstrated the potential power of the Internet in presenting an alternative to the two major parties.

Primary elections are a fact of political life, but insofar as they create competition within a political party and encourage candidates to reveal negative aspects of each other's professional or personal lives, they can weaken the party's eventual nominee when he or she faces opponents in the general election. Because party organizations always want the candidate who is most likely to win the election nominated under the party banner, they try to exert control over the primary election process in several ways. First, state laws govern party ballot access—literally, who can actually get on the primary election ballot. The relationship between elite state party members and state legislators is very close, so the party controls the gate by determining how open or restrictive ballot access is for candidates seeking to run for office on the party label. Second, although party organizations remain technically neutral during the primary election season, they can steer donors toward their preferred candidates and away from candidates who do not agree with their goals. As a consequence, individuals who are perceived as weak or as not loyal to the party may run into major roadblocks set up by the party organization.

The Presidential Nomination.

The process by which each party nominates its presidential candidate has evolved from one that was concentrated in the hands of a small group of elites to the modern process that allows millions of voters to participate directly in choosing the party's presidential nominee.

In a presidential primary, voters cast a vote for a particular candidate, but what they are really doing is choosing delegates who will support that nominee at the party's national nominating convention. In a presidential **caucus**, which serves the same nominating purpose, the process is less formal and more personal in that party members meet together in town halls, schools, and even private homes to choose a nominee. Each state is awarded a number of delegates to the convention by the national party organization based largely on the number of Electoral College votes the state has, but also on the

Connections:
Do you think that the presidential nomination process in 2012 was fair?

caucus: *Meeting of party members in town halls, schools, and private homes to select a presidential nominee.*

Barack Obama made history as the first African American presidential nominee of any major party and then as the first African American president. His selection for vice president, former Senator Joe Biden, had been an early contender for the 2008 Democratic nomination but quickly dropped out. President Obama and Vice President Biden were again endorsed to run as a team by the Democratic Party at the Democratic Convention in North Carolina in 2012.

winner-take-all system: *Electoral system in which whoever wins the most votes in an election wins the election.*

proportional representation: *An electoral system that assigns party delegates according to vote share in a presidential primary election or that assigns seats in the legislature according to vote share in a general election.*

Connections: How does proportional representation affect the dynamics of primaries?

size of party support in that state. The candidate who wins a majority of the delegates from the primary and caucus elections is selected at the national convention as the party's nominee for president.

The Democratic Party and Republican Party allocate their delegates within the primaries and caucuses differently. In the 1960s members of underrepresented groups, such as women and African Americans, began calling for a change in the presidential nominating procedures for the Democratic Party. Specifically, they objected to the use of the unit rule, or **winner-take-all system**, which meant that whoever won the majority of primary or state nominating convention votes would win the entire state's delegates. Activists believed that the unit rule allowed conservative white men to dominate the nominating process. For the 1976 election the Democrats formally instituted **proportional representation**, that is, the number of delegates that a candidate receives is based on the percentage of the vote received in the primary or caucus, either at the state level or in each congressional district. In most states, delegates are committed to a candidate before the primary election takes place. The cumulative effect of these reforms was to create a gateway for members of underrepresented groups to exert influence in determining the Democratic Party presidential nominee.

Mitt Romney was the 2012 Republican Party presidential nominee. He was the former governor of Massachusetts and the CEO of Bain Capital; he was also the first Mormon nominated for president. Here, he is seen with his running mate, Paul Ryan, a Republican congressman from Wisconsin, at the Republican Party Convention in Florida, receiving the party's formal endorsement.

Until 2008, the Republican Party had rarely faced an internal demand for more diverse representation, so it had not significantly changed its nominating system. But starting in 2008, the Republican National Committee proposed using proportional representation in its nominating system in the hopes of generating more competition and a lengthier campaign season, both of which would increase turnout and enthusiasm among Republican voters. In 2010, the party formally adopted a hybrid system whereby states that held their primaries before April 1, 2012, award their delegates proportionally, and states holding primaries after that date have the option of using the old or new system.[7] States that did not abide by this system were penalized by losing some of their delegates to the national convention.

The timing of primaries has become an integral part of the presidential nomination strategy. Larry Bartels's work demonstrates that states that hold primaries early in the process exert disproportional influence by giving one or another candidate an early stamp of approval and momentum.[8] Candidates who win in the early primaries can solicit more campaign money and garner more endorsements from key constituent groups than those who lose. It also literally pays off economically to be a state with an early presidential primary because candidates, their staff, and members

Connections: How do primaries allow voters to register their opinions with party leaders about candidates and about party policy positions?

Connections: How does frontloading affect voter equality across states?

frontloading:
Moving a state primary or caucus earlier in the year to increase its influence.

✓ Checkpoint

Can you:

☐ Define political party

☐ Identify the three arenas in which parties operate

☐ Track the party nomination process

of the media spend a disproportionate amount of time in the state before the primary, generating income for local businesses. Traditionally, the two earliest presidential contests have been the New Hampshire primary and the Iowa caucus; in 2012 both were held in January. Even though these are relatively small states, the fact that they have the first two presidential contests for each major party makes them disproportionately influential in generating publicity and momentum for the winners.[9] Other states have responded by trying to schedule their primaries as early as possible, but both the Republican and Democratic Parties have discouraged these **frontloading** efforts because they minimize the role of voters in states that hold their primaries and caucuses later in the process.

The Dynamics of Early Party Development

› Which issues divided the first political parties

Political parties in 2013 seem very well organized, as if they have existed as long as the nation itself. But parties were not intended to be part of the original fabric of the political system. Today, rather than the narrow organizations that the Framers feared, there are two large parties that each include a broad swath of the electorate and must make internal compromises to stay unified. In this section, we trace the background to these developments.

Political Factions: Federalist versus Antifederalist

Connections: Given the Framers' views on factions and political parties, do you think the development of parties has been good or bad for American democracy?

James Madison, writing in *Federalist Papers* 10 and 51 (see the Appendix), predicted the rise of factions, groups of individuals who share a common political goal and ally with each other on a temporary basis to accomplish that goal. Madison recognized that factions would be a natural outgrowth of different interests among citizens and that there was little government could do to stop them without denying citizens important civil liberties. Although factions were not considered the same thing as political parties of the kind that had emerged in Britain, the Framers also feared that both factions and parties might encourage divisions in the young democracy that could threaten its existence.

Yet factions emerged even before the Constitution was adopted. In the debate over ratification (see Chapter 2, The Constitution), those who argued for the Constitution called themselves Federalists. They believed that a stable federal government that could collect tax revenue, raise and maintain an army and navy, regulate foreign and domestic trade, and stabilize currency would make the American democratic experiment a success. Opponents of a strong national government, however, viewed the future of the United States in terms of loosely affiliated but sovereign states that governed themselves, managing their own tax policies and internal security. These were the Antifederalists.

Ultimately, the Federalist viewpoint triumphed, and the Constitution was ratified. But the debate did not end there. The nation's first president, George Washington (1789–97), formed a government that included proponents of a strong national government (led by Alexander Hamilton and John Adams) and strong state governments (led by Thomas Jefferson). Tensions between the factions accelerated after John Adams's (1797–1801) election as president.

Connections: Relate the modern Democratic and Republican Parties to the viewpoints of the Federalists and the Antifederalists. Which party comes closest to which viewpoint?

Thomas Jefferson, Andrew Jackson, and the Emergence of the Democratic Party

After winning the election of 1800, Thomas Jefferson (1801–1809) used his victory to transform his fledgling political party into a viable long-term organization known as the Democratic-Republicans (most candidates shortened the name to Republican), while the supporters of Adams and Hamilton united around the Federalist Party.[10]

Despite their electoral success and lack of opposition, the Democratic-Republicans themselves grew divided. The conflict was led by Andrew Jackson, an ambitious politician who wanted to take the party to a new level of inclusiveness and use that wider reach to become president. Jackson, from Tennessee, had served in both the House and the Senate, but he made his national reputation during the War of 1812, especially as the hero of the Battle of New Orleans. After his military service ended, Jackson returned to Congress and attempted to win the presidential nomination of the Democratic-Republicans in 1824.[11] At that time, presidential nominations were decided by party caucuses in Congress, and Jackson was challenging John Quincy Adams, the son of President John Adams. Although the congressional party caucus nominated William H. Crawford of Georgia, fewer than a third of the members of the party showed up to cast their votes, reflecting a lack of consensus around a majority candidate. Consequently, there was no clear choice among the Democratic-Republicans in the election of 1824, and no one won a majority in the Electoral College. The outcome then had to be determined by the House of Representatives, which selected Adams (for this process, see Chapter 10, Elections, Campaigns, and Voting).

By 1828 the nomination process had been taken over by party members in state legislatures who voted for their preferred nominees either in the legislature or at state party conventions. By locating the nomination process in the states instead of in Congress, parties were enlarging the number of people involved in making the decision about who could run for president well beyond the electors in the Electoral College or even the members of the House of Representatives. Jackson wanted states to open the voting process to as many people as possible by eliminating such barriers to voting as property ownership requirements. In 1828, using a grassroots state-level strategy to attract both the support of state legislators and the voters themselves, Jackson worked closely with Martin Van Buren, a powerful New York politician, to again challenge Adams for the nomination of the Democratic-Republicans; this time, he won the nomination and the presidential election.

By 1832, the end of Jackson's first term in office, politics had changed in fundamental ways because of the nation's rapid geographic and population growth.[12] The Jackson-led Democrats emerged as a large grassroots majority political party, and Jackson used all the powers of the presidency to strengthen his political party around the country. In the meantime, the anti-Jackson wing of the old Democratic-Republicans had taken the name National Republicans. In the presidential election of 1832, the National Republicans nominated Henry Clay, a U.S. senator from Kentucky, to run against Jackson, but Jackson was victorious.

Although Henry Clay lost that election to Jackson, he returned to the Senate and started laying the groundwork for a new political party that would oppose Jackson's policies. He encouraged members of the National Republicans to join forces with others who opposed Jackson and to form the Whig Party, which objected to what they viewed as Jackson's abuse of presidential power for partisan gains. From 1832 to 1856, the Democrats and the Whigs dominated American politics and presidential elections. However, the issue of slavery soon emerged to shake up the party balance.

The Antislavery Movement and the Formation of the Republican Party

The Democratic Party's general strategy for opening a larger gateway for citizen participation in politics inadvertently encouraged alternate groups and political parties to emerge on the political scene. In 1833 William Lloyd Garrison, a white journalist, formed the American Anti-Slavery Society to press for the abolition of slavery. Former slave Frederick Douglass and other African Americans in the North also led efforts to end slavery, and the abolitionist movement grew large and vocal enough to pressure the Democrats and Whigs to take a formal position on slavery, especially the extension of slavery into western territories.

Further complicating party politics were smaller third parties that arose in the North, some explicitly antislavery. As frequently happens in American politics, however, third parties are absorbed into larger parties; the Liberty Party was absorbed into a larger coalition of groups, led by the Free Soilers, that opposed the expansion of slavery in the territories. Meeting in Ripon, Wisconsin, in 1854, these groups were also joined by some antislavery northern Democrats, and the modern Republican Party was born. Six years later, the Republican Party had consolidated its support and elected Abraham Lincoln (1861–65) to the presidency.

Shortly after Lincoln's election, seven southern states seceded from the union. On April 12, 1861, the Confederates fired on the federal government's fort in Charleston Harbor, and the Civil War began. Four more southern states seceded, leaving the Republicans in complete control of Congress. On January 1, 1863, in issuing the Emancipation Proclamation (see Chapter 5, Civil Rights), Lincoln publicly affirmed that ending slavery was a fundamental aim of the war. The Confederacy dissolved after the war ended in 1865, but southerners resented northerners and the Republican Party because of both the South's physical and economic losses and the continued occupation of the South by northern troops. Since that time, the Democrats and the Republicans have been the nation's two major political parties.

Party Loyalty and Patronage

Andrew Jackson set an example of how to build a political party organization using government resources. Just as Jackson worked to expand the electorate, he sought to expand the size of the federal government in order to increase the number of federally funded jobs his party could control. Whoever controlled the jobs associated with these federal programs could also demand political allegiance from those who filled them. By the late nineteenth century a system emerged whereby the politician became the "patron" of the businessmen and workers who were on the payrolls of the federal or the state governments. Jobs built party loyalty, and those hired often had to declare their political allegiance to the politician who arranged for the job and promise to vote for him. Such a system is commonly referred to as a **patronage system**.

As the government expanded, so did the party organization. At each level—federal, state, and local—there were parallel party committees. Parties became the top-down organizations they are today, with a national committee, state committees, and local chapters at the county, ward, town, or precinct level. At each level, leaders who had power within the party acted as party bosses, controlling the distribution of public funds and rewarding supporters and withholding funds from opponents. Voter support in this kind of system became known as machine politics because it ran like a well-oiled machine.

The expansion of party machines was fueled by a huge influx of new immigrants in the late nineteenth century who mostly settled in large cities of the North and Midwest. Democratic bosses in these cities recognized that immigrants, once naturalized, would be a major source of new voters and courted their loyalty through patronage. In turn, parties served as a type of gateway for immigrants to become integrated into American political life. As city populations increased at a much faster rate than rural populations, Democrats gained political power in cities, while Republican power in the North and Midwest tended to be concentrated in rural areas.

Connections: Do you see the patronage system still at work today in American politics? Explain.

patronage system:

Political system in which government programs and benefits are awarded based on political loyalty to a party or politician.

Reform and the Erosion of Party Control

A critical factor in the success of machine politics was party control of voting. In contrast to today's system—in which states manage most aspects of elections, including ballot design and ballot counting—local parties in the late nineteenth century printed their own ballots, called party strip ballots, which listed only their candidates, and gave them to voters on their way into the polling places. In many places, party officials counted the votes as well, further manipulating the voting process to their advantage.

However, three developments eroded party organizations' control over government jobs and elections: the creation of a merit-based system of government employment, the introduction of ballot reforms, and a change in the way nominees for elected office were selected. All three reforms were led by Progressives, coalitions of Democrats and Republicans who believed that government had been captured by corrupt elites who were using government resources to enrich themselves.

In 1883 the Pendleton Act reformed the civil service by requiring that government jobs be filled based on merit, not on political connections (see Chapter 13, The Bureaucracy, for more on the civil service). This was the first of several laws that slowly transformed the federal bureaucracy from a corrupt insider organization to a neutral, policy-based organization.[13]

 Australian ballot: *Voting system in which state governments run elections and provide voters the option of choosing candidates from multiple parties; also called the secret ballot.*

Voting procedures were also reformed between 1888 and 1911 as states adopted the so-called **Australian ballot** system, which originated in Australia in 1858, to replace the party strip ballots[14] (see Figure 9.2). The Australian ballot system introduced the secret ballot; each ballot listed all of the candidates from all of the parties who were running for office, and voters marked their choices in private. In addition, poll watchers and ballot counters were expected to perform their tasks without favoring a specific party and without intimidating voters. This reform greatly reduced party boss control over election outcomes.[15]

Last, Progressives launched grassroots campaigns for direct primaries run by the state for nominating party candidates. These primaries aimed to replace the nomination of candidates in local and state party conventions, which were typically dominated by party bosses. Although states were relatively slow to adopt direct primaries, eventually this system became the dominant means of choosing party candidates. The effect of direct primaries was to greatly reduce the control that party bosses and machines had over the choices offered in elections. As party bases broadened, leaders turned their attention to finding ways to keep coalitions of voters together.

Checkpoint

Can you:

☐ Explain the differences between the Federalists and the Antifederalists

☐ Describe the events that opened up the presidential nomination process

☐ Explain how the Republican Party formed

☐ Connect patronage and party power

☐ Describe reforms that reduced party power

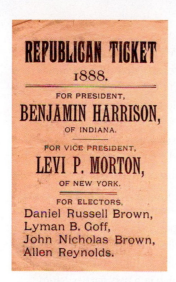
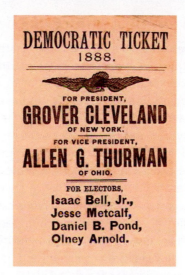
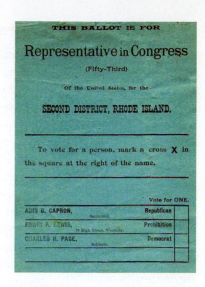

FIGURE 9.2 Ballot Reform.

On the left are examples of party strip ballots used in Rhode Island in 1888. These types of ballots were printed by political parties and handed to voters on election day. They gave a voter no opportunity to split the vote among different parties. On the right is an example of the so-called Australian ballot. Like this ballot used in Rhode Island in 1892, Australian ballots were printed by state governments rather than by political parties. They listed all candidates for elected office, not just candidates from a single party, and therefore allowed a voter to split the vote among different parties.

Source: Russell J. DeSimone and Daniel C. Schofield, "Rhode Island Election Tickets: A Survey," Technical Services Department Faculty Publications (Kingston: University of Rhode Island, 2007), *Private collection, Russell J. DeSimone and Daniel C. Schofield.*

The Effects of a Two-Party System

> **Why two parties dominate the U.S. political system**

Following the Civil War, party divisions ran largely along geographic lines, with Republicans dominant in the Northeast and West, and Democrats dominant in the South and increasingly in the nation's largest cities. Today, the Democratic and Republican Parties have reversed their geographic strongholds, but the two-party system remains intact. In this section we examine the effects of a two-party system not only on citizens' choices but also on the ways that government can respond. We also examine the reasons why the United States, even before the Civil War, never had more than two major parties, and we explore the role of the third parties that have occasionally arisen to challenge two-party dominance.

Limited Political Choice

In any conversation about a political issue, there will likely be more than two opinions expressed. It might seem logical, therefore, that a large democracy like the United States should have as many political parties as there are diverse viewpoints. But the United States has only two major parties, and they stand in stark contrast to each other. Scholars have debated whether this two-party system adequately reflects the range of views among citizens.

In 1957 the scholar Anthony Downs argued that voters whose views fall between the two parties were actually represented in a two-party system. His **median voter theorem** proposed that, in a two-party race, if voters select candidates on the basis of ideology and everyone participates equally, the party closer to the middle will win. As candidates from each party seek to attract a majority of votes, and because most voters fall in the middle of the ideological spectrum, both parties move toward a compromise, or middle position. In this way moderates have a great deal of potential political influence in a two-party system.[16]

Nevertheless, the impact of ideologically extreme campaign activists and interest groups that align with a party can pressure parties and candidates to move away from the center.[17] In today's highly partisan atmosphere, it seems as though the political center has almost entirely disappeared. Each party appears to be so dominated by its more extreme wing that there is little opportunity within each to make moderate views known or to compromise. The current two-party system increasingly appears to contradict Downs's expectations about convergence to the middle. In regions where one party is dominant, elected officials may not be responsive to voters from the other party.

The Structural Limits

Despite its limitations, the two-party system is built into the American electoral system, as the political scientist Maurice Duverger explains: The American electoral system is a **single-member plurality system**, in which one legislative seat represents citizens who live in a geographically defined district.[18] To win that seat, a candidate usually needs only a **plurality** of votes, not a pure **majority**, that is, more votes than any other candidate, but not necessarily 50 percent plus 1. Because there is only one seat to be won in a district, voters have become accustomed to choosing between candidates from the two major parties.

Other electoral systems work differently. Many democracies assign the number of seats a party wins according to proportional representation, based on the percentage of votes it receives in a particular election. This type of electoral system encourages smaller parties to form around specific issues and to field candidates for office. Voters are likewise encouraged to support smaller parties. With so many parties fielding candidates, no single party is likely to receive a majority, and parties govern by forming coalitions (see Global Gateways: Proportional Representation Electoral Systems).

median voter theorem: *Theory that, in a two-party race, if voters select candidates on the basis of ideology and everyone participates equally, the party closer to the middle will win.*

Connections: Do you think the major political parties reflect the views of citizens? If not, what can be done to change that?

single-member plurality system: *Electoral system that assigns one seat in a legislative body to represent citizens who live in a defined area (a district) based on which candidate wins the most votes.*

plurality vote: *Vote in which the winner needs to win more votes than any other candidate.*

majority vote: *Vote in which the winner needs to win 50 percent plus 1 of the votes cast.*

globalgateways

Proportional Representation Electoral Systems

In contrast to the U.S. single-member plurality system, many nations in Europe and in Central and Latin America have proportional representation electoral systems. This system assigns multiple seats to a geographic district according to the proportion of votes a political party receives in an election. In this system, there are rewards for forming more than two parties because parties that receive even a small percentage of the vote—for example, 10 percent—are likely to be awarded seats in the legislature. The legislatures typically have coalition majorities, where members from different parties agree on policies and form a working majority. In this way, proportional representation grants multiple parties the power to make policy and deliver benefits to voters.

There are trade-offs in terms of participation, responsiveness, and accountability in each type of electoral system. Single-member plurality electoral systems tend to produce fewer political parties, which reduces the number of opinions that can be actively represented in a political system. Two-party systems also encourage strict partisanship among officeholders and discourage bipartisanship. On the other hand, this stark contrast allows voters to more easily hold their elected officials accountable.

Proportional representation systems produce multiple parties and greater diversity of representation. However, this system tends to produce coalition government, because no party can gain a straight majority. Coalitions encourage compromise among parties, but it is also true that the parties that make up the coalition can withdraw at any time, and so the ruling government is potentially unstable.* In addition, voters cannot easily identify which party in the coalition should be rewarded or blamed for government policies, so accountability is more difficult than in single-member plurality systems.

- **How does a proportional representation electoral system translate votes into legislative power in the government?**

- **Why are governments established under proportional representation systems inherently unstable?**

*Ko Maeda and Misa Nishikawa, "Duration of Party Control in Parliamentary and Presidential Governments," *Comparative Political Studies* 39 (2006): 352–74.

Connections: Do the political parties provide citizens with opportunities for debate on the issues? Do the political parties reflect citizens' views?

In the United States, however, the single-member plurality system encourages a two-party system, and the two-party system in turn encourages political debates that ask Americans to take a "for" or an "against" position on an issue. During an election, there is little effort to arrive at the middle ground, although there is often debate within a party as to what its position will be. In fact, the two-party system works to transfer the battleground from between parties to within parties. Each party—rather than government itself—is a coalition.

The Role of Third Parties

In one sense, a two-party system stands as a gate that blocks the emergence of alternative viewpoints and reduces the choices available to voters in terms of perspectives on how to govern. On the other hand, when the two parties together do not offer policy proposals that a significant number of voters want to see enacted, third parties form. These third parties can mount challenges so significant that the major parties are compelled to act, often by incorporating the third party's policy proposal into their platforms.

Ross Perot was given credit for using his United We Stand Party to force the two major party candidates in 1992, President George H. W. Bush (1989–93) and William Jefferson (Bill) Clinton (1993–2001), to address the federal deficit, the amount by which annual government spending exceeds incoming revenue. During the 2000 election, Ralph Nader ran for president on the Green Party ticket, promoting a platform that called for stronger environmental and consumer protections. In addition, both the Libertarian Party and the Constitution Party have put forth presidential candidates in recent elections. For a list of significant parties in American politics, see Figure 9.3.

Third parties thus present an alternative to the two dominant political parties. However, an alternative party can also act as a spoiler for major party candidates and can, as a consequence, alienate potential voters. Some Democratic Party activists argued that if Ralph Nader had not run for president on the Green Party ticket in 2000 and had not received 97,488 votes in the state of Florida, Albert Gore Jr. would have been elected president instead of George W. Bush.[19] Although Nader did not win in 2000, 2004, or 2008, his messages of change and open government were echoed by Democratic presidential candidate Barack Obama in his successful 2008 presidential campaign.

Connections: What are the benefits and the risks of voting for a third-party candidate?

Third parties can also be an influential force at lower levels of government. For example, in 2010 and 2012, the Tea Party movement was very effective at supporting challengers to incumbents in primary elections in the Republican Party or supporting a third candidate in the general election. Its message was fiscal responsibility, lower taxes, and paying down the national debt, and it was successful in electing members of Congress. Members of the Tea Party movement were also active in the Republican nominating process in 2012 and were vocal in demanding that the Republicans commit to their

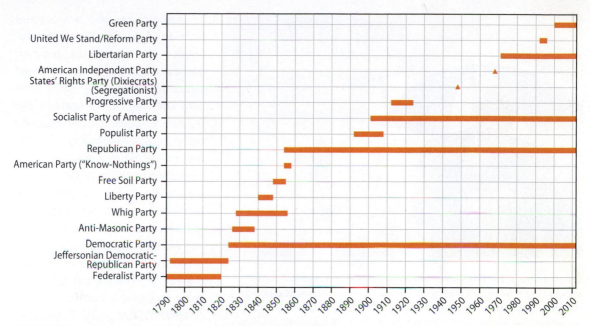

FIGURE 9.3 American Political Parties, 1789–2012.

Note that the Democratic Party is the nation's oldest political party. The graph shows it beginning under President Andrew Jackson, but some argue that it actually began with President Thomas Jefferson's Democratic-Republicans.

© CENGAGE LEARNING

concerns. The Tea Party movement, though not officially a political party, illustrates how third parties can force the two major political parties to be more responsive to the policy concerns of voters generally. When they are large enough, these groups have the potential to move the party platforms in new directions and, in turn, to change federal laws.[20]

Obstacles to Third Parties and Independents

Because third-party candidates can act as spoilers, the two major parties do everything they can to discourage them, from challenging signatures for ballot access in court to preventing them from participating in presidential debates. The Democrats and Republicans have controlled state legislatures and Congress for so long that they have successfully established gates within state electoral laws that favor a two-party system over a multiple-party system. In addition, without the backing of a major party to get out the vote, collect campaign contributions, and arrange for media coverage, most third-party and Independent candidates do not stand much chance of being elected. Consequently, voters who consider themselves Independents do not have the opportunity to vote for candidates who might be closest to them in terms of policy preferences.

Connections:
Should laws that discourage third parties be changed? What would be the effects in terms of government responsiveness?

Candidates who are elected from third parties have little influence in legislatures because parties shape the internal power structure there. The party that wins the majority of seats in the legislature becomes the majority party and consequently controls the legislative process. Once the legislative session begins, members are asked to express their opinions in subcommittees, committees, and on the floor by voting with or against their party's proposed legislation, and it is rare that an alternative to the major party proposal is considered (see Chapter 11, Congress). Those who are elected as Independents, such as Senator Bernie Sanders (I-Vt.), have no party organization to join in the legislature. Independents must pledge to support one of the two major parties in order to sit on committees and perform their other responsibilities as legislators. When he was elected to the Senate in 2006, Sanders chose to caucus with the Democrats.

Senator Bernie Sanders, an Independent representing the state of Vermont, is known as a liberal who advocates for economic equality. He first went to Congress as a member of the House in 1990 after serving as the mayor of Burlington. Because there is no Independent party organization in the Senate, Senator Sanders associates himself with the Democrats in order to receive his committee assignments. Here, Senator Sanders is seen outside the Capitol in 2012 at a rally for programs that help people with disabilities live on their own.

BILL CLARK/CQ ROLL CALL/GETTY IMAGES

Connections: What are the advantages and disadvantages of being an Independent?

 Checkpoint

Can you:

☐ Explain the median voter theorem

☐ Describe how a single-member plurality system encourages two parties

☐ Summarize the role third parties have played in American politics

☐ Survey the obstacles to third parties and Independent candidates

☐ Explain how interest groups and political parties have become more closely aligned

Challenges to Party Power from Interest Groups

In addition to challenges from third parties, the two major parties face challenges from established interest groups and from broader social groups formed at the grassroots of American politics (see Chapter 8, Interest Groups). These groups and movements draw attention to each party's failings in specific issue areas and engage in activities from staging protest rallies to nominating alternative candidates to run in primaries in order to get parties to move closer to the policy positions the group or movement advocates. For example, unions such as the Service Employees International Union (SEIU) and environmental groups such as the Sierra Club are generally supportive of the Democratic Party, whereas business groups such as the Chamber of Commerce and the National Rifle Association are supportive of the Republican Party.

Party Alignment and Ideology

> **How to define partisan affiliation and ideology**

Throughout U.S. history, there have been long stretches of time during which the party affiliations of voters remained stable, but there have also been key elections in which parties lost or gained significant blocs of voters. Scholars have tried to identify the factors that explain why voters make large, permanent shifts from one party to another. Shifts in party allegiance can occur when there is an external shock to the nation, such as an economic depression or a foreign military attack. Shifts can also occur when public attitudes change considerably and one party appears to respond more quickly to those changes than another.

The Parties after the Civil War

Following the Civil War, as we have seen, the Republicans were dominant in the Northeast and West, and the Democrats were dominant in the South and increasingly in large cities with big immigrant populations. This **party alignment**—voters identifying with a party in repeated elections—was relatively stable until 1896, when a number of smaller parties challenged the Republican and Democratic Parties. The Republican Party emerged from that election with a victory, and the smaller parties faded from the national political scene.

From 1896 to 1932, the basic geographic pattern of party alignment stayed the same, but the combination of the stock market crash of October 24, 1929, a global depression that followed, and a drop in worldwide agricultural prices brought political trouble to the Republican Party. By 1932 voters in every part of the country were ready for a change, not only in political leadership but also in the entire approach to government.

party alignment: *Voter identification with a political party in repeated elections.*

The New Deal and the Role of Ideology in Party Politics

During the election of 1932, voters were exposed to a new political ideology, or set of consistent political views, about the way that the federal government could work. Today's voters might describe themselves as liberal or conservative, but voters before 1932 typically identified themselves with a political party. In that election year, Franklin Delano Roosevelt (1933–45), governor of New York State, ran for president on a platform designed to reverse the effects of the Great Depression. The idea that the federal government would help individuals to help themselves was transformative in American politics. The Democratic Party platform resonated with voters, and Roosevelt won the election.

Connections: Should the federal government help individuals to help themselves?

In his campaign for president in 1932, Franklin Delano Roosevelt introduced an innovative campaign platform. "I pledge you," he said, "I pledge myself, to a new deal for the American people." The term "New Deal" came to describe federal programs that took an active role in helping individual citizens find jobs, save for retirement, and benefit from fair working conditions.

After he took office, Roosevelt championed a vast array of new government programs referred to as the New Deal. These programs were designed to help individuals who were jobless, homeless, or otherwise in financial need. In addition, Roosevelt built a coalition of white southerners, working-class ethnic northerners, liberal advocates for socialist policies, and northern African Americans who had previously been Republicans. This was a radical shift for African Americans, who since the Civil War had followed the party of Abraham Lincoln and shunned the Democrats, whom they associated with racism and slavery. This electoral coalition was large but fragile, and to maintain it Roosevelt engaged in a great deal of political balancing and a wide distribution of government benefits.

In supporting the New Deal, voters came to accept the ideological viewpoint that government involvement in the economic aspects of individuals' lives was legitimate and, on balance, a good thing. As noted in Chapter 1, this perspective on government serves as a foundation for the modern definition of a liberal. Today the liberal viewpoint builds on the New Deal perspective by favoring government redistribution of income through higher taxes on the wealthy to provide social benefits, such as health care, unemployment insurance, and welfare payments to the poor. Those who opposed the New Deal are the forefathers of the modern conservatives, who believe in lower taxes and less government involvement in economic life.

In the aftermath of 1932, the two parties transformed. The Democrats changed from a party that believed in states' rights, low taxes, and little government intervention in individuals' lives to the party that created a large social safety net that relied on the federal government to ensure personal economic stability. The Republicans changed from a party that believed in a strong central federal government and in intervention in the economy when necessary to the party of a strictly limited federal government and fiscal responsibility. Alongside these opposing economic viewpoints, modern liberals and conservatives also differ on social issues, including abortion, gun control, affirmative action, prayer in school, and same-sex marriage.

Voters responded to these partisan and ideological changes by changing their own party allegiances over time, essentially producing a **realignment** of the electorate. In the broadest sense, Democrats today generally support expanding the size of government to accomplish specific policy goals, even if it means raising taxes, and support liberal social values. In contrast, Republicans generally support limiting the size of government by keeping taxation and regulation of the economy to a minimum and support preserving conservative social values.

Civil Rights, the Great Society, and Nixon's Southern Strategy

The Democratic and Republican Parties remained divided mainly along this economic dimension until the early 1960s, when the Democratic Party established itself as the party of civil rights for African Americans. During the presidency of Lyndon Baines Johnson (1963–69), the Civil Rights Act of 1964, the Voting Rights Act of 1965, the Department of Housing and Urban Development Act of 1965, and the Fair Housing Act of 1966 were all signed into law. These acts gave the federal government strong enforcement powers to guarantee African Americans the fullest extent of the civil rights afforded to every American and served as a key gateway for full political participation by African Americans. Johnson's policies brought a second dimension to liberal ideology: Now the federal government was granted the power not only to help individuals in need economically, but also to take affirmative steps to overrule state and local governments to prevent discrimination on all levels. As noted in Chapter 5, the government's role evolved from preventing unequal treatment under the law to ensuring equality in all walks of life, from education to employment to housing.

Today African Americans remain the most loyal of any demographic constituency in the Democratic Party. In 2008, 95 percent of African American voters chose the Democratic candidate, Barack Obama, who was elected as

Connections: How does the realignment that followed the election of 1932 echo the divisions between the Federalists and the Antifederalists? Or is the political ideology of the modern era entirely different?

Connections: Which perspective comes closest to your own views—liberal or conservative?

realignment: *Long-term shift in voter allegiance from one party to another.*

the nation's first African American president.[21] In 2010, a non-presidential election year, 89 percent of African American voters cast their ballots for Democratic candidates for Congress.[22]

The Johnson administration also expanded federal programs that granted aid to individuals and to state and local governments in the areas of health care, education, housing, job training, and welfare to families with children. This set of policies was called the Great Society and was founded on the idea that federal expansion would strengthen American society by helping all citizens reach their potential. By expanding the reach of the federal government this way, Johnson reinforced the liberal ideological underpinnings of the Democratic Party.

Connections: What would the Federalists think of the federal government today? What would the Antifederalists think?

As this shift in Democratic policies occurred, Republicans saw a new opportunity to attract support from voters who opposed the expansion of the federal government into race relations or the regulation of the economy. Beginning with the campaign of Barry Goldwater in 1964 and continuing with those of Richard M. Nixon (1969–74) in 1968 and of Ronald Reagan (1981–89) in 1980, the Republicans employed a so-called southern strategy, presenting themselves to southern white voters as holding views on civil rights and race that were opposite those of the Democrats.

Although Republicans did not sanction racism and discrimination, they made it clear that they would not take the same strong steps as the Democrats to impose federal law on states to remedy these problems. Republicans extended their philosophy of limited government intervention by asserting that each state was responsible for enforcing civil rights and that the federal government was overstepping its bounds by interfering at the state and local levels. At the same time, Republicans opposed the Great Society policies as too expensive, and they were philosophically opposed to the federal government giving so much aid directly to individuals without asking for something in return. In this way, the Republican Party continued to move toward a more conservative ideology that sought to limit the federal government's powers and programs.

The Reagan Revolution and Conservative Party Politics

In 1980 Ronald Reagan, former Republican governor of California, defeated the incumbent President Jimmy Carter (1977–81), a Democrat, partly by appealing to those who opposed the Supreme Court's legalization of abortion in *Roe v. Wade* (1973). Reagan's campaign offered a consistent conservative ideology that focused on limiting the size of the federal government, opposing abortion, and allowing religious prayer in public schools, which had been prohibited by the Supreme Court ruling in *Engel v. Vitale* in 1962.[23]

His strategy was designed to attract conservative Democrats who were alienated by their party's position on abortion and to attract the growing numbers of active evangelical Christian voters, especially in the South.

Reagan also took advantage of the instability in foreign relations that marked Jimmy Carter's four years in office. Reagan campaigned on a strong defense and tough foreign policy that actively promoted freedom, and he made it clear that, under his administration, the United States would work to undermine the Communist political and economic system that was dominant in the Soviet Union, eastern Europe, and Cuba.

These issues brought Reagan the support of many working-class, ethnic, northern voters and southern white voters. It was in large part due to these voters—subsequently called Reagan Democrats—that Ronald Reagan won the presidential election of 1980.

Although the Republicans dominated the presidency for the next twelve years, many of the voters who supported Republicans at the national level stayed loyal to the Democrats in congressional, state, and local elections, especially in the South. This split-ticket voting made it hard for parties to sustain complete voter allegiance at all levels of elected office.

Reagan's vice president, George H. W. Bush, elected president in 1988, had to work with a Democratic-controlled House and Senate. While in office, President Bush was confronted with a very large budget deficit and subsequently approved deficit reduction legislation that raised some taxes and also raised voter anger, particularly among Republican voters who had supported him in 1988. Not only did the Republican Party have a central belief that taxes should be as low as possible, but Bush had promised that he would not raise taxes—in his nomination acceptance speech at the Republican National Convention, where he said, "Read my lips: No new taxes." When Ross Perot entered the race as a third-party candidate to emphasize fiscal responsibility, he took voter support away from Bush, who lost his reelection bid to Clinton.

> **Connections:** What are the advantages and disadvantages of split-ticket voting? Is it best to be an Independent?

© ROBERT MAASS/CORBIS

In his acceptance speech at the Republican National Convention in 1988, George H. W. Bush promised not to raise taxes. "Read my lips," he famously said, "No new taxes." It was a campaign promise he came to regret in 1990, when he agreed with Congress to raise taxes and decrease government spending to reduce the federal budget deficit.

The Modern Partisan Landscape

Bill Clinton was governor of Arkansas when he successfully ran for president in 1992. As had Reagan, Clinton changed his party's direction with a campaign platform that advocated dropping opposition to the death penalty, being more open to free trade, and promising a middle-class tax cut. These policies moved the Democrats away from liberal policies, but Clinton still ran under the established Democratic Party label. Clinton thus appealed to a wider range of voters, and he was able to recapture some electoral territory the Democrats had lost in the southern states.

In office, however, Clinton lost popularity by veering away from core issues such as the middle-class tax cut and economic growth to address socially liberal policies on abortion and gays in the military, which he had given far less emphasis to on the campaign trail. Clinton also proposed a stimulus package of government spending and the creation of a major federal health care program for the uninsured. At the time, voters perceived these policies as too liberal, and they caused conflict among liberal, moderate, and conservative members of the Democratic Party. The conflict grew intense enough that it prevented the Democratic majority in Congress from passing key legislative measures, and the public nature of the infighting made it appear as if the Democrats were not capable of governing efficiently. These political missteps set the stage for a Republican Party resurgence.

In the 1994 midterm congressional elections, Republicans took control of both the House and the Senate for the first time since 1954. Led by Newt Gingrich, a Republican House member from Georgia, the Republicans put forth a party platform called the Contract with America, which promised ten major policy initiatives, such as a balanced federal budget and less federal regulation. Every Republican candidate for the House signed it, and by coordinating candidates this way, the Republican Party presented a single national message to voters about what it would do if it won control of Congress. In addition, Gingrich strategically targeted seats in the South that were held by conservative Democrats, trying to appeal to the same set of southern voters who elected Ronald Reagan. Republican efforts were successful, finally overcoming the split-ticket voting of southern voters who had previously voted Democratic in congressional elections.[24]

At the presidential level, George W. Bush, the son of former President George H. W. Bush and a conservative Republican governor of Texas, built on the momentum of the Republicans to launch a bid for the presidency in 1999. Josh McKoon's first paid job on a presidential campaign was working for Bush in South Carolina to get out the college-age vote. The presidential election of 2000 was highly controversial because there were irregularities in the vote count in several states, including Florida, which were ultimately resolved by the Supreme Court. It was also an election in which the candidate with the greatest number of popular votes, Democrat Al Gore, was defeated by the candidate with the greatest number of Electoral College delegates.

In 2004 the Democratic Party had to try to regroup and present a viable alternative to lure back the voters it had seemingly lost. At that time, nearly

Connections:
Is realignment a generational change of the social contract?

50 percent of voters identified themselves as Democrats or leaning Democratic, 40 percent identified themselves as Republicans or leaning Republican, and 10 percent did not identify with either party.[25] Despite the Democrats' seeming partisan edge, Bush was reelected in 2004 by a much greater margin than in 2000; his victory was in large part viewed as a result of his strong stance on terrorism after the September 11, 2001, terrorist attacks and his successful tax cut politics.

In 2006 the Democrats began to regain electoral momentum with voters who self-identified as Democrats but had not been voting that way in recent elections, as well as with Independent voters. In the congressional and gubernatorial elections held that year, the Democrats made sufficient gains in districts and states that had been narrowly or moderately leaning Republican to regain control of the House of Representatives and Senate. But one election does not constitute voter realignment. That year, there were powerful short-term forces, such as corruption scandals and the Iraq War, that put voters in a particularly sour mood toward incumbent Republicans.

The results of the 2008 elections were a sign that the party landscape was shifting again[26] (see Figure 9.4). Clearly the election of an African American president is a significant turning point in race relations; Barack Obama received 43 percent of the white vote in 2008, 2 percentage points higher than white candidate John Kerry received in 2004.

However, when voters give one party majority party control of the White House and Congress, they have high expectations for a strong governing track record. In one way, that is what political scientists mean by **responsible parties**; if the parties offer voters clear choices, voters can hold the party in charge responsible for policy outcomes. When President Obama and the Democrats took charge of government in 2009, they faced some of the greatest economic challenges since the Great Depression, ongoing wars in Iraq and Afghanistan, and the task of trying to make health insurance available to all Americans. The 2010 congressional midterm elections were the first opportunity that voters had to register their satisfaction or dissatisfaction with the president and his party and they did so by giving Republicans control of the House of Representatives and electing more Republicans to the Senate. The Democratic losses and Republican gains showed the responsible party system in action, because voters held the incumbent majority party accountable for its performance on the economy, health care, and the ongoing wars.

The elections of 2010 were also important for party politics more generally because the influence of the Tea Party movement pushed the Republican Party further to the right on issues of taxes, health care, and federal spending. The Tea Party movement's success in defeating incumbent Republicans in primaries and in electing Republicans who espoused more conservative views

 responsible parties: *Parties that take responsibility for offering the electorate a distinct range of policies and programs, thus providing a clear choice.*

Connections: Do political parties help voters hold government responsible? Why?

Connections: What are the advantages and disadvantages of responsible parties?

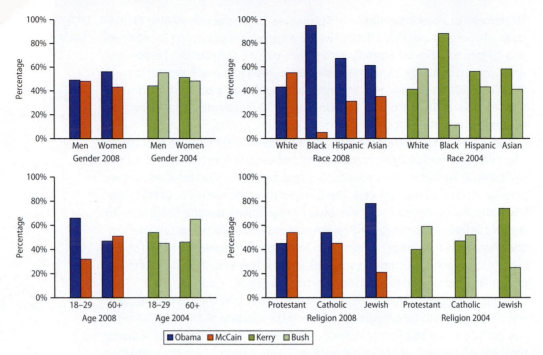

FIGURE 9.4 Votes for President in 2004 and 2008, by Demographic Group.

Patterns of support among voters can change from one election to the next, depending on the candidate the party chooses as its nominee.

Source: *New York Times*, http://elections.nytimes.com.

Connections: Is partisanship taking precedence over policy making? What can be done about that?

Connections: Are consensus and compromise good or bad for American democracy? Give examples.

created a more polarized and less effective governing environment in Congress (see Chapter 6, Figure 6.6). It also cemented opposition to President Obama to the point that Republicans who suggested compromise with the president were threatened with primary challenges and outright opposition in the general election. The 2012 campaigns were notable for the conservative positions adopted by Republican candidates at all levels of government on illegal immigration, access to contraception and abortion, and federal spending.

There is a trade-off between responsible party government and bipartisan cooperation; where there is one, there is almost never the other. In 2011–12, the two major parties were more divided on nearly every important issue than at any time since the Civil War.[27] Members of Congress from opposite parties rarely communicate directly with each other anymore; instead, they take to the airwaves on cable TV and Twitter to criticize each other. Elected officials from each party draw such sharp distinctions between themselves and their partisan opponents that voters in

2012 expressed concerns that the federal government had ceased to function. For most of that year, congressional approval ratings hovered around 14 percent, nearly the lowest congressional approval ratings on record.[28]

Despite the wide divide between the two major parties, within each party members do not always agree on issues and party leaders are not always able to forge internal cooperation. Elected officials are constantly exposed to a wide range of opinions, and they face pressures to respond both to the voters and to party elites. In addition, party activists are able to track elected officials and monitor how well they adhere to the party's policies. Although increased participation in the deliberation of important issues is a welcome development in a democracy, it makes it hard to represent constituents, toe the party line, and still be able to compromise when necessary to enact good public policy.

Checkpoint

Can you:

☐ Explain how voters align and realign with political parties

☐ Describe the impact of the New Deal on political ideology

☐ Explain how the Democratic Party came to be seen by African Americans as the party that supported civil rights

☐ Recall how Ronald Reagan's campaign strategy appealed to conservative Democrats

☐ Describe the general shift in the ideological core of the Democratic and Republican Parties since 1994

Political Parties and Public Policy: Immigration

Political parties lay out their platforms during the campaign season, and elections serve as a key link between parties and policy outcomes. The extent to which candidates honor their party's platform can differ, depending on external conditions and the opportunities available to them. Not every element of a party platform can be enacted into law, but lawmakers, from the president to state legislators, recognize that they must try to address the issues raised in their campaign platforms to retain the trust of voters (see Chapter 10).

Among the most contentious issues in the public policy sphere is the question of immigration reform—for both legal and illegal immigration. Immigration has fueled U.S. population growth since the nation's founding. In 2010 there were 39,956,000 foreign-born people in the United States—12.9 percent of the total population. The largest percentage of foreign-born people come from Latin America (mostly Mexico), followed by people from Asia and then Europe.[29] Immigration laws serve simultaneously as gates regulating entry into the United States and as gateways to eventual citizenship. For those individuals who entered the United States illegally and have put down roots, there is no current pathway to legal citizenship available. However, children who are born to illegal immigrants living in the United States are legal citizens because of the Fourteenth Amendment to the Constitution.

The Legal Immigration Process

For the most part, the main political parties do not hold core differences on legal immigration policy. The legal immigration process is jointly administered by the Department of State and the U.S. Citizenship and Immigration Services (USCIS), an agency of the Department of Homeland Security. Immigrants seeking to come to the United States apply for visas, which are granted by the Department of State; once they arrive, their journey toward citizenship is overseen by USCIS.[30] To come to the United States with the intention of staying on a permanent basis, individuals can apply for a general immigration visa, a family relations visa, or an employment visa. The Immigration and Nationality Act of 1990 sets an annual limit of between 416,000 and 675,000 on these types of visas; in addition, 50,000 visas are set aside for people born in countries that have recently had the lowest numbers of immigrants to the United States.[31] In 2010, 476,049 individuals entered the United States as legal permanent residents.[32]

To become a naturalized citizen, an immigrant must first apply to be a legal permanent resident (LPR) of the United States, a step known as getting a green card, which is the permanent resident card issued to those who are eligible. (The green card is no longer green, but the name has remained.) To get a green card, an individual must secure a sponsor who will attest that the individual has some means of financial support. The individual must also take a medical exam and secure proof of employment if he or she intends to hold a job in the United States. This last criterion can present a significant barrier to permanent residency: The federal government requires an individual seeking permanent residence to have talents or skills for a particular job that a current U.S. citizen could not provide. To become a fully naturalized U.S. citizen, a green card holder must reside in the United States continuously for at least five years; be able to read, write, and speak English; pass a citizenship test on the history and government of the United States (see Chapter 5); and pledge support for the United States.[33]

Connections: Should a democracy have any barriers to legal immigration?

The Debate over Illegal Immigration

There are significant differences between the Republican and Democratic Parties on the issue of illegal immigration, and pressure to reform immigration laws to address this issue has mounted because of the high numbers of individuals who have entered the United States outside the legal immigration

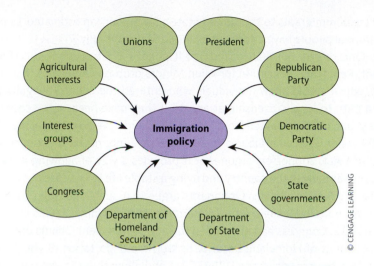

Unions

President

Agricultural interests

Republican Party

Interest groups

Immigration policy

Democratic Party

Congress

State governments

Department of Homeland Security

Department of State

© CENGAGE LEARNING

process. Republicans tend to hold that individuals who broke the law to enter the United States must be forced to return to their country of origin and apply for legal immigration status. Democrats tend to believe that individuals who arrived illegally but have since established productive lives should be legally incorporated into society and have the opportunity to be full and active citizens.

However, there are variations on these positions within both political parties, and members of both parties have at times worked together to address the issue of illegal immigration. The last major piece of legislation to deal specifically with illegal immigration was the 1986 Immigration Reform and Control Act, which passed with bipartisan support and was signed into law by President Ronald Reagan. The act granted amnesty, or forgiveness, to almost 2.8 million individuals who had entered the country illegally and wished to stay as legal residents.[34] Since then, amnesty has been extended to specific groups of illegal residents from Latin America and Haiti, and amnesty is still available to anyone who was eligible under the 1986 law but has not yet filed for legal residence. Proponents of amnesty argue that giving illegal residents legal status makes it possible for them to earn fair wages, participate in politics, and pay taxes on their earnings. Without amnesty, proponents argue, these families are torn apart when parents are forced to leave the United States while their children, born in the United States and therefore citizens, stay in this country. Opponents of immigration reform argue that the 1986 amnesty program only encouraged more people to enter the United States illegally and any extension of amnesty will only do the same. In addition, they argue that illegal immigrants take away jobs from workers who are here legally because the illegal immigrants are willing to work for lower wages and employers do not pay Social Security tax on these wages. What is certain is that the 1986 reform bill did not stem the flow of illegal immigrants to the United States. Since then, an estimated 12 million additional people have entered the United States illegally.

One reform bill that looked like it might have traction is the Development, Relief, and Education for Alien Minors proposal, known as the DREAM Act, which would allow individuals who entered the country illegally to get on a path to legal citizenship at age 16 if they have been in the country for five years, have graduated from high school, and have no criminal record.[35] In 2009, when President Obama took office, he announced his support for the DREAM Act. Supporters argue that it provides a way of allowing individuals who are already in the country and living a stable life to increase their chances to be productive citizens. Opponents argue that such a bill will be an incentive for more individuals with children to enter the United States illegally. By June 2012, Congress had not passed the act, so President Obama ordered the Department of Homeland Security to stop the deportation of young people who met the criteria of the DREAM Act and allow them to apply for temporary work permits. Although it did not create a full path to citizenship, President Obama's action did partially implement the policy goals of the act.[36]

State and Local Action on Illegal Immigration

Connections:
Should states and the federal government share jurisdiction over immigration?

States and localities, especially those along the border with Mexico, have tried to address illegal immigration in their own ways. States with Republican-dominated legislatures have taken more punitive action than those controlled by Democrats. The most publicized effort took place in Arizona, where in April 2010 Republican Governor Jan Brewer signed a law, S.B. 1070, that allowed police officers to ask about immigration status when they stopped individuals for another police matter. Under the law, it was a crime to fail to show documentation establishing legal residence in the United States, and police officers could hold someone until their immigration status was verified.[37] Later that year, the U.S. Justice Department sued to get the law struck down in federal court on the basis that the state was infringing on the proper role of the federal government on immigration. The federal district court judge in the case issued an injunction against this provision of the law, and the injunction was subsequently upheld by the Ninth Circuit Court of Appeals. The Supreme Court agreed to hear the case, *Arizona v. United States*, in 2012 and subsequently struck down most provisions of the law because it assumed state powers over immigration that are granted to the federal government. The Court allowed states to confirm people's immigration status while enforcing other laws.[38]

Not all state responses to illegal immigration have been punitive. For example, California, Texas, and New Mexico have each adopted policies that allow illegal immigrants to receive private and public aid to attend state colleges and universities. Their justification is that it is better to educate residents who are in the United States so that they can contribute to society than it is to put up gates against their educational and economic advancements. What is notable is that California has a Democratic governor, and Texas and New Mexico have Republican governors. In 2012, Governor Rick Perry (R-Tex.) came under attack in the Republican presidential primaries for his more moderate support of educational programs available to illegal immigrants. To some, his position was a major reason he dropped out of the race. During the 2012 election, Republican Party presidential nominee Governor Mitt Romney called for stricter enforcement of immigration laws and border control to prevent people from entering the country illegally.

Ultimately it will be a major challenge for policy makers in both major political parties to construct a holistic immigration policy that is both fair and practical. Although there is general agreement within the core membership of each party, there are enough dissenting voices on how to best cope with illegal immigration that a clear policy choice between the parties may not emerge. One factor that might affect the future of immigration reform is the growing number of Latinos in the United States who typically express strong opposition to punitive measures on illegal immigration. As the number of Latino voters grows, the United States may see more convergence on a single policy position by the parties in an effort to win this increasingly important voting bloc.

When President Obama visited Arizona on January 25, 2012, Governor Jan Brewer greeted him at the airport and appeared to scold the president. This photograph of her pointing her figure at him was immediately picked up by the national media. During the visit, Obama and Brewer discussed the issue of border control and illegal immigration, but their conversations were overshadowed by the outcry over this photograph, which critics of Arizona's law used as exemplifying intolerance on the issue.

aplia Construct Your Own Policy

1. Construct an immigration policy that treats potential immigrants from all foreign countries equally while maintaining a total limit on yearly immigration.

2. Design an amnesty program for illegal immigrants who currently work and live in the United States that does not also encourage illegal immigration in future years.

   For more on the policy-making process, see Chapter 1.

Connections: In the immigration debate, do you side with the Republicans, the Democrats, or neither?

Political Parties and Democracy

Focus Questions Revisited

- How do political parties shape the choices voters face in local, state, and federal elections?

- In what ways do political parties allow voters to hold their elected officials accountable for the policies they produce?

- How do political parties respond to changes in public opinion on key issues?

- Do political parties enable all citizens to participate equally in self-government, or do they help give more power to some people, and less to others? Explain.

- Are political parties a gate or a gateway to democracy?

Political parties, which emerged in the nation's first decade, now play a major role in American democracy. The Democrats and the Republicans together claim the allegiance of more than 90 percent of voters when one includes strong identifiers and voters who consistently lean toward one party.[39] Political parties determine the choices voters have at the polls by crafting the laws that allow candidates to be on the ballot and overseeing the primaries that allow voters to choose candidates. Parties also recruit candidates for elected office, raise funds for campaigns, register voters, and organize get-out-the-vote drives. In sum, parties shape the selection of candidates who seek, run for, and win elected office.

Do political parties make it easier for voters to hold elected officials accountable? Party platforms tell voters what candidates intend to do if elected, and voters can compare their actions against their campaign pledges. If pledges and policies match up, voters typically reelect the officials; if they do not, voters can vote for the opponents in the next election. One advantage of clear lines between the parties is that it makes the job of monitoring the government easier for the average voter. However, such clear divisions also bring the disadvantages of conflict and stalemate that make bipartisan policy making difficult.

Parties do a mixed job of promoting equal political participation among all citizens. On the one hand, they are a gateway to participation because membership in a political party is free and citizens can work a little or a lot on behalf of the party. Primaries and caucuses give every party member a say in determining who will represent the party in elected office, and they force candidates who seek the party's endorsement to shape their campaign platforms according to party voters' preferences. Because voters are free to join and leave political parties as frequently as they wish, parties are always seeking to represent their members' viewpoints.

But parties can discourage political participation by putting obstacles in the way of third-party formation. The U.S. party system is structured around two major parties, and even though third parties have arisen at various times, they are quickly subsumed or defeated by one of the two major parties. The two-party system reduces major policy issues to two-sided questions, when in fact the complexity of these issues warrants multiple perspectives. The problem for democracy is that there is no formal venue for presenting multiple perspectives in elections or in the governing institutions.

The larger question is whether the twenty-first-century U.S. party system fulfills the role of enabling widespread participation in the governing process. In terms of responding to changes in public opinion, political parties fall short of meeting their responsibilities as agents of democratic government. They are large, entrenched organizations with multiple layers—federal, state, and local—that can differ in their viewpoints on specific issues. The breadth of the national parties makes it difficult to reach internal consensus on issues at every level of government.

The combination of intra-party divisions with interparty polarization and conflict has produced a party-dominated democracy that is not consistently responsive to voters' interests and opinions. However, in a democracy, power rests on winning elections, and for that parties will always depend on voters like you, who hold the power to change them by staying loyal or switching allegiance.

gatewaystolearning

Top Ten to Take Away

1. Political parties are the broadest and most open gateway to participation in American politics. (pp. 270–271)
2. They have one primary purpose: to win elections in order to control government power and implement their policies. (p. 271)
3. Parties organize the electorate by giving them choices of policies and candidates, and they also organize Congress and state legislatures into cohesive groups that consistently vote for the policies that they promise in their platforms. (pp. 271–274)
4. Parties nominate candidates for office in primary elections, which are open to all voters, although in some states voters must affiliate with a party before voting. (pp. 274–278)
5. The basic division between the Federalists and the Antifederalists over the ratification of the Constitution survived into the Washington administration to become factions; by the time of Jefferson's election in 1800, the factions had become political parties. (pp. 278–279)
6. Between 1800 and the Civil War, various parties rose and fell, but since the end of the war the two major

parties—the Democratic Party and the Republican Party—have dominated the American political system. (pp. 279–282)
7. The effects of the two-party system are to limit voter choices to "for" and "against" and to discourage third parties, although the issues third parties arise to address are frequently adopted by one of the major political parties. (pp. 283–288)
8. Voter realignments occur when the parties readjust the focus of their policies, typically as a result of a major event such as an economic depression or a military conflict. (pp. 289–297)
9. Since Franklin D. Roosevelt's New Deal of the 1930s, liberals have generally aligned with the Democratic Party and conservatives with the Republican Party. (pp. 289–291)
10. The modern political landscape is marked by a partisan divide, with the parties taking on starker opposing positions and ramping up rhetoric to the point that voters sometimes wonder if partisanship is taking precedence over policy making. (pp. 293–297)

Key Concepts

Australian ballot (p. 282). How did the Australian ballot reduce the party boss's control over election outcomes?

ballot (p. 274). What types of ballots were used before electronic voting?

caucus (p. 275). How is a caucus different from a primary?

frontloading (p. 278). What is frontloading and how does influence primary outcomes?

general election (p. 274). What is the role of parties in general elections?

majority vote (p. 284). What is the difference between plurality and majority vote?

median voter theorem (p. 284). Why does the median voter theorem contribute to limited political choice?

national committees (p. 273). What are the responsibilities of the national committees?

party alignment (p. 289). Is party alignment stable today?

party caucus (p. 272). Which form of the party—party in the electorate, party in government, party as an organization—are party caucuses affiliated with and why?

party platform (p. 271). What role do party platforms play in electoral politics?

patronage system (p. 281). How did the patronage system strengthen political parties?

plurality vote (p. 284). How does plurality voting encourage third parties?

political parties (p. 271). How are political parties a gateway to democracy?

primary election (p. 274). When did primaries first emerge in U.S. politics?

proportional representation (p. 276). How does proportional representation work?

realignment (p. 291). What precipitates a realignment?

responsible parties (p. 295). How does a responsible party system produce accountability?

single-member plurality system (p. 284). Why does a single-member plurality system promote a two-party system?

winner-take-all system (p. 276). What are the advantages and disadvantages of a winner-take-all system?

Your Virtual Tutor
Master What You Need to Know and Test Yourself.

Learning Outcomes

WHAT YOU NEED...

To Know	To Test Yourself	To Participate
How political parties evolved in American politics	• Define political party • Identify the three arenas in which parties operate • Track the party nomination process	• Consider how political parties shape politics • Choose to join a party • Design a system that allows the greatest number of voters to participate in choosing the party nominee
Which issues divided the first political parties	• Explain the differences between the Federalists and the Antifederalists • Describe the events that opened up the presidential nomination process • Explain how the Republican Party formed • Connect patronage and party power • Describe reforms that reduced party power	• Evaluate the importance of a strong central government to democracy • Reflect on ways to broaden the grassroots base for modern political parties • Consider whether party power should be further reduced
Why two parties dominate the U.S. political system	• Explain the median voter theorem • Describe how a single-member plurality system encourages two parties • Summarize the role third parties have played in American politics • Survey the obstacles to third parties and independent candidates • Explain how interest groups and political parties have become more closely aligned	• Assess whether the 2012 elections prove that the party closer to the middle wins • Consider whether the parties accurately reflect voters' views • Debate whether the formation of third parties should be the only way to transform the public issue agenda
How to define partisan affiliation and ideology	• Explain how voters align and realign with political parties • Describe the impact of the New Deal on political ideology • Explain how the Democratic Party came to be seen by African Americans as the party that supported civil rights • Recall how Ronald Reagan's campaign strategy appealed to conservative Democrats • Describe the general shift in the ideological core of the Democratic and Republican Parties since 1994	• Evaluate the value of stable party alignments in the political process • Understand the modern definitions of *liberal* and *conservative* • Consider the lasting impact of a strategic presidential campaign on party alignment • Survey the current partisan landscape

GATEWAYS TO LEARNING   **305**

> **"** *It's within your power to change the system. Don't ever feel that you're not capable of leading in our democracy.* **"**

Maya Torralba, University of Science and Arts of Oklahoma, Chickasha

CLASS 1932

COURTESY OF MAYA TORRALBA

COURTESY OF UNIVERSITY SCIENCE AND ARTS, OKLAHOMA

10 Elections, Campaigns, and Voting

As a senior political science major at the University of Science and Arts of Oklahoma in Chickasha, Maya Torralba might have focused, like many seniors, on grades and a job search, but she instead turned her efforts to helping her community. As a Native American—a member of the Kiowa tribe and also of Comanche and Wichita descent—she was less worried about her personal prospects than about the prospects for young women in her hometown of Anadarko, a city in central Oklahoma where Native Americans form a near majority. She knew that these teenagers were battling drug abuse, teen pregnancy, and a general lack of hope. "They feel like they don't fit into society," Torralba explains. Through the Community Esteem Project that she established in 2008 as a fellow with Young People For, a leadership initiative of the People for the American Way Foundation, Torralba has sought to empower these young women. "I want to show the ladies the power that Native women have had within themselves throughout history," she explains.

The program has taught teenagers how to make traditional regalia and has brought them together with elder women who talk about their life experiences and overcoming obstacles associated with the loss of Native culture. "What I found," says Torralba, "is that the girls have a defeatist mentality in their education and academic work. They don't feel like they can achieve good grades or finish school." Through the Community Esteem Project, the young women of Anadarko

aplia Need to Know

- What ideas molded the Framers' thinking about elections
- What the steps in presidential campaigns are
- What issues shape presidential campaigns
- What the steps in congressional campaigns are
- What issues shape congressional campaigns
- Why there are battles over ballot access
- Who tends to turn out in American elections
- How low turnout is in American elections
- What important forms of participation there are other than voting

are reconnecting with their heritage. They are learning that "they don't have to 'fit' anywhere," says Torralba. "They make their own spot by going back to their traditions."

Native empowerment has been a theme of Torralba's life. She helps with the Anadarko UNITY Council, does research for the Celebrate Native Health Grant, and volunteers for an Indians for Indians radio program. She and her brother started an online radio station, Radio Kiowa, to help Native American children learn their indigenous languages. Torralba believes that voting is a gateway to Native empowerment. In the summer of 2006, she led voter registration drives at Native events in western Oklahoma and made sure that registered voters got to the polls in November. She was also active in the 2008 get-out-the-vote drive.

Torralba's commitment to helping her community demonstrates that the gateways to participation at the local level are wide open. As a student, she balanced schoolwork, family life (she and her husband have three young children), and community service. She also recognized the gates that seemed to stand in the way of a strong civic life, especially for Native Americans. But she knew, too, that if people voted, their voices would be heard, and that if young women believed in themselves,

they would invest in their communities. Self-esteem, she believes, builds community esteem.

In 2010, Torralba pursued another gateway by running for the Oklahoma state legislature. Although she did not win the election, she ran a courageous campaign that relied very little on money. Instead, she went door to door, seeking votes from local communities in Oklahoma such as Anadarko, Binger, and Verden. Her "shoe leather" campaign drew attention for its energy.[1]

Democracy thrives when citizens dedicate themselves to their communities. For democracy to work, it is essential that citizens be involved in public life in ways that advance both self-interest and civic interest. Participation makes the system responsive. Voting is the most important gateway to participation, but as Torralba's community-focused work attests, it is only one of the ways that active citizens can make their communities better. In this chapter, we examine how elections, campaigns, and voting work, asking whether, and how, these institutions promote government responsiveness and equality for citizens. The chapter also addresses other forms of participation that help hold government accountable, including protests and the rise of e-participation. Finally, we look at recent and future public policy concerning participation and voting.

FocusQuestions

- In what ways do elections encourage accountability and responsiveness in government?
- How does citizen equality work, or not work, in elections and campaigns?
- Do laws that regulate the financing of campaigns impede or advance equality and accountability in elections?
- Do young citizens participate enough to make the system responsive to their preferences? What about other groups?
- In what ways are elections, campaigns, and voting gateways to American democracy? What are the gates?
- How do other forms of participation, besides voting, serve as gateways to democracy? Are they more or less effective than voting?

The Constitutional Requirements for Elections

> **What ideas molded the Framers' thinking about elections**

Given the importance of elections to the democratic process, it is surprising that the Constitution says so little about them, primarily setting up barriers against direct democracy. Only the House of Representatives was to be elected directly by the people. In elections for the president and for the Senate, the public's role was indirect and complex. Today, senators are elected directly by the people. Presidential elections also give citizens more say in the process, but these contests continue to be shaped by constitutional requirements that serve as a gate between the people and the presidency. In this section, we explain the constitutional requirements for American elections as background for understanding the ways in which presidential and congressional campaigns are run.

Presidential Elections

The constitutional rules governing the selection of the president reflect three fundamental themes that guided the Framers' thinking. First, the states were given broad discretion on key matters regarding presidential elections to ensure their importance and to counterbalance the power of the national government. Second, the Framers designed the presidency with George Washington in mind and did not spell out all aspects in great detail, including elections. Over time, the details were filled in. Third, the presidency was envisioned as being above party politics, doing what was right for the nation rather than supporting one faction over another. That assumption went awry early on, and parties formed almost from the start.

The Electoral College. The means by which the president of the United States is elected was born of compromise between the interests of the states and the interests of the people, yielding a system that even today is indirect and confusing. The formal selection of the president is in the hands of electors, who collectively constitute the **Electoral College**.

The Constitution gave state legislatures the responsibility of deciding how best to choose electors. Because state legislators were, for the most part, elected by the people, this arrangement gave the public an indirect say in the choice. The idea was that the state legislatures would serve as gatekeepers against rash or ignorant voters. There was little support among the Framers for letting the people choose the president directly. Today the people of each state, not the members of state legislatures, choose the electors in an arrangement that has given citizens a new gateway for influence (see Figure 10.1).

Connections:
Why did the Framers set up gates against popular participation in elections?

Connections: Why did the Framers give so much authority over presidential elections to the states?

Electoral College: *The presidential electors, selected to represent the votes of their respective states, who meet every four years to cast the electoral votes for president and vice president.*

Electoral votes per state = number of senators (2) + number of representatives
Total number of electoral votes = 538
Majority needed to elect the president = 270

Citizens go to the polls and vote on the Tuesday after the first Monday in November.

↓

Votes are counted by the states.

↓

In each state, the candidate receiving the most votes is the winner.

↓

Each state appoints the winner's electors to the Electoral College.

↓

The electors meet in their respective state capitals and vote for the winner on the Monday after the second Wednesday in December.

↓

Congress meets in joint session to count the electoral votes and announce the next president.

Each state's number of electors for the 2012 election, allocated on the basis of the 2010 census.

Note: In every state but two the winner of the popular vote takes all of the electoral votes. Maine and Nebraska allocate votes by congressional district and so can split their electoral votes.

FIGURE 10.1 How the Electoral College Works.

© CENGAGE LEARNING

The electors, however, remain the formal decision makers for choosing the president. Before the election, each party lines up electors for its candidate. In the 2012 presidential elections, both Mitt Romney and Barack Obama chose people they could trust to be loyal to them. This is important because many states allow electors to vote their conscience; they are not bound by the results of the election in their state. However, electors who deviate from the candidate to whom they are pledged are rare.

Each state receives a number of electoral votes equal to its number of senators and members of the House of Representatives. The minimum is three, because every state has at least one House member and two senators. In all but two states, all the state's electoral votes are allocated to the candidate who finishes first in the voting. This winner-take-all system means that if a candidate wins California by just a single vote, that candidate gets all fifty-five of the state's electoral votes. The two exceptions are Nebraska and Maine, which allocate votes by congressional district and so can split

Connections: Is the winner-take-all system fair?

their electoral votes. In 2008 Barack Obama won one congressional district in Nebraska, securing one of Nebraska's five electoral votes. This was the only time either state split its votes.

To win the presidency, a candidate needs to win a majority (270) of the 538 electoral votes (538 is the total of 435 representatives and 100 senators plus 3 votes from the District of Columbia, whose residents can vote for president but do not have representation in Congress). If no one wins a majority of electoral votes, the election is thrown into the House of Representatives. At this point, each state delegation gets a single vote, and the candidate who wins a majority of the states becomes the next president. That last happened in 1824.

Problems with the Electoral College.

The Electoral College has never worked as the Framers envisioned, as an institution that would allow a group of independent decision makers to get together in the many states and deliberate over who would make the best president. The Framers viewed the presidency as a contest between individuals, not between political parties, and in the first four presidential elections (1789, 1792, 1796, and 1800), electors cast ballots for their top two choices; the winner became president, and the second-place finisher became vice president. The process ignored the parties of the candidates; the goal was to select the most qualified person. In 1796 the process yielded John Adams (1797–1801) as president and his chief rival, Thomas Jefferson, as vice president. Just imagine Mitt Romney becoming Barack Obama's vice president!

Problems increased in 1800, when political parties had fully emerged. Thomas Jefferson and Aaron Burr, both running as Democratic-Republicans, received the same number of Electoral College votes, even though everyone knew that Jefferson was seeking the presidency and Burr the vice presidency. Because there was no outright majority in the Electoral College and Burr would not concede, a lengthy battle in the House ensued, lasting thirty-seven ballots before Thomas Jefferson (1801–1809) won the presidency. The Twelfth Amendment, adopted in 1804, fixed this problem by combining the vote for president and vice president into one ballot, with the person running for each office named.

Another source of problems in the system was that states were free to set their own rules for selecting electors. Further, there was no agreed-upon time for holding these elections. States also frequently changed their methods of selecting electors. Now states hold elections all on the same day—the first Tuesday after the first Monday in November—and electors meet in December to choose the next president. The outcome in December is now largely a formality, a relic of the Framers' constitutional design.

> **Connections:** How did the emergence of political parties change the way the Framers hoped elections would work?

> **Connections:** What inequalities does state control of elections introduce?

Electoral College Reform.

The biggest problem with the Electoral College occurs when winning the nation's popular vote does not automatically translate into a win in the Electoral College, meaning that the individual who received fewer votes could become the president. This happened in the 1824, 1876, 1888, and 2000 presidential elections. Such outcomes raise questions about equality; because of the Electoral College, votes in some states matter more than votes in others. The votes citizens cast in Alaska have more than twice the influence of those cast in Texas.[2] If a democracy rests on the idea of majority rule—that is, the candidate with the most support in the public wins the election—then four or five presidential elections (about 10 percent) have been undemocratic.

Some may wonder why the country does not just change the rules to select the president through the popular vote. This method would appear more democratic because all votes would be treated equally. But the current system has some advantages. For example, the Electoral College system encourages candidates to secure support in all corners of the country, not just in areas with dense populations. A system of popular votes would privilege Los Angeles over New Hampshire. In America's federal system, the states do matter. Eliminating the Electoral College would decrease the role of the states, dampening the significance of state interests. There are also practical problems. Doing away with the Electoral College through a constitutional amendment would be difficult, because it is unlikely that three-quarters of the states, needed to ratify an amendment, would support such a reform. Small states see merit in the system.

Connections:
Should the Electoral College be eliminated? What would be the consequences?

The 2000 Presidential Election.

Because elections are a centerpiece of democracy, it is important for them to be viewed as fair. The events surrounding the 2000 presidential election tested the credibility of the American electoral process. The margin between Vice President Albert Gore Jr. and George W. Bush (2001–2009) was razor thin. In the popular vote, Gore received nearly 600,000 more votes than Bush—just a 0.5 percentage point difference (48.4 percent to 47.9 percent). The number of electoral votes did not identify a winner on election night because the state of Florida was too close to call, and without that state's electoral votes, neither candidate had the necessary 270 votes. Bush led in Florida by 537 votes out of 5.8 million votes cast—a 0.0001 percent difference. Demands for a recount ensued, and the Florida recount revealed how difficult it is to produce an accurate vote count. A series of court cases resulted in a Supreme Court decision that determined the outcome of the election (see Supreme Court Cases: *Bush v. Gore*).

AP PHOTO/MARTA LAVANDIER

Election workers in Miami manually recount votes while representatives of both parties observe. The 2000 Florida recount was fraught with difficulty, and a series of court cases regarding the election culminated in a Supreme Court decision on December 12 that halted the recount and essentially made George W. Bush the winner of the election.

supremecourtcases

Bush v. Gore (2000)

QUESTION: Does Florida's subjective recount mechanism violate equal protection of the law? If so, should there be a recount using more objective standards?

ORAL ARGUMENT: December 11, 2000 (listen at http://www.oyez.org/cases)

DECISION: December 12, 2000 (read at http://www.findlaw.com/casecode/supreme.html)

OUTCOME: Yes, Florida's recount procedures violate the equal protection clause (7–2), and no, there is insufficient time to conduct a recount (5–4).

The presidential election of 2000 came down to Florida's electoral votes. The candidate who won the state—Republican Governor George W. Bush of Texas or Democratic Vice President Al Gore—would win the election. The early counts were excruciatingly close, with the news networks first calling the election for Gore, then declaring it undecided, then declaring Bush the winner, and then putting it back in the undecided column.

Due to the closeness of the race, an automatic machine recount took place. Bush led Gore by 537 votes out of nearly 6 million cast. Because elections, even for federal office, are administered under state law, Gore went to state court in Florida, asking for a hand recount in four counties that would require election officials in those counties to determine, from each ballot, the intent of the voter. In punch card ballots, the machine will not read a ballot unless the chad—the area that is to be punched out by the voter—is completely removed. But a hand count might be able to determine the voter's intent from a "hanging" or "dimpled" or "pregnant" chad—indented but not sufficiently punched out so as to break off or even break the corners.

The Florida Supreme Court ruled for Gore by a 4–3 vote on December 8. Bush then filed suit in federal court, claiming that the standard of the intent of the voter that Florida used, which could mean different standards by different officials, was so arbitrary as to violate the equal protection clause. The Bush legal team asked for an injunction, an order blocking further recount. Both the U.S. District Court and the U.S. Court of Appeals rejected Bush's request. Bush then appealed to the Supreme Court.

The Supreme Court agreed to hear the case, and on December 9, it decided, by a 5–4 vote, to halt the recount before the Court's decision. The Court heard oral arguments on December 11 and announced its decision at 10:00 P.M. on December 12.

The Supreme Court ruled by a 7–2 vote that the absence of specific standards for gauging the intent of the voter was so arbitrary as to violate the equal protection clause. The Court also declared by a 5–4 vote that Florida's legislature intended all recounts to be completed by December 12, thus making a recount impossible.

The dissenters declared that the machinery of running elections is a state question that should not involve the federal courts; that the Court's prior interpretation of the equal protection clause has allowed differential treatment as long as there is no intent to discriminate against certain groups; and that the Court's December 12 deadline was never stated in Florida law.

Vice President Gore conceded the election the next day.

- **Why was the Supreme Court so rushed in its decision?**
- **In what way did Florida's recount plan violate equality?**

Many votes had not been counted in Florida, and some had been counted for the wrong candidate. Citizens across the country lost faith in American elections. Nearly one in five voters had doubts about whether his or her vote had been counted.[3] Only 32 percent thought there was "a fair and accurate vote count in Florida."[4] In January 2001, just a few days before George W. Bush was to be sworn in as president, only 51 percent of the public felt he had won the presidency "legitimately."[5] More than 60 percent wanted to do away with the Electoral College.[6]

Since that time, the public's confidence has been restored. By 2008 only one in twenty Americans had doubts about whether his or her vote had been counted. The 2000 election raised distrust in the short run but did little lasting damage to the nation's electoral institutions.

Connections: Was the outcome of the 2000 presidential election fair? Does it matter if it was fair?

Congressional Elections

The constitutional guidelines for congressional elections also reflect the compromise between the interests of the states and the interests of the people. The Framers intended that the Senate would bring state interests to bear on the legislative process, while they intended that the House would represent the people. Each state, regardless of size, has two senators, while representatives are elected from congressional districts within states whose boundaries are adjusted to accommodate changes in population. Senators serve staggered six-year terms, while House members serve two-year terms.

Senate Elections. The Constitution originally gave the choice of senators to state legislatures. Again the Framers inserted a gate between the people and those who were to serve their interests in the Senate. In the late nineteenth century, however, Progressive reformers argued that the people ought to have a direct say in the election of senators. This reform became a reality with the adoption of the Seventeenth Amendment in 1913. However, there are still barriers against overwhelming change in the composition of the Senate because Senate elections are staggered; only one-third of senators are up for election at a time. This arrangement ensures that the Senate is insulated from large shifts in public sentiment.

Connections: How do differences in term lengths and constituencies affect how senators and House members behave?

House Elections and Redistricting. In contrast to the Senate, the entire House of Representatives is up for election every two years. Also in contrast to the Senate, House members have always been elected directly by the people.

The Constitution requires that representatives be apportioned, within each state, according to population, which is counted every ten years in a census. As the population grew, the House also grew; in 1929 the number of representatives was capped at 435. A member now represents, on average, more than 700,000 people, as set by the 2010 census.

Every ten years, new district lines are drawn following a census. Depending on patterns of population growth or decline, states win or lose congressional seats with each new census. State legislatures are responsible for drawing the district lines in a process known as **redistricting**. While the official aim of redistricting is to try to keep districts equal in terms of population, the majority party in the state legislature tries to construct each district in such a way as to make it easier for its candidates to win congressional seats. Although citizens are not required to disclose party affiliation in the census, past voting patterns give parties a strong indication of where they have the advantage. A main limitation of this redistricting process is that the boundaries of the district must be contiguous (uninterrupted).

Redistricting has also been used as a tool to achieve greater minority representation in the House of Representatives. Following passage of the Voting Rights Act in 1965, some states sought to dilute the effect of minority voters by drawing district lines so as to split their voting strength. In 1982 amendments to the Voting Rights Act forbade this practice, and in response state legislatures created majority-minority districts, in which African Americans or Hispanics would constitute a majority of the voters in the

redistricting: *Process whereby state legislatures redraw the boundaries of congressional districts in the state to make them equal in population size.*

Connections: Do majority-minority districts help advance equality or introduce inequalities?

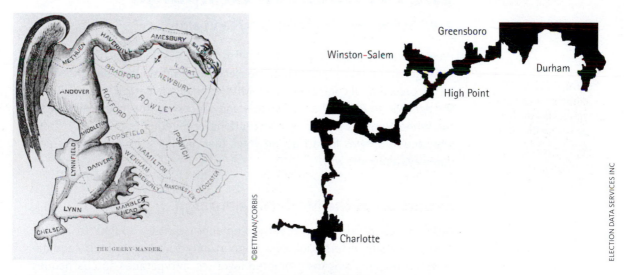

©BETTMAN/CORBIS

ELECTION DATA SERVICES INC

The term *gerrymander* comes from the salamander-shaped district in Massachusetts (above left), which Governor Elbridge Gerry approved following the census of 1810. Political rivals denounced the blatant seeking of political advantage that had produced such an oddly shaped congressional district, and the taunt stuck, passing into common usage in politics. Nevertheless, gerrymandered districts remain. In 1991 a North Carolina redistricting was designed to create a district with African Americans in the majority (above right). Federal courts later ruled that North Carolina had to revise these district lines so that the congressional district was more compact.

gerry-mandering:

Redistricting that blatantly benefits one political party over the other or concentrates (or dilutes) the voting impact of racial and ethnic groups.

district, thereby increasing the possibility of their electing African American or Hispanic candidates. In the past decade, however, the federal courts have ruled that state legislatures overemphasized the racial composition of these districts to the point that the districts made no geographic sense. As a result, current guidelines on redistricting call for the consideration of race in drawing district lines, but not to the extreme that it has been employed in the past.

Any change to the size and shape of a district can have political implications because shifts in its partisan makeup alter which party might be able to capture the seat. For these reasons, there are major battles over the composition of districts. The politicization of drawing districts is called **gerrymandering**. Chapter 11, Congress, provides more details about this process and explains how different compositions of districts can alter the kind of gateway congressional elections offer.

✓ **Checkpoint**

Can you:

☐ Summarize the constitutional requirements for presidential and congressional elections

The Presidential Campaign

> ❭ **What the steps in presidential campaigns are**

Connections: Do presidential campaigns ensure that the best person for the office wins?

Presidential campaigns capture the interest of the vast majority of Americans. In September 2012, 83 percent of the electorate paid at least some attention to the presidential contest between Mitt Romney and Barack Obama.[7] From the decision to run to the final victory and concession speeches, the road to the White House is shaped by constitutional requirements, interparty struggles, and strategies for attracting votes that highlight the many gates and gateways along the way.

Evolution of the Modern Campaign

Although candidates in the early nineteenth century sought to appear aloof, their supporters took every opportunity to advance their candidacies. Buttons and slogans promoted favorites, and parades and barbeques sought to convince the undecided. Participation had much more of a social component than it does now. Many observers argue that the high rate of voting in the late nineteenth century reflected the fact that campaigns were often fun.[8]

By the early twentieth century, presidential contenders began to campaign actively, too, and campaigning started earlier and earlier. The 2012 presidential campaign officially began in early 2011, when the former

Republican governor of Minnesota, Tim Pawlenty, formed an exploratory committee for president, announcing his intentions in a video released through Facebook.[9] Pawlenty's bid for the Republican nomination did not last long, however, as he dropped out later that year. Starting in fall 2011, President Obama was also frequently on the road, seeking support and raising money. Many have expressed concern over what has been called the permanent campaign,[10] a worry that politicians, especially presidents, spend too much time working toward reelection and not enough time governing. Some argue that if politicians spent more time governing and less time running for elections, the nation would be better off. Nevertheless politicians must win elections to be able to govern, and constant campaigning may be an indication of responsiveness.

The Decision to Run and the Invisible Primary

The decision to seek the presidency is a serious one and not an easy one to make. Every move a major candidate makes is discussed and analyzed by the press and political pundits. Presidential campaigns are pressure cookers, perhaps appropriately, because the office is demanding. The American public wants to know whether a candidate has the toughness to serve as commander-in-chief and the wisdom to sort out the best policies.

Once a candidate decides to run for president, he or she enters what is called the **invisible primary**. No votes are cast, but candidates are jockeying for position so they can be ready to do well in the initial primaries and caucuses. They must line up party support, financial backing, and credibility with journalists in the news media. Candidates who can get attention from the news media can raise more money and secure more endorsements from party leaders. Running for election relies heavily on momentum.

Incumbent presidents usually win their party's nomination for a second term. If that part of the contest is a struggle, it is a sign that the incumbent is in trouble, and he usually goes on to lose the general election. But when the seat is open—when an incumbent is in his second term or decides not to run again—a battle unfolds. These struggles often involve seven or eight serious contenders seeking the nomination. The 2008 election was unusual because both nominations were open, meaning that neither the sitting president nor the sitting vice president was seeking the nomination—a situation that had last occurred in 1952. As a result, twelve major candidates competed for the nomination in the two major parties. In 2012, President Obama faced no primary challengers from within the Democratic Party.

On the Republican side, there were nine serious contenders for the 2012 presidential nomination. As in the previous four decades, this phase of the campaign tends to favor party insiders—candidates with deep ties

Connections: Were you satisfied with the option you were offered in 2012, a choice between Barack Obama or Mitt Romney?

 invisible primary: *Period just before the primaries begin during which candidates attempt to capture party support and media coverage.*

JOE RAEDLE/GETTY IMAGES

The battle for the 2012 Republican presidential nomination was highly competitive and witness to frequent debates. Newt Gingrich (left of center) was particularly good in these settings.

to major party leaders who are not challenging the existing party leadership. Mitt Romney is a classic example. Many outsiders were hoping to knock off the former governor of Massachusetts, but his support from the party establishment helped him fend off his challengers and secure the Republican nomination.

The Caucuses and Primaries

To win a party's nomination, a candidate must secure a majority of delegates to the national party convention. The national party allocates delegates to each of the fifty states (plus the District of Columbia, Guam, and Puerto Rico) and sets guidelines on how the states may choose their delegates. If a state does not follow the guidelines, the party can refuse to accept its delegates at the national convention. This situation arose in 2012, when Florida and Arizona did not receive the normal allocation of delegates because they failed to follow the rules set by the Republican National Committee.[11]

About 70 percent of the states use some form of primary election in which citizens go to the polling booths and vote for their favorite party candidates. The other 30 percent use caucuses, which are something like town meetings. During the Iowa caucus, the nation's first and most famous caucus, each party requires people to attend a meeting of about two hours in which they indicate their preferences and then try to convince those who are undecided to join a particular candidate's group. Because caucuses demand more time from voters, participation is usually low.

The National Convention

Following the primary season, each party meets in a national convention. Before the 1960s, conventions were often exciting because it was far from clear who would be the nominee. In 1924, for example, it took the Democrats 124 ballots to decide on their nominee. But by the 1960s, conventions began to be televised, so the parties wanted to ensure that they were orderly. Party leaders instituted rule changes designed to increase the odds that the likely nominee would be known well in advance of the convention. Convention planners could then stage the event to emphasize party unity, rather than discord, to impress television viewers.

Today, party conventions usually last for four days and provide a chance for activists and party leaders to get together to discuss strategy and policy behind the scenes. The highlight of these four days is the acceptance speech, in which the party's nominee has a chance to speak directly to the nation, laying out a vision for the country. Also in front of the cameras, the party's platform, stating its plan for government, is formally adopted. Because one party dominates the news for these four days, the convention is both an advertisement for the party and its candidate and an important springboard for the fall campaign.

Checkpoint

Can you:

☐ Compare and contrast presidential campaigns

☐ State the importance of the invisible primary to candidate momentum

☐ Explain how caucuses and primaries work

☐ Tell what happens at the national conventions

Issues in Presidential Campaigns

❯ **What issues shape presidential campaigns**

Citizen participation in American politics peaks during presidential campaigns. Supporters and people who are undecided have the chance to attend rallies, hear speeches, read commentary, and watch the never-ending advertisements on television. Because the campaigns are important gateways for public participation, we look in particular at fundraising and campaign strategies that make public engagement possible but may also introduce inequalities.

Fundraising and Money

Of course, no one could run for president without funding. How candidates raise money, how much money they raise, and the influence of money in presidential elections have been concerns of Congress and voters for decades, especially as the amount of spending on campaigns has risen sharply. Some believe these huge sums inject inequalities into presidential campaigns, as it seems candidates who lack personal fortunes and established fundraising operations are less likely to be able to compete.

In 1971 Congress tried to put candidates on an equal financial footing and make them less beholden to special interests by passing the Federal Election Campaign Act (FECA). This law transformed the way campaigns are conducted and monitored, as it requires candidates and political parties to disclose their campaign financial records. In 1974 Congress amended the law to set strict limits on how much money could be contributed by individuals and parties to campaigns, and more important, created the Federal Election Commission as an independent agency to monitor campaign finance.[12] Under the rules, candidates seeking their party's nomination are given public funds for the campaign in the form of matching funds: a dollar amount equal to the amount the candidates raise from private contributors, with a limit per individual contributor and an overall cap. In 2012 the limit per contributor was $2,500 in the primary and $2,500 in the general campaign;[13] the cap was $45.6 million for the primary and $91.2 million for the general election.[14]

The rules for the public financing of presidential nomination campaigns are complicated, as they are designed to ensure that candidates are serious contenders before receiving matching funds. First, candidates must raise at least $5,000 in twenty states from donations that are less than $500 each. Then they must get at least 10 percent of the vote in two consecutive primaries or they lose eligibility; to reestablish it, they must get 20 percent of the vote in a subsequent primary. These standards are hard to meet when the field of candidates is crowded, and they discourage third-party candidates from running. Even if candidates remain eligible, matching funds pose constraints in addition to the cap, as a candidate can spend only a certain amount of money per state. This constraint produces odd behavior. For example, because the New Hampshire primary is the first and perhaps the most important primary, candidates want to invest heavily in it. Yet under matching funds, they face a spending limit in the state, so they might spend the night in a hotel in an adjoining state, Vermont or Maine, to avoid having to charge that expense against the New Hampshire limit.

Since the 1970s, candidates and their contributors—including interest groups and corporations—have sought ways to fund campaigns within the FEC regulations and by finding loopholes they can exploit. Some contributors have amplified their impact by bundling—that is, by amassing individual contributions. Others have formed political action committees (PACs) with the express purpose of donating money to candidates who agree with their political agenda, although these amounts are also limited—in some cases $5,000 per candidate (see Chapter 8, Interest Groups). In 2002 the McCain-Feingold Bipartisan Campaign Reform Act adjusted the FEC regulations by raising the legal contribution allowances for campaigns; prohibiting political parties from accepting and spending unlimited amounts of money directly on campaigns (a loophole in the old rules); restricting the ability of interest groups to run issue ads without fully identifying themselves; and prohibiting them from running such ads within thirty days of a primary and sixty days of a general election.[15]

But the FEC rules matter far less now. Since 2000, presidential candidates have started to forego matching funds in their quest for the nomination. One reason is to be able to spend money in states important to the contest without regard to FEC limits. But primarily they believe they can raise (and spend) more money if they do not accept federal matching funds. In 2000 George W. Bush believed he could raise much more than the $40 million allowed and, foregoing matching funds, raised $70 million before the first primary.[16]

In the 2008 general election, John McCain used public funds, receiving about $80 million from the government, but Barack Obama opted out of

Connections: What are the pros and cons of laws that regulate campaign finance?

general election funding for the first time since the system began in 1976. By so doing, he had access to far more money than did McCain. Over the course of the yearlong campaign, he spent $730 million, breaking all previous fundraising records. McCain spent $333 million dollars during that same period, a huge amount by historical standards, but dwarfed by Obama's spending (see Figure 10.2 for total spending). In the 2012 presidential election, no serious candidates used federal funds in the primaries, raising and spending their own money instead.

During the 2012 election cycle, the 2010 Supreme Court's ruling in *Citizens United v. Federal Election Commission* (2010) (see Supreme Court Cases in Chapter 8) also increased campaign fundraising amounts and spending, as it undid many of the restrictions formerly placed on corporations and unions. One consequence was the rise of **Super PACs**, which—unlike PACs—can raise funds from corporations, unions, interest groups, and individuals without legal limits.[17] These organizations are not allowed to coordinate directly with the candidates they support, but often those who run a Super PAC are friends and former aides to the candidates, making the distinction questionable.

In the 2012 Republican presidential primary alone, Romney's Super PACs spent more than $46 million, and many observers credit this money for helping him secure the Republican nomination.[18] During the entire presidential campaign, Super PACs spent a staggering $629 million in an effort to determine the next president.[19]

Many observers worry about the influence of money on the election process and believe that these huge amounts raise questions about fairness and equality, as people who have money will have more gateways than those who do not. But even with bundling, the $5,000 total limit does offer some important constraints. It is impossible to "buy" a candidate with $5,000. In addition, the money is being spent on getting candidates' messages out to the public and building organizations to get out the vote. It can be argued that putting money into the system informs people and activates them to participate.[20] Campaign spending stimulates interest in the election, and that is also a public benefit. Last, some of the Super PACs allowed candidates such as Newt Gingrich and Rick Santorum to stay in the 2012 primary contests a

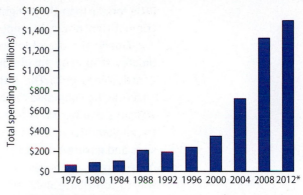

*As of October 1, 2012.

FIGURE 10.2 **Total Spending by Presidential Candidates, 1976–2012.**

Spending in presidential campaigns has shown a steady increase over the last four decades, with big increases in the last two elections. By election day 2012, spending by presidential candidates had risen to about $1.8 billion.

Source: From "Presidential Fundraising and Spending 1976-2008." Center for Responsive Politics, 2008. Copyright © 2008 by Center for Responsive Politics. Reproduced by permission. www.opensecrets.org. The source for 2012 is opensecrets.org, fec.gov, and http://elections.nytimes.com/2012/campaign-finance.

Super PACs: *Independent groups that can raise unlimited amounts of money from individuals, labor unions, and corporations and can spend it to support or oppose political candidates but cannot coordinate directly with candidates or political parties.*

Connections: Are presidential campaigns too expensive?

little longer than they might have otherwise. That outcome ensures greater competition, not less competition.[21]

Finally, the rise of Internet fundraising has made it worthwhile for candidates to pursue small contributions—as small as $15—rather than large contributions only. The Internet has made small donations cost-effective, encouraging candidates to broaden their base of contributors. By setting up websites that permit online donations, candidates do not need to pay people to call potential voters or knock on doors. They just need to maintain the websites and ensure that lots of people know about them. The Internet has given more people a gateway to be part of the electoral process by offering them a way to contribute small amounts of money.

The real problem with Super PACs and the issue ads they sponsor is that voters do not always know where the money is coming from. Under the new campaign rules, there is less transparency. Thus it is possible for one or two wealthy donors to fund a Super PAC, and to the extent that the Super PAC's issue ads impact an election outcome, some observers contend that these results distort the electoral process.

Swing States

Although partisanship is extremely high, swing voters still exist—people who do not fall into either the Republican or Democratic camp—and so do **swing states** that might vote either Democratic or Republican in an election. Parties avidly pursue swing voters during a presidential election, as they can swing the results one way or the other. In the past, swing voters have constituted about 20 percent of the electorate, but that share has been falling. Six months before the November 2012 election, only about 10 percent of the electorate was undecided, and the share fell to about 5 percent during the fall campaign.[22]

More important for campaign strategy are the swing states, which can mean the difference between victory and defeat. Because of the Electoral College's winner-take-all system, presidential candidates invest time and effort only in states that they can win. In 2012, for example, it made no sense for Mitt Romney to campaign in New York, a reliably Democratic state that he could not win. But both Romney and Barack Obama campaigned hard in Pennsylvania—a **battleground state** that each thought he had a chance to win. In 2012 other key battleground states were Florida, Iowa, Ohio, Nevada, and Wisconsin.

Citizens in these states got lots of attention (see Figure 10.3). Nearly 90 percent of campaign visits in 2000, 2004, and 2008 were to battleground states.[23] Citizens in these states were well informed and increasingly interested in the campaign. But the strategy of pursuing votes in swing states yields an important inequality, for citizens in non-swing states do not get such attention, and interest in the campaign lags, especially among the poor. According to one estimate, "the seven battleground states targeted by both major parties

Connections: Are presidential campaigns fair?

swing states: *States that are not clearly pro-Republican or pro-Democrat and therefore are of vital interest to presidential candidates, as they can determine election outcomes.*

Connections: Do you live in a swing or a battleground state? What is the impact on you?

battleground state: *State in which the outcome of the presidential election is uncertain and in which both candidates invest much time and money, especially if its votes are vital for a victory in the Electoral College.*

contained only 18% of the nation's population" in 2004, "with another 24% residing in states that were classified as leaning, but not quite safe."[24] That means that about 60 percent of the public did not get the benefits of a campaign in 2004. Much the same was true in 2012.

Microtargeting

Since the 1960s, when consumer behavior became a popular field of study, direct marketers have refined the practice of gathering detailed information about different cross sections of consumers to sell their products.[25] Today, the technique of **microtargeting** has become a boon to political parties and electoral campaigns. By identifying and tracking potential supporters, campaign strategists can design specific political messages tailored for each of the voting profiles developed from the data. In the 2012 campaign, both Mitt Romney and Barack Obama microtargeted Latino voters, believing that this growing block of voters was critical to the election outcome.[26]

As a campaign strategy, microtargeting has begun to replace traditional polling techniques and precinct-by-precinct get-out-the-vote drives (see Chapter 6, Public Opinion). By combining information from polling surveys with political participation and consumer information obtained from data-gathering companies like Acxiom and InfoUSA, political parties and campaigns can establish profiles of the many different types of voters and the issues they support. The resulting database can then be "mapped" to get a geographic depiction of the trends in voting habits and political interests of different voters. Each party works with its own large database: The Democrats have "VoteBuilder," and the Republicans have "Voter Vault."[27] This strategy takes a person-by-person view of the electorate rather than a view of the electorate en masse. So, instead of targeting a broad category like women, campaigns can now focus on categories like "married iPhone owners in their 40s with a master's degree who shop at Costco."[28]

Campaign Issues

Campaigns are very much shaped by issues. Many observers think that the personalities of the candidates dictate the race, but that view is not consistent with the evidence. Between 1960 and 2000, for example, 56 percent of

FIGURE 10.3 Visits by Presidential Candidates to Battleground States, 2000–2008.

Presidential candidates pay much more attention to the competitive states, a pattern that continued in 2012.

Source: Daron R. Shaw, *The Race to 270: The Electoral College and the Campaign Strategies of 2000 and 2004* (Chicago: University of Chicago Press, 2006) . Copyright © 2006 by University of Chicago Press. All rights reserved. Reproduced by permission; figures for 2008 provided by Daron R. Shaw.

> **Connections:** What is your microtargeting profile? Can the category predict how you will vote?

 microtargeting: *Gathering detailed information on cross sections of the electorate to track potential supporters and tailor political messages for them; also called narrowcasting.*

valence issues: *Noncontroversial or widely supported campaign issues that are unlikely to differ among candidates.*

position issues: *Political issues that offer specific policy choices and often differentiate candidates' views and plans of action.*

wedge issue: *Divisive issue focused on a particular group of the electorate that candidates use to gain more support by taking votes away from their opponents.*

the content of advertising in presidential campaigns involved policy, with 26 percent concerning the personal traits of the candidates, and the remaining 18 percent focusing on general values such as freedom, hard work, and patriotism.[29] In 2008 the economy dominated the discussion between John McCain and Barack Obama. According to one estimate, more than 50 percent of the appeals made by these contenders dealt with the economy alone.[30] The economy was the main issue in 2012 as well.

To understand how issues influence campaigns, political scientists have drawn a distinction between **valence issues** and **position issues**.[31] A valence issue is a vague claim to a goal, such as "a strong economy," "improved education," or "greater national security." These are goals all candidates talk about and voters seek: No candidate has ever opposed a strong economy or called for less national security. Valence issues provide limited insight into the policies a candidate might pursue once in office. A position issue is different. Here candidates adopt views that allow voters to understand specific plans for government. Two examples from the 2012 campaign are Barack Obama's support for increasing taxes on the wealthy and Mitt Romney's opposition to the health care reform law passed in 2010. Because views on position issues may drive some votes away, presidential candidates rely more heavily on valence issues than on position issues. According to one study, about three-quarters of their TV ads highlight valence issues.[32]

Because campaigns are competitive struggles for votes, candidates look for ways to secure extra votes while maintaining existing support. This dynamic is especially true for candidates who trail because they need to find some way to break up the support for the candidate in the lead. One strategy is to use a **wedge issue** that has the potential to break up the opposition's coalition.[33] Wedges usually involve controversial policy concerns, such as abortion and same-sex marriage, that divide people rather than build consensus. In 2012, the Democrats sought to use various gender issues as wedges against the Republicans, including debates over contraception and equal pay.[34]

Polls and Prediction Models

Political scientists have developed prediction models that yield specific estimates of the vote share in presidential elections. The goal is to provide a general understanding of who wins and why. In 2008, eight of the nine models predicted an Obama win. Some thought he would win narrowly (predicting 50.1 percent), while others anticipated a major landslide (predicting 58.2 percent). Nate Silver (see Chapter 6) called it right, too, predicting the outcomes in 49 of the 50 states correctly. In 2012, Silver's predictions were also accurate. He viewed Florida as a true toss-up on the eve of the election.[35]

The best prediction models use some combination of the following key structural factors:

1. The economy. What is the condition of the economy? A strong economy leads voters to support the incumbent party. A struggling economy gives an edge to the challenger.
2. Presidential popularity. How popular is the sitting president? An unpopular president will hurt the chances for his party's candidate.
3. The incumbent party's time in office. How long has the incumbent party controlled the presidency? The American public has shown a consistent preference for change. A party that has been in power for a long time usually has made enough mistakes to lead citizens to vote for the other side.

Considering these factors, one could have predicted that 2012 would be a close race because the economy was struggling. Although incumbent presidents tend to win reelection, their chance for success decreases if the economy is weak. In a process called **retrospective voting**, voters tend to judge incumbents on their performance and vote accordingly.[36] At the same time, Barack Obama was reasonably popular and respected, and these qualities, coupled with voters' reluctance to oust incumbent presidents, contributed to his victory.

 **retrospective voting:** *Theory that voting is driven by a citizen's assessment of an officeholder's performance since the last election.*

 Checkpoint

Can you:
- ☐ Track trends in fundraising for presidential campaigns
- ☐ Describe the impact of the Electoral College on presidential campaigns
- ☐ Compare and contrast valence issues and position issues
- ☐ Describe the role of negativity in campaign strategies
- ☐ Name the key factors in predicting who wins the presidential election

Congressional Campaigns

> **What the steps in congressional campaigns are**

Nearly all congressional campaigns start with a primary election at which the party's official candidate is selected. The general election then follows.

The Decision to Run and the Primaries

People who choose to run for Congress are usually visible residents of their district or state. Often they already hold local or state-level elected offices. They might be school board members, city council members, or state legislators. Many grew up in the district or state and can claim long-standing ties to it. Contenders with strong local roots can organize core supporters who volunteer time, and often money, to advance their candidacies.

Although candidates do not have to declare their intention to run for Congress until about a year before the election, both incumbents—those already holding the office—and challengers generally begin campaigning nearly two years before election day. For House members, that means that the campaign never stops—yet

Congressman Aaron Schock (R-Ill.) campaigns for reelection in May 2010 in Burns, Illinois.

COURTESY AARON SCHOCK

midterm elections: *Congressional elections held between the presidential elections.*

another manifestation of the permanent campaign. The contests that occur in between the four-year presidential election cycles are called **midterm elections**.

Party primaries nearly always determine which candidate will gain the party endorsement for a House or Senate seat. To win the primary election, a candidate generally shapes campaign messages to please core party members in the district or state. For Democrats, that typically means slanting toward a more liberal set of policies and, for Republicans, toward a more conservative set of policies.

The Fall Campaign

Following the primaries, the two winning candidates often revise their campaign messages to attract more moderate voters. Anthony Downs explained this shift in message with the median voter theorem, which argues that candidates in their quest for votes should adopt moderate positions on issues. If one candidate fails to do so, the other candidate can move to the center, winning a majority of votes and the election.[37] To win the general election, candidates usually need votes from party members as well as from Independents and members of the opposing party. It is for these reasons that elections are often battles over the so-called middle.

Connections: Did you vote in the 2010 midterm election? Why or why not?

Elections to the House of Representatives typically focus more on local issues intrinsic to the district and less on national programs and issues. Senate elections pay more attention to national issues because the Senate is viewed as more nationally focused. In elections where an incumbent is running, the contest becomes an evaluation of his or her performance in office compared to what the challenger promises to do if elected.

✓ Checkpoint

Can you:
- ☐ Describe midterm elections
- ☐ Relate how candidates try to win election

Issues in Congressional Campaigns

> ❯ **What issues shape congressional campaigns**

Congressional elections do not draw as much attention as presidential elections, but they involve many of the same issues. Money and fundraising are concerns, and again the FEC sets limits. Voters almost always reelect House and Senate members, so whether congressional elections actually serve to hold Congress accountable is a question for American democracy. Voters know less about these candidates than about the candidates in presidential elections, suggesting perhaps that there is not much accountability. Nevertheless, the composition of Congress changes in response to conditions in the country. If times are good, voters reward the party that controls the presidency. In general, the pattern of Republican and Democratic gains and losses indicates that voters hold members of Congress accountable and that Congress is, therefore, a responsive institution.

Fundraising and Money

A key element in launching and running a congressional campaign is fundraising. Federal campaign finance laws set the same limits on congressional elections as on presidential elections: An individual could contribute up to $2,500 to a candidate for the primary election in 2012 and the same amount for the general election. Individuals can contribute to candidates in different races, up to a total of $46,200 for primaries and the same amount for general election campaigns. Candidates also raise money from PACs, which are limited to donating $5,000 for a primary election, and $5,000 for a general election, to a single candidate.[38] In the 2010 midterm elections, a challenger had to raise, on average, about $1.5 million to win a seat in the House of Representatives, and an incumbent had to raise, on average, $1.3 million to keep his or her seat. For Senate races, a successful challenger had to raise, on average, $9.1 million and an incumbent $10.5 million to win the contest. Losing Senate incumbents spent on average $16.5 million in their unsuccessful bid for reelection.[39]

The Role of Political Parties

Of other sources of financial support available to candidates, the most important is the political party. Parties are forbidden by campaign finance laws from actively coordinating a specific individual's congressional or senatorial campaign, but local parties can engage in general activities, such as voter registration drives, partisan rallies, and get-out-the-vote efforts on election day.

National parties are also forbidden from directly coordinating with individual campaigns, but they can do much to help their candidates win. They can pay for campaign training for candidates and their staff members, hold general party fundraisers, and buy campaign advertisements that attack the opposing candidate so long as they do not mention their party's candidate. They can also share lists of campaign donors and party members who are likely to volunteer time to candidates' campaigns.

Both the Democratic and Republican Parties have congressional campaign organizations designed to recruit and support candidates for the House and Senate. These committees can choose to be more or less supportive of incumbents seeking reelection, depending on how loyal the incumbents have been to the party. Individuals can contribute to these committees in addition to making donations to the candidates themselves, although an individual is limited to $25,000 in donations to a single party campaign committee.[40]

 **vanishing marginals:** *Trend marking the decline of competitive congressional elections.*

 **safe seat:** *Seat in Congress considered to be reliably held by one party or the other.*

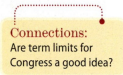 **Connections:** Are term limits for Congress a good idea?

Incumbency Advantage

Incumbents almost always win,[41] and in the last two decades, more than 70 percent of House incumbents won by 60 percent or more of the vote[42] (see Figure 10.4). Since the 1960s the number of competitive races has been in decline, a trend called **vanishing marginals**. Fewer and fewer congressional elections are competitive. Noncompetitive districts are often referred to as **safe seats**. The high rates of incumbent reelection may indicate that incumbents are doing a good job, especially with constituent services that build support with voters (see also Chapter 11). Or they might raise concerns about whether elections really foster accountability. The 2012 election told much the same story. Congress remained unpopular, but most incumbents easily won reelection. Concerns about incumbency advantage have led some observers to fear a lack of accountability and to call for term limits, which would force members to retire after serving a maximum number of terms.

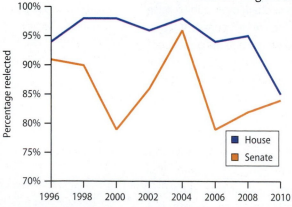

FIGURE 10.4 **Reelection Rates of Incumbents in Congress, 1996–2010.**

Source: Center for Responsive Politics, "Historical Elections: Reelection Rates over the Years." Copyright © 2012 by Center for Responsive Politics. Reproduced by permission. www.opensecrets.org; Bruce Oppenheimer.

More turnover actually occurs in the House than the 90 percent reelection rate suggests. Members often engage in strategic retirement, deciding not to run for reelection when the outcome is likely to be unfavorable. It is unclear what reelection rates exactly mean. For example, the lower reelection rates of senators do not imply that the Senate is more responsive than the House. Instead, the gap may be a function of differences between the two chambers. A seat in the Senate, the upper house, is a more coveted position than a seat in the House, and Senate races generally attract higher-quality challengers than do House races. Better challengers yield more competitive elections and more defeats for incumbents. The ability of challengers to do better in Senate races than in House races is also related to the additional media attention these races receive; quite simply, voters learn more about the challengers. Finally, the difference in terms—six years as opposed to two—may indicate that House members stay in closer touch with constituents than do senators, and their constituents re-elect them.[43] Incumbents also win reelection at high rates because they are known commodities to their constituents. Name recognition for House and Senate incumbents is often higher than 80 percent. Senate challengers do better than House challengers, but still about a quarter of the electorate does not recognize their names.[44] Compare these percentages to those of the 2012 presidential election, in which only 1 percent of the public claimed not to know the name of Mitt Romney, who was challenging President Obama.[45]

Recent evidence suggests that members of Congress may be the beneficiaries of the migration of Americans, as well. That is, incumbency advantage appears to be increasing because districts are becoming "deep red" (Republican) and "deep blue" (Democrat) due to people's decisions about where to live. The assumption is that a Republican who has a choice to live, for example, in San Francisco or Dallas, will tend to choose Dallas because it offers a political culture more in line with his or her preferences. In this sense, because of the redrawing of district lines and the desire of individuals to live near people with similar values and political leanings, congressional districts are becoming heavily Democratic or heavily Republican. The result is that fewer races are competitive and incumbents are more successful.[46]

Relative Lack of Interest

Voting rates in congressional elections, particularly in midterm elections, are always lower than in presidential elections. Presidential elections are high-stimulus elections, whereas congressional elections are low-stimulus. As a result, voting is driven largely by two major forces: partisanship and incumbency. Voters follow party identification and vote for their party's candidates. And, as we have seen, voters also tend to vote for incumbents. There is also the effect of **presidential coattails**—that is, a popular president running for reelection brings additional party candidates into office. Voters going to the polls in high-stimulus elections to vote for president cast ballots for other members of the party for lower-level offices. While scholars debate this effect, it is clear that the partisan makeup of Congress reflects the popularity of the president or presidential candidate.[47]

Much has been written on the exact mechanisms that drive voters and congressional elections. While there is disagreement over the specifics, it is clear that the composition of Congress changes in response to economic conditions. When there are good times, the president's party benefits. When times are bad, the president's party suffers.

Connections: If Congress is supposed to be the branch closest to the people, why do congressional campaigns generate less interest than do presidential campaigns?

 presidential coattails: *Effect of a popular president or presidential candidate on congressional elections, boosting votes for members of his party.*

✓ Checkpoint

Can you:

☐ Explain how fundraising needs restrain candidates

☐ Describe the role of political parties in congressional campaigns

☐ Give reasons for incumbency advantage

☐ Explain the relationship between the outcome of midterm elections and public opinion of the president

The Practice and Theory of Voting

> Why there are battles over ballot access

Americans enjoy near universal opportunities to vote. Despite the widespread belief in the importance of elections for democratic institutions, some Americans have argued that voting rights should not be universal. Voting, in short, is a gateway to power, so there are always battles over who gets access to the ballot.

The Constitution and Voting

The Constitution is nearly silent on the rules about voting in elections, leaving such choices to the states. As Article I, Section 4 of the Constitution states, "The Times, Places and Manner of holding Elections for Senators and Representatives, shall be prescribed in each State by the Legislature thereof." The Constitution does spell out in some detail the workings of the Electoral College, which chooses the president. However, differing state rules lead to inequalities among the states, making it easier to vote in some states than in others.

Competing Views of Participation

Debates about voting and the removal of obstacles to voting have often centered on whether potential voters would be qualified to cast ballots. Too much voter participation might create too many demands on government, making government less able to respond. It seems that those opposed to removing obstacles to voting feared that too much democracy could be bad for democracy.[48]

> **Connections:** Can you think of any reason why a citizen should not be allowed to vote?

We label these ideas the Hamiltonian model of participation. Alexander Hamilton represents a perspective that sees risks in greater participation and, thus, favors a larger role for elites. In this model, not only would the quality of the decision be diluted by more participation, but government would be less able to advance the national interest because it would be responding to uninformed voters. In stark contrast is the Jeffersonian model, which holds that more participation yields a more involved and engaged public and that, in turn, produces better outcomes.[49] In other words, democracy thrives with more democracy. Thomas Jefferson had more faith than Hamilton did in the people's ability and worried that excessive reliance on elites would make government less responsive to its citizens.

> **Connections:** Do you lean toward the Hamiltonian or the Jeffersonian model of participation?

Figure 10.5 offers a summary of these competing views. Proponents of the Hamiltonian model do seek accountability, but they place much more faith in the ability of elites than in the ability of the general public to make the right decisions. The people, they contend, are often uninformed and cannot make the best choices. In contrast, proponents of the Jeffersonian model want to see more participation, believing that the people can be trusted and that getting more people involved will push government to be more responsive to the people's interests. They contend that if certain groups of people are disenfranchised, government will be less responsive. People may not be well informed about politics, but if they have a chance to be involved, they will become better informed. An informed citizenry that actively participates in politics will ensure that government is both accountable and responsive.

Obviously the Jeffersonian model holds equality as an important political value, whereas the Hamiltonian model places more emphasis on efficient and effective outcomes. These competing visions of citizen involvement have played out in nearly all debates about expanding the opportunity for more citizens to cast ballots. In the course of the nation's history, proponents and opponents of expanding the right to vote have each achieved victories. Although the overall trend has been constant expansion, the contest has been fraught with conflict—not only debate in Congress and the courts but also violence in the streets, as the following section will attest.

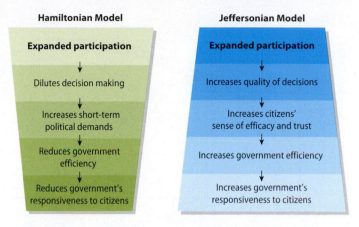

FIGURE 10.5 Hamiltonian and Jeffersonian Models of Participation.

© CENGAGE LEARNING

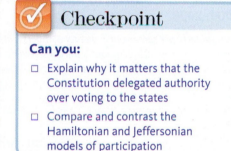

Checkpoint

Can you:

☐ Explain why it matters that the Constitution delegated authority over voting to the states

☐ Compare and contrast the Hamiltonian and Jeffersonian models of participation

Who Votes?

> **Who tends to turn out in American elections**

Voting is an important gateway to influence, but not everyone has the inclination or the desire to participate. Failure to vote has real implications for the political process; it affects which representatives govern and make laws, and who governs has policy consequences that affect everyone in the United States. Low **turnout** raises questions about government's responsiveness, and unequal turnout by various demographic groups suggests that government's response is unequal, too. Low turnout among young people, for example, in contrast to older Americans, means that elected officials may give more attention to issues affecting senior voters, such as Social Security, than to issues affecting younger voters, such as the costs of education. Figure 10.6

turnout: *Share of all eligible voters who actually cast ballots.*

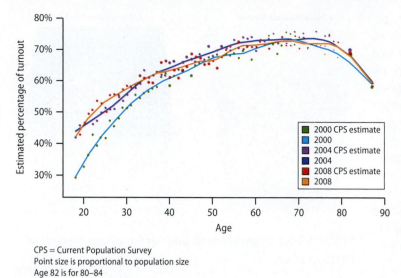

CPS = Current Population Survey
Point size is proportional to population size
Age 82 is for 80–84
Age 87 is for 85 and up

FIGURE 10.6 **Turnout by Age in Presidential Elections, 2000–2008.**

Young voters have turned out in greater numbers in the last two presidential elections, but their rate of turnout is still considerably lower than that of people over 30, decreasing the likelihood that government will be responsive to their interests.

Source: Charles Franklin, "Turnout by Age, 2000–2008," Understanding Political Numbers, p. 36. PollsAndVotes .com, accessed September 13, 2012, http://pollsandvotes.com/PaV/wp-content/uploads/2012/04/ FranklinVisExamples.pdf. Copyright © 2008 by Charles Franklin. Reproduced by permission.

documents that the youngest voters have the lowest turnout and that voters turn out more often as they age, until they reach about age 75. In this section, we examine turnout rates generally and then look at turnout rates by various demographic groups.

Turnout

Even with widespread opportunity to cast ballots and shape the course of government, Americans often choose not to vote. In 1996 fewer than half of eligible voters (about 48 percent) took the time to vote. In 2008 the rate of participation improved to more than 57 percent. But presidential elections are high-stimulus events. In midterm congressional elections, which are low-stimulus elections, turnout is usually less than 40 percent. For primary elections during presidential nominations, turnout is even lower. For local school board elections, the electorate is even smaller: Often fewer than 10 percent of eligible citizens vote in such contests. A general assessment of turnout in the United States is offered later in the chapter. Here, we turn to the demographics of turnout (see Figure 10.7).

The Demographics of Turnout

Connections: Why do better-educated, better-paid, and older people vote at higher rates than less-educated, more poorly paid, and younger people? What is the effect on government?

Given the important power that voting brings in a democracy, a central question becomes, Who votes? Do various demographic groups vote in equal proportions? If not, what are the consequences for government responsiveness?

The data below suggest that people who are most likely to vote tend to be better educated, better paid, and older than those who are unlikely to vote. There are some modest race and gender differences, but when scholars control for differences in education and income, differences in race pretty much disappear.[50] The key lesson is that the driving force of participation is the development in young people of the kinds of skills and habits that prepare an individual for active citizenship.

Race and Ethnicity. Whites have a slightly higher rate of participation than do blacks. By 2008, 66 percent of whites and 65 percent of African Americans reported voting. Barack Obama's campaign clearly engaged the African American community.

Other minority groups participate less frequently. About 47 percent of Asian Americans vote.[51] Native Americans appear to have the lowest rate of turnout, although precise estimates have been difficult to gather.[52] Latinos vote less frequently than do whites or blacks, at about 50 percent, but Latino voting rates are increasing and will become a more significant force in U.S. elections. In 1988 Latinos constituted less than 4 percent of voters. Twenty years later, the proportion had more than doubled to nearly 8 percent.[53]

In general, turnout rates among ethnic minorities tend to be below the average for the entire country. Part of the reason is that members of minority groups are likely to have lower incomes, and lower income generally means lower turnout. Many are not eligible to vote because they are not citizens. This is especially true for Asians and Latinos.

Sex. Women turn out at a slightly higher rate than men, by perhaps 3 to 5 percentage points. 66 percent of women reported voting in 2008 compared to 62 percent of men.[54] The gender gap is important in American politics, but it relates to the tendency of women to support Democrats over Republicans, not to the difference in turnout between women and men, which is much smaller and less consequential.

Age. Age affects rates of participation. Turnout peaks once voters are about 60 years old (see Figure 10.6). Even when differences in education and income are controlled for, participation remains higher for older Americans. In 2004 around 70 percent of citizens older than 65 claimed to have voted. The proportion is just 47 percent for those 24 and younger, and it is even lower for those 21 and younger. Such findings are tied to the fact that younger citizens are often more mobile and less integrated into the community than are older citizens.[55]

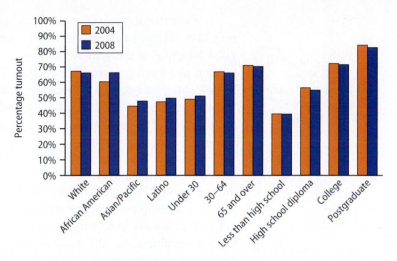

FIGURE 10.7 **Turnout by Demographic Group in Presidential Elections, 2004 and 2008.**

Source: Michael P. McDonald, "2008 Current Population Survey Voting and Registration Supplement," United States Elections Project, April 6, 2009, http://elections.gmu.edu; Doug Hess, "Analysis of the 2008 Current Population Survey (CPS) Voter and Registration Supplement," Project Vote, April 8, 2009, http://www.projectvote.org/.

Connections: What can you do to get young people in your community to vote? Why is it important?

It is worth noting that participation by the very youngest voting-age citizens (18–29) climbed to more than 51 percent in 2008, from 49 percent in 2004. Nearly all of this gain was among young blacks, whose rate of participation jumped 9 percentage points between 2004 and 2008 (from 49 percent to 58 percent). Just a decade earlier, turnout among youths had hovered around 30 percent.[56] One has to be cautious in making too much of this surge, but it does suggest that younger people become more active in politics in certain contests.

Income.   The higher one's income, the more likely one is to vote. More income generally means that the person has more at stake and thus more reason to vote. People with higher incomes are also likely to be in environments in which politics is frequently discussed and that provide greater opportunities for learning about the political process. Political knowledge is strongly correlated with the propensity to vote.

Data from the U.S. Census Bureau in Figure 10.8 strongly confirm this relationship. In 2008 about 75 percent of people with total family incomes between $100,000 and $150,000 reported that they went to the polls. For people whose incomes fell in the range that represents the annual median family income in America—$40,000 to $50,000—turnout was 58 percent. For the least-well-off (those earning less than $15,000), the proportion who claimed to have voted was 41 percent.

Education.   Although race and ethnicity, sex, age, and income have some effects on the propensity of people to vote, the number of years of formal

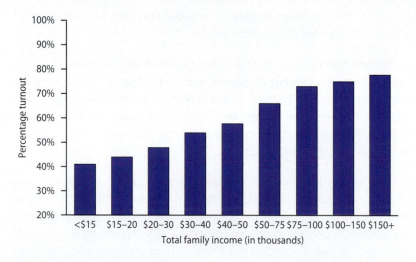

FIGURE 10.8 **Turnout by Income in the 2008 Presidential Election.**

Source: U.S. Census Bureau.

TABLE 10.1 Turnout by Education in Presidential Elections, 1988–2008

Years of Education	1988	1992	1996	2000	2004	2008
			Turnout			
8 years or fewer	37%	35%	30%	27%	24%	23%
Less than high school	41%	41%	34%	34%	34%	27%
High school	55%	58%	49%	49%	50%	50%
Less than college	65%	69%	61%	60%	66%	65%
College or more	78%	81%	73%	72%	74%	73%

Source: Harold Stanley and Richard Niemi, *Vital Statistics on American Politics* (Washington, D.C.: CQ Press, 2009).

education seems to be the most important influence. Social science research has documented the connection between education and voting.[57] The youngest voting-eligible citizens (18- to 24-year-olds) who have college degrees have turnout rates 13 percentage points higher than the rates of older citizens (65 to 75) who do not have a high school education.[58] Table 10.1 shows the propensity to vote by educational level from 1988 to 2008. The gap between people with the least education and those with the most is 50 percentage points in 2008, a huge difference. Nearly three-fourths of college-educated people vote, whereas less than a quarter of those with just a grade school education do so.

The relationship between education and voting may not be as simple as these data suggest, however. New evidence indicates that going to college does not matter as much as childhood socialization, which imbues the values of citizenship and similarly affects the decision to attend college. It is not, therefore, spending four years in college that makes college graduates more likely to vote; rather, it is having been raised in an environment that stresses the importance of education that shapes willingness to vote.[59]

 **Checkpoint**

Can you:

☐ Generalize about turnout in the United States

☐ Identify the characteristics of individuals who are more likely to vote

Assessing Turnout

❯ How low turnout is in American elections

As this chapter has established, most Americans do not vote in most elections. Even in presidential elections, for which turnout is highest, only slightly more than half of eligible voters go to the polls. In this section we assess turnout in the United States. Is it too low for responsive and responsible government? Even more important, does turnout increase the prospects of governmental action that ensures equality?

Is Turnout Low?

Connections:
What does it mean for democracy when only 41 percent of Americans vote in midterm elections?

There is a widespread belief among political scientists, political observers, and journalists that turnout in American elections is low. When just 41 percent of the American public took the time to vote in the 2010 congressional elections, the concern about low turnout expressed in these books seems justified. Even with all the attention and interest surrounding the 2008 presidential elections, turnout of the voting-age population was about 57 percent.[60] Such data strike many as disappointing. But further investigation of turnout can offer a different way to interpret the situation.

The United States Compared to Other Democracies.

Compared to other democracies, turnout in the United States is low. Between 1945 and 2008, the average rate of turnout in U.S. presidential elections was 56 percent,[61] while in other democracies it was 90 percent or more. These numbers compel an assessment of why U.S. turnout is so low.

Connections:
Should the United States adopt compulsory voting?

One reason has to do with the rules for voting. Australia has compulsory voting—citizens are required by law to vote. Those who do not vote must pay a $20 fine, and the fine increases to $50 if the nonvoter does not answer the Australian Election Commission's inquiry about why he or she did not vote. New Zealand requires all citizens to register to vote. In most of the countries of western Europe, the government is responsible for registering citizens to vote. In the United States, by contrast, both voting and registering are voluntary, and only about 70 percent of the public is registered. That means that nearly one-third of potentially eligible voters cannot cast votes on election day even if they want to do so.

Another reason has to do with the convenience of voting. Most European countries lessen the costs of voting by allowing it to take place on Sunday. In the United States voting takes place on Tuesday, a workday for most people. Federal law stipulates that the first Tuesday after the first Monday in November is the day on which voting for president and members of Congress will take place, and most states have also selected Tuesdays as the day for voting in primaries and in state and local elections. The costs of voting are increased because people may be at work and may have difficulty finding the time to vote. With more costs to voting, turnout is lower in the United States than in many European democracies. This discussion highlights the importance of considering the context of each election.

According to one estimate, turnout in the United States would be 27 percentage points higher (or more than 80 percent) if the nation had laws and rules that foster voting.[62] At the least, this figure suggests that comparisons of turnout in various democracies require a careful accounting of the rules and institutions that shape the willingness of citizens to go to the polls.

Trends in Turnout.   A second way turnout in American elections looks problematic is the trend over the last fifty years. One of the lines in Figure 10.9 (see page 338) represents the percentage of turnout in presidential elections measured against the **voting-age population (VAP)**, the number of those old enough to vote. In the United States all citizens 18 or older constitute the VAP. The graph shows that there has been an overall decline in voting since 1960, despite a recent upswing. This pattern is much the same for midterm elections.

This downward trend becomes more worrisome in light of rising levels of education since 1960, as education is one of the strongest predictors of turnout. Even though education levels have increased over the last fifty years (see Table 10.1 on page 335), the rate of participation in elections has not increased.

These data have led political scientists to study why fewer Americans seem to be voting.[63] Explanations have varied. One explanation looks at the difference between those who enter the electorate and those who leave. The concept of **generational replacement** describes a trend in which older voters who pass away are replaced in the electorate by less reliable young voters.[64] It is very difficult, however, to sort out generational differences from changes in self-interest. That is, do older voters turn out to vote because of the generation they were part of, or because they are older and have more experience in dealing with politics, or because they want to protect their interests or expand the benefits that directly affect them, such as Medicare and low payments for prescription drugs?

A second explanation has been the decline of party organizations.[65] Local parties have been less able to turn out the vote on election day than they were in the late nineteenth and early twentieth centuries, and therefore the voting rate has declined. Some scholars have estimated that half of the decline in turnout can be attributed to the drop in mobilization efforts.[66]

A third explanation for declining turnout is the increasingly harsh tone of political campaigns. Some argue that negative campaigns have fueled voter apathy. It is clear that negative advertising on TV often fosters voters' disgust with politics. About 80 percent of people say they do not like these campaign tactics.[67] Initial studies suggested that negative campaigns could decrease turnout by about 5 percentage points.[68] In addition, there is clear evidence that negativity in campaigns has been on the rise since the 1960s, so there has been an apparent correlation between the two trends.[69] Scholars and pundits rushed to endorse this hypothesis. But subsequent studies have called the hypothesis into question.[70] A harsh campaign is likely to be competitive, and competitive campaigns draw interest and therefore increase turnout. Further, negative attacks can activate partisanship, which also increases turnout. An attack ad by the Republicans can remind their supporters

voting-age population (VAP): *Used to calculate the rate of participation by dividing the number of voters by the number of people in the country who are 18 and over.*

generational replacement: *Cycle whereby younger generations replace older generations in the electorate.*

Connections: What effect do negative ads have on you?

why they oppose the Democrats, giving them more reason to participate. A recent comprehensive study of all research on this topic shows clearly that negativity is not responsible for lowering turnout.[71]

The Voting-Eligible Population Measure.

Two political scientists, Michael McDonald and Samuel Popkin, offer a fourth explanation by arguing that turnout has not declined over the last thirty years: The VAP measure has been in error because it does not take into account increases in the number of immigrants and convicted felons who are ineligible to vote. Over the last thirty years, there has been a steep increase in the number of illegal immigrants. With the sagging economy of the last few years, the numbers have declined, but even so, in 2011 the number of illegal immigrants was estimated to be nearly 12 million (or about 4 percent of the population).[72] Over the last twenty years there has also been nearly a threefold increase in the number of people in prison (from 585,000 to 1.6 million), reflecting tougher sentencing in American courts of law.[73]

McDonald and Popkin correct for these trends by introducing a new measure called the **voting-eligible population (VEP)**. The top line in Figure 10.9

🔑 **voting-eligible population (VEP):** *Used to calculate the rate of participation by dividing the number of voters by the number of people in the country who are eligible to vote rather than just of voting age.*

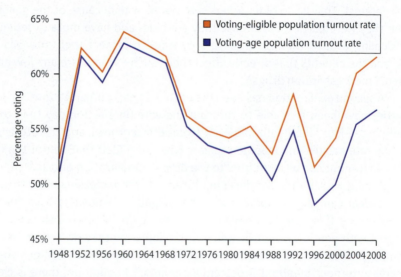

FIGURE 10.9 **Presidential Turnout Rates, 1948–2008.**

The VAP measure is the traditional approach to assessing turnout, dividing the number of voters by the voting-age population. The VEP seeks to correct for overcounting in the voting-age population by removing noncitizens and people in jail who are not eligible to vote. Until 1972 this correction made only a modest difference. But given the surge of immigration and the growth in the number of convicted felons since then, the VEP measure is more accurate. Turnout in the 2004 and 2008 elections is actually comparable to turnout in the 1950s and 1960s.

Source: "Presidential Turnout Rates, 1948-2008," United States Elections Project, accessed August 16, 2012, http://elections .gmu.edu/voter_turnout.htm. Copyright © 2012 by Michael McDonald. Reproduced by permission.

presents the VEP estimates for turnout. It indicates that aggregate turnout in the 2008 presidential election was actually about 62 percent. By this measure, turnout has not declined over the last thirty years. In fact, turnout is now a full 10 percentage points higher than in the presidential election of 1948, when it was 52 percent. These revised estimates put a new spin on what has been perceived as a problem with U.S. elections, suggesting that Americans are not less willing to vote than in the past or than citizens in other democracies.[74]

Do Turnout Rates Promote Inequality?

Voting is a hallmark of democratic politics and is certainly a cherished American value. The idea is simple. Each person has one vote, and each vote should be equal. The fact that those who are better educated or better off participate at a greater rate is a potential source of concern (see Table 10.1 and Figure 10.8). That the wealthy are more likely to vote than the poor is an especially troubling trend because the income gap between the rich and the poor is increasing.[75] As the rich become richer, they become better able to contribute more money to parties and candidates.[76] Such donations only further advance their potential influence.

> **Connections:** Do Americans have equality in voting? Explain.

That individuals with more resources participate more is not a new idea. Its implications have fueled much speculation but were supported by little evidence until 2008, when Larry Bartels provided a systematic account of the impact of these differences. Focusing on the behavior of U.S. senators, Bartels shows that they respond more to the rich, less to people of middle income, and not at all to the poor.[77] It makes sense that politicians respond to people who participate and do not respond to those who do not. That is why it is so important for people to get involved in politics. It is also why the increasing rate of participation in the last decade or so is good news.

Checkpoint

Can you:

☐ Explain why turnout is lower in the United States than in some other democracies

☐ Address the issue of turnout and inequality

Participation beyond Voting

> **What important forms of participation there are other than voting**

Voting is by far the most common form of participation. But in a democracy, citizens have opportunities to express their views in other ways. In fact, voting is a very constrained form of participation: Voters select one person from a limited set of candidates. There is no way to tell from a single vote whether the citizen agrees or disagrees with the candidate on the key issues of the day. But the American political system gives individuals the opportunity to express their preferences and the intensity of those preferences in other ways.

> **Connections:** Aside from voting, how have you participated in politics and civic life?

Although far fewer Americans join political campaigns or protest movements, both are important gateways for the expression of political views.

Campaigns give citizens a chance to talk about politics, volunteer, promote issues they care about, and make financial donations to candidates and causes. The weeks leading up to an election allow candidates and interest groups to connect with the public. The campaign is an important gateway that allows the public to influence politics and politicians to influence the public. As a result, political scientists try to understand the motivations for people's involvement in campaigns and the nature of their involvement. Do Americans try to influence other citizens? According to a survey done in 2010, more than 50 percent of Americans indicate that they "frequently" discuss politics or current events with "family and friends."[78]

Connections:
Why is the right to protest important for democracy?

Protest Politics

Political protests are an important means of expressing opinions and bringing about change. The Boston Tea Party, in which protesters dumped tea into Boston Harbor rather than support the British government-backed monopoly, is perhaps the first and most famous American protest.

Connections:
What does today's Tea Party movement have in common with the Boston Tea Party?

Most recently, the Tea Party movement has recast American politics. It began with protests against the nearly $800 billion stimulus package, which Congress passed in 2009 in the hopes of ending the steep economic downturn that began in 2008. The protests quickly coalesced into a movement that became active in politics. During the 2010 midterm elections, a number of Tea Party–backed candidates were elected to office, including Senator Rand Paul (R-Ky.). The movement played a key role in the 2012 Republican nomination and continues to shape American politics, especially within the Republican Party.[79] Tea Party supporters were not happy with the nomination of Mitt Romney,[80] but his choice of Paul Ryan to be his vice presidential running mate mitigated Tea Party activists' doubts about Romney's commitment to their issues.

In general, very few Americans participate in protests. Overall,

HALEY/SIPA/AP IMAGES

In 2009–10, critics of taxes, big government generally, and government spending in the stimulus bill and the health care reform act came together to label their protests Tea Parties. Shown here on April 17, 2010, Tea Party supporters take part in the second annual tea-throwing event at the Choptank River Fisher Pier in Trappe, Maryland.

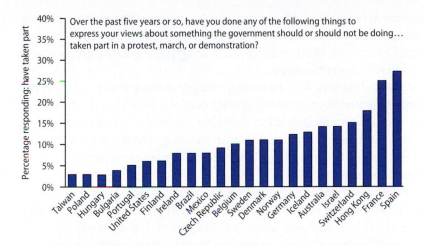

FIGURE 10.10 **Protests and Demonstrations in Twenty-Three Democracies, 2001–2004.**

Source: Surveys by Comparative Studies of Electoral Systems, 2001–2004, accessed July 5, 2012, http://www.cses .org/resources/results/POP_Oct2005_1.htm. Copyright © 2005 by Comparative Studies of Electoral Systems. Reproduced by permission.

only about 5 percent of Americans claim to have participated in a "protest, march, or demonstration" over the last five years. Australians report a willingness to engage in such activities that is three times greater than that of Americans, and in Spain and France about 25 percent of the citizenry claim to have done so[81] (see Figure 10.10). High rates of protest activities in other democracies can be attributed to strong labor parties—some of them socialist and Communist—that make protests common and symbolic. One expert on European protests comments that they are "more fun in Europe than [in the United States], having the feel of attending the county fair."[82]

Connections: What does the fact that few Americans participate in protests mean? That they are satisfied with government?

E-Participation

In the past decade, many Americans have engaged in politics through e-mail and the Internet. It is easier and cheaper to send an e-mail message to a member of Congress than to write a letter, and Americans do so with increasing frequency. In 1998 members of Congress received more than 23 million e-mails; two years later that number had doubled to 48 million.[83] The use of e-mail to contact members of Congress has surely exploded over the last decade, underscoring the ease and convenience of e-mail and transforming the way voters communicate with politicians. Members of Congress facilitate this gateway by encouraging citizens through their websites to contact them via e-mail.[84]

Beyond e-mail, people express their opinions through blogs. As Chapter 7, The News Media and the Internet, demonstrates, blogs have become an

Connections: What is the effect of new technologies on voting and participation?

important way to share information and to influence the political process. Candidates now hire their own bloggers in an effort to influence the direction of these exchanges. Most recently, politicians have started to use Twitter to share information with people.

Participating in politics by writing a blog or responding in writing to one and by using other e-communications will continue to rise. In 2010, about 15 percent of Americans claimed to read political blogs.[85] Readers of political blogs do participate in politics more than non-blog readers, but whether that difference is due to the reading of blogs or just a preexisting desire to participate is far from clear.[86]

The Internet has also transformed fundraising and campaign involvement. Candidates have made use of the Internet and have developed websites and various outreach programs. The Internet is a means to gather small contributions cheaply, as Barack Obama's 2008 campaign for president exemplified. Obama broke all records for fundraising during the primary season, raising $32 million in January 2008, $28 million of it via the Internet.[87] As the campaign progressed, Obama started to rely more on fundraising in person, but his campaign still made extensive use of the Internet.[88] In fact, David Plouffe, Obama's campaign manager, argued in 2009 that the ability to raise money through the Internet was a key ingredient in Obama's winning the election.[89]

Checkpoint

Can you:

- ☐ Survey the effectiveness of protest politics

- ☐ Describe new trends in participation made possible by the Internet

Voting and Participation and Public Policy: Voting Laws and Regulations

The rules surrounding voting alter participation rates. Policy making regarding voting is undertaken at both the federal and state levels. State governments continue to manage most voting laws and procedures, although the federal government steps in to prevent discrimination at the polls. Both state and federal governments are committed to increasing participation by making voting as easy as possible. At the same time, both work to prevent voter fraud. Thus, policy making regarding voting has the effect of both expanding and potentially contracting turnout. This section reviews policies that have altered the way voting works in the United States.

Reforms to Voting Laws in the 1890s

Rules matter, as the institutional model of voting suggests. Any change in the laws governing voting (or any process related to voting) will alter how that process works. A classic example of the power of rules can be found in the late nineteenth century, when the Progressives called for a series of reforms to the voting process to end corrupt practices. The reforms affected who was eligible to vote and the way people actually voted. In other words, they altered who participated in elections.

Corrupt voting practices needed to end. Turnout in some cities exceeded 100 percent, meaning that not only were some people voting who should not have been, but also that some were voting multiple times. Party members often rounded up people and brought them, in sequence, to various polling precincts around the city, making sure they voted in each one. Someone who had died would remain on the rolls, and the party machine would "allow" that person to vote. This corrupt practice has been referred to as graveyard voting.[90]

In response to these excesses, Progressives called for voter registration.[91] The idea was that voters would have to preregister with a government official to be placed on an official list of voters. The list would be updated when someone died, and it would be used at the polls on election day to ensure that a potential voter had the right to vote and had not already voted. This reform spread rapidly. Today, all states except North Dakota require voter registration.

Voter registration laws prevented outright fraud at the polls. An additional consequence was that they prevented immigrants from voting. Party machines had benefited greatly from the support of immigrants in city elections, and many of the newcomers to America who came in great numbers in the late nineteenth and early twentieth centuries were among those whom parties encouraged to vote multiple times. But the new registration laws made voting a two-step process, requiring potential voters to document, before the election, that they met the conditions for voting. Voter registration added a new gate to the system. While it reduced fraud, decreased the strength of the party machines, and pleased Americans who were worried about the impact of immigrants, it caused an overall decline in turnout. In 1888 turnout in presidential elections stood at 81 percent. By 1912 it had fallen to 59 percent. It is surely true that the 81 percent turnout was inflated due to corrupt voting practices, but the introduction of voter registration had negative effects on participation.[92]

Another important change in voting rules in the 1890s was the adoption of the Australian ballot, also known as the secret ballot (see Figure 9.2 in Chapter 9, Ballot Reform). In the early nineteenth century, voting was public and was often done by "party strips." That is, voters would enter a polling

Connections: If you are a registered voter, what was your experience with registration? Was it a gate or a gateway?

Connections: How can government prevent fraud and still encourage citizens to vote?

precinct and ask for a ballot from one party or the other, thereby indicating their preferences. It was easy to cast and count such ballots, but voters were also subjected to pressure from party bosses. Those who operated the polling precincts would know how voters planned to vote by observing which party strip they requested. The introduction of the secret ballot meant that voters faced less intimidation. But voting also became more complicated. Voters now could choose candidates for each office separately; they no longer had automatic access to party line voting as they did with the strip ballot. With a more complicated process, once again turnout declined. Despite decreasing turnout, the secret ballot has become a cornerstone of American democracy.

The National Voter Registration Act and Voter Identification

In 1993 Congress sought to streamline voter registration procedures so that more Americans would exercise their right to vote, at least in federal elections. The National Voter Registration Act, commonly known as the "Motor Voter" law, requires states to allow citizens to register to vote at the same time they apply for or renew their driver's licenses. This law also requires states to inform citizens who are removed from the approved voter rolls and limits removal to a change of address, conviction for a felony, and, of course, death. These requirements responded to charges that local governments, controlled by political parties, improperly removed voters from the voter rolls without their knowledge; under the guise of updating voter registration lists, officials of one party were disqualifying voters who would tend to vote for the other party's candidates. The 1993 law imposes criminal penalties on anyone who tries to coerce or intimidate voters on their way to the polling place or tries to prevent registered voters from casting their ballots.[93]

Connections:
Should government take steps to increase voting? Why?

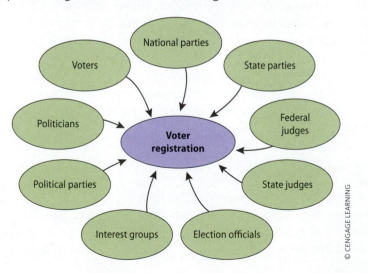

© CENGAGE LEARNING

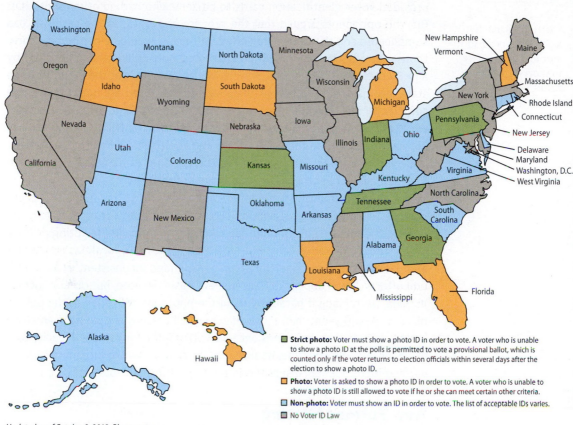

Updated as of October 2, 2012. Please note:

- Enforcement of Pennsylvania's voter ID law has been postponed until 2013 by a state judge.
- Alabama will become a photo ID state in 2014 if its new law receives pre-clearance under Section 5 of the Voting Rights Act.
- Mississippi, South Carolina, and Texas have new strict photo ID laws that may take effect before November 2012 if they receive pre-clearance under Section 5 of the Voting Rights Act.
- Wisconsin's new strict photo ID law was held unconstitutional on March 12, 2012. It could take effect before November 2012 if that ruling is reversed by a higher court.

FIGURE 10.11 Voter Identification Requirements, 2012.

Source: © Cengage Learning, data from National Conference of State Legislatures, http://www.ncsl.org/legislatures -elections/elections/voter-id.aspx.

To avoid voter fraud, many states have instituted voter identification requirements (see Figure 10.11). Their implementation on election day has been controversial. Opponents of Indiana's 2005 photo identification law sought to block its implementation through a lawsuit. The fundamental issue in this case was whether state laws that were intended to prevent voter fraud had the result of preventing citizens who were legally entitled to vote from doing so because they lacked proper identification. Indiana argued that the requirement of a photo ID was not unduly burdensome because the state provided voter identification cards to citizens who had no other photo IDs. But the opponents argued that the process of getting such a card was too complicated and that the overall effect of the law would be to disenfranchise thousands of citizens. In 2008 the Supreme Court upheld the Indiana law by a 6–3 vote. Justice John Paul Stevens wrote on behalf of the majority, "The state interests identified as justifications for [the law] are both neutral and sufficiently strong to require us to reject" the lawsuit. Justice David Souter wrote in dissent that the law "threatens to impose nontrivial burdens on the voting right of tens of thousands of the state's citizens."[94] Four years later, the issue was still not settled. On May 1, 2012, the American Civil Liberties Union filed suit against Pennsylvania's new strict voter ID law.[95]

With the Hamiltonian and Jeffersonian views of voting in mind, it is important to decide what standards should be imposed for citizens to vote. Clearly, the federal government has taken steps to make the voting process easier and more convenient. But ultimately states and localities administer and oversee elections, and states have responded inconsistently to the federal efforts. Some appear to have made it easier to vote, but others, such as Indiana, have made it harder by requiring photo identification at the polling place. It would seem that, in a democracy, all citizens should have an equal opportunity to cast their votes because voting is the fundamental mechanism by which we hold government accountable. As states introduce more laws regarding identification, disparities in the opportunity to vote may be growing.

New Forms of Voting

As indicated above, some states are experimenting with laws that make voting easier. Some have instituted early voting, allowing voters to cast ballots before the Tuesday on which a general election is held. This flexibility helps working people, who might find it difficult to vote on a Tuesday. Other states, such as Oregon, have started to make use of a **vote-by-mail (VBM) system**. Voters get ballots in the mail two weeks before the election, giving them a chance to research the candidates and cast their ballots. They can make their choices at home and avoid long lines at the polling booth. This innovation, proponents argue, lowers the cost of voting, and there is some evidence it has increased participation. In 2004, 87 percent of registered voters in Oregon voted—the highest rate in the nation.[96] But California has had less success with voting by mail.

Nevertheless, new technologies, including the Internet and cell phones, may be used in the future, and they could make it easier for some people to vote—elderly and disabled, for example—thus increasing turnout. However, opponents of using these technologies argue that they would be too susceptible to voter fraud for two reasons: First, there would be no way to identify the person who is casting the vote, unless citizens are given individual pin codes or use their Social Security numbers. Given the number of Internet security breaches, opponents argue that such a system would not guard personal privacy. Second, votes at polling places are counted by election officials, but Internet and cell phone voting data would likely be collected and counted by computer servers, which are vulnerable to hacking and other security breaches.

 Construct Your Own Policy

1. Devise a voting system that would prevent fraud without requiring pre-registration.
2. Construct a national program that would provide voting incentives for the young and the poor.

   For more on the policy-making process, see Chapter 1.

Elections, Campaigns, Voting, and Democracy

The United States government has lasted more than two centuries. This longevity is not an accident. It is attributable in large part to the fact that Americans have, collectively, taken the time to participate. There have been many barriers, from limited suffrage to rules that discourage voting. But the long-term trend has been increased participation, and that speaks to the health of American democracy. Now suffrage—the right to vote—is available to all citizens except those convicted of a felony.[97] The rate of voting in the United States is not as low as many observers tend to assert. Further, looking at participation more broadly, Americans do more than just vote in elections. They are engaged in political campaigns and in making their communities better at the local level. The Internet offers a world of possibilities for greater amounts and different forms of participation.

American elections and the campaigns that precede them are the means by which citizens participate in selecting those who will govern them. It is inevitable that they are at the center of concerns about American democracy. Many observers worry that campaigns are too long, that

Focus Questions Revisited

- In what ways do elections encourage accountability and responsiveness in government?
- How does citizen equality work, or not work, in elections and campaigns?
- Do laws that regulate the financing of campaigns impede or advance equality and accountability in elections?
- Do young citizens participate enough to make the system responsive to their preferences? What about other groups?
- In what ways are elections, campaigns, and voting gateways to American democracy? What are the gates?
- How do other forms of participation, besides voting, serve as gateways to democracy? Are they more or less effective than voting?

candidates spend too much money, and that the voters are not well informed. These concerns often focus on the fairness of the process and of the outcome. In the long term, the process has worked reasonably well. In the short term, it is those who lose who see the process as unfair.

Indeed, there is a danger to a democracy from a distortion in turnout; the rich participate more than the poor, and this gap seems to be growing. With nonvoters being poorer and less educated, their failure to participate may help explain why government is not as responsive to their needs. Put another way, the government may be overly responsive to the needs of the well-off. This disparity in responsiveness threatens the underpinnings of a democratic and egalitarian society. If the political system responds to one segment of the population and systematically ignores other segments, general support for democracy, based on principles of fairness, could drop significantly.

With the Internet's growing influence, there may be other dangers to democracy. Wealthier citizens have more access to the information and resources on the Internet and therefore become even more informed and better able to make government responsive to their needs. The rich have always had advantages, but their advantages may be growing. At the same time, the Internet might be used to extend participation. As recent presidential campaigns have demonstrated, this technology can be used to expand the number of contributors to include people who have only a few dollars to contribute or who might want to show up at a local meeting to learn about an issue of relevance to them.

Let us now return to Figure 10.5 (page 331), which offered two models of participation. The Hamiltonian model argued that more participation is not always a good thing and that government works best with limited involvement from the public. The Jeffersonian model contended that greater participation improves both the quality of the input and the lives of citizens. Within our book's gateway approach, the participatory model of voting has more appeal than the elite model. Democracy becomes more responsive, more accountable, and more equal if more people participate. The cycle is reinforcing. Citizens themselves need to do all they can to encourage participation; doing so is in their self-interest and their civic interest. Democracy rests on the active and healthy participation of the citizenry. In other words, as the number of gateways increase, so does the quality of American civic life.

The general lesson is that elections and campaigns, although imperfect, provide a real chance to ensure government responsiveness. Candidates seek the support of the public through speeches, ads, press releases, and other methods of campaigning. The public digests that information and chooses a candidate. People's votes are a blunt instrument, but they help to forge accountability. If elected officials want to stay in office, they need to act in a way that will increase the chances of continued support. Of course, the party out of office would like to get back in, and it, too, seeks the support of the public. It is through this competitive struggle that American democracy works. Critics worry that the public does not know many of the details of candidates and their platforms, and that is clearly true. But the American public should not be underestimated. That the country has not only survived for more than two centuries, but thrived, suggests just the opposite. The fact that the public collectively seems to act in reasonably coherent ways is testimony to political scientist V. O. Key's classic observation that "voters are not fools."[98]

gatewaystolearning

Top Ten to Take Away

1. Today senators are elected directly by the people, and presidential elections give the people more influence, but the Electoral College enhances the influence of small states over states with large populations and affects the strategy of presidential campaigns; the candidate with the highest number of popular votes sometimes does not win the presidency. (pp. 309–314)

2. Strategies for winning states crucial to winning the electoral vote introduce inequalities. (pp. 319–323)

3. Each state has two senators. House members represent state congressional districts whose lines are redrawn every ten years following the census to make the population represented roughly equal. (pp. 314–316)

4. Election outcomes in Congress correspond strongly with incumbent advantages. (pp. 328–329)

5. The federal government regulates the financing of campaigns to help equalize opportunities to run for federal office. (pp. 319–322)

6. The Constitution gives states authority over the "Times, Places and Manner of holding Elections." State rules vary, introducing some inequalities in access. (p. 330)

7. Because voting shapes the outcome of elections and the conduct of government, there have always been debates over who gets access to the ballot. The Hamiltonian model and the Jeffersonian model debate the effects of voting participation. (pp. 330–331)

8. Unequal turnout by various demographic groups suggests that government's response is unequal. (pp. 331–335, 339)

9. Americans participate in the political system in other ways, including participating in political campaigns and protests that call attention to causes, and, engaging in political debates, fundraising, and political campaigns on the web. (pp. 339–342)

10. Voter registration helps prevent fraud in elections but also poses a gate that decreases turnout. (pp. 342–347)

Key Concepts

battleground state (p. 322). Why do presidential candidates focus on battleground states?

Electoral College (p. 309). Is the Electoral College a gate or a gateway to democracy?

generational replacement (p. 337). What changes in turnout can be expected as young people become eligible to vote and older citizens no longer can?

gerrymandering (p. 316). Does gerrymandering weaken responsiveness?

invisible primary (p. 317). What is the importance of the invisible primary?

microtargeting (p. 323). Why do politicians engage in microtargeting?

midterm elections (p. 326). What is the relationship between the outcome of midterm elections and sitting presidents?

position issues (p. 324). Why are position issues uncommon in campaigns?

presidential coattails (p. 329). Do presidential coattails enhance government responsiveness?

redistricting (p. 315). What is the difference between redistricting and gerrymandering?

retrospective voting (p. 325). How does retrospective voting encourage responsiveness by elected leaders?

safe seat (p. 328). Are safe seats a sign of government responsiveness or unresponsiveness?

super PACs (p. 321). What was the effect of super PACs on the 2012 presidential election?

swing states (p. 322). Is your state a swing state?

turnout (p. 331). Evaluate the trends in turnout over the last thirty years.

valence issues (p. 324). Why are valence issues common in campaigns?

vanishing marginal (p. 328). Why do vanishing marginals mean elections are less competitive?

vote-by-mail (VBM) system (p. 346). Why might VBM increase turnout?

voting-age population (VAP) (p. 337). How is VAP different from VEP?

voting-eligible population (VEP) (p. 338). Explain the merits of this measure.

wedge issue (p. 324). Why do politicians like to use wedge issues?

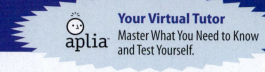

Your Virtual Tutor
Master What You Need to Know and Test Yourself.

aplia

Learning Outcomes

WHAT YOU NEED...

To Know	To Test Yourself	To Participate
What ideas molded the Framers' thinking about elections	• Summarize the constitutional requirements for presidential and congressional elections	• Argue that the constitutional requirements for elections create citizen inequality
What the steps in presidential campaigns are	• Compare and contrast presidential campaigns • State the importance of the invisible primary to candidate momentum • Explain how caucuses and primaries work • Tell what happens at national conventions	• Debate whether the permanent campaign increases government responsiveness or impairs performance • Attend a caucus or vote in a primary • Watch the national conventions and decide if they are informative or propaganda
What issues shape presidential campaigns	• Track trends in fundraising for presidential campaigns • Describe the impact of the Electoral College on presidential campaigns • Compare and contrast valence issues and position issues • Name the key factors in predicting who wins the presidential election	• Evaluate the role of money in presidential elections • Assess whether the Electoral College creates citizen inequality • Critique the applicability of prediction models for the 2012 presidential election
What the steps in congressional campaigns are	• Describe midterm elections • Relate how candidates try to win election	• Critique the applicability of the median voter theorem to the 2012 congressional elections
What issues shape congressional campaigns	• Explain how fundraising needs restrain candidates • Describe the role of political parties in congressional campaigns • Give reasons for incumbency advantage • Explain the relationship between the outcome of midterm elections and public opinion of the president	• Decide if campaigns are too expensive • Decide if incumbents are too entrenched
Why there are battles over ballot access	• Explain why it matters that the Constitution delegated authority over voting to the states • Compare and contrast the Hamiltonian and Jeffersonian models of participation	• Debate the relationship between citizen voting and democratic government
Who tends to turn out in American elections	• Generalize about turnout in the United States • Identify the characteristics of individuals who are more likely to vote	• Critique citizen equality in light of turnout
How low turnout is in American elections	• Explain why turnout is lower in the United States than in some other democracies • Address the issue of turnout and inequality	• Evaluate whether low turnout invalidates the idea of self-government • Assess whether higher turnout among the wealthy than among the poor has an impact on public policy
What important forms of participation there are other than voting	• Survey the effectiveness of protest politics • Describe new trends in participation made possible by the Internet	• Participate in a protest or an Internet movement, or interview someone who has, to assess the role of citizen participation in a democracy

"The future of our nation is held in the hands of our youth, and we must do all we can to prepare them for the competitive, international job market they will enter."

Nydia Velázquez,
University of Puerto Rico,
Río Piedras, San Juan

11

Congress

As a young girl, Nydia Velázquez had to convince her family to let her start school early. By age 16 she was already a student at the University of Puerto Rico. Her major—political science—was no surprise to her family, because her father, a sugarcane cutter, had long been a political activist. He founded a political party in Yabucoa, where the family lived; and, Nydia remembered, dinner conversations were full of talk about workers' rights. She credits him with passing on to her a strong social conscience. "I always wanted by be like my father," she told the *New York Times*.

After graduating with honors in 1974, Velázquez pursued a master's degree in political science at New York University and went on to serve as a legislative aide to African American Congressman Ed Towns, from New York. She also worked as the director of the Department of Puerto Rican Community Affairs for the governor of Puerto Rico and, like her father, was a community activist on behalf of Latinos, organizing massive voter registration drives in the New York City area.

But the key element in Velázquez's story is how she won a seat in the U.S. House of Representatives in 1992. Running in a newly created congressional district that was designed to include a majority of Latino voters, she faced challenges from other Latino candidates and from a white former congressman seeking to reclaim his seat. During her campaign, she and her volunteers went door to door in the district's poorest neighborhoods to register voters and ask for their support. On election day she emerged victorious with the help of thousands of Latino voters, and she has never forgotten them. "Her biggest commitment," reports an observer, "is to her district and her 'pueblo'—the Latino community she says has historically been shut off from access to power and information." With her election, Nydia Velázquez did not just win

aplia Need to Know

- **How Congress has developed**
- **What the powers of Congress are**
- **How Congress is structured**
- **How a law is made in Congress**
- **What a member of Congress does**

a seat in Congress; she gave the Latino residents of her district a voice in national policy making that they never had before.[1]

In the House, Congresswoman Velázquez has been a strong advocate on behalf of Latinos, especially Latino women, as well as of the Chinese and African American residents in her district. She has focused on immigration issues and on strengthening ties with Latin America. She has spoken out against English-only laws because, she argues, Latinos need both Spanish and English in their early years of education to overcome language barriers and become full citizens. Congresswoman Velázquez has served as chair of the House Committee on Small Business. She is a senior member of the House Financial Services Committee and has served as chair of the Congressional Hispanic Caucus. She believes that economic empowerment for the working poor is her district's chief challenge, and her position in Congress gives her the opportunity to bring home federal dollars, in the form of projects and grants, to provide economic and political opportunities for her constituents.

As a protector of her constituents who never forgets her roots, Velázquez has been reelected ten times. Her very presence in Congress helps advance the cause of equality; she represents a series of firsts: first in her family to graduate from college, first Puerto Rican woman elected to Congress, first Latina to chair a House committee. She believes her background as a Puerto Rican woman helps her to better address the needs and concerns of people of all ethnicities because she shares their experiences.

In this chapter, we explain how members of Congress navigate the gates and gateways embedded in the legislative branch to best serve the interests of their constituents. The fact that members of Congress must repeatedly return home to ask the voters to reelect them helps to keep them responsive to their constituents, who hold them accountable for the policies they enact into law. But the process of congressional representation—that is, of putting good ideas into practice as law—is difficult and complex. There are structural gates embedded in a separation of powers system of government and in a democratic legislative process that encourages competition among groups with conflicting interests. Navigating this terrain is not easy, but Nydia Velázquez's efforts on behalf of her district show how an individual member of Congress can be an advocate as well as a legislator.

FocusQuestions

- How are members of Congress held accountable, both individually and for the collective output of Congress as a whole?
- In what ways is Congress responsive as a decision-making body? How does Congress address the pressing needs of the American people?
- What opportunities are there for the average person to influence the policy process in Congress? Is Congress accessible to citizens equally?
- How do the institutional structures in the House of Representatives and those in the Senate work as gates blocking the enactment of legislation? Are there any gateways in these chambers that can help overcome these obstacles? Why did the Framers set up the legislative branch this way?
- Is Congress a gate or a gateway to democracy?

Congress as the Legislative Branch

〉 How Congress has developed

In Chapter 2, The Constitution, we discussed the ideas of representation that shaped the Framers' thinking. They believed that a democratic government had to be responsive and accountable to the people. In such a government, leaders would not inherit power; rather, they would be chosen by the people at regular intervals, and these elections would be the key way that voters would hold government officials accountable for their actions. The Framers of the Constitution designed Congress to be the legislative branch of the federal government. At the same time, they wanted the process of lawmaking to be complex and deliberative so that members of Congress would not succumb to impulsive actions that might harm constituents or violate fundamental constitutional rights. Over time, Congress has increased the scope and range of its powers, but the added responsibilities have added a layer of complexity that makes it harder than ever to pass laws.

> **Connections:** Is Congress a gateway to democracy, or a gate?

Representation and Bicameralism

Essential to understanding how Congress facilitates representation in the American democracy is to recognize that it is bicameral, that is, it is divided into two separate chambers: the House of Representatives and the Senate. This structure reflects the Framers' fear that the power of the legislative branch might grow to the point where it could not be controlled by the other two branches. Because the legislative branch is closest to the people—its

ISTOCKPHOTO

The Framers created the House of Representatives and the Senate as separate chambers of Congress, but both are located in the U.S. Capitol. In this view from the National Mall, the Senate chamber is on the left, and the House chamber is on the right. There are six office buildings for members of Congress and their staff members, three on each side of the Capitol.

members represent specific population groups, by region, and can be removed by election—the Framers believed that Congress would have a democratic legitimacy that neither the executive nor the judicial branches would possess.

The solution, according to James Madison, was to divide the legislature into two parts that would check each other. The House of Representatives would be a large body that reflected population size within states and was directly elected frequently (every two years), and the Senate would be an elite chamber, with two senators for every state regardless of population size elected by state legislatures for six-year terms. This arrangement guaranteed that large states could not overwhelm smaller states in determining the content of laws. The specific differences between the two parts of Congress are discussed next.

Connections: What did the Framers do to control Congress's power?

Constitutional Differences between the House and Senate

To accomplish Madison's goal, the Constitution establishes four key differences between the two chambers of Congress: qualifications for office, mode of election, terms of office, and constituencies (see Table 11.1).

Qualifications for Office. To serve as a member of the House of Representatives, an individual must be at least 25 years old, reside in the state that he or she represents, and have been a U.S. citizen for seven years before running for office. For the Senate, an individual must be at least 30 years old, reside in the state he or she represents, and have been a U.S. citizen for nine years before running for office. Senators are expected to be older and to have lived in the United States for a longer period of time than House members because the Framers believed those characteristics would make the Senate the more stable partner in the legislative process.

No provision in the Constitution delineates a specific race, gender, income level, or religion as a prerequisite for serving in Congress. Twenty-first-century

TABLE 11.1 Comparison of House and Senate Service

	House	Senate
Minimum age	25 years old	30 years old
Citizenship	7 years	9 years
Term of office	2 years	6 years
Geographic constituency	District	State
Redistricting	Every 10 years	—
Mode of election until 1914	Direct	Indirect through state legislatures
Mode of election after 1914	Direct	Direct

© CENGAGE LEARNING

Congresses have been much more diverse, with female, African American, Hispanic, Pacific Islander, and Native American members in the House. Nevertheless, note that women held only 17 percent of the seats in the 112th Congress (House and Senate combined), although they constituted 51 percent of the nation's population. Congress is still predominantly white and male.[2] The average House and Senate member is older than 56. House members tend to serve an average of five terms (ten years) and Senators an average of two terms (twelve years).[3] The twenty-first-century House has included members from the Protestant, Catholic, Jewish, Greek Orthodox, Mormon, Buddhist, Quaker, and—for the first time—Muslim faiths. The religious background of senators has been slightly less varied but has also included members from the Protestant, Roman Catholic, Mormon, and Jewish faiths.[4]

House members have more varied prior experience than their Senate colleagues. A majority of House members served in their state legislatures before coming to Congress; others were mayors, law enforcement officers, teachers, doctors, ministers, radio talk show hosts, accountants, business owners, and even four airline pilots. Just as House members use state legislatures as stepping-stones, senators use the House of Representatives to launch their bids for the Senate. In the 112th Congress, forty-nine senators had previously served in the House of Representatives, and others had been mayors, governors, and attorneys general or had held executive branch positions.

Mode of Election.   House members are elected directly by citizens. Senators are elected directly as well, but that is a more recent development. From 1789 to 1914, the mode of election for the Senate was indirect: Citizens voted for members of their state legislatures, who then selected the U.S. senators. The House was supposed to be more immediately responsive to the opinions of the people, but the Framers designed the Senate to insulate senators from the direct voice of the people, in other words, to make them less directly responsive to the people. The mode of election for the Senate was changed to direct in 1913 with the ratification of the Seventeenth Amendment.

Terms of Office.   A term of office is the length of time that an elected official serves before facing the voters again in an election. The term of office for House members is two years, and the term of office for U.S. senators is six years. The difference in term of office leads to key differences in how each chamber operates. House members have a shorter amount of time to demonstrate their effectiveness before they face reelection, so the House of Representatives as a whole is usually in a greater hurry to pass legislation than is the Senate. Senators know they have six years before they have to face their voters, so they have a bit more flexibility in working out disagreements among their constituents and balancing constituents' interests against the interests of the nation as a whole. Because senators know they have a longer time in which to establish a good reputation among their home state voters, the Senate takes more time to deliberate over legislation.

In any given election year, the entire membership of the House of Representatives must face the voters, but only one-third of senators stand for reelection. To this day, the maximum number of senators who stand for regularly scheduled reelection in the same year is thirty-four (out of a possible hundred), thereby ensuring that a majority of the Senate is never up for reelection at the same time as the entire House of Representatives.[5] This electoral condition reinforces the stability of the Senate's membership; it also limits the electoral incentives for House and Senate members to cooperate with one another to pass legislation.

Constituencies.   A constituency is the set of people that officially elects the House or Senate member; in the United States, constituency is defined geographically. Each member of the House of Representatives represents a congressional district with established geographic boundaries within the state (except for seven states with populations so small that they have just one congressional district).

In 1789 the average size of a congressional district was about 30,000 people, and the average size of a state was about 300,000 people; in 2012, a congressional district had about 711,000 people, and the nation's largest state, California, had approximately 38 million residents.[6] Because the Framers knew that the country's population would change, they required a count, or census, of the population every ten years. Following the census, the number of congressional districts in each state would be adjusted to reflect population changes. The House started with 65 members and, when capped by Congress at 435 in 1929, had increased by 670 percent.[7] Congress was concerned that if the House grew any larger it would not be possible to conduct legislative business.[8] Today, because there is an absolute limit on the total number of House members, population growth or decline has a direct bearing on a state's representation, increasing or decreasing the state's number of representatives and thus its relative influence in the House.

Geographic boundaries on constituencies have a direct impact on congressional representation. A member of the House is responsive to the needs of the residents of a district, but a U.S. senator is responsive to the needs of the residents of an entire state. As a result, members of the House and Senate from the same state can react differently to the same issue.

Redistricting.   Only the House of Representatives is subject to redistricting, which is the redrawing of the boundaries of congressional districts in a state to make them approximately equal in population size. Because the size of the House is limited to 435, the overall number of congressional seats per state must be adjusted following a census if there have been population changes. Based on

Connections:
Which congressional district do you live in? Which congressional district is your college in?

the state's allocation of congressional districts, the state legislature redraws the districts, and the only real limitation on redistricting is that the boundaries of the district must be contiguous (uninterrupted). During redistricting, the majority party in the state legislature tries to influence the process to construct each district in such a way that a majority of voters favors its party, thereby making it easier for its candidates to win, in a process known as gerrymandering.

Redistricting has also been used as a tool to achieve greater minority representation in the House of Representatives following the theory of descriptive representation, whereby an individual represents a constituency not just in terms of geography but also in terms of race or ethnicity. The Voting Rights Act of 1965 prohibits states and political subdivisions from denying or abridging "the right of any citizen of the United States to vote on account of race or color"; it was later amended to protect the voting rights of non-English-speaking minorities—referring to Latinos—as well. This act is discussed in detail in Chapter 5, Civil Rights; here we focus on the fact that many states initially responded to the law by redrawing congressional districts to group minority voters in a way that would deny them the voting strength to elect a minority member of Congress. In 1982 Congress amended the Voting Rights Act to prevent this kind of manipulation. In response, some state legislatures created so-called majority-minority districts in which African Americans or Latinos would constitute a majority of the voters and would have enough votes to elect an African American or Latino candidate.[9] The New York district from which Congresswoman Velázquez was first elected was one of them. Current guidelines on redistricting call for the consideration of race in drawing district lines, but not to the extreme that it was employed in the past.[10]

Because representation in the Senate is related to state boundaries, not to population size, some scholars have argued that the Senate is less responsive than the House. As we explore later in this chapter, the rules of the Senate amplify this imbalance of influence by granting each senator equal power to delay or block legislation. As a result, a senator who represents a state like Wyoming, with fewer than six hundred thousand people, can prevent the passage of a policy that might benefit a state like California, with 38 million people.

Connections: How do majority-minority districts provide a gateway for better representation of minority interests?

Connections: With each state having the same number of senators, what are the consequences for citizen equality across small and large states?

 **Checkpoint**

Can you:
- ☐ Explain the reasons for and consequences of bicameralism
- ☐ Explain the constitutional differences between the House and Senate

The Powers of Congress

〉 What the powers of Congress are

The Framers granted Congress powers that were necessary to construct a coherent and forceful federal government. Some of these, such as the power to tax and to regulate commerce among the states, had been denied to Congress under the Articles of Confederation, and their absence had weakened the new republic. At the same time, the Framers worried that the legislative branch would grow too powerful. So they limited the powers of Congress to a list in Article I, Section 8 of the Constitution, together with a few stated responsibilities in other sections. The following discussion highlights the most important powers of Congress. It also examines the ways that Congress has used its constitutional powers to expand its role in the policy-making system and ways that Congress, as the legislative branch, is balanced and checked by the executive and judicial branches.

Taxation and Appropriation

Congress has the power "To lay and Collect Taxes." In a division of this important power, the Constitution states that all bills for raising revenue should originate in the House of Representatives, but the Senate "may propose or concur with Amendments, as on other Bills." Initially, the Framers thought that tax revenue would come primarily from levies placed on imported goods. As the industrial economy grew, so did the need for government services and programs that cost money. With the Sixteenth Amendment, ratified in 1913, Congress gained the power "to lay and collect taxes on incomes," whatever the source. This amendment overturned prohibitions on certain types of income taxes.

Paralleling the power to tax, Congress also has the power to spend—"to pay the Debts and to provide for the common Defence and general Welfare." The general welfare clause has proven to be a major means by which Congress's power has expanded. Congress **appropriates** (or allocates) federal monies on programs it **authorizes** (or creates) through its lawmaking power. This "power of the purse" has been instrumental in the expansion of Congress's relative strength among the branches of government.[11] The Constitution also gives Congress the authority to borrow money, to coin money, and to regulate its value, and it requires a regular accounting of revenue and expenditures of public money.

War Powers

The Constitution gives Congress authority to "provide for the common Defence." In reality, the war powers are shared with the president. For example, Congress has the sole power to declare war, but this power is typically used only after the president has requested a declaration of war. In many cases, the president may ask Congress for specific authorization to take military action; under its power of taxation and appropriation, Congress has the authority to fund or refuse to fund military operations. Relations between Congress and the president over war powers have sometimes been harmonious, but in recent decades they have become contentious. The struggle between the president and Congress over the war powers is examined in detail in Chapter 12, The Presidency.

Connections: How have the powers of Congress increased? Why did they increase?

Connections: Why do you think the Framers gave the House, rather than the Senate, the authority to originate revenue bills?

appropriate: *Congress's power to allocate a set amount of federal dollars for a specific program or agency.*

authorize: *Congress's power to create a federal program or agency and set levels of federal funds to support that program or agency.*

Regulation of Commerce

The Constitution gave Congress an important power that it did not have under the Articles of Confederation: the power "to regulate Commerce with foreign Nations, and among the several States, and with the Indian Tribes." Using the power in this commerce clause, Congress established a national set of laws regulating commerce that are applicable to all states equally.[12] In time, the authority to regulate interstate commerce has allowed Congress to expand its power to the point that almost no economic activity is beyond its reach. In the name of regulating interstate commerce, Congress has passed laws that permit the federal government to break up monopolies, protect labor unions, set a minimum wage, and outlaw racial discrimination by businesses and commercial enterprises. In 2012, the Court ruled that Congress's requirement, set forth in the Patient Protection and Affordable Care Act, that individuals purchase health insurance went beyond Congress's commerce clause authority but upheld most of the Act as within Congress's taxing authority.

Appointments and Treaties

In recognition of the Senate's perceived wisdom and stability, the Framers gave the Senate, and not the House, the power of advice and consent. In the appointment of high-level executive branch appointees, such as cabinet secretaries and ambassadors, this power allows the Senate to evaluate the qualifications of a presidential nominee and, by majority vote, to approve or reject the nominee. Similarly, the appointment of all federal judges, from district courts to the Supreme Court, is subject to the approval of the Senate (see Chapter 14, The Judiciary, for more details on this process). Additionally, the Senate acts as a check on the president's power to make treaties with foreign nations: Treaties must be approved by a two-thirds vote or they fail to take effect (see Chapter 12 for more on treaty negotiation and ratification). The advice and consent role of the Senate acts as a gateway for citizen influence over

> **Connections:** Why did the Framers give the Senate the power of advice and consent?

ALEX WONG/GETTY IMAGES

The Senate exercises its advice and consent powers when it holds hearings on presidential nominees and then votes to approve or reject them. In the summer of 2009, senators questioned President Barack Obama's first Supreme Court nominee, Sonia Sotomayor, an appeals court judge from New York. She was confirmed on August 6, 2009, by a vote of 68 to 31.

presidential appointments and treaties because senators are more likely to block appointments and treaties that they believe are unpopular with their constituents.

Impeachment and Removal from Office

Congress's ultimate check on the executive and judicial branches is its power to remove officials and judges from office by impeachment. The president, vice president, and high-level officials are subject to impeachment for "Treason, Bribery, or other high Crimes and Misdemeanors." This power is rarely used. In Chapter 12 we examine the two cases in which presidents have been impeached, but not removed from office.

The process of impeachment and removal from office takes place in two steps. First, a majority of the House of Representatives votes to bring formal charges against the president or other federal official, an action called impeachment. Then the Senate conducts the trial, with the chief justice of the United States presiding in the case of the president's impeachment, and votes to convict or acquit. If two-thirds of the senators present vote to convict, the president or the federal official will be removed from office.

Lawmaking

Congress, as the legislative branch, is responsible for lawmaking. Unlike the enumerated powers listed at the beginning of Article I, Section 8 and explained above, the final paragraph of Section 8 gives Congress broad authority "to make all Laws which shall be necessary and proper for carrying into Execution the foregoing Powers." In combination with the general welfare clause and the commerce clause, this necessary and proper clause allows Congress a great deal of leeway to carry out its responsibilities under the assumption that additional powers are implied in these clauses, although not explicitly stated in the Constitution. Over time, Congress has made full use of this flexibility to expand its authority in a wide range of areas, such as regulating interstate railroads, establishing civil rights protections, funding school lunch programs, limiting greenhouse gases, and providing student loans. Essentially, if an argument can be made that a service or program is important for the nation, Congress has used its powers to create that service or program.

Authorization of Courts

In Article I the Constitution also gives Congress the power to "constitute Tribunals inferior to the Supreme Court." Article III, the section on the judiciary, reiterates congressional control by saying that Congress may "ordain and establish" courts at levels lower than the Supreme Court. In 1789 Congress used this power to pass the Judiciary Act, which established federal district courts and circuit courts of appeal. Today, there are ninety-four district courts and thirteen appellate circuits.[13]

The federal judicial branch asserted more authority over the other two branches in the Supreme Court case of *Marbury v. Madison* (1803; see Chapter 2). This case established judicial review, which is the federal judiciary's power to declare laws passed by Congress as unconstitutional. The *Marbury* decision gave the courts the power to interpret the Constitution and determine how congressional laws (and even executive branch actions) conform to its explicit language and its intent (see Chapter 14 for further explanation of this decision).

In recent years the Senate has tried to reassert its influence over the federal courts through the nomination process.[14] As we discuss later in the chapter, individual senators can try to stall or block presidential nominees for federal judgeships with whom they disagree on key constitutional questions.

Oversight

Once a bill becomes a law, the executive branch, headed by the president, is supposed to carry out the law according to Congress's wishes. But the executive branch is a bureaucracy with many departments and agencies that have authority to implement laws. The sheer size and complexity of the federal bureaucracy make it difficult for Congress to determine whether laws are being administered according to the intent behind them (see Chapter 13, The Bureaucracy, for more details). Over time, Congress has asserted its oversight authority to monitor the ways in which the executive branch implements law.

Members of Congress engage in oversight activities in several ways. They hold hearings with cabinet officials and bureaucrats to analyze how well programs are working, and they frequently invite members of the public to describe how federal programs operate in their communities. In cases of special investigations or suspected wrongdoing by members of the executive branch, Congress can legally require members of the administration to testify. In some instances, Congress convenes special committees to investigate actions involving members of the president's staff or even the president himself. In these ways, members of Congress provide a gateway for the people to constantly monitor and hold the federal government accountable for how it implements the law.

> **Connections:** Think about the power to investigate. Which branch should have this power?

Checkpoint

Can you:

- ☐ State what the general welfare clause allows Congress to do
- ☐ Recall why war powers are shared with the president
- ☐ Define the commerce clause and explain its power
- ☐ Explain the power of advice and consent
- ☐ Describe the process of impeachment
- ☐ Compare and contrast the enumerated and implied powers
- ☐ Explain Congress's role in the authorization of courts
- ☐ Characterize how Congress uses its powers of oversight on the other two branches

The Organization of Congress

〉 How Congress is structured

The House and the Senate have evolved into very different institutions by virtue of their differences in size, rules, structure, and responsibilities. The Constitution establishes few guidelines for how the House and Senate should operate, so it was left to the members to determine how to choose their leaders and how much power to give them. Some aspects of leadership are shared by the House and Senate, but there are important differences in the amount of power each grants to its leaders. Notably, the power of political parties to shape policy is vastly different in each chamber.

The Role of Political Parties

Connections: Are political parties in the House too powerful? Are they a gate or a gateway to passing legislation?

In today's political world, political parties seem natural and intrinsic to the organization of Congress. Indeed members of Congress align more closely with their political parties in the House and Senate than in any time in the past 100 years (see Figure 6.6). As scholars Sarah Binder and Eric Schickler each show, not until after the Civil War did the House change its internal rules to give the majority party the ability to get its preferred policies passed over the objections of the minority party.[15] Since then, party affiliation and party loyalty have become the defining features of how policy is made in the House of Representatives.

With a rise in party strength at the district level, House members were increasingly judged on the performance of their party in office, and elections became centered on gaining majority control of the chamber. If the majority party could pass policies that it favored and prevent those who disagreed with them (the minority party) from gaining any power, majority party members could return to their districts and claim credit for being effective legislators.

Although the Senate also became more party-oriented at the end of the nineteenth century, its members never changed the rules of the chamber to give the majority party complete dominance. Because the number of senators has remained small, it is still possible to conduct legislative business in a personal manner, and each senator exerts individual influence over policy outcomes. In this age of increased polarization, voters weigh a senator's ideology and party affiliation more heavily than they used to, but it is still not as important as in House elections. Consequently, senators have had fewer incentives to hand over their individual powers to a single party leader to accomplish party goals.

Connections: What evidence of compromise and cooperation do you see in the Senate today?

The Senate has remained small enough that each individual senator can wield relatively equal amounts of power. As a result, members of the minority party in the Senate have far more power in the policy-making process than do their counterparts in the House.[16] In essence, getting any legislation passed in the Senate usually requires compromise and cooperation among all senators—majority and minority party members—in one way or another. We discuss the role of political parties and partisanship in the health care reform overhaul in the policy section at the end of this chapter.

The House of Representatives

As is the case with any large organization, success requires leadership. To maximize party cohesion, members of the House meet in a party caucus ("to caucus" literally means "to gather") of the members of their political party. Each party's caucus chooses its party leaders: For the majority party, the top party leader is the Speaker of the House, and for the minority party, it is the minority leader.

The Speaker of the House.   **Speaker of the House** is the only formal leadership position written into the Constitution. Article I, Section 2 states that "the House of Representatives shall chuse their Speaker and other Officers," but there the official description ends. The Speaker is elected by a majority of House members every two years, on the first day of the first session of each new Congress.

The leadership styles of Speakers vary according to how much power the rank-and-file party members want to give to their leaders. The ability of the Speaker to make the most of party power depends a great deal on how unified the party is on any given issue, or a whole range of issues, and on whether he or she represents the same party as the president. In the 112th Congress, Speaker John Boehner, with an opposite party president, had the most difficulty holding his majority party together on votes related to federal spending and deficit reduction. On these issues he faced both an internal party division and a small wing of the Republican majority that did not want to cooperate with President Barack Obama under any circumstances (see Chapters 1 and 12).

Whether he or she works with a same- or an opposite-party president, the Speaker's most important responsibility is to maintain power in the House for the majority party, and that means getting the members of the majority party reelected. To do so, the Speaker supports a set of policies that he or she believes are popular with voters, and he or she tries to get those policies enacted into law. For example, during the consideration of health care reform in the House, the Democrats shared the goal of passing a health care reform bill, so they allowed the Speaker to use all the tools at her disposal to get the bill passed. The Democrats suffered big losses in the 2010 elections, in part due to voter backlash on this issue. For Speaker Boehner, the 2012 elections represented his first test of holding onto power in the

 Speaker of the House:
Constitutional and political leader of the House.

Connections: Why is the Speaker of the House so powerful? Why is the person who holds this position third in line in presidential succession, after the vice president?

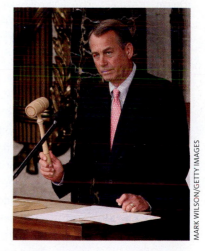

MARK WILSON/GETTY IMAGES

John Boehner (R-Ohio) replaced Nancy Pelosi (D-Calif.) as Speaker in 2011 after the Republicans won control of the House in the 2010 elections. Boehner has faced more internal party division than Pelosi did, but the Republicans still managed to hold on to the House in the 2012 elections.

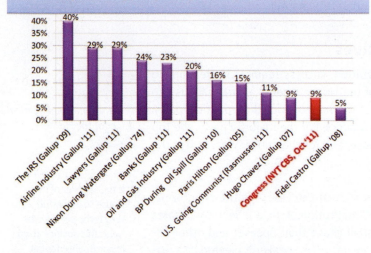

The Popularity of Congress Today
Other Approval Ratings, Compared Against Congressional Approval at 9%

Bar chart values:
- The IRS (Gallup '09): 40%
- Airline Industry (Gallup '11): 29%
- Lawyers (Gallup '11): 29%
- Nixon During Watergate (Gallup '74): 24%
- Banks (Gallup '11): 23%
- Oil and Gas Industry (Gallup '11): 20%
- BP During Oil Spill (Gallup '10): 16%
- Paris Hilton (Gallup '05): 15%
- U.S. Going Communist (Rasmussen '11): 11%
- Hugo Chavez (Gallup '07): 9%
- Congress (NYT CBS, Oct '11): 9%
- Fidel Castro (Gallup, '08): 5%

FIGURE 11.1 **The Popularity of Congress, 2011.**

Congressional popularity fell to such low levels in 2011 that even members of Congress pointed it out. In a speech to the Senate, Senator Michael Bennet (D-Colo.) used this chart to show colleagues that voters viewed them as unfavorably as they viewed Venezuelan dictator Hugo Chavez and only slightly more favorably than they viewed Fidel Castro, the former dictator of Cuba.

Source: As presented by Senator Michael Bennet (D-Colo.).

House majority leader: *Leader of the majority party in the House and second in command to the Speaker.*

House minority leader: *Leader of the minority party in the House.*

House, and he focused his efforts on bringing bills to the House floor on issues such as federal aviation, transportation, and insider trading in Congress, all of which he knew had support within Congress and were popular with voters. Both former Speaker Nancy Pelosi, the first female Speaker of the House, and Boehner share the dubious distinction of presiding over Congresses with some of the lowest approval ratings ever recorded[17] (see Figure 11.1).

House Party Leaders. The **House majority leader**, as second in command, works with the Speaker to decide which issues the party will consider. He or she also coordinates with committee leaders on holding hearings and reporting bills to the House floor for a vote. The House majority leader must strike a compromise among many competing forces, including committee chairs and external interest groups. He or she is also expected to raise a significant amount of campaign contributions for party members, and that role produces more pressure to appease as many interest groups as possible. The majority leader also has nine majority whips to help "whip up" support for the party's preferred policies and keep lines of communication open between the party leadership and the rank-and-file membership. The majority leader and whips work hard to track members' intended votes—in a process called the whip count—because they want to bring to the floor only those bills that will pass; any defeat on the floor could weaken voter confidence in the majority party.[18]

The minority party in the House is the party that has the largest number of House members who are not in the majority party. The highest-ranking member of the minority party is the **House minority leader**, and his or her main responsibility is crafting the minority party's position on an issue and serving as the public spokesperson for the party. If the minority party is the same as the president's party, the House minority leader is also expected to garner support for the president's policies among minority party members. The House minority leader works with minority whips who are responsible for keeping all the minority members in line with the party's public positions.

The challenge for the minority party in the House of Representatives is that it has very little institutional power; the majority party uses its numerical advantage to control committee and floor actions. Because of its institutional disadvantages, the minority party in the modern House of Representatives rarely has the power to stop majority party proposals from passing. Minority party members can vote no, but their real power lies in making speeches, issuing press releases, and stirring up grassroots opposition to majority party proposals.

Connections:
Does the institutional structure of the House promote party dominance? Responsible lawmaking? What can be done about the structure of Congress?

The Senate

The Senate has always been a smaller chamber than the House because it is based on the number of states in the union and does not adjust according to population growth. The Senate majority leader has fewer formal powers to advance the party's agenda compared to the Speaker of the House. Because the Senate never grew to be as large and unwieldy as the House, the individual members have rarely seen the benefit of giving up power to party leaders to make the Senate run efficiently or enact the party's agenda.

President Pro Tempore.

Article I, Section 3 of the Constitution states that the vice president shall be the president of the Senate, but in his absence the Senate may appoint a president pro tempore (temporary president) to preside over the Senate. For most of the Senate's history, the vice president presided over the Senate, and his main functions were to recognize individual senators who wished to speak and to rule on which procedural motions were in order on the Senate floor. The vice president can also break a tie vote in the Senate, a power that can give the president's party control of the outcome on the floor. But in the 1950s the vice president became more active in executive branch business and less active in the Senate. Subsequently, the Senate began appointing the oldest serving member from the majority party as the president pro tempore to serve as the temporary presiding officer. The president pro tempore is closely advised by the Senate parliamentarian, who is responsible for administering the rules of the Senate.

Senate Party Leaders.

The majority party elects the **Senate majority leader**, but unlike the Speaker of the House, this position is not written into the Constitution. The job of the Senate majority leader is to make sure the Senate functions well enough to pass legislation. To accomplish that goal, the Senate majority leader tries to craft legislation as close to the preferred policies of his or her party as possible, necessitating a great deal of compromise and the "power of persuasion."[19]

Senate majority leader: *Leader of the majority party in the Senate.*

Connections:
Does the institutional structure of the Senate promote party dominance? Responsible lawmaking? Individual careers? What can be done about the structure of Congress?

Senate minority leader: *Leader of the minority party in the Senate.*

Still, the Senate majority leader does have several formal powers. For instance, he or she is the official scheduler of Senate business and is always recognized first to speak on the Senate floor. Being recognized first, before any other senator, gives the majority leader the power to control the floor and prevent any other senator from speaking. But because the Senate majority leader relies on the senators' voluntary cooperation to conduct the business of the Senate, there are limits on how tough he or she can be on Senate colleagues. If a Senate majority leader tries to bully senators, they might retaliate by constantly using their individual floor powers to delay or block key legislation.

The **Senate minority leader** is the leader of the minority party in the Senate and is expected to represent minority party senators in negotiations with the majority leader on which bills are brought to the Senate floor and under what circumstances. Similar to the House counterpart, the Senate minority leader's job is to organize minority party senators into a coherent group that can present viable alternatives to the majority party's proposals.

The extended leadership structure of the Senate looks similar to that of the House (see Figure 11.2). It consists of an assistant majority leader, majority and minority whips, and conference chairs, all of whom are responsible for uniting the senators in their respective parties and crafting legislative proposals that can garner enough support to pass the Senate.

The Committee System

Almost all legislation that passes the House or Senate goes through a committee. The House and Senate are organized into separate committees to deal with the different issues that fall under the purview of the federal government. The party that has the majority in the entire House or Senate also has the majority of seats on each committee, and the committee chair is chosen from the majority party, with the approval of the party caucus. Typically, each House member or senator gives the party leadership a list of desired committee assignments, and the leadership assigns committee seats according to seniority and the availability of seats on specific committees.

The House and Senate each have several types of committees. A standing committee is a permanent committee with the power to write legislation and report it to the full chamber. Select committees, joint committees, and special committees are usually focused on a more narrow set of issues, such as aging or tax policy, but none has the same legislative clout and authority as a standing committee. In the House, there are twenty standing committees, and the average House committee has forty-three members. In the Senate, there are sixteen standing committees, and the average Senate committee has twenty members.[20] The committee system is the central hub of legislative activity in Congress. Committees hold hearings to consider members' bills, to conduct oversight of the executive branch, or to draw attention

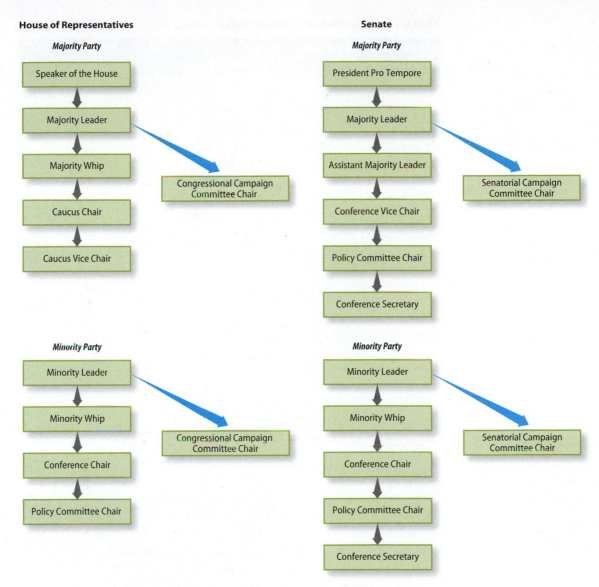

House of Representatives

Majority Party

Speaker of the House
↓
Majority Leader → Congressional Campaign Committee Chair
↓
Majority Whip
↓
Caucus Chair
↓
Caucus Vice Chair

Minority Party

Minority Leader → Congressional Campaign Committee Chair
↓
Minority Whip
↓
Conference Chair
↓
Policy Committee Chair

Senate

Majority Party

President Pro Tempore
↓
Majority Leader → Senatorial Campaign Committee Chair
↓
Assistant Majority Leader
↓
Conference Vice Chair
↓
Policy Committee Chair
↓
Conference Secretary

Minority Party

Minority Leader → Senatorial Campaign Committee Chair
↓
Minority Whip
↓
Conference Chair
↓
Policy Committee Chair
↓
Conference Secretary

FIGURE 11.2 The Structure of Party Leadership in Congress.

Each chamber of Congress has its own separate party leadership structure designed to help party leaders keep rank-and-file members united and accomplish the party's policy goals.
© CENGAGE LEARNING

to a pressing issue. Committees also write the legislation that is eventually considered on the House and Senate floors. Table 11.2 lists the standing committees in each chamber.

During committee hearings, committee members literally hear testimony on the content and impact of a bill from other members of Congress, executive branch officials, interest groups, businesses, state and local government

TABLE 11.2 Standing Committees in Congress

House of Representatives (20 committees)	Senate (16 committees)
Agriculture	Agriculture, Nutrition, and Forestry
Appropriations	Appropriations
Armed Services	Armed Services
Financial Services	Banking, Housing, and Urban Affairs
Budget	Budget
Education and the Workforce	Health, Education, Labor, and Pensions
Energy and Commerce	Commerce, Science, and Transportation Energy and Natural Resources Environment and Public Works
Foreign Affairs	Foreign Relations
Homeland Security	Homeland Security and Governmental Affairs
Oversight and Government Reform	
House Administration	Rules and Administration
Judiciary	Judiciary
Natural Resources	
Transportation and Infrastructure	
Rules	
Science, Space, and Technology	
Small Business	Small Business and Entrepreneurship
Ethics	
Veterans' Affairs	Veterans' Affairs
Ways and Means	Finance

Source: U.S. House of Representatives, http://www.house.gov; and Senate, http://www.senate.gov. See the committee membership lists.

Connections: How do hearings serve as gateways?

officials, and citizens' groups. For the public, hearings are a direct gateway for influence on members of Congress because important information is conveyed in a public setting. Committee hearings serve five basic functions for members of Congress: They draw attention to a current problem or issue that needs public attention, inform committee members about the consequences of passing a specific bill, convey constituents' questions and concerns about an issue, exert oversight of the executive branch to determine whether congressional intent is being honored, and provide an arena in which individual members make speeches to attract media attention that is often used later in a campaign as evidence that the member is doing his or her job. Committee chairs decide which bills receive hearings and which go on to **markup**, a meeting in which committee members write the version of the bill that they may send to the entire chamber for a vote. In both the hearing and markup process, the committee chair gives preference to the views of the majority party members of the committee.

Committee chairs have powerful roles. The chair is typically the majority party member who has the most seniority (longest time) on the committee. However, the Speaker or the Senate majority leader reserves the right to suggest a less senior member as chair if he or she believes that person will better serve the party's interests. The term **ranking member** signifies the member of the committee from the minority party with the greatest seniority.

Until 1994 there was no limit on the number of terms that committee chairs could serve. However, in 1995 the Republican majorities in the House and the Senate adopted six-year consecutive term limits on chairs. Limiting the tenure of committee chairs makes it harder for them to amass long-term individual power, so the Speaker retains more control over the committees' legislative agendas. In 2007, when the Democrats took the majority in the House and Senate, House Democrats retained term limits, but Senate Democrats did not; in January 2009 House Democrats eliminated term limits on committee chairs.[21] The Republicans reinstituted the term limit rule when they assumed control of the House in the 112th Congress, although they exempted the chair of the House Rules Committee (discussed below) from term limits.

When Congresswoman Velázquez served as chair of the House Committee on Small Business in the 110th Congress, she scheduled hearings to

markup: *Process by which bills are literally marked up, or written by the members of the committee.*

ranking member: *Leader of the minority party members of a committee.*

AP PHOTO/SUSAN WALSH

Chairs of House and Senate committees hold hearings to explore key issues of concern to their constituents and to the nation as a whole. They also use their position to advance legislation they believe will accomplish their own and their party's policy goals. Here Nydia Velázquez chairs the House Committee on Small Business during a hearing on October 28, 2008.

draw attention to budget cuts in key programs that provided loans to owners of small businesses in low-income areas and helped minorities start their own businesses.[22] These types of federal programs are essential to Congresswoman Velázquez's constituents, and she used her position as committee chair to draw attention to their needs.

In general, when a bill is referred to a committee, it is assigned to a subcommittee, a smaller group of committee members who focus on a specific subset of the committee's issues. Subcommittees can consider legislation, but only the full committee can report a bill to the chamber floor for consideration. In 1973 the House expanded the number of subcommittees and subcommittee chairs, largely as a result of the efforts of young representatives who wanted to enact policies that older committee chairs opposed. By creating more subcommittees, the House created smaller centers of power in which individual members could exert influence over the content of legislation.[23] The Senate did not make similar changes; each senator already had individual power and did not see the need to make changes in the committee structure.

Advocacy Caucuses

In addition to committees in the House and Senate, there are also advocacy caucuses, groups whose members have a common interest and work together to promote it. Members might have similar industries located in their districts and states, such as coal mining; or share a background, such as the Congressional Black Caucus or the Hispanic Caucus; or hold similar opinions on issues, such as abortion or land conservation. Members join an advocacy caucus because it gives them an opportunity to work closely with colleagues to represent specific interests and to draw attention to issues of concern to them and to their constituents. Many advocacy caucuses are bipartisan, that is, both Democrats and Republicans join as members. Advocacy caucuses are important to the interactions of Congress because they bring together members from different parties and regions that might not otherwise work closely with each other.[24]

Advocacy caucuses have no formal legislative power, but they can be influential on a bill, especially in the House, because they represent a bloc of members who could vote together in support or opposition. As an alternative to joining a caucus, senators can join together in a temporary coalition and call a press conference to draw attention to the group, industry, or issue that unites them. Senators can also join a congressional caucus even though it is lodged in the House. When he was a senator from Illinois (2005–2008), Barack Obama joined the Congressional Black Caucus.

> **Connections:** How do advocacy caucuses counteract the role of parties in Congress? How can they be a gateway for citizen influence?

Checkpoint

Can you:

☐ Describe the role parties play in Congress

☐ Explain the role of party leaders in the House of Representatives

☐ Compare and contrast the functioning of the Senate and House

☐ State how the committee system works

☐ Identify the role of advocacy caucuses in Congress

The Lawmaking Process

> **How a law is made in Congress**

In this section, we examine the lawmaking process. The process by which a policy proposal becomes a bill and then a law is long and winding, and the Framers designed it deliberately to ensure that laws were reasonable and well thought out. The gates against passage are almost too successful. In the 111th Congress (2009–2010), for example, members introduced 6,562 public bills in the House of Representatives and 4,059 public bills in the Senate. Of the total of 10,621 public bills, Congress enacted only 336—or 3 percent—into law.[25] It requires compromise and cooperation for a bill to become a law. For an overview of the process, see Figure 11.3.

The Procedural Rules of the House and Senate

Just as the roles of political parties and leaders differ in the House and Senate, so do the internal rules of these chambers. Over time, House and Senate members have adopted different procedures for considering legislation, and these procedures can make compromise between the two chambers more difficult.

The House Committee on Rules.

To proceed from committee to the House floor, all bills must pass through the House Rules Committee. Because the House is so large, bills cannot proceed to the floor from committee unprotected; otherwise, the number of legislative amendments that could be offered by the 435 members of the House would overwhelm lawmaking.

The Rules Committee maintains control before the bill goes to the floor by issuing a rule dictating how many amendments may be considered. A closed rule means that no amendments may be offered; a modified closed rule allows a few amendments; and an open rule, as its name suggests, allows any number of amendments. The most typical rule is a modified closed rule, which allows the minority party to offer at least one alternative to the bill supported by the majority party. The rule is voted on by all members of the House; if it is approved, debate on the bill begins. If the rule is defeated, the bill is returned to the House Rules Committee or the originating committee for further consideration.

The majority party has learned over time how to use the Rules Committee to maintain policy advantages over the minority party. The majority party uses its numerical advantage on the Rules Committee (8–4 in the 112th Congress) to structure floor debate to limit the minority party's opportunity to amend or change a bill. The Speaker appoints all the majority party members to the Rules Committee, and they are expected to use their powers to advance the party's preferred version of a bill.

Connections:
Do the procedural rules of the House and Senate serve as gates or gateways to legislation? Why would there be gates that prevent Congress from fulfilling its fundamental responsibility to pass laws?

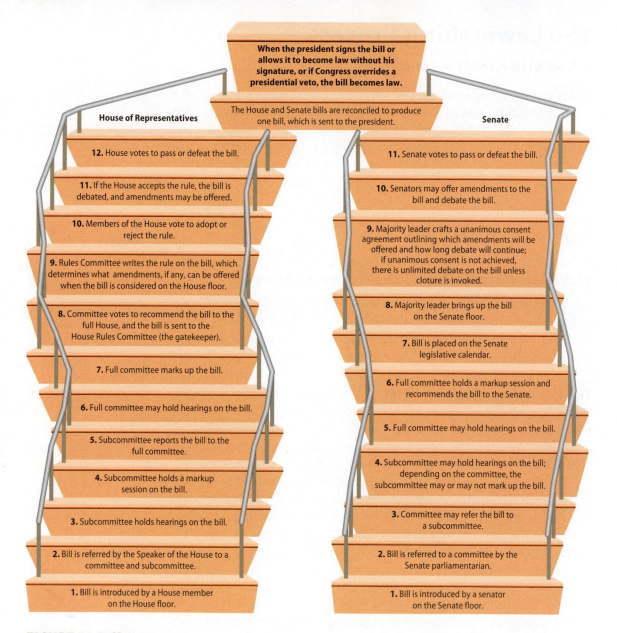

When the president signs the bill or allows it to become law without his signature, or if Congress overrides a presidential veto, the bill becomes law.

The House and Senate bills are reconciled to produce one bill, which is sent to the president.

House of Representatives

12. House votes to pass or defeat the bill.

11. If the House accepts the rule, the bill is debated, and amendments may be offered.

10. Members of the House vote to adopt or reject the rule.

9. Rules Committee writes the rule on the bill, which determines what amendments, if any, can be offered when the bill is considered on the House floor.

8. Committee votes to recommend the bill to the full House, and the bill is sent to the House Rules Committee (the gatekeeper).

7. Full committee marks up the bill.

6. Full committee may hold hearings on the bill.

5. Subcommittee reports the bill to the full committee.

4. Subcommittee holds a markup session on the bill.

3. Subcommittee holds hearings on the bill.

2. Bill is referred by the Speaker of the House to a committee and subcommittee.

1. Bill is introduced by a House member on the House floor.

Senate

11. Senate votes to pass or defeat the bill.

10. Senators may offer amendments to the bill and debate the bill.

9. Majority leader crafts a unanimous consent agreement outlining which amendments will be offered and how long debate will continue; if unanimous consent is not achieved, there is unlimited debate on the bill unless cloture is invoked.

8. Majority leader brings up the bill on the Senate floor.

7. Bill is placed on the Senate legislative calendar.

6. Full committee holds a markup session and recommends the bill to the Senate.

5. Full committee may hold hearings on the bill.

4. Subcommittee may hold hearings on the bill; depending on the committee, the subcommittee may or may not mark up the bill.

3. Committee may refer the bill to a subcommittee.

2. Bill is referred to a committee by the Senate parliamentarian.

1. Bill is introduced by a senator on the Senate floor.

FIGURE 11.3 How a Bill Becomes a Law.

© CENGAGE LEARNING

filibuster: *Tactic of extended speech designed to delay or block passage of a bill in the Senate.*

Agenda-Setting Tools in the Senate. The Senate does not have a gatekeeper committee like the Committee on Rules in the House, and all senators have the power to try to amend legislation on the floor. The tool that they use is Rule XIX of the Standing Rules of the Senate, which grants senators the right to speak on the Senate floor. Over time, senators have used this right to make speeches, offer amendments to bills, object to consideration of a bill on the floor, or engage in **filibusters**, extended debates that members start with the purpose of delaying or even preventing the passage of bills.[26] All senators in the majority and the minority parties can use the filibuster. Throughout Senate history, a wide range of bills, from civil rights legislation to product liability legislation, have been delayed or defeated by filibusters.[27]

The only way to stop a filibuster is by invoking **cloture**, a motion to end debate that requires a supermajority of sixty votes to pass. Once cloture has been invoked on a bill, no more than thirty additional hours of debate are permitted. All amendments must be germane to the bill's issues, and a time for a final vote is set.

In addition, Senate rules no longer require those seeking to block a bill to speak continuously on the floor. Senators who oppose a bill can merely state their intention to filibuster, and that will be sufficient to block the bill from consideration on the floor. Senators also use the threat of a filibuster to block the president's judicial nominations at all levels, a practice that has come under increasing scrutiny. Filibusters of this type are an expression of partisanship or ideology, and they can disrupt the operation of the federal courts.[28] To counteract the filibuster in recent years, the Senate has resorted to a two-track system in which a bill that is being filibustered can be set aside to allow the Senate to proceed to other bills. But even with this two-track system, the filibuster has imposed substantial costs on the Senate, both in terms of the legislation that has failed to pass and the legislation that could not be brought to the floor.

Some scholars have argued that the filibuster has been used too frequently as a way of blocking action on important public policies and is not a legitimate democratic instrument of power. Others argue that filibustering is a responsive and effective means of representation in Congress; if there is intense opposition to a bill in a senator's state, or from a minority of voters nationwide, the senator may consider it a responsibility to block the bill's passage.[29]

Without a gatekeeper like the House Committee on Rules and with the constant threat of a filibuster, there are few restrictions on a bill when it comes to the Senate floor. When the Senate majority leader wishes to bring a bill up for consideration, he or she must ask unanimous consent of every senator. Consequently, the Senate typically operates under **unanimous consent agreements** to establish guidelines for debating a bill. Senators strike a deal about how a bill will be debated on the Senate floor, how and when amendments will be offered, how much time will be allocated to debate and vote on amendments, and at what time on what date the final vote on the complete bill will take place. Senators have accepted this form of limitation on their rights to amend or block a bill because it requires their consent and enables the Senate to move forward and pass key legislation.

Nevertheless, a senator can object to a unanimous consent request to bring a bill to the Senate floor in a practice known as a **hold**. A hold is a less drastic measure than a filibuster, but it can be used by any senator to delay a bill for a minimum of twenty-four hours. The majority leader can circumvent a hold by

cloture: *Vote that can stop a filibuster and bring debate on a bill to end.*

Connections: Is the filibuster a legitimate means of protecting minority rights?

unanimous consent agreement: *Agreement among all one hundred senators on how a bill or presidential nomination will be debated, changed, and voted on in the Senate.*

hold: *Power available to a senator to prevent the unanimous consent that allows a bill or presidential nomination to come to the Senate floor, which can be broken by invoking cloture (sixty votes).*

requesting a vote on cloture; if sixty senators agree, the Senate proceeds to consider the bill. Typically, senators hold up bills to extract concessions from Senate leaders or from the administration on the legislation being considered. They also use the hold to draw increased attention to a bill or to delay a presidential nominee whom they oppose, in the hope that public opposition will develop.

Legislative Proposals

The lawmaking process starts with an idea. Ideas for legislation can come from a number of sources, including constituents, interest groups, local or national newspaper stories, state or local governments, staff members, and the members' own personal interests.[30] When an idea is agreed on, the House or Senate member's staff consults with the Office of Legislative Counsel, which turns the general outlines of a bill into the technical language that will alter the U.S. Code, the set of federal laws that governs the United States. After approving the final legal language of a bill, the member introduces the bill into the respective chamber (House or Senate), an action known as bill sponsorship. Once a bill is introduced, other members can sign on to be cosponsors (sponsorship of legislation is discussed in more detail later in this chapter). In reality, many freestanding bills that are introduced separately are later incorporated into larger omnibus bills that are passed by Congress. Combining bills into omnibus legislation can be useful, especially in periods of divided government. These big bills allow Congress to pass numerous provisions that might not pass if each was presented separately.[31]

Connections: How do omnibus bills make accountability more difficult?

Committee Action

After a member introduces a bill, it is referred to one or more committees or subcommittees that have jurisdiction over its subject matter. The first step in getting the bill enacted into law is to secure a hearing on a bill in subcommittee or full committee. In general, a committee tends to act first on bills that are sponsored by the chair of the committee, then on those sponsored by the subcommittee chairs, and last on bills sponsored by regular members of the committee. If the sponsor is not on the committee to which the bill is assigned, it is much harder to get action on the bill. This arrangement also makes sense because committee members are more likely to have expertise on the issues covered by the committee than are other legislators, so their bills are taken more seriously by their fellow committee members.[32] In rare cases, however, as a result of intense interest group lobbying or media pressure, a committee might hold a hearing on a bill sponsored by someone who is not a committee member, but the committee typically drafts its own bill to address the same issue.

After the hearings, the committee may move to the markup. At this point, the stakes intensify in terms of what the bill will ultimately look like, so the stakeholders in the policy process try to exert influence. Once the full committee approves a bill, it and an accompanying committee report are sent to the full House or Senate for consideration by all members.

Floor Action and the Vote

When a bill is sent to the full House or Senate—commonly known as "going to the floor"—all the members of the chamber gather to debate and vote on it. Debate takes different forms in each chamber. In the House, it is heavily structured, and most members are allowed no more than five minutes to speak on a measure, leaving almost no time for actual deliberation among members. But in the Senate, as noted earlier, there are few limits on the time allowed for members to speak on an issue on the floor. If the Senate is operating under a unanimous consent agreement or cloture, time is limited; otherwise, senators can make speeches and even engage in active debate on an issue for much longer than their House counterparts. Unfortunately for the current political system, real debate rarely occurs on the floor; instead, representatives and senators use their opportunity to speak to make partisan speeches or to direct their remarks to their constituents back home.

During a roll call vote, the clerks of the House or Senate call the name of each member, who registers his or her vote electronically. Members cast up or down votes on legislation (to pass or reject), to table (set aside) legislation, or to approve a motion to recommit (send it back to committee with instructions to rewrite it). In addition to individually recorded votes, general voice votes can be taken when a consensus exists and there is no perceived need to record each member's vote.

A roll call vote is the most fundamental way that a member of Congress represents constituents. When members of Congress cast their votes, they can act as trustees who exercise independent judgment about what they believe is best for the people or as delegates who do exactly as the people wish. Over time, congressional representation has evolved into a hybrid of both types of representation; thus, members of Congress act as both trustees and delegates. Roll call voting is therefore a key gateway for citizen influence in the legislative process.

Scholars have long characterized roll call voting by partisan dimension and by ideological or spatial dimension, because in the past both the Democratic and Republican parties contained both liberals and conservatives.[33] Currently, the vast majority of Democratic members are liberal, and the vast majority of Republican members are conservative. Consequently, scholars now can examine roll call voting through both the partisan and ideological lens simultaneously. They confirm that most members of the House and Senate vote along party lines; in the 111th Congress, 88 percent of House members and 90 percent of Senate members voted with their party.[34] In today's Congress, leaders frame the content of bills and the choices for roll call votes along the lines of party platforms and ideology. Essentially, they are engaging in what is called message politics, designing legislation to push members into casting votes that may later be used in campaigns against them.[35] This framework reflects a responsible parties system (see Chapter 9, Political Parties) in which

Connections: What is the purpose of floor debate? Does it change minds and votes?

Connections: Who are your representatives and senators? Do you want them to be trustees or delegates?

voters can clearly distinguish Democratic and Republican legislative policy goals. Although the increased emphasis on partisanship makes it easier for citizens to more clearly hold Congress accountable, it decreases the likelihood of bipartisan cooperation and makes passing legislation more difficult.

Conference Committee

For a bill to become law, the House and Senate have to pass an identically worded version of it to send to the president for signature. The last stage in the congressional legislative process takes place when the House and Senate meet in conference committee to resolve any differences in the versions that passed each chamber. The Speaker of the House and the Senate majority leader typically appoint the chairs and ranking members from the committees that originated the bills, plus other members who have been active on the bill. If the bill is very important to the party leaders, they also have the power to appoint themselves to the committee. If the conferees can reach agreement, the conference committee issues a conference report that must be voted on by the entire House and Senate. Because the conference report represents the end of the negotiation process between the two chambers, members cannot offer amendments to change it. However, if a majority of members of the House or Senate are displeased with the final results of the conference, they can defeat the report outright or vote to instruct the conference committee to revise the agreement.

In the past twenty years, Congress has decreased its use of conference committees. Instead, party leaders take on the responsibility of producing a final bill themselves. In choosing this path, they concentrate power in the hands of fewer members of Congress than in the traditional conference committee system.[36] Although this alternative provides a more streamlined way of legislating, it also acts as a gate against input from committee members who wish to represent their constituents' views on the final version of the bill.

The Budget Process and Reconciliation

Although the federal government tries to spend about as much money as it takes in from revenues, it does not typically succeed. Instead, it usually runs a **federal budget deficit**, which requires it to borrow money to meet all its obligations (see Table 11.3 and Figure 1.8). Although the process is complex, essentially this means that the federal government pays interest on outstanding loans, and the loans and interest that accumulate over time constitute the **national debt**.

The modern Congress operates under a budget process created in the Congressional Budget and Impoundment Control Act of 1974, which was enacted to give Congress more power over the federal budget.[37] The act created the House and Senate Budget Committees and the Congressional Budget Office so that Congress could construct its own budget blueprint as an alternative to the president's annual budget.

federal budget deficit:
Difference between the amount of money the federal government spends in outlays and the amount of money it receives from revenues.

national debt:
Sum of loans and interest that the federal government has accrued over time to pay for the federal deficit.

TABLE 11.3 Federal Budget Deficits and the National Debt (in billions of dollars), 1970–2012

Year	Revenues	Outlays	Total Deficit	National Debt
1970	192.8	195.6	−2.8	380.9
1975	279.1	332.3	−53.2	541.9
1980	517.1	590.9	−73.8	909.0
1985	734.0	946.3	−212.3	1,817.4
1990	1,032.0	1,253.0	−221.0	3,206.3
1995	1,351.8	1,515.8	−164.0	4,920.6
2000	2,025.2	1,789.0	236.2	5,628.7
2005	2,153.6	2,472.0	−318.3	7,905.3
2009	2,104.6	3,518.2	−1,413.6	11,875.8
2012	2,468.6	3,795.5	−1,326.9	16,350.9

Source: Table 7.1, Federal Debt at the End of Year: 1940–2017, U.S. Budget for FY 2013; Table 1.1—Summary of Receipts, Outlays, and Surpluses or Deficits (−): 1789–2017, http://www.whitehouse.gov/omb/budget/Historicals/.

The federal government's fiscal year begins on October 1 and ends on September 30, and the key aspect of the budget process (see Figure 11.4) is that the congressional budget, known as the **concurrent budget resolution**, is supposed to be approved by both chambers by April 15. Because the budget resolution does not have the force of law, it is not sent to the president for his signature. Rather, it serves as general instructions to congressional committees about how much money can be allocated for federal programs in the fiscal year. The authorizing committees take this blueprint into account when they reauthorize existing programs or create new ones, and the appropriations committees in the House and Senate use it to allocate funds in twelve separate bills. They typically begin their work in May in the hope of enacting all appropriations bills by September 30. If Congress and the president fail to agree on any one of the twelve appropriations bills, a **continuing resolution** is enacted that funds the government temporarily while disagreements about spending are worked out.

In recent years, the House of Representatives has passed a budget resolution but the Senate has not. This failure to produce a concurrent budget resolution has left the appropriations process less structured as well. As a result, Congress relies more heavily on continuing resolutions and omnibus funding legislation than on passing separate appropriations bills. Congress's failure to produce a budget resolution makes it harder for voters to hold it accountable for federal budget policy.

The 1974 Budget Act also created a parallel budget bill, known as **reconciliation**, which does require the president's signature. Reconciliation was specifically designed as umbrella legislation to bring all bills that contain

concurrent budget resolution:
Congressional blueprint outlining general amounts of funds that can be spent on federal programs.

continuing resolution:
Measure passed to fund federal programs when the appropriations process has not been completed by September 30, the end of the fiscal year.

Connections: Does the congressional budget process help or hurt deficit reduction efforts?

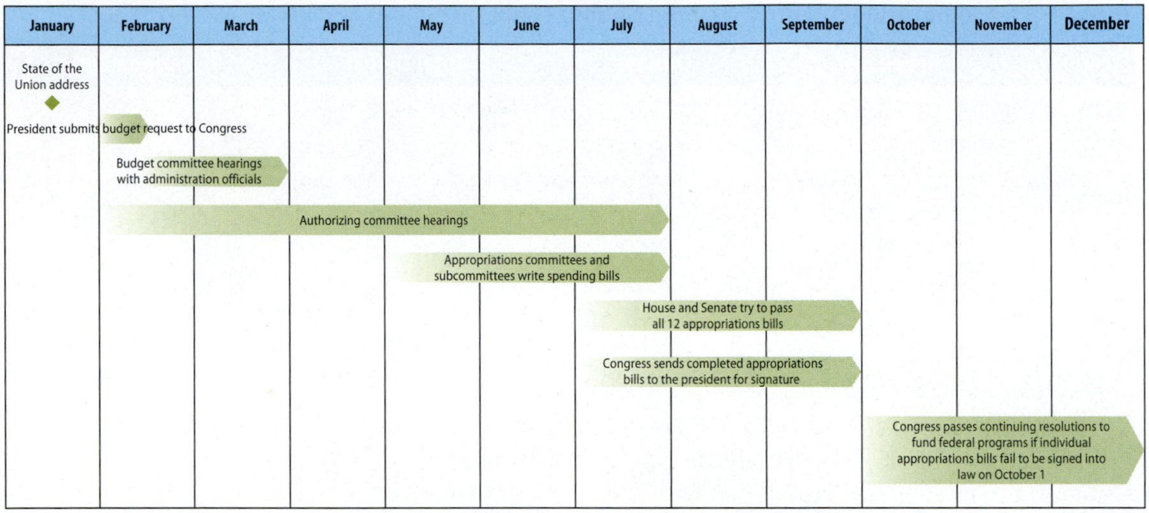

January	February	March	April	May	June	July	August	September	October	November	December

State of the Union address

President submits budget request to Congress

Budget committee hearings with administration officials

Authorizing committee hearings

Appropriations committees and subcommittees write spending bills

House and Senate try to pass all 12 appropriations bills

Congress sends completed appropriations bills to the president for signature

Congress passes continuing resolutions to fund federal programs if individual appropriations bills fail to be signed into law on October 1

FIGURE 11.4 **The Congressional Budget Timeline.**

Congress produces its own blueprint for the federal budget to serve as an alternative to the president's budget and to guide the appropriations process. If necessary, Congress also produces a reconciliation bill to make changes to tax and entitlement programs.

Source: Based on the Budget and Impoundment Control Act of 1974, Title III, Section 300 (Washington, D.C.: U.S. Government Printing Office, 1987), 72.

reconciliation:
A measure used to bring all bills that contain changes in the tax code or entitlement programs in line with the congressional budget.

changes in the tax code or entitlement programs in line with the congressional budget. Entitlement programs, such as Social Security, Medicare, and Medicaid, are considered mandatory because they pay out benefits to individuals based on a specified set of eligibility criteria. When Congress wishes to make a change to one of these programs, it must pass a reconciliation bill. The reconciliation bill has special procedural protections in the Senate: It cannot be filibustered, and it can be debated for no more than twenty hours. A bill that cannot be filibustered was a tempting target for those who wanted to add non-budget-related provisions. Consequently, in 1985 the budget process was modified to include the Byrd rule, which required that reconciliation be used only to reduce the federal deficit, which at the time was $212.3 billion.[38] In subsequent years, the Byrd rule has been interpreted to mean that all provisions of reconciliation must be directly related to the budget.[39]

Despite the Byrd rule, Congress has found ways to use the reconciliation process to pass controversial legislation. Most recently, the Democratic majority in Congress used it to pass part of its comprehensive health care reform, which we discuss below. Both Democrats and Republicans have used the reconciliation process to go beyond changes in the tax code, or to balance the budget, on issues ranging from welfare reform to children's health insurance.[40]

Presidential Signature or Veto, and the Veto Override

In the last step in the legislative process, the bill is sent to the president for his approval or rejection. A president can actively reject, or veto, a bill. If Congress will be going out of session within ten days, the president can wait for the session to end and simply not sign the bill, a practice known as a pocket veto. If Congress remains in session and the president neither vetoes the bill nor signs it, the bill becomes law (see Chapter 12 for more discussion of the presidential use of the veto power).

The veto is a powerful balancing tool for the president against the overreach of Congress; but the Framers also gave Congress the override, the power to overturn a presidential veto with a two-thirds vote in each chamber. When the president vetoes a bill, it is returned to the chamber from which it originated; if two-thirds of the members of that chamber vote to override the veto, it is sent to the other chamber for a vote. A two-thirds vote by each chamber, rather than just a majority vote, is required for an override because the Framers wanted to enable the president to block a bill passed by Congress if he does not believe that it is in the best interest of the nation as a whole. The president can use the veto either to prevent a bill from becoming law or to pressure Congress into making changes that are closer to his policies.[41]

Connections: Why did the Framers give Congress the final say in whether a bill should become a law?

Checkpoint

Can you:

☐ Compare the procedural rules in the House and Senate

☐ State how a bill is proposed

☐ Describe what happens to a bill in committee

☐ Characterize floor action and voting

☐ Explain what happens in conference committees

☐ Identify the key components of the congressional budget process

☐ Define the president's role in the lawmaking process

The Member of Congress at Work

❯ **What a member of Congress does**

The cardinal rule of succeeding in the House or Senate is simple: Never forget where you came from. Representative Nydia Velázquez has shown how a member tries to balance the competing demands of legislating with the core responsibility of serving constituents. The following sections describe exactly what the job of a House or Senate member entails.

Offices and Staff

For all newly elected members in the House and Senate, the first steps are to set up an office and hire staff members. In the House, each representative receives about the same amount of money for office operations. In the Senate, the office budget is determined by the population size of the senator's home state, based on the reasoning that senators from larger states have more constituents and more issues to deal with than their smaller-state colleagues. Most members bring some of their campaign workers to Washington to work on their staffs and try to hire people from their districts or states. New members of Congress also seek out individuals with prior Capitol Hill experience to help orient them to their new surroundings and provide specific issue expertise.

Generally, a member of Congress's Washington office has a chief of staff who oversees the entire office, a scheduler who makes the member's appointments, a press secretary who handles all interactions with the media, and a legislative director who oversees the member's legislative work. In addition, legislative assistants handle specific issues, and legislative correspondents are responsible for answering constituent mail.

House and Senate members aim to be responsive to constituents, and that means providing prompt and extensive constituent services. To do so, they establish district offices in the congressional district for representatives and around the state for senators. These offices help constituents navigate federal agencies if they have difficulty—for example, getting a Social Security check or a passport—and advise constituents on how to win federal contracts. Specific requests for help are assigned to caseworkers. These local offices serve as direct and important links between voters and members of Congress and affect both accountability and responsiveness.[42]

Connections: Have you ever contacted your representative or senators? If so, was it to express an opinion or to ask for help?

Legislative Responsibilities

A successful legislator typically fulfills four responsibilities: securing desired committee assignments and performing committee work, sponsoring and cosponsoring bills, casting votes, and obtaining federal funds for the district or state.

Committee Work.

Just before the start of each new Congress, members are asked which committees they would like to join, and party leaders try to accommodate their wishes, although freshman members rarely get their most favored committees immediately. Freshman members choose committee assignments based on the needs of their district or state, their professional background, their personal experience, and their desire to increase chances for reelection. However, a new senator has to accommodate his or her committee assignment wish list to the reality of the existing committee assignments of the senior senator from the state. All members of the House and Senate try to put themselves in the best possible institutional position to address issues that matter to their constituents.

Committee work consists of attending hearings and participating in markups as well as initiating ideas for legislation for consideration by the committee. Committee members also meet with interest groups, businesses, and citizens' groups that are specifically concerned about bills to be considered in the committee. The extent to which members participate actively in committee business varies according to the local concerns of their constituents, their personal interests, and whether the committee might provide an opportunity for political advancement.[43]

Bill Sponsorship.   Members can sponsor a bill by themselves, or they can ask colleagues to cosponsor bills with them; the higher the number of cosponsors, the greater the show of support for the bill. Members sponsor and cosponsor bills for three important reasons: First, bill sponsorship is an effective tool for giving voters in a district or state a voice in the federal policy-making system. Second, it is a means of staking out specific territory that members can claim as their area of expertise and can be a means of fulfilling campaign promises.[44] Third, it attracts the attention of the media, relevant interest groups, and the press, and thereby can help House and Senate members build their reputations as legislators.

One bill that accomplishes all three goals is H.R. 218, the Stabilizing Affordable Housing for the Future Act, which Congresswoman Velázquez sponsored and introduced on March 20, 2012. This bill proposed an increase in the amount of federally sponsored affordable housing available to citizens with low incomes; it would have directly benefited Velázquez's constituents by equalizing the opportunity for finding affordable housing. The bill fell directly under the jurisdiction of the House Financial Services Committee, of which Congresswoman Velázquez is a member. Although it did not pass, it drew media attention to the national problem of a shortage of affordable housing.

Roll Call Votes.   Each representative and senator is expected to cast a roll call vote on the bills and amendments that reach the floor of the House and Senate. In the House alone, members cast 985 roll call votes during the 111th Congress, and Senators cast 696 roll call votes.[45] Given the large number of roll call votes, voters have difficulty identifying how their members of Congress voted on bills that affect them directly. Because most members of Congress vote the party line, party identification can be helpful in holding members accountable for their roll call votes. If members do not vote the party line, they risk losing the support of party voters in their district or state. However, most members will not vote for a measure that goes against their constituents' opinion or interests. For this reason, majority party leaders try to construct bills that will benefit the constituents of the members of their party.

Federal Funds.   Most members of Congress try to secure federal funds for their districts and states. The effort to carve out some piece of the federal financial pie is typically referred to as "bringing home the bacon" or pork barrel spending, and it can work through funding formulas for federal programs or **earmarks**, which are narrowly defined federally funded projects.[46] One of the most controversial earmarks in recent times was the so-called bridge to nowhere in Alaska championed by the late Senator Theodore (Ted) Stevens

earmark: *Federal dollars devoted specifically to a local project in a congressional district or state.*

(R-Alaska). A bipartisan group of members of Congress, as well as public watchdog groups, raised media awareness about the enormous cost of this bridge. In response, the House and Senate directed the state of Alaska to spend the money allocated for the bridge on more necessary transportation projects.[47] Over the past decade, spending on earmarks has increased; in fiscal year 2010, $16.5 billion was authorized to fund 9,129 earmarks.[48] When the Republicans won control of the House of Representatives, they proposed a total ban on earmarks beginning in 2011, which the Senate also adopted. It is not clear that this ban actually eliminates the kind of localized spending that earmarks directed toward constituents, because now legislators find ways to hide their efforts to direct federal dollars back home. For this reason, it may be that the ban on earmarks actually makes it harder to hold Congress accountable for federal spending.

Despite the conflict over the earmark and federal funding process generally, one could argue that obtaining federal dollars for the district is a form of responsiveness to the local needs of voters. Voters are taxpayers, and members of Congress are simply seeking to bring some of that tax money back home in a directed fashion. On the other hand, many of the projects are not necessary to most voters, and they create waste and inefficiency that can make the federal government less effective.

Communication with Constituents

Congressional representation depends on good communication between constituents and their representatives and senators. Before e-mail and the Internet, members used the franking privilege, which is free mail service, to respond to constituent letters and to send quarterly newsletters as updates on their activities. Today the vast majority of members of Congress use social media to transmit information about their activities to constituents, in addition to hard copy mailings. For example, 81 percent of members of Congress link their official websites to Facebook pages, and 387 members of the House and Senate use Twitter.[49]

To help members stay in touch with their constituents, the federal government pays for House and Senate members to return home to their districts or states approximately thirty-three times a year. These trips home are crucial for building bonds with voters, and members make sure to meet with individuals, speak to local interest groups, attend local parades and business openings, and attract local media coverage.

Cultivating direct links with constituents and making a good impression on them is what the political scientist Richard Fenno calls **home style**, or the way members portray themselves to constituents.[50] Members can choose to emphasize their local work for constituents, or they can emphasize their influence on national policy; some try to do both. Members can be very good at giving charismatic speeches, or they can be quiet, unassuming workers;

Connections:
Federal funds for local projects are often denounced as "pork." How does pork figure in your decision to vote for or against an incumbent?

Connections: What communications have you received from your representative and senators? Have they arrived in the mail or via the Internet?

home style: *The way in which incumbents portray themselves to constituents.*

successful members adapt their home style to the expectations and customs of constituents.

The Next Election

As political scientist David Mayhew explains, members of Congress are always looking ahead to the next election.[51] Elections are the means by which constituents express approval or disapproval of the job members of Congress are doing, and they are the fundamental tool that voters use to hold their members accountable for individual legislative work and the collective performance of their party in office.

The fact is that most incumbents in the House and Senate win reelection. In 2010, 85 percent of all House incumbents and 84 percent of all Senate incumbents won reelection.[52] However, elections in 2010, like 1994, saw more incumbent losses than usual, resulting in a shift in party control in the House; in 1994, losses resulted in a shift of party control in both the House and Senate (see the discussion of congressional elections in Chapter 10, Elections, Campaigns, and Voting).

Congressional campaigns are typically divided into two categories: those with an incumbent seeking reelection, and those with open seats, where no incumbent is seeking reelection. In elections in which an incumbent is running, the contest becomes an evaluation of the job he or she has done in office compared to what the challenger promises to do if elected. Incumbents have major advantages because they have already won at least one election in the district, they are likely to have moderate name recognition, and they have the power to use their congressional offices to provide services to constituents. However, incumbents can also suffer if the reputation of Congress suffers (see Figure 11.5), and so they work to stake out individual reputations that contrast to the institution as a whole.

Consequently, reelection is far from automatic. Part of the incumbent advantage rests on incumbents' efforts to use all their resources to serve their constituents responsively; successful incumbents have a strong motivation to perform well so that they will be reelected. Incumbents also have an electoral incentive to work on behalf of constituents to earn high approval ratings. In addition, if incumbents have any ambition to run for another political office in their state, such as governor, they want to make sure constituents have a good impression of them.

Connections: If an election were held today, would you vote for the incumbent in the House? In the Senate? What would you base your decision on?

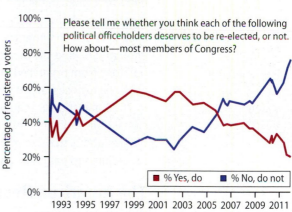

Please tell me whether you think each of the following political officeholders deserves to be re-elected, or not. How about—most members of Congress?

■ % Yes, do   ■ % No, do not

FIGURE 11.5 Voter Opinion of Congressional Incumbents, 1993–2011.

Although congressional incumbents typically enjoy high reelection rates, negative impressions of Congress as an institution can reduce voter support. In 2011, a record low percentage of voters thought members of Congress deserved reelection.

Source: Frank Newport, "Record High Anti-Incumbent Sentiment Toward Congress." Gallup.com, December 9, 2011. Copyright © 2011 Gallup, Inc. All rights reserved. The content is used with permission; however, Gallup retains all rights of republication.

Checkpoint

Can you:

☐ Explain the importance of constituent services

☐ Recall the four legislative responsibilities of congressional members

☐ Describe the key ways in which members of Congress communicate with constituents

☐ State how elections shape the work of members of Congress

Members' concern for their local districts or states can be one of the biggest gates standing in the way of a productive Congress, and frequently the party works to overcome division among its members. Parties provide a collective set of policy goals that will benefit or appeal to party members at the local level. For a member of Congress, however, tying electoral fortunes to the political party can be risky if the majority party falls out of favor with voters who hold it accountable for policy outcomes. Although elections with changes in party majorities are infrequent, they are powerful reminders that incumbents must constantly balance the needs of their constituents with the ideas of their party and stay responsive, or risk losing their bids for reelection.

Congress and Public Policy: Health Care

The central challenge to Congress in carrying out its fundamental responsibility of lawmaking is to find a way to balance the individual interests of its members with the collective need of the nation. Party leaders and committee chairs in each chamber try to write legislation that will attract the support of enough rank-and-file members to pass. At the same time, Congress considers opinions from organized interest groups and, of course, the president, whose approval is necessary to enact laws. The heath care reform legislation passed in 2010 and the subsequent reaction to it reflect the challenges of congressional policy making. Intense lobbying from interest groups, conflicting ideologies about the size of government, and the use of complicated rules and procedures to gain final passage all characterized this policy enactment.

The American Health Care System

The American health care system includes private and public health care insurance components. Most Americans receive health insurance through their employment or purchase it independently from private insurance companies. People over age 65 are covered by Medicare, a federally funded health insurance program, and very-low-income people are covered by Medicaid, a jointly funded health insurance program offered by the federal, state, and local governments.[53] However, in 2011, approximately 48 million Americans did not have access to health insurance, for a variety of reasons: their employer did not offer it; they were self-employed and could not afford to purchase it;

they were unemployed but not poor or old enough to qualify for a government program; or they were deemed ineligible by private insurance companies because they had health conditions that made them high risk and expensive to cover. [54]

Because of its vast scope, health care reform has always attracted intense support and opposition from the many organizations that have stakes in the outcome of reforms. Two central issues have been the availability of health insurance coverage and the cost of health care programs. President Obama promised to address health care reform during his 2008 presidential campaign and followed through by asking Congress, then controlled by the Democrats, to write legislation in the summer of 2009. Although Congress did not meet that deadline, it passed the Patient Protection and Affordable Care Act in 2010.

The health care reform act established a number of new programs, the most notable of which extended health insurance coverage to approximately 32 million uninsured citizens and legal immigrants through an expansion of Medicaid and the provision of federal subsidies to workers to purchase private health insurance.[55] The act provided for increased regulation of private insurance company practices, mandated that individuals carry health insurance, required that young adults under the age of 26 be able to stay on a parent's insurance policy, and banned the denial of health insurance based on a preexisting condition. The bill also increased payment levels to doctors who participate in the Medicaid program and helped senior citizens by closing a loophole in Medicare coverage for prescription drugs.

The process by which health care policy moved from proposal to bill to law was long and winding, as lawmaking always is, and it was especially complicated because of the fragmented nature of America's health care system, party politics and partisanship, and the heightened political rhetoric that surrounded the effort.

Committee Action

Most lawmaking starts in committees and, because the U.S. health care system is so vast and complicated, it comes under the jurisdiction of multiple committees. In 2009, when Representative John Dingell (D-Mich.) introduced the America's Affordable Health Choices Act, the bill fell under the jurisdiction of three different House committees. Henry Waxman (D-Calif.), chair of Energy and Commerce who had a long history of legislative involvement

Connections:
Do you think the government should provide health care coverage for everyone?

Policy discussion occurs in a number of different places in Congress, including in members' offices, in committee rooms, on the House and Senate floors, and among staff members. Such discussion plays an important internal and external role in shaping legislation. Here senators consider health care legislation in committee, with their aides sitting behind them to provide additional information if they need it.

in health care policy, led the coordination effort. Working together, the committees produced an amended version of this bill, which Representative Dingell introduced later that year. The House passed this bill by a vote of 220–215 and sent it to the Senate, because a bill must pass both chambers of Congress to be enacted into law. Key to the House bill was a so-called public option authorizing a federal health insurance program to create competition with private health insurance providers.[56]

In the Senate, the health care bill was also subject to the jurisdiction of multiple committees: the Health, Education, Labor, and Pensions Committee (HELP) and the Finance Committee. The HELP Committee reported its bill, the Affordable Health Choices Act of 2009, to the full Senate in September, and the Senate Finance Committee reported its version of the bill in late October.[57] Senate leaders still had to reconcile this bill with the HELP committee's bill in order for health care reform legislation to pass the Senate. On Christmas Eve the Senate stayed in session for a roll call vote on a compromise version of health care reform titled America's Healthy Future Act of 2009. The bill passed with a vote of 60–39; voting was strictly along party lines.[58] Senate leaders believed they had made great progress, but the bill differed substantially from that passed by the House, notably because it did not contain the public option. This sequence demonstrates the complexity of policy making; changing a policy requires the cooperation and approval of many players, and even when a bill passes one chamber of Congress, it still must pass the other.

Party and Ideological Politics

Health care reform generated strong opinions both in favor of the legislation and against it. Although the Democrats were in the majority, there were divisions within the party on how best to approach this issue. Some Democrats were concerned that the health care bill was too costly and would contribute to an unacceptable level of deficit spending; they valued deficit reduction over the expansion of affordable health care insurance. At the same time, they worried that cuts made in other federal services to pay for the bill would fall disproportionately on rural areas. The debate over health care reform within the Democratic caucus illustrates the constant tension between majority party goals and local concerns in congressional policy making (see Chapter 12 for a discussion of similar tensions in the 112th Congress within the Republican majority in the House over the federal budget deficit and national debt).

The House Republicans, the minority party in 2009, opposed the bill's provisions on both fiscal and ideological grounds. They argued that the bill would raise the deficit, and they opposed a federal mandate that would force individuals to purchase health care insurance because it was tantamount to government interference into individual choice on health care decisions. However, because the minority party has virtually no procedural power to stop the passage of a bill in the House, the Republicans were unable to block the health care bill.

In contrast, the Senate Republicans, despite being the minority party, had the power to filibuster the health care bill on the Senate floor. Technically the Democrats had the sixty votes needed to invoke cloture and shut down a filibuster because the two Independent senators—Joseph Lieberman (I-Conn.) and Bernie Sanders (I-Vt.)—caucused with them. However, in January 2010 they lost their sixtieth vote when Scott Brown, a Republican, was elected to fill the late Senator Edward Kennedy's seat.

Without the necessary sixty votes to invoke cloture, the Democrats feared they could not pass health care. So Democratic leaders in the House and Senate, working with President Obama, came up with an end run around Republican opposition to the bill. They passed health care reform in two stages, using the reconciliation procedure, taking advantage of the fact that reconciliation bills cannot be filibustered and only require a majority (fifty-one votes) to pass. First, the House passed the Senate version of health care, the Patient Protection and Affordable Care Act, by a vote of 219–212 on March 21, 2010, and President Obama signed it two days later. Second, the Health Care and Education Reconciliation Act of 2010, was passed by the Senate (56–43) and the House (220–207) on the same day and signed into law by President Obama. The education part of this bill was included because federal student loan programs have budgetary implications and using the reconciliation process was necessary to revamp those loan programs.

The process of health care reform in the House and Senate starkly illustrates the differences between the two chambers, especially the procedures by which each considers a bill. The House of Representatives uses majority rules and does not give members the opportunity to individually block or delay legislation, so compromise occurs within the majority party more than it does between the majority and minority parties. But in the Senate, the power of the minority party to filibuster makes compromise essential to successful legislating; without it the majority party must resort to invoking cloture and other procedural maneuvers to pass a bill.

Connections: In 2012 the media and public debated this question: Did the health care reform bill involve too much government intervention? What do you think?

Interest Groups and Implementation of the Law

Because of the vast scope of the health care reform effort, hundreds of organizations became involved in lobbying efforts both on Capitol Hill and back home in members' districts and states. These organizations included large employers such as Wal-Mart, large medical associations such as the Federation of American Hospitals, and spending watchdog groups such as the Club for Growth. In fact, 1,541 different organizations reported lobbying on this bill in 2009 alone.[59] Interest group participation was so strong that members of Congress, and even President Obama, spent the second half of 2009 and early 2010 trying to clarify the reform effort and build public support for it.[60]

Interest group involvement did not stop with the passage of the law, and groups used both the legal system and Congress as venues to challenge it. Twenty-six state attorneys general signed onto a lawsuit challenging the constitutionality of the federal health insurance mandate included in the law. Individuals and organizations have also filed cases in federal court to stop or hinder the implementation of the law. Federal judges in different jurisdictions have offered different rulings on the constitutionality of the mandate, and in March 2012, the Supreme Court heard oral arguments on the mandate, as well as other provisions of the act that have been challenged. The Court ruled in June 2012 and upheld the mandate (see Supreme Court Cases: *National Federation of Independent Business et al. v. Sebelius*).

While these challenges were winding their way through the court system, opponents of the bill used the Republican takeover of the House of Representatives in 2010 to try and slow the implementation of the law. The Republicans ran their campaigns in 2010 largely on their opposition to the health care bill, and President Obama more generally, and they interpreted their large victory as a mandate to repeal the act. However, because the Senate was still controlled by Democrats, and President Obama still had two years left in his term of office, there was little chance that a full repeal would pass Congress. Instead, at the urging of groups opposed to the law, the House GOP began a strategy of attaching amendments to legislation that would prevent the Obama administration from issuing the regulations necessary to implement the law. (See Chapter 13 for a broader discussion of the regulatory process.)

One of the most controversial of these amendments dealt with coverage of contraception by insurance companies. In January 2012, the Obama administration issued final regulations as part of the health care law that mandated all employers with health insurance plans provide free contraception to all employees but included an exemption for religious institutions and gave organizations affiliated with religious institutions a year to implement the regulation.[61] Organizations that opposed the use of contraception as part of their central religious beliefs opposed this mandate because, they argued, it violated the separation of church and state. On the other side of the issue,

supremecourtcases

National Federation of Independent Business et al. v. Sebelius (2012)

QUESTION: May Congress impose a mandate to purchase health insurance on those who do not wish to carry it? Did Congress exceed its spending authority with the Medicaid expansions?

ORAL ARGUMENT: March 26–28, 2012 (listen at http://www.oyez.org/cases)

DECISION: June 28, 2012 (read at http://www.findlaw.com/casecode/supreme.html)

OUTCOME: Yes, the authority is within Congress's taxing power (5–4). No, Congress did not exceed its spending authority (5–4).

The Obama administration argued that because the decisions of individuals not to purchase health insurance have a substantial effect on hospitals and insurance companies involved in interstate commerce, Congress has the right to mandate the purchase of such insurance. Those opposed to the act argued that if Congress could make people purchase health insurance because of the substantial effect it has on interstate commerce, why couldn't it make people buy broccoli? The administration then argued that even if the act was not itself a regulation of commerce, it was necessary and proper to the regulation of commerce (see *McCulloch v. Maryland*). Finally, the administration argued that the mandate was a valid exercise of Congress's authority to tax to provide for the general welfare. Opponents responded that the Obama administration insisted that the payments for not purchasing health insurance were a penalty and not a tax, so that members of Congress could not be accused of passing unpopular tax increases. Additionally, opponents claimed that the threat states faced of losing all Medicaid funding if they did not voluntarily expand their Medicaid coverage was coercive, in violation of the Tenth Amendment.

In a complicated decision, Chief Justice John Roberts, joined by the Court's four more conservative justices (Samuel Alito, Anthony Kennedy, Antonin Scalia, and Clarence Thomas), declared that Congress did not have the authority under the commerce clause to mandate that individuals enter the insurance market. Crucially, however, Chief Justice Roberts, joined by the Court's four more liberal justices (Stephen Breyer, Ruth Bader Ginsburg, Elena Kagan, and Sonia Sotomayor), ruled that the penalty for not purchasing insurance could be considered a tax and it was well within Congress's authority.

Finally, by a 5–4 vote with Roberts joining the liberal bloc, the Court upheld the withholding of new funds from states that did not accept the new Medicaid expansion, as well as the rest of the law. All justices except Ginsburg and Sotomayor argued that Congress cannot rescind previously committed funds to states that refuse to accept the new Medicaid requirements, imposing the first limits on Congress's spending power in seventy-five years.

- **Why does it matter whether the payment for not having health insurance is a "penalty" or a "tax"?**

- **What was unusual about the Court's decision involving Congress's spending authority?**

women's groups and activists for reproductive rights defended the provision as ensuring equal health care coverage for women no matter where they worked. In response to the outcry, President Obama clarified that organizations affiliated with religious institutions that oppose contraception would not have to pay directly for this coverage, but that the insurance companies that provided their health insurance would have to cover the cost of it for employees of such organizations.[62]

The issue did not end there. In March 2012, Republican Senator Roy Blunt (R-Mo.) offered an amendment to the federal highway reauthorization bill that would allow employers and insurance companies to refuse to provide specific benefits if they conflicted with their religious beliefs. In the House a minority party member would not have been able to offer such an amendment, but majority and minority party senators are granted much broader individual powers to do so. After heated debate on the Senate floor that lasted for several days, the amendment was defeated by a vote of 51–48.[63] After this defeat, House Speaker Boehner stated that the Republican majority in the House would likely try to attach the amendment to other legislation. This amendment illustrates the way that Congress and interest groups can try to counteract the executive branch's power to implement laws, and it indicates the ways that legislative and executive policy making is complex and intertwined. The internal structure of Congress, the intensity of partisan politics, and the role of citizens and the president all present gates and gateways for legislative policymaking, and the boundaries for action are constantly changing.

 Construct Your Own Policy

1. Construct a health care system that would cover all U.S. citizens but not involve private insurance companies.

2. Create a health care system that would cover all U.S. citizens without any government involvement at all.

   For more on the policy-making process, see Chapter 1.

Congress and Democracy

The composition of Congress has changed considerably over the nation's history. The lawmaking body is five times larger and now includes men and women from a wide range of ethnic, racial, and religious backgrounds. From the standpoint of equality of opportunity in a democracy, the increased diversity in Congress is a positive step.

Is Congress a responsive decision-making body? Individual members clearly work hard to address the concerns of their constituents, both at home in the district or state and in their Washington offices. But Congress as a whole is not always capable of addressing the immediate needs of the nation in a timely fashion. The bicameral nature of the institution, with each chamber's separate rules of operation, makes the legislative process time-consuming and complex. In the House, the majority party almost always succeeds in passing legislation that reflects the party's policy goals. In the Senate, the minority has much greater power to block the majority through the threat of a filibuster, so minority party views are typically incorporated into legislation. These differences offer advantages and disadvantages; if Congress acts too hastily, it can pass harmful legislation, but if it acts too slowly, it can fail to meet its fundamental responsibilities to address issues that citizens care about.

Are individual members of Congress accountable for the collective output of Congress as a whole? Not always. The fundamental difficulty with the representative structure of Congress is that each member is elected separately, so that voters may reelect their own representative or senator but still be unhappy with Congress as a whole. It is too easy for one member of Congress to say to constituents, "I am working hard to help you; it is all those other men and women who are not doing their jobs." Only in the rarest of election years do voters actually hold all the members of the Congress accountable for their collective performance. This lack of collective accountability can be a significant obstacle or gate to Congress's productivity and responsiveness to important policy needs.

Is Congress equal in its treatment of each citizen relative to all others? Because each state has the same number of senators regardless of population size, are the citizens of small states more powerful in the Senate than citizens who live in large states? Are the laws that Congress passes fair and balanced, or do they benefit one group more consistently than another? There are no simple answers to these questions. Some voices in society are louder and more prominent than others, and members of Congress tend to respond to citizens whom they perceive to be supportive, who donate more money, and who vote regularly. In some issue areas, the more prominent members of society win out over citizens who are less active and less visible. It is not clear that Congress sets out to give some people greater advantages than others, but the process of balancing the different individual and regional interests in national policy making produces winners and losers. The fundamental challenge to Congress is to make sure that there are no permanent winners or losers, and the challenge to all citizens is to monitor their members of Congress to be sure they are performing their legislative responsibilities.

Focus Questions Revisited

- How are members of Congress held accountable, both individually and for the collective output of Congress as a whole?

- In what ways is Congress responsive as a decision-making body? How does Congress address the pressing needs of the American people?

- What opportunities are there for the average person to influence the policy process in Congress? Is Congress accessible to citizens equally?

- How do the institutional structures in the House of Representatives and those in the Senate work as gates blocking the enactment of legislation? Are there any gateways in these chambers that can help overcome these obstacles? Why did the Framers set up the legislative branch this way?

- Is Congress a gate or a gateway to democracy?

gatewaystolearning

Top Ten to Take Away

1. The Framers designed Congress as a bicameral legislature so that the House of Representatives and the Senate—with different qualifications for office, modes of election, terms of office, and constituencies—would check and balance each other. (pp. 355–356)

2. Although its enumerated powers are limited, Congress has built on its implied powers to become the powerful legislative branch that it is today. (pp. 359–363)

3. Differences in size, rules, structure, and responsibility have molded the House and the Senate into very different institutions. (pp. 356–359)

4. Political parties play a stronger role in the organization and operation of the House than of the Senate. (pp. 364–367)

5. In the Senate, each member has relatively equal power, and passing legislation requires compromise and cooperation. (pp. 367–368)

6. The procedures through which a bill becomes a law are different in the House and Senate, but each chamber engages in committee work, hearings, floor debate, and voting. Following passage by each chamber individually, a formal conference committee or an informal group of party leaders resolves differences between the two bills to produce a single bill that is presented to the president for signature. (pp. 368–372)

7. If the president vetoes a bill, Congress can override the veto with a two-thirds majority in each house. (p. 381)

8. The process of lawmaking is not smooth or efficient, and there are structural gates against a bill's passage. Lawmaking requires balancing competing interests through cooperation, compromise, and deal-making. (pp. 373–381)

9. In recent years, intense partisanship, including party-line voting and message politics, has decreased the likelihood of bipartisan cooperation and made it more difficult for Congress to pass legislation. (pp. 377–378, 387–389)

10. Members of Congress try to balance the competing demands of legislation and constituent service, and they are always anticipating the next election. A successful legislator seeks to be responsive to constituents by engaging in committee work, sponsoring and voting on bills, and securing federal funds for his or her district or state. (pp. 381–386)

Key Concepts

appropriate (p. 360). What is the difference between appropriation and authorization?

authorize (p. 360). How is authorization a part of Congress's "power of the purse"?

cloture (p. 375). How is cloture invoked?

concurrent budget resolution (p. 379). How is a concurrent budget resolution used by congressional committees?

continuing resolution (p. 379). When is a continuing resolution used?

earmark (p. 383). Why did Congress ban earmarks?

federal budget deficit (p. 378). What causes the federal government to run a budget deficit?

filibuster (p. 374). How does the filibuster give power to individual senators?

hold (p. 375). How is a hold used in relation to unanimous consent agreements?

home style (p. 384). How does a member of Congress use home style to help get reelected?

House majority leader (p. 366). What is the House majority leader's role within the House?

House minority leader (p. 366). What is the role of the House minority leader in policy making when he or she shares the president's party?

markup (p. 371). What is the committee chair's role in relation to markup?

national debt (p. 378). How is the national debt related to the federal budget deficit?

ranking member (p. 371). Who gets to serve as ranking member on a committee?

reconciliation (p. 379). Why was the reconciliation process created?

Senate majority leader (p. 367). What is the primary means through which the Senate majority leader wields power?

Senate minority leader (p. 368). How does the Senate minority leader represent his or her party members?

Speaker of the House (p. 365). What methods does a Speaker use to maintain power?

unanimous consent agreement (p. 375). What does a unanimous consent agreement do?

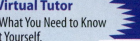

Learning **Outcomes**

WHAT YOU NEED...

To Know	To Test Yourself	To Participate
How Congress has developed	• Explain the reasons for and consequences of bicameralism • Explain the constitutional differences between the House and Senate	• Weigh the gridlock caused by bicameralism against the checks and balances it provides
What the powers of Congress are	• State what the general welfare clause allows Congress to do • Recall why war powers are shared with the president • Define the commerce clause and explain its power • Explain the power of advice and consent • Describe the process of impeachment • Compare and contrast the enumerated and implied powers • Explain Congress's role in the authorization of courts • Characterize how Congress uses its powers of oversight on the other two branches	• Debate whether Congress's power over interstate commerce should be limited but its power over going to war should be strengthened • Consider whether Congress's power over the executive and judicial branches should be expanded
How Congress is structured	• Describe the role parties play in Congress • Explain the role of party leaders in the House of Representatives • Compare and contrast the functioning of the Senate and House • State how the committee system works • Identify the role of advocacy caucuses in Congress	• Evaluate whether advocacy caucuses are effective in representation
How a law is made in Congress	• Compare the procedural rules in the House and Senate • State how a bill is proposed • Describe what happens to a bill in committee • Characterize floor action and voting • Explain what happens in conference committees • Identify the key components of the congressional budget process	• Design a way to change the Senate's rules to limit individual power of senators to filibuster • Map out ways you could influence the content of legislation as it is being considered in Congress • Consider whether Congress is held sufficiently accountable for federal spending
What a member of Congress does	• Explain the importance of constituent services • Recall the four legislative responsibilities of congressional members • Describe the key ways in which members of Congress communicate with constituents • State how elections shape the work of members of Congress	• Determine if your interests are being addressed in Congress • Decide if the congressional workload is too light or too heavy for effective representation

> "I can't stress how important it is to simply get involved. Get into the fight. Do everything you can to get hands-on experience."

Stephanie Cutter, Smith College, Northampton, Massachusetts

STEPHEN CROWLEY/THE NEW YORK TIMES/REDUX

© JIM GIPE 1997

12

The Presidency

As a government and economics major at Smith College, Stephanie Cutter enjoyed politics, but it was her adviser's encouragement that turned interest into involvement. Her work on the 1988 presidential campaign of Michael Dukakis opened a whole new world and, it turned out, a career. After college, she took a job as a receptionist in the Washington office of New York Governor Mario Cuomo, but she shortly returned to presidential campaign work, serving as a staff member on the campaigns of Bill Clinton, John Kerry, and Barack Obama. Campaign work led, in turn, to White House work. For Clinton, Cutter was communications director. For Obama, she has served as chief spokesperson for his transition team, head of communications at the Department of the Treasury, coordinator of press strategy for the nomination of Sonia Sotomayor to the Supreme Court, and coordinator for outreach on health care reform. In late 2011, Cutter became deputy campaign manager for President Obama's 2012 reelection campaign. Between White House assignments, Cutter got a law degree and worked

for Senator Edward Kennedy, First Lady Michelle Obama, and the Democratic National Committee.

Stephanie Cutter's career exemplifies the gateways that open when one gets involved in politics. It also reveals the political networks that talented and hard-working volunteers establish on presidential campaigns and how they use them to secure influential positions in the executive branch. Cutter's specialty is communications. She describes handling the press for political leaders

aplia Need to Know

- What is required to serve as president
- What the powers of the president are and how they are limited
- How executive influence has grown over time
- Why the president is so powerful during wartime
- How the White House is organized
- What defines a great president

as "a game of Ping-Pong," planning press briefings and fielding questions from the news media, in an effort to get the president's message out. Her skills at this game offer insight into the management of the modern presidency and into the importance of presidential agendas and citizen response.[1]

In this chapter we examine how the president governs and how responsive he can be to the people. We look at his constitutional powers and the way he uses the executive power to achieve his policy goals. We also look at the limits on presidential power. As presidential scholar Charles Jones has argued, successful presidents work within a separation of powers system and alongside the legislative and judicial branches.[2] The most successful presidents are strong leaders with clear policy visions and excellent communication and negotiation skills. In the twenty-first century the American president has to implement existing law and, equally important, leads the effort to turn his policy goals into law and achieve his vision for the nation.

FocusQuestions

- In what ways is the president held accountable both individually and for the collective economic, military, and social condition of the nation?
- How responsive is the presidency as a democratic office? How can the president address the vital public policy concerns of the American people?
- What opportunities are there for the average citizen to influence the decisions of the president?
- What powers does the president have to ensure equality across all citizens?
- Is the modern presidency a gate or a gateway to democracy?

Presidential Qualifications

❯ What is required to serve as president

The American presidency was invented at the Constitutional Convention in 1787. The Framers had no definitive models to help them determine what sort of person should serve as a democratically elected head of state because nations were still ruled by monarchs whose power to rule was hereditary. But the Framers had George Washington, the hero of the Revolutionary War, in mind for the office, and he helped shape the idea of what a president should be. Still, they left the qualifications as open as possible, and men with diverse experiences have served as president.

Constitutional Eligibility and Presidential Succession

Article II, Section 1 of the Constitution states that the president must be a natural-born citizen (or a citizen at the time the Constitution was adopted), at least 35 years old, and a resident of the United States for at least fourteen years. The original Constitution did not specify eligibility for the vice presidency, as the person who came in second in the vote for president would be vice president. But in 1800 Thomas Jefferson (1801–1809) and Aaron Burr ended up in a tie in the Electoral College when in fact supporters wanted to elect them as a team, with Jefferson as president and Burr as vice president. The Twelfth Amendment, ratified in 1804, changed the process so that candidates are elected for president and vice president separately. The amendment also directs that the vice president must meet the same eligibility requirements as the president and that electors cannot vote for both a president and a vice president from the elector's home state. This requirement makes it difficult for parties to nominate presidents and vice presidents from the same state.

The Constitution also states that when the president is removed from office by death, resignation, or inability to perform the duties of the office, the vice president becomes president. It stipulates that if neither the president nor the vice president is able to complete the elected term, Congress should designate a successor by law. In 1792 Congress passed the Presidential Succession Act, which designated the president pro tempore of the Senate as next in line, and then the Speaker of the House. In 1886 Congress changed the order of succession to include only cabinet secretaries in the sequence in which the cabinet departments were created, starting with the State Department, Treasury Department, War Department, and attorney general, who is the head of the Justice Department (for more on cabinet departments, see Chapter 13, The Bureaucracy). In 1947 Congress changed presidential succession once again, putting the order of succession as vice president, Speaker of the House, and president pro tempore, followed by the cabinet secretaries, starting with the secretary of state and again following in order the dates of the departments' creation.

There was no constitutional provision for replacement of the vice president, and in the course of the nation's history the office has occasionally been vacant, as it was after Vice President Andrew Johnson (1865–69) assumed the presidency in 1865, following Abraham Lincoln's (1861–65) death. Eventually, the Twenty-Fifth Amendment, ratified in 1967, required the president to nominate a replacement vice president, who must be approved by a majority vote of the House and the Senate. The first vice president to assume office in this manner was Gerald R. Ford, nominated by President Richard M. Nixon (1969–74) in 1973, following the indictment and subsequent resignation of Vice President Spiro T. Agnew. The amendment also allows for a temporary transfer of power from the president to the vice president in cases of incapacity when invoked by either the president or vice president and a majority of the cabinet. To date, only the president has invoked this clause and then only when he has had to have surgery that would require sedation. In contrast, no one invoked the clause when President Ronald Reagan (1981–89) was shot in a failed assassination attempt

Connections: How do term limits make the president less responsive to public opinion?

FIGURE 12.1 Constitutional Amendments That Pertain to the Presidency.

Color Code: Structure

Twelfth	1804	Requires that electors cast separate votes for president and vice president and specifies requirements for vice presidential candidates
Twentieth	1933	Declares that presidential term begins on January 20 (instead of March 4)
Twenty-Second	1951	Limits presidents to two terms
Twenty-Fifth	1967	Specifies replacement of the vice president and establishes the position of acting president during a president's disability

© CENGAGE LEARNING

in 1981; Vice President George H. W. Bush stood in for him at official functions and meetings for approximately two weeks but did not serve as the official acting president during this time. Another constitutional amendment, the Twenty-Second (1951), limits the president to two elected terms. For a list of constitutional amendments that pertain to the presidency, see Figure 12.1.

Term limits enforce turnover and open opportunity for new leadership, but they also act as a gate that prevents voters from reelecting a popular president whom they want to keep in office. Because a president in his second term cannot seek reelection, he is commonly referred to as a **lame duck**. Lawmakers know that the president's time in office is limited, so they are less likely to cooperate or compromise with him. On the other hand, a president who wants to chart a policy course that is unpopular may be more likely to do so when he does not have to face the voters. Lame duck status therefore has the advantage of giving the president more political freedom, but the disadvantage of making him less directly responsive to public opinion.

The clearest path to the White House is through the office of the vice president, but most presidents have some combination of service in the military, in a state legislature or as governor, in the U.S. House of Representatives and Senate, and in a prior presidential administration. There are advantages and disadvantages for presidents, depending on their prior experience. Lyndon Baines Johnson (1963–69) was very successful in passing his domestic policy agenda in large part due to his experience as a House member, U.S. senator, and Senate majority leader. His prior experience taught him crucial negotiating skills with members of Congress, and he used his skills to their fullest extent. In contrast, Jimmy Carter (1977–81) was generally considered to have failed in getting his domestic policy agenda enacted because of his lack of experience in Washington. He came to the White House from the governor's mansion in Georgia, where he exercised executive power with little challenge from the legislature. When he faced a Congress that did not embrace his agenda, he lacked the negotiating skills to be successful. Of course, no single set of qualifications or experiences can guarantee success as a

lame duck:
Term-limited official in his or her last term of office.

president. When voters cast their ballots for president, they take a leap of faith that the person who wins will be trustworthy, accountable, and responsive to their needs and will implement the laws equally for every citizen. For a list of the presidents of the United States, see Table 12.1.

TABLE 12.1 The Presidents of the United States, 1789–2012

	President	Term Dates	Party	Prior Experience
1	George Washington	1789–97		General
2	John Adams	1797–1801	Federalist	Vice president
3	Thomas Jefferson	1801–1809	Democratic-Republican	Vice president, secretary of state
4	James Madison	1809–17	Democratic-Republican	Secretary of state, U.S. House, state legislator
5	James Monroe	1817–25	Democratic-Republican	Secretary of war, secretary of state, U.S. Senate
6	John Quincy Adams	1825–29	Democratic-Republican	Secretary of state, U.S. Senate
7	Andrew Jackson	1829–37	Democrat	U.S. Senate, general, U.S. House
8	Martin Van Buren	1837–41	Democrat	Vice president, U.S. Senate
9	William Henry Harrison	1841 (died in office)	Whig	U.S. Senate, general, territorial governor
10	John Tyler	1841–45	Whig	Vice president, U.S. Senate, governor, U.S. House
11	James K. Polk	1845–49	Democrat	Governor, U.S. House
12	Zachary Taylor	1849–50 (died in office)	Whig	General
13	Millard Fillmore	1850–53	Whig	Vice president, U.S. House
14	Franklin Pierce	1853–57	Democrat	U.S. Senate, U.S. House, state legislator
15	James Buchanan	1857–61	Democrat	Secretary of state, U.S. Senate, U.S. House
16	Abraham Lincoln	1861–65 (died in office)	Republican; National Union	U.S. House
17	Andrew Johnson	1865–69	Democrat; National Union	Vice president, U.S. Senate, U.S. House
18	Ulysses S. Grant	1869–77	Republican	General
19	Rutherford B. Hayes	1877–81	Republican	Governor, U.S. House, general
20	James A. Garfield	1881 (died in office)	Republican	U.S. Senate, general, U.S. House, state legislator
21	Chester A. Arthur	1881–85	Republican	Vice president, collector of the port of New York
22	Grover Cleveland	1885–89	Democrat	Governor, mayor

TABLE 12.1 (Continued)

	President	Term Dates	Party	Prior Experience
23	Benjamin Harrison	1889–93	Republican	U.S. Senate
24	Grover Cleveland	1893–97	Democrat	President, governor, mayor
25	William McKinley	1897–1901 (died in office)	Republican	Governor, U.S. House
26	Theodore Roosevelt	1901–1909	Republican	Vice president, governor
27	William Howard Taft	1909–13	Republican	Secretary of war, governor general of the Philippines, federal judge
28	Woodrow Wilson	1913–21	Democrat	Governor, university president
29	Warren G. Harding	1921–23 (died in office)	Republican	U.S. Senate, lieutenant governor, state legislator
30	Calvin Coolidge	1923–29	Republican	Vice president, governor
31	Herbert Hoover	1929–33	Republican	Secretary of commerce
32	Franklin Delano Roosevelt	1933–45 (died in office)	Democrat	Governor, assistant secretary of the navy, state legislator
33	Harry S. Truman	1945–53	Democrat	Vice president, U.S. Senate
34	Dwight D. Eisenhower	1953–61	Republican	University president, general
35	John F. Kennedy	1961–63 (died in office)	Democrat	U.S. Senate, U.S. House
36	Lyndon Baines Johnson	1963–69	Democrat	Vice president, U.S. Senate, U.S. House
37	Richard M. Nixon	1969–74 (resigned)	Republican	Vice president, U.S. Senate, U.S. House
38	Gerald R. Ford	1974–77	Republican	Vice president, U.S. House
39	Jimmy Carter	1977–81	Democrat	Governor, state legislator
40	Ronald Reagan	1981–89	Republican	Governor, actor
41	George H. W. Bush	1989–93	Republican	Vice president, CIA director, U.S. House
42	William J. Clinton	1993–2001	Democrat	Governor, state attorney general
43	George W. Bush	2001–2009	Republican	Governor
44	Barack Obama	2009–	Democrat	U.S. Senate, state legislator

The Expansion of the Presidency

President George Washington (1789–97) had the enormous responsibility of setting the standard for how a president should govern in a democracy, and he was very careful not to infuse the office with airs of royalty or privilege. The Framers anticipated that the executive branch would be led by one person whose primary responsibility would be the defense of the United States. As commander of the Continental Army during the Revolutionary War, Washington had military experience, but he was also a cautious and thoughtful statesman who wanted to establish a precedent for how the chief executive should operate.

In the course of the nineteenth century, from the presidencies of Thomas Jefferson, to Andrew Jackson (1829–37), to Abraham Lincoln, and finally to William McKinley (1897–1901), the nation grew in size, population, and economic power. The job of the chief executive grew accordingly, but, though increasingly demanding and complex, it remained essentially focused on national defense and economic growth. In the twentieth century, however, the United States became a leading international military and economic power. Historian and presidential adviser Arthur Schlesinger Jr. used the term **imperial presidency** to describe the power of the president to speak for the nation on the world stage and to set the policy agenda at home.[3] Schlesinger's view suggests that as long as the United States is engaged in military conflicts all over the world to promote and protect its interests, the president will be considered the most important figure in American politics.

imperial presidency: *Power of the president to speak for the nation on the world stage and to set the policy agenda at home.*

Connections: What defines an imperial presidency?

 Checkpoint

Can you:

☐ State the constitutional qualifications and succession requirements for the presidency

☐ Explain what is meant by imperial presidency

Presidential Power: Constitutional Grants and Limits

> **What the powers of the president are and how they are limited**

As we saw in Chapter 11, Congress, the Framers enumerated Congress's powers, both to assert powers that were missing under the Articles of Confederation, such as the powers to collect taxes and to regulate commerce, and to constrain the branch they anticipated would be the most powerful. The Framers expected the executive branch to be smaller and less powerful and did not believe it necessary to enumerate the executive powers as they did the legislative powers (see Table 12.2). Instead, in the very first sentence of Article II, they "vested" the president with a general grant of "executive Power" and then, later in the article, stated certain additional powers and responsibilities. The general grant of executive power has allowed the presidency to become the powerful office it is today. In this section, we look at the constitutional sources of the president's powers, the ways in which presidents have sought to expand their constitutional powers, and the ways in which the other branches, especially Congress, act to check and balance the president.

TABLE 12.2 A Comparison of Legislative and Executive Authority under the Constitution

While the Constitution grants specific legislative authority to Congress, it provides a general grant of authority to the president that does not require specific enumerated grants of power. Nor is there an executive equivalent of Article I, Section 9, which specifically limits congressional authority.

	Legislative	Executive
Authority	"All legislative Powers herein granted shall be vested in a Congress of the United States"	"The executive Power shall be vested in a President of the United States"
Specific Powers	Article I, Section 8, including: • lay and collect taxes • provide for the common defense • regulate interstate and foreign commerce • authorize courts • set uniform rules for naturalization and bankruptcy • establish post offices • make all laws that are "necessary and proper" for carrying out the listed powers	Article II, Section 2, including: • act as commander in chief of armed forces • grant pardons • make treaties • receive foreign ministers • appoint ambassadors, judges, cabinet-level officials Article II, Section 3: • ensure that the laws are faithfully executed Article I, Section 7: • veto legislation
Limits on Power	Explicit limits on powers: Article I, Section 9, including: • no bills of attainder • no ex post facto laws • no titles of nobility Bill of Rights: • substantive limits of the First through Eighth Amendments Ninth Amendment: • enumeration of rights does not grant general authority Tenth Amendment: • people and states retain reserved powers not granted to Congress	Mostly through checks and balances: • veto override • Senate confirmation on appointments • Senate Treaty ratification • removal by impeachment

© CENGAGE LEARNING

Commander in Chief

commander in chief: *Leader of the armed forces of the United States.*

The president is the **commander in chief** of the armed forces of the United States, which includes the Army, Navy, Air Force, Marine Corps, and Coast Guard, plus their Reserve and National Guard units. An elected commander in chief, rather than an appointed military officer, is a distinctly important element of American democracy. The president directs all war efforts and military conflict. Congress, however, has the power to officially declare war and to authorize funding for the war effort. Because the war powers that are divided between the president and Congress are so contentious, we examine them later in the chapter.

Power to Pardon

The president has the power to grant clemency, or mercy, for crimes against the United States, except in the case of impeachment from federal office. Clemency is a broad designation that includes a **pardon**, which is forgiving an offense altogether, and a commutation, which is shortening a federal prison sentence; in general, pardoning someone is considered a more sweeping act of clemency than commuting a sentence.

Treaties and Recognition of Foreign Nations

The president or his designated representative has the power to negotiate and sign treaties with foreign nations, but he must do so with the "Advice and Consent of the Senate," as specified by the Constitution. For a treaty to be valid, two-thirds "of the Senators present" must approve. The requirement that the Senate approve treaties serves as a gateway for public input into presidential actions and as a gate that blocks a president's attempt to reach agreements with foreign nations. Today, with the expansion of globalization, the president's representatives negotiate treaties over a wide range of areas, such as military alliances, human rights accords, environmental regulations, and trade policies (see Global Gateways: The World Trade Organization and Global Trade). The president also enters into executive agreements, which do not require Senate approval and tend to be less expansive in scope than treaties.

The president's authority in foreign affairs includes the power to "receive Ambassadors and other public Ministers," which allows the president to recognize the legitimacy of foreign regimes. Such decisions are frequently based on the internal political system of the foreign nation.

Appointments and Judicial Nominations

The president has the power to appoint all federal officers, including cabinet secretaries, heads of independent agencies, and ambassadors. The presidential appointment process has two steps: nomination, and subsequent approval by a majority of the Senate. The appointed officers are typically referred to as political appointees, and they are expected to carry out the president's political and policy agenda (in contrast to civil servants, who are hired through a merit-based system and are politically neutral; see Chapter 13). During Senate recesses, the president can make appointments that will expire when the Senate officially adjourns at the close of a Congress (adjourns *sine die*), unless the appointee is subsequently confirmed. Presidents have

Connections: Why is it important that the commander in chief of the U.S. military is a civilian?

pardon: *Full forgiveness for a crime.*

Connections: Should the president have the power to pardon? What impact does this power have on citizen equality?

globalgateways

The World Trade Organization and Global Trade

One of the areas in which the president can exercise his power is through global trade because the executive branch negotiates trade agreements, which are then approved by Congress. With globalization, trade has become increasingly important to the U.S. domestic economy in two ways. First, as U.S. companies expand by manufacturing and selling goods overseas, they press the president to forge trade agreements with other countries. Likewise, foreign companies have started to locate in the United States, and this development makes it all the more important for the president to remove trade barriers that might deter investment in the United States.

From 1948 to 1994, world trade was governed by the General Agreement on Tariffs and Trade (GATT), which was the gateway through which nations set up trade agreements, sometimes bilaterally but frequently on a multi-country basis. The first round of GATT involved only 23 nations; in 1994, at the final round, 123 nations participated. That year these nations agreed to form the World Trade Organization (WTO), a neutral body responsible for settling trade disputes among member countries.*

* Information in this paragraph is from the World Trade Organization, http://www.wto.org. For more on trade politics, see Jeanne J. Grimmett, *Why Certain Trade Agreements Are Approved as Congressional-Executive Agreements Rather Than as Treaties*, CRS Report for Congress, 97-896 (Washington, D.C.: Congressional Research Service, November 3, 2011), http://www.fas.org/sgp/crs/misc/97-896.pdf.

U.S. membership in the WTO presents an opportunity and a challenge to presidential power. On the one hand, it provides a means for resolving trade disputes, but, on the other, it constrains the United States, which must abide by WTO rulings even when they are detrimental to U.S. trade interests.

Another check on the president's power is the requirement that Congress approve global trade agreements. Moreover, because Congress is elected by the people, it serves as a gateway for public opinion to influence global trade. Indeed, Congress has required that trade agreements include environmental protections and meet certain labor standards to ensure that the countries doing business with the United States follow the same rules as U.S.-based companies.

- **Should the president be able to use unilateral action when it comes to trade agreements with foreign nations?**
- **Is U.S. involvement in international trade organizations such as the World Trade Organization good for American democracy?**

sometimes used recess appointments to bypass the Senate, as President Obama did in appointing Richard Cordray director of the Consumer Financial Protection Bureau in 2012 (for more on this bureau, see Chapter 13). The president also nominates judges in the federal judicial system, from district court level to the Supreme Court, and they too must receive majority approval in the Senate. In recent years, this process has become more ideological and contentious; rather than considering only qualifications for the job, presidents and members of the Senate also consider a nominee's ideological views on key issues such as abortion (see Chapter 14, The Judiciary, for more information on the nomination process). As with the treaty process, the Senate's advice and consent role in appointments and nominations is a gateway for citizen influence.

The president has the power to fire federal officers, but not to remove judges, who can be removed only by impeachment. Even though they have the formal power to do so, presidents rarely remove cabinet members because that would entail an admission of error in making the appointment in the first place.

Connections:
Consider the Senate's power to check the president in making treaties and appointments. What are the costs and benefits of this power sharing in terms of government efficiency and responsiveness?

Veto and the Veto Override

The president has an important role in the enactment of legislation. He has the power to **veto** bills passed by Congress before they become law by refusing to sign them and sending them back to the chamber in which they originated with his objections. If Congress will be going out of session within ten days, he can simply not sign the bill, a practice known as a **pocket veto**. In cases in which the president refuses to sign the bill and Congress remains in session, the bill is enacted into law.

To counter the power of the veto, the Framers gave Congress the veto override, the power to overturn a presidential veto with a two-thirds vote in each chamber. Because the two-thirds threshold is higher than the majority vote needed to pass a bill in the first place, it is difficult for Congress to overcome presidential opposition to a bill. The high threshold reinforces the power of the president in blocking congressional action and so serves as a gateway for presidential influence in the legislative process. One could also see the veto as a gate that legislation must pass through to become law, which can be unlocked only with a congressional supermajority.

The veto is the most direct way that the president checks the power of Congress. Presidents use the veto power either to prevent a bill from becoming law or to pressure Congress into making changes to bring the bill closer to his policies and his view of the national interest.[4] In recent decades Congress has learned to get around the threat of a presidential veto by passing omnibus bills that include provisions affecting a number of issue areas. These bills are costly to veto because they affect a wide range of voters and generate a lot of public support, so they give Congress an advantage in negotiating with the president.[5]

veto: *Authority of the president to block legislation passed by Congress. Congress can override a veto by a two-thirds majority in each chamber.*

pocket veto: *Automatic veto that occurs when Congress goes out of session within ten days of submitting a bill to the president and the president has not signed it.*

omnibus bill: *One very large bill that encompasses many separate bills.*

Presidents naturally tend to veto more bills when Congress is controlled by the opposite party, a condition known as divided government. The president may use the threat of a veto to get members of Congress to produce legislation closer to his policy positions.[6]

Other Powers

The president works within this framework of formal powers and constraints to lead the nation, and in doing so becomes the chief agenda setter for domestic and foreign policy. In a later section of this chapter, we discuss agenda setting in more detail; here it is important to note that, over time, smaller tasks assigned to the president in the Constitution have evolved into powerful tools for influencing legislation. One tool is the **State of the Union address**, which is authorized in Article II, Section 3: The president "shall from time to time give to the Congress Information of the State of the Union, and recommend to their Consideration such Measures as he shall judge necessary and expedient." Nothing in this passage requires the president to inform Congress on a yearly basis or to do so in person. Over the last century, presidents have turned this obligation into an opportunity to outline a broad policy agenda for the nation. That same passage also says that the president "may, on extraordinary Occasions convene both Houses, or either of them." Thus the president can call Congress into a special session to consider legislation or to hear him deliver an important speech.[7]

Congress's Ultimate Check on the Executive: Impeachment

Congress has general oversight of the executive branch (a power discussed in Chapters 11 and 13), but its ultimate check on the president is its power to remove him from office. Article II, Section 4 of the Constitution stipulates that the president, vice president, and all civil officers (including cabinet secretaries and federal judges) are subject to removal for "Treason, Bribery, or other high Crimes and Misdemeanors." Should these officers be removed from office, they may be subject to normal criminal charges and proceedings, where applicable.

The process of removal begins with **impeachment** in the House of Representatives. Typically, the House Judiciary Committee investigates charges and recommends to the full House whether to impeach or not. If the House votes to impeach a federal officer, the Senate holds a trial, and if the president is impeached, the chief justice of the Supreme Court presides. If two-thirds of the senators vote to convict, the official is removed from office.

At the highest level of federal office, two presidents—Andrew Johnson and Bill Clinton—have been impeached, but neither was convicted by the Senate, and both remained in office. Impeachment resolutions have been

---

Connections: How does the veto power give the president influence in the legislative process?

Connections: Have you watched a State of the Union address? What do you think its purpose was? What did you learn from it?

State of the Union address: *Speech on the condition of the country given by the president to Congress every January.*

impeachment: *Process whereby the House brings charges against the president or another federal official that will, upon conviction by the Senate, remove him or her from office.*

introduced by individual members of the House of Representatives against other presidents, but they were not acted on. The case of Richard M. Nixon shows that the threat of impeachment can be enough to remove a president from office. Knowing he was about to be impeached, Nixon resigned instead. In addition to charges of wrongdoing, partisan disagreements can influence some members of Congress in their votes to move forward with impeachment proceedings.

As the following discussion of these cases will show, impeachment is a rarely used but powerful instrument that makes it possible for Congress to hold the president accountable for his actions. In a democratic nation guided by the rule of law, all citizens are equally obligated to obey the laws of the land, including the president.

Andrew Johnson.

The first presidential impeachment case was against President Andrew Johnson. A Democratic senator from Tennessee who had remained loyal to the Union, Johnson was elected as Lincoln's vice president in 1864 and succeeded to the presidency following Lincoln's assassination in 1865. Johnson repeatedly vetoed Reconstruction acts passed by the Republican-controlled Congress, but his vetoes were overridden.[8] His secretary of war, Edwin Stanton, stood with the Republicans, but Johnson could not dismiss him because in 1867 Congress had passed, over Johnson's veto, the Tenure of Office Act, which prevented a president from firing a cabinet member without the Senate's approval. When Johnson suspended Stanton, the Senate responded by refusing to confirm the suspension. On February 21, 1868, Johnson fired Stanton outright, contending that the Tenure of Office Act was unconstitutional.[9]

Impeachment proceedings against Johnson had already begun based on charges of usurpation of power; and when Johnson violated the Tenure of Office Act, the full House moved to approve eleven articles of impeachment against him by a vote of 126–47. The trial in the Senate began on March 30, and on May 16 the Senate voted 35 to convict (and 19 to acquit), one vote short of the two-thirds necessary to remove Johnson from office.[10] On May 26 the Senate voted on two more articles of impeachment but again failed to convict, so it dropped all remaining charges, and the trial ended. President Johnson served out his term until March 1869. In 1887 Congress repealed the Tenure of Office Act.

Richard M. Nixon.

President Richard M. Nixon was embroiled in a serious scandal known as Watergate, after the name of a complex in Washington where the Democratic National Committee had its headquarters. It was there that the scandal began with a break-in on June 17, 1972. In August the *Washington Post* reported that the bank account of one of the five men caught in the act and arrested had $25,000 in funds originally given to the Nixon 1972 reelection campaign.[11]

Connections: Think about the impeachments and the near-impeachment described here. What was the basis for impeachment in each case?

Connections: What should happen when the president breaks the law?

Nixon denied any connection and was reelected in the fall, but all the while he and his aides were working to cover up the fact that his reelection committee had ordered the break-in to install listening devices on Democratic Party phones. Two *Washington Post* reporters, Bob Woodward and Carl Bernstein, continued to investigate the story (see Chapter 7, The News Media and the Internet). As connections between Nixon and the break-in were revealed, several of his aides were convicted of conspiracy, burglary, and wiretapping, and others resigned. In May 1973 the Senate's newly formed Watergate Committee began televised hearings on the Watergate break-in and cover-up, and the Justice Department appointed Archibald Cox as the special prosecutor in charge of the Watergate investigation.

In the months that followed, a Nixon staffer revealed that the president had tape-recorded all of his White House conversations, and both the Senate Watergate Committee and the House Judiciary Committee formally issued subpoenas demanding that Nixon turn over the recordings. The turning point in what became known as the Watergate scandal came on Saturday, October 20, 1973, when President Nixon asked his attorney general, Elliot Richardson, to fire Archibald Cox and abolish the office of special prosecutor entirely. Richardson refused, as did the deputy attorney general. Both resigned. Solicitor General Robert Bork, next in command, then carried out the president's wishes. What had been a struggle for information became a question of obstruction of justice by the president.

Connections: In a democracy, should the president have executive privilege?

executive privilege:

President's right to engage in confidential communications with his advisers.

President Nixon turned over a limited number of tapes, but there was an eighteen-and-a-half-minute gap on one tape, and Congress wanted to know what was discussed during that time and why it was erased. The administration claimed that the tape was erased by mistake. During the next months, Nixon released only partial transcripts and said that others were protected by **executive privilege**—the president's right to engage in communications with his advisers that he does not have to reveal. The justification for this privilege is that the president must make difficult choices and, without the guarantee of privilege, may not receive or deliver the fullest information in the course of his deliberations.

The Supreme Court created an exception to this privilege in *United States v. Nixon* when on July 24, 1974, it unanimously ruled that executive privilege is not absolute and must give way when the government needs the information for a trial. The tapes showed that Nixon and his aides had conspired to cover up the Watergate break-in. Three days later the House Judiciary Committee approved three articles of impeachment against Nixon.[12] With the full House of Representatives ready to vote on the articles, President Nixon resigned on August 9, 1974.

In 1975 Nixon's successor, former Vice President Gerald R. Ford (1974–77), pardoned Nixon of all federal offenses he might have committed. The Watergate scandal had a negative impact on the American presidency, raising public mistrust of the office and of the federal government more generally.

William Jefferson Clinton.

The most recent case of impeachment involved President William Jefferson (Bill) Clinton (1993–2001).[13] In 1979 then-Arkansas Governor Clinton and his wife Hillary formed a real estate company called Whitewater with some business associates. After Clinton was elected president in 1992, his foes pushed for an investigation into the Whitewater dealings, and in January 1994 public pressure led the attorney general to authorize

Stemming from charges that he lied under oath in his testimony in the Paula Jones case, President Bill Clinton was impeached by the House of Representatives on December 19, 1998. In a trial that began the following month in the Senate, presided over by Chief Justice William Rehnquist, the president was acquitted.

an investigation by an independent counsel into these dealings. The first independent counsel was Robert Fiske, but he was perceived to be less than vigorous in pursuit of the investigation, and in August 1994 he was replaced by Kenneth Starr.[14]

Meanwhile, in an unrelated event, a woman named Paula Jones, who had met with then Governor Clinton in an Arkansas hotel room in 1991, had filed a sexual harassment suit against him. President Clinton's lawyers moved to prevent the lawsuit from proceeding while he was still in office.[15] That case, *Jones v. Clinton*, made its way to the Supreme Court, which on May 27, 1997, ruled that a sitting president has no immunity from a civil suit arising from acts occurring before he took office and that Jones's lawsuit could proceed. In the course of their work, Jones's lawyers uncovered information alleging that Clinton had engaged in a sexual affair with a White House intern named Monica Lewinsky. Independent counsel Kenneth Starr found out about Lewinsky and her possible testimony in the Jones case, and he won permission to question the president about the affair. In essence, he was trying to secure evidence about whether President Clinton had committed perjury (lied under oath) about his relationship with Lewinsky during his deposition in the Jones trial.

Starr concluded that there was sufficient evidence that Clinton had committed perjury, and on September 9, 1998, he released his report to members of the House of Representatives. On October 8 the House approved

Connections: Should the president be subjected to civil lawsuits while he is in office? State the reasons for your answer.

Connections: In the impeachment process, what evidence do you see of checks and balances?

Checkpoint

Can you:

☐ Characterize the presidential power of commander in chief

☐ Compare pardon and commutation

☐ Describe the role of the Senate in the president's power to negotiate and sign treaties

☐ Recall the steps to presidential appointments

☐ Survey the power of the veto

☐ Explain how the State of the Union address has evolved as a tool for the president

☐ Compare and contrast examples of impeachment (or impending impeachment)

an impeachment inquiry, and on December 19 the House debated four articles of impeachment against President Clinton for two counts of perjury, one count of obstruction of justice, and one count of abuse of power, subsequently voting to impeach Clinton on one count each of perjury and obstruction of justice.[16] The formal phase of the trial began in the Senate on January 7, 1999, and lasted until February 8, when voting fell far short of the two-thirds (sixty-seven) vote necessary to convict President Clinton of the two charges against him. He was acquitted and served out the remainder of his second term. Ironically, the original Whitewater investigation that had led to the impeachment proceedings failed to unearth solid evidence that President Clinton or his wife Hillary committed any crime.

Impeachment is not a power to be used lightly, but it does serve as a gateway for the public, through its elected officials in Congress, to hold the president, cabinet officials, and federal judges accountable for abuses of power.

The Growth of Executive Influence

〉 How executive influence has grown over time

Connections:
What should be done about the growth of executive power? Is it a problem for checks and balances among the separate branches?

With all the formal constitutional restrictions on the president, one has to wonder how the modern presidency became so powerful. The answer lies in the general grant of executive power and the constitutional provision that the president "take Care that the Laws be faithfully executed," which he promises to do when he takes the oath of office. Presidents have found ways to unlock the enormous powers inherent in these constitutional provisions to expand their informal powers over policy making and implementation. The president's veto power and Congress's power to override and to impeach the president counteract each other and help ensure that each branch remains responsive to its governing responsibilities. However, Congress has no formal means to balance and check the president's growing executive power, though at times the judicial branch has been able to do so.

Presidential Directives and Signing Statements

presidential directive:
Official instructions from the president regarding federal policy.

Presidents use the executive power to issue **presidential directives** that give specific instructions on a federal policy and do not require congressional approval. Recent presidents have used this unilateral power much more frequently than previous presidents, especially under conditions of divided government or interbranch policy conflict.[17] <mark>Presidential directives might take the form of executive orders, proclamations, or military orders. They are the primary way that presidents shape policy implementation, and they</mark> are the instruments presidents use to act quickly in national emergencies.[18]

The best-known type of directive is the **executive order**, which can be used for a wide range of purposes. Typically, executive orders instruct federal employees to take a <mark>specific action</mark> or <mark>implement a policy in a particular way.</mark> Some scholars argue that executive orders are an important source of "independent authority" that is used solely at the discretion of the president.[19] Even though presidents since Washington have issued executive orders, the orders were not officially numbered until 1862 and not published in the *Federal Register* until 1935.[20]

In 1957 President Dwight D. Eisenhower (1953–61) used a combination of executive orders, proclamations, and military orders to enforce school integration in Little Rock, Arkansas. Following the 1954 and 1955 *Brown v. Board of Education* Supreme Court rulings that struck down the practice of segregation in public schools, the governor of Arkansas, Orval Faubus, called up the Arkansas National Guard to block nine African Americans from attending Central High School in Little Rock. President Eisenhower responded by issuing a proclamation calling on the governor to cease and desist, and when the governor ignored the proclamation Eisenhower issued Executive Order 10730 to send the 101st Airborne Division to Little Rock to ensure that the students would be allowed into the school (see also the Supreme Court Case, *Cooper v. Aaron,* in Chapter 14). He also used his authority as commander in chief to take command of the Arkansas National Guard and order it to assist in the school's integration. Eisenhower intervened because he believed it was his obligation as president to enforce the laws of the land as set forth by the rulings of the Supreme Court.[21]

In foreign and military affairs, presidents can issue presidential directives on national security, which have a similar purpose to executive orders but are not published in the *Federal Register*. These directives can announce specific sanctions against individuals who are considered enemies of the United States

 executive order: *Presidential directive that usually involves implementing a specific law.*

© BETTMANN/CORBIS

In September 1957, in a move that demonstrated federal power over state power as well as the authority of the commander in chief, President Dwight D. Eisenhower sent the 101st Airborne Division to Little Rock, Arkansas, to protect nine African American students attempting to attend previously all-white Central High School. He also nationalized the Arkansas National Guard for the same purpose.

or make larger statements about U.S. policy toward a foreign country. President George W. Bush (2001–2009) used this power frequently in what he described as a war on terror and in the conduct of the wars in Afghanistan and Iraq. For example, he issued an order in 2001 to create military tribunals that would try suspected enemy combatants and terrorists, rather than allowing them to be tried in a regular military court. He also created a special subcategory called homeland security presidential directives, which are not as widely publicized as other directives and deal only with homeland security policy.

When a president signs a bill into law, he can issue **signing statements**, written remarks that reflect his interpretation of the law that are not required or authorized by the Constitution. Signing statements can be classified as non-constitutional and constitutional (see Table 12.3). Nonconstitutional statements are typically symbolic, celebrating the passage of the law or providing technical instructions for implementing a new law. Constitutional statements are more serious in that the president uses them to indicate a disagreement with Congress on specific provisions in the law. In constitutional signing statements, the president may go so far as to refuse to implement specific provisions of laws. This kind of statement is a challenge to Congress's constitutional authority to legislate.[22] Even when the presidency and the Congress are controlled by the same party, signing statements can be used to shift the implementation of policy toward presidential preferences. President Barack Obama recognized the controversy over signing statements, and he issued a memorandum early in his administration stating that he would use signing statements "to address constitutional concerns only when it is appropriate to do so as a means of discharging my constitutional responsibilities."[23] In issuing this memorandum, President Obama was trying to alleviate concerns about abusing executive power but at the same time preserving the presidential power to interpret legislation that is inherent in signing statements. As of September 2012, President Obama had issued twenty-one signing statements and 143 executive orders.[24]

Presidential directives and signing statements create tension between the president and Congress and between the president and the judiciary because they are an expansion of presidential power. At times they have been deemed illegal.[25] Many presidents, from Lincoln to Franklin Delano Roosevelt to George W. Bush, have taken temporary actions that

signing statements:
Written remarks issued by the president when signing a bill into law that often reflect his interpretation of how the law should be implemented.

Connections: What limits can Congress, the courts, and/or the American people place on the president?

TABLE 12.3 **Presidential Signing Statements, 1969–2008**

President	Nonconstitutional	Constitutional	Total
Richard M. Nixon	111 (94.9%)	6 (5.1%)	117
Gerald R. Ford	123 (89.8%)	14 (10.2%)	137
Jimmy Carter	198 (86.8%)	30 (13.2%)	228
Ronald Reagan	165 (66.3%)	84 (33.7%)	249
George H. W. Bush	106 (46.5%)	122 (53.5%)	228
William Jefferson Clinton	294 (77.4%)	86 (22.6%)	380
George W. Bush	32 (19.9%)	129 (80.1%)	161
Total	1,029 (68.6%)	471 (31.4%)	1,500

Source: Michael J. Berry, "Controversially Executing the Law: George W. Bush and the Constitutional Signing Statement," *Congress and the Presidency* 36 (2009): 252. Copyright © 2009 by Taylor and Francis, reprinted by permission of the publisher, Taylor & Francis, Ltd. http://www.tandf.co.uk/journals

have violated constitutional rights in the name of national security, from suspending *habeas corpus* to interning Japanese Americans to eavesdropping on U.S. citizens (see Chapter 4, Civil Liberties, and Chapter 5, Civil Rights, for expanded discussions of these actions). Judging the merit of such actions is difficult because ==citizens have to decide whether the president is acting in good faith on behalf of the country or seeking to expand his own power and agenda.==

Power to Persuade

Presidents understand that communicating well with the public is essential to building support for their policies. They also face the challenge of using their personal reputations and negotiating skills to generate support among members of Congress. President Theodore Roosevelt (1901–1909) described the office of the president as a **bully pulpit**, where presidents could use the attention associated with the office to make a public argument in favor of or against a policy.[26] The key to using the bully pulpit effectively is to explain a policy in simple and accessible terms, to get the public's attention, and to frame an issue in a way that is favorable to the president's policy position. Using the bully pulpit can accomplish the president's goals only if he already has a receptive audience. In today's highly partisan and divided political climate, there is no guarantee that the president's detractors will listen to his message.[27]

A president's relationship with the members of the news media is a crucial factor in successful communication, and it has evolved dramatically over time. Samuel Kernell, a presidential media scholar, argues that over the last seventy years, presidents have increased the extent to which they control their interactions with the press. Press conferences are one important way of sustaining a relationship with the news media, and presidents have tried to use them to their advantage. Some presidents are more comfortable with the press than others. Press conferences are somewhat risky because, unlike speeches, presidents do not control the content of the questions that are asked, and they can sometimes make unrehearsed statements that have political consequences. In addition to press conferences and televised speeches, President Obama used new technologies to bypass the media and speak directly to the people. Recognizing that many voters get their news and political information from sources such as cable TV and Twitter instead of from traditional network television, he created a blog on the White House website, posted videos of his speeches, and sent mass e-mails to citizens who inquired about specific proposals.[28]

bully pulpit: *Nickname for the power of the president to use the attention associated with the office to persuade the media, Congress, and the public to support his policy positions.*

Connections: Does the bully pulpit serve as a communication gateway between the president and citizens?

© BETTMANN/CORBIS

President Theodore Roosevelt was a larger-than-life figure who challenged corporate monopolies, sought to strengthen U.S. international power, and increased federal efforts at land conservation. He was known for using the office of the president as a bully pulpit to persuade the public to support his policies.

In conjunction with public outreach, the president also tries to personally persuade members of Congress and other policy makers to support his policies. Political scientist Richard Neustadt has argued that this <mark>personal persuasion</mark> is the root of presidential power. Several factors affect a president's power to persuade, notably his professional reputation and his approval ratings.[29] A presidential approval rating is usually expressed as the percentage of the American people who say the president is doing a good job. A president's professional reputation is a combination of his prior experience and the steps he takes throughout his term. When a president comes to the Oval Office with executive experience or a strong reputation as a productive legislator, he is likely to have a reservoir of respect from members of Congress, the public, and the media. That reservoir can become depleted if the president makes missteps and is not successful with his legislative agenda.

Lawmakers are more likely to pass a president's policy proposals when his approval rating is high, and they are less cooperative when the president is unpopular. Members of Congress pay attention to presidential approval ratings because national polls are a barometer of public opinion. Members of Congress from districts or states in which a majority of voters chose the incumbent president generally want to support him. It follows, then, a large presidential electoral victory will yield a greater number of supportive members of Congress. Even members of Congress from districts that did not support the incumbent president want to be careful in the way that they oppose a popular president for fear of looking unpatriotic or unresponsive to majority public opinion. Public approval can be essential to presidential policy success, which is why the president tries to maintain public support throughout his years in the White House[30] (see Chapter 6, Public Opinion, for more on presidential approval ratings and presidential effectiveness).

To be persuasive, a president has to balance his own policy preferences with those of members of Congress and convince the American public that he is leading the country in the right direction.[31] The stakes can be very high for presidents as they navigate the legislative process (see Chapter 11). The president's need to be responsive to public opinion serves as a gateway for influence by the public on his decision making.

Connections: Has the increased emphasis on job approval ratings strengthened the power of the public to hold the president accountable?

Agenda Setting

As the chief executive officer of the entire federal government, the president has an obligation and an opportunity to work with Congress to set the foreign and domestic policy agenda for the nation, from determining how to configure military strength, to overseeing economic growth, to ensuring the health and safety of individual citizens. The president has formal and informal advantages over Congress in directing the federal agenda toward his policy preferences, starting with the fact that he is the sole occupant of his elected office, as compared with 535 members of the House and Senate. Consequently, the president has the power to focus the nation's attention on his ideas and policy proposals.

In dealing with foreign powers, the president is **head of state** and commander in chief of the military. As head of state, the president oversees a vast organization of employees in the State Department and the office of the U.S. Trade Representative, who lay the groundwork for negotiations with foreign leaders on issues ranging from nuclear weapons control to trade policy. Upon their recommendation, the president proposes new treaties or revisions to existing agreements as needed. Ultimately, the president is the public face of and the authority behind U.S. foreign policy decisions. He must establish working relationships with foreign leaders and demonstrate an understanding of how other nations' political systems operate, especially the extent to which the executive power is placed in one person or shared, as it is in parliamentary systems.

Because the president is presumed to serve the best interest of the entire nation, the American public frequently supports most of his foreign policies— at least initially. The main congressional counterweights to the president's powers in these areas are the power of the Senate to ratify treaties and the power of Congress to appropriate money for federal programs, including foreign aid and diplomatic programs. These congressional powers come in the form of responses to the president's proposals. Congress can have some influence on the president's foreign policy agenda through hearings and press statements, but if the president is able to persuade the public to support his positions, he is typically able to forge his own path on foreign policy.

In the area of domestic policy, the president uses the State of the Union address, the federal budget, the power to make executive appointments, the bully pulpit, the executive power to implement laws, and the veto power as his agenda-setting tools. He issues his federal budget in early February, shortly after he delivers the State of the Union address. The budget is a blueprint that indicates his spending priorities for all areas of the federal government. Congress does not have to abide by this budget, and Congress frequently ignores it and constructs its own federal budget (see Chapter 11 for a discussion of the budget). All measures that raise taxes and spend federal money can be

AP PHOTO/CHARLES DHARAPAK

The president, as head of state, engages in direct diplomacy with foreign leaders in a number of different settings. Such formal functions expose world leaders to elite members of the American political and economic arenas. These events can serve to enhance diplomatic relations between the United States and its allies. In this state dinner in May 2010, President and Mrs. Obama welcomed Felipe Calderón, who was then president of Mexico, and his wife Margarita.

head of state: *Title given to the president as national leader.*

Connections: Evaluate the effectiveness of the president's agenda-setting tools.

vetoed by the president, and, as we have seen, the veto or the threat of a veto gives the president a means of exerting pressure on Congress to follow his budget priorities.

The president engages in domestic policy agenda setting in other ways as well. For example, as in the case of President Obama and health care, presidents can propose legislation that changes existing programs or creates new ones and ask Congress to consider his suggestions. He can also be even more proactive by issuing presidential directives that direct the bureaucracy to implement laws as he sees fit. The president's major speeches, press conferences, interviews, social media communication, and travels always command media attention, so he has a constantly open forum to try to persuade voters to support his proposals.[32]

Checkpoint

Can you:

☐ Recall the different types of presidential directives

☐ List the tools available to a president as he uses his power to persuade

☐ Describe how the president can set the public agenda

The President in Wartime

> **Why the president is so powerful during wartime**

As executive branch powers have grown, presidents have increasingly come into conflict with the judicial branch and Congress, especially in times of national crisis and war (see also Chapter 4). In this section, we examine the power struggle between the president and Congress over war powers, which the Constitution divides between the two branches, and the power struggle between the president and the judiciary on the scope of presidential powers and civil liberties. It is crucial to understand that the balance of power among the three branches of the federal government is constantly evolving in response to changing internal and external conditions.

Connections: What powers should the president have during wartime?

Power Struggles between the President and Congress

The Constitution gives Congress the power to declare war, but it has been the practice for presidents to first formally ask Congress for a declaration of war. Once Congress declares war, the president as commander in chief has the authority to direct the conflict. Through its constitutional powers in Article I, Section 8 to "to raise and support Armies" and "to provide and maintain a Navy," Congress retains the power to cut off the flow of money for the war effort. Generally, the president and Congress have worked together in times of military conflict, but in the late 1960s, opposition to the Vietnam War brought about significant divisions between the executive and legislative branches over war powers.

Vietnam and the War Powers Act. Vietnam had been a divided nation since 1954, with Communist forces controlling North Vietnam and anti-Communists controlling South Vietnam, and a civil war had erupted between them. President Dwight D. Eisenhower and then-Presidents John F. Kennedy (1961–63) and Lyndon Baines Johnson believed that containing Communism and keeping the North Vietnamese Communists from taking over South Vietnam were important, but the U.S. troop buildup was slow at first. In 1964, however, President Johnson presented evidence to Congress that the North Vietnamese were attacking U.S. ships on patrol duty in international waters in the Gulf of Tonkin off the shore of North Vietnam. Johnson asked Congress for the authority to fight back, and Congress responded with the Tonkin Gulf Resolution, stating that "The Congress approves and supports the determination of the President, as Commander in Chief, to take all necessary measures to repel any armed attack against the forces of the United States and to prevent further aggression."[33] Congress passed the resolution with only two dissenting votes, few restrictions, and no time limit on how long the United States would stay involved in the conflict.[34]

By 1968 the United States had more than five hundred thousand troops in Vietnam, and the conflict was commonly referred to as the Vietnam War, although there was never a formal declaration of war by Congress. The conflict had become highly unpopular. That year, Richard M. Nixon was elected president and promised to end the Vietnam War; however, he actually broadened the conflict to the neighboring countries of Cambodia and Laos in his efforts to win the war.

By 1971 Congress had repealed the Tonkin Gulf Resolution, and, following the Paris Peace Accords signed in January 1973, U.S. troops were withdrawn from Vietnam. In October 1973 Congress passed a more formal proposal to limit presidential authority to engage in military conflict. This **War Powers Act** states that the president cannot send troops into military conflict for more than a total of ninety days without seeking a formal declaration of war, or authorization for continued military action, from Congress. President Nixon vetoed the act, but Congress overrode the veto.

The War Powers Act was ostensibly a gate that would stand in the way of a president's decision to launch a war without first gauging congressional support. Although the act tried to clarify presidential authority and limits, the scholar Louis Fisher argues that it is flawed because the ninety-day limit does not begin until the president has officially reported the troop engagement to Congress. A president could send troops into a conflict and not report it to Congress, thereby avoiding a trigger of the War Powers Act.[35] In addition, the act did not really give Congress the power to end a military conflict except by denying all funding for it, as it ultimately did with Vietnam. However, if there is considerable public support for an ongoing military engagement, the president can make the case that it is too dangerous to cut off all funding,

 War Powers Act: *1973 act that provides that the president cannot send troops into military conflict for more than a total of ninety days without seeking a formal declaration of war, or authorization for continued military action, from Congress.*

and Congress would be reluctant to cut off funding when troops were still in the field and could be harmed. The irony of the War Powers Act is that it gives presidents an incentive to seek a declaration of war or authorization to use military force, after which time Congress loses much of its control of the operation of the conflict.[36] In other words, once Congress gives the president permission to go to war, it is next to impossible for Congress to stop the war.[37]

The Iraq War. In the past decade, Congress and the president have struggled over several military conflicts. The Iraq War began in 2003 but its origins date back to August 1990, when Iraq, led by Saddam Hussein, invaded Kuwait. This act of aggression prompted multilateral military action known as the Gulf War, which aimed to push Iraq out of Kuwait. The Gulf War was short-lived; as part of the peace settlement, Iraq was prohibited from developing weapons of mass destruction and was required to submit to constant UN monitoring.

By 2002 it had become increasingly difficult for UN inspectors to accurately assess Iraq's capabilities for producing weapons of mass destruction. Although there had been no concrete evidence of such weapons, President George W. Bush argued that a preemptive strike against Iraq was necessary to preserve the security of the United States. In accordance with the War Powers Act, President Bush asked Congress for a resolution authorizing military action. On October 10, 2002, the House of Representatives approved a joint resolution that gave the president the authority to use all military force to "defend the national security of the United States."[38] The Senate approved the resolution the next day by a vote of 77–23.

The Iraq War was launched on March 19, 2003; Saddam Hussein was captured in December 2003 and was tried and hanged for war crimes. Nevertheless, instability in Iraq continued. By 2006, with violence in Iraq at a high level, the Democrats in Congress—many of whom had initially supported the war—withdrew their support and called for the return of all U.S. troops and an end to the war.

As of January 2009, the three dominant groups in Iraq—the Sunnis, the Shiites, and the Kurds—were operating under a parliamentary system of government. Over the next two years, President Obama and the U.S. government worked with the Iraqis to end the war and transfer full governmental control to them. On August 31, 2010, President Obama announced the end of the nation's formal combat involvement, and by the end of December 2011 the last official military personnel departed from Iraq.

JOE RAEDLE/GETTY IMAGES

The United States was engaged in the Iraq War from 2003 to 2011; 4,489 military personnel were killed and 32,229 were injured during the course of the conflict. In November 2011, some of the last remaining U.S. troops left Iraq.

The Afghanistan War.

Although the Iraq war was over, the Afghanistan war was ongoing. The war in Afghanistan began after the September 11, 2001, terrorist attacks were traced back to al-Qaeda operatives harbored by the Afghan Taliban regime. President George W. Bush addressed Congress on September 20, 2001, indicating that the Taliban would be held responsible for the attacks, and in October the United States and its allies launched a military action on Afghanistan designed to find those responsible for the 9/11 attacks and bring down the Taliban regime. Although the Taliban regime was subsequently toppled and a new leader, Hamid Karzai, was elected and later reelected, the Taliban has mounted a resurgence in Afghanistan. In 2009 President Obama, as commander in chief, responded to resurgent Taliban-sponsored attacks on U.S. troops and civilian Afghans by ordering a surge of thirty thousand additional troops to Afghanistan, bringing the total there to nearly a hundred thousand.[39] In the next two years, as the number of American and Afghan casualties increased, public support for the war decreased, and it was hard for President Obama to maintain U.S. involvement there.

On May 1, 2011, President Obama announced that Osama bin Laden, who had claimed to be the head of al-Qaeda and the coordinator of the 9/11 attacks, had been killed in a military operation in Pakistan. With the death of bin Laden, public support for the war diminished further. In 2012, President Obama and Secretary of Defense Leon Panetta announced their intention to work with the Afghanistan government to reduce the number of U.S. troops in Afghanistan at a faster rate, withdrawing all U.S. troops by 2014.

Uprisings in Arab States.

Ongoing military conflicts such as those in Iraq and Afghanistan have spillover effects that can limit the president's flexibility in responding to conflicts in other foreign nations. Protests in 2011 in Tunisia, Egypt, Syria, and Libya—known as the Arab Spring—offer an example. The United States got involved only in Libya. When in March 2011 President Obama authorized the use of air strikes and drones in conjunction with NATO forces, he was acting to help enforce a United Nations Security Council resolution that authorized international military action to stop the Libyan leader, Muammar al-Qaddafi, from committing violence against his own people. The decision to intervene in Libya was controversial given ongoing involvement in Afghanistan, so Obama gave a national address to explain his decision and inform the American people that U.S. ground troops would not be deployed. Nevertheless, he was criticized from both sides of the political spectrum. The president moved forward anyway, and by October 2011 the rebel forces had prevailed and Qaddafi was killed as he resisted capture.[40]

Unlike Libya, President Obama did not propose intervening in the Syrian conflict, although the United States did support a UN resolution condemning the violence committed by President Bashar al-Assad's regime against protesters. That resolution was vetoed by Russia and China, and without multilateral

Connections: How much responsibility should Presidents Bush and Obama assume for the Iraq and Afghanistan Wars, respectively? Does Congress have shared responsibility in those conflicts?

or congressional support for intervention, Obama lacked the same justification for entering that conflict as he had in the case of Libya.[41]

The tension between the presidency and Congress over war powers compels the president to make the case to Congress and the American people that military action is necessary. As President George W. Bush learned, an unpopular war can erode a president's popularity and effectiveness (see Chapter 6).

Power Struggles between the President and the Judiciary

Power struggles between the president and the judiciary in wartime generally focus on civil liberties. In this chapter we have noted many limits on presidential actions and now discuss judicial attempts to restrict presidential powers.

The most recent clashes between the president and the judiciary over wartime powers arose during President George W. Bush's declared war on terror. Following 9/11, President Bush greatly expanded the powers of the executive branch of government. Specifically, he created separate military tribunals to try captured terrorists, claimed exemption from the Geneva Convention rules on the treatment and detainment of prisoners, and authorized the National Security Agency to monitor conversations of suspected terrorists with residents of the United States without obtaining warrants. President Bush's justification was that, as commander in chief, he had the foremost responsibility to protect American citizens and actions taken for that purpose should not be subject to the approval of Congress or the courts.

Congressional action and Supreme Court decisions constrained most of these presidential actions. In 2004 the Supreme Court's *Hamdi v. Rumsfeld* decision rejected Bush administration attempts to deny *habeas corpus* protections to an enemy combatant who was a U.S. citizen because federal law prohibits such denial to U.S. citizens.[42] That same day the Court also rejected the administration's authority to deny *habeas corpus* to an enemy combatant who was not a U.S. citizen.[43] The Bush administration then established special military tribunals to review the detention of enemy combatants at Guantanamo Bay, but the Court rejected the authority of the tribunals because Congress had not authorized them.[44] The Court rejected congressional and presidential efforts to limit the Court's jurisdiction to hear such appeals, claiming that those limits did not apply to cases that had been filed before Congress passed the law. Even when Congress and the president authorized tribunals, the Supreme Court declared that neither Congress nor the president has the authority to suspend the writ of *habeas corpus*, which the Constitution allows only during "Cases of Rebellion or Invasion."[45] Thus, in cases involving terrorism, the Court has put gates in the way of Congress and the president in their efforts to restrict civil liberties in the name of national security. (For a broader discussion of the balance between laws against terrorism and civil liberties, see Chapter 4.)

Connections: What limits should the judiciary impose on presidential actions in wartime? Give examples.

Connections: How are acts of terrorism different from or the same as acts of war? How should the president, Congress, and the judiciary respond to terrorist attacks?

Two days after President Obama was inaugurated, he issued three executive orders requiring a complete evaluation of all policies related to interrogation, detention, and military tribunals for military prisoners, and he ordered an immediate stop to practices that constituted torture under international law.[46] At the same time, he declared his intent to close the detention center at Guantanamo Bay, but not in a way that would put U.S. citizens at risk from terrorism threats. Because of security concerns about sending prisoners back to their home countries, that process has taken longer than expected. In May 2009 President Obama decided that the United States would continue the use of military tribunals to prosecute terrorism suspects so long as they were guaranteed fundamental constitutional rights in the process. In May 2012, the trial of five suspects in the 9/11 attacks began in a military tribunal in Guantanamo Bay, but the suspects refused to acknowledge the authority of the tribunal or to respond to any of the military judge's questions; their behavior illustrates the complexities of trying foreign nationals in the United States.

Checkpoint

Can you:

☐ Track trends in the struggle between the president and Congress over war powers

☐ Describe issues in the struggle between the president and the judiciary in wartime

The Organization of the Modern White House

> **How the White House is organized**

The way that a president organizes the Executive Office and the cabinet reveals a great deal about his management style as well as his policy preferences. The president relies on his White House advisers for policy recommendations. The modern president has the challenge of encouraging cooperation between political appointees and members of the civil service and making sure that employees in each category are held accountable for their decisions.

The Executive Office of the President

The president runs a large organization known as the Executive Office of the President (EOP), a loosely knit unit of several key organizations that report directly to him. These include the White House Office, the Office of Management and Budget (OMB), the National Security Council (NSC), and the Council of Economic Advisers (CEA). Each office has influence over budgetary, military, and economic policies. Stephanie Cutter worked in the EOP when she served on the communications staff for Presidents Clinton and Obama.

The growth of the president's staff in the past seventy-five years is stunning. President Franklin D. Roosevelt established the Executive Office of the

Connections: How does the Executive Office of the President reflect individual management styles?

President. At that time there were about sixty people working in the EOP; under President Obama, there were nearly eighteen hundred.[47]

In general, a tightly organized White House staff organization yields a productive presidency, and the chief of staff is central to that effort in several ways. He serves as a gatekeeper by controlling the flow of staff and paperwork and focuses the president's attention on key issues. The chief of staff also monitors the coherence of presidential policies across cabinet departments and can serve as a referee for disagreements among members of the president's senior staff. Last, he can be important in forming bridges between the president and Congress.

Connections:
President Harry S. Truman had a sign on his desk that read "The Buck Stops Here." What did it mean?

When a president fails to get his agenda approved, he may respond by changing his senior staff. In its first two years, Bill Clinton's administration was viewed as chaotic and inefficient and not adept at dealing with Congress. In November 1994 Republicans took control of the House and Senate largely by portraying Democratic Party government (the Democrats controlled Congress as well as the presidency) as a failure. Clinton's response to the electoral losses of his own party was to replace his chief of staff, Thomas McLarty, his childhood friend from Arkansas, with Leon Panetta, a former congressman with considerable legislative experience. Panetta brought order and discipline to the White House, and Clinton was able to produce enough popular policies to win reelection.

Another important element in presidential productivity is staff continuity, and new presidents often bring former executive branch personnel into their administrations. These staff members bring personal experience to a new president's organization. They also bring policy expertise that will help bolster the president in dealing with members of Congress who specialize in specific policy areas.

The Office of the Vice President

Traditionally, the office of the vice president has not had many important responsibilities. It was not until the twentieth century that vice presidents were chosen by presidential candidates to enhance their electoral prospects, and even then, once they were in office, they were given little more than ceremonial tasks. However, with the increasing complexity and international significance of the presidential role following World War II, President Dwight D. Eisenhower assigned his vice president, Richard M. Nixon, the task of traveling around the world to meet with foreign leaders. Twenty years later Walter Mondale, President Jimmy Carter's vice president, expanded the role of the office by serving as a close adviser to the president on issues ranging from national security to domestic policy.[48] Al Gore, vice president to President Clinton, took on responsibility for specific issues, including federal efficiency, science and technology, and global warming.

Each vice president tries to carve out a role that he is most comfortable with and that the president finds acceptable. During the eight years of the George W. Bush administration, for example, Vice President Richard Cheney assumed a prominent role in the nation's military and foreign policy. He had been secretary of defense under Bush's father, George H. W. Bush (1989–93), and oversaw the Gulf War. Cheney was widely perceived to be highly influential on such issues as the Iraq War, antiterrorism policies, and energy development. The fact that George W. Bush relied so heavily on Cheney to make key decisions elevated the power, visibility, and even controversy of the role of the vice president.[49] Joseph Biden, who served as vice president under President Obama, was also given considerable responsibility for foreign affairs. Ultimately, however, the people hold the president accountable for the actions and policies of his administration; even if a vice president exerts influence, it is the president who bears responsibilities for the outcomes.

Connections:
What constitutional responsibilities does the vice president have? What authority should he have?

Checkpoint

Can you:

☐ Track the growth of the executive staff

☐ Explain how the role of the vice president has evolved over time

Presidential Greatness

> **What defines a great president**

President Obama is the forty-fourth president of the United States. The men who came before him served with varying degrees of success as leaders in foreign and domestic policy. Presidential leadership is judged by whether a president is able to get his preferred policies passed by Congress and enacted into law and by how well he oversees the bureaucracy to make the government run effectively and efficiently.

The American people like to rank their presidents, and scholars also assess presidential greatness, looking at the clarity of a president's vision for policy, his communication and negotiation skills, and the effectiveness of his use of presidential powers, especially the general grant of executive power. Good presidents do not have to excel in every one of these categories, but they have to compensate for a weakness in one area with greater strength in another. Stephen Skowronek argues that presidents have opportunities to continue the policies of their predecessors or forge new paths, but that a president's success is often determined by external events, such as a terrorist attack or a global economic downturn.[50] The scholar Aaron Wildavsky suggests that there are actually "two presidencies": a foreign policy presidency and a domestic policy presidency.[51] On foreign policy, the president often must work quickly and in private, as negotiations must be conducted discretely. Domestic politics rarely require immediate action and usually entail open debate, with many citizens and interest groups vested in the outcome.[52]

Connections:
Name two presidents you think should be called great.

The following discussion focuses on three presidents who are frequently singled out for their impact on domestic and foreign policy: Franklin Delano Roosevelt, a Democrat from a wealthy, elite New York family; Lyndon Baines Johnson, a Democrat from a very poor Texas family; and Ronald Reagan, a Republican from a middle-class family in Illinois.[53] Each had strengths and weaknesses, and each knew how to maximize his greatest asset—intellect, negotiating skills, public communications—to try to accomplish his goals.

Franklin Delano Roosevelt (1933–45): The New Deal and World War II

When Franklin Delano Roosevelt (FDR) took office in 1933, the nation was experiencing the Great Depression. Unemployment had reached 25 percent, and Americans, many of them homeless and hungry, were suffering. To combat the effects of the depression, FDR had a clear policy vision, which he called the **New Deal**. In the first three years of his presidency, he succeeded in getting Congress to pass legislation that radically altered the size and shape of the federal government. His immediate need was to find a way to get cash into the hands of individual citizens, but he opposed handouts. Instead, he created job programs, including the Conservation Corps, the Works Progress Administration, and the Tennessee Valley Authority, all of which both employed and trained workers.

FDR also expanded the government's role in regulating the economy. The creation of the Securities and Exchange Commission and other laws relating to banking and finance helped restore confidence in banks and the stock market. The National Labor Relations Act established federal oversight of working conditions, labor standards, and labor disputes. This legislation brought the government and the business and labor sectors closer together. The Social Security program, a pension program to which workers contributed through a payroll tax that was also paid by employers, further entwined business and government.

Franklin Roosevelt used the bully pulpit and advanced the use of communication technology in the office of the president. He invented the fireside chat, a radio address to voters explaining the reasoning behind his governing decisions. Because fewer than half of all Americans owned radios at this time, FDR also turned the chats into newsreels that were shown in movie theaters. Ever since, presidents have found direct communications with voters to be an effective governing device.[54] President Roosevelt was also open and available to the Washington press corps, and his very first press conference in 1933 was a success. As a media-savvy president, FDR created the formal position of White House press secretary.[55]

New Deal:
Franklin Delano Roosevelt's program for ending the Great Depression through government intervention in the economy and development of a set of safety-net programs for individuals.

Connections:
Identify one of Franklin Roosevelt's successes and one of his failures.

THE WHITE HOUSE HISTORICAL ASSOCIATION (WHITE HOUSE COLLECTION)

Franklin Delano Roosevelt

Roosevelt took a personal role in negotiating legislative deals with members of the House and Senate, which were controlled by the Democrats. He allowed his staff to lay out the conditions for a compromise, but Roosevelt would finish the negotiations himself.[56] During his first five years in office, Roosevelt had great success in getting legislation through Congress. But in 1937 he overstepped by proposing to expand the size of the Supreme Court. The Court had struck down several of Roosevelt's favored policies, often by closely divided votes, and his so-called Court-packing plan would have allowed him to appoint additional justices and secure a majority favorable to him. Congress rejected Roosevelt's attempt to circumvent the checks and balances, and after that his relationship with Congress began to falter.

On December 7, 1941, Japan attacked the United States at Pearl Harbor in Hawaii, drawing the United States into World War II. From that point on, foreign affairs dominated Roosevelt's presidency, but the New Deal legislation of the previous decade laid the groundwork for the modern structure of domestic programs in the United States.

Lyndon Baines Johnson (1963–69): The Great Society and Vietnam

President Lyndon B. Johnson (LBJ) focused his mission on improving race relations and ending poverty because he believed they stood in the way of social, political, and economic progress. Most of his programs, which he called the **Great Society**, built on the infrastructure of FDR's New Deal, but they went much further in connecting the individual to the federal government. Johnson believed that as president he had an obligation to try to guarantee civil rights to all Americans.[57] In the area of race relations, he persuaded Congress to pass the Civil Rights Act of 1964, the Voting Rights Act of 1965, and the Fair Housing Act of 1968, which together formed a powerful set of laws protecting the rights of African Americans and subsequently the rights of other minority groups as well (see Chapter 5).

LBJ believed that it was possible for people to work very hard but still remain poor and that poor people were severely disadvantaged in terms of education, access to jobs, and affordable housing. He transformed the relationship between the individual and the federal government into one that included pure need, rather than merit based on work. He created two major federal health insurance programs: Medicaid, a health insurance program for the poor, and Medicare, a health insurance program for the elderly. He was also responsible for creating the Food Stamp Program, the School Lunch Program, Head Start, the Job Corps, and the Elementary and Secondary Education Act.

Great Society:
Lyndon Johnson's program for expanding the federal social welfare programs in health care, education, and housing and for ending poverty.

Connections:
Identify one of Lyndon Johnson's successes and one of his failures.

THE WHITE HOUSE HISTORICAL ASSOCIATION (WHITE HOUSE COLLECTION)

Lyndon Baines Johnson

Johnson was not a skilled communicator or comfortable giving speeches, and he did not come across well on television, which by this time had succeeded radio as the dominant form of political communication. He compensated for his lack of communication skills by relying more heavily on his very strong negotiation skills. From his prior experience as a member of Congress and Senate majority leader, Johnson understood how to convince members of Congress that it was in their best interests to pass legislation. Johnson made sure that his programs would benefit all poor people, white and black, rural and urban. By creating wide eligibility criteria, Johnson almost guaranteed that every congressional district in the country would receive some benefit from the programs. For example, both Medicaid and Medicare legislation included subsidies to rural hospitals and to big inner-city hospitals for services and capital expenditures such as improving facilities and building new ones. School lunch programs benefited schoolchildren as well as farmers, who sold the federal government their meat, milk, cheese, and grains at a guaranteed price, so they always had a market.

Johnson also used his presidential powers to distribute and award federal contracts and federal funds to key members of Congress and key state officials in return for their support of his programs. He understood that if a member of Congress needed to explain his vote in support of a liberal bill, he could do so more easily if he could point to some other federal benefit he had secured, such as a bridge, a Navy or Army base, or a new hospital wing.

Although Johnson's personal relationship with the press and the public started out reasonably well, as U.S. involvement in the Vietnam War escalated the press began to distrust him, and many journalists believed he was not being candid with them and the American people about the war. By the end of his presidency, Johnson's relationship with the press was downright hostile. In fact, negative reporting on the progress of the Vietnam War, combined with significant health concerns, was among the reasons that Johnson ultimately chose not to seek reelection, a decision he announced on March 31, 1968. Lyndon Johnson died five years later, on January 22, 1973.

Ronald Reagan (1981–89): The Reagan Revolution and the End of the Cold War

President Ronald Reagan's vision of the relationship between the individual and the federal government was different from the views of Roosevelt and Johnson, and it is invoked to this day by conservative Republicans seeking to limit the size and scope of the federal government. Reagan believed that the New Deal and the Great Society had combined to weaken individual initiative and responsibility. When he took office, he mounted an aggressive campaign to scale back federal programs that provided benefits to individuals without asking for anything in return.

Tax cuts were the first thing on Reagan's agenda for two reasons. First, he believed that if taxes went down, the economy would flourish. Second, he knew that if tax revenue went down and spending increased, federal deficits would be created. These deficits would serve as justification for proposing cuts in entitlement programs, such as Social Security, Medicaid, and Aid to Families with Dependent Children (replaced in 1996 by the Temporary Aid to Needy Families program). Entitlement programs put a strain on the federal budget, especially as the number of people living in poverty grew and the elderly lived longer. Reagan managed to make cuts in the programs for the poor and elderly by restricting eligibility for benefits, but he did not succeed in dismantling them.

THE WHITE HOUSE HISTORICAL ASSOCIATION (WHITE HOUSE COLLECTION)

Ronald Reagan

At the same time Reagan was implementing his domestic policy vision, he was also implementing his foreign policy vision. He took a firm stand against the Soviet Union, which he perceived as a direct threat to the United States and as a major promoter of Communism throughout the world. The defense buildup he ordered set off a military spending race that strained the Soviets' state-controlled economy to the breaking point. By the end of Reagan's second term, it was clear that the Soviet Union was moving toward collapse and could no longer control its satellite nations in eastern Europe. Reagan's foreign policy was arguably an important factor in the end of Communism and the Cold War.

Ronald Reagan is referred to as the "Great Communicator" because he came across very well on television; as a former actor, he was able to give engaging, persuasive, and even comforting speeches. In January 1986, when the space shuttle *Challenger* blew up shortly after takeoff as millions of Americans watched their TVs in horror, Reagan's words eased the national pain: "The crew of the space shuttle *Challenger* honored us by the manner in which they lived their lives. We will never forget them, nor the last time we saw them, this morning, as they prepared for their journey and waved goodbye and slipped the surly bonds of earth to touch the face of God."[58] The power of speech cannot be overestimated in an analysis of presidential success because it is the most basic way that the president tries to connect with the people.

President Reagan delegated much of the actual negotiating over policy to staff members. He also enhanced the power of the director of the Office of Management and Budget to negotiate with Congress on budgetary matters. Reagan and his staff were frequently successful in these negotiations, but on issues on which they were at a public disadvantage, Reagan knew when to compromise. During his last two years in office, he worked with a Democratic-controlled Congress to pass trade legislation, welfare reform, and the first comprehensive AIDS funding and treatment bill. Although Reagan enjoyed relatively consistent popularity and was perceived as highly responsive to his base of supporters, his record came under greater scrutiny

Connections:
Identify one of Ronald Reagan's successes and one of his failures.

Connections:
Describe the legacy of Franklin Roosevelt, of Lyndon Johnson, and of Ronald Reagan. How did each change the presidency?

Checkpoint

Can you:

☐ Explain how Franklin Delano Roosevelt had such a large impact on public policy

☐ Recall the programs of the Lyndon B. Johnson's Great Society and how they were passed

☐ Describe the impact of Ronald Reagan on the economy with his support of tax cuts

after he left office because his policies produced higher federal budget deficits and reduced funding for programs for the disadvantaged.

The example of Reagan, in the context of Roosevelt and Johnson, shows how the office of the presidency can shape domestic and foreign policy for future generations. Thirty-five years after Roosevelt died and eleven years after Johnson left office, Reagan ran for president on a campaign platform of scaling back the New Deal and the Great Society. In turn, Reagan left a conservative political legacy about the limited role of the federal government that remains a powerful rallying cry for Republicans today.

The President and Public Policy: Taxing and Spending

All presidents confront a vast policy landscape, but their performance with regard to the nation's economy is a primary point on which they are judged. Although presidents have only limited influence on the economy, they are held accountable for it. What the president can influence is taxation and government spending, which involves many important policies. In the section that follows, we describe his direct and indirect roles in implementing economic policy.

Tax Policy

Congress has the power to raise or lower federal taxes, but the executive branch has always been responsible for managing federal taxes and spending. The Internal Revenue Service, a unit of the Department of the Treasury, monitors the payment of federal taxes. Americans pay a wide range of federal taxes in addition to income tax, including Medicare and Social Security taxes, corporate taxes, and customs fees (taxes on imported goods). The federal government also collects taxes on gasoline, cigarettes, wireless phones, and airline tickets.

The problem that modern presidents face is the complexity of the tax code itself. Some economists argue for reform, claiming that business decisions and job growth are too closely tied to tax incentives rather than to the marketplace. In 1986, President Reagan worked with Congress to enact the Tax Reform Act, which tried to streamline the tax code. However, he left office in 1989 with a substantial federal deficit, and the next two presidents, George H. W. Bush and Bill Clinton, ultimately had to raise taxes to balance the federal budget. In 1998, the federal government achieved a budget surplus, and when Bill Clinton left office in January 2001, this surplus stood at $236 billion. When President George W. Bush took office in 2001, he followed through on his campaign pledge to cut taxes and worked with Congress to enact a major tax cut that same year.

The constant revising of the tax code and the changing levels of federal spending create a less than predictable economic environment. With tax policy so complicated, it becomes increasingly difficult for the president to be equally responsive to all citizens, corporations, and lobbyists who have a stake in the tax code.

In turn, it has become harder for citizens to hold the president accountable for spending their tax dollars. Moreover, because the president shares the power to shape the federal budget with Congress, working with Congress on the budget can be a source of frustration for the president.

Fiscal Policy and Monetary Policy

Government can use fiscal policy to intervene in the economy by manipulating the money supply through taxing and spending. More spending or lower taxes increase the money supply, while lower spending or more taxes decrease the money supply. In times of severe economic crises, the president may support a policy of increasing the money supply to ward off a recession. Alternatively, an increase in prices can cause workers to demand raises. Higher wages will lead to even larger increases in prices, setting off inflation. In this case, the president may support a decrease in the money supply to ward off or reduce the extent of inflation.

But the president is limited in his power to directly influence the nation's economic conditions because monetary policy is under the control of the **Federal Reserve Board**, an independent agency that serves as the nation's central bank, increasing or decreasing the money supply by changing the reserve requirements—the amount of cash reserves that banks must keep on hand (see Table 12.4). When the Federal Reserve increases reserve requirements, banks have less money to lend, and the money supply decreases. When the Federal Reserve decreases reserve requirements, banks have more money to lend, and thus the money supply increases. The Federal Reserve Board also controls the money supply through the discount rate, which is the interest rate that the Federal Reserve charges other banks on loans. When the discount rate is lower, banks are not able to charge high interest rates on the money they lend to consumers and businesses.

To control the flow of money in the economy, Congress created the Federal Reserve in 1913 as a system of twelve regional banks in one national

Federal Reserve Board:

Independent regulatory commission that affects the money supply by setting the reserve requirements of member banks, establishing a discount rate for loans to member banks, and buying or selling government securities.

TABLE 12.4 Comparison of Tax and Monetary Policy

Actions by Congress and the president affect fiscal policy, while actions by the Federal Reserve Board affect monetary policy.

Type of Policy	Policy Maker	Action	Direct Effect	Effect on Money Supply
Fiscal	Congress, president	Increase spending or cut taxes	Consumers have more money to spend.	Increases
	Congress, president	Decrease spending or increase taxes	Consumers have less money to spend.	Decreases
Monetary	Federal Reserve Board	Increase reserve requirement	Banks have less money to loan.	Decreases
	Federal Reserve Board	Decrease reserve requirement	Banks have more money to loan.	Increases
	Federal Reserve Board	Increase the discount rate	Loans are more expensive.	Decreases
	Federal Reserve Board	Decrease the discount rate	Loans are less expensive.	Increases

© CENGAGE LEARNING

banking system. The Federal Reserve System is led by a seven-member board of governors, each nominated by the president and confirmed by the Senate. Members serve fourteen-year terms, and the president selects the board chair, who serves a four-year term. The chair of the Federal Reserve is Ben Bernanke, who serves until January 2014. He was first nominated and confirmed under President George W. Bush and renominated and confirmed under President Obama.

Although the president can name people to the Federal Reserve, he cannot fire them if they promote monetary policy that differs from his preferred path. His only power over them comes from the nomination process, especially choosing the chair. Fair or not, the president does not have a lot of power over the Federal Reserve, but he is held accountable by voters for the success or failure of the board's policies.

Presidential Intervention in the Economy

Beginning with Theodore Roosevelt and accelerating under Franklin Roosevelt, presidents have led federal intervention in the economy—regulating business practices, ensuring workplace safety, overseeing banking and finance, and constructing a safety net of retirement, unemployment, and disability benefits. When the economy is weak, there is pressure on the president to take extraordinary steps to address it. This is what Franklin Roosevelt did during the Great Depression and what Barack Obama did during the years 2009–11 in response to a deep recession. A recession is typically defined as a downturn in economic activity, with declines in employment levels, income, retail spending, and industrial production. The recent recession was attributed largely to inflated housing prices, irresponsible lending by banks, and excessive borrowing by consumers, all of which led to widespread foreclosures and the collapse of major sectors of the financial and construction industries. When people lose jobs, consumer spending declines, forcing business and industry to cut back production and lay off workers.

When President Obama took office in 2009, he faced an enormous set of pressures relating to the recession. The decisions he made must be understood in the context of partisan policies on taxes and spending. Republican presidents have typically wanted to lower all taxes, a policy that provides less revenue to the federal government and subsequently decreases federal spending. Democratic presidents have typically wanted to cut taxes for individuals with lower incomes and to raise taxes on wealthier citizens to support federal programs. But raising taxes during a recession is widely believed to have a negative impact on consumer spending and job growth.

President Obama responded to the economic crisis by adopting a mixed strategy on taxes and spending. He continued President George W. Bush's TARP program, which effectively bailed out banks, and he instituted a bailout program for the auto industry. Additionally, he worked with Congress to enact an $800 billion stimulus bill that was a combination of spending increases favored by Democrats and tax credits (which amount to tax cuts) favored by Republicans to increase the money supply. In 2010, Obama and Congress extended Bush's tax cuts for two years. As noted in Chapter 11, Obama also promoted health care reform, signing legislation passed by Congress that required all individuals to purchase health care insurance. Some argue that this mandate amounts to a tax increase for individuals who currently do not have health insurance, but supporters of health care reform argue that if everyone has health insurance, taxpayers will not be subsidizing the cost of medical care for the uninsured and the total cost of federal funded health care will be reduced. In 2012, the Supreme Court heard arguments on the constitutionality of the mandate and ruled that it was within the taxing power of Congress.

The Federal Deficit and the National Debt

Although many experts credit President Obama's policies with warding off an even deeper recession, or depression, they greatly increased the federal deficit, which in turn increased the national debt. As we note in Chapter 11, the federal deficit is the difference between the amount of money that the government takes in and the amount of money that the government spends. When the federal government runs a deficit, it must borrow money to make up the shortfall. Consequently, the federal government pays interest on this borrowed money, and the combined amount of the borrowed money and the interest that accumulate over time constitute the national debt.

There are two components to the federal debt: public debt, which is the money that comes from issuing debt instruments, such as U.S. Treasury bonds, that investors buy with a promise of getting a set amount of interest on the bonds at a later date; and intragovernment-held debt, which is the amount of money that the federal government borrows from itself when it transfers money from one program to another or uses built-up reserves in one program as collateral for borrowing. The **debt ceiling** is a cap on the amount of money that Congress authorizes the president to borrow to pay the federal government's bills. Before 1917, there was no legal limit on the government's ability to issue such debt. However, to fund operations for World War I, Congress passed the Second Liberty Bond Act, which allows the federal government to issue longer-term debt so long as Congress issues its approval for doing so.[59] Consequently, the president must ask to raise the debt ceiling and cannot do so without congressional approval.

When President Obama took office, he inherited a federal deficit of $1.4 trillion and a total national debt of $11.9 trillion dollars (see Figure 1.8); both were the cumulative effect of past presidential policy making, including the Bush tax cuts and the Iraq and Afghanistan wars. During the first two years of the Obama administration, the national debt climbed to $13.5 trillion.[60] In the 2010 midterm congressional elections, the Tea Party movement became active within the Republican Party in order to strengthen the GOP's existing commitment to reduce taxes and federal spending. When the Republicans won control of the House of Representatives, those members who were elected with Tea Party support stayed adamant in their position against raising the debt ceiling.

The issue of the federal debt ceiling rose to the forefront of American politics in May 2011, when the Obama administration requested an increase in the debt limit from $14.3 to $16.7 trillion because it anticipated that the national debt would rise beyond its legal cap by August 2011. The $14.3 trillion constituted 93 percent of U.S. Gross Domestic Product (GDP). Republicans viewed that as dangerously high, so the Republican-controlled House of Representatives rejected that request and Republicans made it clear that they would not approve a debt ceiling increase without decreases in federal spending. This was the first time that Congress had actually refused to raise the debt ceiling. The issue was very serious because the federal government relies on debt as a means of financing programs, and those programs would have to be cut if the government could no longer borrow money.

debt ceiling:
The congressionally authorized limit on federal borrowing.

In July 2011, President Obama proposed a "grand bargain" that would have cut the debt by $4 trillion over ten years with a combination of spending reductions and increased taxes. Republicans in the House, led by members affiliated with the Tea Party movement, rejected any plan that included tax increases. A standoff ensued, and policy makers, the business community, and the media voiced fear that the United States government might default on its financial obligations for the first time in its history. The standoff was broken on July 31, 2011, when the president, Senate leaders, and Speaker Boehner agreed on a plan that would raise the debt ceiling by $2.4 trillion over the course of the next year but would require the same amount in cuts to federal spending over the subsequent ten years, with an initial cut of $900 billion from the federal budget. The bill created a bipartisan supercommittee with members from the House and Senate that was directed to create a long-term budget reduction plan to be voted on by Congress by the end of 2011. The committee failed to reach agreement, so automatic cuts in federal spending were scheduled to take place in January 2013 unless an alternative plan was adopted.

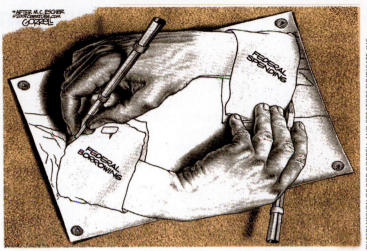

BY PERMISSION OF BOB GORRELL AND CREATORS SYNDICATE, INC.

As this sequence of events reveals, the president does not have sole power over any element of the national economy; he shares power with the Federal Reserve and Congress. This shared power arrangement can be a gate against efficient and responsive policy making in these areas, especially in times of divided party government. It takes enormous skill and strategy on the part of the president to forge the cooperation that is necessary to effect positive change in the areas of taxing and spending.

aplia Construct Your Own Policy

1. How would you change the current tax system to generate more revenue in a fair way?
2. What programs would you cut or eliminate to reduce the federal deficit and pay down the national debt?

For more on the policy-making process, see Chapter 1.

The Presidency and Democracy

Focus Questions Revisited

- In what ways is the president held accountable both individually and for the collective economic, military, and social condition of the nation?

- How responsive is the presidency as a democratic office? How can the president address the vital public policy concerns of the American people?

- What opportunities are there for the average citizen to influence the decisions of the president?

- What powers does the president have to ensure equality across all citizens?

- Is the modern presidency a gate or a gateway to democracy?

From George Washington to Barack Obama, the presidency has evolved from an institution with strictly limited responsibilities to the large and powerful institution it is today. Certainly the Framers would be surprised by the growth of the presidency, and they might wonder whether the executive branch is too focused on serving the president individually and not focused enough on the needs of citizens more generally.

Nevertheless, the president operates in a separation of powers system, and laws must be passed with the cooperation of Congress, so the president cannot be rewarded or blamed entirely for the federal government's policies.[61] Voters can render their direct verdict on the president's job performance when they choose whether to reelect him, provided he runs for a second term. Voters also indirectly register their opinions in congressional midterm elections, which focus on members of the House and Senate but are also interpreted as judgments on the president's record. In cases of very serious wrongdoing, Congress has the power to impeach and convict the president, but the threshold for impeachment is extremely high, and it happens very rarely. No president has ever been convicted and removed from office after being impeached.

Overall, it is difficult for the average citizen to hold the president personally accountable for his actions. Surrounded by so many staff members, a president does not give ordinary citizens much chance to influence him, nor does he often make himself available to be responsive to citizen needs. Given the vast size of the nation and security concerns for the president's safety, it is not easy for citizens to convey their opinions directly to the president. In the course of the nation's history, presidents have grown less accessible to the average voter. However, technological innovations as simple as fast airplane travel and, more recently, e-mail, texting, and social networking websites provide many more modes of communication between voters and the president or the president's staff. Although the president will not meet most of the people he represents, each town meeting he holds and public speech he gives is an opportunity for an exchange of views. And the job of presidential staff is to keep him as well informed on public opinion as possible.

Despite the limited opportunities for accountability, presidents do tend to be responsive to public opinion over the course of their time in office, although less so in the second term. However, each president strives for success and wants to leave behind a legacy that is respected and honored. In the modern age, presidents are considered their political party's leaders, and they want their records to reflect well on other elected officials from their party. All presidents see it as their responsibility to do what they believe to be best for the country, even in the face of opposition from the media, the public, and Congress. At times, this opposition can result in a less effective president than some might want, but the operation of checks and balances on presidential power accords with the Framers' vision of presidential leadership.

Overall, the modern presidency acts as both a gate and a gateway to democracy at the same time. It is a gate in that the president oversees a very large federal government that can be complex and difficult to change in response to public needs. It is a gateway in that any natural-born citizen can run for the most powerful office in the land, and although wealth, education, and connections are extremely helpful in winning, they are not prerequisites for victory. The men who have been elected president have come from a wide range of economic, educational, and professional backgrounds. With the election of an African American president, major entry barriers to the presidency have been broken; one might argue that the path to the White House is more open than ever before.

gateways**to**learning

1. The American presidency was an innovation in governance. As the nation grew, the presidency grew accordingly. Today the president speaks for the nation on the world stage and sets the policy agenda at home. (pp. 398–401)

2. As the nation has grown in size, population, and economic power, the job of the chief executive has also grown, resulting in the expansion of presidential power and creating what has become known as the imperial presidency. (pp. 402–403)

3. Among the president's constitutional powers are those associated with being commander in chief. The president also has the power to pardon, to negotiate and sign treaties and recognize foreign nations, to veto bills passed by Congress, and to appoint federal officers. (pp. 403–408)

4. Congress's ultimate check on the executive is the power to impeach and remove from office. (pp. 408–412)

5. The Constitution vests the president with a general grant of executive power and requires that he "take Care that the Laws be faithfully executed." These responsibilities have been used by presidents to vastly increase presidential power. (p. 412)

6. The president uses his executive power to issue presidential directives. He also uses the office to persuade the people and Congress and to set the agenda for domestic and foreign policy. (pp. 412–418)

7. As presidential power has grown, the president has come into increasing conflict with the other two branches of government, particularly during wartime. (pp. 418–423)

8. The Executive Office of the President has great influence over budgetary, military, and economic policies. The role of vice president has grown in recent years. (pp. 423–425)

9. Presidential leadership is generally judged on how successful a president is in getting his preferred policies passed into law and in getting the bureaucracy to be effective and efficient. Americans also judge their presidents on their communication and negotiation skills. (pp. 425–426)

10. Presidents' performance with regard to the nation's economy is a primary point on which they are judged, although they have limited influence over it. (pp. 430–435)

Key **Concepts**

bully pulpit (p. 415). Give examples of presidents using the bully pulpit.

commander in chief (p. 404). What are the responsibilities of the commander in chief?

debt ceiling (p. 434). Why has the debt ceiling recently caused contention?

executive order (p. 413). Give an example of when the president used an executive order to exercise his independent authority.

executive privilege (p. 410). What is the basis for executive privilege?

Federal Reserve Board (p. 431). What is the Federal Reserve Board?

Great Society (p. 427). How did Johnson's Great Society expand the role of government in society?

head of state (p. 417). How does the president function as head of state?

impeachment (p. 408). Is impeachment an effective check on executive power?

imperial presidency (p. 403). What defines an imperial presidency?

lame duck (p. 400). Why are legislators less likely to cooperate with a lame-duck president?

New Deal (p. 426). How did Roosevelt's New Deal expand the role of the government in the economy?

omnibus bill (p. 407). Why are omnibus bills harder to veto?

pardon (p. 405). What does a presidential pardon mean?

pocket veto (p. 407). How is a pocket veto different from a regular veto?

Your Virtual Tutor
Master What You Need to Know
and Test Yourself.

presidential directive (p. 412). What are the forms a presidential directive can take?

signing statements (p. 414). How has the use of signing statements increased the powers of the presidency?

State of the Union address (p. 408). How has the use of the State of the Union address evolved from its creation in the Constitution?

veto (p. 407). How can Congress counteract the president's veto power?

War Powers Act (p. 419). How did the events of the Vietnam War lead to the passage of the War Powers Act?

Learning Outcomes

WHAT YOU NEED...

To Know	To Test Yourself	To Participate
What is required to serve as president	• State the constitutional qualifications and succession requirements for the presidency • Explain what is meant by imperial presidency	• Discuss ways to open the pathways to the presidency
What the powers of the president are and how they are limited	• Characterize the presidential power of commander in chief • Compare pardon and commutation • Describe the role of the Senate in the president's power to negotiate and sign treaties • Recall the steps to presidential appointments • Survey the power of the veto • Explain how the State of the Union address has evolved as a tool for the president • Compare and contrast examples of impeachment (or impending impeachment)	• Evaluate the president's power over the military • Design a way to make appointments and judicial selection less partisan • Evaluate the role of partisanship in impeachment
How executive influence has grown over time	• Recall the different types of presidential directives • List the tools available to a president as he uses his power to persuade • Describe how the president can set the public agenda	• Determine whether you think the presidency has become too powerful
Why the president is so powerful during wartime	• Track trends in the struggle between the president and Congress over war powers • Describe issues in the struggle between the president and the judiciary in wartime	• Design a way to broaden Congress's power to limit intervention in foreign conflicts • Evaluate the importance of civil liberties in wartime
How the White House is organized	• Track the growth of the executive staff • Explain how the role of the vice president has evolved over time	• Evaluate whether the vice president should be given an expanded set of formal powers
What defines a great president	• Explain how Franklin D. Roosevelt had such a large impact on public policy • Recall the programs of Lyndon B. Johnson's Great Society and how they were passed • Describe the impact of Ronald Reagan on the economy with his support of tax cuts	• Develop criteria for judging presidents • Describe the ideal president for the twenty-first century

Get involved. You have no idea what you can accomplish until you become unstoppable. . . . If I had a nickel for every time someone said we would fail I would never have to work again.

Kate Hanni,
College of the Redwoods,
Eureka, California

13

The Bureaucracy

When Kate Hanni was a student at the College of the Redwoods, she was a theater arts major who dreamed of being a rock star—"to be in front of a gazillion people with their lighters on," as she put it. Today she is a different kind of rock star, founder and head of the Coalition for an Airline Passengers' Bill of Rights (FlyersRights .org), which claimed a major victory in December 2009 when the Department of Transportation ruled that domestic airlines must allow passengers who have been stuck on a stranded plane for more than three hours to get off the plane, and again in August 2011, when that rule was extended to international airlines that operate in the United States for delays lasting more than four hours.

Hanni had not planned to be a political activist. For years, she was a successful real estate broker in Napa County, California, who enjoyed spending time with family and friends and still sang on occasion with her rock band, the Toasted Heads. But on December 29, 2006, her life took a new direction. With 134 other passengers, she and her family were stranded for nine hours and sixteen minutes in a jet parked at the Austin, Texas, airport. There was little food or water, and the lavatories reeked. "People got so angry they were talking about busting through the emergency exits," Hanni recalled. "I was fuming. It was imprisonment."

When Hanni got home, she drafted an online petition demanding legal rights for airline passengers. The following month, when an ice storm at New York's Kennedy International Airport stranded thousands of passengers in planes for up to eleven hours, her cause took off. She gave up her real estate business, and she and her husband took out a line of credit on their house to build a website. Soon her petition had eighteen thousand signatures, and people in her e-mail network wrote

aplia Need to Know

- **What the bureaucracy does**
- **What the essential elements of a bureaucracy are**
- **How the bureaucracy developed over time**
- **How the bureaucracy is both accountable and responsive, and how it can fail**

to Congress and the Federal Aviation Administration and posted videos of the stranded flight experience on YouTube. Hanni got media attention, promoting passengers' rights in radio and TV interviews. Her coalition gained support from airline labor unions, air traffic controller unions, and consumer groups. She talked her congressman, Mike Thompson (D-Calif.), into introducing legislation. In September 2007 Hanni staged a "strand-in" near the Capitol in Washington, with a tent outfitted to resemble the interior of an airplane and invitations to members of Congress to see what it felt like to be trapped. As the movement's theme song, she got the Toasted Heads to rewrite the Animals' 1965 hit, "We've Gotta Get Out of This Place."

In response, the airlines fought back by claiming that conditions were not as bad as reported. The Air Transport Association argued that deplaning would only cause delays and cancellations and might compromise passenger safety. A version of Congressman Thompson's bill passed the House, but a similar bill introduced by Barbara Boxer (D-Calif.) did not pass the Senate. New York and California passed airline passenger laws, but a federal court of appeals struck down New York's law on the grounds that only the federal government has the authority to regulate airline service.

In the end, that's exactly what happened. On December 21, 2009, Transportation Secretary Ray LaHood announced new airline regulations. After two hours on the tarmac, airlines must give passengers food and water. After three hours, they must let them off or face stiff fines—$27,500 per passenger. In an e-mail to supporters, an elated Hanni called the regulations "an early Christmas present" but reminded them that "we're not done yet!" Citing fees for checked bags and chronically delayed or canceled flights, she continues to push for passenger rights legislation and is actively involved in the debate over body scanners.[1]

The story of Kate Hanni is remarkable because she, as an ordinary citizen, demanded that the federal government live up to its responsibility of ensuring the safe travel of passengers. She took matters into her own hands and used the gateways of citizen influence on policy making to draw attention to the issue. Her activism got the Federal Aviation Administration, a subdivision of the Department of Transportation, to respond.

In this chapter we examine the cabinet-level departments, agencies, and other organizations that constitute the executive branch. We look at their structure, characteristics, rationale, procedures, accountability, and responsiveness to citizens' concerns. A fundamental question for students of American government is whether the sprawling nature of the bureaucracy makes it a gate or a gateway to effectively serving the people.

FocusQuestions

- How does the federal bureaucracy play a role in responding to the individual needs of ordinary citizens?
- How does the structure of the federal bureaucracy shape the way policies are implemented?
- What powers does the bureaucracy have to ensure that federal policies are administered equally across all citizens?
- How can the average citizen influence the decisions of the bureaucracy?
- Is the bureaucracy a gate or a gateway to democracy? Explain.

The American Bureaucracy

› **What the bureaucracy does**

Just mention the word *bureaucracy*, and most people roll their eyes and utter phrases like "red tape" or "slow as molasses." Of all the components of American government, the bureaucracy is most likely to be perceived as annoying and daunting, as a gate against getting things done. Of all the components of American government, the bureaucracy is also the most likely to have a direct impact on citizens' lives. Most Americans have never met a president or a member of Congress or a federal judge, but every American has likely interacted with an employee of the government. Whether the interaction involves showing identification to a TSA agent in the airport or waiting in line at the post office, the rules and regulations of the federal bureaucracy present numerous opportunities for frustration.

Bureaucracies generally are not afforded much respect because they seem so complicated and impenetrable, and bureaucrats are often portrayed as faceless robots who merely enforce the rules. Yet enforcing the rules is the bureaucracy's job; as an extension of the presidency, bureaucratic implementation is how the president executes the law. Rules must be enforced equally across all citizens.

Despite the well-known problems associated with bureaucracies, organization is essential to modern government. In the late nineteenth century the German sociologist Max Weber described bureaucracies as highly rational organizations that enabled large numbers of people to get difficult jobs done efficiently.[2] If the federal bureaucracy does not seem efficient today, that may be because of the enormous responsibilities it bears, not only to implement complex policy and law established by the president and Congress, but also to do so in a way that is orderly, predictable, fair, equal for all citizens, and transparent. The formal aspects of bureaucratic structure promote accountability, while the informal operations—the bureaucratic culture—determine how well the organization carries out its own mission and how well it interacts with other organizations. We discuss these elements in detail to draw a practical road map, not only to understanding the federal government, but to actually make it work better for ordinary citizens.

What Is the Bureaucracy?

The **bureaucracy** is the large collection of executive branch departments, agencies, boards, commissions, and other government organizations that carry out the responsibilities of the federal government. At first, the nation did not require many employees to fulfill the government's duties, which were limited to large national issues such as defense, tariffs on imported goods, and settling western lands. As the nation's lands and economy grew, so did

Connections: What federal employees have you come in contact with in the past? What was the most recent experience like?

Connections: What is your impression of the federal bureaucracy? Which branch of government do you think works best? Which works least well?

bureaucracy: *Executive branch departments, agencies, boards, and commissions that carry out the responsibilities of the federal government.*

the need for a more complex structure at the federal level to oversee government activities. These responsibilities are established by laws passed by Congress and signed by the president, but for execution they often entail expertise, so the legislature relies on specialists—the bureaucrats—to write the **regulations** that implement the law.

In 2012 the number of federal employees, including the armed services, totaled almost 4.3 million people.[3] The jobs of federal employees vary widely. A national park ranger is a federal employee, as is a border patrol officer, a bridge designer with the Army Corps of Engineers, an accountant with the Securities and Exchange Commission, and a lawyer with the Department of Justice. For every federal job classified as "professional," there are also staff jobs, including clerks, office managers, janitors, mechanics, and delivery personnel, who keep the bureaucracy running. Skills and specialties in almost any type of work can be a gateway to employment in the federal government, which we discuss in more detail later in the chapter.

One simple way to understand the basic structure of the bureaucracy is to imagine a piece of furniture called a cabinet that stores different types of items in different drawers. It is no accident that the term *bureaucracy* has *bureau* at its base, an old-fashioned term for a cabinet. President Thomas Jefferson (1801–1809) had a separate room in the White House that he called his cabinet, and the centerpiece of the room was a long table with drawers on each side that served as his desk, in which he stored all important federal papers according to issue area.[4] President Barack Obama could not fit all the paperwork of the federal bureaucracy in a single desk, but the idea of compartmentalizing federal responsibilities has endured over time. Today, a president builds a **cabinet**—his set of key advisers who are responsible for the areas under their jurisdiction. As noted in Chapter 12, The Presidency, the cabinet is distinct from the president's White House staff,

OFFICIAL WHITE HOUSE PHOTO BY CHUCK KENNEDY

On April 20, 2009, President Obama posed in the East Room of the White House with Vice President Joe Biden and other members of his cabinet.

which works directly for the president, because cabinet members oversee entire departments constructed to implement federal policy. For example, President Obama appointed Janet Napolitano as secretary of the Department of Homeland Security based on her experience with border control as governor of Arizona. Most cabinet members are **cabinet secretaries** and head executive departments, but presidents may select additional advisers for cabinet-rank status.

Constitutional Foundations

The word *bureaucracy* does not appear in the U.S. Constitution, but the foundations of the federal bureaucracy can be traced to a few key sentences in Article II that relate to the powers of the president.

Appointments. Article II, Section 2 gives the president the power to "nominate, and by and with the Advice and Consent of the Senate,...appoint...all other Officers of the United States, whose Appointments are not herein otherwise provided for, and which shall be established by Law." This section goes on to state that Congress can "by Law vest the Appointment of such inferior Officers, as they think proper, in the President alone, in the Courts of Law, or in the Heads of Departments." Thus the discussion of the president's appointment power implies the existence of executive departments.

Opinions on Federal Policies. Article II, Section 2 references the executive branch more directly when it authorizes the president to "require the Opinion, in writing, of the principal Officer in each of the executive Departments, upon any subject relating to the Duties of their respective Offices." The Framers envisioned that the president would manage a staff of federal officers who would oversee executive departments managing the operations of government.

Execution of the Laws. Article II, Section 3 gives the president broad powers to "take Care that the Laws be faithfully executed." At the same time that the Framers wanted to make sure that the president would follow the intent of Congress, they also gave him wide discretion in how he carried out the laws. This broad executive power is the foundation for the growth of the federal bureaucracy as well as for the growth of the presidency, as we saw in Chapter 12.

The Structure of the Bureaucracy

For more than two centuries the federal bureaucracy has been changing, growing, and developing into today's interlinked set of organizations that implement federal policy. Some organizations are vast, such as the executive departments, and some are small advisory boards and commissions. Coordinating the authority and operations of these different types of organizations is a significant challenge for the executive branch as it carries out its constitutional duties. The structure of the U.S. bureaucracy is not unique, nor are the challenges it faces. Bureaucratic organization is essential for the operation of modern governments and organizations, as a look at the bureaucracy in the United Nations indicates (see Global Gateways: The United Nations Bureaucracy).

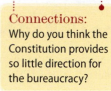

Connections:
Why do you think the Constitution provides so little direction for the bureaucracy?

CHRIS SLANE/CARTOONSTOCK

The United Nations Bureaucracy

As the most important international governmental organization, the United Nations is a gateway for peace by acting as a neutral forum where nations can attempt to resolve conflicts before they lead to violence. Founded at the end of World War II, the United Nations today has 193 member nations, each of which pays dues. It has grown into a large and complex governmental organization with a bureaucratic system that aims to carry out the policies on which the member nations agree.

As the UN bureaucracy has grown in size and complexity, there have been increasing complaints of inefficiency and corruption. Corruption and inefficiency can serve as a gate against effective governance and undermine the legitimacy of the UN as a global organization.

- **Is the lack of transparency in the United Nations' bureaucracy damaging to its mission?**
- **Do you think the United States' bureaucracy has any of the problems that the United Nations' bureaucracy suffers from?**

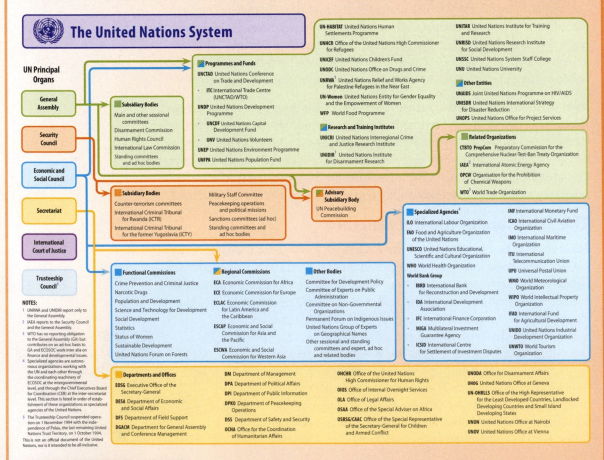

UNITED NATIONS BUREAUCRACY.

Source: "The United Nations System," United Nations, accessed July 19, 2012, http://www.un.org/en/aboutun/structure/pdfs/un_system_chart_colour_sm.pdf.

Executive Departments. Today there are fifteen executive, or cabinet-level, departments in the federal bureaucracy. A cabinet department is an executive branch organization led by a cabinet secretary appointed by the president. Cabinet departments are responsible for implementing laws and policies in specific areas, and the job of the secretary is to oversee implementation, provide advice to the president about the issues under the department's control, and develop an annual budget for the department. Congress has the authority to create a cabinet department, but once it is created, it is under the control and supervision of the president as head of the executive branch. Table 13.1 lists each department, the year it was created, its website, and its number of employees.

Each cabinet department consists of subdivisions arranged in a hierarchical form to divide up its tasks and theoretically maximize efficiency and responsiveness. Figure 13.1 shows how the Department of Health and Human Services (HHS) is organized. This organizational chart makes it clear

TABLE 13.1 Cabinet Departments, 2012

Department	Year Established	Website	Employees (in thousands)
State	1789	http://www.state.gov	32.4
Treasury	1789	http://www.treasury.gov	108.2
Defense (originally, War)	1789	http://www.dod.gov	764.3
Interior	1849	http://www.interior.gov	70.4
Agriculture	1862	http://www.usda.gov	93.3
Justice	1870	http://www.justice.gov	117.9
Commerce	1903	http://www.commerce.gov	140.5
Labor	1913	http://www.labor.gov	17.4
Housing and Urban Development	1965	http://www.hud.gov	9.4
Transportation	1966	http://www.transportation.gov	57.7
Energy	1977	http://www.energy.gov	16.5
Education	1979	http://www.education.gov	4.3
Health and Human Services	1980	http://www.hhs.gov	70.1
Veterans Affairs	1989	http://www.va.gov	302.3
Homeland Security	2003	http://www.dhs.gov	187.5

Source: The White House, http://www.whitehouse.gov; The White House, Office of Management and Budget, *Analytical Perspectives, Budget of the U.S. Government FY 2013* (Washington, D.C.: U.S. Government Printing Office, 2012), Table 11-2, Total Federal Employment, p. 120, accessed June 26, 2012, http://www.whitehouse.gov/omb/budget/Analytical_Perspectives. For the history of each department, see the websites listed above.

that each department has many subdivisions, or layers, each assigned a specific federal policy to implement. HHS is one of the largest cabinet departments. It oversees three hundred programs, with 70,100 employees and a budget of $871.9 billion.[5] This massive and complex organization is necessary to respond to the needs of all the individuals affected by the programs that HHS manages.

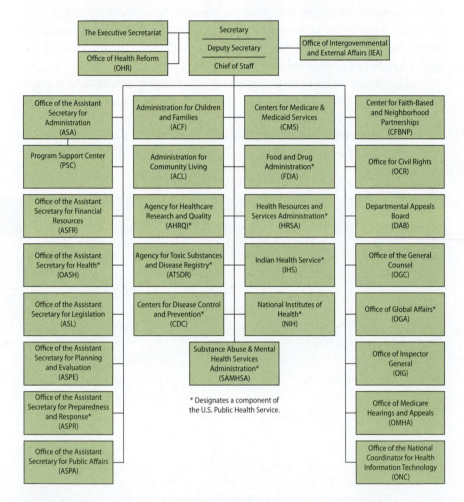

FIGURE 13.1 Organizational Chart of the Department of Health and Human Services.

Cabinet departments are complex hierarchical organizations with layers of authority and sublevel agencies that have jurisdiction over specific federal programs and policies. This organizational chart of the Department of Health and Human Services shows sublevel agencies with lines of responsibility.

Source: U.S. Department of Health and Human Services, Organizational Chart, accessed June 27, 2012, http://www.hhs.gov /about/orgchart.

For example, HHS is responsible for administering the Children's Health Insurance Program (CHIP), which supplies funding to state governments to provide health insurance coverage for children living in working families that are not able to afford private health insurance and are also not poor enough to receive benefits through the Medicaid program. Created in 1965, Medicaid is a government-funded health insurance program for individuals in poverty, and it falls under the jurisdiction of the Centers for Medicaid and Medicare Services (http://www.cms.hhs.gov), a division of HHS. Medicaid is strictly limited to people at specific income levels, and millions of children are not eligible for health care insurance under this program. To care for the health of these children, Congress created CHIP in 1997, but it expired in 2007, and President George W. Bush (2001–2009) and the Democratic-controlled Congress could not agree on a reauthorization plan. Consequently, states were limited in the coverage they could offer to children in 2007–2008. Without continued permission and federal funds to offer medical services to eligible children, the states had no choice but to pull back. On February 3, 2009, Congress passed the Children's Health Insurance Program Reauthorization, and President Obama signed the legislation the next day, extending this program to 11 million children.[6]

The responsibilities of HHS grew even broader when President Obama signed the Patient Protection and Affordable Care Act into law on March 23, 2010. Because HHS oversees Medicaid, Medicare, and other federal health-related programs, it bears the bulk of the responsibility to implement the new programs associated with this legislation. For example, HHS tries to remedy deficiencies in the Medicare prescription drug program for senior citizens and inform citizens about expanded eligibility for health insurance through Medicaid. It also coordinates health insurance exchanges, works with states to enhance existing state-based insurance programs, and joins with other federal agencies to encourage wellness and disease prevention programs.[7] CHIP and health care reform are two examples of federal policy that are implemented by a cabinet department, in conjunction with state governments.

Other Types of Federal Organizations.   In addition to cabinet-level departments, there are numerous independent organizations that constitute the federal government, including agencies, commissions, administrations, boards, corporations, and endowments (see Table 13.2). These organizations vary by structure, mission, and degree of independence from the president. For example, the **Office of Management and Budget (OMB)** has final authority over the entire federal budget, and each agency and department must submit its proposed budget to OMB for approval before it is included in the president's official proposed budget. The OMB's director is part of the president's cabinet, although OMB is not a cabinet department. Additionally, all regulations must go through OMB before they take effect.

Office of Management and Budget (OMB): *Federal agency that oversees the federal budget and all federal regulations.*

TABLE 13.2 Selected Independent Agencies and Commissions, 2012

Department	Year Established	Website	Employees (in thousands)
Environmental Protection Agency (EPA)	1970	http://www.epa.gov	17.1
Equal Employment Opportunity Commission (EEOC)	1965	http://www.eeoc.gov	2.4
General Services Administration (GSA)	1949	http://www.gsa.gov	13.2
National Aeronautics and Space Administration (NASA)	1958	http://www.nasa.gov	18.4
National Labor Relations Board (NLRB)	1935	http://www.nlrb.gov	1.7
National Science Foundation (NSF)	1950	http://www.nsf.gov	1.4
Nuclear Regulatory Commission (NRC)	1974	http://www.nrc.gov	4.0
Office of Personnel Management	1978	http://www.opm.gov	5.7
Peace Corps	1961	http://www.peacecorps.gov	1.1
Securities and Exchange Commission (SEC)	1935	http://www.sec.gov	3.9
Small Business Administration (SBA)	1953	http://www.sba.gov	3.4
Social Security Administration (SSA)	1935	http://www.socialsecurity.gov	65.4

Source: The White House, http://www.whitehouse.gov; The White House, Office of Management and Budget, *Analytical Perspectives, Budget of the U.S. Government FY 2013* (Washington, D.C.: U.S. Government Printing Office, 2012), Table 11-2, Total Federal Employment, p. 120, accessed June 26, 2012, http://www.whitehouse.gov/omb/budget/Analytical_Perspectives. For Peace Corps, see p. 926 of the *Budget of the U.S. Government FY 2013.*

 **independent agency:** *Federal organization that has independent authority and does not operate within a cabinet department.*

The Environmental Protection Agency (EPA) is an **independent agency**, a type of federal organization established by Congress with authority to regulate an aspect of the economy or a sector of the federal government. Independent agencies do not operate within a cabinet department. Congress designs such agencies to operate with their own authority. The EPA has a unique role in the federal government, with responsibility for preserving the quality of the air, water, and land. It can issue regulations and create policy—as it did on greenhouse gas emissions in January 2010; its regulations are subject to OMB approval, just like regulations from any cabinet department. A federal regulatory commission is an agency typically run by a small number of officials, known as commissioners, who are appointed by the president for fixed terms and are responsible for overseeing a sector of the economic or political arena. One example is the Securities and Exchange Commission (SEC), which is responsible for monitoring all business practices involving the stock market. The SEC has five commissioners who serve staggered five-year terms and manage 3,900 employees.[8] The SEC oversees the work of accountants, stockbrokers, hedge fund managers, financial advisers, and small business owners. It has legal authority to demand information from these professionals, impose fines for bypassing investment rules, and even bring formal charges for serious violations of the law.

A federal administration is responsible for running a federal program or overseeing specific areas of federal responsibility. The Federal Aviation Administration (FAA), as we saw at the beginning of this chapter, is located within the Department of Transportation and is responsible for overseeing the entire airline industry and setting the requirements and guidelines for safe travel. It has approximately 42,500 employees, including air traffic controllers and safety inspectors.[9] Its stated mission is "to provide the safest, most efficient aerospace system in the world."[10] This is a huge responsibility, and the internal complexity of the FAA makes it difficult for air travelers such as Kate Hanni to find the right office to contact about a problem. Her efforts to get the FAA to respond to travelers' needs are therefore all the more inspiring.

A federal board typically has a more narrow scope of authority but can possess the power to require changes in operating procedures and to suggest fines. It usually consists of individuals appointed for a specific term and who, ideally, have expertise in the area of the board's jurisdiction. For example, the National Transportation Safety Board (NTSB) is responsible for investigating transportation-related accidents such as the emergency landing of US Airways flight 1549 in January 2009; dubbed the "Miracle on the Hudson," the jetliner's engines lost power after encountering a flock of geese. There were no fatalities, and only a few injuries, in that water landing. When-

Connections: Why would the government fund a for-profit railroad?

AP PHOTO/STEVEN DAY

ever an accident involves any form of transportation, one of the NTSB's five board members is appointed to oversee an investigation of the event. When the investigation is completed, the agency issues a report that includes findings about the accident's cause and recommendations for avoiding a similar event. Despite its authority in these investigations and its members' knowledge of safe transportation practices, the NTSB does not have the power to issue federal regulations.

A federal corporation is a type of federal organization similar to a private business in that it provides a service or commodity for a price to the public, but it also receives federal funding. For example, the National Railroad Passenger Corporation, better known as Amtrak, is essentially a for-profit railroad, but it receives federal funding and is subject to federal restrictions and controls.

A national endowment is also a type of federal organization that uses funds specifically allocated to promote a public good or service.

The National Transportation Safety Board investigates the causes of transportation accidents, such as the bird strike that forced US Airways Flight 1549 to land in the Hudson River on January 15, 2009. Not all accidents have such fortunate outcomes, and the NTSB makes recommendations for preventing similar accidents in the future.

The National Endowment for the Arts, for example, was created to support scholarship and art that would be available to the general public, but it does not have any formal responsibility to monitor private- and public-sector activities in a specific set of issue areas. Because endowments are funded by the federal government, they are expected to serve as gateways for the expression of a wide range of viewpoints and perspectives in the work that they support.

Core Components of the Bureaucracy

> **What the essential elements of a bureaucracy are**

All these bureaucratic organizations share four core components that determine how government implements policy and, more immediately, how government responds to the individual needs of citizens. These components are a mission, a hierarchical decision-making process, expertise, and a bureaucratic culture.

Mission

Each federal agency has a stated mission that defines its role and responsibilities within the federal bureaucracy. For example, the mission of the Department of Health and Human Services is stated on its website:

> THE DEPARTMENT OF HEALTH AND HUMAN SERVICES (HHS) is the United States government's principal agency for protecting the health of all Americans and providing essential human services, especially for those who are least able to help themselves.[11]

A mission statement is important as the public face of the department, and it is the measure by which members of Congress and the general public can hold the department accountable for the success or failure of its efforts.

Hierarchical Decision-Making Process

To carry out its mission, every federal organization has a hierarchical decision-making process that structures the way policy is implemented. The hierarchy of authority in a bureaucracy means that an employee's decision on the implementation of policy is reviewed at each higher level in the organization. For example, HHS contains the following levels of authority, in ascending order: bureau chief, assistant secretary, deputy secretary, secretary. Each of these officials puts his or her expert input into policy implementation and then sends the decision up to the next level for approval. Not every department uses these levels of authority in the same way, but each leads up to the secretary, who is responsible for all of the policy decisions that come out of a department, and, ultimately, to the president.

The hierarchical decision-making process has advantages and disadvantages. It ensures that the unit responds consistently and predictably. The process also requires careful consideration of a policy before it is implemented. These two structural characteristics, taken together, are designed to ensure that policies are administered equally across citizens. However, this same hierarchical structure can present an obstacle to speedy decision making. Despite efforts to streamline the process, the step-by-step review of decision making inevitably slows down the implementation of federal laws.

Expertise

Fundamental to the core of the federal bureaucracy is the presumption that the people who hold bureaucratic positions have expertise in the issue areas they oversee and implement. This expertise can come from a number of sources. Individuals can enter the bureaucracy at the lowest possible levels and stay in their jobs long enough to acquire knowledge about federal programs. An employee might have worked in a particular industry, such as nuclear energy, and then have brought his or her preexisting knowledge to the bureaucracy as a mid-level employee. Other bureaucrats may have studied a federal policy area in academia or at policy think tanks and then may have been offered government positions. Congress, with members who chaired or served on relevant congressional committees, is a major source of cabinet secretary appointments.

Bureaucratic Culture

The fourth core component of a bureaucracy is bureaucratic culture. As one political scientist explained, "Every organization has a culture, that is, a persistent, patterned way of thinking about the central tasks of and human relationships within an organization. Culture is to an organization what personality is to an individual. Like human culture it is passed on from one generation to the next."[12] Fundamental to bureaucratic culture is the constant drive to self-perpetuate; employees in a bureaucratic organization want to preserve their jobs and their influence in the policy-making system. For this reason, bureaucratic culture can act as a gate that prevents efficiency and responsiveness in government because it can create situations in which employees in different organizations duplicate tasks, counterbalance one another's efforts, and ultimately fail to accomplish their agency's or department's mission.

At its worst, bureaucratic failure can result in a terrible loss of life, as in the case of the terrorist attacks of September 11, 2001. Many politicians,

Connections:
How important is a hierarchical decision-making process to government responsiveness and citizen equality?

Connections:
What are the causes of bureaucratic failure?

members of the media, and citizens blamed the federal agencies that oversee intelligence gathering—the Federal Bureau of Investigation (FBI), the Central Intelligence Agency (CIA), and the National Security Agency (NSA)—for failing to uncover and prevent the attacks. Each agency detected warning signs of such an attack, but the agencies did not work together. The bureaucratic culture of each agency was insular and distrustful, and lack of coordination among them resulted in an intelligence failure.[13]

To remedy the lack of coordination among the nation's national security and disaster relief agencies, Congress created the cabinet-level Department of Homeland Security in 2003. The hope was that a single large federal organization, presumably with one culture and one overarching mission, would be more effective. The new department consolidated several key units that had been operating independently, including the Coast Guard, U.S. Citizenship and Immigration Services, Customs Service, Secret Service, and Federal Emergency Management Agency, and also created new intelligence offices that would try to serve as bridges between the FBI and the CIA. However, the department was not functioning well enough to coordinate the government's response to Hurricane Katrina in 2005, where, once again, warnings of possible catastrophe—the National Weather Service and the Army Corps of Engineers had both reported that the levees might break and flood New Orleans—went unheeded. As in the case of the 9/11 attacks, key federal emergency agencies failed to coordinate with one another. In particular, the inexperience of the director and top aides of the Federal Emergency Management Agency was blamed for the loss of life and property that occurred during and after Hurricane Katrina.[14]

Other types of disasters do not involve as large a loss of life but still reflect mismanagement of risk by the government. In 2010 the Deepwater Horizon oil rig exploded in the Gulf of Mexico near Louisiana, killing eleven workers and unleashing approximately 4.9 million barrels of oil into Gulf waters.[15] The oil rig was leased by the British-owned company BP. At first it appeared that the oil spill would be contained, but the rig sank, creating complications in the cleanup effort, and the oil spill grew larger and approached U.S. shores from Florida to Texas. This bureaucratic failure began in the office of the Minerals Management Service, the agency in the Department of the Interior that gave BP permission to drill without first requiring assessments from other federal agencies, specifically the National Oceanic and Atmospheric Administration, about the risks to endangered species in the area, as well as the overall probability of an accident similar to the one that occurred.[16] This lack of coordination has proved costly to the environment and to the people who live along the shores of the Gulf of Mexico. As a result of the disaster, the chief federal bureaucrat responsible for overseeing offshore drilling resigned, as did the head of the Minerals Managements Service. President Obama responded by issuing an executive order to form a commission to investigate the failure, instituted a temporary ban on all offshore drilling projects, and addressed the nation to explain how the federal government was addressing the crisis. On October 12, 2010, he lifted the ban on offshore drilling but put greater safeguards into permit approval and safety guidelines.[17] In 2012, BP agreed to a $7.8 billion settlement with individuals who claimed economic and medical hardship as a result of the spill.[18]

Although the disasters discussed above were brought about by entirely different circumstances, a common lack of communication and expert direction exposed the inherent dangers of a flawed bureaucratic culture. If such failings are serious enough, the president may ultimately be held accountable for them.

One counteracting force to the drawbacks of bureaucratic culture and its tendency to block cooperation among agencies is bureaucratic reputation. Federal agencies want to develop good reputations for their effective implementation of federal policy. Most people take pride in the jobs they do, and bureaucrats are no different. In addition, good reputations are important to the political process, because they enhance an agency's ability to prevent interference in its decision making from outside forces, such as interest groups, Congress, and the media.[19]

Connections: What are the advantages of a government job? What are the disadvantages?

> ## Checkpoint

Can you:

- Explain how the mission of a bureaucracy shapes its goals
- State the advantages and disadvantages of the hierarchical decision-making process
- Characterize bureaucratic expertise
- Describe bureaucratic culture

The Historical Evolution of the Bureaucracy

> **How the bureaucracy developed over time**

The federal bureaucracy is as old as the nation itself, but it has evolved in ways that the Framers would barely recognize. Although they understood that the population would increase and the country's borders would expand, they could never have imagined that the federal government would have so many responsibilities and be so integral to citizens' daily lives. Over time, in tandem with economic, social, and technological developments, Congress passed laws creating new executive departments and other bureaucratic organizations. Here we trace the growth of the federal bureaucracy and the development of professional staff positions to implement federal policy.

Connections: What made the bureaucracy grow? Is it too big?

The Expansion of Executive Branch Departments

The first departments created by Congress in 1789 were State, Treasury, and War. The attorney general also sat on the president's cabinet, though he did not yet head a department. In addition, the Post Office, first created in 1775 by the Continental Congress to serve the vital function of establishing communication routes among the colonies, became a permanent government organization in 1794.[20] Through these organizations, Congress intended to fulfill the constitutional responsibilities set forth in Article I, Section 8—to regulate commerce among the states and with foreign nations, to provide for defense, to collect taxes and borrow money, and to establish post offices and post roads.

In 1849 Congress created the Department of the Interior, consolidating under its direction several organizations that regulated the sale and development of federal lands and the management of Indian affairs. The Department of Agriculture was established in 1862 in response to the importance of the agricultural sector in the nation's economy and to the hardships caused by crop and price fluctuations. To address these hardships, Congress created crop subsidies that remain in place today. In 1870 the Office of the Attorney General, first set up in 1793, was transformed into the Department of Justice, which employed lawyers to handle the legal business of the nation and managed all prosecutions and suits in which the United States had an interest.

As with the Departments of the Interior and Agriculture, the next two departments, Commerce and Labor, represented economic concerns. Congress addressed them by creating a single department in 1903, but within a decade the issues of child safety and workers' standards became so important that Congress divided the department, giving Labor its own cabinet status. This sequence was paralleled later in the twentieth century by the creation of the Department of Health, Education, and Welfare in 1953 and its subsequent division into two departments—the Department of Education, created in 1979 to coordinate programs dealing with elementary, secondary, and postsecondary education, and the Department of Health and Human Services in 1980 to oversee health care and welfare programs, such as Medicare and Medicaid. Legislation enacted in 1947 and expanded on in 1949 transformed the War Department into the Department of Defense, coordinating the Army, Navy, and Air Force. In 1965, Congress created the Department of Housing and Urban Development to oversee federal programs designed to build more affordable housing for people with low incomes and to help restore inner cities that were losing residents. The Department of Transportation was created in 1966, following a decade of interstate highway building authorized by the Highway Act of 1956. Increases in trucking also put pressure on the federal government to maintain highways and regulate business and labor practices in trucking and the air travel industry. As a direct response to the energy crisis of the early 1970s, the Department of Energy was created in 1977 to promote fuel conservation as well as the development of alternatives to fossil fuels, including nuclear, ethanol, and solar power.

In 1989 the Department of Veterans Affairs was created with the support of President George H. W. Bush (1989–93). It elevated the Veterans

Administration, which oversaw a separate federally funded health care system for veterans, to a cabinet-level department intended to give visibility and support to veterans' critical needs. Finally, as noted earlier, Congress created the Department of Homeland Security in 2003 in a direct response to the widely perceived intelligence failures associated with the terrorist attacks of 9/11.

Connections: The expansion of executive departments reflects the growth of the nation. What do you think will be the next executive department created?

Regulatory Agencies and Other Organizations

In addition to the formal cabinet departments, the executive branch contains numerous regulatory agencies and other organizations that are responsible for administering the details of laws in specific areas, as well as for overseeing the practices of businesses and individuals involved in all facets of economic and political life. Agencies such as the Federal Aviation Administration, the Food and Drug Administration, and the Federal Trade Commission serve as gateways for the federal government to respond to citizens in targeted ways and on a localized level, and they are especially important in ensuring safety and economic fairness for citizens in daily life. Among the concerns these agencies address are highway and air travel, food inspection and product labeling, and the practices of banks and the stock market.

From Patronage to the Civil Service

For the nation's first forty years, jobs in the executive branch were filled by wealthy elites who had personal political and social connections to members of Congress and the president.[21] But President Andrew Jackson (1829–37) used the executive powers of the president to appoint people from wider social and economic backgrounds to federal positions. He also demanded political loyalty from federal employees; to get a job in the Jackson administration, one had to be an active political supporter of Jackson and the Democratic Party. This arrangement, in which the politician appoints employees who pledge loyalty to him, is generally referred to as the patronage system. Jackson's political enemies called it the spoils system, charging Jackson with awarding jobs to political friends in the manner of the saying "To the victor belong the spoils."

For most of the nineteenth century, Congress and the president shared the patronage power; the president allowed members of Congress to recommend individuals for government posts. With each election in which a different party assumed office, there was a large turnover in staff. The federal patronage system allowed politicians to manipulate federal programs and positions for political and private gain.[22]

As the nation grew larger and the economy more complex, the federal bureaucracy needed more expertise and stability. The assassination of President James A. Garfield in 1881 by an individual who had sought, but had not received, a federal job caused a public outcry against patronage in

Pendleton Act:
1883 act that established a merit- and performance-based system for federal employment.

Civil Service Commission:

Created by the Pendleton Act to administer entrance exams for the federal civil service and set standards for promotion based on merit.

Connections: How did the merit-based civil service improve the job performance of federal employees?

merit system:
System of employment under which employees are chosen and promoted based on merit.

civil service: *The non-partisan federal workforce employed to carry out government programs and policies.*

political appointees:
Federal employees appointed by the president with the explicit task of carrying out his political and partisan agenda.

career civil servants: *Federal employees who are hired through a merit-based system to implement federal programs and who are expected to be neutral in their political affiliations.*

government employment. Although the assassin had had no direct contact with Garfield, he evidently held the president responsible for his failure to secure a federal job. In response, Congress passed the **Pendleton Act**, which was signed into law by President Chester A. Arthur (1881–85) on January 16, 1883. It was the first of the reforms that slowly changed the federal bureaucracy from a corrupt and partisan insider organization to a neutral, policy-based organization.[23]

The Pendleton Act created the **Civil Service Commission** to administer entrance exams for the federal civil service and set job requirements and promotion standards based on a **merit system** and performance, not political affiliation. At first the civil service covered only a small fraction of federal jobs; the rest were controlled primarily by powerful members of Congress who used their influence to direct federal jobs to loyal supporters. But over time, successive presidents wrested more control over the federal bureaucracy from Congress by issuing executive orders to classify a greater percentage of jobs as merit-based and as part of the **civil service**. By 1897, 50 percent of federal jobs were covered by the civil service, and by 1951, 88 percent of federal jobs were civil service jobs.[24] The remaining federal employees are **political appointees** appointed by the president to carry out his political and partisan agenda within the federal policy-making system.

Career Civil Service

Career civil servants are nonpolitical personnel who must pass an exam to secure their jobs and compete on an equal playing field with anyone else who has the same credentials. For the number of executive branch employees, and other members of the federal workforce, see Figure 13.2. The vast majority of executive branch employees are located in the metropolitan Washington, D.C., area.[25] In general, federal civil service employees fall into three categories: blue-collar, white-collar, and senior executive positions. Blue-collar jobs consist of "craft, repair, operator, and laborer jobs," and employees in this category are under the Federal Wage System, which sets pay levels associated with specific jobs.[26] White-collar workers fill a wide range of professional positions ranging from clerks and administrative assistants to engineers, informational technology specialists, and lawyers. These types of jobs are governed by the General Schedule (GS), which has fifteen grades or levels of pay assigned according to level of responsibility and work experience. In 2012, for example, the entry-level pay was $17,803 for GS 1 and $99,628 for GS 15.[27] Executive-level management employees are governed by the Senior Executive Service guidelines, which generally follow the GS pay scale. All federal employees are subject to performance evaluations and may receive gradual raises, promotions up the career ladder, and incentive and merit bonuses for outstanding job performance.

Some departments and agencies are staffed by career employees who are not in the civil service but nonetheless operate under similar structures. For example, the State Department oversees a corps of diplomats known as Foreign Service officers who are sent all over the world to manage U.S. embassies and consulates. To join the Foreign Service, one must meet certain qualifications and pass an entrance exam, similar to the procedure for entering the civil service generally. However, the Foreign Service has its own pay scale and promotion criteria. As mentioned earlier in the chapter, there is a wide range of areas in which the federal government offers employment opportunities, and each department and agency tries to recruit qualified young people.

Due to the specific nature of their responsibilities, the CIA and the FBI also have their own career tracks with separate requirements. So do the Library of Congress, the Smithsonian Institution, and the National Institutes of Health. These personnel work under merit systems; they are hired, retained, and promoted through a standardized system of performance review, and politics are not officially considered. Although politics may permeate any workplace, the civil service is designed to protect employees from partisanship, and employees are expected to be objective as they carry out their job responsibilities. Civil servants remain in their positions from one administration to the next, and they cannot be asked to resign for partisan reasons.

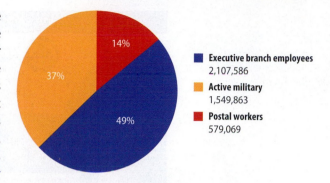

FIGURE 13.2 Distribution of Federal Government Workforce, 2012.

Federal employment is divided into several categories: executive branch, active military forces, and the U.S. Postal Service.

Source: The White House, Office of Management and Budget, *Analytical Perspectives, Budget of the U.S. Government FY 2013* (Washington, D.C.: U.S. Government Printing Office, 2012), Table 11.2, Total Federal Employment, p. 120, accessed June 27, 2012, http://www.whitehouse.gov/omb/budget/Analytical_Perspectives.

Political Appointees

Political appointees, unlike civil servants, get their jobs because they are members of the same party that controls the executive branch, they have connections to politically powerful people, or they have served in a prior presidential administration. Political appointees can occupy a wide range of positions, from cabinet secretary to commissioner to administrator. Although it is uncommon, political appointees can also come from the opposition party, especially when they have particular expertise in a policy area or a president wants continuity in department leadership early in his administration. This was the case with Secretary of Defense Robert Gates, who served in the George W. Bush administration and was asked to stay on by President Barack Obama; Gates served until June 2011 and was replaced by Leon Panetta, who had been serving as director of the Central Intelligence Agency. No matter

WWW.CAREERS.STATE.GOV

WWW.FBIJOBS.GOV

Federal departments and agencies present career opportunities for individuals and make that information known on their websites. The websites of the U.S. Department of State and the Federal Bureau of Investigation display various routes for employment and different types of jobs.

Source: U.S. Department of State, "Careers Representing America," accessed June 27, 2012, http://www.careers.state.gov; Federal Bureau of Investigation, "Careers," accessed June 27, 2012, http://www.fbijobs.gov.

their personal views, political appointees are expected to carry out the president's policy agenda.[28]

Political appointees can come from a variety of backgrounds. Typically they are members of the president's inner circle or campaign team, have served as congressional committee chairs, or have served in former presidential administrations. In some cases, they come from the private sector. There are advantages and disadvantages to the president in choosing people from any of these backgrounds. Sometimes a president's trusted campaign advisers are not talented administrators; sometimes members of the private sector find government work too frustrating. Presidents try to make the best choices possible, but occasionally a cabinet secretary is replaced during a presidential term, especially if he or she has become a lightning rod for a broader controversy or an unpopular position. When a president is reelected for a second term, he customarily requests the resignations of his entire cabinet and then chooses which resignations to accept and which to reject. This custom gives presidents the opportunity to change policy direction and bring fresh perspectives into the executive branch at the start of a second term.

Top-level political appointees require Senate confirmation, and that number has risen from 73 under Franklin Delano Roosevelt (1933–45) to 499 for President Obama.[29] But there are hundreds of other jobs that are considered political appointments.

In 1978 President Jimmy Carter (1977–81) created the **Senior Executive Service (SES)**, experienced personnel who can be assigned by the president to senior management positions throughout the federal bureaucracy. For SES positions, the president generally chooses career civil service employees who have shown expertise in their jobs, but he also has the authority to bring in individuals from the private sector. The SES provides a layer of administration over federal programs that is directed by the president, infusing the federal bureaucracy with political perspectives that can clash with the goal of objective implementation of federal policy. Since 1980 the total number of political appointees has averaged about three thousand.[30] Although that may not seem like a high number compared to the total federal workforce, the category of political appointee has been used successfully by many presidents to expand their direct influence within the bureaucracy.

Private-Sector Contract Workers

In addition to civil service employees and political appointees, the federal government hires thousands of individuals and companies from the private sector to administer programs and carry out tasks associated with specific policies. These companies can range from nonprofit community organizations, to midsize security firms, to large health care conglomerates. They are not under the direct control of the federal bureaucracy, but they carry out

Connections: What are two gateways to becoming a presidential appointee?

Connections: How much authority should the president have over executive branch employees?

Senior Executive Service (SES): *Senior management personnel in the federal government appointed by the president.*

crucial tasks for it. During the administration of William Jefferson (Bill) Clinton (1993–2001), Vice President Albert Gore Jr. took on the job of revamping the bureaucracy. His Reinventing Government plan sought to reduce the complexity and size of the federal bureaucracy by contracting out the provision of key services and administration of federal programs. Other presidents had made similar efforts, but President Clinton was the first Democrat since the 1930s to suggest that some of the services provided by the federal government could be more efficiently done by the private sector. In addition, incentive programs were put in place to reward federal civil servants for efficiency, in the same way that employees in the private sector receive bonuses.

President George W. Bush continued this trend of contracting out the performance of government tasks to private companies. For example, during the Iraq War, the federal government contracted with major construction companies to work with the Army Corps of Engineers to rebuild war-torn areas of Iraq. It also contracted with private security firms to provide additional security for U.S. diplomatic and civilian personnel in both Iraq and Afghanistan. At home, much of the actual administration and provision of benefits under the Medicare and Medicaid programs is carried out by large private health maintenance organizations (HMOs).

There are costs and benefits to the privatization of federal services. One concern is that the federal government does not have close **oversight** over the quality, experience, or job performance of the employees who work in the private companies. Although company employees have an incentive to do their jobs well, fraud, waste, and abuse can go undetected for years because of the lack of direct federal oversight. Sometimes the federal government ends up paying more for the provision of services through private contractors than it would if federal employees administered the program directly. The benefit of using private firms is that they do not technically count as additional federal employees, so when they are used, the overall size of the federal workforce appears smaller. In some cases, it is more efficient to use a private firm that has expertise in an area to provide a service at a lower cost than to use permanent employees and achieve the same outcome.

Bureaucrats and Politics

The civil service was created to protect federal employees from partisan politics, but by 1939 it had become clear that political influence was still rampant throughout the bureaucracy, not only at the federal level but at state and local levels as well. In response, Congress passed the Hatch Act, which prohibited government employees from working on political campaigns, using their positions to solicit campaign donations, or promoting candidates for

Connections: Are there government services that should not be contracted out to the private sector?

oversight: *Powers of Congress to monitor how the executive branch implements the laws.*

elected office. This mandated separation of politics from the bureaucracy was designed to eliminate the last vestiges of patronage. It took pressure off bureaucrats, who could tell campaigning politicians that they were prohibited from engaging in certain political activities. In 1993 the Hatch Act Reform Amendments (HARA) significantly loosened restrictions on political activities by government employees as long as the activities occurred while they were off duty. Now political appointees are explicitly allowed to engage in political activities on behalf of the president so long as the costs for these activities are not paid with tax dollars. However, bans on political activities remain in force for employees in law enforcement and intelligence agencies as well as for employees of the Federal Election Commission, which monitors federal campaign activities.[31]

Conflict between civil servants, who take a programmatic approach and aim to make programs work efficiently over the long term, and political appointees, who want to carry out the president's partisan agenda while the president is in office, was addressed by the Civil Service Reform Act of 1978. President Jimmy Carter proposed the act to encourage cooperation between political appointees and civil servants and to make sure that each was held accountable for decision making. The act created the Office of Personnel Management (OPM) to oversee both categories of federal employees. The OPM, under the direct control of the Executive Office of the President, can expand the number of political appointees and reduce the number of career civil servants. With more politically appointed personnel in the bureaucracy, presidents assert greater control over how federal policy is formulated and implemented. To preserve the essential political neutrality of the career civil service, the act also created the Merit Systems Protection Board, which ensures that the protections afforded to career civil servants through the merit system remain in place.

Nevertheless, bureaucrats do face conflicting pressures when Congress is controlled by one political party and the executive branch is controlled by the other political party, a condition known as divided government. Under divided government, federal bureaucrats are frequently caught in the middle because they are pressured by Congress to implement policy one way and by political appointees in their agencies to implement policy in a different way. Objectively, policy is supposed to be implemented in a manner that will produce the most efficient and responsive results, but trying to please two powerful bosses can result in inefficient and ineffective policy. Fortunately, the career nature of the civil service, with its built-in protections against political pressure, helps mitigate the negative consequences of divided government. In addition, because career civil servants frequently outlast presidents and some members of Congress, they have a longer-term perspective on the impact of their decisions.

Connections: Should there be a gate that blocks government employees from engaging in certain kinds of political activities? Would such a gate compromise citizen equality?

Connections: Why was the civil service designed so that employees remain in place despite turnover in the presidency and in Congress?

At the same time, bureaucrats tend to form long-term working relationships with members of Congress and even with interest group lobbyists in the policy areas in which they specialize. In Chapter 8, Interest Groups, we explored the concepts of iron triangles (see Figure 8.2 on page 256) and issue networks, both of which are used to describe these relationships. Bureaucrats want to maximize their longevity as administrators of federal programs, so they try to be as responsive as possible to the other members of the network, and each member constantly shares information with the others.[32] Critics of iron triangles and issue networks argue that they contribute to the inefficiency of the federal government because they sustain programs that may be duplicative or outdated, and they may encourage corruption within the government. However, given the 24-7 news cycle and the amount of government information available on the Internet, the public, the media, and watchdog groups are able to monitor such relationships, and they are now more transparent than ever before. Nevertheless, iron triangles are another indication that, despite the protections of a merit-based civil service, politics will always influence, to some degree, the bureaucrats who implement federal policy.

Checkpoint

Can you:

- ☐ Equate the establishment of cabinet departments with developments in the U.S. economy and society
- ☐ Describe what regulatory agencies do
- ☐ Explain how and why the civil service evolved
- ☐ Survey the types of jobs career civil servants perform
- ☐ Recall why political appointees have increased in number over time
- ☐ Explain the growth of the use of private-sector contract workers
- ☐ Describe how Congress has attempted to protect the bureaucracy from partisan politics

Accountability and Responsiveness in the Bureaucracy

> **How the bureaucracy is both accountable and responsive, and how it can fail**

Typically, the power of the vote in regularly scheduled elections is used to monitor elected officials, but there are no ways for the average voter to register an opinion about the collective job performance of employees of the federal bureaucracy. Because the bureaucracy varies by type of agency, size of agency, and type of employee, it is difficult for citizens to evaluate job performance and hold bureaucrats collectively accountable for their actions. At the individual level, the job performance of civil servants is reviewed by supervisors at regular intervals, and political appointees can be removed by the president if he is unhappy with their work. But democracy requires that citizens be able to hold their entire government accountable for the policies it implements, and there is no readily available mechanism for the public to hold civil servants accountable for their job performance. There are, however, certain

Connections:
Is it easy or hard for citizens to hold the bureaucracy accountable for its actions? Why?

standards and procedures that Congress has put in place to hold the bureaucracy accountable and encourage responsiveness. Legal challenges to regulations are another means by which the bureaucracy can be held accountable.

The Roles of the Legislative and Judicial Branches

Congress contributes to the accountability and responsiveness of the bureaucracy through its oversight of implementation and its so-called power of the purse. Congressional committees with jurisdiction in a set of issue areas can request that agency and cabinet officials testify before them to explain the way they implement programs under their jurisdiction.[33] For example, when officials at the General Services Administration spent more than $820,000 on a conference in Las Vegas in 2010, their own inspector general raised questions. Members of Congress followed up by calling officials in to testify about this inappropriate use of taxpayer dollars. As a result of congressional inquiry and public outrage, two top GSA deputies who attended the conference were forced to resign their positions.[34] More striking was the fact that the chief administrator of GSA, who had not been involved in the conference, chose to resign because she accepted responsibility for failing to oversee her employees. When Congress exercises its oversight power, and an agency becomes viewed as incompetent, it risks budget and personnel cuts, being rolled into a larger agency, or being dissolved altogether.

Another way Congress can hold the bureaucracy accountable is through its powers to authorize and appropriate. Authorization and appropriation hearings give Congress a chance to evaluate federal agencies and to withhold or reduce funds if there are dissatisfactions. Agency heads are fully aware of this congressional power, and it is a key reason that they take congressional opinion into account when they implement federal programs. Congressional influence of this type thus serves as a gateway for the public—which elects members of Congress—to hold the bureaucracy accountable for its actions.

The judicial branch, too, helps hold the bureaucracy accountable. The courts can serve as effective monitors of implementation because they are a gateway for groups adversely affected by a federal regulation to argue their case against it. Typically, the courts intervene when there is a dispute between Congress and the executive on the interpretation of a law, and not when the two branches agree.

Efficiency and Transparency

One of the biggest challenges a bureaucratic organization faces is carrying out its mission efficiently while maintaining transparency to the American public. A chronic complaint about the bureaucracy is that it is slow. Yet issuing rules and regulations takes so long because the process solicits input from all sectors, including members of Congress, businesses and industries that are being regulated, and average citizens with a stake in the issue. The government can justify the slowness of the decision-making process on the grounds that it considers many points of view in implementing policy. Unfortunately, inclusiveness comes at the expense of efficiency.

In addition, the issues related to food and drug safety, transportation safety, working conditions, and antiterrorism measures can be matters of life and death. Citizens expect the federal government to act in their best interests, but such issues require caution, and caution can lead to delay. On the other hand, if the government fails to make its practices transparent and does not consider all the implications of its decisions, citizens may lose trust in government.

Connections:
Why is transparency important in a democracy?

These concerns were part of the rationale behind a series of bills designed to open up the workings of the federal bureaucracy to the general public. In 1966 the Freedom of Information Act established a procedure by which ordinary citizens can directly request documents and reports from the federal government by paying a nominal fee, so long as the documents are not classified. Access to a classified document or report is automatically restricted to federal employees who hold security clearances and have a legitimate need to see the document. In times of military conflict, such as during the Vietnam and Iraq Wars, presidents typically restrict access to public documents relating to war efforts. In response to the mistrust of the federal government that grew out of the Vietnam War and the Watergate scandal, in 1976 Congress enacted the Government in the Sunshine Act, which tried to increase transparency by requiring government agencies to hold open forums to allow the public to comment on their decisions, regulations, and performance.

To highlight the tension between efficiency and transparency, let us consider the Food and Drug Administration. One of the agency's most important responsibilities is monitoring pharmaceutical development from the initial testing of drugs to final approval for widespread use. Even before a drug is submitted to the FDA for approval, pharmaceutical companies have conducted three phases of clinical trials—experiments and applications on human subjects that measure the efficacy and safety of the drug. If the drug shows promise, the company submits a New Drug Application to the FDA. If agency employees agree that the clinical trial results are reliable, the FDA forms a review panel whose members have different types of expertise about the potential effects of the drug. The panel serves as a gateway for nonemployees of the agency to participate in the drug approval process. Members of the panel consider all the results of the trials and offer opinions as to whether the drug can be approved for sale. Ultimately, the FDA makes the final decision.

This process illustrates the trade-off between efficiency and transparency.[35] When a new drug is effective against disease, the public wants access to that drug as soon as possible. However, every new drug has unforeseen side effects, some of which may not be visible in the short term, so the more information the FDA has, the more likely the drugs it approves for the market will be safe. Forming review committees with members from outside the agency is one way of collecting a wide range of information about the possible impacts of the drug. Yet this process is time-consuming; the more participants, the more slowly it moves. Like many federal agencies, then, the FDA must weigh the cost of efficient decision making against the cost of approving a drug before it has been thoroughly tested.

At times the FDA has approved a drug that has later proved to have unacceptably dangerous side effects. The agency has then reversed the approval and issued a public health advisory warning of the side effects. When the FDA issues such an advisory to the public, the manufacturer usually withdraws the drug from the market.

The issue of transparency is especially highlighted when the federal government enacts large spending bills, such as the stimulus bill that President Obama signed into law in February 2009. The nearly $800 billion bill authorized a combination of spending and tax cuts, including funds for infrastructure, education, extension of unemployment benefits, and tax breaks for homeowners and businesses. The challenge confronting the federal bureaucracy in implementing this bill was getting the funds to recipients as quickly as possible while at the same time enforcing federal program rules and being clear about where the money was going.[36] Critics of the bill pointed to the huge amount of money involved and questioned the practical effect that the stimulus funds could have on the economy because of the length of time it would take to distribute the money according to standard federal practices. President Obama responded by saying that he would consider revamping standard bureaucratic practices to streamline the process of distributing the funds. However, such streamlining could reduce accountability and transparency. President Obama, aware of the importance of transparency to voters, created a website (http://www.recovery.gov) that pinpointed how and where the funds were distributed, down to a block on a street.

> **Connections:** What is more important, transparency or efficiency?

Whistleblowing

Most federal employees are careful, dedicated, and hardworking. However, as in all organizations run by human beings, there can be inefficiency, error, abuse of power, and corruption. Each federal agency has an Office of Inspector General (IG) that monitors the activities of the agency's employees. But unless a wrongdoing is identified and brought to the IG's attention, it frequently goes unpunished.

To encourage more candid disclosure of wrongdoing in federal agencies, Congress passed the Whistleblower Protection Act in 1989 to protect **whistleblowers**, government employees who report mismanagement,

 **whistle-blowers:** *Employees who report mismanagement, corruption, or illegal activity within their agencies.*

Connections: Are private contractors working for the government likely to be whistleblowers? Why or why not?

corruption, or illegal activity within their agencies.[37] Before the passage of this act, whistleblowers had no real protection against reprisals from their colleagues, especially from those at higher levels of authority. The act established grievance and appeal procedures for employees who believe they have been retaliated against for reporting wrongdoing in their agencies. In 2010, Congress extended protections to employees in the financial services industry who act as whistleblowers.

Bureaucratic Failure

Whether whistleblowers come from inside or outside the federal government, it is up to the federal government to respond to them in an effective fashion. Unfortunately, there are serious cases in which a government agency has failed to respond. What happens when an entire agency fails to accomplish its mission? The Securities and Exchange Commission (SEC) did just that in the case of the fraudulent activities of investor and financial manager Bernard Madoff.

One of the realities of federal management and oversight is that a federal agency or a congressional committee needs to be aware of a problem in order to address it. The Madoff scandal is an example of bureaucratic and congressional oversight after the fact. In December 2008 Madoff confessed to engaging in fraudulent investment practices over the span of thirty years, costing individual investors (many of whom were retirees who lost their life savings), financial management firms, and charitable foundations an estimated $50 billion. Simply put, Madoff collected money, known as ==principal,== from the investors, but at some point he stopped investing the money in real companies. Although he paid dividends (profits from investments) to his clients, the money came from new clients, not from investments; to maintain the scheme, he had to continue to recruit wealthy investors. When the financial crisis hit in 2008, some of his wealthy investors demanded large sums of their principal back, but Madoff did not have the money to return to them. Madoff confessed his scheme to his sons, who reported him to the authorities; he was subsequently tried and convicted of financial fraud and sentenced to 150 years in prison.

Connections: What can be done about lack of responsiveness by the bureaucracy?

MARIO TAMA/GETTY IMAGES

In June 2009, 71-year-old financial investment manager Bernard Madoff was sentenced to 150 years in prison for fraud. His financial scam was estimated to have cost investors close to $50 billion.

Madoff's investment activities should have been more closely monitored by the SEC, which was accused of not doing its job properly. The SEC had been warned about Madoff repeatedly over a ten-year period by Harry Markopolos, an investment fund manager. Markopolos contacted a Boston regional SEC officer about Madoff's scheme in 2000, after he tried to replicate Madoff's stated earnings and could not find any sound way to do so. Over the next six years, Markopolos actively tried to get the SEC to act, but the agency did not start an inquiry into Madoff's dealings until 2006. Even then, following interviews of Madoff and some of his business associates, SEC lawyers found no wrongdoing and dropped the case.[38]

When the House Banking Committee questioned SEC commissioners about why they had acted as a gate against investigating Madoff and, more important, why they found no wrongdoing, they had little to say. As a general explanation, they said that the SEC was understaffed and ill-equipped to investigate such a massive fraud. In a hearing held on February 4, 2009, Congressman Gary Ackerman (D-N.Y.) said the following to the SEC commissioners:

MARK WILSON/GETTY IMAGES

A private citizen turned whistleblower, Harry Markopolos tried to inform the SEC that Bernard Madoff was a fraud and that his financial dealings were unsound, but the agency did not act on his warnings. On February 4, 2009, Markopolos testified during a House Financial Services Committee hearing.

> *Your mission you said was to protect investors and detect fraud quickly. How'd that work out? What went wrong? . . . You have single-handedly diffused the American public of any sense of confidence in our financial markets if you are the watchdogs. You have totally and thoroughly failed in your mission. Don't you get it? . . . You forfeited your right to investigate by not doing it. Certainly not doing it properly or adequately. . . . What happened here? That's a question.*[39]

How could such major financial dealings go unnoticed, even with information provided over time by a very determined private citizen? The SEC's failure to monitor and prevent such fraud and the lack of congressional intervention until it was too late illustrate the limits of the federal bureaucracy as well as of congressional oversight.

The dual responsibilities of accountability and responsiveness in the federal bureaucracy require the bureaucracy to do its job well enough to protect citizens from physical and financial harm. Unfortunately, the American people are so familiar with the failures of the federal bureaucracy that its successes are overlooked. The fact that 314 million people live in relative peace and security; experience safe and reasonable working conditions; trust that the medications they take are well tested; travel on trains, buses, and planes without incident; drink clean water; and receive their mail every day is a testament to the ways in which the federal bureaucracy meets its obligations. It is up to the voters to hold their elected officials—in Congress as well as the president—accountable for the performance of the federal bureaucracy.

Checkpoint

Can you:

☐ Explain ways the legislative and judicial branches can check the bureaucracy

☐ Examine how the need for bureaucratic efficiency and transparency can counteract each other

☐ Describe what it means to be a whistleblower

☐ Relate the consequences of bureaucratic failure

The Bureaucracy and Public Policy: The Regulatory Process and Oversight of the Financial Sector

The federal bureaucracy has grown, in part, because Congress has continually responded to changes in the economy and society that have required government action. But what happens if Congress fails to respond adequately to developments in a policy area? The absence of regulation of an industry or policy area is itself a type of policy, because the government is essentially allowing activity to continue without oversight. The deep recession that began in 2008 revealed the consequences of Congress's inadequate regulation of new developments in banks and financial markets. This section examines the events that led to the recession, the legislation promoted by the president and passed by Congress to address the problem, and the process by which the bureaucracy has been trying to implement the law. For background on the policy-making process, see Chapter 1, and especially Figure 1.4, which provides a broad overview of this process, from problem identification through policy proposals to implementation. There we identified key stakeholders in the policy process, including the president, Congress, political parties, interest groups, and, of course, voters. Here we get more specific by tracking how problems that are identified generate solutions that are enacted into law and then put into practice.

The Onset of the Financial Crisis and Recession

Several policy developments converged to cause the recession. From 1998 to 2007, the federal government deregulated the banking and investment industries. At the same time, the Federal Reserve, the primary organization responsible for controlling the flow of money[40] (see Chapter 12), lowered interest rates, and Congress set a priority on homeownership by encouraging banks to make mortgage loans available to low-income families. As a consequence, many people who did not have the personal savings typically required for a mortgage were able to purchase homes. Loans made to lower-income individuals—called "sub-prime" loans—were risky because if these people encountered any economic hardship at all, their ability to pay their monthly mortgage payments would likely be compromised. Nonetheless, banks began packaging these loans and selling them as investment opportunities. In other

Connections: Should most people own their own homes? Should government policy promote homeownership?

words, instead of holding onto the loans and receiving the interest, the banks sold groups of them to investors who hoped to receive the interest on the loans as return on their investments.

This type of investment was a new invention, and Congress, not recognizing its importance, did not take steps to regulate it. Serious problems arose in 2008 when the economy started to falter, and individuals could not sustain their mortgage payments. At first, sub-prime loans made up a large share of mortgage defaults. As the recession worsened, however, individuals at all income levels—some of whom had lost their jobs—failed to keep up with their mortgage payments and went into foreclosure, often losing their homes as a consequence. With so many people defaulting, investors' returns on investment disappeared, and with so many properties foreclosed, property values declined. As a result, major banking institutions lost billions of dollars and became less willing to make loans for housing, businesses, and consumer purchases, including automobile loans. This sad series of events deepened the recession.

Connections: What caused the recession that began in 2008? Who or what was to blame?

Responses by the President and Congress

The breadth of the U.S. financial crisis was staggering, and elected officials, policy makers, and businesses all feared that the economy would sink into depression if steps were not taken to intervene. In 2008 alone, at least 2.3 million properties were put into foreclosure proceedings, an increase of 81 percent from the previous year; Nevada, Florida, and California led the nation in the number of foreclosures.[41] Lehman Brothers, founded in 1850 and the nation's fourth largest bank, collapsed in September 2008 under the weight of bad investments and mortgage defaults; its 25,000 employees were suddenly unemployed.[42] The nation had not seen this rapid an economic descent since the Great Depression.

The Troubled Asset Relief Program.

In late fall 2008, President George W. Bush and Congress responded by enacting the Emergency Economic Stabilization Act, which broadened the federal government's powers to support and regulate the banking industry. The act created the Troubled Asset Relief Program (TARP), commonly called the "bank bailout." It authorized $700 billion to subsidize banks by purchasing packaged loans that had lost their value because of consumer defaults. The condition that the government imposed on this rescue was that banks had to resume lending to businesses and individuals and to repay the government loans with interest. When President Obama took office in January 2009, more than $300 billion of TARP money had been set aside to be distributed to banks, but lending had not loosened up and members of Congress and voters began to wonder whether taxpayer money was being spent wisely. When the public learned that several of the companies receiving bailout money had given multimillion-dollar bonuses to their employees and continued to plan lavish retreats and purchase corporate jets, anger at banks and financial institutions—symbolized by Wall Street—intensified.

Public pressure built quickly on Congress and the president to hold the banks accountable, and Congress reacted by holding oversight hearings in both the House and Senate Banking Committees. On February 11, 2009, the House Banking Committee asked the chief executive officers of eight of the nation's largest banks that received TARP money to come together and explain how they had used the funds to increase lending and dispose of bad assets. It is this type of forum that Congress uses to exercise its oversight function, and it was all the more important to do so at this time because the government was deciding whether to distribute more funds to banks. Persuaded that it was necessary to aid the economy, the Obama administration and Congress agreed to continue the program. Ultimately, supporters of TARP argued that it was successful in warding off greater financial disaster, helping the economy recover, and returning a profit to the federal government. As of 2012, the Treasury Department revised the costs associated with TARP: $245 billion had been distributed, $230 billion had been repaid, and the government made $34 billion in profits from the program.[43]

The Making Home Affordable Program.

As part of the financial recovery effort, in March 2009 the federal government created a $75 billion loan modification program, Making Home Affordable (MHA).[44] The program, administered jointly by the Treasury and the Housing and Urban Development departments, aimed to educate struggling homeowners about viable options for keeping their homes. These included loan modifications for homeowners who were employed and a separate program for the unemployed that lowered mortgage payments or postponed them for at least a year.[45]

Making Home Affordable was the government's first step in protecting consumers from the market forces that were buffeting the financial sector. It did not, however, change financial regulations or implement new ones to stop the risky financial instruments that caused the problem in the first place. Thus President Obama and the Democratic Congress took an additional step.

The Dodd-Frank Act and the Consumer Financial Protection Bureau.

To protect consumers from bearing the brunt of actions by banks and financial institutions in the future, in 2010 Congress and President Obama worked to pass comprehensive financial reform. The Dodd-Frank Wall Street Reform and Consumer Protection Act passed the House on June 30, 2010, with a vote of 237–192.[46] Less than a month later Dodd-Frank passed the Senate with a vote of 60–39.[47] This legislation made a number of important changes designed to place the banking industry under greater federal

regulatory process: *System of rules that govern how a law is implemented; also called the rule-making process.*

Administrative Procedures Act (APA): *1946 act that provides a consistent blueprint for all federal organizations to issue regulations.*

supervision and protect against future financial crises. It prohibits banks and other companies from engaging in unethical lending practices, such as offering high-interest mortgages and credit cards to individuals who do not have incomes or assets to afford them. It requires banks to set aside large sums of money to guard against losses from risky or highly unprofitable investments. Additionally, the law requires large banks to organize their investment practices as separate entities apart from their more traditional banking functions, so if investments, such as derivatives and credit-default swaps, go bad, the entire bank will not be put at risk.[48] All these provisions illustrate the way the president and Congress as institutions try to adapt to the invention of new products, services, and economic practices. Opponents of regulation, however, including major banks and financial institutions affected by the legislation, argued that the new law interferes with the free market, and, during a recession, could slow down recovery.[49]

The law also created a new Consumer Financial Protection Bureau, an independent bureau within the Federal Reserve, to ensure that banking and credit-related businesses operate in a way that is transparent and fair to consumers and businesses alike through enforcement and consumer education.[50] The bureau is still very new, and in 2012 regulations designed to activate new consumer protections had just begun to be issued.

The Regulatory Process and the Implementation of the Dodd-Frank Act

For a law such as Dodd-Frank to be implemented, there must be rules to instruct policy makers, government officials, and businesses in the private sector. The formal responsibility for policy implementation falls to the bureaucracy in what is commonly called the **regulatory process** (see Figure 13.3). The current framework for the regulatory process has its foundation in the **Administrative Procedures Act (APA)** that Congress passed in 1946 to provide a consistent blueprint for all federal agencies in the issuing of regulations. In 1947 the *Attorney General's Manual on the Administrative Procedure Act* was issued to explain APA guidelines. Although it has been modified over the years, the APA is still the predominant blueprint for the federal regulatory process.

The federal government typically issues regulations when a law is first enacted and when a new circumstance or policy need arises that requires updates to the way the law is implemented. One such circumstance might be a change in the political control of the White House. Frequently, an incoming president of a different party issues new regulations to reverse the previous administration's policies. More commonly, a new president instructs federal agencies and the OMB to revise existing regulations to better reflect his policy preferences. The president can also influence policy by issuing signing

Connections:
Why is the regulatory process so complicated?

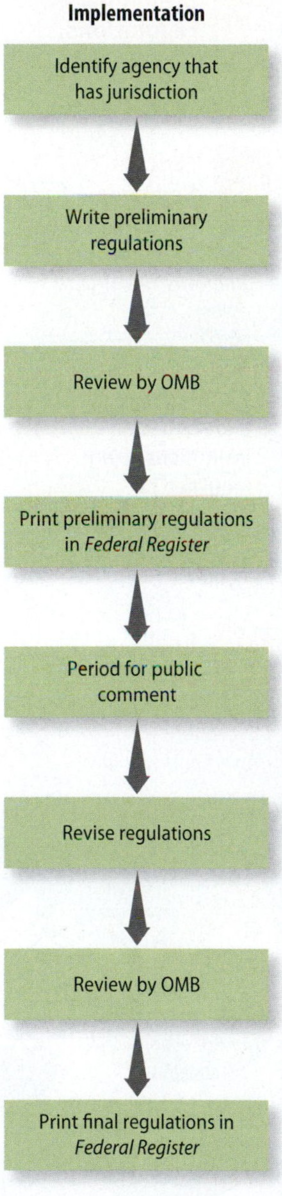

Implementation

Identify agency that has jurisdiction

Write preliminary regulations

Review by OMB

Print preliminary regulations in *Federal Register*

Period for public comment

Revise regulations

Review by OMB

Print final regulations in *Federal Register*

FIGURE 13.3 The Regulatory Process.

© CENGAGE LEARNING

statements that reflect his interpretation of what the law should accomplish (see Chapter 12).

The bureaucracy makes these rules, using the regulatory process that begins with identifying the agency that has jurisdiction. In the case of the Dodd-Frank Act, some of the regulations are (and will be) created by the Consumer Financial Protection Bureau, while others may be given to other agencies such as the Federal Reserve or cabinet departments such as Housing and Urban Development (HUD). The agency in charge will then offer **preliminary regulations** during which the political appointees of the agency will determine whether they are in line with the president's policy views. Although the bureaucracy is theoretically supposed to be insulated from direct political pressure, the reality is that the president's policies are considered during this process.

When there is some agreement on the content of the preliminary regulations, they are submitted to the Office of Information and Regulatory Affairs (OIRA) within the OMB for approval to be printed in the *Federal Register*, the official published record of all executive branch rules, regulations, and orders. As noted previously, the OMB must review all regulations before they take effect. When preliminary regulations appear in the *Federal Register*, a period for public comment is defined (typically outlined in the originating legislation) ranging from thirty to ninety days. During this period, ordinary citizens, interest groups, and relevant industries and businesses can submit their opinions to the agency about the regulations. In addition, the agency or its local affiliate can hold public hearings in locations across the country to solicit opinions on the regulations. These public hearings were a particularly important part of the regulatory process for the Dodd-Frank Act. The Federal Reserve allows for a public comment period for a minimum of sixty days, and as of December 2011, it had held more than three hundred meetings with outside parties and consumer groups in order to solicit a wide range of opinions on the regulations issued to begin the implementation of the act.[51]

Based on all the responses it receives, the responsible agency—in this case, the Consumer Financial Protection Bureau and the Federal Reserve—revises the preliminary draft regulations and issues **final regulations**. These are once again sent to the OMB and then are published in the *Federal Register* thirty days in advance of taking formal effect. Once the final regulations are issued, the program is officially ready to be implemented (see Figure 13.4).

preliminary regulations: *Draft instructions for implementing a law.*

Federal Register: Official *published record of all executive branch rules, regulations, and orders.*

Connections:
Should the financial institutions being regulated be permitted to influence public policy?

final regulations: *Final version of the instructions for implementing a law.*

Federal Register /Vol. 77, No. 64 /Tuesday, April 3, 2012 /Notices P.**20011**

BUREAU OF CONSUMER FINANCIAL PROTECTION

[Docket No. CFPB–2012–0014]
RIN 3170–AA06

Fair Credit Reporting Act Disclosures

AGENCY: Bureau of Consumer Financial Protection.

ACTION: Notice regarding charges for certain disclosures under the Fair Credit Reporting Act.

SUMMARY: The Bureau of Consumer Financial Protection ("Bureau") announces that the ceiling on allowable charges under Section 612(f) of the Fair Credit Reporting Act ("FCRA") will increase from $11.00 to $11.50 effective April 3, 2012. The Bureau is required to increase the $8.00 amount referred to in Section 612(f)(1)(A)(i) of the FCRA on January 1 of each year, based proportionally on changes in the Consumer Price Index ("CPI"), with fractional changes rounded to the nearest fifty cents. The CPI increased 40.75 percent between September 1997, the date the FCRA amendments took effect, and September 2011. This increase in the CPI, and the requirement that any increase be rounded to the nearest fifty cents, results in a maximum allowable charge of $11.50.

DATES: Effective April 3, 2012.

Fair Credit Reporting Act Disclosures

FIGURE 13.4 Fair Credit Reporting Act Disclosures.

The federal government issues regulations in the Federal Register *that serve as guidelines for citizens and businesses in following federal law. The guidelines shown here pertain to how much credit-rating organizations can charge customers seeking their individual credit reports.*

Source: "Fair Credit Reporting Act Disclosures," *Federal Register,* April 3, 2012, https://www.federalregister.gov/articles/2012/04/03/2012-7916/fair-credit-reporting-act-disclosures.

The Creation of the Consumer Financial Protection Bureau

The regulatory process is time-consuming. The Dodd-Frank Act was signed into law on July 21, 2010, but it took a year for the Consumer Financial Protection Bureau to begin operations. The delay was due to a provision in the law that required that a director be confirmed before any regulations could be issued. Opponents of the law in the Senate blocked President Obama's first nominee and were delaying action on the second nominee when, in January 2012, the president appointed Richard Cordray as the bureau's first director as a recess appointment.[52] Some of the most important parts of the law, such as the regulations to ensure that lenders do not give mortgages to people who cannot repay them as well as restrictions on high-cost loans, will not be implemented for quite some time. The final rules ensuring more stringent regulations for lenders in approving loans were not due until January 2013, and the final rules on the restrictions for high-cost loans were not expected until January 21, 2013.[53]

The regulatory process is never easy, and delays are common, but the implementation of the Dodd-Frank Act has been especially complex because it involves the overhaul and installment of financial regulations and the establishment of a new agency. The act has a wide impact, ranging from protecting homeowners to safeguarding consumers against unfair credit and debit card fees. The regulatory process has been prolonged by another factor as well—the degree of coordination required among the other agencies involved, including the Federal Reserve and the Securities and Exchange Commission.[54] Finally, the public comment periods and the backlash from financial institutions have made the process even more complicated, with many vigorously opposing the regulations that will force them to adopt new practices to achieve fairness and transparency. As of September 4, 2012, only 131 of the 398 regulations had been finalized,[55] demonstrating that laws that are a gateway for consumer protection may have to work past the gates that the regulatory process, interest group lobbying, and partisan politics might put in their way.

 Construct Your Own Policy

1. Design three reforms that would provide consumer protections for credit card use.

2. Develop a system whereby the federal government would lend money directly to individuals wanting buy their own homes, instead of working through private banks.

For more on the policy-making process, see Chapter 1.

The Bureaucracy and Democracy

The federal government that started with three cabinet departments has grown to include fifteen cabinet departments and many powerful independent agencies. The federal bureaucracy, including the armed services, employs nearly 4.3 million people. Their jobs affect the lives of every citizen, from the quality of the food they eat, to the safety of the highways they drive, to the purity of the water they drink.

In some important ways, the federal bureaucracy has become far more responsive to the needs of average individuals in the course of the nation's history, especially in the areas of social benefits, health care, environmental protection, and civil rights enforcement. The federal bureaucracy has tried to be more transparent in its operations by placing comprehensive information on the Internet for the public to access at any time. However, as the responses to Hurricane Katrina in 2005 and the Gulf Oil Spill of 2010 show, there have been notable and serious failures in the government's responses to disasters, especially in areas with higher concentrations of poor and rural residents.

The structure of the bureaucracy includes many gates against speedy implementation of federal policy. The fact that there are so many layers of authority even within one agency, much less an entire cabinet department, adds considerable delay to the process of policy implementation. Multiple agencies can have jurisdiction over the same federal program or share responsibility for responding to natural disasters such as hurricanes. Such overlap can lead to miscommunication and to competition over authority and power. The hierarchy and procedural barriers that come with a large federal bureaucracy can stand in the way of efficient government.

At the same time, the rules and guidelines governing decision making in the bureaucracy are designed to ensure equal implementation of the law, which is a crucial element of a democracy. Americans expect federal laws to be applied in a consistent manner, with openness and vigilant congressional and public oversight. Understanding how laws are implemented, especially the gateways through which federal regulations are issued and enforced, gives citizens the power to hold the government accountable.

Citizens like Kate Hanni and Harry Markopolos have the opportunity, in a democracy, to pressure the government to be responsible and implement the laws with vigor in all areas. But one might also argue that advocates should not be needed to ensure that the bureaucracy works with efficiency and transparency. Hanni and Markopolos both experienced frustration in trying to navigate the gateways of the bureaucracy. Fortunately, they were persistent in their efforts to overcome obstacles. Their experiences are indicative of both the gates and gateways that the bureaucracy presents for citizen involvement in policy implementation.

Focus Questions Revisited

- How does the federal bureaucracy play a role in responding to the individual needs of ordinary citizens?

- How does the structure of the federal bureaucracy shape the way policies are implemented?

- What powers does the bureaucracy have to ensure that federal policies are administered equally across all citizens?

- How can the average citizen influence the decisions of the bureaucracy?

- Is the bureaucracy a gate or a gateway to democracy? Explain.

Top Ten to Take Away

1. The bureaucracy is the collection of executive branch departments, regulatory agencies, and other organizations that carry out the responsibilities of the federal government. Today nearly 4.3 million people, including those in the armed services, work for the federal government. (pp. 443–444)

2. Each bureaucratic organization has a clear mission, a hierarchical decision-making process, an area of expertise, and a bureaucratic culture. Aside from cabinet departments, there are various types of organizations within the bureaucracy, some designed to be more or less independent of the president. (pp. 452–455)

3. The constitutional foundations for the bureaucracy include the president's power to nominate and appoint officers of executive departments, from whom he may request advice. The bureaucracy is also based in the president's broad grant of executive power. (pp. 445–452)

4. Since 1789 the bureaucracy has grown from three to fifteen executive departments as government's responsibilities have grown, primarily in the area of the economy. The first regulatory agency was established in 1887 to regulate railroad practices. (pp. 455–457)

5. Federal employment has developed from a corps of wealthy elites with political connections to members of the Congress and the president into a merit- and performance-based civil service designed to be protected from political influence. (pp. 457–462)

6. The president appoints cabinet secretaries and other high-level political appointees who are expected to carry out the president's agenda. (pp. 462–464)

7. Following a consistent regulatory process, agencies draft regulations, which are open to comment by citizens, members of Congress, interest groups, and relevant businesses and industries before they are finalized. (pp. 470–476)

8. Congress exercises influence over policy through its oversight responsibilities and power to authorize and allocate funds. Lawsuits can involve the judicial branch in the interpretation of public policy. (pp. 457, 464)

9. The bureaucracy is subject to criticism for acting slowly, but in a democracy the need for efficiency is counterbalanced by the need for transparency. Reform efforts have improved transparency by providing protections for whistleblowers. (pp. 464–469)

10. The policy-making process and regulatory process together exemplify government responsiveness and accountability to citizens even as they also reflect the concerns of competing interests. (pp. 470, 476)

Key Concepts

Administrative Procedures Act (APA) (p. 473). What role does the APA play in the regulatory process?

bureaucracy (p. 443). Is the bureaucracy a gate or a gateway to democracy?

cabinet (p. 444). What departments make up the cabinet?

cabinet secretaries (p. 444). What do cabinet secretaries do?

career civil servants (p. 458). How do career civil servants move up the career ladder?

civil service (p. 458). Why is the civil service important to implementing federal law fairly and equitably?

Civil Service Commission (p. 458). What role does the Civil Service Commission play in overseeing federal employment practices?

Federal Register (p. 474). How does the *Federal Register* encourage citizen input and ensure transparency?

final regulations (p. 474). When are final regulations administered?

independent agency (p. 450). How is an independent agency different from a cabinet department?

merit system (p. 458). Compare the merit system with the patronage system.

Office of Management and Budget (p. 449). What is the OMB's role in the regulatory process?

oversight (p. 462). How does congressional oversight serve as a check on the bureaucracy?

Pendleton Act (p. 458). What is the significance of the Pendleton Act?

political appointees (p. 458). How do political appointees implement the president's policies?

preliminary regulations (p. 474). What purpose do preliminary regulations serve?

regulations (p. 444). Explain the role of regulations in the policy-making process.

regulatory process (p. 473). Is the regulatory process responsive enough to the interests and concerns of citizens, business, and Congress?

Senior Executive Service (SES) (p. 461). How can the Senior Executive Service be used to expand a president's influence in the bureaucracy?

whistleblowers (p. 467). Does the government provide enough incentives and protections to whistleblowers?

Learning Outcomes

WHAT YOU NEED...

To Know	To Test Yourself	To Participate
What the bureaucracy does	• Define bureaucracy • Explain how the Constitution provides a basis for bureaucratic power • Describe the structure of the federal bureaucracy	• Recognize how the federal government affects your daily life • Evaluate how well bureaucrats serve the people • Consider whether the bureaucracy is too large to be responsive
What the essential elements of a bureaucracy are	• Explain how the mission of a bureaucracy shapes its goals • State the advantages and disadvantages of the hierarchical decision-making process • Characterize bureaucratic expertise • Describe bureaucratic culture	• Evaluate the degree of accountability associated with a bureaucratic mission • Design a bureaucracy that is more efficient and responsive
How the bureaucracy developed over time	• Equate the establishment of cabinet departments with developments in the U.S. economy and society • Describe what regulatory agencies do • Explain how and why the civil service evolved • Survey the types of jobs career civil servants perform • Recall why political appointees have increased in number over time • Explain the growth of the use of private-sector contract workers • Describe how Congress has attempted to protect the bureaucracy from partisan politics	• Evaluate the bureaucracy in terms of government responsiveness • Assess why merit-based employment is better than patronage in a democracy • Consider whether you would like to work for the government • Evaluate the accountability of private-sector contract workers
How the bureaucracy is both accountable and responsive, and how it can fail	• Explain ways the legislative and judicial branches can check the bureaucracy • Examine how the need for bureaucratic efficiency and transparency can counteract each other • Describe what it means to be a whistleblower • Relate the consequences of bureaucratic failure	• Understand how you can influence the bureaucracy • Evaluate the importance of offering protection to whistleblowers

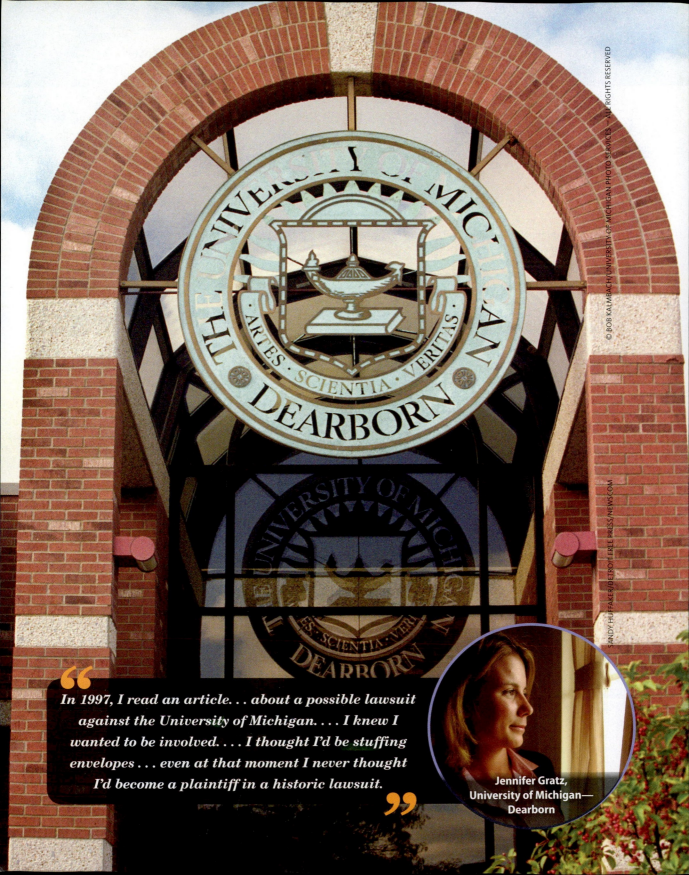

" *In 1997, I read an article. . . about a possible lawsuit against the University of Michigan. . . . I knew I wanted to be involved. . . . I thought I'd be stuffing envelopes . . . even at that moment I never thought I'd become a plaintiff in a historic lawsuit.* "

Jennifer Gratz, University of Michigan— Dearborn

14

The Judiciary

"The envelope was way too thin," thought Jennifer Gratz, a high school senior in the class of 1995 at Southgate Anderson High School, in Southgate, Michigan. Despite graduating in the top 5 percent of her class, having a 3.8 (out of 4.0) GPA, and receiving a score of 25 out of 36 (83rd percentile) on her ACT, she had received a wait-list letter and ultimately a rejection letter from her first choice for college, the University of Michigan.

Elsewhere in Michigan, Barbara Grutter, a mother of two in her mid-40s who had decided to attend law school, did not get admitted to her first and only school choice. Despite a 3.8 undergraduate GPA and a score of 161 out of 180 (86th percentile) on her LSAT, she, too, was wait-listed and ultimately denied admission to the law school at the University of Michigan.

Gratz and Grutter then took a step that most students do not take; they chose to sue the school that rejected them. Each challenged the university's affirmative action policies, which gave underrepresented minority students preferential advantages in admissions compared to whites with similar GPAs and standardized test scores. The preference at the undergraduate college, for example, was equivalent to a full point on a 4-point GPA scale. That is, a student from an underrepresented minority group with a 2.8 GPA would have the same chance of admission as a middle-class white student with a 3.8 GPA. Gratz and Grutter claimed that these policies denied

aplia Need to Know

- **What the judicial branch does**
- **How the Supreme Court has expanded and contracted national powers**
- **How federal judges get selected**
- **How state and lower federal courts operate**
- **What procedures the Supreme Court uses for deciding cases**

them "equal protection of the laws" as guaranteed by the Fourteenth Amendment. Instead of an equal opportunity to gain admission to the university of their choice, they were, as individuals, disadvantaged. Supporters of affirmative action, on the other hand, claim that affirmative action policies enhance equality generally by increasing the chances that the university student body as a whole better represents the population as a whole. The consequence is a greater equality of outcome.

Gratz and Grutter received legal assistance from the Center for Individual Rights, a conservative legal group that actively sought students looking to fight affirmative action. Both lawsuits named Lee Bollinger, the president of the University of Michigan, as the respondent. They sought admission to the respective colleges (the undergraduate college for Gratz, and the law school for Grutter) and an end to the colleges' use of race as a criterion for admission. Meanwhile Gratz, although disappointed not to attend Michigan's flagship Ann Arbor campus, had enrolled in one of the school's regional campuses, the University of Michigan–Dearborn.[1]

In this chapter, we track the *Gratz* and *Grutter* cases all the way to the Supreme Court. Lawsuits such as these provide a gateway for one individual to have an enormous impact on the political system of the United States. The Supreme Court ultimately delivered a set of decisions that upheld the affirmative action plan of the law school but found constitutional violation in the plan of the undergraduate college. As these cases help show, the judicial system of the United States, because of its authority to rule on the constitutionality of federal and state laws and policies, has an extraordinary amount of power in the American political system. The Supreme Court, as the highest court in the land, decides not only whether affirmative action may be allowed, but also decides other issues, such as whether health insurance can be mandated, abortion can be prohibited, or the death penalty inflicted. The justices on the Court make important decisions that affect the lives of individuals and the policies of the nation at large despite the fact that they are not elected by the people and cannot be removed from office if the people disagree with the decisions that they make. Thus we examine, too, the controversial role and power of the judiciary in a democracy.

FocusQuestions

- Why is the apparently simple requirement of providing "equal protection of the laws" more difficult than it seems?
- In what ways do the federal courts lack traditional means of accountability?
- How are courts, nevertheless, responsive?
- Do citizens have equal access to the justice system? Does the justice system treat them equally?
- Is the judiciary a gate or a gateway to democracy?

The Role and Powers of the Judiciary

› **What the judicial branch does**

The job of courts is to resolve legal disputes. The American legal system is based largely on the English system, the system that the colonists were familiar with. The legal system under the Constitution kept many of the same practices but added some innovations.

English Legal Traditions

Resolution of legal disputes follows an **adversary process**. In an adversarial system, each party, usually represented by an attorney, presents its version of events, with virtually all attempts to slant information short of lying under oath deemed acceptable. According to a noted Supreme Court scholar, "The underlying assumption is that two persons arguing, as partisanly as possible, will produce the fairest decision."[2]

While in some cases a judge decides which side in such legal battles is correct, a group of ordinary citizens more usually determines the outcome. The right to trial by jury dates back in England to the Magna Carta (1215), where it replaced trial by ordeal, the practice of subjecting people to drowning or burning to see if they were innocent. Trial by jury is crucial to liberty, for it inserts a gate of citizen judgment between the accused person and the government that protects the accused from arbitrary detention and unjust punishment. It also provides a gateway of citizen involvement through juror participation.

Trials involve questions of fact (for example, did the University of Michigan set different standards for white and minority students?) and questions of law (for example, do such differing standards violate the Fourteenth Amendment?). Trial court decisions about questions of fact are presumed to be valid because the trial judge or the jury directly hears the evidence in the case. But because trial courts sometimes make mistakes about questions of law, the American legal system has followed the British practice by allowing **appeals** from trial court rulings. In the U.S. federal system, the **courts of appeals** and the Supreme Court hear appeals, which involve issues of law. These courts do not retry the facts as established by the trial court.

Trials resolve two distinct types of disputes. In a **criminal case**, the government prosecutes an individual for breaking the law. Criminal cases are based almost exclusively on prohibitions on behavior written into statutes (laws) passed by federal, state, or local legislatures. In a **civil suit**, a plaintiff, such as Jennifer Gratz, sues a defendant, such as the University of Michigan, to enforce a right or to win monetary damages. The U.S. Constitution

adversary process: *Confrontational legal process under which each party presents its version of events.*

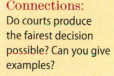
Connections: Do courts produce the fairest decision possible? Can you give examples?

appeal: *Legal proceeding whereby the decision of a lower court on a question of law can be challenged and reviewed by a higher court.*

courts of appeals: *Intermediate federal courts that are above the district courts and below the Supreme Court.*

criminal case: *Government prosecution of an individual for breaking the law.*

civil suit: *Lawsuit by a person, organization, or government against another person, organization, or government.*

guarantees jury trials in all criminal cases and in all civil suits for amounts higher than $20. Today, Congress limits access to the federal courts in monetary civil suits to claims of $75,000 or more. Suits for lesser amounts must go to state courts.

Criminal law is based on statutory authority, but statutory authority cannot cover all possible civil disputes between individuals. Many disputes are actions that no legislative authority could have ever imagined. When there are gaps in statutory law, courts rely on judge-made law known as **common law**. Common law requires judges to accept and rely on previous decisions (if each judge makes his or her own decisions on each case, there can be no common law). Thus, British royal judges developed the practice of reaching decisions based on **precedents**, or the previous decisions of other royal judges. Deciding cases based on precedents means that similar cases are decided similarly. Precedent is perhaps the most fundamental feature of English and American law. Because similar cases get decided similarly, following precedent promotes greater equality, predictability, and stability in law.

Constitutional Grants of Power

Article III of the Constitution establishes the judicial branch of government. It briefly refers to a Supreme Court of the United States and grants Congress the authority to create lower courts at its discretion. The Constitution grants the federal courts the authority to hear "cases" or "controversies," which the Supreme Court has interpreted to require that people who initiate lawsuits have standing, that is, have suffered a harm that the law arguably protects. Standing is a gate that limits access to the judicial system by requiring real disputes involving legally recognized harms, not hypothetical cases.

Because the Constitution says so little about the judicial branch, one of the early acts of the First Congress, the Judiciary Act of 1789, established 13 **district (trial) courts** and 3 circuit courts with both trial and appellate authority that serve at an intermediate level between the district courts and the Supreme Court. Today, there are 667 district court judges serving in 94 separate district courts and 179 court of appeals judges serving in 13 intermediate appellate circuits.[3]

The lawful authority of a court to hear a case is its **jurisdiction**. In general, jurisdiction for any federal court requires either that the case involve federal law (including the Constitution and treaties); that the parties include the United States, ambassadors, or other public ministers; or that the parties are residents of different states. These latter suits are called diversity suits. As for the Supreme Court, the Constitution further divides its jurisdiction into original jurisdiction, that is, authority to hear a case directly from a petitioning party (as in a trial), and appellate jurisdiction, authority to hear cases on appeals from lower courts. Specifically, the Supreme Court has original jurisdiction in "all Cases affecting Ambassadors, other public Ministers

common law:
Judge-made law in England and the United States that results from gaps in statutory law.

precedent:
Practice of reaching decisions based on the previous decisions of other judges.

Connections: If you recognize an injustice but have not been harmed by it, how can you get government to respond?

district courts:
Federal trial courts at the bottom of the federal judicial hierarchy.

jurisdiction:
Lawful authority of a court to hear a case.

and Consuls, and those in which a State shall be Party" (Article III, Section 2). The Constitution then declares that "in all the other Cases" properly before the Court, it would have appellate jurisdiction subject to such exceptions and regulations that Congress shall make.

The Constitution grants the president the authority to nominate judges, but these nominations are subject to the advice and consent of the Senate. Judges confirmed by the Senate serve during "good behavior," which, short of impeachment, essentially means a life term. The House has impeached only one Supreme Court justice, Samuel Chase (1805), in an attempt by the Democratic-Republicans to remove an ardent Federalist from the bench. The Senate rejected every charge against Chase (just three votes short of the required two-thirds majority on one of the counts),[4] establishing a custom crucial to judicial independence that judges would not be removed due to partisan disagreements with their decisions.

The Constitution grants the federal courts the authority to hear cases of law and equity—cases in which the litigant filing suit seeks specific action by the party being sued rather than monetary damages. Cases of law and equity can involve (1) the common law when there are gaps in legislative authority; (2) statutory interpretation, where the courts have to determine what Congress meant by a statute (for example, is discrimination on the grounds of pregnancy included in the prohibition on sex discrimination in the Civil Rights Act of 1964?), and (3) constitutional interpretation, where the courts must decide whether a law or practice violates a provision of the Constitution, such as the Fourteenth Amendment's guarantee of equal protection of the laws.

Constitutional interpretation brings forth the greatest power of the federal judiciary, judicial review. This power is not explicitly in the Constitution, but it is a power that Alexander Hamilton, the author of *Federalist* 78, expected would belong to the courts.[5] Judicial review is the power of courts to declare actions of Congress, the president, or state officials unconstitutional and therefore void. The Supreme Court used this extraordinary power to rule on the Michigan affirmative action cases in 2003. The Supreme Court granted itself the power of judicial review in the case of *Marbury v. Madison* (1803).

Marbury v. Madison

The *Marbury* case arose out of the election of 1800, which resulted in the defeat of President John Adams (1797–1801) by Thomas Jefferson (1801–1809). It also resulted in the defeat in Congress of Adams's Federalist Party by Jefferson's Democratic-Republicans. Days before the Jeffersonians took control of government, the defeated Federalists, seeking to maintain some power, passed the Judiciary Act of 1801. This act created many new judgeships that presumably would be filled by Federalists nominated by outgoing President Adams and confirmed by the outgoing Federalist Senate.

judicial independence: *Ability of judges to reach decisions without fear of political retribution.*

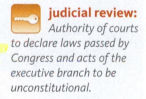

judicial review: *Authority of courts to declare laws passed by Congress and acts of the executive branch to be unconstitutional.*

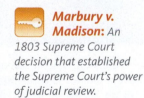

Marbury v. Madison: *An 1803 Supreme Court decision that established the Supreme Court's power of judicial review.*

One of those judges was William Marbury. In the hectic final hours of the Adams administration, Secretary of State John Marshall, who had recently been confirmed as chief justice of the Supreme Court, failed to deliver Marbury's judicial commission, thus preventing Marbury from assuming his position. After Jefferson's presidential term began, Marbury requested that Jefferson's secretary of state, James Madison, deliver the commission, but Madison refused. Marbury then took his case directly to the Supreme Court, seeking a writ of *mandamus,* an order compelling Madison to deliver the commission. Marbury believed that the Judiciary Act of 1789 gave the Supreme Court original jurisdiction to hear cases involving writs of *mandamus*.

Connections: How does "less is more" apply to the decision in *Marbury*?

The decision of the Supreme Court, written by Chief Justice John Marshall, unanimously decreed that Marbury had a legal right to his commission, but the Supreme Court could not order Madison to provide it because the Court did not have jurisdiction to hear the case. The Court did not have jurisdiction, Marshall wrote, because the section of the Judiciary Act of 1789 that expanded the Court's original jurisdiction to cover writs of *mandamus* was unconstitutional. The decision was brilliant. In declaring that the Court did not have jurisdiction to hear the case, Marshall established that the Court has the power to decide whether a law passed by Congress is valid under the Constitution.

In asserting the authority to declare acts of Congress to be unconstitutional, the Court noted that if Congress passes a law that violates a provision of the Constitution, either that law is valid or the constitutional provision is valid, but not both. So, argued the Court, if the Constitution specifically limits the Supreme Court's original jurisdiction to certain types of cases, but Congress passes legislation to expand it beyond those cases, either the legislation expanding jurisdiction is valid or the constitutional limit on jurisdiction is valid. Which is it? And who gets to decide?

Although it is obvious to us today that the Constitution is supreme over regular legislation, that relationship was not as clear in 1803. In *Marbury v. Madison,* Chief Justice Marshall clarified that the Constitution must be supreme and that regular laws cannot overrule

STOCK MONTAGE/GETTY IMAGES

John Marshall was the nation's fourth chief justice and the first one to make an impact. His decisions, starting with *Marbury v. Madison* (1803), strengthened the judicial branch specifically and the federal government generally. Not only did he set forth the power of judicial review, but in a series of decisions during thirty-four years on the Court, he crafted a broad interpretation of the Constitution that expanded the scope of national power and ensured the uniformity of federal law.

constitutional requirements: "It is emphatically the province of the judicial department to say what the law is."[6] In short, Marshall was interpreting the Constitution to say that the Court has the power to interpret the meaning of the rules laid down by the Constitution's Framers and to hold those rules supreme over legislative acts passed by Congress. More than two hundred years later, this decision stands as the foundation of judicial power in the United States (see Supreme Court Cases in Chapter 2, The Constitution). Since that time, approximately 120 nations have adopted this constitutional arrangement, but in 1803 it was an innovative departure even from the British system of justice (see Global Gateways: Judicial Review).

Checkpoint

Can you:

- ☐ Summarize the U.S. legal traditions derived from English legal traditions
- ☐ Restate what the Constitution says about the organization and powers of the federal judiciary
- ☐ Explain *Marbury v. Madison* and its importance

Historical Trends in Supreme Court Rulings

> **How the Supreme Court has expanded and contracted national powers**

In *Federalist* 78, Alexander Hamilton described the judiciary as "the least dangerous branch" because it has no power over the sword or the purse. But due to the power of judicial review, the Supreme Court has actually played a major role in dividing authority between the nation and state, between Congress and the president, and between government, whether state or local, and the people.

Expansion of National Power under the Marshall Court

During George Washington's administration (1789–97), the Supreme Court had so little power or status that its first chief justice, John Jay, resigned to become governor of New York. Not until the fourth chief justice, John Marshall, did the Court begin to establish itself as a major player in national politics. The Marshall Court (1801–1835; Courts are often named after the sitting chief justice) did so not only by affirming its power of judicial review in the *Marbury* case, but also by setting forth a broad interpretation to the scope of national power in the cases of *McCulloch v. Maryland* (1819) and *Gibbons v. Ogden* (1824) and by limiting the authority of state judiciaries in a series of decisions culminating in *Cohens v. Virginia* (1821; see Supreme Court Cases in Chapter 3, Federalism).[7]

The decision in *McCulloch v. Maryland* expanded national power in two ways: by granting the national government the right to create a bank through

Connections: In *Marbury*, the Court established its power over laws made by Congress. Why, then, did the Marshall Court also expand Congress's power?

globalgateways

Judicial Review

The notion of judicial review arguably began in England in 1610 when Lord Coke declared in Dr. Bonham's Case that "when an act of parliament is against common right and reason, or repugnant, or impossible to be performed, the common law will control it, and adjudge such act to be void."* The case, though, involved an unlawful imprisonment, not an unconstitutional law, so Lord Coke was only speaking hypothetically.

Judicial review did not catch on in Great Britain for two reasons. First, unlike the United States, where Congress's powers are limited, Parliament is supreme. Second, Great Britain does not have a written constitution, thus depriving courts of a basis to declare that a law is unconstitutional.

* Dr. Bonham's Case, 8 Co. Rep. 114 (Court of Common Pleas [1610]).

The United States thus became the first modern nation to establish judicial review, but until recently few countries followed this practice. Today, with greater attention to human rights around the world, most countries have moved toward some form of judicial review.

In the United Kingdom, with full sovereignty resting in Parliament, American-style judicial review does not exist. But Britain has shown some movement in that direction. The newly created British Supreme Court cannot overturn Parliamentary laws but can issue "declarations of incompatibility" when laws violate the European Convention on Human Rights. Such a declaration does not void the law, but it can be used to embarrass Parliament into changing the law. It is still up to Parliament, however, to change the incompatible law.

Great Britain also has power-sharing agreements with Scotland and Northern Ireland. If Parliament passes laws that violate these agreements, British courts may be unwilling to enforce them.

- **Why were more countries adopting judicial review in the late twentieth century than before that time?**

- **How are rights protected in countries without judicial review?**

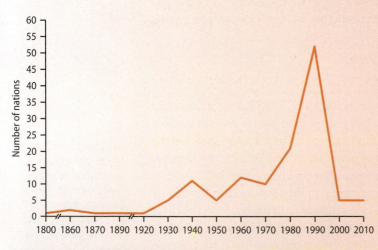

NUMBER OF NATIONS ADOPTING JUDICIAL REVIEW, 1800–2010.

Source: Tom Ginsberg, *Judicial Review in New Democracies: Constitutional Courts in Asian Cases* (Cambridge, U.K.: Cambridge University Press, 2003); Robert Maddex, *Constitutions of the World* (Washington, D.C.: CQ Press, 1995); *CIA World Factbook*; Tom Ginsburg and Mila Versteeg, "The Global Spread of Judicial Review: An Empirical Analysis" (manuscript, 2012), and various national supreme court websites.

the necessary and proper clause, and by limiting state power by denying the states the authority to tax activities of the national government. Similarly, in *Gibbons v. Ogden*, the Court took an expansive view of national power, declaring that the commerce clause, which granted the national government the authority to regulate commerce "among the several States," would be broadly defined to include not just the shipping of goods across state lines but also the economic activities within a state that concern other states. As in *McCulloch*, what the Constitution grants as a legitimate object of national authority (here, interstate commerce) could not be regulated by a state.

This supremacy of federal law over state law is explicitly stated in the Constitution's supremacy clause. But the fact that federal law is supreme over state law does not necessarily answer whether the national courts or the state courts get the final say over what federal law means. In decisions made necessary by state court refusals to abide by its initial decisions, the Supreme Court declared that federal courts have the final say over what federal law means, establishing the federal judiciary as supreme over state judiciaries on questions of national law. These cases, culminating in *Cohens v. Virginia*, are not as famous as *Marbury* and *McCulloch*, but they have been essential in preventing the sort of divisions that would arise if state judges had the final say on what federal tax laws, or, for example, the Affordable Care Act (Obamacare), meant in their home states.

By establishing judicial review, expanding national power, and ensuring the uniformity of federal law, the Marshall Court set the United States on the path to a strong and unified nation.

Limits on National Power, 1830s to 1930s

Starting in the 1830s the Supreme Court began limiting national power over slavery and, later, civil rights, as well as governmental efforts to regulate the economy. Although the Constitution permitted slavery, the justices did not address the issue directly until the case of *Dred Scott v. Sandford* (1857).[8] As noted in Chapter 5, Civil Rights, the Supreme Court declared that no black person could be an American citizen and that Congress did not have the authority to regulate slavery in the territories. The decision inflamed the tensions over slavery that soon led to the outbreak of the Civil War.

Following the war, Congress proposed and the states ratified the Fourteenth Amendment, which overturned the *Scott* case by making "all persons born in the United States . . . citizens of the United States." The amendment further prevented states from denying any person due process of law or the equal protection of the laws and from abridging the privileges or immunities of citizens of the United States. The amendment granted Congress the means to enforce the amendment's commands by appropriate legislation, thus adding to Congress's enumerated powers.

The Supreme Court interpreted these clauses narrowly, thus limiting national power. For example, the *Slaughterhouse Cases* gave a restricted interpretation of the privileges or immunities clause that states could not abridge, holding that the clause protects the right of access to the seat of government, the right to pass freely from state to state, and the right to demand the protection of the federal government on the high seas or abroad, but little more.[9] Through precedent, the limited reading of the clause largely remains in effect today.

Connections: Why did the Court reduce or limit federal power in this era?

In *United States v. Cruikshank*, the Supreme Court reversed federal charges against the perpetrators of the Colfax massacre (see Chapter 5), arguing that the right to enforce the due process clause gave Congress the authority to act only against states, not against individuals.[10] Similarly, in the *Civil Rights Cases,* the Court refused to grant Congress the authority to prohibit discrimination by private individuals under the equal protection clause, declaring that state-sponsored inequality was all that the amendment prohibited.[11] But when the states actively discriminated against blacks by mandating segregated facilities, the Court allowed this too, under the separate-but-equal doctrine (see Chapter 5), which the Court established in the 1896 case *Plessy v. Ferguson*.[12] In addition, for more than fifty years, neither the Court nor the segregated states paid attention to whether separate facilities were actually equal.

The Supreme Court limited national authority in the economy, too. Following the Civil War, as the shift in the American economy from agriculture to industry accelerated, powerful business and industrial interests sought to limit attempts by Congress and the states to regulate economic activity and labor. The Supreme Court generally backed business and industrial interests by setting up barriers to regulation. It promoted laissez-faire, the belief that the government should not intervene in the economy, through two constitutional doctrines. First, when Congress attempted to regulate the economy, the Court narrowly read the commerce clause, declaring that economic regulation was to be left to the states. But when states tried to regulate the economy, the Court, siding with business interests, prohibited states from regulating businesses under its reading of the Fourteenth Amendment's due process clause.

Connections: If a right is not explicitly stated in the Constitution, should it be protected?

Strengthened National Power, 1930s to the Present

Following the onset of the Great Depression in 1929, citizens called on the states and the national government to try to regulate the economy and to assist workers, but the Supreme Court held firm in creating a constitutional gate that declared much of the economic legislation passed in the early years of the Franklin Delano Roosevelt administration (1933–45) unconstitutional. Under pressure from Congress and Roosevelt, the Court eventually opened a gateway by allowing the federal and state governments greater leeway in regulating the economy. During this same period, the Court began restricting state government limits on civil rights and liberties, while strengthening national power to protect civil rights.

Economic Regulation.

Elected president in 1932 on a platform of economic recovery and reform, Franklin Roosevelt saw several pieces of his New Deal legislation—which aimed to alleviate the nation's economic hardships—struck down by the Court, often by closely divided votes. After his 1936 reelection, Roosevelt struck back at the Court, proposing a so-called Court-packing plan that would have allowed him to appoint a new justice for every justice older than 70 who failed to resign. This scheme would have increased the Court's size to fifteen and guaranteed judicial support for his economic plans.

In the historic "switch in time that saved nine," two of the moderate backers of the Court's laissez-faire policies, Owen Roberts and Chief Justice Charles Evans Hughes, proved themselves responsive to the hostile political environment facing the Court. They began to change their votes, providing majorities for both national and state plans to regulate the economy, thereby removing the need for Roosevelt's controversial Court-packing plan. In a series of cases decided in 1937, the Court upheld minimum wage laws and the right of unions to organize and bargain collectively as within the powers of Congress to regulate under the commerce clause. In *Wickard v. Filburn*, the Court went so far as to declare that wheat grown by a farmer on his own farm for consumption on his own farm was produced in interstate commerce, because of the effect that the wheat, and all similarly grown wheat, would have on the marketplace.[13] The implication of this decision was clear: If such wheat was involved in interstate commerce, then virtually all economic activity involves interstate commerce and thus falls within the regulatory powers of Congress. In 2012, the Supreme Court chose not to expand the *Wickard* precedent, holding that that the decision not to engage in commerce by not purchasing health insurance, fell beyond the reach of the commerce clause.[14]

Increased Protections for Civil Liberties and Civil Rights.

With the government's authority over the economy established, cases before the Court dealt increasingly with questions of civil rights and civil liberties. As noted in Chapter 4, Civil Liberties, paving the way for closer scrutiny of these rights were Court decisions incorporating various provisions of the Bill of Rights, making them binding on the states. This selective incorporation doctrine began slowly, with First Amendment rights among the few incorporated before the 1950s. The doctrine expanded during the liberal Warren Court (1953–69), which made most of the criminal procedure guarantees of the Bill of Rights binding on the states.

Outside of incorporation, the Warren Court greatly expanded the interpretation of liberties involving the First Amendment, equal protection, the right to privacy, and criminal procedure. In First Amendment cases, the Court protected the speech rights of those advocating violence against religious and racial minorities, the press rights of newspapers against libel suits by

Connections: Do you think justices over the age of 70 should be allowed to stay on the Supreme Court? Is appointment for life a good or a bad idea?

public figures, and the right to publish allegedly obscene materials as long as they had even the slightest amount of redeeming social value. It also limited prayer and Bible readings in the schools.[15] Regarding equal protection, beyond the momentous *Brown v. Board of Education* decision striking at segregation (see Supreme Court Cases, Chapter 5), the Court launched a reapportionment revolution, striking down arrangements in which some congressional or state legislative districts had ten or twenty times the population of other districts. Setting forth a "one person, one vote" requirement, the Court demanded equality in the number of citizens represented in each legislative district.[16] The Warren Court also created a right to privacy that is not explicitly in the Constitution, striking down a Connecticut statute that prohibited any person—including married couples—from using birth control and any person—including doctors—from counseling patients on such use.[17] Finally, regarding criminal justice, the Warren Court demanded that evidence obtained by police in violation of the Fourth Amendment's protection against unreasonable searches or seizures should be excluded at trial (the exclusionary rule) and that subjects in custody not be interrogated without being informed of their right to remain silent and have an attorney (the so-called *Miranda* warnings, after the plaintiff in the case).[18]

In 1968 Republican presidential candidate Richard M. Nixon attacked the Supreme Court for "hamstringing the peace forces in our society and strengthening the criminal forces."[19] Nixon (1969–74) won the election and was able to appoint four new justices to the Court, including Chief Justice Warren Burger. But with greater social acceptance of racial integration and police acceptance of the *Miranda* warnings, neither the more conservative Burger (1969–86) nor Rehnquist (1986–2005) Courts undid what the liberal Warren Court had done. For a summary of the Supreme Court's leading decisions, see Table 14.1.

While school desegregation originally meant allowing children to go to their neighborhood school regardless of race, such desegregation did little in places where whites and blacks lived in separate areas. In such areas, neighborhood schools would still be segregated. To remedy this situation, the Burger Court allowed children to be bused away from their neighborhood schools to increase integration. The Burger Court also established abortion rights, limited the death penalty, protected women's rights under the equal protection clause of the Fourteenth Amendment, and, in a precursor to the *Gratz* and *Grutter* lawsuits, first allowed affirmative action at colleges and universities.[20] On the other hand, the Burger Court chose not to extend equal protection rights to the unequal funding of school districts and, in the criminal justice area, limited the reach of the exclusionary rule and the *Miranda* warnings.[21] It also limited presidential authority in *United States v. Nixon*, declaring that the Nixon administration could not withhold tapes related to the Watergate scandal.[22] This decision and the evidence from the tapes led directly to Nixon's resignation (see Chapter 12, The Presidency).

Although conservative, the Rehnquist Court, over Chief Justice William Rehnquist's dissent, first extended privacy rights to homosexual conduct[23] (see *Lawrence v. Texas,* Chapter 6, Public Opinion). On the other hand, the Rehnquist Court limited, however slightly, the scope of abortion rights and cut back, again only slightly, the scope of congressional authority under the commerce clause and sovereign immunity (see Chapter 3). It also issued split decisions in the *Gratz* and *Grutter* cases.[24] And perhaps most important, as

TABLE 14.1 Leading Decisions of the Marshall, Taney, Warren, Burger, and Rehnquist Courts

Court	Case (Year)	Description
Marshall (1801–1835)	*Marbury v. Madison* (1803)	Established judicial review
	McCulloch v. Maryland (1819)	Used implied powers to allow Congress to establish a national bank
	Cohens v. Virginia (1821)	Declared that federal courts have final say on meaning of federal law
	Gibbons v. Ogden (1824)	Established expansive interpretation of commerce clause
Taney (1836–1864)	*Dred Scott v. Sandford* (1857)	Stated that "negroes of the African race" cannot be citizens and that Congress cannot prohibit slavery in the territories
Warren (1953–1969)	*Brown v. Board of Education* (1954)	Prohibited segregation of public schools
	Wesberry v. Sanders (1964)	Required equality in the size of legislative districts
	New York Times v. Sullivan (1964)	Made it very difficult for public officials to sue newspapers for libel
	Miranda v. Arizona (1966)	Required that criminal defendants be told of their rights
	Griswold v. Connecticut (1965)	Established the right to privacy
Burger (1969–1986)	*Reed v. Reed* (1971)	Granted women rights under the equal protection clause
	New York Times v. United States (1971)	Set extremely high bar for government censorship of newspapers
	Roe v. Wade (1973)	Extended privacy rights to cover abortion rights
	United States v. Nixon (1974)	Required President Richard M. Nixon to hand over incriminating evidence in Watergate case
	Regents v. Bakke (1978)	Allowed universities to use race-based affirmative action admissions
Rehnquist (1986–2005)	*Planned Parenthood v. Casey* (1992)	Cut back but did not eliminate abortion rights established in *Roe v. Wade*
	Bush v. Gore (2000)	Ended the Florida presidential recount with George W. Bush holding a small lead, leading to Al Gore's concession
	Lawrence v. Texas (2003)	Extended privacy rights to homosexual conduct
	Gratz/Grutter v. Bollinger (2003)	Upheld race-based affirmative action as long as racial considerations are made on a case-by-case basis

Checkpoint

Can you:

- ☐ Describe the ways in which the Marshall Court expanded national power

- ☐ Explain how the Supreme Court acted to limit equality between the 1830s and 1930s

- ☐ Discuss what might have led the Supreme Court to accept greater national authority starting in 1937

noted in Chapter 10, Elections, Campaigns, and Voting, it ended the dispute over the 2000 presidential election with its decision in *Bush v. Gore*.[25]

The Roberts Court has been decidedly pro-business, hearing more such cases than previous courts and ruling on them in a decidedly pro-business direction.[26] It protected Walmart against a large discrimination lawsuit.[27] Even more important, it ruled that corporations have the same speech rights as citizens, enabling corporations to spend unlimited amounts of money on political campaigns.[28] On the other hand, the Court upheld Obama's health care plan in 2012, in what was not the conservative position in the case.[29]

The Appointment Process for Federal Judges and Justices

› **How federal judges get selected**

Among the important consequences of the George W. Bush presidency (2001–2009) was his nomination of two Supreme Court justices who share his conservative ideology, John Roberts and Samuel Alito. Given the importance of John Marshall, Earl Warren, and other justices to the nation, Supreme Court nominations may be among the most important decisions a president makes.[30] Indeed, it was Roberts who saved President Obama's health care law (see Supreme Court Cases in Chapter 11, Congress). Article II of the Constitution, however, says no more about appointments of judges and justices than that the president shall nominate federal judges "with the Advice and Consent of the Senate." As procedures have evolved, the president and the Senate accommodate each other on district court appointments, but there is some Senate resistance at the appeals court level. At the Supreme Court level, presidential nominees face intense scrutiny by the Senate, which often reflects concerns by citizens and interest groups.

Connections:
Describe the lasting impact of Supreme Court appointments.

The District Courts

When a vacancy occurs in a district court, the president selects a nominee, but with awareness of how the senators from the state in which the court is located might react. Before the nomination is announced, presidential staff members consult with the state's senators if they are members of the president's party; if one of them is opposed to the nomination, he or she can invoke the norm of senatorial courtesy and receive the support of other members of the Senate in blocking that nominee. When the two senators are from different parties, the senator from the president's party sometimes offers the other senator a percentage of the appointments, hoping the favor will be returned if the other party wins the presidency.

This norm is enhanced by the practice of the chair of the Judiciary Committee of sending "blue slips," so-called because of the color of the paper, to the senators of the president's party of a nominee's home state, asking whether they approve of the choice. Without a positive response, the Judiciary Committee generally will not hold a hearing on the nominee; with no hearing, there is no vote. Even with a positive response to the blue slip, the Judiciary chair may choose not to hold a hearing, particularly if he or she is of the opposite party of the president.

Sonia Sotomayor, who would go on to become President Barack Obama's first Supreme Court nominee, received her district court nomination during the presidency of Republican George H. W. Bush (1989–93) due to an appointment-sharing deal between New York's two senators, Republican Alfonse D'Amato and Democrat Daniel Patrick Moynihan. Like the president, senators use a variety of criteria in naming district court judges, including ideology, qualifications, and the rewarding of party loyalty.[31]

Patrick Duggan, the district court judge in the *Gratz* case, and Bernard Friedman, the judge in the *Grutter* case, had fairly similar backgrounds. Both parlayed campaign work for the Republican Party into state court judgeships, and both received federal court nominations from President Ronald Reagan (1981–89).

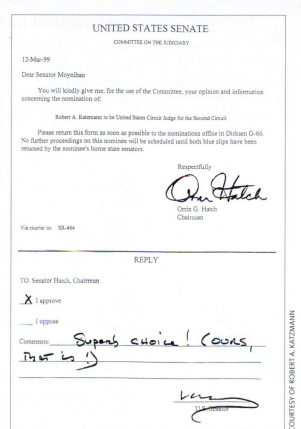

Senator Daniel Patrick Moynihan (D-N.Y.) signed a blue slip approving the appointment of Robert Katzmann to the Second Circuit Court of Appeals. The Xerox copy that Judge Katzmann gave us was white.

Confirmation of district court judges is generally routine, with nearly 90 percent of nominees between the administration of Jimmy Carter (1977–81) and George H. W. Bush approved.[32] With an increasingly partisan confirmation environment following the 2010 elections, and a Democratic majority in the Senate but not enough votes to end filibusters, the confirmation rate during the Obama administration was closer to 43 percent.[33] Following the nomination, the Senate Judiciary Committee conducts hearings on nominees. At the hearings, the American Bar Association (ABA), an organized interest group representing the nation's attorneys, evaluates the merits of nominees. District court nominees may also be requested to testify. If the Judiciary Committee approves the nomination, it moves to the Senate floor for a vote. Unless the vote is blocked by a filibuster, a majority is all that is needed for approval.[34]

The Courts of Appeals

Connections: Is the judicial appointment process fair?

The formal process of appointment of court of appeals judges is the same as that of district court judges, but the greater authority of court of appeals judges means that the Senate and outside interest groups pay much closer attention to the president's nominees. While court of appeals judges formally represent multiple states, seats are informally considered to belong to particular states. Thus, senatorial courtesy still applies.

Connections: Should judicial appointments be subject to partisanship?

Senate Democrats twice blocked the nomination of future Chief Justice John Roberts, a conservative Republican, to the U.S. Court of Appeals. President George H. W. Bush first nominated Roberts in 1991, but the Democrats never gave Roberts a hearing, thereby killing the nomination. Ten years later, President George W. Bush renominated Roberts to the court of appeals, and again the Democrats in charge of the Judiciary Committee did not provide a hearing. Only after a third nomination in 2003, at which point Republicans controlled the Senate (and thus the Judiciary Committee), did Roberts receive a hearing and a vote. Of course Republicans withheld hearings from many of President William Jefferson (Bill) Clinton's nominees when they controlled the Senate during his administration (1993–2001), including the future Supreme Court justice Elena Kagan after Clinton nominated her to the D.C. Court of Appeals in 1999. Overall, the Senate has failed to confirm more than 20 percent of court of appeals nominees since Jimmy Carter's administration, with the overwhelming majority being blocked at the Judiciary Committee.[35] In 2010 Senate Republicans began extensive use of holds, a process by which a single senator can block the unanimous consent agreements by which the Senate operates, to delay votes on many of President Obama's nominees.[36] These holds are similar to filibusters in that they can be overcome only with the sixty votes it takes to invoke cloture (see Chapter 11).

The Supreme Court

Connections: Should judges be appointed without regard to race, ethnic background, gender, or religion?

Given the Supreme Court's authority, the appointment of a Supreme Court justice is a high-stakes affair with extensive media coverage, interest group mobilization, public opinion polls, and the occasional scandal. Presidents also use Supreme Court appointments for electoral advantage. Presidential candidate Ronald Reagan promised to nominate the first woman to the Court and did so with his 1981 appointment of Sandra Day O'Connor. Fear that George W. Bush would get credit for nominating the first Latino to the Supreme Court was one of the factors that led Democratic interest groups to oppose Miguel Estrada's court of appeals nomination,[37] and he was thus denied the judicial experience that would be important for a Supreme Court nomination. President Obama received credit for nominating the first Hispanic to the Supreme Court with Sonia Sotomayor's appointment in 2009.

Though electoral advantage certainly influences presidential decisions, presidents also try to choose nominees who are close to them ideologically, hoping to shape the direction of the Court for years to come. Ronald Reagan had this in mind when he nominated the conservatives Robert Bork (whom a Democratic-controlled Senate rejected) and Antonin Scalia (whom a Republican-controlled Senate approved), and George W. Bush did when he named conservatives John Roberts and Samuel Alito.

In recent times, nominees for the Supreme Court always receive hearings from the Senate Judiciary Committee. These hearings include testimony by the ABA on the qualifications of the nominee, comments by organized interests for and against the nominee, and testimony by the nominee.

Figure 14.1 presents the number of interest groups supporting and opposing nominees at Judiciary Committee hearings since 1969. As can readily be seen, there has been a substantial growth in interest group involvement in Supreme Court nominations, largely due to the crucial role that the Court plays in so-called values issues such as abortion, the death penalty, and affirmative action. Lobbying by interest groups can substantially influence senators' votes for and against nominations.[38]

Connections:
What are the effects of televising congressional hearings?

While the Judiciary Committee can kill a nomination by refusing to report it to the Senate floor, the committee has reported every recent Supreme Court nominee, even when the recommendation is negative, as it was in 1987 for Robert Bork (9–5 against). An outspoken conservative, Bork answered questions about his legal beliefs directly, openly discussing his opposition to the right to privacy. The result was a 58–42 vote against him by the full Senate. Since the Bork rejection, nominees have dodged questions about their beliefs. Recently, they have stated that it would be improper to answer any questions about any issue that might conceivably come before the Court.

Once the nomination is on the floor, senators debate the pros and cons of the nominee until the vote is set. Floor votes can be postponed indefinitely through a filibuster, a tactic used with increasing frequency for court of appeals nominees.

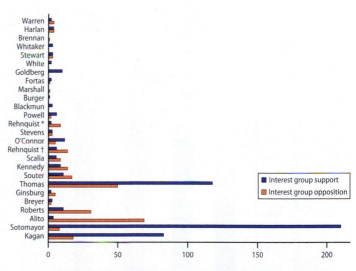

* Represents the support/opposition for Justice Rehnquist's nomination for associate justice.
† Represents the support/opposition for Justice Rehnquist's nomination for chief justice.

FIGURE 14.1 **Number of Interest Groups Supporting and Opposing Supreme Court Nominees in Senate Judiciary Committee Hearings, 1970–2010.**

Source: Derived from GPO Access, "Senate Committee on the Judiciary: Supreme Court Nomination Hearings." Jeffrey A. Segal, © Cengage Learning.

The confirmation process has also become a much more partisan process over the years. In recent nominations, highly qualified conservatives such as Antonin Scalia received unanimous support from Democrats and Republicans and liberal Ruth Bader Ginsburg received unanimous support from Democrats and overwhelming support from Republicans, but opposition party senators frequently oppose nominees. While Chief Justice John Roberts, nominated by Republican George W. Bush, received unanimous support from Republicans, Senator Barack Obama and 17 other Democrats opposed him. Similarly, while Elena Kagan, nominated by Democratic President Obama, received nearly unanimous support from Democrats (57 out of 58), only 5 (out of 41) Republicans supported her.

Among opposition party senators, ideology can be decisive. In the Roberts vote, only 25 percent of liberal Democrats supported him whereas more than 80 percent of more moderate Democrats did so. With Kagan, however, opposition was below 20 percent for both moderate Republicans (14 percent) and more conservative Republicans (10 percent) (see Figure 14.2). Constituent preferences matter too:[39] Only one of the Republicans who voted for Kagan came from a state that Obama lost in 2008.

The nominees' perceived qualifications are no less important than ideology. While the high-quality nominees of recent years—Kagan, Sotomayor, Alito, and Roberts—all received substantial opposition, the Senate confirmed all of them. Lower-qualified nominees have long faced decisive trouble. Generally, lower-qualified nominees receive substantially fewer votes than their

> **Connections:**
> Should public opinion affect judicial appointments?

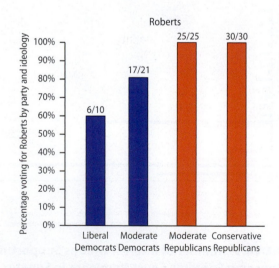
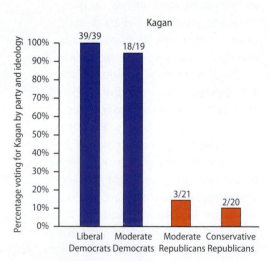

FIGURE 14.2 **Partisanship and Ideology in the Roberts and Kagan Votes.**

Source: Votes and ideology from Keith Poole and Howard Rosenthal, http://www.voteview.com. Jeffrey A. Segal, © Cengage Learning.

more highly qualified counterparts. The number is still enough to pass under normal circumstances, particularly if the president's party controls the Senate. When the president's party does not control the Senate, the Senate often rejects a poorly qualified nominee. Strong concern about her lack of qualifications is among the reasons that led one of George W. Bush's nominees, Harriet Miers, to withdraw her nomination.

In a Court long dominated by white males, Clarence Thomas (1991) was only the second African American to serve; Thurgood Marshall (1967), a distinguished litigator for the National Association for the Advancement of Colored People (NAACP) who argued *Brown v. Board of Education* (1954) before the Court, was the first. The Senate has confirmed 112 justices to seats on the Supreme Court. Of those 112, only 4—Sandra Day O'Connor (1981), Ruth Bader Ginsburg (1993), Sonia Sotomayor (2009), and Elena Kagan (2010)—have been female. Sotomayor is the first and only Hispanic. By some measures, the current Supreme Court, with three women, one African American, and one Hispanic, is the most diverse ever.

It is also the case that the first thirty-two nominations went to Protestants, long the dominant religious group in American politics. Today, in a sign that the gateways to prominent positions have opened dramatically, the Court has six Roman Catholic justices, three Jewish justices, and no Protestants.

This diversity matters in a number of ways, both on lower courts and at the Supreme Court.[40] Supreme Court justice Sandra Day O'Connor, for example, understood sex discrimination well. After graduating second in her class from Stanford Law School, no law firm in California offered her a job as an attorney, but one did offer her a secretarial position. Given that the Court has tremendous discretion about which cases to hear, greater diversity means that the Court may be more responsive to the issues that matter most to an increasingly diverse national population. Historic appointments such as O'Connor's can also have an influence on how their colleagues vote.[41] As more women serve on the U.S. Supreme Court, the bias found against female attorneys might lessen.[42]

On the other hand, for the first time in history, not one member of the Supreme Court held elective office prior to service on the Court. This lack of experience in electoral politics might play into their decisions striking down campaign finance laws (see *Citizens United v. Federal Election Commission*, in Chapter 8, Interest Groups). The educational background of the current justices also is fairly narrow. Every one of them attended either Harvard or Yale Law School. Professionally, only Sotomayor served as a trial judge, and all the justices except Kagan came to the Supreme Court from federal appeals courts. This narrowness of background has not always been the case. In the past, many Supreme Court nominees graduated from modestly ranked

Connections: Does diversity on the Court matter? Should the Supreme Court be age diverse?

Checkpoint

Can you:

☐ Explain senatorial courtesy

☐ Describe issues in nominations to courts of appeals

☐ Discuss the ways in which partisanship and ideology influence Supreme Court nominations

law schools, and the justices often came to the Court from governorships, cabinet positions, the Senate, and private practice. To people who believe that the justices simply make decisions that are commanded by the Constitution, this narrowness does not matter. But to those who believe that just as experience with discrimination helps judges understand civil rights complaints, experience in the executive or legislative branches helps judges understand the constraints operating on those branches, the lack of this form of diversity hurts both the Court and the nation.

State and Lower Federal Courts

❯ How state and lower federal courts operate

While the Supreme Court is the highest court in the United States, it hears only a small percentage of the cases filed in federal court. Litigants might insist that they will take a case all the way to the Supreme Court, but the overwhelming majority of federal cases are resolved in the district courts, which conduct civil and criminal trials. Cases appealed from the district courts go to one of the U.S. Courts of Appeals, in which three-judge panels usually decide cases. From those panels, losing litigants can appeal cases to the entire circuit for an *en banc* ("by the full court") hearing, or they can appeal directly to the U.S. Supreme Court (see Figure 14.3).

State Courts in the Federal Judicial System

Each state has its own judicial system, and unless a case involves federal law or the type of parties that create federal jurisdiction, cases get resolved in state courts, each of which has its own hierarchy of trial and appellate courts. Cases that involve federal issues that begin in one of the fifty separate state court systems can be appealed to the federal court system in one of two ways. First, criminal defendants who have exhausted their state appeals, that is, have gone through their last appeal at the state level, can file a writ of *habeas corpus* with a U.S. District Court, which then allows the court to determine whether one or more of the defendant's federal legal rights have been violated. Second, any parties who have exhausted their state appeals can file a request for review, known as a **petition for a writ of *certiorari***, directly with the Supreme Court.

 **petition for a writ of certiorari:** *Request to the Supreme Court that it review a lower court case.*

The District Courts

The Judiciary Act of 1789 established thirteen district courts for the thirteen states. Today, there are ninety-four districts. Many states have more than one

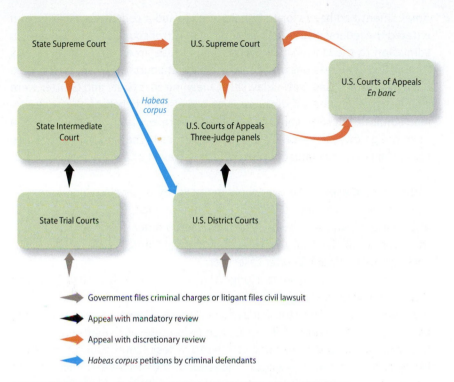

Government files criminal charges or litigant files civil lawsuit

Appeal with mandatory review

Appeal with discretionary review

Habeas corpus petitions by criminal defendants

FIGURE 14.3 Judicial Organization in the United States.

Source: Adapted from Lee Epstein, Jeffrey A. Segal, Harold J. Spaeth, and Thomas G. Walker, *The Supreme Court Compendium*, 5th ed. (Washington, D.C.: CQ Press, 2010), Figure 7-3. Copyright © 2010 by CQ Press. All rights reserved. Reproduced by permission.

district, but no district covers more than one state. Districts that cover only part of a state receive geographical names, such as the Northern District of Illinois. Altogether there are 667 district judgeships. Many districts have only one judge, but the Southern District of New York has 28, and the Central District of California has 27. Nevertheless, with rare exceptions, district judges oversee trials alone, not in panels.

Trials in the district courts are either criminal or civil. In civil suits, plaintiffs (the parties bringing the suit) often request monetary damages to compensate for harm done to them, such as by a broken contract or a defective product. When rights are alleged to have been violated, they may ask that the practice be stopped. Litigants filed more than 282,000 civil suits in the district courts in 2010, and the federal government commenced nearly 78,000 criminal prosecutions.[43]

When Gratz and Grutter sued the University of Michigan over its admissions policies, the first stop for each was the U.S. District Court. Both had standing to sue, as their rejections by the university were real injuries, and because they claimed that their rights to equal protection under the Fourteenth

Amendment had been violated, their cases raised a constitutional issue and entered the federal court system. Gratz and Grutter sought not only their own admission to the University of Michigan, but also an end to the university's use of race in admissions decisions. The district courts allowed both suits to move forward as **class action lawsuits**, meaning that Gratz and Grutter were suing not only on behalf of themselves but also on behalf of all people denied admission at Michigan on account of their race. Class action lawsuits can open the gateways of access to groups of citizens in the same circumstances, thus broadening the impact over the possible result of an individual lawsuit.

class action lawsuit: *Lawsuit filed by one person on behalf of that person plus all similarly situated people.*

Civil Procedure.

The overwhelming majority of lawsuits filed in federal court settle out of court with a negotiated agreement between the plaintiff and the defendant. In 2010 the district courts commenced slightly more than three thousand civil trials. Of these, nearly two-thirds were bench (nonjury) trials, as the *Gratz* and *Grutter* cases were.

Once a case is assigned to a judge, the next step in a civil suit is discovery. Discovery grants each side access to information relevant to its suit held by the other side. Crucial to the *Gratz* and *Grutter* suits were University of Michigan documents showing differential admission rates for whites and minorities who had similar grades and standardized test scores. During discovery, the attorneys for each side can also question witnesses for the other side in a process known as deposition. Following discovery, litigants file briefs with the court, laying out their arguments.

Outside interests can file *amicus curiae* ("friend of the court") briefs, stating their concerns in a case.[44] The most influential *amicus* briefs are those filed in the name of the United States, as represented by the Office of the **Solicitor General** in the Justice Department.[45] In the *Gratz* and *Grutter* cases, the Clinton administration filed briefs in favor of the University of Michigan, which argued that affirmative action was necessary to obtain a diverse student body. General Motors also filed a brief in favor of the university's affirmative action program, stating that it needed a diverse pool of highly qualified attorneys, managers, and the like. Eventually, Microsoft and nineteen other Fortune 500 companies signed briefs supporting the university.[46]

Trial courts make determinations as to fact and as to law, whereas appellate courts generally make determinations only as to law, applying the facts as determined by the trial court. That would normally mean that it would be up to the district court to determine factually whether race played a role in admissions at Michigan and how much of a role it played. Then it would decide as a matter of law whether that role was allowable or not. The parties in the *Gratz* and *Grutter* cases made the decision a bit easier for the judges, for the University of Michigan readily admitted—indeed, strongly defended—its use of race in admissions. Therefore, the question for the trial judge was not a question of fact, but a question of law: Does the equal protection clause of

solicitor general: *Official in the Justice Department who represents the president in federal court.*

Connections:
How important is a diverse student body on your campus? How important is a diverse workforce? What is your experience?

the Fourteenth Amendment prohibit the use of race as a factor in
university admissions?

While trial judges or juries
have nearly complete discretion
in deciding questions of fact, they
are constrained by the courts
above them on questions of law. In
affirmative action, the key precedent was the 1978 Supreme Court
decision in *Regents of the University of California v. Bakke*.[47] A divided Court ruled in *Bakke* that the
University of California's quota
system of reserving a certain number of seats for minorities was unconstitutional, but that a system
in which race was a "plus" in admissions could be justified due to
the benefits that a diverse student
body provides all the students (see
Chapter 5).

Barbara Grutter was in her 40s when she applied to law school. The
mother of two children, she also ran a consulting business. In this
photo, Jennifer Gratz listens on the right.

In December 2000 Judge Duggan ruled in the *Gratz* case that the point
system used by the university—in which each applicant could receive up to
150 points, including 20 for being from an underrepresented minority group—
was a valid and necessary means of obtaining a diverse student body. On the
other hand, Judge Friedman ruled in March 2001 that the law school's use
of race in admissions violated the Constitution, finding that it was an "enormously important factor" in admissions, and not the mere plus approved by
the Supreme Court in *Bakke*. The University of Michigan appealed Friedman's
decision to the Sixth Circuit Court of Appeals, while the Center for Individual
Rights backed Gratz's appeal to the same circuit.

Connections:
Should race be a
factor in university
admissions?

Criminal Procedure.

Beyond civil cases like the Michigan affirmative
action suits, trial courts also conduct criminal trials. A criminal prosecution
begins with an alleged violation of federal criminal law. In the U.S. federal
system, states have primary authority over law enforcement, but the federal
government frequently prosecutes drug, weapons, and immigration cases,
plus other crimes that involve interstate commerce or the instrumentalities
of the federal government, such as the post office and government buildings.

The clearance rate for state and federal crimes—that is, the percentage
of reported crimes in which someone is arrested, charged, and turned over
for prosecution—is highest for violent crimes (47 percent in 2009) but much

plea bargain:
Agreement by a criminal defendant to plead guilty in return for a reduced sentence.

Connections:
Do plea bargains make efficiency more important than justice?

lower for property crimes such as burglary (18.6 percent).[48] Under the Constitution, an accused criminal in a federal court has a right to indictment by a grand jury, a specially empanelled jury consisting of between sixteen and twenty-three citizens who determine whether the government has sufficient evidence to charge the suspect with a crime. In the rare occasions in which a grand jury chooses not to indict, the suspect is freed.

Following indictment, the accused is arraigned, or informed of the charges against him or her, and asked to enter an initial plea of guilty or not guilty. About 90 percent of federal criminal cases are resolved through **plea bargains**, in which the accused plead guilty, usually in exchange for reduced charges or lesser sentences.[49] This arrangement greatly enhances the ability of trial courts to deal with large criminal caseloads.

In the small number of cases that proceed to trial, the accused has the right to a trial by jury but is free to request a bench trial, in which the judge decides guilt or innocence. A jury in a federal felony case consists of twelve individuals who must reach a verdict unanimously. (Neither twelve people nor unanimity is required in a state court.) The accused can appeal a guilty verdict, but the double jeopardy clause of the Constitution prohibits the government from appealing a verdict of not guilty. If the accused is found guilty, the judge determines the sentence based on guidelines that depend on the nature of the offense, the number of prior convictions, and other factors as recommended by the U.S. Sentencing Commission. In death penalty cases, the decision on the punishment is left to the jury. That is, following a guilty verdict, the jury hears new testimony by the prosecutor and defense attorney about whether death is the appropriate punishment.

The Courts of Appeals

Sitting hierarchically above the ninety-four district courts are the U.S. Courts of Appeals. Congress has divided the Courts of Appeals into eleven numbered circuits plus a circuit for the District of Columbia and a "federal circuit" that hears appeals from specialized lower courts that deal with patents and customs (see Figure 14.4). Each of the numbered courts of appeals has jurisdiction over several states. The number of judgeships in each circuit ranges from six to twenty-nine. Regardless of the number of judgeships, randomly assigned three-judge panels usually hear appeals from the district courts.

The courts have mandatory jurisdiction over cases appealed to them. That is, if a losing party from the district court appeals to the appropriate court of appeals, the court must hear the case. Because the circuit courts are in the middle of the federal judicial hierarchy, cases can be both appealed to the court of appeals and appealed from the court of appeals (see Figure 14.3). Appeals from a court of appeals can happen in two ways. First, losing litigants

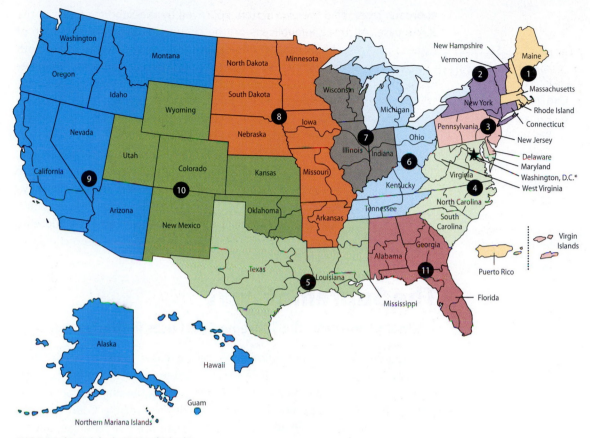

*U.S. Court of Appeals for the District of Columbia
The Federal Circuit Court, in Washington, D.C., hears appeals in trade and patent cases.

FIGURE 14.4 **U.S. Courts of Appeals and U.S. District Courts.**

Source: © Cengage Learning, data from United States Courts, Court Locator, http://www.uscourts.gov/court_locator.aspx.

at the court of appeals who believe that the three-judge panel that heard their case did not represent the judgment of the circuit as a whole can request an *en banc* review. Alternatively, losing litigants can request review by the Supreme Court. In both cases, further review is at the discretion of the court that is being petitioned.

Given the importance of the *Grutter* and *Gratz* cases, they made it through the U.S. Court of Appeals in anything but a normal manner. Rather than a hearing with a three-judge panel, possibly followed by *en banc* and/or Supreme Court review, the Center for Individual Rights, which represented Gratz and Grutter, requested and was granted an immediate *en banc* review. On May 14, 2002, the Sixth Circuit ruled in favor of the university in the law school case by a 5–4 vote. The **majority opinion** argued that the law school's

majority opinion: *Opinion of a court laying out the official position of the court in the case.*

approach resembled the plus system approved by the Supreme Court in the *Bakke* case. All three Republicans on the circuit sided with Grutter; five of the six Democrats sided with the university, consistent both with generally greater support among Democrats than Republicans for equality of outcome over equality of opportunity and with evidence that such attitudes often influence judicial decisions. Not surprisingly, Barbara Grutter appealed the decision to the Supreme Court.

On October 1, 2002, ten months after oral arguments, the court of appeals still had not issued its ruling in the undergraduate case. In an unusual step, Gratz's attorneys asked the Supreme Court to bypass the court of appeals and rule directly on their appeal. On December 1 the Supreme Court accepted review in both cases.

Checkpoint

Can you:

☐ Explain how state court cases can end up in federal court

☐ Give an overview of the responsibilities and procedures in district courts

☐ Give an overview of the responsibilities and procedures in courts of appeals

The Supreme Court

❯ **What procedures the Supreme Court uses for deciding cases**

The Supreme Court's procedure in handling cases consists of deciding whether to grant review and, if review is granted, of receiving briefs, hearing oral arguments, deciding who wins, and writing the majority opinion. If desired, justices who do not agree with the decision of the Court majority (that is, the decision about who wins the case) can write dissenting opinions. Those who agree with the majority opinion on who should win but differ as to the reasoning can write concurring opinions. The majority opinion, however, stands as the precedent for lower court judges to apply in similar cases dealing with the same issue.

Granting Review

Each year about eight thousand losing litigants ask the Supreme Court to review their cases. The vast majority of appeals to the Supreme Court come in the form of petitions for writs of *certiorari*, often shortened to petitions for "cert." The Supreme Court's decision to grant cert is purely discretionary, but its rules suggest that a grant of cert is more likely when a lower court resolves issues of law differently from the way other lower courts have or issues a decision that conflicts with decisions of the Supreme Court. The Supreme Court is also more likely to grant review when the government of the United States, represented by the solicitor general's office, requests it, either as a petitioning party or as *amicus curiae*. The filing of *amicus* briefs by other parties can also be important to the Court, as it signals that the case involves important questions of public policy.[50]

The large number of petitions for cert prevents the justices from fully reviewing each one. Instead, they rely on their clerks, who are usually recent law school graduates, to write summaries. Most of the justices' chambers have joined the "cert pool," which splits the cert petitions among the clerks of the justices in the pool.

The large number of petitions also prevents the justices from fully discussing each one. Rather, the chief justice passes around a "discuss list," a set of cases he thinks worthy of discussion. Any justice can add any other case to the list if he or she wishes. Cases not on the discuss list are automatically denied cert, leaving the lower court's decision as final. The justices then meet in conference to consider each of the cases on the discuss list. The Court grants cert through a **rule of four**. That is, although five votes constitute a majority, the Court will agree to hear a case if any four justices vote to grant cert. Overall, the Court grants only about 1 percent of cert petitions, leaving the lower court decision as final in the remaining 99 percent of the cases.

The justices' votes on petitions for *certiorari* remain secret unless a justice leaves his or her papers to the public, as justices sometimes do after they retire. To date, the justices' votes in the *Gratz* and *Grutter* cases are unavailable, but the importance of the issue plus a split between the Sixth Circuit Court upholding affirmative action and an earlier Fifth Circuit decision striking it down at the University of Texas made a grant highly likely.[51] On December 2, 2002, the Court granted review to both cases.

rule of four:
Supreme Court rule that grants review to a case if as few as four of the justices support review.

Oral Arguments

Following a grant of cert, the justices receive written briefs from the litigants explaining why their position should win. Other parties may file *amicus curiae* briefs urging the Court to affirm or reverse the lower court decision. While the Clinton administration sided with the university at the district court level in the *Gratz* and *Grutter* cases, the George W. Bush administration switched sides and asked the Supreme Court to strike down the law school and undergraduate admissions programs. On the other hand, seventy-four organizations filed *amicus* briefs supporting the university, which, until the 2012 health care decision,[52] was the most ever in a Supreme Court case.

Parties normally receive thirty minutes each for oral argument, although the justices frequently interrupt with questions. The quality of these arguments varies enormously, and, not surprisingly, can influence which party wins.[53] Oral arguments in the *Gratz* and *Grutter* cases, as well as in hundreds of other cases, are available at http://www.oyez.org.

Connections:
Should the federal government be allowed to try to influence a court decision?

The Decision

Within a few days of oral argument, the justices meet in conference to vote on the merits of the case, that is, to decide which side wins, and to assign a justice to write the Opinion of the Court in the case. If the chief justice is in the majority, he determines who will write the opinion. If the chief justice is not in the majority, the assignment is made by the senior justice who is in the majority.

Assigning a justice to write the Opinion of the Court—which explains the Court's justification for its decision and sets guidelines for other courts to follow—does not mean that a majority opinion will result. If a justice writes an opinion siding with one side, and other justices agree with the result (that is, agree on who wins) but not with the reasoning, they can concur in the judgment. That means that they are not joining the Opinion of the Court. Such justices will typically write a **concurring opinion** that explains their reasoning or join the concurring opinion of another justice. Justices who disagree with the result reached by the majority can write a **dissenting opinion** explaining why they believe the Court's decision was in error. If, due to a combination of concurring and dissenting justices, fewer than five justices join the Opinion of the Court, that opinion becomes a plurality judgment rather than a majority opinion. Plurality judgments have less value as precedents than majority opinions.

The conference on the affirmative action cases revealed a split in the justices' preferences: 5–4 in favor of the law school program, but 6–3 against the undergraduate program. As Figure 14.5 shows, four conservative justices thought that both the undergraduate and the law school affirmative programs violated the Fourteenth Amendment and were unconstitutional, whereas the three most liberal justices thought that both programs were acceptable because of the university's compelling interest in creating a diverse student body and the narrow tailoring of the affirmative action programs to meet that interest. Justices Sandra Day O'Connor and Stephen Breyer were the swing justices. They agreed that diversity constituted a compelling interest but did not believe that the undergraduate program, which automatically gave a set number of points to minority applicants, was narrowly tailored to meet that interest. They thus voted with the more conservative justices to strike the undergraduate program. But O'Connor and Breyer voted with the liberals to uphold the law school program, which overall gave strong preferences to underrepresented minorities but was more careful in considering the importance of race in each individual's application.

Though Gratz won her case, she had by this point graduated from a different Michigan campus, the University of Michigan–Dearborn. The University of Michigan changed its admissions procedures to be more like the law school's: Race would still be used as an admissions factor, but there would be no automatic point total added just because of an applicant's race.

Supreme Court Impact

The fact that the Supreme Court issues a decision does not necessarily mean that government officials charged with implementing it will comply. The courts have no power of enforcement. The Court's school desegregation decision in

concurring opinion: *Opinion that agrees with the results of the majority opinion (that is, which party wins) but sets out a separate rationale.*

dissenting opinion: *Opinion that disagrees with the majority opinion as to which party wins.*

Connections:
Should Gratz have won her case? Should Grutter?

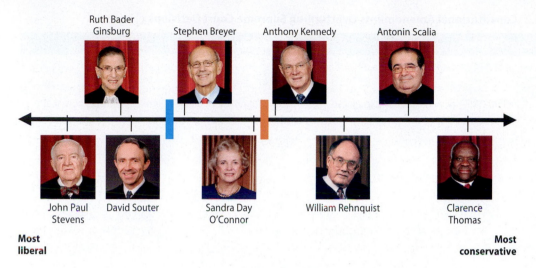

Ruth Bader Ginsburg   Stephen Breyer   Anthony Kennedy   Antonin Scalia

John Paul Stevens   David Souter   Sandra Day O'Connor   William Rehnquist   Clarence Thomas

Most liberal

Most conservative

FIGURE 14.5 Ideology and Votes of Supreme Court Justices in the *Gratz* and *Grutter* Cases.

The justices are aligned from most liberal to most conservative. The six justices to the right of the blue line voted with Gratz to strike the undergraduate affirmative action program at the University of Michigan. The five justices to the left of the brown line voted with the University of Michigan in upholding the law school's affirmative action program.

Source for justices' ideology: Martin-Quinn Scores, http://mqscores.wustl.edu/. Jeffrey A. Segal, © Cengage Learning. *Photos:* Ginsburg, Breyer, Kennedy, Scalia, Stevens, and Thomas by Steve Petteway, Collection of the Supreme Court of the United States; Souter by Joseph Bailey, National Geographic Society, Courtesy of the Collection of the Supreme Court of the United States; O'Connor by Dane Penland, Smithsonian Institution, Collection of the Supreme Court of the United States; Rehnquist by Dane Penland, Smithsonian Institution, Collection of the Supreme Court of the United States.

Brown, for example, met with massive resistance from supporters of segregation: Elected officials urged disobedience, local boards of education ignored the decision, and lower courts complied with the decision halfheartedly at best. All the while, citizens rallied in the streets in opposition (see Chapter 12).

Additionally, many types of court decisions can be overturned by Congress, state legislatures, or other legislative mechanisms such as state-level referenda. When a court's decision is based on the meaning of a statute (for example, is carbon dioxide considered a pollutant under the Clean Air Act?), Congress can simply overturn the court's decision if it disagrees with the court's conclusion.

In the constitutional realm, if the Court declares that a practice is not unconstitutional, as in the affirmative action case, that practice can still be prohibited through the legislature or, if the state allows, through a referendum. So when the Supreme Court rules that affirmative action is not prohibited by the Constitution, that does not mean that the university is required to implement an affirmative action program or that the state is required to allow such a program. Following the Supreme Court decision in her case, Jennifer Gratz used the gateway provided by Michigan's initiative procedure, organizing a

Connections: How are court decisions enforced? Would government work better if the courts had the power of enforcement?

Connections: Did the Michigan ballot initiative undermine justice or help ensure it?

TABLE 14.2 Constitutional Amendments Overturning Supreme Court Decisions

Supreme Court Decision	Amendment
Chisolm v. Georgia (1793) allowed citizens to sue other states in federal court.	Eleventh Amendment (1795) establishes sovereign immunity for states.
Dred Scott v. Sandford (1857) denied citizenship to African Americans.	Fourteenth Amendment (1868) makes all people born in the United States citizens of the United States.
Minor v. Happersett (1874) denied voting rights to women.	Nineteenth Amendment (1920) guarantees women the right to vote.
Pollock v. Farmers' Loan and Trust (1895) limited Congress's authority to tax income.	Sixteenth Amendment (1913) grants Congress the authority to tax income from whatever source derived.
Oregon v. Mitchell (1970) prompted Congress to set the voting age at 18 for all elections. The case struck the law as applied to state elections.	Twenty-Sixth Amendment (1971) sets the voting age at 18 for all elections.

statewide proposal in Michigan that banned the use of race, gender, or ethnicity for admissions or hiring in higher education. The initiative passed decisively in November 2006 by a 58 percent to 42 percent margin. Thus, despite the Supreme Court's decision in the affirmative action cases, affirmative action in admissions is illegal at all public colleges in Michigan, including the University of Michigan. With three of the five justices from the 5–4 *Grutter* majority having left the Court, the Court will revisit the constitutionality of race-based affirmative action in the 2012–13 term.

On the other hand, when the Supreme Court declares that the Constitution prohibits an activity, legislatures find that prohibition difficult to overturn. For example, when the Court declared that Congress did not have the authority to set the voting age at 18 for state elections, the only recourse was for Congress and the states to pass a constitutional amendment overturning that decision. Only five of the Supreme Court's constitutional decisions have ever been overturned via amendment (see Table 14.2). While relatively more of the Court's statutory decisions get overturned by Congress, such instances are still fairly rare.

In addition, most Supreme Court decisions are complied with, even when the consequences for the losing litigants are serious. Following the Supreme Court's Watergate decision, President Richard M. Nixon turned over the Watergate tapes, even though doing so meant the end of his presidency.[54] Following the Supreme Court's decision in reapportionment cases, state legislatures reapportioned their states, even though it meant that many of the legislators would be reapportioned out of their seats.[55] Similarly, states stopped prosecuting doctors for providing abortions following *Roe v. Wade*.[56]

 Checkpoint

Can you:

☐ Explain how cases reach the Supreme Court

☐ Describe the process of oral argument

☐ Survey how the Court reaches and issues decisions

☐ Discuss the impact Court decisions do and do not have

The Judiciary and Public Policy: Affirmative Action and Judicial Activism and Restraint

An overly simple view of American politics holds that the legislative branch makes the law, the judicial branch interprets the law, and the executive branch enforces the law. But the president can issue executive orders, and executive branch agencies can issue regulations that often are indistinguishable from legislation. The legislative branch holds hearings on executive branch agencies that often focus on how those agencies enforce the law. The job of the courts is to interpret the law, but in doing so they often appear to go beyond mere interpretation and get actively involved in policy making. Supporters and critics of the *Roe* abortion decision often agree that the decision, which established different degrees of abortion rights depending on the trimester of the pregnancy (see Chapter 4), reads more like the making of policy than the interpretation of law.

We now consider two broad approaches to understanding judicial policy making: a legal approach and an extralegal approach. We look at affirmative action policy in particular and then examine the consequences for a democracy of the reliance on extralegal factors by an unelected judiciary.

Connections: In the *Gratz* and *Grutter* cases, was government responsive? Did the decisions help ensure equality?

The Legal Approach

According to the legal approach, justices base their decisions on legally relevant materials, such as prior court precedents, the plain meaning of the text of the law under consideration, and the intent of the framers of the law.

As we explained earlier in the chapter, precedent means a reliance on the prior decisions of the Court. In the *Grutter* case the Court accepted the arguments from the *Bakke* case that the government had a compelling interest in achieving a diverse student body but concluded that systems that establish racial quotas go too far. Reliance on precedent creates stability in law: Decisions change gradually rather than abruptly. Reliance on precedent also generates a degree of equality and fairness. Lower courts are bound by Supreme Court precedents, but the Supreme Court does not necessarily consider itself strictly bound to its own precedents. Otherwise there would be no growth in the law.

Beyond precedent, legal-based approaches consider the plain meaning of the law being interpreted. However, while a textual approach makes some

Connections: On what should judges and justices base their decisions?

issues perfectly clear, it does not necessarily answer whether affirmative action plans designed to increase diversity or fair representation in an unequal society violate equal protection of the law.

Justice Clarence Thomas often argues for decision making based on the intent of the Framers. This approach places the meaning of the Framers ahead of the literal meaning of the words that they wrote. However, in many circumstances it is difficult to know what the Framers meant or what they would have thought if they could have envisioned modern American society.

The Extralegal Approach

Legal approaches often fail to provide a good indicator of what the Supreme Court will do. Alternatively, we can consider extralegal approaches to Supreme Court decision making, which go beyond the legal factors that courts are supposed to consider. The most important extralegal considerations include the justices' own preferences and strategic considerations based on the preferences of others.

The Justices' Preferences.
Recall from the affirmative action cases that the four most conservative justices voted to strike both the undergraduate and the law school plans, the three most liberal justices voted to uphold both, and two justices in the middle voted to uphold the law school program but to strike the undergraduate program. (For the ideology of the justices currently on the Court, see Figure 14.6.)

This sort of relationship between the justices' ideology and their votes is fairly common. But because Supreme Court scholars cannot obtain information from the justices themselves about their ideology, they use indirect measures. As Figure 14.7 shows, there exists a very strong relationship between the justices' ideology and their votes once on the Court.[57] Note, however, that this strong relationship does not necessarily apply to state courts or lower federal courts, both of which must follow precedents established by the Supreme Court, at least on matters of federal law.

Strategic Considerations.
Justices cannot behave solely on the basis of their ideological preferences but must consider the preferences of other justices as well. Negotiations over the content of the majority opinion are a routine part of Supreme Court decision making.[58] In addition, a justice may need to consider the preferences of other actors in the political environment. For example, the efforts of President Franklin Roosevelt to pack the Court in the face of the Court's rejection of his New Deal programs assuredly played a role in the Court's subsequent approval of such programs.

Affirmative Action

The term *affirmative action* first made its way into federal policy through Executive Order 10925, signed by President John F. Kennedy (1961–63) in 1961.

Connections: What role should ideology play in judicial decisions? What role does it play?

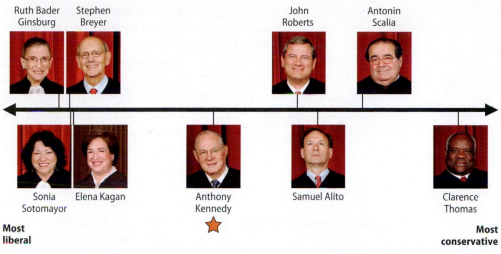

Ruth Bader Ginsburg   Stephen Breyer   John Roberts   Antonin Scalia

Sonia Sotomayor   Elena Kagan   Anthony Kennedy   Samuel Alito   Clarence Thomas

Most liberal

⭐

Most conservative

⭐ = Median (swing) justice

FIGURE 14.6 **Estimated Ideology of the Supreme Court Justices, 2012.**

Although liberalism and conservatism mean different things at different times, liberalism on the Supreme Court is usually associated with support for women and minorities in civil rights cases, support for governmental authority in economic cases, support for defendants and convicts in criminal cases, and support for individuals claiming abridgment of rights in First Amendment and privacy cases. Conservatism is associated with the opposite values. The figure shows the ideology of the Court as measured at the end of the 2011–12 term. Justice Kennedy, with no one particularly close to him on his left or his right, is the swing justice by a substantial margin. In other words, when he votes liberally, the four more liberal colleagues probably will also vote liberally, and when he votes conservatively, the four more conservative colleagues probably will vote conservatively as well. Nevertheless, in the 2012 health care case, Kennedy voted to strike the law on all issues while Chief Justice John Roberts voted to uphold the law on the taxing issue. Overall, though, Kennedy is in the majority more than any other justice.

Source: *Judicial liberalism:* Lee Epstein, Jeffrey A. Segal, Harold J. Spaeth, and Thomas G. Walker, *The Supreme Court Compendium*, 5th ed. (Washington, D.C.: CQ Press, 2010), Table 6-4. *Justices' ideology:* Martin-Quinn Scores, http://mqscores.wustl.edu/. Jeffrey A. Segal, © Cengage Learning. *Photos:* Steve Petteway, Collection of the Supreme Court of the United States.

The order required federal contractors to "take affirmative action to ensure that applicants are employed, and that employees are treated during employment, without regard to their race, creed, color, or national origin."[59] In 1964 the Civil Rights Act, while generally prohibiting discrimination on account of race or sex, specifically allowed preferential treatment for Native Americans living on or near reservations. Today federal funding acts for education, defense, and transportation routinely grant contracting preferences for minority- and female-owned business. The Department of Education interprets the nondiscrimination provisions of the Civil Rights Act to encourage voluntary affirmative action plans that help achieve a diverse student population.[60]

As the *Gratz* and *Grutter* cases show, the courts have a major role in this process, balancing equality of opportunity against affirmative action policies

Connections:
Which is more important, equality of opportunity or equality of outcome?

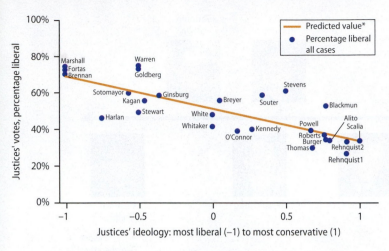

*Predicted value is the percentage of time the justice is predicted to vote liberally given his or her ideology.

Note: Rehnquist 1 indicates his term as an associate justice; Rehnquist 2 indicates his term as chief justice.

FIGURE 14.7 Justices' Votes by Their Ideology, 1953–2010.

This graph plots justices' ideology (shown from left to right) against the percentage of times justices voted in a liberal direction (shown from top to bottom). It is clear that the most conservative justices, such as Rehnquist and Burger (among those further to the right in the graph), voted in a liberal direction far less often than the more liberal justices, such as Fortas, Marshall, and Brennan (who are on the left of the graph).

Source: Justices' ideology: Data updated and backdated by Jeffrey Segal from Jeffrey Segal and Albert Cover, "Ideological Values and the Votes of Supreme Court Justices," *American Political Science Review* 83 (1989): 557–65. *Justices' votes:* Lee Epstein, Jeffrey A. Segal, Harold J. Spaeth, and Thomas G. Walker, *The Supreme Court Compendium,* 5th ed. (Washington, D.C.: CQ Press, 2010). Jeffrey A. Segal, © Cengage Learning.

> **Connections:** Is the judicial branch, as Hamilton said, "the least dangerous branch"? Defend your answer.

judicial activism:
Decisions that go beyond the what the law requires made by judges who seek to impose their own policy preferences on society through their judicial decisions.

aimed at providing greater equality of outcome. Given the play of extralegal factors in such decisions, are judges, in fact, policy makers?[61] When the Supreme Court decides for the nation that affirmative action programs are allowed as long as they provide individualized assessments of students' records, they are making policy. The fact that this is not merely interpretation of the law is supported by the fact that the justices' ideological preferences overwhelmingly explain their votes on the Court.

But we might reach a different conclusion regarding the lower courts. Consider a district court judge faced with a suit by a white student to gain admission to a university that has an affirmative action program similar to the Michigan law school program. The judge applies the precedent from *Grutter* and rejects the student's challenge. Although that judge has made a decision that is crucial to the student, both the scope of the decision (which applies only to that student) and the low level of discretion involved in reaching it (the judge felt bound by the Supreme Court precedent in *Grutter*) make this sort of behavior distinct from policy making.

Activism and Restraint

Because judges are unelected and serve for life, they are not accountable to the people in the same way that presidents and members of Congress are. Nevertheless, they have an extraordinary power—the power of judicial review. Judicial review allows an unelected branch of government to strike the laws and actions of the elected branches of government—Congress and the president. This authority by the judicial branch is questionable in a democracy, where the people are supposed to have the final say.

The Supreme Court first held an act of Congress unconstitutional in 1803, and then did not hold another one unconstitutional until 1857. Since that time, however, the Court has struck down 166 congressional laws, slightly more than one per year, with seven laws struck down in 1935 during the height of the Court's battle with the New Deal (see Figure 14.8). Since 1986 the Court has struck down nearly three times as many state and municipal laws (101) as federal laws (39).[62]

Given the undemocratic nature of judicial review, politicians frequently decry **judicial activists**, judges who go beyond what the law requires and seek to impose their own policy preferences on society through their decisions. These critics insist that judges should act with **judicial restraint**, that is, judges should respect the decisions of other branches or, through the concept of precedent, the decisions of earlier judges.

Contemporary research suggests that justices respect the decisions of legislatures and earlier judges when those decisions are consistent with the justices' ideology. Thus, for example, liberal justices such as Ginsburg and Breyer overwhelmingly vote to uphold liberal precedents[63] or federal laws favored by liberals.[64] But when conservative precedents or laws favored by conservatives are under consideration, liberal justices are more than willing to strike them. Similarly, conservative justices such as Scalia and Thomas overwhelmingly vote to uphold conservative precedents or the constitutionality of federal laws favored by conservatives. But when precedents are liberal in direction or when liberals favor the laws under review, conservative justices are more than willing to strike them.

© CENGAGE LEARNING

Connections:
Is judicial review a problem for democracy?

judicial restraint:

Decisions by judges respecting the decisions of other branches or, through the concept of precedent, the decisions of earlier judges.

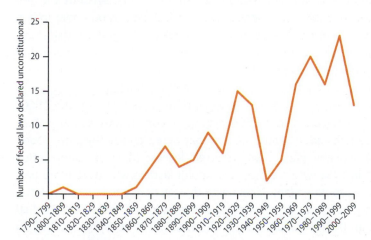

FIGURE 14.8 **Number of Federal Laws Declared Unconstitutional, 1790–2009.**

The Supreme Court declared one federal law unconstitutional in the 2010 term and one in the 2011 term.

Source: Harold W. Stanley and Richard G. Niemi, eds., *Vital Statistics on American Politics*, 3rd ed. (Washington, D.C.: CQ Press, 1992); Lawrence Baum, *The Supreme Court*, 8th ed. (Washington, D.C.: CQ Press, 2004), 170, 173; Harold J. Spaeth, Lee Epstein, Andrew D. Martin, Jeffrey A. Segal, and Thomas W. Walker, The Supreme Court Database, http://scdb.wustl.edu. Jeffrey A. Segal, © Cengage Learning.

Connections: How do elections affect judicial decisions? Should they?

The vast majority of justices are restrained toward laws and precedents that they agree with ideologically but are quite willing to overturn laws and precedents that they are distant from ideologically. One of the consequences of presidential elections is that the president gets to choose which judges will make judicial policy in the United States.

Construct Your Own Policy

1. Construct an employment policy that maintains equal opportunity but does not explicitly consider race, ethnicity, or gender.
2. Revise the judicial nomination and confirmation process to reduce the emphasis on ideology as a legitimate consideration.

For more on the policy-making process, see Chapter 1.

The Judiciary and Democracy

The judicial system of the United States promotes the equal right of participation by allowing a single individual who has been harmed by a law to challenge its constitutionality. People who have financial resources or who can find support from organized interests may fare better than those who have to act on their own. The action may not be successful. Nevertheless, the judiciary provides a separate gateway to the political system, one that is different in kind from the gateway to the legislative or executive branch. By filing a suit through the judiciary, a single individual can have an enormous influence on the American political system.

Representative democracy requires government to be accountable and responsive to the public. Yet the judicial branch is not accountable in any meaningful way: Even if the public is dissatisfied with judges' decisions, judges are unlikely to be removed from office. Yet this does not mean that the Court is not responsive to the public or to the public's representatives. Responsiveness can happen through four different gateways.

The first gateway is through the electoral process.[65] During the 1960s the Warren Court made a series of decisions on contentious issues such as criminal procedure and religious freedom that were significantly more liberal than many Americans might have preferred. Richard M. Nixon campaigned for president in 1968 with promises to appoint justices who were more pro-police and less pro-defendant. Nixon won the election and, in his first term, appointed four justices, all of whom were more conservative on criminal procedure than the rest of the Court. The result was a conservative shift in

Supreme Court decisions in criminal cases that mirrored public preferences as expressed in the 1968 election.

Second, in cases in which the Court is unresponsive to congressional preferences, Congress can threaten the Court's institutional authority. During the Civil War, Congress took away the Court's appellate jurisdiction over *habeas corpus* appeals. In the 1930s Franklin Roosevelt threatened to dilute the Court by adding six new members. In both cases, the Court backed down and responded favorably to congressional (and thus, presumably, public) preferences.

The third gateway is through current events, which can move public opinion and judges' behavior in the same direction. As society became more progressive on women's rights and other issues, judges, who themselves are members of society, became more progressive on those issues, too. Immediately after the attacks of September 11, 2001, Americans were increasingly willing to allow the government to examine personal mail and Internet activity (see Chapter 6), and judges moved in the same direction.

Fourth, judges might believe that they have an obligation to rule consistently with public opinion, even if they are not subject to electoral sanctions. It is probably no accident that the Supreme Court's split decision in the Michigan affirmative action cases reflected America's ambivalence about whether equality meant treating everybody exactly the same or whether, to promote equality of outcomes, underrepresented groups should be given advantages in admissions. Justice O'Connor, who split the difference over what can be done in the name of equal protection in the *Gratz* and *Grutter* cases, has spoken often about the need of the Supreme Court not to vary too far from public preferences.

That argument cuts both ways. As Justice Robert Jackson declared in a 1943 case striking down mandatory flag salutes, "The very purpose of a Bill of Rights was to withdraw certain subjects from the vicissitudes of political controversy, to place them beyond the reach of majorities and officials and to establish them as legal principles to be applied by the courts. One's right to life, liberty, and property, to free speech, a free press, freedom of worship and assembly, and other fundamental rights may not be submitted to vote; they depend on the outcome of no elections."[66] If justices are responsive, it is not because the Constitution's framework encourages it; it is because they choose to be.

Focus Questions Revisited

- Why is the apparently simple requirement of providing "equal protection of the laws" more difficult than it seems?

- In what ways do the federal courts lack traditional means of accountability?

- How are courts, nevertheless, responsive?

- Do citizens have equal access to the justice system? Does the justice system treat them equally?

- Is the judiciary a gate or a gateway to democracy?

gateways to learning

Top Ten to Take Away

1. The American legal system is based on the English system, following an adversary process, guaranteeing a right to trial by jury, and depending on common law in the absence of statuary authority. (pp. 483–484)

2. The Constitution established the Supreme Court. Congress has created federal district courts and courts of appeals. The Supreme Court has both original jurisdiction and appellate jurisdiction. (pp. 484–485)

3. Through the power of judicial review established in *Marbury v. Madison*, the Supreme Court has the authority to declare laws and executive actions unconstitutional and thus void. In this decision and others, the Marshall court set the United States on the path to a strong and unified nation. (pp. 485–488)

4. Through the Court's history, its interpretations have expanded, then contracted, and once again expanded national powers, especially with regard to economic regulation. After a long and slow start, the Court has also moved, fairly consistently, toward greater protections of equality. (pp. 488–494)

5. The president appoints federal judges with the advice and consent of the Senate. The higher the court, the more likely the Senate is to scrutinize nominees and refuse consent on the basis of nominees' ideology and/or qualifications. (pp. 494–496)

6. The Supreme Court has increasingly diversified with respect to religion, race, and gender. This more-equal access to the Supreme Court may also make the Court more responsive to an increasingly diverse nation. (pp. 496–500)

7. District courts conduct civil and criminal trials, while courts of appeals hear appeals from district courts. Cases from the courts of appeals can be appealed to the Supreme Court. (pp. 500–506)

8. Supreme Court decisions are made by a majority, though the justices sometimes write concurring opinions that agree with the majority but give a different rationale. The minority who disagree may write dissents. (pp. 506–510)

9. Judicial policy making can be explained by both legal and extralegal approaches, with legal approaches having more sway at lower levels and extralegal approaches at higher levels, where judicial activism can be problematic for a democracy. (pp. 511–516)

10. Although the Supreme Court is not directly accountable to the public, it is to some degree responsive to public opinion. (pp. 516–517)

Key Concepts

adversary process (p. 483). How does the adversary process seek to discover truth?

appeal (p. 483). What sort of questions can generally be appealed to a higher court?

class action lawsuit (p. 502). How do class action lawsuits promote equality in the legal system?

civil suit (p. 483). Why do civil suits exist?

common law (p. 484). What led to the development of common law?

concurring opinion (p. 508). Why might a justice concur in an opinion rather than dissent?

courts of appeals (p. 483). What is the role of the U.S. courts of appeals?

criminal case (p. 483). What is the most likely outcome when a criminal case is filed?

dissenting opinion (p. 508). How might dissenting opinions influence the public's view of the Supreme Court?

district courts (p. 484). What is the role of the U.S. District Courts?

judicial activism (p. 515). How do judges who are judicial activists behave?

judicial independence (p. 485). Why does the United States need judicial independence?

judicial restraint (p. 515). What is the evidence for the practice of judicial restraint at the Supreme Court level?

judicial review (p. 485). How does judicial review create the countermajoritarian difficulty?

jurisdiction (p. 484). What generally happens if a court does not have jurisdiction to hear a case?

majority opinion (p. 505). Why is the majority opinion so important for the Supreme Court?

Marbury v. Madison (p. 485). What doctrine did the *Marbury* case establish?

petition for a writ of *certiorari* (p. 500). How often are petitions for writs of *certiorari* granted?

plea bargain (p. 504). Why is plea bargaining so prevalent?

precedent (p. 484). Why is a general rule for the following of precedent essential to justice?

rule of four (p. 507). How does the rule of four work?

solicitor general (p. 502). What is the role of the solicitor general?

Learning Outcomes

WHAT YOU NEED...

To Know	To Test Yourself	To Participate
What the judicial branch does	• Summarize the U.S. legal traditions that derive from English legal traditions • Restate what the Constitution says about the organization and powers of the federal judiciary • Explain *Marbury v. Madison* and its importance	• Assess whether courts are gateways to citizen influence and to justice • Determine the extent to which judicial review is consistent with democratic government
How the Supreme Court has expanded and contracted national powers	• Describe the ways in which the Marshall Court expanded national power • Explain how the Supreme Court acted to limit equality between the 1830s and 1930s • Discuss what might have led the Supreme Court to accept greater national authority starting in 1937	• Understand why it is important for courts to protect minority rights
How federal judges get selected	• Explain senatorial courtesy • Describe issues in nominations to courts of appeals • Discuss the ways in which partisanship and ideology influence Supreme Court nominations	• Consider the merits of diversity in the courts
How state and lower federal courts operate	• Explain how state court cases can end up in federal court • Give an overview of the responsibilities and procedures in district courts • Give an overview of the responsibilities and procedures in courts of appeals	• Understand what would happen if federal courts could not review state court decisions on questions of federal law • Evaluate whether average citizens are able to use the gateway of filing lawsuits
What procedures the Supreme Court uses for deciding cases	• Explain how cases reach the Supreme Court • Describe the process of oral argument • Survey how the Court reaches and issues decisions • Discuss the impact Court decisions do and do not have	• Identify the gateways that make the federal judiciary more responsive to public wishes • Read and critique a recent majority opinion (http://supreme.lp.findlaw.com) • Evaluate why and whether Supreme Court decisions might have limited impacts

The Declaration of
Independence

In Congress, July 4, 1776

The Unanimous Declaration
of the Thirteen United States of America

When, in the course of human events, it becomes necessary for one people to dissolve the political bands which have connected them with another, and to assume, among the powers of the earth, the separate and equal station to which the laws of nature and of nature's God entitle them, a decent respect to the opinions of mankind requires that they should declare the causes which impel them to the separation.

We hold these truths to be self-evident: That all men are created equal; that they are endowed by their Creator with certain unalienable rights; that among these are life, liberty, and the pursuit of happiness; that, to secure these rights, governments are instituted among men, deriving their just powers from the consent of the governed; that whenever any form of government becomes destructive of these ends, it is the right of the people to alter or to abolish it, and to institute new government, laying its foundation on such principles, and organizing its powers in such form, as to them shall seem most likely to effect their safety and happiness. Prudence, indeed, will dictate that governments long established should not be changed for light and transient causes; and accordingly all experience hath shown that mankind are more disposed to suffer, while evils are sufferable, than to right themselves by abolishing the forms to which they are accustomed. But when a long train of abuses and usurpations, pursuing invariably the same object, evinces a design to reduce them under absolute despotism, it is their right, it is their duty, to throw off such government, and to provide new guards for their future security. Such has been the patient sufferance of these colonies; and such is now the necessity which constrains them to alter their former systems of government. The history of the present King of Great Britain is a history of repeated injuries and usurpations, all having in direct object the establishment of an absolute tyranny over these states. To prove this, let facts be submitted to a candid world.

He has refused to assent to laws, the most wholesome and necessary for the public good.

He has forbidden his governors to pass laws of immediate and pressing importance, unless suspended in their operation till his assent should be obtained; and, when so suspended, he has utterly neglected to attend to them.

He has refused to pass other laws for the accommodation of large districts of people, unless those people would relinquish the right of representation in the legislature, a right inestimable to them, and formidable to tyrants only.

He has called together legislative bodies at places unusual, uncomfortable, and distant from the depository of their public records, for the sole purpose of fatiguing them into compliance with his measures.

He has dissolved representative houses repeatedly, for opposing, with manly firmness, his invasions on the rights of the people.

He has refused for a long time, after such dissolutions, to cause others to be elected; whereby the legislative powers, incapable of annihilation, have returned to the people at large for their exercise; the state remaining, in the mean time, exposed to all dangers of invasions from without and convulsions within.

He has endeavored to prevent the population of these states; for that purpose obstructing the laws for naturalization of foreigners; refusing to pass others to encourage their migration hither, and raising the conditions of new appropriations of lands.

He has obstructed the administration of justice, by refusing his assent to laws for establishing judiciary powers.

He has made judges dependent on his will alone, for the tenure of their offices, and the amount and payment of their salaries.

He has erected a multitude of new offices, and sent hither swarms of officers to harass our people and eat out their substance.

He has kept among us, in times of peace, standing armies, without the consent of our legislatures.

He has affected to render the military independent of, and superior to, the civil power.

He has combined with others to subject us to a jurisdiction foreign to our constitution, and unacknowledged by our laws, giving his assent to their acts of pretended legislation:

For quartering large bodies of armed troops among us:

For protecting them, by a mock trial, from punishment for any murders which they should commit on the inhabitants of these states;

For cutting off our trade with all parts of the world;

For imposing taxes on us without our consent;

For depriving us, in many cases, of the benefits of trial by jury;

For transporting us beyond seas, to be tried for pretended offenses;

For abolishing the free system of English laws in a neighboring province, establishing therein an arbitrary government, and enlarging its boundaries, so as to render it at once an example and fit instrument for introducing the same absolute rule into these colonies;

For taking away our charters, abolishing our more valuable laws, and altering fundamentally the forms of our governments;

For suspending our own legislatures, and declaring themselves invested with power to legislate for us in all cases whatsoever.

He has abdicated government here, by declaring us out of his protection and waging war against us.

He has plundered our seas, ravaged our coasts, burned our towns, and destroyed the lives of our people.

He is at this time transporting large armies of foreign mercenaries to complete the works of death, desolation, and tyranny already begun with circumstances of cruelty and perfidy scarcely paralleled in the most barbarous ages, and totally unworthy the head of a civilized nation.

He has constrained our fellow-citizens, taken captive on the high seas, to bear arms against their country, to become the executioners of their friends and brethren, or to fall themselves by their hands.

He has excited domestic insurrections among us, and has endeavored to bring on the inhabitants of our frontiers the merciless Indian savages, whose known rule of warfare is an undistinguished destruction of all ages, sexes, and conditions.

In every stage of these oppressions we have petitioned for redress in the most humble terms; our repeated petitions have been answered only by repeated injury. A prince, whose character is thus marked by every act which may define a tyrant, is unfit to be the ruler of a free people.

Nor have we been wanting in our attentions to our British brethren. We have warned them, from time to time, of attempts by their legislature to extend an unwarrantable jurisdiction over us. We have reminded them of the circumstances of our emigration and settlement here. We have appealed to their native justice and magnanimity; and we have conjured them, by the ties of our common kindred, to disavow these usurpations, which would inevitably interrupt our connections and correspondence. They, too, have been deaf to the voice of justice and of consanguinity. We must, therefore, acquiesce in the necessity which denounces our separation, and hold them, as we hold the rest of mankind, enemies in war, in peace friends.

We, therefore, the representatives of the United States of America, in General Congress assembled, appealing to the Supreme Judge of the world for the rectitude of our intentions, do, in the name and by the authority of the good people of these colonies, solemnly publish and declare, that these United Colonies are, and of right ought to be, FREE AND INDEPENDENT STATES; that they are absolved from all allegiance to the British crown, and that all political connection between them and the state of Great Britain is, and ought to be, totally dissolved; and that, as free and independent states, they have full power to levy war, conclude peace, contract alliances, establish commerce, and do all other acts and things which independent states may of right do. And for the support of this declaration, with a firm reliance on the protection of Divine Providence, we mutually pledge to each other our lives, our fortunes, and our sacred honor.

John Hancock, *President and delegate from Massachusetts*

Georgia
Button Gwinnett
Lyman Hall
George Walton

North Carolina
William Hooper
Joseph Hewes
John Penn

South Carolina
Edward Rutledge
Thomas Heyward Jr.
Thomas Lynch Jr.
Arthur Middleton

Maryland
Samuel Chase
William Paca
Thomas Stone
Charles Carroll of Carrollton

Virginia
George Wythe
Richard Henry Lee
Thomas Jefferson
Benjamin Harrison
Thomas Nelson Jr.
Francis Lightfoot Lee
Carter Braxton

Pennsylvania
Robert Morris
Benjamin Rush
Benjamin Franklin
John Morton
George Clymer
James Smith
George Taylor
James Wilson
George Ross

Delaware
Caesar Rodney
George Read
Thomas McKean

New York
William Floyd
Philip Livingston
Francis Lewis
Lewis Morris

New Jersey
Richard Stockton
John Witherspoon
Francis Hopkinson
John Hart
Abraham Clark

New Hampshire
Josiah Bartlett
William Whipple
Matthew Thornton

Massachusetts
Samuel Adams
John Adams
Robert Treat Paine
Elbridge Gerry

Rhode Island
Stephen Hopkins
William Ellery

Connecticut
Roger Sherman
Samuel Huntington
William Williams
Oliver Wolcott

The Constitution
of the United States

We the People of the United States, in Order to form a more perfect Union, establish Justice, insure domestic Tranquility, provide for the common defence, promote the general Welfare, and secure the Blessings of Liberty to ourselves and our Posterity, do ordain and establish this Constitution for the United States of America.

Article I.

Section 1.   All legislative Powers herein granted shall be vested in a Congress of the United States, which shall consist of a Senate and House of Representatives.

Section 2.   The House of Representatives shall be composed of Members chosen every second Year by the People of the several States, and the Electors in each State shall have the Qualifications requisite for Electors of the most numerous Branch of the State Legislature.

No Person shall be a Representative who shall not have attained to the age of twenty five Years, and been seven Years a Citizen of the United States, and who shall not, when elected, be an Inhabitant of that State in which he shall be chosen.

Changed by the Fourteenth Amendment, Section 2.

Representatives and direct Taxes shall be apportioned among the several States which may be included within this Union, according to their respective Numbers, which shall be determined by adding to the whole Number of free Persons, including those bound to Service for a Term of Years, and excluding Indians not taxed, three fifths of all other Persons. The actual Enumeration shall be made within three Years after the first Meeting of the Congress of the United States, and within every subsequent Term of ten Years, in such Manner as they shall by Law direct. The Number of Representatives shall not exceed one for every thirty Thousand, but each State shall have at Least one Representative; and until such enumeration shall be made, the State of New Hampshire shall be entitled to chuse three, Massachusetts eight, Rhode-Island and Providence Plantations one, Connecticut five, New-York six, New Jersey four, Pennsylvania eight, Delaware one, Maryland six, Virginia ten, North Carolina five, South Carolina five, and Georgia three.

When vacancies happen in the Representation from any State, the Executive Authority thereof shall issue Writs of Election to fill such Vacancies.

The House of Representatives shall chuse their Speaker and other Officers; and shall have the sole Power of Impeachment.

Section 3. The Senate of the United States shall be composed of two Senators from each State, chosen by the Legislature thereof, for six Years; and each Senator shall have one Vote.

Changed by the Seventeenth Amendment

Immediately after they shall be assembled in Consequence of the first Election, they shall be divided as equally as may be into three Classes. The Seats of the Senators of the first class shall be vacated at the Expiration of the second Year, of the second Class at the Expiration of the fourth Year, and of the third Class at the Expiration of the sixth Year, so that one third may be chosen every second Year; and if Vacancies happen by Resignation, or otherwise, during the Recess of the Legislature of any State, the Executive thereof may make temporary Appointments until the next Meeting of the Legislature, which shall then fill such Vacancies.

Changed by the Seventeenth Amendment.

No Person shall be a Senator who shall not have attained to the Age of thirty Years, and been nine Years a Citizen of the United States, and who shall not, when elected, be an Inhabitant of that State for which he shall be chosen.

The Vice President of the United States shall be President of the Senate, but shall have no Vote, unless they be equally divided.

The Senate shall chuse their other Officers, and also a President pro tempore, in the Absence of the Vice President, or when he shall exercise the Office of President of the United States.

The Senate shall have the sole Power to try all Impeachments. When sitting for that Purpose, they shall be on Oath or Affirmation. When the President of the United States is tried the Chief Justice shall preside: And no Person shall be convicted without the Concurrence of two thirds of the Members present.

Judgment in Cases of Impeachment shall not exceed further than to removal from Office, and disqualification to hold and enjoy any Office of honor, Trust or Profit under the United States: but the Party convicted shall nevertheless be liable and subject to Indictment, Trial, Judgment and Punishment, according to Law.

Section 4. The Times, Places and Manner of holding Elections for Senators and Representatives, shall be prescribed in each State by the Legislature thereof; but the Congress may at any time by Law make or alter such Regulations, except as to the Places of chusing Senators.

The Congress shall assemble at least once in every Year, and such Meeting shall be on the first Monday in December, unless they shall by Law appoint a different Day.

Changed by the Twentieth Amendment, Section 2.

Section 5. Each House shall be the Judge of the Elections, Returns and Qualifications of its own Members, and a Majority of each shall constitute a

Quorum to do Business; but a smaller number may adjourn from day to day, and may be authorized to compel the Attendance of absent Members, in such Manner, and under such Penalties as each House may provide.

Each House may determine the Rules of its Proceedings, punish its Members for disorderly Behaviour, and, with the Concurrence of two thirds, expel a Member.

Each House shall keep a Journal of its Proceedings, and from time to time publish the same, excepting such Parts as may in their Judgment require Secrecy; and the Yeas and Nays of the Members of either House on any question shall, at the Desire of one fifth of those Present, be entered on the Journal.

Neither House, during the Session of Congress, shall, without the Consent of the other, adjourn for more than three days, nor to any other Place than that in which the two Houses shall be sitting.

Amplified by the Twenty-Seventh Amendment.

Section 6. The Senators and Representatives shall receive a Compensation for their Services, to be ascertained by Law, and paid out of the Treasury of the United States. They shall in all Cases, except Treason, Felony and Breach of the Peace, be privileged from Arrest during their Attendance at the Session of their respective Houses, and in going to and returning from the same; and for any Speech or Debate in either House, they shall not be questioned in any other Place.

No Senator or Representative shall, during the Time for which he was elected, be appointed to any civil Office under the Authority of the United States, which shall have been created, or the Emoluments whereof shall have been encreased during such time; and no Person holding any Office under the United States, shall be a Member of either House during his Continuance in Office.

Section 7. All Bills for raising Revenue shall originate in the House of Representatives; but the Senate may propose or concur with Amendments as on other Bills.

Every Bill which shall have passed the House of Representatives and the Senate, shall, before it become a Law, be presented to the President of the United States; If he approve he shall assign it, but if not he shall return it, with his Objections to that House in which it shall have originated, who shall enter the Objections at large on their Journal, and proceed to reconsider it. If after such Reconsideration two thirds of that House shall agree to pass the Bill, it shall be sent, together with the Objections, to the other House, by which it shall likewise be reconsidered, and if approved by two thirds of that House, it shall become a Law. But in all such Cases the Votes of both Houses shall be determined by yeas and Nays, and the Names of the Persons voting for and against the Bill shall be entered on the Journal of each House respectively. If any Bill shall not be returned by the President within ten Days (Sundays excepted) after it shall have been presented to him, the Same shall be a Law, in like Manner, as if he had signed it, unless the Congress by their Adjournment prevent its Return, in which Case it shall not be a Law.

Every Order, Resolution, or Vote to which the Concurrence of the Senate and House of Representatives may be necessary (except on a question of Adjournment) shall be presented to the President of the United States; and before the Same shall take Effect, shall be approved by him, or being disapproved by him, shall be repassed by two thirds of the Senate and House of Representatives, according to the Rules and Limitations prescribed in the Case of a Bill.

Section 8. The Congress shall have Power To lay and Collect Taxes, Duties, Imposts and Excises, to pay the Debts and provide for the common Defence and general Welfare of the United States; but all Duties, Imposts and Excises shall be uniform throughout the United States.

To borrow Money on the credit of the United States;

To regulate Commerce with foreign Nations, and among the several States, and with the Indian Tribes;

To establish an uniform Rule of Naturalization, and uniform Laws on the subject of Bankruptcies throughout the United States;

To coin Money, regulate the Value thereof, and of foreign Coin, and fix the Standard of Weights and Measures;

To provide for the Punishment of counterfeiting the Securities and current Coin of the United States;

To establish Post Offices and post Roads;

To promote the Progress of Science and useful Arts, by securing for limited Times to Authors and Inventors the exclusive Right to their respective Writings and Discoveries;

To constitute Tribunals inferior to the Supreme Court;

To define and punish Piracies and Felonies committed on the high Seas, and Offences against the Law of Nations;

To declare War, grant Letters of Marque and Reprisal, and make Rules concerning Captures on Land and Water;

To raise and support Armies, but no Appropriation of Money to that Use shall be for a longer Term than two Years;

To provide and maintain a Navy;

To make Rules for the Government and Regulation of the land and naval Forces;

To provide for calling forth the Militia to execute the Laws of the Union, suppress Insurrections and repel Invasions;

To provide for organizing, arming, and disciplining, the Militia, and for governing such Part of them as may be employed in the Service of the United States, reserving to the States respectively, the Appointment of the Officers, and the Authority of training the Militia according to the discipline prescribed by Congress;

To exercise exclusive Legislation in all Cases whatsoever, over such District (not exceeding ten Miles square) as may, by Cession of Particular States,

General welfare clause gives Congress the power to tax to provide for the general welfare.

Commerce clause gives Congress the power to regulate commerce with foreign nations, with Indian tribes, and among the various states.

and the Acceptance of Congress, become the Seat of the Government of the United States, and to exercise like Authority over all Places purchased by the Consent of the Legislature of the State in which the Same shall be, for the Erection of Forts, Magazines, Arsenals, dock-Yards and other needful Buildings;—And

To make all Laws which shall be necessary and proper for carrying into Execution the foregoing Powers, and all other Powers vested by this Constitution in the Government of the United States, or in any Department or Officer thereof.

Necessary and proper clause gives Congress the power to pass all laws necessary and proper to the powers enumerated in Section 8.

Section 9. The Migration or Importation of such Persons as any of the States now existing shall think proper to admit, shall not be prohibited by the Congress prior to the Year one thousand eight hundred and eight, but a Tax or duty may be imposed on such Importation, not exceeding ten dollars for each Person.

The Privilege of the Writ of Habeas Corpus shall not be suspended, unless when in Cases of Rebellion or Invasion the public Safety may require it.

No bill of Attainder or ex post facto Law shall be passed.

Changed by the Sixteenth Amendment.

No Capitation, or other direct, Tax shall be laid, unless in Proportion to the Census or Enumeration herein before directed to be taken.

No Tax or Duty shall be laid on Articles exported from any State.

No Preference shall be given by any Regulation of Commerce or Revenue to the Ports of one State over those of another; nor shall Vessels bound to, or from, one State, be obliged to enter, clear or pay Duties in another.

No Money shall be drawn from the Treasury, but in Consequence of Appropriations made by Law; and a regular Statement and Account of the Receipts and Expenditures of all public Money shall be published from time to time.

No Title of Nobility shall be granted by the United States: And no Person holding any Office of Profit or Trust under them, shall, without the Consent of the Congress, accept of any present, Emolument, Office, or Title, of any kind whatever, from any King, Prince, or foreign State.

Section 10. No State shall enter into any Treaty, Alliance, or Confederation; grant Letters of Marque and Reprisal; coin Money; emit Bills of Credit; make any Thing but gold and silver Coin a Tender in Payment of Debts; pass any Bill of Attainder, ex post facto Law, or Law impairing the Obligation of Contracts, or grant any Title of Nobility.

No State shall, without the Consent of the Congress, lay any Imposts or Duties on Imports or Exports, except what may be absolutely necessary for executing its inspection Laws; and the net Produce of all Duties and Imposts, laid by any State on Imports or Exports, shall be for the Use of the Treasury of the United States; and all such Laws shall be subject to the Revision and Control of the Congress.

No State shall, without the Consent of Congress, lay any Duty of Tonnage, keep Troops, or Ships of War in time of Peace, enter into any Agreement or Compact with another State, or with a foreign Power, or engage in War, unless actually invaded, or in such imminent Danger as will not admit of delay.

Article II.

Section 1. The executive Power shall be vested in a President of the United States of America. He shall hold his Office during the term of four Years, and, together with the Vice President, chosen for the same Term, be elected, as follows

Vesting clause gives the president the executive power.

Each State shall appoint, in such Manner as the Legislature thereof may direct, a Number of Electors, equal to the whole Number of Senators and Representatives to which the State may be entitled in the Congress: but no Senator or Representative, or Person holding an Office of Trust or Profit under the United States, shall be appointed an Elector.

The Electors shall meet in their respective States, and vote by Ballot for two Persons, of whom one at least shall not be an Inhabitant of the same State with them-selves. And they shall make a List of all the Persons voted for, and of the Number of Votes for each; which List they shall sign and certify, and transmit sealed to the Seat of the Government of the United States, directed to the President of the Senate. The President of the Senate shall, in the Presence of the Senate and House of Representatives, open all the Certificates, and the Votes shall then be counted. The Person having the greatest Number of Votes shall be the President, if such Number be a Majority of the whole Number of Electors appointed; and if there be more than one who have such Majority, and have an equal Number of Votes, then the House of Representatives shall immediately chuse by Ballot one of them for President; and if no Person have a Majority, then from the five highest on the List the said House shall in like Manner chuse the President. But in chusing the President, the Votes shall be taken by States, the Representation from each State having one Vote; a quorum for this Purpose shall consist of a Member or Members from two thirds of the States, and a Majority of all the States shall be necessary to a Choice. In every Case, after the Choice of the President, the Person having the greatest Number of Votes of the Electors shall be the Vice President. But if there should remain two or more who have equal Votes, the Senate shall chuse from them by Ballot the Vice President.

Changed by the Twelfth Amendment.

The Congress may determine the Time of chusing the Electors, and the Day on which they shall give their Votes, which Day shall be the same throughout the United States.

No Person except a natural born Citizen, or a Citizen of the United States, at the time of the Adoption of this Constitution, shall be eligible to the Office of President; neither shall any person be eligible to that Office who shall not have attained to the Age of thirty five Years, and been fourteen Years a Resident within the United States.

In Case of the Removal of the President from Office, or of his Death, Resignation, or Inability to discharge the Powers and Duties of the said Office, the Same shall devolve on the Vice President, and the Congress may by Law provide for the Case of Removal, Death, Resignation or Inability, both of the President and Vice President, declaring what Officer shall then act as President, and such Officer shall act accordingly, until the Disability be removed, or a President shall be elected.

The President shall, at stated Times, receive for his Services, a Compensation, which shall neither be encreased nor diminished during the Period for which he shall have been elected, and he shall not receive within that Period any other Emolument from the United States, or any of them.

Before he enter on the Execution of his Office, he shall take the following Oath or Affirmation:—"I do solemnly swear (or affirm) that I will faithfully execute the Office of President of the United States, and will to the best of my Ability, preserve, protect and defend the Constitution of the United States."

Section 2. The President shall be Commander in Chief of the Army and Navy of the United States, and of the Militia of the several States, when called into the actual Service of the United States; he may require the Opinion, in writing, of the principal Officer in each of the executive Departments, upon any Subject relating to the Duties of their respective Offices, and he shall have Power to grant Reprieves and Pardons for Offences against the United States, except in Cases of Impeachment.

He shall have Power, by and with the Advice and Consent of the Senate, to make Treaties, provided two thirds of the Senators present concur; and he shall nominate, and by and with the Advice and Consent of the Senate, shall appoint Ambassadors, other public Ministers and Consuls, Judges of the supreme Court, and all other Officers of the United States, whose Appointments are not herein otherwise provided for, and which shall be established by Law: but the Congress may by Law vest the Appointment of such inferior Officers, as they think proper, in the President alone, in the Courts of Law, or in the Heads of Departments.

The President shall have Power to fill up all Vacancies that may happen during the Recess of the Senate, by granting Commissions which shall expire at the End of their next Session.

Section 3. He shall from time to time give to the Congress Information of the State of the Union, and recommend to their Consideration such Measures as he shall judge necessary and expedient; he may, on extraordinary Occasions, convene both Houses, or either of them, and in Case of Disagreement between them, with Respect to the Time of Adjournment, he may adjourn them to such Time as he shall think proper; he shall receive Ambassadors and other public Ministers; he shall take Care that the Laws be faithfully executed, and shall Commission all the Officers of the United States.

Section 4. The President, Vice President and all civil Officers of the United States, shall be removed from Office on Impeachment for, and Conviction of, Treason, Bribery, or other high Crimes and Misdemeanors.

Article III.

Section 1. The judicial Power of the United States, shall be vested in one supreme Court, and in such inferior Courts as the Congress may from time to time ordain and establish. The Judges, both of the supreme and inferior Courts, shall hold their Offices during good Behaviour, and shall, at stated Times, receive for their Services, a Compensation, which shall not be diminished during their Continuance in Office.

Section 2. The judicial Power shall extend to all Cases, in Law and Equity, arising under this Constitution, the Laws of the United States, and Treaties made, or which shall be made, under their Authority;—to all Cases affecting Ambassadors, other public Ministers and Consuls;—to all Cases of admiralty and maritime Jurisdiction;—to Controversies to which the United States shall be a Party;—to Controversies between two or more States;—between a State and Citizens of another State;—between Citizens of different States;—between Citizens of the same State claiming Lands under Grants of different States, and between a State, or the Citizens thereof, and foreign States, Citizens or Subjects.

> Changed by the Eleventh Amendment.

In all Cases affecting Ambassadors, other public Ministers and Consuls, and those in which a State shall be Party, the supreme Court shall have original Jurisdiction. In all the other Cases before mentioned, the supreme Court shall have appellate Jurisdiction, both as to Law and Fact, with such Exceptions, and under such Regulations as the Congress shall make.

The Trial of all Crimes, except in Cases of Impeachment, shall be by Jury; and such Trial shall be held in the State where the said Crimes shall have been committed; but when not committed within any State, the Trial shall be at such Place or Places as the Congress may by Law have directed.

Section 3. Treason against the United States, shall consist only in levying War against them, or in adhering to their Enemies, giving them Aid and Comfort. No Person shall be convicted of Treason unless on the Testimony of two Witnesses to the same overt Act, or on Confession in open Court.

The Congress shall have Power to declare the Punishment of Treason, but no Attainder of Treason shall work Corruption of Blood, or Forfeiture except during the Life of the Person attainted.

Article IV.

Section 1. Full Faith and Credit shall be given in each State to the public Acts, Records, and judicial Proceedings of every other State. And the Congress may by general Laws prescribe the Manner in which such Acts, Records and Proceedings shall be proved, and the Effect thereof.

> **Full faith and credit clause** requires states to accept civil proceedings from other states.

Privileges and immunities clause requires states to treat nonresidents equally to residents.

Fugitive slave clause required states to return runaway slaves; negated by the Thirteenth Amendment.

Guarantee clause provides a federal government guarantee that the states will have a republican form of government.

Section 2. The Citizens of each State shall be entitled to all Privileges and Immunities of Citizens in the several States.

A person charged in any State with Treason, Felony, or other Crime, who shall flee from Justice, and be found in another State, shall on Demand of the executive Authority of the State from which he fled, be delivered up, to be removed to the State having Jurisdiction of the Crime.

No Person held to Service or Labour in one State, under the Laws thereof, escaping into another, shall, in Consequence of any Law or Regulation therein, be discharged from such Service or Labour, but shall be delivered up on Claim of the Party to whom such Service or Labour may be due.

Section 3. New States may be admitted by the Congress into this Union; but no new State shall be formed or erected within the Jurisdiction of any other State; nor any State be formed by the Junction of two or more States, or Parts of States, without the Consent of the Legislatures of the States concerned as well as of the Congress.

The Congress shall have Power to dispose of and make all needful Rules and Regulations respecting the Territory or other Property belonging to the United States; and nothing in this Constitution shall be so construed as to Prejudice any Claims of the United States, or of any particular State.

Section 4. The United States shall guarantee to every State in this Union a Republican Form of Government, and shall protect each of them against Invasion; and on Application of the Legislature, or of the Executive (when the Legislature cannot be convened) against domestic Violence.

Article V.

The Congress, whenever two thirds of both Houses shall deem it necessary, shall propose Amendments to this Constitution, or, on the Application of the Legislatures of two thirds of the several States, shall call a Convention for proposing Amendments, which, in either Case, shall be valid to all Intents and Purposes, as Part of this Constitution, when ratified by the Legislatures of three fourths of the several States, or by Conventions in three fourths thereof, as the one or the other Mode of Ratification may be proposed by the Congress; Provided that no Amendment which may be made prior to the Year One thousand eight hundred and eight shall in any Manner after the first and fourth Clauses in the Ninth Section of the first Article; and that no State, without its Consent, shall be deprived of its equal Suffrage in the Senate.

Article VI.

All Debts contracted and Engagements entered into, before the Adoption of this Constitution, shall be as valid against the United States under this Constitution, as under the Confederation.

This Constitution, and the Laws of the United States which shall be made in Pursuance thereof; and all Treaties made, or which shall be made, under the Authority of the United States, shall be the Supreme Law of the Land; and the Judges in every State shall be bound thereby, any Thing in the Constitution or Laws of any State to the Contrary notwithstanding.

Supremacy clause makes federal law supreme over state laws.

The Senators and Representatives before mentioned, and the Members of the several State Legislatures, and all executive and judicial Officers, both of the United States and of the several States, shall be bound by Oath or Affirmation, to support this Constitution; but no religious Test shall ever be required as a Qualification to any Office or public Trust under the United States.

Article VII.

The Ratification of the Conventions of nine States, shall be sufficient for the Establishment of this Constitution between the States so ratifying the Same.

Done in Convention by the Unanimous Consent of the States present the Seventeenth Day of September in the Year of our Lord one thousand seven hundred and Eighty seven and of the Independence of the United States of America the Twelfth In witness whereof We have hereunto subscribed our Names,

George Washington, *President and deputy from Virginia*

Delaware
George Read
Gunning Bedford Jr.
John Dickinson
Richard Bassett
Jacob Broom

Maryland
James McHenry
Daniel of St. Thomas Jenifer
Daniel Carroll

Virginia
John Blair
James Madison Jr.

North Carolina
William Blount
Richard Dobbs Spaight
Hugh Williamson

South Carolina
John Rutledge
Charles Cotesworth Pinckney
Charles Pinckney
Pierce Butler

Georgia
William Few
Abraham Baldwin

New Hampshire
John Langdon
Nicholas Gilman

Massachusetts
Nathaniel Gorham
Rufus King

Connecticut
William Samuel Johnson
Roger Sherman

New York
Alexander Hamilton

New Jersey
William Livingston
David Brearley
William Paterson
Jonathan Dayton

Pennsylvania
Benjamin Franklin
Thomas Mifflin
Robert Morris
George Clymer
Thomas FitzSimons
Jared Ingersoll
James Wilson
Gouverneur Morris

[The first ten amendments, known as the Bill of Rights, were ratified in 1791.]

First Amendment

Establishment clause prohibits governmental establishment of religion.

Free exercise clause protects the free exercise of religion.

Congress shall make no law respecting an establishment of religion, or prohibiting the free exercise thereof; or abridging the freedom of speech, or of the press; or the right of the people peaceably to assemble, and to petition the Government for a redress of grievances.

Second Amendment

A well regulated Militia, being necessary to the security of a free State, the right of the people to keep and bear Arms, shall not be infringed.

Third Amendment

No Soldier shall, in time of peace be quartered in any house, without the consent of the Owner, nor in time of war, but in a manner prescribed by law.

Fourth Amendment

Double jeopardy clause prevents the government from retrying someone for a crime after an initial acquittal.

Self-incrimination clause protects people from having to testify against themselves at trial.

Due process clause prevents the federal government from denying any person due process of law.

Takings clause requires just compensation when the government seizes private property for a public purpose.

The right of the people to be secure in their persons, houses, papers, and effects, against unreasonable searches and seizures, shall not be violated, and no Warrants shall issue, but upon probable cause, supported by Oath or affirmation, and particularly describing the place to be searched, and the persons or things to be seized.

Fifth Amendment

No person shall be held to answer for a capital, or otherwise infamous crime, unless on a presentment or indictment of a Grand Jury, except in cases arising in the land or naval forces, or in the Militia, when in actual service in time of War or public danger; nor shall any person be subject for the same offence to be twice put in jeopardy of life or limb; nor shall be compelled in any criminal case to be a witness against himself, nor be deprived of life, liberty, or property, without due process of law, nor shall private property be taken for public use, without just compensation.

Sixth Amendment

In all criminal prosecutions, the accused shall enjoy the right to a speedy and public trial, by an impartial jury of the State and district wherein the crime shall have been committed, which district shall have been previously ascertained by law, and to be informed of the nature and cause of the accusation; to be confronted with the witnesses against him; to have compulsory process for obtaining witnesses in his favor, and to have Assistance of Counsel for his defence.

Seventh Amendment

In Suits at common law, where the value in controversy shall exceed twenty dollars, the right of trial by jury shall be preserved, and no fact tried by a jury, shall be otherwise reexamined in any Court of the United States, than according to the rules of the common law.

Eighth Amendment

Excessive bail shall not be required, nor excessive fines imposed, nor cruel and unusual punishments inflicted.

Cruel and unusual punishment clause prohibits cruel and unusual punishments.

Ninth Amendment

The enumeration in the Constitution, of certain rights, shall not be construed to deny or disparage others retained by the people.

Tenth Amendment

The powers not delegated to the United States by the Constitution, nor prohibited by it to the States, are reserved to the States respectively, or to the people.

Reserve powers clause reserves to the states or to the people those powers not delegated to the United States.

Eleventh Amendment (1798)

The Judicial power of the United States shall not be construed to extend to any suit in law or equity, commenced or prosecuted against one of the United States by Citizens of another State, or by Citizens or Subjects of any Foreign State.

Twelfth Amendment (1804)

The Electors shall meet in their respective states and vote by ballot for President and Vice President, one of whom, at least, shall not be an inhabitant of the same state with themselves; they shall name in their ballots the person voted for as President, and in distinct ballots the person voted for as Vice President, and they shall make distinct lists of all persons voted for as President, and of all persons voted for as Vice President, and of the number of votes for each, which lists they shall sign and certify, and transmit sealed to the seat of the government of the United States, directed to the President of the Senate;—The President of the Senate shall, in the presence of the Senate and House of Representatives, open all the certificates and the votes shall then be counted;—The person having the greatest number of votes for President, shall be the President, if such number be a majority of the whole number of Electors appointed; and if no person have such majority, then from the persons having the highest numbers not exceeding three on the list of those voted for as President, the House of Representatives shall choose immediately, by ballot, the President. But in choosing the President, the votes shall be taken by states, the representation from each state having one vote; a quorum for this purpose shall consist of a member or members from two-thirds of the states, and a majority of all the states shall be necessary to a choice. And if the House of Representatives shall not choose a President whenever the right of choice shall devolve upon them, before the fourth day of March next following, then the Vice President shall act as President, as in the case of the death or other constitutional disability of the President.—The person having the greatest number of votes as Vice President, shall be the Vice President, if such number be a majority of the whole number of Electors appointed, and if no person have a majority, then from the two highest numbers on the list, the Senate shall choose the Vice President; a quorum for the purpose shall consist of two-thirds of the whole number of Senators, and a majority of the whole number shall be necessary to a choice. But no person constitutionally ineligible to the office of President shall be eligible to that of Vice President of the United States.

Changed by the Twentieth Amendment, Section 3.

Thirteenth Amendment (1865)

Section 1. Neither slavery nor involuntary servitude, except as a punishment for crime whereof the party shall have been duly convicted, shall exist within the United States, or any place subject to their jurisdiction.

Section 2. Congress shall have power to enforce this article by appropriate legislation.

Fourteenth Amendment (1868)

Citizenship clause makes all persons born in the United States citizens of the United States and of the state in which they reside.

Privileges or immunities clause prohibits states from abridging certain fundamental rights.

Due process clause prevents state governments from denying any person due process of law.

Equal protection clause prevents states from denying any person the equal protection of the laws.

Section 1. All persons born or naturalized in the United States and subject to the jurisdiction thereof, are citizens of the United States and of the State wherein they reside. No State shall make or enforce any law which shall abridge the privileges or immunities of citizens of the United States; nor shall any State deprive any person of life, liberty, or property, without due process of law; nor deny to any person within its jurisdiction the equal protection of the laws.

Section 2. Representatives shall be apportioned among the several States according to their respective numbers, counting the whole number of persons in each State, excluding Indians not taxed. But when the right to vote at any election for the choice of electors for President and Vice President of the United States, Representatives in Congress, the Executive and Judicial officers of a State, or the members of the Legislature thereof, is denied to any of the male inhabitants of such State, being twenty-one years of age, and citizens of the United States, or in any way abridged, except for participation in rebellion, or other crime, the basis of representation therein shall be reduced in the proportion which the number of such male citizens shall bear to the whole number of male citizens twenty-one years of age in such State.

Changed by the Nineteenth and Twenty-Sixth Amendments.

Section 3.   No person shall be a Senator or Representative in Congress, or elector of President and Vice President, or hold any office, civil or military, under the United States, or under any State, who, having previously taken an oath, as a member of Congress, or as an officer of the United States, or as a member of any State legislature, or as an executive or judicial officer of any State, to support the Constitution of the United States, shall have engaged in insurrection or rebellion against the same, or given aid or comfort to the enemies thereof. But Congress may by a vote of two-thirds of each House, remove such disability.

Section 4.   The validity of the public debt of the United States, authorized by law, including debts incurred for payment of pensions and bounties for services in suppressing insurrection or rebellion, shall not be questioned. But neither the United States nor any State shall assume or pay any debt or obligation incurred in aid of insurrection or rebellion against the United States, or any claim for the loss or emancipation of any slave; but all such debts, obligations and claims shall be held illegal and void.

Section 5.   The Congress shall have power to enforce, by appropriate legislation, the provisions of this article.

Fifteenth Amendment (1870)
Section 1.   The right of citizens of the United States to vote shall not be denied or abridged by the United States or by any State on account of race, color, or previous condition of servitude.

Section 2.   The Congress shall have power to enforce this article by appropriate legislation.

Sixteenth Amendment (1913)
The Congress shall have power to lay and collect taxes on incomes, from whatever source derived, without apportionment among the several States, and without regard to any census or enumeration.

Seventeenth Amendment (1913)

The Senate of the United States shall be composed of two Senators from each State, elected by the people thereof, for six years; and each Senator shall have one vote. The electors in each State shall have the qualifications requisite for electors of the most numerous branch of the State legislatures.

When vacancies happen in the representation of any State in the Senate, the executive authority of such State shall issue writs of election to fill such vacancies: *Provided*, That the legislature of any State may empower the executive thereof to make temporary appointments until the people fill the vacancies by election as the legislature may direct.

This amendment shall not be so construed as to affect the election or term of any Senator chosen before it becomes valid as part of the Constitution.

Eighteenth Amendment (1919)

Repealed by the Twenty-First Amendment.

Section 1. After one year from the ratification of this article the manufacture, sale, or transportation of intoxicating liquors within, the importation thereof into, or the exportation thereof from the United States and all territory subject to the jurisdiction thereof for beverage purposes is hereby prohibited.

Section 2. The Congress and the several States shall have concurrent power to enforce this article by appropriate legislation.

Section 3. This article shall be inoperative unless it shall have been ratified as an amendment to the Constitution by the legislatures of the several States, as provided in the Constitution, within seven years from the date of the submission hereof to the States by the Congress.

Nineteenth Amendment (1920)

The right of citizens of the United States to vote shall not be denied or abridged by the United States or by any State on account of sex.

Congress shall have power to enforce this article by appropriate legislation.

Twentieth Amendment (1933)

Section 1. The terms of the President and Vice President shall end at noon on the 20th day of January, and the terms of Senators and Representatives at noon on the 3rd day of January, of the years in which such terms would have ended if this article had not been ratified; and the terms of their successors shall then begin.

Section 2. The Congress shall assemble at least once in every year, and such meeting shall begin at noon on the 3d day of January, unless they shall by law appoint a different day.

Section 3. If, at the time fixed for the beginning of the term of the President, the President elect shall have died, the Vice President elect shall become President. If a President shall not have been chosen before the time fixed for the beginning of his term, or if the President elect shall have failed to qualify, then the Vice President elect shall act as President until a President shall have qualified; and the Congress may by law provide for the case wherein neither a President elect nor a Vice President elect shall have qualified, declaring who shall then act as President, or the manner in which one who is to act shall be selected, and such person shall act accordingly until a President or Vice President shall have qualified.

Section 4. The Congress may by law provide for the case of the death of any of the persons from whom the House of Representatives may choose a President whenever the right of choice shall have devolved upon them, and for the case of the death of any of the persons from whom the Senate may choose a Vice President whenever the right of choice shall have devolved upon them.

Section 5. Sections 1 and 2 shall take effect on the 15th day of October following the ratification of this article.

Section 6. This article shall be inoperative unless it shall have been ratified as an amendment to the Constitution by the legislatures of three-fourths of the several States within seven years from the date of its submission.

Twenty-First Amendment (1933)

Section 1. The eighteenth article of amendment to the Constitution of the United States is hereby repealed.

Section 2. The transportation or importation into any State, Territory, or possession of the United States for delivery or use therein of intoxicating liquors, in violation of the laws thereof, is hereby prohibited.

Section 3. This article shall be inoperative unless it shall have been ratified as an amendment to the Constitution by conventions in the several States, as provided in the Constitution, within seven years from the date of the submission hereof to the States by the Congress.

Twenty-Second Amendment (1951)

Section 1. No person shall be elected to the office of the President more than twice, and no person who has held the office of President, or acted as President, for more than two years of a term to which some other person was elected President shall be elected to the office of the President more than once. But this Article shall not apply to any person holding the office of President when this Article was proposed by the Congress, and shall not prevent any person who may be holding the office of President, or acting as President, during the term within which this Article becomes operative from holding the office of President or acting as President during the remainder of such term.

Section 2.   This Article shall be inoperative unless it shall have been ratified as an amendment to the Constitution by the legislatures of three-fourths of the several States within seven years from the date of its submission to the States by the Congress.

Twenty-Third Amendment (1961)

Section 1.   The District constituting the seat of Government of the United States shall appoint in such manner as the Congress may direct:

A number of electors of President and Vice President equal to the whole number of Senators and Representatives in Congress to which the District would be entitled if it were a State, but in no event more than the least populous State; they shall be in addition to those appointed by the States, but they shall be considered, for the purposes of the election of President and Vice President, to be electors appointed by a State; and they shall meet in the District and perform such duties as provided by the twelfth article of amendment.

Section 2.   The Congress shall have power to enforce this article by appropriate legislation.

Twenty-Fourth Amendment (1964)

Section 1.   The right of citizens of the United States to vote in any primary or other election for President or Vice President, for electors for President or Vice President, or for Senator or Representative in Congress, shall not be denied or abridged by the United States or any State by reason of failure to pay any poll tax or other tax.

Section 2.   Congress shall have power to enforce this article by appropriate legislation.

Twenty-Fifth Amendment (1967)

Section 1.   In case of the removal of the President from office or of his death or resignation, the Vice President shall become President.

Section 2.   Whenever there is a vacancy in the office of the Vice President, the President shall nominate a Vice President who shall take office upon confirmation by a majority vote of both Houses of Congress.

Section 3.   Whenever the President transmits to the President pro tempore of the Senate and the Speaker of the House of Representatives his written declaration that he is unable to discharge the powers and duties of his office, and until he transmits to them a written declaration to the contrary, such powers and duties shall be discharged by the Vice President as Acting President.

Section 4. Whenever the Vice President and a majority of either the principal officers of the executive departments or of such other body as Congress may by law provide, transmit to the President pro tempore of the Senate and the Speaker of the House of Representatives their written declaration that the President is unable to discharge the powers and duties of his office, the Vice President shall immediately assume the powers and duties of the office as Acting President.

Thereafter, when the President transmits to the President pro tempore of the Senate and the Speaker of the House of Representatives his written declaration that no inability exists, he shall resume the powers and duties of his office unless the Vice President and a majority of either the principal officers of the executive department[s] or of such other body as Congress may by law provide, transmit within four days to the President pro tempore of the Senate and the Speaker of the House of Representatives their written declaration that the President is unable to discharge the powers and duties of his office. Thereupon Congress shall decide the issue, assembling within forty-eight hours for that purpose if not in session. If the Congress, within twenty-one days after receipt of the latter written declaration, or, if Congress is not in session, within twenty-one days after Congress is required to assemble, determines by two-thirds vote of both Houses that the President is unable to discharge the powers and duties of his office, the Vice President shall continue to discharge the same as Acting President; otherwise, the President shall resume the powers and duties of his office.

Twenty-Sixth Amendment (1971)
Section 1. The right of citizens of the United States, who are eighteen years of age or older, to vote shall not be denied or abridged by the United States or by any State on account of age.

Section 2. The Congress shall have power to enforce this article by appropriate legislation.

Twenty-Seventh Amendment (1992)
No law varying the compensation for the services of the Senators and Representatives shall take effect, until an election of Representatives shall have intervened.

Federalist Papers
10 and 51

10

James Madison

November 22, 1787

To the People of the State of New York

Among the numerous advantages promised by a well constructed Union, none deserves to be more accurately developed than its tendency to break and control the violence of faction. The friend of popular governments, never finds himself so much alarmed for their character and fate, as when he contemplates their propensity to this dangerous vice. He will not fail therefore to set a due value on any plan which, without violating the principles to which he is attached, provides a proper cure for it. The instability, injustice and confusion introduced into the public councils, have in truth been the mortal diseases under which popular governments have every where perished; as they continue to be the favorite and fruitful topics from which the adversaries to liberty derive their most specious declamations. The valuable improvements made by the American Constitutions on the popular models, both ancient and modern, cannot certainly be too much admired; but it would be an unwarrantable partiality, to contend that they have as effectually obviated the danger on this side as was wished and expected. Complaints are every where heard from our most considerate and virtuous citizens, equally the friends of public and private faith, and of public and personal liberty; that our governments are too unstable; that the public good is disregarded in the conflicts of rival parties; and that measures are too often decided, not according to the rules of justice, and the rights of the minor party; but by the superior force of an interested and over-bearing majority. However anxiously we may wish that these complaints had no foundation, the evidence of known facts will not permit us to deny that they are in some degree true. It will be found indeed, on a candid review of our situation, that some of the distresses under which we labor, have been erroneously charged on the operation of our governments; but it will be found, at the same time, that other causes will not alone account for many of our heaviest misfortunes; and particularly, for that prevailing and increasing distrust of public engagements, and alarm for private rights, which are echoed from one end of the continent to the other. These must be chiefly, if not wholly, effects of the unsteadiness and injustice, with which a factious spirit has tainted our public administrations.

By a faction I understand a number of citizens, whether amounting to a majority or minority of the whole, who are united and actuated by some common impulse of passion, or of interest, adverse to the rights of other citizens, or to the permanent and aggregate interests of the community.

There are two methods of curing the mischiefs of faction: the one, by removing its causes; the other, by controlling its effects.

There are again two methods of removing the causes of faction: the one by destroying the liberty which is essential to its existence; the other, by giving to every citizen the same opinions, the same passions, and the same interests.

It could never be more truly said than of the first remedy, that it is worse than the disease. Liberty is to faction, what air is to fire, an aliment without which it instantly expires. But it could not be a less folly to abolish liberty, which is essential to political life, because it nourishes faction, than it would be to wish the annihilation of air, which is essential to animal life, because it imparts to fire its destructive agency.

The second expedient is as impracticable, as the first would be unwise. As long as the reason of man continues fallible, and he is at liberty to exercise it, different opinions will be formed. As long as the connection subsists between his reason and his self-love, his opinions and his passions will have a reciprocal influence on each other; and the former will be objects to which the latter will attach themselves. The diversity in the faculties of men from which the rights of property originate, is not less an insuperable obstacle to a uniformity of interests. The protection of these faculties is the first object of Government. From the protection of different and unequal faculties of acquiring property, the possession of different degrees and kinds of property immediately results: and from the influence of these on the sentiments and views of the respective proprietors, ensues a division of the society into different interests and parties.

The latent causes of faction are thus sown in the nature of man; and we see them every where brought into different degrees of activity, according to the different circumstances of civil society. A zeal for different opinions concerning religion, concerning Government and many other points, as well of speculation as of practice; an attachment to different leaders ambitiously contending for pre-eminence and power; or to persons of other descriptions whose fortunes have been interesting to the human passions, have in turn divided mankind into parties, inflamed them with mutual animosity, and rendered them much more disposed to vex and oppress each other, than to co-operate for their common good. So strong is this propensity of mankind to fall into mutual animosities, that where no substantial occasion presents itself, the most frivolous and fanciful distinctions have been sufficient to kindle their unfriendly passions, and excite their most violent conflicts. But the most common and durable source of factions has been the various and unequal distribution of property. Those who hold, and those who are without property, have ever formed distinct interests in society. Those who are creditors, and those who are debtors, fall under a like discrimination. A landed interest, a manufacturing interest, a mercantile interest, a monied interest, with many lesser interests, grow up of necessity in civilized nations, and divide them into different classes, actuated by different sentiments and views. The regulation of these various and interfering interests forms the principal task of modern Legislation, and involves the spirit of party and faction in the necessary and ordinary operations of Government.

No man is allowed to be a judge in his own cause; because his interest would certainly bias his judgment, and, not improbably, corrupt his integrity. With equal, nay with greater reason, a body of men, are unfit to be both judges and parties, at the same time; yet, what are many of the most important acts of legislation, but so many judicial determinations, not indeed concerning the rights of single persons, but concerning the rights of large bodies of citizens; and what are the different classes of legislators, but advocates and parties to the causes which they determine? Is a law proposed concerning private debts? It is a question to which the creditors are parties on one side, and the debtors on the other. Justice ought to hold the balance between them. Yet the parties are and must be themselves the judges; and the most numerous party, or, in other words, the most powerful faction must be expected to prevail. Shall domestic manufactures be encouraged, and in what degree, by restrictions on foreign manufactures? are questions which would be differently decided by the landed and the manufacturing classes; and probably by neither, with a sole regard to justice and the public good. The apportionment of taxes on the various descriptions of property, is an act which seems to require the most exact impartiality; yet, there is perhaps no legislative act in which greater opportunity and temptation are given to a predominant party, to trample on the rules of justice. Every shilling with which they over-burden the inferior number, is a shilling saved to their own pockets.

It is in vain to say, that enlightened statesmen will be able to adjust these clashing interests, and render them all subservient to the public good. Enlightened statesmen will not always be at the helm: Nor, in many cases, can such an adjustment be made at all, without taking into view indirect and remote considerations, which will rarely prevail over the immediate interest which one party may find in disregarding the rights of another, or the good of the whole.

The inference to which we are brought, is, that the *causes* of faction cannot be removed; and that relief is only to be sought in the means of controlling its *effects*.

If a faction consists of less than a majority, relief is supplied by the republican principle, which enables the majority to defeat its sinister views by regular vote: It may clog the administration, it may convulse the society; but it will be unable to execute and mask its violence under the forms of the Constitution. When a majority is included in a faction, the form of popular government on the other hand enables it to sacrifice to its ruling passion or interest, both the public good and the rights of other citizens. To secure the public good, and private rights, against the danger of such a faction, and at the same time to preserve the spirit and the form of popular government, is then the great object to which our enquiries are directed: Let me add that it is the great desideratum, by which alone this form of government can be rescued from the opprobrium under which it has so long labored, and be recommended to the esteem and adoption of mankind.

By what means is this object attainable? Evidently by one of two only. Either the existence of the same passion or interest in a majority at the same time, must be prevented; or the majority, having such co-existent passion or interest, must be rendered, by their number and local situation, unable to concert and carry into effect schemes of oppression. If the impulse and the opportunity be suffered to coincide, we well know that neither moral nor religious motives can be relied on as an adequate control. They are not found to be such on the injustice and violence of individuals, and lose their efficacy in proportion to the number combined together; that is, in proportion as their efficacy becomes needful.

From this view of the subject, it may be concluded, that a pure Democracy, by which I mean, a Society, consisting of a small number of citizens, who assemble and administer the Government in person, can admit of no cure for the mischiefs of faction. A common passion or interest will, in almost every case, be felt by a majority of the whole; a communication and concert results from the form of Government itself; and there is nothing to check the inducements to sacrifice the weaker party, or an obnoxious individual. Hence it is, that such Democracies have ever been spectacles of turbulence and contention; have ever been found incompatible with personal security, or the rights of property; and have in general been as short in their lives, as they have been violent in their deaths. Theoretic politicians, who have patronized this species of Government, have erroneously supposed, that by reducing mankind to a perfect equality in their political rights, they would, at the same time, be perfectly equalized and assimilated in their possessions, their opinions, and their passions.

A republic, by which I mean a government in which the scheme of representation takes place, opens a different prospect, and promises the cure for which we are seeking. Let us examine the points in which it varies from pure democracy, and we shall comprehend both the nature of the cure and the efficacy which it must derive from the union.

The two great points of difference, between a democracy and a republic, are, first, the delegation of the government, in the latter, to a small number of citizens, elected by the rest; secondly, the greater number of citizens, and greater sphere of country, over which the latter may be extended.

The effect of the first difference is, on the one hand, to refine and enlarge the public views, by passing them through the medium of a chosen body of citizens, whose wisdom may best discern the true interest of their country, and whose patriotism and love of justice, will be least likely to sacrifice it to temporary or partial considerations. Under such a regulation, it may well happen, that the public voice, pronounced by the representatives of the people, will be more consonant to the public good, than if pronounced by the people themselves, convened for the purpose. On the other hand the effect may be inverted. Men of factious tempers, of local prejudices, or of sinister designs, may by intrigue, by corruption, or by other means, first obtain the suffrages, and then betray the interest of the people. The question resulting is, whether small or extensive republics are most favorable to the election of proper guardians of the public weal, and it is clearly decided in favor of the latter by two obvious considerations.

In the first place, it is to be remarked that, however small the republic may be, the representatives must be raised to a certain number, in order to guard against the cabals of a few; and that however large it may be, they must be limited to a certain number, in order to guard against the confusion of a multitude. Hence, the number of representatives in the two cases not being in proportion to that of the constituents, and being proportionally greatest in the small republic, it follows, that if the proportion of fit characters be not less in the large than in the small republic, the former will present a greater option, and consequently a greater probability of a fit choice.

In the next place, as each Representative will be chosen by a greater number of citizens in the large than in the small Republic, it will be more difficult for unworthy candidates to practise with success the vicious arts, by which elections are too often carried; and the suffrages of the people being more free, will be more likely to center on men who possess the most attractive merit, and the most diffusive and established characters.

It must be confessed, that in this, as in most other cases, there is a mean, on both sides of which inconveniences will be found to lie. By enlarging too much the number of electors, you render the representatives too little acquainted with all their local circumstances and lesser interests; as by reducing it too much, you render him unduly attached to these, and too little fit to comprehend and pursue great and national objects. The Federal Constitution forms a happy combination in this respect; the great and aggregate interests being referred to the national, the local and particular, to the state legislatures.

The other point of difference is, the greater number of citizens and extent of territory which may be brought within the compass of Republican, than of Democratic Government; and it is this circumstance principally which renders factious combinations less to be dreaded in the former, than in the latter. The smaller the society, the fewer probably will be the distinct parties and interests composing it; the fewer the distinct parties and interests, the more frequently will a majority be found of the same party; and the smaller the number of individuals composing a majority, and the smaller the compass within which they are placed, the more easily will they concert and execute their plans of oppression. Extend the sphere, and you take in a greater variety of parties and interests; you make it less probable that a majority of the whole will have a common motive to invade the rights of other citizens; or if such a common motive exists, it will be more difficult for all who feel it to discover their own strength, and to act in unison with each other. Besides other impediments, it may be remarked, that where there is a consciousness of unjust or dishonorable purposes, communication is always checked by distrust, in proportion to the number whose concurrence is necessary.

Hence it clearly appears, that the same advantage, which a Republic has over a Democracy, in controlling the effects of factions, is enjoyed by a large over a small Republic—is enjoyed by the Union over the States composing it. Does this advantage consist in the substitution of Representatives, whose enlightened views and virtuous sentiments render them superior to local prejudices, and to schemes of injustice? It will not be denied, that the Representation of the Union will be most likely to possess these requisite endowments. Does it consist in the greater security afforded by a greater variety of parties, against the event of any one party being able to outnumber and oppress the rest? In an equal degree does the increased variety of parties, comprised within the Union, increase this security? Does it, in fine, consist in the greater obstacles opposed to the concert and accomplishment of the secret wishes of an unjust and interested majority? Here, again, the extent of the Union gives it the most palpable advantage.

The influence of factious leaders may kindle a flame within their particular States, but will be unable to spread a general conflagration through the other States: a religious sect, may degenerate into a political faction in a part of the Confederacy but the variety of sects dispersed over the entire face of it, must secure the national Councils against any danger from that source: a rage for paper money, for an abolition of debts, for an equal division of property, or for any other improper or wicked project, will be less apt to pervade the whole body of the Union, than a particular member of it; in the same proportion as such a malady is more likely to taint a particular county or district, than an entire State.

In the extent and proper structure of the Union, therefore, we behold a Republican remedy for the diseases most incident to Republican Government. And according to the degree of pleasure and pride, we feel in being Republicans, ought to be our zeal in cherishing the spirit, and supporting the character of Federalists.

PUBLIUS

51

James Madison

February 6, 1788

To the People of the State of New York

To what expedient then shall we finally resort for maintaining in practice the necessary partition of power among the several departments, as laid down in the constitution? The only answer that can be given is, that as all these exterior provisions are found to be inadequate, the defect must be supplied, by so contriving the interior structure of the government, as that its several constituent parts may, by their mutual relations, be the means of keeping each other in their proper places. Without presuming to undertake a full development of this important idea, I will hazard a few general observations, which may perhaps place it in a clearer light, and enable us to form a more correct judgment of the principles and structure of the government planned by the convention.

In order to lay a due foundation for that separate and distinct exercise of the different powers of government, which to a certain extent, is admitted on all hands to be essential to the preservation of liberty, it is evident that each department should have a will of its own; and consequently should be so constituted, that the members of each should have as little agency as possible in the appointment of the members of the others. Were this principle rigorously adhered to, it would require that all the appointments for the supreme executive, legislative, and judiciary magistracies, should be drawn from the same fountain of authority, the people, through channels, having no communication whatever with one another. Perhaps such a plan of constructing the several departments would be less difficult in practice than it may in contemplation appear. Some difficulties however, and some additional expense, would attend the execution of it. Some deviations therefore from the principle must be admitted. In the constitution of the judiciary department in particular, it might be inexpedient to insist rigorously on the principle; first, because peculiar qualifications being essential in the members, the primary consideration ought to be to select that mode of choice, which best secures these qualifications; secondly, because the permanent tenure by which the appointments are held in that department, must soon destroy all sense of dependence on the authority conferring them.

It is equally evident that the members of each department should be as little dependent as possible on those of the others, for the emoluments annexed to their offices. Were the executive magistrate, or the judges, not independent of the legislature in this particular, their independence in every other would be merely nominal.

But the great security against a gradual concentration of the several powers in the same department, consists in giving to those who administer each department, the necessary constitutional means, and personal motives, to resist encroachments of the others. The provision for defense must in this, as in all other cases, be made commensurate to the danger of attack. Ambition must be made to counteract ambition. The interest of the man must be connected with the constitutional rights of the place. It may be a reflection on human nature, that such devices should be necessary to control the abuses of government. But what is government itself but the greatest of all reflections on human nature? If men were angels, no government would be necessary. If angels were to govern men, neither external nor internal controls on government would be necessary. In framing a government which is to be administered by men over men, the great difficulty lies in this: You must first enable the government to control the governed; and in the next place, oblige it to control itself. A dependence on the people is no doubt the primary control on the government; but experience has taught mankind the necessity of auxiliary precautions.

This policy of supplying by opposite and rival interests, the defect of better motives, might be traced through the whole system of human affairs, private as well as public. We see it particularly displayed in all the subordinate distributions of power; where the constant aim is to divide and arrange the several offices in such a manner as that each may be a check on the other; that the private interest of every individual, may be a sentinel over the public rights. These inventions of prudence cannot be less requisite in the distribution of the supreme powers of the state.

But it is not possible to give each department an equal power of self defense. In republican government the legislative authority, necessarily, predominates. The remedy for this inconveniency is, to divide the legislature into different branches; and to render them by different modes of election, and different principles of action, as little connected with each other, as the nature of their common functions, and their common dependence on the society, will admit. It may even be necessary to guard against dangerous encroachments by still further precautions. As the weight of the legislative authority requires that it should be thus divided, the weakness of the executive may require, on the other hand, that it should be fortified. An absolute negative, on the legislature, appears at first view to be the natural defense with which the executive magistrate should be armed. But perhaps it would be neither altogether safe, nor alone sufficient. On ordinary occasions, it might not be exerted with the requisite firmness; and on extraordinary occasions, it might be prefidiously abused. May not this defect of an absolute negative be supplied, by some qualified connection between this weaker department, and the weaker branch of the stronger department, by which the latter may be led to support the constitutional rights of the former, without being too much detached from the rights of its own department?

If the principles on which these observations are founded be just, as I persuade myself they are, and they be applied as a criterion, to the several state constitutions, and to the federal constitution, it will be found, that if the latter does not perfectly correspond with them, the former are infinitely less able to bear such a test.

There are moreover two considerations particularly applicable to the federal system of America, which place that system in a very interesting point of view.

First. In a single republic, all the power surrendered by the people, is submitted to the administration of a single government; and usurpations are guarded against by a division of the government into distinct and separate departments. In the compound republic of America, the power surrendered by the people, is first divided between two distinct governments, and then the portion allotted to each, subdivided among distinct and separate departments. Hence a double security arises to the rights of the people. The different governments will control each other; at the same time that each will be controlled by itself.

Second. It is of great importance in a republic, not only to guard the society against the oppression of its rulers; but to guard one part of the society against the injustice of the other part. Different interests necessarily exist in different classes of citizens. If a majority be united by a common interest, the rights of the minority will be insecure. There are but two methods of providing against this evil: The one by creating a will in the community independent of the majority, that is, of the society itself, the other by comprehending in the society so many separate descriptions of citizens, as will render an unjust combination of a majority of the whole, very improbable, if not impracticable. The first method prevails in all governments possessing an hereditary or self appointed authority. This at best is but a precarious security; because a power independent of the society may as well espouse the unjust views of the major, as the rightful interests, of the minor party, and may possibly be turned against both parties. The second method will be exemplified in the federal republic of the United States. While all authority in it will be derived from and dependent on the society, the society itself will be broken into so many parts, interests and classes of citizens, that the rights of individuals or of the minority, will be in little danger from interested combinations of the majority. In a free government, the security for civil rights must be the same as for religious rights. It consists in the one case in the multiplicity of interests, and in the other, in the multiplicity of sects. The degree of security in both cases will depend on the number of interests and sects; and this may be presumed to depend on the extent of country and number of people comprehended under the same government. This view of the subject must particularly recommend a proper federal system to all the sincere and considerate friends of republican government: Since it shows that in exact proportion as the territory of the union may be formed into more circumscribed confederacies or states, oppressive combinations of a majority will be facilitated, the best security under the republican form, for the rights of every class of citizens, will be diminished; and consequently, the stability and independence of some member of the government, the only other security, must be proportionally increased. Justice is the end of government. It is the end of civil society. It ever has been, and ever will be pursued, until it be obtained, or until liberty be lost in the pursuit. In a society under the forms of which the stronger faction can readily unite and oppress the weaker, anarchy may as truly be said to reign, as in a state of nature where the weaker individual is not secured against the violence of the stronger: And as in the latter state even the stronger individuals are prompted by the uncertainty of their condition, to submit to a government which may protect the weak as well as themselves: So in the former state, will the more powerful factions or parties be gradually induced by a like motive, to wish for a government which will protect all parties, the weaker as well as the more powerful. It can be little doubted, that if the state of Rhode Island was separated from the confederacy, and left to itself, the insecurity of rights under the popular form of government within such narrow limits, would be displayed by such reiterated oppressions of factious majorities, that some power altogether independent of the people would soon be called for by the voice of the very factions whose misrule had proved the necessity of it. In the extended republic of the United States, and among the great variety of interests, parties and sects which it embraces, a coalition of a majority of the whole society could seldom take place on any other principles than those of justice and the general good; and there being thus less danger to a minor from the will of the major party, there must be less pretext also, to provide for the security of the former, by introducing into the government a will not dependent on the latter; or in other words, a will independent of the society itself. It is no less certain than it is important, notwithstanding the contrary opinions which have been entertained, that the larger the society, provided it lie within a practicable sphere, the more duly capable will be of self government. And happily for the *republican cause,* the practicable sphere may be carried to a very great extent, by a judicious modification and mixture of the *federal principle.*

Publius

Glossary

A

actual malice Supreme Court test for libel of a public figure, in which the plaintiff must prove that the publisher knew the material was false or acted with reckless disregard of whether it was true or false.

adversary process Confrontational legal process under which each party presents its version of events.

affirmative action Policies that support greater equality, often by granting racial or gender preferences in hiring, education, or contracting.

agenda setting Ability of the media to affect the way people view issues, people, or events by controlling which stories are shown and which are not.

amendment Formal process of changing the Constitution.

Antifederalists Those who opposed the new proposed Constitution during the ratification period.

appeal Legal proceeding whereby the decision of a lower court on a question of law can be challenged and reviewed by a higher court.

appropriate Congress's power to allocate a set amount of federal dollars for a specific program or agency.

approval rating Job performance evaluation for the president, Congress, or other public official or institution that is generated by public opinion polls and is typically reported as a percentage.

Articles of Confederation Initial governing authority of the United States, 1781–88.

Australian ballot Voting system in which state governments run elections and provide voters the option of choosing candidates from multiple parties; also called the secret ballot.

authorize Congress's power to create a federal program or agency and set levels of federal funds to support that program or agency.

autocracy System of government in which the power to govern is concentrated in the hands of an individual ruler.

B

ballot List of candidates who are running for elected office; used by voters to make their choice.

battleground state State in which the outcome of the presidential election is uncertain and in which both candidates invest much time and money, especially if its votes are vital for a victory in the Electoral College.

Bill of Rights First ten amendments to the Constitution, which provide basic political rights.

Brown v. Board of Education 1954 Supreme Court decision striking down segregated schools.

bully pulpit Nickname for the power of the president to use the attention associated with the office to persuade the media, Congress, and the public to support his policy positions.

bureaucracy Executive branch departments, agencies, boards, and commissions that carry out the responsibilities of the federal government.

C

cabinet Set of executive departments responsible for carrying out federal policy in specific issue areas.

cabinet secretaries Heads of cabinet departments and chief advisers to the president on the issues under their jurisdiction.

capitalism Economic system in which businesses and key industries are privately owned and in which individuals, acting on their own or with others, are free to create businesses.

career civil servants Federal employees who are hired through a merit-based system to implement federal programs and who are expected to be neutral in their political affiliations.

caucus Meeting of party members in town halls, schools, and private homes to select a presidential nominee.

checks and balances Government structure that authorizes each branch of government (executive, legislative, and judicial) to share powers with the other branches, thereby holding some scrutiny of and control over the other branches.

citizens' groups Groups that form to draw attention to purely public issues that affect all citizens equally.

citizenship Full-fledged membership in a nation.

civil liberties Those rights, such as freedom of speech and religion, that are so fundamental that they are outside the authority of government to regulate.

civil rights Set of rights centered around the concept of equal treatment that government is obliged to protect.

Civil Rights Act Prohibits discrimination in employment, education, and places of public accommodation (1964).

civil service The non-partisan federal workforce employed to carry out government programs and policies.

Civil Service Commission Created by the Pendleton Act to administer entrance exams for the federal civil service and set standards for promotion based on merit.

civil suit Lawsuit by a person, organization, or government against another person, organization, or government.

class action lawsuit Lawsuit filed by one person on behalf of that person plus all similarly situated people.

clear and present danger test First Amendment test that requires the state to prove that there is a high likelihood that the speech in question would lead to a danger that Congress has a right to prevent.

cloture Vote that can stop a filibuster and bring debate on a bill to end.

commander in chief Leader of the armed forces of the United States.

commerce clause Gives Congress the power to regulate commerce with foreign nations, with Indian tribes, and among the various states (Article I, Section 8).

common law Judge-made law in England and the United States that results from gaps in statutory law.

compelling interest test Standard frequently used by the Supreme Court in civil liberties cases to determine whether a state has a compelling interest for infringing on a right and whether the law is narrowly drawn to meet that interest.

compulsory voting Practice that requires citizens to vote in elections or face punitive measures such as community service, fines, or imprisonment.

concurrent budget resolution Congressional blueprint outlining general amounts of funds that can be spent on federal programs.

concurrent powers Powers held by both the national and state governments in a federal system.

concurring opinion Opinion that agrees with the results of the majority opinion (that is, which party wins) but sets out a separate rationale.

confederal system System of government in which ultimate authority rests with the regional (for example, state) governments.

confidence interval Statistical range, with a given probability, that takes random error into account.

Connecticut Compromise Compromise on legislative representation whereby the lower chamber is based on population and the upper chamber provides equal representation to the states.

conservatives Individuals who distrust government, believing that free markets offer better ways than government involvement to improve people's livelihood. In the social sphere, conservatives have more faith in government's ability to enforce traditional values.

constitution Document or set of documents that establish the basic rules and procedures for how a society shall be governed.

Constitutional Convention Meeting in 1787 at which twelve states intended to revise the Articles of Confederation but ended up proposing an entirely new Constitution.

content-neutral Free speech doctrine that allows certain types of regulation of speech, as long as the restriction does not favor one side or another of a controversy.

continuing resolution Measure passed to fund federal programs when the appropriations process has not been completed by September 30, the end of the fiscal year.

countermajoritarian difficulty Alexander Bickel's phrase for the tension that exists for representative government when unelected judges have the power to strike laws passed by elected representatives.

Court-packing plan President Franklin Roosevelt's proposal to add new justices to the Supreme Court so that the Court would uphold his policies.

courts of appeals Intermediate federal courts that are above the district courts and below the Supreme Court.

criminal case Government prosecution of an individual for breaking the law.

D

debt ceiling The congressionally authorized limit on federal borrowing.

Declaration of Independence 1776 document declaring American independence from Great Britain and calling for equality, human rights, and citizen participation.

democracy System of government in which the supreme power is vested in the people and exercised by them either directly or indirectly through elected representatives.

direct democracy Form of democracy in which political power is exercised directly by citizens.

dissenting opinion Opinion that disagrees with the majority opinion as to which party wins.

district courts Federal trial courts at the bottom of the federal judicial hierarchy.

Dred Scott v. Sandford 1857 Supreme Court decision declaring that blacks could not be citizens and Congress could not ban slavery in the territories.

dual federalism Doctrine holding that state governments and the federal government have almost completely separate functions.

E

earmark Federal dollars devoted specifically to a local project in a congressional district or state.

economic interest group Group formed to advance the economic status of its members.

egalitarianism Belief in human equality that disdains inherited titles of nobility and inherited wealth.

Electoral College The presidential electors, selected to represent the votes of their respective states, who meet every four years to cast the electoral votes for president and vice president.

enumerated powers Powers expressly granted to Congress by the Constitution.

equality of opportunity Expectation that citizens may not be discriminated against on account of race, gender, or national background and that every citizen should have an equal chance to succeed in life.

equality of outcome Expectation that equality is achieved if results are comparable for all citizens regardless of race, gender, or national background or that such groups are proportionally represented in measures of success in life.

Equal Pay Act Prohibits different pay for males and females for the same work (1963).

equal protection clause Prevents states from denying any person the equal protection of the laws (Fourteenth Amendment).

establishment clause First Amendment clause prohibiting governmental establishment of religion.

exclusionary rule Supreme Court rule declaring that evidence found in violation of the Fourth Amendment cannot be used at trial.

executive order Presidential directive that usually involves implementing a specific law.

executive privilege President's right to engage in confidential communications with his advisers.

exit polls Polls that survey a sample of voters immediately after exiting the voting booth to predict the outcome of the election before the ballots are officially counted.

expectation of privacy test Supreme Court test for whether Fourth Amendment protections apply.

F

faction Defined by Madison as any group that places its own interests above the aggregate interests of society.

federal budget deficit Difference between the amount of money the federal government spends in outlays and the amount of money it receives from revenues.

federalism System of government in which sovereignty is constitutionally divided between national and state governments.

Federalist Papers Series of essays written by James Madison, Alexander Hamilton, and John Jay arguing for the ratification of the Constitution; today a leading source for understanding the Constitution.

Federalists Initially, those who supported the Constitution during the ratification period; later, the name of the political party established by supporters of Alexander Hamilton.

Federal Register Official published record of all executive branch rules, regulations, and orders.

Federal Reserve Board Independent regulatory commission that affects the money supply by setting the reserve requirements of member banks, establishing a discount rate for loans to member banks, and buying or selling government securities.

filibuster Tactic of extended speech designed to delay or block passage of a bill in the Senate.

final regulations Final version of the instructions for implementing a law.

501(c)(3) organizations Tax-exempt groups that are prohibited from lobbying or campaigning for a party or candidate.

Founders The people who were involved in establishing the United States, whether at the time of the Declaration of Independence or the writing of the Constitution.

Framers The people who were involved in writing the Constitution.

framing Ability of the media to influence public perception of issues by constructing the issue or discussion of a subject in a certain way.

free exercise clause First Amendment clause protecting the free exercise of religion.

free rider problem Problem faced by interest groups when a collective benefit they provide is so widespread and diffuse that members and nonmembers alike receive it, reducing the incentive for joining the group.

frontloading Moving a state primary or caucus earlier in the year to increase its influence.

fugitive slave clause Required states to return runaway slaves; negated by the Thirteenth Amendment (Article IV, Section 2).

G

gender gap Differences in the political attitudes and behavior of men and women.

general election Election in which voters choose their elected officials.

general welfare clause Gives Congress the power to tax to provide for the general welfare (Article I, Section 8).

generational replacement Cycle whereby younger generations replace older generations in the electorate.

gerrymandering Redistricting that blatantly benefits one political party over the other or concentrates (or dilutes) the voting impact of racial and ethnic groups.

grassroots movement Group that forms in response to an economic or political event but does not focus on only one issue.

graveyard voting Corrupt practice of using a dead person's name to cast a ballot in an election.

Great Society Lyndon Johnson's program for expanding the federal social welfare programs in health care, education, and housing and for ending poverty.

H

hard news Political news coverage, traditionally found in the printed press, that is more fact-based, opposed to more interpretive narratives and commentary.

head of state Title given to the president as national leader.

hold Power available to a senator to prevent the unanimous consent that allows a bill or presidential nomination to come to the Senate floor, which can be broken by invoking cloture (sixty votes).

home style The way in which incumbents portray themselves to constituents.

House majority leader Leader of the majority party in the House and second in command to the Speaker.

House minority leader Leader of the minority party in the House.

I

ideological interest groups Groups that form among citizens with the same beliefs about a specific issue.

impeachment Process whereby the House brings charges against the president or another federal official that will, upon conviction by the Senate, remove him or her from office.

imperial presidency Power of the president to speak for the nation on the world stage and to set the policy agenda at home.

implied powers Powers not expressly granted to Congress but added through the necessary and proper clause.

incorporate Process of applying provisions of the Bill of Rights to the states.

independent agency Federal organization that has independent authority and does not operate within a cabinet department.

Independents Individuals who do not affiliate with either of the major political parties.

interest groups Groups of citizens who share a common interest—a political opinion, a religious or ideological belief, a social goal, or an economic characteristic—and try to influence public policy to benefit themselves.

invisible primary Period just before the primaries begin during which candidates attempt to capture party support and media coverage.

iron triangle Insular and closed relationship among interest groups, members of Congress, and federal agencies.

issue network View of the relationship among interest groups, members of Congress, and federal agencies as more fluid, open, and transparent than that described by the term iron triangle.

J

Jim Crow laws Southern laws that established strict segregation of the races and gave their name to the segregation era.

judicial activism Decisions that go beyond the what the law requires made by judges who seek to impose their own policy preferences on society through their judicial decisions.

judicial branch The branch of the federal government that interprets the laws.

judicial independence Ability of judges to reach decisions without fear of political retribution.

judicial restraint Decisions by judges respecting the decisions of other branches or, through the concept of precedent, the decisions of earlier judges.

judicial review Authority of courts to declare laws passed by Congress and acts of the executive branch to be unconstitutional.

jurisdiction Lawful authority of a court to hear a case.

L

lame duck Term-limited official in his or her last term of office.

Lawrence v. Texas 2003 Supreme Court case extending the right to privacy to homosexual behavior.

Lemon test Test for determining whether aid to religion violates the establishment clause.

levels of conceptualization Measure of how ideologically coherent individuals are in their political evaluations.

libel Publishing false and damaging statements about another person.

liberals Individuals who have faith in government to improve people's lives, believing that private efforts are insufficient. In the social sphere, liberals usually support diverse lifestyles and tend to oppose any government action that seeks to shape personal choices.

libertarians Those who generally believe that government should refrain from acting to regulate either the economy or moral values.

lobbying Act of trying to persuade elected officials to adopt a specific policy change or maintain the status quo.

M

majority opinion Opinion of a court laying out the official position of the court in the case.

majority rule Idea that a numerical majority of a group should hold the power to make decisions binding on the whole group; a simple majority.

majority vote Vote in which the winner needs to win 50 percent plus 1 of the votes cast.

Marbury v. Madison An 1803 Supreme Court decision that established the Supreme Court's power of judicial review.

markup Process by which bills are literally marked up, or written by the members of the committee.

mass media News sources, including newspapers, television, radio, and the Internet, whose purpose is to provide a large audience with information about the nation and the world.

McCulloch v. Maryland 1819 Supreme Court decision upholding the right of Congress to create a bank.

median voter theorem Theory that, in a two-party race, if voters select candidates on the basis of ideology and everyone participates equally, the party closer to the middle will win.

merit system System of employment under which employees are chosen and promoted based on merit.

microtargeting Gathering detailed information on cross sections of the electorate to track potential supporters and tailor political messages for them; also called narrowcasting.

midterm elections Congressional elections held between the presidential elections.

Miller test Supreme Court test for determining whether material is obscene.

minimal effects model View of the media's impact as marginal, since most people seek news reports to reinforce beliefs already held rather than to develop new ones.

minority rights Idea that majority should not be able to take certain fundamental rights away from those in the minority.

Missouri Plan Process for selecting state judges whereby the original nomination is by appointment and subsequent retention is by a retention election.

moderates Individuals who are in the middle of the ideological spectrum and do not hold consistently strong views about whether government should be involved in people's lives.

monarchy System of government that assigns power to a single person who inherits that position and rules until death.

muckraking Journalistic practice of investigative reporting that seeks to uncover corruption and wrongdoing.

N

national committee Top level of national political parties; coordinates national presidential campaigns.

national debt Sum of loans and interest that the federal government has accrued over time to pay for the federal deficit.

natural (unalienable) rights Rights that every individual has and that government cannot legitimately take away.

necessary and proper clause Gives Congress the power to pass all laws necessary and proper to the powers enumerated in Section 8 (Article I, Section 8).

negativity Campaign strategy of telling voters why they should not vote for the opponent and of highlighting information that raises doubts about the opponent.

New Deal Franklin Delano Roosevelt's program for ending the Great Depression through government intervention in the economy and development of a set of safety-net programs for individuals.

news media Subset of the mass media that provide the news of the day, gathered and reported by journalists.

nonattitudes Sources of error in public opinion polls in which individuals feel obliged to give opinions when they are unaware of the issue or have no opinions about it.

nongovernmental organizations (NGOs) Organizations independent of governments that monitor and improve political, economic, and social conditions throughout the world.

not-so-minimal effects model View of the media's impact as substantial, occurring by agenda setting, framing, and priming.

nullification Right of states to invalidate acts of Congress they believe to be illegal.

O

Office of Management and Budget (OMB) Federal agency that oversees the federal budget and all federal regulations.

oligarchy System of government in which the power to govern is concentrated in the hands of a powerful few, usually wealthy individuals.

omnibus bill One very large bill that encompasses many separate bills.

order Political value in which the rule of law is followed and does not permit actions that infringe on the well-being of others.

override Congress's power to overturn a presidential veto with a two-thirds vote in each chamber.

oversight Powers of Congress to monitor how the executive branch implements the laws.

P

pardon Full forgiveness for a crime.

party alignment Voter identification with a political party in repeated elections.

party caucus Group of party members in a legislature.

party identification Psychological attachment to a political party; partisanship.

party platform Document that lays out a party's core beliefs and policy proposals for each presidential election.

patronage system Political system in which government programs and benefits are awarded based on political loyalty to a party or politician.

Pendleton Act 1883 act that established a merit- and performance-based system for federal employment.

penny press Newspapers sold for a penny, initiating an era in which the press began to rely on circulation and advertising for income and not on political parties.

permanent campaign Charge that presidents and members of Congress focus more on winning the next election than on governing.

petition for a writ of *certiorari* Request to the Supreme Court that it review a lower court case.

plea bargain Agreement by a criminal defendant to plead guilty in return for a reduced sentence.

pluralism Political system in which competing interests battle over the direction and content of important policy making.

pluralist View of democratic society in which interest groups compete over policy goals and elected officials are mediators of group conflict.

plurality vote Vote in which the winner needs to win more votes than any other candidate.

pocket veto Automatic veto that occurs when Congress goes out of session within ten days of submitting a bill to the president and the president has not signed it.

polarization Condition in which differences between parties and/or the public are so stark that disagreement breaks out, fueling attacks and controversy.

policy agenda The second step in the policy-making process, in which a problem that has been identified gets the attention of policy makers.

policy diffusion Process by which policy ideas and programs initiated by one state spread to other states.

policy enactment The fourth step in the policy-making process, in which Congress passes a law that authorizes a specific governmental response to the problem.

policy evaluation The final step in the policy-making process, in which the policy is evaluated for its effectiveness and efficiency; if changes are needed, the issue is placed back on the policy agenda, and the cycle starts again.

policy formulation The third step in the policy-making process, in which those with a stake in the policy area propose and develop solutions to the problem.

policy implementation The fifth step in the policy-making process, in which the executive branch develops the rules that will put the policy into action.

political action committees (PACs) Groups formed to raise and contribute funds to support electoral candidates and that are subject to campaign finance laws.

political appointees Federal employees appointed by the president with the explicit task of carrying out his political and partisan agenda.

political culture A shared way of thinking about community and government and the relationship between them.

political equality The idea that people should have equal amounts of influence in the political system.

political ideology Set of coherent political beliefs that offers a philosophy for thinking about the scope of government.

political trust Extent to which people believe the government acts in their best interests.

politics Process by which people make decisions about who gets what, when, and how.

populists Those who oppose concentrated wealth and adhere to traditional moral values.

position issues Political issues that offer specific policy choices and often differentiate candidates' views and plans of action.

power elite Small handful of decision makers who hold authority over a large set of issues.

precedent Practice of reaching decisions based on the previous decisions of other judges.

preliminary regulations Draft instructions for implementing a law.

presidential coattails Effect of a popular president or presidential candidate on congressional elections, boosting votes for members of his party.

presidential directive Official instructions from the president regarding federal policy.

primary election Election in which voters select the candidates who will run on the party label in the general election; also called direct primary.

priming Process whereby the media influence the criteria the public uses to make decisions.

prior restraint Government restrictions on freedom of the press that prevent material from being published.

private discrimination Discrimination by private individuals or businesses.

private goods Goods or benefits provided by government in which most of the benefit falls to the individuals, families, or companies receiving them.

problem identification The first step in the policy-making process, in which a problem in politics, the economy, or society is recognized as warranting government action.

propaganda model Extreme view of the media's role in society, arguing that the press serves the interest of the government only, driving what the public thinks about important issues.

proportional representation An electoral system that assigns party delegates according to vote share in a presidential primary election or that assigns seats in the legislature according to vote share in a general election.

public discrimination Discrimination by national, state, or local governments.

public goods Goods or benefits provided by government from which everyone benefits and from which no one can be excluded.

public opinion Aggregate of individual attitudes or beliefs about certain issues or officials.

public policy Intentional actions of government designed to achieve a goal.

push polls Polls that are designed to manipulate the opinions of those being polled.

R

race to the bottom Situation in which states compete with one another to lower protections and services below the level they might otherwise prefer.

rally-around-the-flag effect Surge of public support for the president in times of international crisis.

random sample Method of selection that gives everyone who might be selected to participate in a poll an equal chance to be included.

ranking member Leader of the minority party members of a committee.

rationality Acting in a way that is consistent with one's self-interest.

realignment Long-term shift in voter allegiance from one party to another.

reconciliation A measure used to bring all bills that contain changes in the tax code or entitlement programs in line with the congressional budget.

Reconstruction The period from 1865 to 1877 in which the former Confederate states gained readmission to the Union and the federal government passed laws to help the emancipated slaves.

redistricting Process whereby state legislatures redraw the boundaries of congressional districts in the state to make them equal in population size.

regulations Guidelines issued by federal agencies for administering federal programs and implementing federal law.

regulatory process System of rules that govern how a law is implemented; also called the rule-making process.

representative democracy Form of democracy in which citizens elect public officials to make political decisions and formulate laws on their behalf.

republic Form of government in which power derives from citizens, but public officials make policy and govern according to existing law.

reserve powers Powers retained by the states under the Constitution.

responsible parties Parties that take responsibility for offering the electorate a distinct range of policies and programs, thus providing a clear choice.

retrospective voting Theory that voting is driven by a citizen's assessment of an officeholder's performance since the last election.

revolving door Movement of members of Congress, lobbyists, and executive branch employees into paid positions in each other's organizations.

right of association Right to freely associate with others and form groups, protected by the First Amendment.

right of petition Right to ask the government for assistance with a problem or to express opposition to a government policy, protected by the First Amendment.

right to privacy Constitutional right inferred by the Court that has been used to protect unlisted rights such as sexual privacy and reproductive rights, plus the right to end life-sustaining medical treatment.

Roe v. Wade 1973 Supreme Court case extending the right to privacy to abortion.

rule Guidelines issued by the House Rules Committee that determine how many amendments may be considered for each bill.

rule of four Supreme Court rule that grants review to a case if as few as four of the justices support review.

rule of law Legal system with known rules that are enforced equally against all people.

S

safe seat Seat in Congress considered to be reliably held by one party or the other.

secession Act of seceding, or formally withdrawing, from a nation-state.

seditious libel Conduct or language that incites rebellion against the authority of a state.

selective benefits Benefits offered exclusively to members of an interest group.

selective exposure Process whereby people secure information from sources that agree with them, thus reinforcing their beliefs.

selective incorporation Doctrine used by the Supreme Court to make those provisions of the Bill of Rights that are fundamental rights binding on the states.

selective perception Process whereby partisans interpret the same information differently.

self-government Rule by the people.

Senate majority leader Leader of the majority party in the Senate.

Senate minority leader Leader of the minority party in the Senate.

Senior Executive Service (SES) Senior management personnel in the federal government appointed by the president.

separate-but-equal doctrine Supreme Court doctrine that upheld segregation as long as there were equivalent facilities for blacks.

separation of powers Government structure in which authority is divided among branches (executive, legislative, and judicial), with each holding separate and independent powers and areas of responsibility.

signing statements Written remarks issued by the president when signing a bill into law that often reflect his interpretation of how the law should be implemented.

single-issue groups Groups that form to present one view on a highly salient issue that is intensely important to members, such as gun control or abortion.

single-member plurality system Electoral system that assigns one seat in a legislative body to represent citizens who live in a defined area (a district) based on which candidate wins the most votes.

social contract Theory that government has only the authority accorded it by the consent of the governed.

socialism Economic system in which the government owns major industries.

socialization Impact and influence of one's social environment on the views and attitudes one carries in life, a primary source of political attitudes.

soft news News stories focused less on facts and policies than on sensationalizing secondary issues or on less serious subjects of the entertainment world.

solicitor general Official in the Justice Department who represents the president in federal court.

Speaker of the House Constitutional and political leader of the House.

special interests Set of groups seeking a particular benefit for themselves in the policy process.

stakeholders Participants in the policy-making system who seek to influence the content and direction of legislation.

state action Action by a state, as opposed to a private person, that constitutes discrimination and therefore is an equal protection violation.

State of the Union address Speech on the condition of the country given by the president to Congress every January.

Stonewall riots Street protest in 1969 by gay patrons against a police raid of a gay bar in New York; the protest is credited with launching the gay rights movement.

Super PACs Independent groups that can raise unlimited amounts of money from individuals, labor unions, and corporations and can spend it to support or oppose political candidates but cannot coordinate directly with candidates or political parties.

supremacy clause Makes federal law supreme over state laws (Article VI).

swing states States that are not clearly pro-Republican or pro-Democrat and therefore are of vital interest to presidential candidates, as they can determine election outcomes.

symbolic speech Actions, such as burning the flag, that convey a political message without spoken words.

T

term limits Rule restricting the number of terms an elected official can serve in a given office.

three-fifths compromise Compromise over slavery at the Constitutional Convention that granted states extra representation in the House of Representatives based on their number of slaves at the ratio of three-fifths.

tracking polls Polls that seek to gauge changes of opinion of the same sample size over a period of time, common during the closing months of presidential elections.

turnout Share of all eligible voters who actually cast ballots.

U

unanimous consent agreement Agreement among all one hundred senators on how a bill or presidential nomination will be debated, changed, and voted on in the Senate.

unions Interest groups of individuals who share a common type of employment and seek better wages and working conditions through collective bargaining with employers.

unitary system System of government in which ultimate authority rests with the national government.

V

valence issues Noncontroversial or widely supported campaign issues that are unlikely to differ among candidates.

valid secular purpose Supreme Court test that allows states to ban activities that infringe on religious practices as long as the state has a nonreligious rationale for prohibiting the behavior.

vanishing marginals Trend marking the decline of competitive congressional elections.

veto Authority of the president to block legislation passed by Congress. Congress can override a veto by a two-thirds majority in each chamber.

vote-by-mail (VBM) system Method of voting in an election whereby ballots are distributed to voters by mail, and voters complete and return the ballots by mail.

voter registration Enrollment required prior to voting to establish eligibility.

voting-age population (VAP) Used to calculate the rate of participation by dividing the number of voters by the number of people in the country who are 18 and over.

voting-eligible population (VEP) Used to calculate the rate of participation by dividing the number of voters by the number of people in the country who are eligible to vote rather than just of voting age.

Voting Rights Act Gives the federal government the power to prevent discrimination in voting rights (1965).

W

War Powers Act 1973 act that provides that the president cannot send troops into military conflict for more than a total of ninety days without seeking a formal declaration of war, or authorization for continued military action, from Congress.

watchdog Role of the press in monitoring government actions.

wedge issue Divisive issue focused on a particular group of the electorate that candidates use to gain more support by taking votes away from their opponents.

whistleblowers Employees who report mismanagement, corruption, or illegal activity within their agencies.

winner-take-all system Electoral system in which whoever wins the most votes in an election wins the election.

women's suffrage movement Movement to grant women the right to vote.

writ of *habeas corpus* Right of individuals who have been arrested and jailed to go before a judge, who determines whether their detention is legal.

Y

yellow journalism Style of journalism in the late nineteenth century characterized by sensationalism intended to capture readers' attention and increase circulation.

Endnotes

Chapter 1

1. This story was compiled from Tim Craig and Michael D. Shear, "Allen Quip Provokes Outrage, Apology," *Washington Post*, August 15, 2006, A1; Fredrick Kunkle, "Fairfax Native Says Allen's Words Stung," *Washington Post*, August 25, 2006, B1; S. R. Sidarth, "I Am Macaca," *Washington Post*, November 12, 2006, B2; and telephone and e-mail interviews with S. R. Sidarth, December 25 and 28, 2009, conducted for this textbook; the chapter-opening quotation is from the December 25, 2009, interview.

2. International Social Survey Program, as cited in Russell Dalton, *The Good Citizen* (Washington, D.C.: CQ Press, 2007), 144; Morley Winograd and Michael D. Hais, *Millennial Makeover: MySpace, YouTube and the Future of American Politics* (New Brunswick, N.J.: Rutgers University Press, 2008), 260–63. The caption for the photo on page 5 is drawn from this source.

3. Dalton, *Good Citizen*, 153.

4. Larry Bartels, *Unequal Democracy* (Princeton, N.J.: Princeton University Press, 2008); David Cay Johnston, "The Gap between Rich and Poor Grows in the United States," *New York Times*, March 29, 2007. The caption for the photo on page 6 is drawn from these sources: U.S. census data; Merrill Goozner, "Top 1 Percent Got Lion's Share of Income," *Fiscal Times*, March 5, 2012, http://www.thefiscaltimes.com/Blogs/Gooz-News/2012/03/05/Top-1-Percent-Got-Lions-Share-of-Income-Gains-in-2010.aspx; and Emmanuel Saez, "Striking It Richer: The Evolution of Top Incomes in the United States (Updated with 2009 and 2010 Estimates)," *Pathways Magazine* (Winter 2008): 6–7, http://www.stanford.edu/group/scspi/_media/pdf/pathways/winter_2008/Saez.pdf.

5. "Americans' Approval of Congress Drops to Single Digits," *New York Times*, October 25, 2011, http://www.nytimes.com/interactive/2011/10/25/us/politics/approval-of-congress-drops-to-single-digits.html.

6. "Obama Ratings Historically Polarized," *Gallup Politics*, January 27, 2012, accessed April 10, 2012, http://www.gallup.com/poll/152222/Obama-Ratings-Historically-Polarized.aspx.

7. The White House, Office of Management and Budget, Table 7.1, Federal Debt at the End of Year: 1940–2017, U.S. Budget for FY 2013, accessed April 10, 2012, http://www.whitehouse.gov/omb/budget/Historicals/.

8. Charles Beard, *American Government and Politics* (New York: Macmillan Company, 1915), 18.

9. Edmund Burke, *Reflections on the Revolution in France*, in *The Portable Edmund Burke*, ed. Isaac Kramnick (New York: Viking, 1999), 32.

10. John Adams to John Taylor, April 15, 1814, in *The Political Writings of John Adams: Representative Selections*, ed. George Peek Jr. (New York: Hackett Publishing, 2003), 67.

11. Quoted in David McCullough, *John Adams* (New York: Simon and Schuster, 2001), 68.

12. See Josiah Ober, *Mass and Elite in Democratic Athens* (Princeton, N.J.: Princeton University Press, 1991).

13. Harold Lasswell, *Politics: Who Gets What, When, How* (New York: McGraw-Hill, 1936).

14. Bryan D. Jones and Frank M. Baumgartner, *The Politics of Attention* (Chicago: University of Chicago Press, 2005).

15. David Remnick, "The President's Hero," *New Yorker*, February 2, 2009, http://www.newyorker.com/talk/comment/2009/02/02/090202taco_talk_remnick.

16. Barack Obama, Inaugural Address, January 20, 2009, http://www.whitehouse.gov/blog/inaugural-address.

17. The White House, "Making College More Affordable," February 24, 2009, accessed April 10, 2012, http://www.whitehouse.gov/issues/education/higher-education.

18. Tom Robinson, "SAFRA One Year Later," *University Business*, June 1, 2011, http://universitybusiness.com/article/safra-one-year-later.

19. Darrell M. West, Grover J. Whitehurst, and E. J. Dionne Jr., "Invisible: 1.4 Percent Coverage for Education Is Not Enough," Brookings.edu, December 2, 2009, accessed April 10, 2012, http://www.brookings.edu/research/reports/2009/12/02-education-news-west.

20. The White House, Office of Management and Budget, Table 7.1, Federal Debt at the End of Year: 1940–2017, U.S. Budget for FY 2013, accessed April 10, 2012, http://www.whitehouse.gov/omb/budget/Historicals/.

21. Brian Koenig, "Survey Examines Politics of Occupy Wall Street Movement," *New American*, November 3, 2011, http://thenewamerican.com/usnews/politics/item/9829-survey-examines-politics-of-occupy-wall-street-movement.

22. James Madison to W. T. Barry, "Epilogue: Securing the Republic," August 4, 1822, in *The Founders' Constitution*, ed. Philip B. Kurland and Ralph Lerner (Chicago: University of Chicago Press, 1986), accessed April 25, 2012, http://press-pubs.uchicago.edu/founders/documents/v1ch18s35.html.

Chapter 2

1. This story was compiled from an article in the May 8, 1992, issue of *USA Today* and an e-mail interview with Gregory Watson on January 29, 2010, conducted for this textbook. The chapter-opening quotation is from that interview.

2. Gordon S. Wood, *The American Revolution* (New York: Modern Library Chronicles, 2002), 39.

3. Robert Middlekauff, *The Glorious Cause: The American Revolution, 1763–1789* (New York: Oxford University Press, 1982), 231.

4. Thomas Paine, *Common Sense* (Philadelphia, 1776), USHistory.org, accessed April 10, 2012, http://www.ushistory.org/paine/commonsense/sense4.htm.

5. Articles of Confederation, Article IX, Paragraph 5, U.S. Constitution Online, accessed April 10, 2012, http://www.usconstitution.net/articles.html#Article9.

6. Historical Census Browser, University of Virginia, Geospatial and Statistical Data Center, accessed April 10, 2012, http://mapserver.lib.virginia.edu/.

7. Middlekauff, *Glorious Cause*, 624.

8. William Riker, "The Heresthetics of Constitution Making," *American Political Science Review* 78 (1984): 1–16.

9. See "Variant Texts of the Plan Presented by William Patterson," in *Debates in the Federal Convention of 1787 Reported by James Madison*, ed. Gaillard Hunt and James B. Scott (New York: 1920), 102–4, quoted by the Avalon Project, Yale University, Lillian Goldman Law Library, accessed April 10, 2012, http://avalon.law.yale.edu/18th_century/patexta.asp.

10. "1790 Census of Slave and Free Population," U.S. Census of Population and Housing, Historical Census Browser, University of Virginia, Geospatial and Statistical Data Center, accessed April 10, 2012, http://mapserver.lib.virginia.edu/.

11. Quoted in Max Farrand, *The Framing of the Constitution of the United States* (New Haven, Conn.: Yale University Press, 1913), 1:486–87.

12. See Allison M. Martens, "Reconsidering Judicial Supremacy: From the Counter-Majoritarian Difficulty to Constitutional Transformations," *Perspectives on Politics* 5 (2007): 447–59.

13. James Madison, "*Federalist* 39," in *The Federalist Papers*, U.S. Constitution Online, accessed May 3, 2012, http://www.constitution.org/fed/federa39.htm.

14. Brutus, "Antifederalist 1," U.S. Constitution Online, accessed May 10, 2012, http://www.constitution.org/afp/brutus01.htm.

15. Ibid.

16. "To Bill of Rights or Not To Bill of Rights," *Behind the Constitution* (blog), July 18, 2011, http://tjofftherecord.wordpress.com/tag/jamesmadison/.

17. James Madison, "*Federalist* 41," in *The Federalist Papers*, U.S. Constitution Online, accessed April 10, 2012, http://www.constitution.org/fed/federa41.htm.

18. *Wickard v. Filburn*, 317 U.S. 111 (1942).

19. *National Federation of Independent Business v. Sebelius*, 11–393 (2012).

20. Brian J. Gaines, "Popular Myths about Popular Vote–Electoral College Splits," *PS: Political Science & Politics* 34 (March 2001): 70–75.

21. *Furman v. Georgia*, 408 U.S. 238 (1972).

22. *Gregg v. Georgia*, 428 U.S. 153 (1976).

23. "States with and without the Death Penalty," Death Penalty Information Center, accessed April 10, 2012, http://www.deathpenaltyinfo.org/states-and-without-death-penalty.

24. "Federal Death Penalty," Death Penalty Information Center, accessed April 10, 2012, http://www.deathpenaltyinfo.org/federal-death-penalty?scid=29&did=147.

25. David Baldus, Charles A. Pulaski Jr., and George Woodworth, *Equal Justice and the Death Penalty* (Boston: Northeastern University Press, 1990).

26. *McCleskey v. Kemp*, 481 U.S. 279 (1987).

27. *Roper v. Simmons*, 543 U.S. 551 (2005); *Kennedy v. Louisiana*, 554 U.S. 407 (2008).

28. Innocence Project, "27 Years Later, Donald Gates Is Declared Innocent," *Innocence Blog*, last modified December 23, 2009, http://www.innocenceproject.org/Content/27_Years_Later_Donald_Gates_is_Declared_Innocent.php.

29. *District Attorney's Office v. Osborne*, 174 L. Ed. 2d 38 (2009).

30. See Alexander Keyssar, *The Right to Vote* (New York: Basic Books, 2000), 17.

Chapter 3

1. This story was written by Dana K. Glencross of Oklahoma City Communtiy College and compiled from information on the Oklahoma County website, http://www.oklahomacounty.org; Bryan Painter, "Local community service project helps area SHINE," *The Oklahoman*, October 11, 2010, 1A; Bryan Painter, "Community Service Project helps area SHINE," *The Oklahoman*, November 14, 2010, 9J; and telephone and e-mail interviews with Brian Maughan, February 29, March 28, and April 5, 2012, conducted for this textbook; chapter-opening quotation from March 13, 2012, e-mail.

2. Colin Bonwick, *The American Revolution* (Charlottesville: University of Virginia Press, 1991), 194.

3. "The First Political Cartoons," Archiving Early America, accessed April 13, 2012, http://www.earlyamerica.com/earlyamerica/firsts/cartoon/.

4. James Madison, Virginia (Randolph) Plan as Amended (National Archives Microfilm Publication M866, 1 roll), The Official Records of the Constitutional Convention, Records of the Continental and Confederation Congresses and the Constitutional Convention, 1774–1789, Record Group 360, National Archives, accessed April 27, 2012, http://www.ourdocuments.gov/doc.php?flash=true&doc=7.

5. William Riker, *Federalism: Origin, Operation, Significance* (Boston: Little Brown, 1964), 5.

6. *Cohens v. Virginia*, 19 U.S. 264 (1821).

7. *Arizona v. United States*, 11–182 (2012).

8. *Chisolm v. Georgia*, 2 U.S. 419 (1793).

9. Elinor Ostrom, *Governing the Commons: The Evolution of Institutions for Collective Action* (New York: Cambridge University Press, 1990), 106–10.

10. *McCulloch v. Maryland*, 17 U.S. 316 (1819).

11. *Gibbons v. Ogden*, 22 U.S. 1 (1824).

12. Scott Basinger, "Regulating Slavery: Deck-Stacking and Credible Commitment in the Fugitive Slave Act of 1850," *Journal of Law, Economics, and Organization* 19 (2003): 307.

13. *Dred Scott v. Sandford,* 60 U.S. 393 (1857).

14. Morton Grodzins, *The American System: A New View of the Government of the United States* (New York: Rand McNally, 1966), 8.

15. *United States v. E.C. Knight Co.*, 156 U.S. 1 (1895).

16. Wendy J. Schiller, "Building Careers and Courting Constituents: U.S. Senate Representation, 1889–1924," *Studies in American Political Development* 20 (2006): 1.

17. *Carter v. Coal Co.*, 298 U.S. 238 (1936).

18. *United States v. Butler*, 297 U.S. 1 (1936).

19. *National Labor Relations Board v. Jones & Laughlin Steel Corporation*, 301 U.S. 1 (1937).

20. *United States v. Darby Lumber Company*, 312 U.S. 100 (1941).

21. Grodzins, *American System*, 8–9.

22. *Brown v. Board of Education*, 347 U.S. 483 (1954).

23. Sean Nicholson-Crotty, "Rational Election Cycles and the Intermittent Political Safeguards of Federalism," *Publius: The Journal of Federalism* 38 (2008): 295–314.

24. Timothy Conlon, *New Federalism: Intergovernmental Reform from Nixon to Reagan* (Washington D.C.: Brookings Institution, 1988).

25. "Ronald Reagan, First Inaugural Address," January 20, 1981, American Rhetoric, accessed April 13, 2012, http://www.americanrhetoric.com/speeches/ronaldreagandfirstinaugural.html.

26. Tim Conlan and John Dinan, "Federalism, the Bush Administration, and the Transformation of American Conservatism," *Publius: The Journal of Federalism* 37 (2007): 279–303.

27. Scott F. Abernathy, *No Child Left Behind and the Public Schools* (Ann Arbor: University of Michigan Press, 2007), 23.

28. Clifford Rechtschaffen, "Sidestepping Regulations: On Environment, Bush Ignores Federalism," *San Francisco Chronicle,* August 18, 2003, http://www.sfgate.com/cgi-bin/article.cgi?f=/c/a/2003/08/18/ED255899.DTL.

29. Conlan and Dinan, "Federalism," 280.

30. John Schwartz, "Obama Seems to Be Open to a Broader Role for States," *New York Times,* January 29, 2009, http://www.nytimes.com/2009/01/30/us/politics/30federal.html/; "DEA Pot Raids Go On; Obama Opposes," *Washington Times,* February 5, 2009, http://www.washingtontimes.com/news/2009/feb/05/dea-led-by-bush-continues-pot-raids/?page=1.

31. David M. Herszenhorn, "Recovery Bill Gets Final Approval," *New York Times,* February 13, 2009, http://www.nytimes.com/2009/02/14/us/politics/14web-stim.html.

32. *United States v. Lopez*, 514 U.S. 549 (1995).

33. *National Federation of Independent Business v. Sebelius*, 11–393 (2012).

34. *Alden v. Maine,* 527 U.S. 706 (1999).

35. *College Savings Bank Florida v. Florida Prepaid*, 527 U.S. 666 (1999).

36. *Board of Trustees v. Garrett,* 531 U.S. 356 (2001).

37. *Gonzales v. Raich*, 545 U.S. 1 (2005).

38. *National Federation of Independent Business v. Sebelius*, 11–393 (2012).

39. *The Partial Veto in Wisconsin,* Information Bulletin 04-1 (Madison: State of Wisconsin Legislative Reference Bureau, 2004), http://legis.wisconsin.gov/lrb/pubs/ib/04ib1.pdf.

40. *Constitutional Amendment to Be Considered by Wisconsin Voters, April 1, 2008,* Wisconsin Briefs from the Legislative Reference Bureau 08-4 (Madison: State of Wisconsin Legislative Reference Bureau, 2008), accessed April 25, 2012, http://legis.wisconsin.gov/lrb/pubs/wb/08wb4.pdf.

41. Michael Cooper, "Budget Is Job of Governor, Judges Rule," *New York Times,* December 17, 2004.

42. Melinda Gann Hall, "Constituent Influence in State Supreme Courts: Conceptual Notes and a Case Study," *Journal of Politics* 49 (1987): 1117–24; Gregory A. Huber

and Sanford C. Gordon, "Accountability and Coercion: Is Justice Blind When It Runs for Office?," *American Journal of Political Science* 48 (2004): 247–63.

43. *Republican Party of Minnesota v. White*, 536 U.S. 765 (2002).

44. *Pay to Play: How Big Money Buys Access to the Texas Supreme Court* (Austin, Tex.: Texans for Public Justice, 2001), http://info.tpj.org/docs/2001/04/reports/paytoplay/paytoplay.pdf.

45. *Caperton v. Massey Coal Co.* 173 L. Ed. 2d 1208 (2009).

46. U.S. Census Bureau, "Local Government and Public School Systems by Type and State: 2007," accessed May 5, 2012, http://www.census.gov/govs/go/index.html.

47. National Conference of State Legislatures, "Initiative, Referendum, and Recall," NCSL.org, accessed April 13, 2012, http://www.ncsl.org/legislatures-elections/elections/initiative-referendum-and-recall-overview.aspx.

48. "Notable," *Ballotwatch* 2 (September 2010): 1.

49. Frances E. Lee, "Bicameralism and Geographic Politics: Allocating Funds in the House and Senate," *Legislative Studies Quarterly* 29 (2004): 185–213.

50. U.S. Census Bureau, *Federal Aid to States for Fiscal Year 2010* (Washington, D.C.: Government Printing Office, 2011), x, accessed May 2, 2012, http://www.census.gov/prod/2011pubs/fas-10.pdf.

51. Ibid., 10.

52. Valentino Larcinese, Leonzio Rizzo, and Cecilia Testa, "Allocating the U.S. Federal Budget to the States: The Impact of the President," *Journal of Politics* 68 (2006): 447–56.

53. *New State Ice Co. v. Liebmann*, 285 U.S. 262 (1932) at 311. See Andrew Karch, *Democratic Laboratories: Policy Diffusion among the American States* (Ann Arbor: University of Michigan Press, 2007).

54. Craig Volden, "States as Policy Laboratories: Emulating Success in the Children's Health Insurance Program," *American Journal of Political Science* 50 (2006): 294–312.

55. Chris Koski, "Greening America's Skylines: The Diffusion of Low-Salience Policies," *Policy Studies Journal* 38 (2010): 93–117.

56. Michael Mintron and Sandra Vergari, "Policy Networks and Innovations Diffusion: The Case of State Education Reforms," *Journal of Politics* 60 (1998): 126–48.

57. Christopher Stream, "Health Reform in the States: A Model of State Small Group Health Insurance Market Reforms," *Political Research Quarterly* 52 (1999): 499–525.

58. Frederick J. Boehmke and Richard Witmer, "Disentangling Diffusion: The Effects of Social Learning and Economic Competition on State Policy Innovation and Expansion," *Political Research Quarterly* 57 (2004): 39–51.

59. Robert R. Preuhs, "State Policy Components of Interstate Migration in the United States," *Political Research Quarterly* 52 (1999): 527–47.

60. David M. Konisky, "Regulatory Competition and Environmental Enforcement: Is There a Race to the Bottom?," *American Journal of Political Science* 51 (2003): 853.

61. *Shapiro v. Thompson*, 394 U.S. 618 (1969); *Saenz v. Roe*, 526 U.S. 489 (1999).

62. Craig Volden, "The Politics of Competitive Federalism: A Race to the Bottom in Welfare Benefits?," *American Journal of Political Science* 46 (2006): 352–63.

63. John Adams, "Dissertation on Canon and Feudal Law," in *The Political Writings of John Adams*, ed. George A. Peek Jr. (Indianapolis: Hackett Publishing, 2003), 4.

64. Frank Johnson, Lei Zhou, and Nanae Nakamoto, *Revenues and Expenditures for Public Elementary and Secondary Education: School Year 2008–09 (Fiscal Year 2009)* (Washington, D.C.: National Center for Education Statistics, 2011), 2, accessed April 13, 2012, http://nces.ed.gov/pubs2011/expenditures/.

65. Michael B. Berkman and Eric Plutzer, *Ten Thousand Democracies* (Washington D.C.: Georgetown University Press, 2005).

66. U.S. Census Bureau, *Public Education Finances: 2009* (Washington, D.C.: U.S. Government Printing Office, 2011), 8, accessed April 13, 2012, http://www2.census.gov/govs/school/09f33pub.pdf.

67. Michael W. Giles, "HEW versus the Federal Courts: A Comparison of School Desegregation Enforcement," *American Politics Quarterly* 3 (1975): 81–90.

68. Zero to Three: National Center for Infants, Toddlers, and Families, *Federal Agencies Responsible for Implementing Programs Affecting Infants and Toddlers* (Washington, D.C.: Zero to Three, n.d.), accessed April 13, 2012, http://zttcfn.convio.net/site/DocServer/Federal_Agencies.pdf?docID=1689&AddInterest=1159.

Chapter 4

1. This story was compiled from interviews with R. Stephanie Good in 2011 and 2012 conducted for this textbook, from which the chapter-opening quotation is also taken.

2. Brutus, "*Antifederalist* 2," U.S. Constitution Online, accessed May 9, 2012, http://www.constitution.org/afp/brutus02.htm.

3. *West Virginia State Board of Education v. Barnette*, 319 U.S. 624 (1943).

4. *Schenck v. United States*, 249 U.S. 47 (1919).

5. *Barron v. Baltimore*, 32 U.S. 243 (1833); Zechariah Chafee Jr., *Free Speech in the United States* (Cambridge, Mass.:

Harvard University Press, 1967); *Gilbert v. Minnesota*, 254 U.S. 325 (1920).

6. Judith A. Baer, *Equality under the Constitution* (Ithaca, N.Y.: Cornell University Press, 1983).

7. *Chicago B & Q Railway Company v. Chicago*, 166 U.S. 226 (1897).

8. *Gitlow v. New York*, 268 U.S. 652 (1925).

9. *Palko v. Connecticut*, 302 U.S. 319 (1937).

10. *Schenck v. United States,* 249 U.S. 47 (1919); *Debs v. United States,* 249 U.S. 211 (1919).

11. *Hirota v. MacArthur*, 338 U.S. 197 (1948).

12. *Hamdan v. Rumsfeld,* 548 U.S. 557 (2006).

13. Robert McMillan, "Obama Administration Defends Bush Wiretapping," *PC World,* July 15, 2009, http://www.pcworld.com/article/168502/obama_administration_defends_bush_wiretapping.html.

14. Daphne Eviatar, "Promises, Promises: President Obama's NDAA Signing Statement," *Human Rights* First (blog), January 4, 2012, http://www.humanrightsfirst.org/2012/01/04/promises-promises-president-obamas-ndaa-signing-statement/.

15. Charlie Savage, "U.S. Law May Allow Killings, Holder Says," *New York Times,* March 5, 2012.

16. *Brandenburg v. Ohio*, 395 U.S. 444 (1969).

17. David L. Hudson Jr., "Hate Speech and Campus Speech Codes," First Amendment Center, September 13, 2002, accessed May 9, 2012, http://www.firstamendmentcenter.org/hate-speech-campus-speech-codes.

18. *UWM Post v. Board of Regents of the University of Wisconsin,* 774 F. Supp. 1163 (1991).

19. Kermit L. Hall, "Free Speech on Public College Campuses," First Amendment Center, last modified April 29, 2012, accessed May 9, 2012, http://archive.firstamendmentcenter.org/speech/pubcollege/overview.aspx.

20. Alan Charles Kors and Harvey Silvergate, *The Shadow University: The Betrayal of Liberty on America's Campuses* (New York: Free Press, 1998).

21. Ibid.

22. *UWM Post v. Board of Regents of the University of Wisconsin,* 774 F. Supp. 1163 (1991).

23. *Virginia v. Black*, 538 U.S. 343 (2003).

24. *Tinker v. Des Moines School District,* 393 U.S. 503 (1969). The quotation in the caption on page 110 is from this decision, at 506.

25. *Bland et al. v. Roberts* (E.D. Va. Apr. 24, 2012).

26. *United States v. O'Brien*, 391 U.S. 367 (1968).

27. *Hill v. Colorado,* 530 U.S. 703 (2000).

28. *West Virginia Board of Education v. Barnette*, 319 U.S. 624 (1943).

29. *Texas v. Johnson*, 491 U.S. 397 (1989).

30. *Morse v. Frederick,* 551 U.S. 393 (2007).

31. *Grayned v. City of Rockford*, 408 U.S. 104 (1972).

32. *New York Times v. United States,* 403 U.S. 713 (1971).

33. *United States v. Progressive*, 467 F. Supp. 990 (1979).

34. See http://www.wikileaks.org.

35. Adam Liptak and Brad Stone, "Judge Shuts Down Web Site Specializing in Leaks," *New York Times*, February 20, 2008.

36. *Miller v. California*, 413 U.S. 15 (1973).

37. *Jenkins v. Georgia*, 418 U.S. 153 (1974).

38. *New York v. Ferber*, 458 U.S. 747 (1982).

39. *Ashcroft v. Free Speech Coalition*, 535 U.S. 234 (2002).

40. *Reno v. American Civil Liberties Union*, 521 U.S. 844 (1997).

41. *Brown v. Entertainment Merchants Association*, 180 L. Ed. 2d 708 (2011).

42. *United States v. Stevens*, 176 L.Ed.2d 435 (2010).

43. *Roberts v. United States Jaycees*, 468 U.S. 609 (1984).

44. *Boy Scouts v. Dale*, 530 U.S. 640 (2000).

45. *Rosenberger v. University of Virginia*, 515 U.S. 819 (1995).

46. *Church of Lakumi Babalu Aye v. City of Hialeah*, 508 U.S. 520 (1993).

47. *Reynolds v. United States*, 98 U.S. 145 (1878).

48. *Employment Division v. Smith*, 494 U.S. 872 (1990).

49. *City of Boerne v. Flores*, 521 U.S. 507 (1997), at 536.

50. *Hosanna-Tabor Evangelical Lutheran Church and School v. Equal Employment Opportunity Commission,* (No. 10-553, 2012).

51. See "Rethinking the Incorporation of the Establishment Clause: A Federalist View," *Harvard Law Review* 105 (1992): 1700.

52. *Everson v. Board of Education*, 330 U.S. 1 (1947).

53. *Lemon v. Kurtzman*, 403 U.S. 602 (1971).

54. *Engel v. Vitale*, 370 U.S. 421 (1962); *Abington School District v. Schempp*, 374 U.S. 203 (1963).

55. *Epperson v. Arkansas*, 393 U.S. 97 (1968).

56. *Edwards v. Aguillard*, 482 U.S. 578 (1987).

57. *Lee v. Weisman*, 505 U.S. 577 (1992).

58. *Santa Fe Independent School District v. Doe*, 530 U.S. 290 (2000).

59. *Board of Education v. Allen*, 392 U.S. 236 (1968).

60. *Meek v. Pittenger*, 421 U.S. 349 (1975).

61. *District of Columbia v. Heller*, 554 U.S. 570 (2008).

62. *McDonald v. Chicago*, 561 U.S. 3025 (2010).

63. *Florence v. County of Burlington*, 10-945 (2012).

64. *Schneckloth v. Bustamonte*, 412 U.S. 218 (1973).

65. See Jeffrey A. Segal, "Predicting Supreme Court Decisions Probabilistically: The Search and Seizure Cases, 1962–1981," *American Political Science Review* 78 (1984): 801.

66. *California v. Ciraolo*, 476 U.S. 207 (1986).

67. *Kyllo v. United States*, 533 U.S. 27 (2001).

68. *Virginia v. Moore*, 553 U.S. 164 (2008).

69. *United States v. Jones*, Docket 10-1259 (2012).

70. *Vernonia School District 47J v. Acton*, 515 U.S. 646 (1995); *National Treasury Union v. Von Raab*, 489 U.S. 656 (1989); *Chandler v. Miller*, 520 U.S. 305 (1997).

71. *Mapp v. Ohio*, 367 U.S. 643 (1961).

72. Priscilla H. Machado Zotti, *Injustice for All: Mapp v. Ohio and the Fourth Amendment* (New York: Peter Lang, 2005).

73. *Miranda v. Arizona*, 384 U.S. 436 (1966).

74. *Dickerson v. United States*, 530 U.S. 428 (2000).

75. *Powell v. Alabama*, 287 U.S. 45 (1932).

76. *Gideon v. Wainwright*, 372 U.S. 335 (1963).

77. *Argersinger v. Hamlin*, 407 U.S. 25 (1972).

78. *Griswold v. Connecticut*, 381 U.S. 479 (1965).

79. *Eisenstadt v. Baird*, 405 U.S. 438 (1972).

80. Gerald Rosenberg, *The Hollow Hope* (Chicago: University of Chicago Press, 1991), 262.

81. *Roe v. Wade*, 410 U.S. 113 (1973).

82. *Planned Parenthood of Southeastern Pennsylvania v. Casey*, 505 U.S. 833 (1992).

83. Lori A. Ringhand and Paul M. Collins Jr., "May It Please the Senate: An Empirical Analysis of the Senate Judiciary Committee Hearings of Supreme Court Nominees, 1939–2009" (University of Georgia School of Law Research Paper Series, Paper No. 10-12, 2010).

84. *Bowers v. Hardwick*, 478 U.S. 186 (1986).

85. National Opinion Research Center, General Social Survey, University of Chicago.

86. *Lawrence v. Texas*, 539 U.S. 558 (2003).

87. *Cruzan v. Director, Missouri Department of Health*, 497 U.S. 261 (1990), at 278.

88. *Washington v. Glucksberg*, 521 U.S. 702; *Vacco v. Quill*, 521 U.S. 793 (1997).

89. *In the Matter of Waller v. The City of New York*, Supreme Court, New York County, 112957/11 (2011).

90. Ibid.

91. *West Virginia State Board of Education v. Barnette*, 319 U.S. 624 (1943).

92. Robert Dahl, "Decision-Making in a Democracy: The Supreme Court as a National Policy-Maker," *Journal of Public Law* 6 (1957): 279–95.

93. Anthony Lewis, *Freedom for the Thought That We Hate: A Biography of the First Amendment* (New York: Basic Books, 2007).

94. John L. Sullivan, James Pierson, and George Marcus, *Political Tolerance and American Democracy* (Chicago: University of Chicago Press, 1973); James L. Gibson, "Enigmas of Intolerance: Fifty Years after Stouffer's *Communism, Conformity, and Civil Liberties*," *Perspectives on Politics* 4 (March 2006): 22.

95. August 2007 Freedom Forum Survey, retrieved May 13, 2012, from the iPOLL Databank, The Roper Center for Public Opinion Research, University of Connecticut.

Chapter 5

1. This story has been compiled from Juan Williams, *Eyes on the Prize: America's Civil Rights Years, 1954–1965* (New York: Penguin Books, 1987), 130–31, and, generally, 122–61; Michael Westmoreland-White, "Diane Nash (1938–): Unsung Heroine of the Civil Rights Movement," August 22, 2010, accessed May 10, 2012, http://pilgrimpathways.wordpress.com/2010/08/22/peacemaker-profiles-2-diane-nash/; Linda T. Wynn, "Diane Judith Nash (1938–): A Mission for Equality, Justice, and Social Change," in *Tennessee Women: Their Lives and Times*, ed. Sarah Wilkerson Freeman and Beverly Greene Bond (Athens: University of Georgia Press, 2009), 281–304; interview with Diane Nash, November 12, 1985, accessed May 10, 2012, http://www.teachersdomain.org/resource/iml04.soc.ush.civil.nash; the chapter-opening quotation is from this interview.

2. See Alexander Keyssar, *The Right to Vote* (New York: Basic Books, 2000), 20 (women) and 164 (Native Americans).

3. Senator Lyman Trumbull, quoted in Judith Baer, *Equality under the Constitution* (Ithaca, N.Y.: Cornell University Press, 1983), 96.

4. Ronald Dworkin, *Taking Rights Seriously* (Cambridge, Mass.: Harvard University Press, 1978), 272–78.

5. Quoted in Steven M. Gillon and Cathy D. Matson, *The American Experiment*, 2nd ed. (Boston: Houghton Mifflin, 2006), 61.

6. *Dred Scott v. Sandford*, 60 U.S. 393 (1857).

7. *United States v. Cruikshank*, 92 U.S. 542 (1876).

8. Ronald Walters, "'The Association Is for the Direct Attack': The Militant Context of the NAACP Challenge to *Plessy*," *Washburn Law Journal* 43 (Winter 2004): 329.

9. *Plessy v. Ferguson*, 163 U.S. 537 (1896).

10. California Alien Land Law (1913).

11. Vicki L. Ruiz, "South by Southwest: Mexican Americans and Segregated Schooling, 1900–1950," *OAH Magazine of History* 15 (Winter 2001): 23–27, http://www.oah.org/pubs/.

12. *Westminster School District v. Mendez*, 161 F.2d 774 (1947).

13. Ruiz, "South by Southwest."

14. Quoted in Renata Fengler, "Abigail and John Adams Discuss Women and Republican Government: 1776," part of the "Documenting American History" project, University of Wisconsin–Green Bay, last modified July 29, 2009, accessed April 25, 2012, http://www.historytools.org/sources/Abigail-John-Letters.pdf.

15. Keyssar, *Right to Vote*.

16. E. Susan Barber, comp., "One Hundred Years toward Suffrage: An Overview," Library of Congress, National American Woman Suffrage Association Collection, accessed May 14, 2012, http://memory.loc.gov/ammem/naw/nawstime.html.

17. Peter H. Schuck and Rogers M. Smith, *Citizenship without Consent* (New Haven, Conn.: Yale University Press, 1985), 1–2.

18. *Johnson v. M'Intosh*, 21 U.S. 543 (1823), at 569.

19. *Elk v. Wilkins*, 112 U.S. 94 (1884).

20. Smith, *Civic Ideals*, 17.

21. Immigration Act of 1924, 43 Statutes at Large 153.

22. *Korematsu v. United States*, 323 U.S. 214 (1944).

23. David Cole, "No More Roundups," *Washington Post*, June 16, 2004, http://www.washingtonpost.com/wp-dyn/articles/A44875-2004Jun15.html.

24. *Civil Rights Cases*, 109 U.S. 3 (1883); *Shelley v. Kraemer*, 334 U.S. 1 (1948).

25. *Missouri ex rel. Gaines v. Canada*, 305 U.S. 337 (1938); *Sipuel v. Board of Regents of University of Oklahoma*, 332 U.S. 631 (1948); *Sweatt v. Painter*, 339 U.S. 629 (1950).

26. *Bolling v. Sharpe*, 347 U.S. 497 (1954).

27. *Brown v. Board of Education*, 349 U.S. 294 (1955).

28. *Cooper v. Aaron*, 358 U.S. 1 (1958).

29. Gerald N. Rosenberg, *The Hollow Hope: Can Courts Bring about Social Change* (Chicago: University of Chicago Press, 1991), 46–54.

30. *Alexander v. Holmes County Board of Education*, 396 U.S. 1218 (1969).

31. *Browder v. Gayle*, 352 U.S. 903 (1956).

32. Henry Abraham and Barbara Perry, *Freedom and the Court*, 6th ed. (New York: Oxford University Press, 1994), 380. See also David Halberstam, *The Children* (New York: Fawcett Books, 1998), 230–34. The caption for the photo on page 150 was drawn from this source.

33. Martin Luther King Jr., "Letter from Birmingham Jail," April 16, 1963, The King Center, accessed April 25, 2012, http://www.thekingcenter.org/archive/document/letter-birmingham-city-jail-0.

34. Martin Luther King Jr., "The I Have a Dream Speech," August 28, 1963, U.S. Constitution Online, accessed April 25, 2012, http://www.usconstitution.net/dream.html.

35. *Heart of Atlanta Motel v. United States*, 379 U.S. 241 (1964); *Katzenbach v. McClung*, 379 U.S. 294 (1964).

36. *Griggs v. Duke Power Co.*, 401 U.S. 424 (1971).

37. *Wards Cove Packing Co. v. Antonio*, 490 U.S. 642 (1989).

38. *Ricci v. DeStefano* 174 L. Ed. 2d 490 (2009).

39. *Guinn v. United States*, 238 U.S. 347 (1915); *Smith v. Allwright*, 321 U.S 649 (1944).

40. Martin Luther King Jr., "Civil Right No. 1: The Right to Vote," *New York Times Magazine*, March 14, 1965, 26.

41. Lyndon B. Johnson, "We Shall Overcome," March 15, 1965, Voices of Democracy: The U.S. Oratory Project, accessed April 25, 2012, http://voicesofdemocracy.umd.edu/johnson-we-shall-overcome-speech-text/.

42. Pew Hispanic Center, "Dissecting the 2008 Electorate: Most Diverse in U.S. History," Pew Research Center, April 30, 2009, accessed April 25, 2012, http://www.pewhispanic.org/2009/04/30/dissecting-the-2008-electorate-most-diverse-in-us-history/.

43. *Northwest Austin Municipal Utility District No. One v. Holder* 557 U.S. 193 (2009).

44. *Bowers v. Hardwick*, 478 U.S. 186 (1986).

45. *Lawrence v. Texas*, 539 U.S. 558 (2003).

46. Poll conducted by CNN, February 2010, retrieved May 14, 2012, from the iPOLL Databank, The Roper Center for Public Opinion Research, University of Connecticut.

47. *Perry v. Brown*, Ninth Circuit U.S. Court of Appeals, 10-16696 (2012).

48. In September 2011 a CBS News/*New York Times* poll asked, "Which comes closest to your view? . . . Gay couples should be allowed to legally marry. Gay couples should be allowed to form civil unions but not legally marry. There should be no legal recognition of a gay couple's relationship." Of those polled, 38 percent said gay couples should be allowed to legally marry; 27 percent said they should be allowed to form civil unions; 28 percent said there should be no legal recognition; and 7 percent didn't know or did not answer. Data retrieved May 14, 2012, from the iPOLL Databank, The Roper Center for Public Opinion Research, University of Connecticut.

49. Adam Nagourney, "A Watershed Move, Both Risky and Inevitable," *New York Times,* May 10, 2012, A1.

50. Lyndon Johnson, "President Lyndon B. Johnson's Commencement Address at Howard University: 'To Fulfill These Rights,'" June 4, 1965, Lyndon Baines Johnson Library and Museum, accessed April 25, 2012, http://www.lbjlib.utexas .edu/johnson/archives.hom/speeches.hom/650604.asp.

51. *Regents v. Bakke,* 438 U.S. 265 (1978).

52. *Grutter v. Bollinger,* 539 U.S. 306 (2003).

53. *Gratz v. Bollinger,* 539 U.S. 244 (2003).

54. U.S. Equal Employment Opportunity Commission, *The Americans with Disabilities Act: A Primer for Small Business,* last modified February 4, 2004, accessed May 15, 2012, http:// www.eeoc.gov/facts/adahandbook.html#drugalcohol.

55. David A. Harris, "Driving While Black: Racial Profiling on Our Nation's Highways," June 7, 1999, American Civil Liberties Union, accessed April 25, 2012, http:// www.aclu.org/racial-justice/driving-while-black-racial -profiling-our-nations-highways.

56. Ibid.

57. *United States v. Travis,* 837 F. Supp. 1386 (1993); *Derricott v. State of Maryland* 611 A.2d 592 (1992).

58. Poll conducted by Quinnipiac University, October 2011, retrieved March 18, 2012, from the iPOLL Databank, The Roper Center for Public Opinion Research, University of Connecticut.

59. *Plyler v. Doe,* 457 U.S. 202 (1982).

60. Poll conducted by *60 Minutes/Vanity Fair,* August 2010, retrieved March 18, 2012, from the iPOLL Databank, The Roper Center for Public Opinion Research, University of Connecticut.

61. U.S. Equal Employment Opportunity Commission, "Sexual Harassment Charges EEOC & FEPAs Combined: FY 1997–FY 2011," accessed May 23, 2012, http:// www.eeoc.gov/eeoc/statistics/enforcement/sexual _harassment.cfm.

62. U.S. Bureau of Labor Statistics, *Highlights of Women's Earnings in 2010,* Report 1031 (Washington, D.C., July 2011), accessed May 23, 2012, http://www.bls.gov/cps /cpswom2010.pdf.

63. Ibid.

64. *Ledbetter v. Goodyear Tire and Rubber Co.,* 550 U.S. 618 (2007).

65. Ibid., 645.

66. Lilly Ledbetter Fair Pay Act of 2009, Pub. L. No. 111-2, 42 USC 2000e-5 (2009), http://www.gpo.gov/fdsys/pkg /PLAW-111publ2/html/PLAW-111publ2.htm.

67. ABA Section of Labor & Employment Law, *Survey of Recent Cases under the Lily Ledbetter Fair Pay Act,* March 2011, accessed May 23, 2012, http://www2 .americanbar.org/calendar/ll0322-2011-midwinter -meeting/Documents/08_complexlitigation.pdf (on new cases), and U.S. Bureau of Labor Statistics, *Highlights of Women's Earnings,* on continuing pay disparity.

68. King, "Civil Right No. 1."

69. M. V. Hood, Quentin Kidd, and Irwin L. Morris, "The Key Issue: Constituency Effects and Southern Senators' Roll-Call Voting on Civil Rights," *Legislative Studies Quarterly* 26 (2001): 599–621.

70. Royce Carroll, Jeff Lewis, James Lo, Nolan McCarty, Keith Poole, and Howard Rosenthal, "'Common Space' DW-NOMINATE Scores With Bootstrapped Standard Errors (Joint House and Senate Scaling)," Voteview.com, last modified January 22, 2011, accessed May 14, 2012, http://www.voteview.com/dwnomjoint.asp.

Chapter 6

1. This story was compiled from Stephanie Clifford, "Finding Fame with a Prescient Call for Obama," *New York Times,* November 10, 2008; Adam Sternbergh, "The Spreadsheet Psychic," *New York Magazine,* October 12, 2008; James Wolcott, "The Good, the Bad, and Joe Lieberman," *Vanity Fair,* February 2009, 76; and Nate Silver, "Will Young Voters Turn Out for Obama?," *New York Post,* August 10, 2008, http://www.nypost.com/p/news /opinion/opencolumnists/item_cPgKLSN0uPUZunQtyk-kyyN; opening quotation is from the *New York Post* column.

2. Quoted in Harry Jaffa, *The Crisis of the House Divided,* 2nd ed. (Chicago: University of Chicago Press, 1959), 10.

3. See James Bryce, *The American Commonwealth* (New York: MacMillan, 1895), 239.

4. The first scholar to discuss how the public rallies to support the president in time of trouble was John Mueller, *War, Presidents, and Public Opinion* (New York: Wiley, 1970).

5. Quoted in Ted Barrett and Steve Brusk, "Bush: Immigration Bill Will Enforce Borders, Workplaces," CNN,

June 12, 2007, http://edition.cnn.com/2007/POLITICS/06/12/immigration/index.html.

6. A CBS News/*New York Times* poll conducted October 31 to November 2, 2008, indicated that only 20 percent of the public approved of Bush's job as president. Prior to that, Harry Truman (23 percent) and Richard Nixon (24 percent) had been the least popular presidents. Both Truman and Nixon rebounded a bit from those low points as they left office. These data were retrieved April 15, 2012, from the iPOLL Databank, The Roper Center for Public Opinion Research, University of Connecticut.

7. Survey conducted by CBS News/*New York Times*, October 19–24, 2011, retrieved April 15, 2012, from the iPOLL Databank, The Roper Center for Public Opinion Research, University of Connecticut.

8. See Marc Hetherington, *Why Trust Matters* (Princeton, N.J.: Princeton University Press, 2005).

9. See American National Election Studies, "External Political Efficacy Index 1952–2008," *ANES Guide to Public Opinion and Electoral Behavior*, last modified August 16, 2010, accessed April 27, 2012, http://electionstudies.org/nesguide/toptable/tab5b_4.htm.

10. Barack Obama, Inaugural Address, January 20, 2009, http://www.whitehouse.gov/blog/inaugural-address.

11. Survey conducted by Princeton Survey Research Associates International for Pew Research Center for the People & the Press, September 22–25, 2011, retrieved May 12, 2012, from the Pew Research Center.

12. It is hard to know the exact share of people who would support overthrowing the American government because pollsters almost never ask that question. We say "almost never," but in our search of questions asked over the last seventy-five years, we have not found one such question. A database at the Roper Center at the University of Connecticut contains nearly five hundred thousand questions, allowing a detailed search.

13. Erikson and Tedin, *American Public Opinion,* 26.

14. Kathy Frankovic, "The Truth about Push Polls," *CBS News*, February 11, 2009, http://www.cbsnews.com/2100-250_162-160398.html.

15. These data come from 2003 polls retrieved April 15, 2012, from the iPOLL Databank, The Roper Center for Public Opinion Research, University of Connecticut.

16. See Philip E. Converse, "Nonattitudes and American Public Opinion: Comment: The Status of Nonattitudes," *American Political Science Review* 68 (June 1974): 650–60.

17. Pew Research Center for the People & the Press, "Cell Phones and the 2008 Vote: An Update," Pew Research Center, July 17, 2008, accessed April 27, 2012, http://pewresearch.org/pubs/901/cell-phones-polling-election-2008.

18. U.S. Energy Information Administration, Residential Energy Consumption (RECS), 2009 Household Characteristics. Release date: March 28, 2011. Survey data for occupied primary housing units.

19. See also Pew Research Center for the People & the Press, "Polls Face Growing Resistance, but Still Representative," Pew Research Center, April 20, 2004, accessed April 27, 2012, http://people-press.org//2004/04/20/polls-face-growing-resistance-but-still-representative/.

20. Erikson and Tedin, *American Public Opinion,* 121.

21. Pew Internet & American Life Project, "Millennials Will Benefit and Suffer Due to Their Interconnected Lives," Pew Research Center, February 29, 2012, accessed April 27, 2012, http://www.pewinternet.org/Reports/2012/Hyperconnected-lives.aspx?src=prc-headline.

22. See Robert Erikson and Kent Tedin, *American Public Opinion,* 8th ed. (New York: Longman, 2010).

23. This theory comes out of the work of John Zaller, *Nature of Mass Beliefs* (New York: Cambridge University Press, 1992).

24. The classic book that lays out the argument about party identification is Angus Campbell, Philip Converse, Warren Miller, and Donald Stokes, *The American Voter* (New York: Wiley, 1960).

25. Poll conducted by CBS News/*New York Times*, September 20–23, 2001, retrieved April 15, 2012, from the iPOLL Databank, The Roper Center for Public Opinion Research, University of Connecticut.

26. See American National Election Studies, "Party Identification 7-Point Scale 1952–2008," *ANES Guide to Public Opinion and Electoral Behavior*, last modified August 5, 2010, accessed April 27, 2012, http://www.electionstudies.org/nesguide/toptable/tab2a_1.htm.

27. David Brooks, "What Independents Want," *New York Times*, November 5, 2009, A31.

28. John Sides, "Three Myths about Political Independents," *The Monkey Cage* (blog), December 17, 2009, http://www.themonkeycage.org/blog/2009/12/17/three_myths_about_political_in/.

29. Poll conducted by ABC News/*Washington Post*, March 7–10, 2012, retrieved April 15, 2012, from the iPOLL Databank, The Roper Center for Public Opinion Research, University of Connecticut.

30. This way of thinking about the public comes from Philip Converse, "Nature of Belief Systems in Mass Publics," in *Ideology and Discontent,* ed. David Apter (New York: Free Press, 1964).

31. The exact percentage of the public that was literate at the time of the founding is unclear. This percentage reflects the best guess of some historians.

32. *CIA World Factbook*, https://www.cia.gov/library/publications/the-world-factbook/geos/us.html.

33. Paul Lazarsfeld, Bernard Berelson, and Helen Gaudet, *The People's Choice* (New York: Duell, Sloane, Pearce, 1944).

34. Bernard Berelson, Paul F. Lazarsfeld, and William N. McPhee, *Voting: A Study of Opinion Formation in a Presidential Campaign* (Chicago: University of Chicago Press, 1954).

35. Converse, "Nature of Belief Systems in Mass Publics."

36. These data all come from Erikson and Tedin, *American Public Opinion*, 8th ed., 61.

37. See John Zaller, "Monica Lewinsky and the Mainsprings of American Politics," in *Mediated Politics: Communication in the Future of Democracy*, ed. W. Lance Bennett and Robert M. Entman (Cambridge, U.K.: Cambridge University Press, 2001).

38. Stanley Kelley, *Interpreting Elections* (Princeton, N.J.: Princeton University Press, 1983).

39. Christopher Achen, "Mass Political Attitudes and the Survey Response," *American Political Science Review* 69 (1975): 1218–31.

40. Sam Popkin developed this concept in his book *The Reasoning Voter* (Chicago: University of Chicago Press, 1991).

41. "The Polarization of the Congressional Parties," Voteview.com, last modified March 6, 2012, accessed April 27, 2012, http://voteview.com/political_polarization.asp.

42. For a comprehensive account of these data, see Alan Abramowitz and Kyle Saunders, "Is Polarization a Myth?," *Journal of Politics* 70 (2008): 542–55.

43. "Polarization of the Congressional Parties."

44. See Morris Fiorina, *Culture War?* (New York: Longman, 2008).

45. Morris Fiorina, Samuel Abrams, and Jeremy Pope, "Polarization in the American Public," *Journal of Politics* 70 (2008): 558.

46. See Alan Abramowitz, *The Disappearing Center* (New Haven, Conn.: Yale University Press, 2010).

47. Erikson and Tedin, *American Public Opinion*, 8th ed., 193.

48. Ibid., 208.

49. Erikson and Tedin, *American Public Opinion*, 6th ed., 215.

50. Susan Page, "Swing States Poll: A Shift by Women Puts Obama in Lead," *USA Today*, last modified April 2, 2012, http://www.usatoday.com/news/politics/story/2012-04-01/swing-states-poll/53930684/1.

51. Center for American Women and Politics, Eagleton Institute of Politics, Rutgers University, "The Gender Gap: Voting Choices in Presidential Elections," December 2008, accessed May 23, 2012, http://www.cawp.rutgers.edu/fast_facts/voters/documents/GGPresVote.pdf.

52. Survey conducted by ORC International for CNN, September 9–11, 2011, retrieved April 15, 2012, from the iPOLL Databank, The Roper Center for Public Opinion Research, University of Connecticut.

53. Data from American National Election Studies, "Aid to Blacks/Minorities 1970–2008," *ANES Guide to Public Opinion and Electoral Behavior*, last modified August 5, 2010, accessed May 12, 2012, http://www.electionstudies.org/nesguide/2ndtable/t4b_4_1.htm.

54. Data from the 2004 General Social Survey conducted by the National Opinion Research Center (NORC) at The University of Chicago.

55. Carole Jean Uhlaner and F. Chris Garcia, "Latino Public Opinion," in *Understanding Public Opinion*, ed. Barbara Norrander and Clyde Wilcox (Washington, D.C.: CQ Press, 2002).

56. David L. Leal, "Latino Public Opinion," Texas A&M University, Department of Political Science: Project for Equity, Representation, and Justice, accessed April 27, 2012, http://perg.tamu.edu/lpc/Leal.pdf.

57. Marisa Abrajano, R. Michael Alvarez, and Jonathan Nagler, "The Hispanic Vote in the 2004 Presidential Election," *Journal of Politics* 70 (2008): 368–82.

58. Pew Research Center for the People & the Press, "Where the Public Stands on Immigration Reform," Pew Research Center, November 23, 2009, accessed April 27, 2012, http://pewresearch.org/pubs/1421/where-the-public-stands-on-...1.

59. See Norman H. Nie, Jane Junn, and Kenneth Stehlik-Barry, *Education and Democratic Citizenship in America* (Chicago: University of Chicago Press, 1996).

60. Ellen C. Collier, "Instances of Use of United States Forces Abroad, 1798–1993," Naval Historical Center, last modified September 12, 1997, accessed May 12, 2012, http://www.history.navy.mil/wars/foabroad.htm.

61. John Mueller, *War, Presidents, and Public Opinion* (New York: Wiley, 1970).

62. "Presidential Approval Ratings, George W. Bush," Gallup.com, accessed May 12, 2012, http://www.gallup.com/poll/124922/presidential-approval-center.aspx.

63. "The Abu Ghraib Files," *Salon*, March 14, 2006, http://www.salon.com/2006/03/14/introduction_2/.

64. Sarah Mendelson, "The Guantanamo Countdown," *Foreign Affairs*, October 1, 2009.

65. Gallup Poll, April 24–25, 2009, retrieved April 15, 2012, from the iPOLL Databank, The Roper Center for Public Opinion Research, University of Connecticut.

66. V. O. Key, *The Responsible Electorate* (Cambridge, Mass.: Harvard University Press, 1966), 1.

67. Robert S. Erikson, Michael B. MacKuen, and James A. Stimson, *The Macro Polity* (Cambridge, U.K.: Cambridge University Press, 2002).

68. See Key, *Public Opinion and American Democracy*, and Douglas Arnold, *Logic of Congressional Action* (New Haven, Conn.: Yale University Press, 1991).

Chapter 7

1. This story was compiled from the *Daily Kos* website, http://www.dailykos.com/; Christopher Null, "The 50 Most Important People on the Web," *PC World,* March 5, 2007, http://www.pcworld.com/; David M. Ewalt, "The Web Celeb 25," *Forbes,* January 23, 2007, http://www.forbes.com/2007/01/23/internet-fame-celebrity-tech-media-cx_de_06webceleb_0123land.html; *Daily Kos* website's ranking as reported on January 2, 2010, in "Top 15 Most Popular Blogs," eBizMBA, accessed January 2, 2010, http://www.ebizmba.com/articles/blogs; the *Daily Kos* website's ranking as reported for April 2012 on the blog directory page on the Technorati website, http://technorati.com/blogs/directory/politics/uspolitics/; Markos ("Kos") Moulitsas Zúniga, foreword to Lowell Feld and Nate Wilcox, *Netroots Rising: How a Citizen Army of Bloggers and Online Activists Is Changing American Politics* (Westport, Conn: Praeger, 2008), viii, which is the source of the chapter-opening quotation.

2. Herbert Gans, *Democracy and the News* (New York: Oxford University Press, 2003), 1.

3. Pew Research Center's Project for Excellence in Journalism, "A Year in the News," *The State of the News Media 2009: An Annual Report on American Journalism,* accessed May 27, 2012, http://stateofthemedia.org/2009/a-year-in-the-news. See, especially, the section titled, "The Economy Finally Emerges as a Major Story."

4. Bob Woodward and Carl Bernstein, *All the President's Men* (New York: Simon and Schuster, 1994).

5. Thomas E. Patterson, *Out of Order* (New York: Knopf, 1993), 82.

6. *Near v. Minnesota*, 283 U.S. 697 (1931).

7. *New York Times Co. v. United States,* 403 U.S. 713 (1971).

8. Shanto Iyengar, *Media Politics: A Citizen's Guide,* 2nd ed. (New York: W. W. Norton, 2011), 51.

9. See Pew Research Center's Project for Excellence in Journalism's *The State of the News Media 2012: An Annual Report on American Journalism,* http://stateofthemedia.org/2012/, for a range of data documenting this point.

10. Benjamin Franklin, "An Apology for Printers," *Pennsylvania Gazette,* May 27, 1731, reprinted as *An Apology for Printers* (Washington, D.C.: Acropolis Books, 1973).

11. Jeremy D. Mayer, *American Media Politics in Transition* (New York: McGraw Hill, 2007), 81.

12. Michael Schudson and Susan Tifft, "American Journalism in Historical Perspective," in *The Press,* ed. Geneva Overholser and Kathleen Hall Jamieson (New York: Oxford University Press, 2005), 19.

13. Michael Schudson, *Discovering the News: A Social History of American Newspapers* (New York: Basic Books, 1978).

14. William Riker, *The Strategy of Rhetoric: Campaigning for the American Constitution* (New Haven, Conn.: Yale University Press, 1996).

15. Sedition Act, July 14, 1798, U.S. Constitution Online, accessed June 4, 2012, http://www.constitution.org/rf/sedition_1798.htm.

16. See Michael Schudson, *The Sociology of News* (New York: W. W. Norton, 2003), 75.

17. Melvin Laracey, "Who Listened? Political Media Communications by 'Pre-Modern' Presidents" (paper presented at the annual meeting of the Midwest Political Science Association, Chicago, Ill., 2004).

18. James Hamilton, *All the News That's Fit to Sell: How the Market Transforms Information into News* (Princeton, N.J.: Princeton University Press, 2006).

19. See Great Projects Film Company, "Yellow Journalism," Public Broadcast System (PBS), 1999, accessed May 15, 2012, http://www.pbs.org/crucible/journalism.html.

20. Jon Blackwell, "1906: Rumble over 'The Jungle,'" *Trentonian*, http://www.capitalcentury.com/1906.html.

21. Schudson and Tifft, "American Journalism," 17–46.

22. Iyengar, *Media Politics*; American National Election Studies, *ANES Guide to Public Opinion and Electoral Behavior,* http://www.electionstudies.org/nesguide/nesguide.htm.

23. Data retrieved May 1, 2012, from the iPOLL Databank, The Roper Center for Public Opinion Research, University of Connecticut.

24. Theodore H. White, *The Making of the President, 1960* (New York: Atheneum Publishers, 1961).

25. Sidney Krause, *The Great Debates: Kennedy v. Nixon, 1960* (Bloomington: Indiana University Press, 1977). The quotation in the caption on page 213 is from Kennedy's telegram to the NBC board chair, accepting the invitation to debate, quoted in the *Tri City Herald,* July 28, 1960.

26. Schudson and Tifft, "American Journalism," 26.

27. "Internet and Telecommunications Statistics," Chartsbin, accessed May 27, 2012, http://chartsbin.com/view/1886.

28. Charlie Sorrel, "Apple's iPad Sales Accelerate: Three Million Sold in 80 Days," *Gadget Lab* (blog), Wired, June 23, 2010, http://www.wired.com/gadgetlab/2010 /06/apples-ipad-sales-accelerate-three-million-sold-in -80-days.

29. Data available at "Report: Community Journalism in the United States," Bill Lane Center for the American West, Stanford University, last modified August 7, 2011, accessed May 27, 2012, http://www.stanford.edu/group /ruralwest/cgi-bin/drupal/projects/newspapers.

30. For data on news consumption, see *The State of the News Media 2012* report available from the Pew Research Center's Project for Excellence in Journalism at http:// stateofthemedia.org/2012.

31. Alex Jones, *Losing the News* (New York: Oxford University Press, 2009).

32. The data come from a study conducted for the Newspaper Association of America. See "Study: Newspapers Attract 102.8 million U.S. Internet Users," *SFN Blog*, World Association of Newspapers and News Publishers, http:// www.sfnblog.com/2010/10/14/study-newspapers -attract-1028-million-us-internet-users.

33. Bill Mitchell, "Clues in the Rubble: Finding a Framework to Sustain Local News" (Discussion Paper Series, Joan Shorenstein Center on the Press, Politics, and Public Policy, Harvard University, 2010).

34. Geoffrey Cowan, "Leading the Way to Better News" (Discussion Paper Series, Joan Shorenstein Center on the Press, Politics, and Public Policy, Harvard University, 2008), 7.

35. Ibid.

36. See Jones, *Losing the News*.

37. Pew Research Center's Project for Excellence in Journalism, "Audio: How Far Will Digital Go?," *The State of the News Media 2012*, Pew Research Center, accessed May 27, 2012, http://stateofthemedia.org/2012/audio -how-far-will-digital-go/.

38. See David Barker, *Rushed to Judgment* (New York: Columbia University Press, 2002).

39. Pew Research Center's Project for Excellence in Journalism, "Talk Radio," *The State of the News Media 2012*, Pew Research Center, accessed May 28, 2012, http://stateofthemedia.org/2012/audio-how-far-will -digital-go/#talk-radio.

40. No one has studied reasons why liberal talk radio has failed, but we offer some hypotheses here. Thank you to Markus Prior of Princeton University for brainstorming with us on this topic.

41. These data divide the number of viewers by the number of Americans at the time: 226 million in 1980 and 311 million in 2011.

42. Pew Research Center's Project for Excellence in Journalism, "Digital Trends," *The State of the News Media 2009*, Pew Research Center, accessed May 27, 2012, http:// stateofthemedia.org/2009/cable-tv-intro/digital-trends.

43. Nielsen Media Research, cited by the Pew Research Center's Project for Excellence in Journalism, in "Key Findings," *The State of the News Media 2012*, Pew Research Center, accessed May 27, 2012, http://stateofthemedia .org/2012/overview-4/key-findings/.

44. "Jon Stewart's Ratings Are Now Higher Than All of Fox News," *Politicus USA* (blog), June 4, 2011, http://www .politicususa.com/jon-stewart-fox-ratings/.

45. Most of the data presented here came from Pew Research Center's Project for Excellence in Journalism, "Journalism, Satire or Just Laughs? 'The Daily Show with Jon Stewart,' Examined," Journalism.org, May 8, 2008, http://www.journalism.org/node/10961.

46. See this episode, which originally aired on January 12, 2012, at http://www.colbertnation.com/the- colbert-report-videos/405889/january-12-2012 /indecision-2012—colbert-super-pac—coordination- resolution-with-jon-stewart.

47. eBizMBA's ranking of the top fifteen blogs is available at http://www.ebizmba.com/articles/blogs. The rankings shown here were retrieved in April 2012.

48. Eric Lawrence, John Sides, and Henry Farrell, "Self- Segregation or Deliberation? Blog Readership, Participation, and Polarization in American Politics," *Perspectives on Politics* 8, no. 1 (2010): 146.

49. See http://www.drudgereport.com and http://www .rushlimbaugh.com/.

50. See Dylan Tweney, "Controlled Chaos: An Interview with Kos," *Epicenter* (blog), Wired, May 8, 2007, http://blog .wired.com/business/2007/05/controlled_chao.html.

51. Pew Research Center's Project for Excellence in Journalism, "The Year on Blogs and Twitter," *The State of the News Media 2012*, Pew Research Center, accessed May 28, 2012, http://stateofthemedia.org/2012/mobile-devices-and -news-consumption-some-good-signs-for-journalism /year-in-2011/#the-year-on-blogs-and-twitter.

52. Michael Stoner, "Takeaways on the Web, Social Media and Student Recruitment," *CASE Social Media* (blog), Council for Advancement and Support of Education, July 27, 2011, http://case.typepad.com

/case_social_media/2011/07/takeaways-on-the-web
-social-media-and-student-recruitment-.html.

53. Christine B. Williams and Girish J. Gulati, "Social Net-works in Political Campaigns: Facebook and Congres-sional Elections 2006, 2008" (paper presented at the APSA meetings in Toronto, Canada, September 2009).

54. The authors confirmed this fact through their own Face-book accounts.

55. "ABC News Joins Forces with Facebook," ABC News, De-cember 18, 2007, http://abcnews.go.com/Technology /Politics/story?id=3899006&page=1#.T7J9ccXtMVA.

56. Thomas E. Patterson, *Young People and News* (Cambridge, MA: Joan Shorenstein Center on the Press, Politics, and Public Policy, Harvard University, July 2007).

57. Morley Winograd and Michael D. Hais, *Millennial Make-over: MySpace, YouTube and the Future of American Politics* (New Brunswick, N.J.: Rutgers University Press, 2008).

58. Paul Lazarsfeld, Bernard Berelson, and Hazel Gaudet, *The People's Choice* (New York: Columbia University Press, 1944). It is worth noting that the 1940 campaign was probably the worst campaign in which to look for possible media effects. It was the only presidential election in U.S. history in which a sitting president, Franklin Roosevelt, was running for a third term. The stability of preference surely reflected the fact that people had opinions about Roosevelt and that not much would change them one way or the other. In contrast, Senator Obama was not a well -known figure in the 2008 presidential campaign.

59. Angus Campbell et al., *The American Voter* (New York: Wiley, 1960).

60. Survey conducted by ABC News/Washington Post, Janu-ary 13–January 16, 2011, retrieved June 3, 2012, from the iPOLL Databank, The Roper Center for Public Opin-ion Research, University of Connecticut.

61. In political science, the most important book to reshape the field was Shanto Iyengar and Donald R. Kinder, *News That Matters: Television and American Opinion* (Chicago: University of Chicago Press, 1987). Also see Maxwell McCombs and Donald L. Shaw, "The Agenda-setting Function of Mass Media," *Public Opinion Quarterly* 36 (1972): 176–87, and Maxwell McCombs, Donald L. Shaw, and David Weaver, *Communication and Democracy: Ex-ploring the Intellectual Frontiers in Agenda-setting Theory* (Mahwah, NJ: Erlbaum, 1997).

62. Bernard Cohen, *The Press and Foreign Policy* (Princeton, N.J.: Princeton University Press, 1963), 13.

63. Darrell M. West, Grover J. Whitehurst, and E. J. Dionne Jr., "Invisible: 1.4 Percent Coverage for Education Is Not Enough," Brookings.edu, December 2, 2009, accessed May 28, 2012, http://www.brookings.edu/research /reports/2009/12/02-education-news-west.

64. Shanto Iyengar and Jennifer A. McGrady, *Media Politics: A Citizen's Guide* (New York: W. W. Norton, 2007), 216.

65. See Jonathan Ladd, *Why Americans Hate the Media* (Princeton, N.J.: Princeton University Press, 2012).

66. See the Accuracy in Media website at http://www.aim .org.

67. Thomas Patterson, "Political Roles of the Journalist," in *The Politics of the News,* ed. Doris Graber, Denis McQuail, and Pippa Norris (Washington, D.C.: CQ Press, 2000), 3.

68. For a thoughtful discussion of soft news, see Matthew Baum, *Soft News Goes to War: Public Opinion and Ameri-can Foreign Policy in the New Media Age* (Princeton, N.J.: Princeton University Press, 2003), 6–7.

69. Pew Research Center for the People & the Press, "Public Knowledge of Current Affairs Little Changed by News and Information Revolutions," Pew Research Center, April 15, 2007, accessed May 28, 2012, http://www.people-press .org/2007/04/15/public-knowledge-of-current-affairs -little-changed-by-news-and-information-revolutions/.

70. Pew Internet & American Life Project, "Home Broadband Adoption 2009," Pew Research Center, June 17, 2009, accessed May 28, 2012, http://www.pewinternet.org /Reports/2009/10-Home-Broadband-Adoption-2009 .aspx.

71. Damon Poeter, "Pew: Mobile Helping Narrow Digi-tal Divide, But Not for All," *PC Mag,* April 15, 2012, as quoted by the Pew Internet & American Life Project, Pew Research Center, accessed May 28, 2012, http://www .pewinternet.org/Media-Mentions/2012/Pew-Mobile -Helping-Narrow-Digital-Divide-But-Not-For-All.aspx.

72. The argument presented over the next few paragraphs is inspired by the work of Markus Prior, *Post Broadcast De-mocracy* (New York: Cambridge University Press, 2007).

73. Ibid.

74. *Federal Communications Commission v. Pacifica Founda-tion,* 438 U.S. 726 (1978).

75. *FCC v. Fox Television Stations,* 173 L. Ed. 2d 738 (2009).

76. Matthew Lasar, "Supreme Court Remands FCC 'Nipple-gate' Case to Lower Court," *Ars Technica,* May 4, 2009, http://arstechnica.com/tech-policy/2009/05/supreme -court-remands-fcc-nipplegate-case-to-lower-court/.

77. "White House Asks Supreme Court to Consider FCC Appeal of Court Ruling in Janet Jackson Incident," AllAccess.com, April 19, 2012, http://www.allaccess .com/net-news/archive/story/105015/white-house -asks-supreme-court-to-consider-fcc-app.

78. Emma Llansó and Mark Stanley, "Communications De-cency Act," Center for Democracy & Technology, Septem-ber 21, 2011, accessed May 28, 2012, https://www.cdt .org/category/blogtags/communications-decency-act;

79. Liberty Counsel, "Legislative History of COPA," LC.org, accessed June 4, 2012, http://www.lc.org/profamily/copa.pdf.

80. American Civil Liberties Union v. Mukasey, 534 F. 3d 181 (3rd Cir. 2008).

81. The Federal Trade Commission, "Facts for Consumers," 2007. See http://ftc.gov/ for all available information collected by the FTC for consumers.

82. Library of Congress, "An Act to Prevent Child Abduction and the Sexual Exploitation of Children," http://thomas.loc.gov/.

83. Center for Democracy and Technology, "CAN-SPAM Signed into Law," December 16, 2003, https://www.cdt.org/pr_statement/can-spam-signed-law.

84. Richard Pérez-Peña, "Group Plans to Provide Investigative Journalism," *New York Times,* October 15, 2007, http://www.nytimes.com/2007/10/15/business/media/15publica.html.

85. Paul Steiger, "Note on ProPublica's Second Pulitzer Price," *ProPublica,* April 18, 2011, http://www.propublica.org/article/a-note-on-propublicas-second-pulitzer-prize.

Chapter 8

1. This story was compiled from information on the Students for Concealed Carry on Campus website, http://www.concealedcampus.org; Dean A. Ferguson, "Campus Gun Ban Bill Disarmed," *Lewiston Tribune,* February 14, 2008; Suzanne Smalley, "More Guns on Campus?," *Newsweek,* February 15, 2008; Dave Workman, "Magic Monday: Second Win for Gun Rights Posted in Colorado," March 5, 2012, http://www.examiner.com/gun-rights-in-seattle/magic-monday-second-win-for-gun-rights-posted-colorado; and an e-mail interview with Al Baker, April 6, 2010, conducted for this textbook, which is the source of the chapter-opening quotation.

2. Alexis de Tocqueville, *Democracy in America,* ed. J. P. Mayer, trans. George Lawrence (New York: Doubleday & Company, 1969), 193.

3. Interest groups at the state level have even been involved in elections for state judges. See Clive S. Thomas, Michael L. Boyer, and Ronald J. Hrebenar, "Interest Groups and State Court Elections: A New Era and Its Challenges," *Judicature* 87 (2003): 135–49.

4. Rachel Weiner, "Issue 2 Falls, Ohio Collective Bargaining Law Repealed," *The Fix* (blog), *Washington Post,* November 8, 2011, http://www.washingtonpost.com/blogs/the-fix/post/issue-2-falls-ohio-collective-bargaining-law-repealed/2011/11/08/gIQAyZ0U3M_blog.html

5. John Helton and Tom Cohen, "Walker's Wisconsin Win Big Blow to Unions, Smaller One to Obama," CNN, June 6, 2012, http://www.cnn.com/2012/06/05/politics/wisconsin-recall-vote/index.html?hpt=hp_t1.

6. National Right to Work Legal Defense Foundation, Inc., "Right to Work States," accessed May 23, 2012, http://www.nrtw.org/rtws.htm.

7. U.S. Bureau of Labor Statistics, "Union Members Summary," January 27, 2012, accessed May 23, 2012, http://www.bls.gov/news.release/union2.nr0.htm.

8. MoveOn.org, http://front.moveon.org/.

9. American Israel Public Affairs Committee, "About AIPAC," accessed May 23, 2012, http://www.aipac.org/en/about-aipac.

10. Mark R. Amstutz, "Faith-Based NGOs and U.S. Foreign Policy," in *The Influence of Faith: Religious Groups and Foreign Policy,* ed. by Elliot Abrams, 175–87 (Lanham, Md.: Rowman and Littlefield Publishers, 2001); National Council of the Churches of Christ in the USA, http://www.ncccusa.org.

11. American Civil Liberties Union, *Report: Blocking Faith, Freezing Charity,* June 16, 2009, accessed May 23, 2012, http://www.aclu.org/human-rights/report-blocking-faith-freezing-charity.

12. "President Obama Rejects Keystone XL!," *Compass* (blog), Sierra Club, January 18, 2012, http://sierraclub.typepad.com/compass/2012/01/president-obama-rejects-keystone-xl.html.

13. Kay Brilliant, "NEA's Response to Race to the Top," National Education Association, August 21, 2008, accessed May 23, 2012, http://www.nea.org/home/35447.htm.

14. For more information on general lobbying, see Anthony J. Nownes, *Total Lobbying* (New York: Cambridge University Press, 2006).

15. Center for Responsive Politics, "Lobbying Database," OpenSecrets.org, accessed May 23, 2012, http://www.opensecrets.org/lobby/index.php.

16. Ibid.

17. Bart Jansen, "Legislative Summary: Congressional Affairs: Lobbying Practices and Disclosures," *CQ Weekly Online,* January 7, 2008, 39.

18. Gregory Koger and Jennifer N. Victor, "Polarized Agendas: Campaign Contributions by Lobbyists," *PS: Political Science and Politics* 42 (2009): 485–88.

19. U.S. Internal Revenue Service, "Exemption Requirements-Section 501(c)(3) Organizations," accessed May 23, 2012, http://www.irs.gov/charities/charitable/article/0,,id=96099,00.html.

20. *Buckley v. Valeo,* 424 U.S. 1 (1976).

21. See John R. Wright, *Interest Groups and Congress: Lobbying, Contributions, and Influence* (Boston: Allyn & Bacon,

1995, reprinted in Longman Classics Series, 2009); Michelle L. Chin, Jon R. Bond, and Nehemia Geva, "A Foot in the Door: An Experimental Study of PAC and Constituency Effects on Access," *Journal of Politics* 62 (2000): 534–49.

22. *Federal Election Commission v. Wisconsin Right to Life, Inc.,* 551 U.S. 449 (2007).

23. Tocqueville, *Democracy in America,* 514.

24. David Truman, *The Governmental Process: Political Interests and Public Opinion* (New York: Alfred Knopf, 1971).

25. Mancur Olson, *The Logic of Collective Action* (Cambridge, Mass.: Harvard University Press, 1971).

26. Robert Dahl, *A Preface to Democratic Theory* (Chicago: University of Chicago Press, 1956). Also see Robert Dahl, *Who Governs?,* 2nd ed. (New Haven, Conn.: Yale University Press, 2005).

27. C. Wright Mills, *The Power Elite* (New York: Oxford University Press, 1956).

28. Theodore J. Lowi, *The End of Liberalism: Ideology, Policy, and the End of Public Authority* (New York: Norton, 1969).

29. E. E. Schattschneider, *The Semi-Sovereign People* (New York: Holt, Rinehart, and Winston, 1960). Also see E. E. Schattschneider, *Politics, Pressures, and the Tariff* (New York: Prentice-Hall, 1935).

30. On April 1, 2010, the EPA and the Department of Transportation jointly issued the final regulations. See Environmental Protection Agency 40 CFR Parts 85, 86, and 600, Department of Transportation National Highway Traffic Safety Administration, 49 CFR Parts 531, 533, 537 and 538 Light-Duty Vehicle Greenhouse Gas Emission Standards and Corporate Average Fuel Economy Standards; Final Rule. For electronic versions of the rules, see https://www.federalregister.gov.

31. Hugh Heclo, "Issue Networks and the Executive Establishment," in *The New American Political System,* ed. Anthony King (Washington, D.C.: American Enterprise Institute, 1978), 87–124.

32. Robert H. Salisbury, "An Exchange Theory of Interest Groups," *Midwest Journal of Political Science* 13 (1969): 1–32.

33. In *Logic of Collective Action,* Olson labels these *selective incentives* (p. 51).

34. Ibid.

35. DeWayne Wickham, "Group Loses Another Leader, and More Luster," *USA Today,* March 6, 2007, A13; Krissah Thompson, "100 Years Old, NAACP Debates Its Current Role," *Washington Post,* July 12, 2009.

36. AARP, "AARP Consolidated Financial Statements, December 31, 2010 and 2009," accessed May 22, 2012, http://www.aarp.org/content/dam/aarp/about_aarp /annual_reports/2010_aarp_consolidated_financial _statements_12_31_10.pdf.

37. AARP's 2010 operating budget was $1.19 billion. Ibid.

38. Lachlan Markay and Jay Lucas, "Timeline: Keystone's Three Years in Limbo," *The Foundry* (blog), January 19, 2012, http://blog.heritage.org/2012/01/19/timeline -keystones-three-years-in-limbo/.

39. "Keystone XL Pipeline Project," TransCanada, accessed May 22, 2012, http://www.transcanada.com/keystone .html.

40. Environmental Protection Agency, "The Origins of EPA," http://www.epa.gov/aboutepa/history/origins.html.

41. House Energy and Commerce Committee, "Waiting for the Keystone XL Pipeline," accessed May 22, 2012, http://energycommerce.house.gov/keystonexl.shtml.

42. Pierre Bertrand, "Keystone Pipeline: 5 Things You Need to Know," *International Business Times,* January 19, 2012, http://www.ibtimes.com/articles/284582/20120119 /keystone-pipeline-xl-oil-5-things-need.htm; House Energy and Commerce Committee, "Waiting for Keystone XL, Waiting for Jobs," January 4, 2012, accessed May 22, 2012, http://energycommerce.house.gov/news/PRArticle .aspx?NewsID=9180.

43. Ibid.

44. John M. Broder, "TransCanada Renewing Request to Build Keystone Pipeline," *New York Times,* February 27, 2012, http://www.nytimes.com/2012/02/28/science/earth /keystone-pipeline-permit-request-to-be-renewed .html?_r=2&hp.

45. Markay and Lucas, "Timeline."

46. International Brotherhood of Teamsters, "Labor: Keystone XL Is Jobs and Economic Game Changer," October 25, 2010, accessed May 22, 2012, http:// www.teamster.org/content/labor-keystone-xl-jobs -and-economic-game-changer.

47. F. Vincent Vernuccio and Matt Patterson, "Keystone and the Unions," *American Spectator,* February 7, 2012, http://spectator.org/archives/2012/02/07/keystone -and-the-unions.

48. "Endorsements," Tar Sands Action, accessed May 22, 2012, http://www.tarsandsaction.org/category/endorsements/.

49. Ben Geman, "Keystone Backers, Foes Find New Ammo in Report on State Dept. Review Process," *The Hill* (blog), February 9, 2012, http://thehill.com/blogs/e2-wire /e2-wire/209791-keystone-pipeline-backers-foes-find -ammo-in-new-report.

50. "Key Facts on Keystone XL," Tar Sands Action, accessed May 22, 2012, http://www.tarsandsaction.org /spread-the-word/key-facts-keystone-xl/.

51. Kirsten Gillibrand, "Senators Query Secretary Clinton on Pending Decision on TransCanada Tar Sands Pipeline," on Senator Gillibrand's official website, October 29, 2010, accessed May 22, 2012, http://www.gillibrand.senate.gov/newsroom/press/release/senators-query-secretary-clinton-on-pending-decision-on-transcanada-tar-sands-pipeline.

52. Center for Responsive Politics, "Top PACs," OpenSecrets.org, accessed May 23, 2012, http://www.opensecrets.org/pacs/toppacs.php, based on data released by the Federal Election Commission, February 13, 2012.

Chapter 9

1. This story has been compiled from "McKoon State Senate 29," on Georgia State Senator Josh McKoon's website, accessed May 31, 2012, http://www.joshmckoon.com; Larry Gierer, "Local GOP Elects New Chairman, Officers: Attorney Josh McKoon to Take Helm of Party," *Columbus Ledger-Enquirer*, March 31, 2007; Brian McDearmon, "Attorney to Run for GOP Chair: McKoon Seeks Top Post Vacated by Rob Doll," *Columbus Ledger-Enquirer*, February 26, 2007; Chuck Williams, "Republican Josh McKoon Running for Senate District 29 Seat with Abandon, Even with No Opposition Yet," *Columbus Ledger-Enquirer*, March 28, 2010; Liz Buckthorpe, "Inside Story: Senator Josh McKoon," WRBL News, February 15, 2012, http://www2.wrbl.com/news/2012/feb/15/inside-story-senator-josh-mckoon-ar-3237249/; Georgia General Assembly, Legislation, Senator Joshua McKoon, 2011–2012 Regular Session, accessed May 31, 2012, http://www.legis.ga.gov/Legislation/en-US/MemberLegislation.aspx?Member=749&Session=21; phone interview with Josh McKoon, January 28, 2008, and e-mail interview with Josh McKoon, April 29, 2010, both conducted for this textbook. The chapter-opening quotation is from the April 29 e-mail interview.

2. V. O. Key Jr., *Politics, Parties, and Pressure Groups*, 5th ed. (New York: Thomas Y. Crowell Company, 1964).

3. For more information on the informal networking that occurs among party activists, see Gregory Koger, Seth Masket, and Hans Noel, "Partisan Webs: Information Exchange and Party Networks," *British Journal of Political Science* 39 (2009): 633–53.

4. Marjorie Hershey, *Party Politics in America*, 12th ed. (New York: Pearson-Longman, 2007), 159.

5. Americans Elect, http://www.americanselect.org/.

6. Aaron Blake, "Americans Elect: The Third Party's Latest Death Knell," *The Fix* (blog), *Washington Post*, May 15, 2012, http://www.washingtonpost.com/blogs/the-fix/post/americans-elect-the-third-partys-latest-death-knell/2012/05/15/gIQAP4uVRU_blog.html.

7. Republican National Committee, "New Timing Rules for 2012 Republican Presidential Nominating Schedule" as cited by Josh Putnam, "An Update on the 2012 Republican Delegate Selection Rules," *FrontloadingHQ* (blog), February 27, 2011, http://frontloading.blogspot.com/2011/02/update-on-2012-republican-delegate.html.

8. Larry M. Bartels, *Presidential Primaries and the Dynamics of Public Choice* (Princeton, N.J.: Princeton University Press, 1988).

9. Brian G. Knight and Nathan Schiff, "Momentum and Social Learning in Presidential Primaries" (Working Paper W13637, National Bureau of Economic Research, November 2007).

10. John F. Bibby and Brian F. Schaffner, *Politics, Parties and Elections in America*, 6th ed. (Boston: Thomson-Wadsworth, 2008), 24.

11. United States Senate, Office of the Historian, *Biographical Directory of the United States Congress*, http://bioguide.congress.gov.

12. U.S. Census Bureau, "1990 Population and Housing Unit Counts: United States," Table 2, in *1990 Census of Population and Housing*, accessed May 31, 2012, http://www.census.gov/population/www/censusdata/files/table-2.pdf.

13. Sean M. Theriault, *The Power of the People* (Columbus: Ohio State University Press, 2005), Chapter 3.

14. Douglas W. Jones, "The Australian Paper Ballot," in "A Brief Illustrated History of Voting," University of Iowa, Department of Computer Science, 2003, accessed May 31, 2012, http://www.divms.uiowa.edu/~jones/voting/pictures/.

15. Erik J. Engstrom and Samuel Kernell, "Manufactured Responsiveness: The Impact of State Electoral Laws on Unified Party Control of the Presidency and the House of Representatives, 1840–1940," *American Journal of Political Science* 49 (July 2005): 531–49, see 535.

16. Anthony Downs, *An Economic Theory of Democracy* (New York: Harper, 1957).

17. Stuart Elaine Macdonald and George Rabinowitz, "Solving the Paradox of Nonconvergence: Valence, Position, and Direction in Democratic Politics," *Electoral Studies* 17, no. 3 (1998): 281–300.

18. Maurice Duverger, "Public Opinion and Political Parties in France," *American Political Science Review* 46, no. 4 (1952): 1069–78, especially 1071.

19. "Presidential Elections Statistics, 2000, Popular Votes for Ralph Nader (Most Recent) by State," StateMaster.com, accessed May 31, 2012, http://www.statemaster.com/graph/pre_2000_pop_vot_for_ral_nad-2000-popular-votes-ralph-nader.

20. For a detailed discussion of how interest groups interact with parties in campaigning, see Matthew J. Burbank, Ronald J. Hrebenar, and Robert C. Benedict, *Parties, Interest Groups, and Political Campaigns* (Boulder, Colo.: Paradigm Publishers, 2008).

21. "Election Results 2008," *New York Times*, December 9, 2008, http://elections.nytimes.com/2008/results/president/map.html.

22. "Campaign 2010," CBS News, November 2, 2010, http://www.cbsnews.com/election2010/exit.shtml?state=US&jurisdiction=0&race=H&tag=contentBody;electionCenterHome.

23. *Engel v. Vitale*, 370 U.S. 421 (1962).

24. For a broad discussion of the resurgence of Republican conservatives, see Mark A. Smith, *The Right Talk: How Conservatives Transformed the Great Society into the Economic Society* (Princeton, N.J.: Princeton University Press, 2007).

25. Data from the Inter-university Consortium for Political and Social Research (ICPSR) National Election Study 2004, as cited in Hershey, *Party Politics in America*, 32.

26. Scholar Tasha Philpot pointed to underlying shifts as early as 2004. See Tasha S. Philpot, "A Party of a Different Color? Race, Campaign Communication, and Party Politics," *Political Behavior* 26 (2004): 249–70.

27. Nolan McCarty, Keith T. Poole, and Howard Rosenthal, "Party Polarization: 1879–2010," Voteview.com, last modified January 11, 2011, accessed May 31, 2012, http://www.voteview.com/polarized_america.htm.

28. "Congressional Job Approval," RealClearPolitics.com, last modified May 24, 2012, accessed May 31, 2012, http://www.realclearpolitics.com/epolls/other/congressional_job_approval-903.html.

29. Elizabeth Grieco et al., *The Foreign-Born Population in the United States: 2010,* American Community Survey Report ACS-19 (Washington, D.C.: U.S. Census Bureau, May 2012), Table 1, http://www.census.gov/prod/2012pubs/acs-19.pdf.

30. U.S. Citizenship and Immigration Services, "About Us," accessed May 31, 2012, http://www.uscis.gov/aboutus.

31. Randall Monger and James Yankay, *Annual Flow Report: U.S. Legal Permanent Residents: 2010* (Washington, D.C.: Office of Immigration Statistics, Department of Homeland Security, March 2011), 1, http://www.dhs.gov/xlibrary/assets/statistics/publications/lpr_fr_2010.pdf.

32. Ibid., 2.

33. U.S. Citizenship and Immigration Services, "A Guide to Naturalization," last modified March 27, 2012, accessed May 31, 2012, http://www.uscis.gov/natzguide.

34. U.S. Immigration Support: Your Online Guide to U.S. Visas, Green Cards and Citizenship, http://www.usimmigrationsupport.org.

35. Luis Miranda, "Get the Facts on the DREAM Act," *The White House Blog*, December 1, 2010, http://www.whitehouse.gov/blog/2010/12/01/get-facts-dream-act.

36. "Remarks by the President on Immigration," The White House, press release, June 15, 2012, http://www.whitehouse.gov/the-press-office/2012/06/15/remarks-president-immigration.

37. Randal C. Archibold, "Arizona Enacts Stringent Law on Immigration," *New York Times*, April 23, 2010, A1.

38. *Arizona v. United States*, 11-182 (2012).

39. "Party Affiliation," Gallup.com, accessed May 31, 2012, http://www.gallup.com/poll/15370/party-affiliation.aspx.

Chapter 10

1. This story has been compiled from "USAO Student Reaches Out to Anadarko Youth," University of Science and Arts of Oklahoma press release, December 17, 2008, http://www.usao.edu; Dan Klein, "Featured Fellow: Maya Torralba," interview with Maya Torralba, July 2008, http://www.yp4.org; "Okla. House Candidate Goes Door-to-Door," *Native Times*, October 25, 2010, http://www.nativetimes.com/index.php?option=com_content& view=article&id=4478:okla-house-candidate-goes-door-to-door&catid=52&amp=28; a biography of Torralba on the Indigenous Democratic Network website, http://www.indsnlist.org; and an e-mail interview with Maya Torralba, March 23, 2010, conducted for this textbook, which is the source for the chapter-opening quotation.

2. This claim arises from dividing the number of electoral votes by the total number of voters. Alaska had 3 electoral votes and about 317,000 voters in 2008. Texas had 34 electoral votes and more than 8 million voters.

3. Polls conducted by CBS News, December 9–10, 2000, retrieved June 9, 2012, from the iPOLL Databank, The Roper Center for Public Opinion Research, University of Connecticut.

4. Polls conducted by CBS News, December 14–16, 2000, retrieved June 9, 2012, from the iPOLL Databank, The Roper Center for Public Opinion Research, University of Connecticut.

5. Polls conducted by CBS News, January 15–17, 2001, retrieved June 9, 2012, from the iPOLL Databank, The Roper Center for Public Opinion Research, University of Connecticut.

6. Polls conducted by the Gallup Organization for CNN and *USA Today*, November 11–12, 2000, retrieved June 1, 2012, from the iPOLL Databank, The Roper Center for Public Opinion Research, University of Connecticut.

7. Survey conducted by CBS News/*New York Times*, September 8–12, 2012, retrieved September 29, 2012, from the iPOLL Databank, The Roper Center for Public Opinion Research, University of Connecticut.

8. Michael McGerr, *The Decline of Popular Politics* (New York: Oxford University Press, 1986).

9. Jackie Kucinich, "GOP's Tim Pawlenty Exploring 2012 Presidential Run," *USA Today,* March 22, 2011, http://www.usatoday.com/news/politics/2011-03-22-pawlenty22_ST_N.htm.

10. Sidney Blumenthal, *The Permanent Campaign* (New York: Simon and Schuster, 1982).

11. "Campaign 2012: Florida Primary," *Washington Post,* January 31, 2012, http://www.washingtonpost.com/wp-srv/special/politics/primary-tracker/Florida/.

12. Federal Election Commission, "The FEC and Federal Campaign Finance Law: Historical Background," February 2004, accessed June 4, 2012, http://www.fec.gov/pages/brochures/fecfeca.shtml.

13. Federal Election Commission, "How Much Can I Contribute?," FEC.gov, accessed June 4, 2012, http://www.fec.gov/ans/answers_general.shtml#How_much_can_I_contribute.

14. Federal Election Commission, "Presidential Spending Limits for 2012," accessed June 4, 2012, http://www.fec.gov/pages/brochures/pubfund_limits_2012.shtml, accessed May 16, 2012.

15. Federal Election Commission, "Bipartisan Campaign Reform Act of 2002," accessed June 4, 2012, http://www.fec.gov/pages/bcra/bcra_update.shtml.

16. Jim Drinkard, "Let the Fundraising Begin—Again," *USA Today,* March 10, 2000, 14a.

17. Richard Briffault, "Super PACs" (Working Paper 12-298, Columbia Law School, April 16, 2012).

18. Kevin Quealy and Derek Willis, "Independent Spending Totals," *New York Times*, accessed May 18, 2012, http://elections.nytimes.com/2012/campaign-finance/independent-expenditures/totals.

19. http://www.foxnews.com/politics/2012/11/06/super-pacs-flood-2012-campaigns-with-millions-but-impact-still-undecided/.

20. Steven J. Rosenstone and John Mark Hansen, *Mobilization, Participation, and Democracy in America* (New York: Macmillan, 1993).

21. This insightful observation was made by Senator Lamar Alexander to one of the authors on March 16, 2012.

22. Lynn Vavrek, "The A-Little-Bit-Less Undecided," *Campaign Stops* (blog), *The New York Times*, September 20, 2012, http://campaignstops.blogs.nytimes.com/2012/09/20/the-a-little-bit-less-undecided/.

23. Daron R. Shaw, *The Race to 270: The Electoral College and the Campaign Strategies of 2000 and 2004* (Chicago: University of Chicago Press, 2006); figures for 2008 provided by Daron R. Shaw.

24. James G. Gimpel, Karen M. Kaufmann, and Shanna Pearson-Merkowitz, "Battleground States versus Blackout States," *Journal of Politics* 69 (2007): 786–97.

25. Chris Cillizza, "Romney's Data Cruncher," *Washington Post,* September 7, 2007, A1.

26. Thomas B. Edsall, "Let the Nanotargeting Begin," *Campaign Stops* (blog), *New York Times,* April 15, 2012, http://campaignstops.blogs.nytimes.com/2012/04/15/let-the-nanotargeting-begin/.

27. Aaron Blake, "DNC Holds National Training As It Rolls Out New Voter File," *The Hill,* August 15, 2007.

28. Mike Madden, "Barack Obama's Super Marketing Machine," *Salon,* July 16, 2008, http://www.salon.com/2008/07/16/obama_data/.

29. John G. Geer, *In Defense of Negativity* (Chicago: University of Chicago Press, 2006), 59–60.

30. Lynn Vavreck, *The Message Matters* (Princeton, N.J.: Princeton University Press, 2009).

31. Donald Stokes, "Spatial Models of Party Competition," *American Political Science Review* 57 (1963): 368–77.

32. Geer, *In Defense of Negativity*, 105.

33. Sunshine Hillygus and Todd Shields, *The Persuadable Voter* (Princeton, N.J.: Princeton University Press, 2008), 36.

34. Mark Z. Barabak, "Wedge Issues May Boost Obama's Prospects," *Los Angeles Times,* April 27, 2012, http://www.latimes.com/news/nationworld/nation/la-na-campaign-2012-wedge-issues-20120428,0,2706316.story.

35. For predictions about the 2008 and 2012 elections, see Nate Silver's *New York Times* blog, *Five Thirty Eight,* at http://fivethirtyeight.blogs.nytimes.com. For 2012, see especially http://fivethirtyeight.blogs.nytimes.com/2012/11/06/nov-5-late-poll-gains-for-obama-leave-romney-with-longer-odds/.

36. See Morris Fiorina, *Retrospective Voting* (New Haven: Yale University Press, 1980).

37. Anthony Downs, *An Economic Theory of Democracy* (New York: Harper, 1957).

38. Federal Election Commission, *Federal Election Campaign Laws* (Washington, D.C.: Federal Election Commission, April 2008), 56–60, http://www.fec.gov. Note that the contribution levels have been increased slightly to adjust for inflation.

39. Center for Responsive Politics, "Different Races, Different Costs," OpenSecrets.org, accessed June 4, 2012, http://www.opensecrets.org/bigpicture/incad.php?cycle=2010.

40. Federal Election Commission, *Federal Election Campaign Laws.* Note that the contribution levels have been increased slightly to adjust for inflation.

41. Albert Cover, "One Good Term Deserves Another: The Advantage of Incumbency in Congressional Elections," *American Journal of Political Science* 21, no. 3 (1977): 523–41.

42. See Gary C. Jacobson, *The Politics of Congressional Elections,* 8th ed. (Upper Saddle River, N.J.: Prentice Hall, 2012).

43. Richard F. Fenno Jr., *Home Style: Home Members in Their Districts* (Boston: Little, Brown, 1978).

44. See Jacobson, *Politics of Congressional Elections.*

45. Poll conducted by *Fox News,* September 9–11, 2012, retrieved on September 29, 2012, from the iPOLL Databank, The Roper Center for Public Opinion Research, University of Connecticut.

46. Bruce Oppenheimer, "Deep Red and Blue Congressional Districts: The Causes and Consequences of Declining Party Competitiveness," in *Congress Reconsidered,* 8th ed., ed. Lawrence Dodd and Bruce Oppenheimer (Washington, D.C.: CQ Press, 2005), 135–58.

47. Jacobson, *Politics of Congressional Elections.*

48. Samuel Huntington, "The United States," in *The Crisis of Democracy,* ed. Michael Crozier, Samuel Huntington, and Joji Watanuki (New York: NYU Press, 1975), 59–115.

49. Steven E. Finkel "Reciprocal Effects of Participation and Political Efficacy: A Panel Analysis," *American Journal of Political Science* 29, no. 4 (1985): 891–913; Steven E. Finkel, "The Effects of Participation on Political Efficacy and Political Support: Evidence from a West German Panel," *Journal of Politics* 49, no. 2 (1987): 441–64. These articles provide empirical evidence that supports the arguments of Carol Pateman, *Participation and Democratic Theory* (New York: Cambridge University Press, 1970).

50. See Jan Leighley, "Attitudes, Opportunities, and Incentives," *Political Research Quarterly* 48 (1995): 184.

51. Pew Hispanic Center, "Dissecting the 2008 Electorate: Most Diverse in U.S. History," Pew Research Center, April 30, 2009, accessed June 7, 2012, http://www.pewhispanic.org/2009/04/30/dissecting-the-2008-electorate-most-diverse-in-us-history.

52. Mark Hugo Lopez, Emily Kirby, Jared Sagoff and Chris Herbst, *The Youth Vote 2004, with a Historical Look at Youth Voting Patterns, 1972–2004* (Working Paper 35, CIRCLE: The Center for Information & Research on Civic Learning and Engagement, July 2005), http://www.civicyouth.org/circle-working-paper-35-the-youth-vote-2004-with-a-historical-look-at-youth-voting-patterns-1972-2004/.

53. Pew Hispanic Center, "Dissecting the 2008 Electorate."

54. Tom File and Sarah Crissey, *Voting and Registration in the Election of 2008,* (Washington, D.C.: U.S. Census Bureau, May 2010), http://www.census.gov/prod/2010pubs/p20-562.pdf.

55. See Leighley, "Attitudes, Opportunities, and Incentives," 181–209.

56. Thom File and Sarah Crissey, *Voting and Registration in the Election of November 2008* (Washington, D.C.: U.S. Census Bureau, May 2010), http://www.census.gov/prod/2010pubs/p20-562.pdf.

57. See, for instance, Raymond Wolfinger and Steven Rosenstone, *Who Votes?* (New Haven, Conn.: Yale University Press, 1980). There has been much research since the publication of this book, but it remains a leading source on this topic.

58. File and Crissey, *Voting and Registration in the Election of November 2008.*

59. Cindy D. Kam and Carl L. Palmer, "Reconsidering the Effects of Education on Political Participation," *Journal of Politics* 70, no. 3 (2008): 612–31.

60. See United States Election Project, http://elections.gmu.edu/voter_turnout.htm.

61. Ibid.

62. G. Bingham Powell Jr., "American Voter Turnout in Comparative Perspective," *American Political Science Review* 80 (1986): 17–37.

63. This "puzzle of participation" was first discussed by Richard Brody in *The New American Political System,* ed. Anthony King (Washington, D.C.: American Enterprise Institute for Public Policy Research, 1978).

64. Warren Miller, "Puzzle Transformed," *Political Behavior* 14 (1992): 1–43.

65. Rosenstone and Hansen, *Mobilization, Participation, and Democracy in America.*

66. Ibid.

67. Keena Lipsitz, Christine Trost, Matthew Grossman, and John Sides, "What Voters Want from Campaign Communication," *Political Communication* 22 (2005): 337–54.

68. Steven Ansolabehere and Shanto Iyengar, *Going Negative* (New York: Free Press, 1995).

69. Geer, *In Defense of Negativity.*

70. See, for example, Joshua Clinton and John Lapinski, "'Targeted' Advertising and Voter Turnout: An Experimental Study of the 2000 Presidential Election," *Journal of Politics* 66 (2004): 69–96.

71. Richard R. Lau, Lee Sigelman, and Ivy Brown Rovner, "A New Meta-Analysis," *Journal of Politics* 69 (2007): 1176–1209.

72. Julia Preston, "Immigrants Number 11.5 Million," *New York Times,* March 24, 2012, http://www.nytimes.com/2012/03/24/us/illegal-immigrants-number-11-5-million.html.

73. Pew Safety Performance Project, *One in 100: Behind Bars in America 2008* (Washington, D.C.: Pew Center on the States, February 2008), http://www.pewtrusts.org/uploadedFiles/wwwpewtrustsorg/Reports/sentencing_and_corrections/one_in_100.pdf.

74. Michael P. McDonald and Samuel L. Popkin, "The Myth of the Vanishing Voter," *American Political Science Review* 95 (2001): 963–74.

75. See Larry Bartels, *Unequal Democracy* (Princeton, N.J.: Princeton University Press, 2008).

76. Task Force on American Inequality, "American Democracy in an Age of Rising Inequality," American Political Science Association, 2004.

77. Bartels, *Unequal Democracy.*

78. Survey conducted by Social Science Research Solutions for Pew Forum on Religion & Public Life, May 19–June 6, 2010, retrieved June 21, 2012, from the iPOLL Databank, The Roper Center for Public Opinion Research, University of Connecticut.

79. See Theda Skocpol and Vanessa Williamson, *The Tea Party and Remaking of Republican Conservativism* (New York: Oxford University Press, 2012).

80. In a poll conducted by Vanderbilt University in May 2012, Tea Party identifiers were less likely to approve of Mitt Romney than Republicans generally. See http://www.vanderbilt.edu/csdi.

81. Russell J. Dalton, "The Myth of the Disengaged American," *Public Opinion Pros,* October 2005, http://www.cses.org/resources/results/POP_Oct2005_1.htm.

82. Thomas R. Rochon, *Mobilizing for Peace* (Princeton, N.J.: Princeton University Press, 1988).

83. Dennis Johnson, "Communicating with Congress," in *Congress and the Internet,* ed. James A. Thurber and Colton C. Campbell (New York: Prentice Hall, 2003).

84. For one example, see Congressman Jim Cooper's official website at http://www.cooper.house.gov/.

85. Eric Lawrence, John Siodes, and Henry Farrell, "Self-Segregation or Deliberation," *Perspectives on Politics* 8 (2010): 141–57.

86. Ibid., 150–1.

87. Matthew A. Mosk, "Internet Donors Fuel Obama," *Washington Post,* February 7, 2008.

88. Matthew A. Mosk, "In Obama Fundraising, Signs of a Shift from Online to in-Person," *Washington Post,* July 18, 2008.

89. David Plouffe, *The Audacity to Win* (New York: Viking Press, 2009).

90. See James Bryce, *The American Commonwealth* (New York: MacMillan, 1895).

91. For the best account of the importance and impact of registration, see Benjamin Highton, "Voter Registration and Turnout in the United States," *Perspectives on Politics* 2 (2004): 507–15.

92. Ibid.

93. Read about the National Voter Registration Act of 1993 at http://www.justice.gov/crt/about/vot/nvra/activ_nvra.php.

94. *Crawford v. Marion County Election Board,* 553 U.S. 181 (2008). See also Bill Mears, "High Court Upholds Indiana's Voter ID Law," CNN, April 28, 2008, http://articles.cnn.com/2008-04-28/politics/scotus.voter.id_1_voter-impersonation-voter-id-laws-voter-fraud?_s=PM:POLITICS; Linda Greenhouse, "In a 6-to-3 Vote, Justices Uphold a Voter ID Law," *New York Times,* April 29, 2008.

95. American Civil Liberties Union, "Applewhite et al. v. Commonwealth of Pennsylvania, et al.," ACLU, accessed May 19, 2012, http://www.aclupa.org/legal/legaldocket/applewhiteetalvcommonwealt/index.

96. Bill Bradbury, "Vote-by-Mail: The Real Winner Is Democracy," *Washington Post,* January 1, 2005.

97. See Jeff Manza and Christopher Ugge, *Locked Out: Felon Disenfranchisement and American Democracy* (Oxford, U.K.: Oxford University Press, 2007).

98. V. O. Key, *The Responsible Electorate* (Cambridge, Mass.: Harvard University Press, 1966).

Chapter 11

1. This story has been compiled from Congresswoman Nydia Velázquez's official website, http://velazquez.house.gov/index.shtml; Answers.com, "Nydia Velázquez," http://www.answers.com/topic/nydia-vel-zquez-2; Sally Friedman, *Dilemmas of Representation: Local Politics, National Factors, and the Home Styles of Modern U.S. Congress Members* (Albany: State University of New York Press, 2007), 164; and Congresswoman Nydia Velázquez, "Velázquez: President Determined to Lay Foundation for Future Growth," on Congresswoman Velázquez's official website, February 25, 2009, http://velazquez.house.gov/newsroom/2009/pr-2-25-09-Obama-address-to-nation.html, which is the source of the chapter-opening quotation.

2. Center for American Women and Politics, Rutgers University, "Facts on Women in Congress 2011," accessed June 21, 2012, http://www.cawp.rutgers.edu/fast_facts/levels_of_office/Congress-CurrentFacts.php; U.S. Census Bureau, "Population Estimates: National Characteristics: Vintage 2011," Table 3, Annual Estimates of the Resident Population by Sex, Race, and Hispanic Origin for the United States: April 1, 2010 to July 1, 2011, accessed

June 21, 2012, http://www.census.gov/popest/data/national/asrh/2011/index.html.

3. Jennifer E. Manning, *Membership of the 112th Congress: A Profile,* CRS Report for Congress, R41647 (Washington, D.C.: Congressional Research Service, March 1, 2011), accessed June 21, 2012, http://www.senate.gov/reference/resources/pdf/R41647.pdf.

4. Ibid. For a broader discussion of the careers of women legislators in the House, see Jennifer Lawless and Sean Theriault, "Will She Stay or Will She Go? Career Ceilings and Women's Retirement from the U.S. Congress," *Legislative Studies Quarterly* 30 (2005): 581–96.

5. In rare cases in which a senator dies or resigns, an interim replacement is typically chosen by the governor of the state until an election is held to fill the seat.

6. U.S. Census Bureau, "Population Estimates: State Totals: Vintage 2011," Table 1, Annual Estimates of the Population for the United States, Regions, States, and Puerto Rico: April 1, 2010 to July 1, 2011; and Table 2, Cumulative Estimates of Resident Population Change for the United States, Regions, States, and Puerto Rico and Region and State Rankings: April 1, 2010 to July 1, 2011, accessed June 21, 2012, http://www.census.gov/popest/data/state/totals/2011/index.html.

7. After the first census of the new federal government under the Constitution, Congress grew to 105 members in 1792. See Brian Frederick, *Congressional Representation and Constituents: The Case for Increasing the Size of the U.S. House of Representatives* (New York: Routledge, 2010), 23–24.

8. U.S. House of Representatives, "Historical Highlights: The Permanent Apportionment Act of 1929," June 11, 1929, accessed June 21, 2012, http://artandhistory.house.gov/highlights.aspx?action=view&intID=200.

9. For a discussion of representation by Latino members, see Jason P. Casellas, "The Institutional and Demographic Determinants of Latino Representation," *Legislative Studies Quarterly* 34, no. 3 (2009): 399–426; see also David Leal and Frederick M. Hess, "Who Chooses Experience? Examining the Use of Veteran Staff by House Freshmen," *Polity* 36 (2004): 651–64.

10. See *Shaw v. Reno,* 509 U.S. 630 (1993), *Miller v. Johnson,* 515 U.S. 900 (1995), and *Easley v. Cromartie,* 532 U.S. 234 (2001). *Thornburg v. Gingles,* 478 U.S. 30 (1986) provides plaintiffs with a right to force a state to create a majority-minority district if the minority community is large and concentrated enough to form a majority in the district, the minority community votes cohesively, and white voting prevents the minority community from electing its preferred candidate. For a longer discussion of redistricting, see Bernard Grofman, Lisa Handley, and Richard G.

Niemi, *Minority Representation and the Quest for Voting Equality* (New York: Cambridge University Press, 1992).

11. Two prominent works on this point are Richard F. Fenno Jr., *The Power of the Purse: Appropriations Politics in Congress* (Boston: Little, Brown, 1966), and Aaron B. Wildavsky, *The New Politics of the Budgetary Process* (Boston: Addison-Wesley Educational, 1992).

12. Fiona McGillivray, "Trading Free and Opening Markets" in *International Trade and Political Institutions,* ed. Fiona McGillivray, Iain McLean, Robert Pahre, and Cheryl Schonhardt-Bailey (Cheltenham, U.K.: Edward Elgar, 2001), 80–98.

13. United States Courts: Federal Courts, http://www.uscourts.gov/FederalCourts.aspx.

14. Sarah A. Binder and Forrest Maltzman, "Senatorial Delay in Confirming Federal Judges, 1947–1998," *American Journal of Political Science* 46, no. 1 (2002): 190–99.

15. Sarah A. Binder, *Majority Rights, Minority Rule* (New York: Cambridge University Press, 1997); Eric Schickler, *Disjointed Pluralism: Institutional Innovation and the Development of the U.S. Congress* (Princeton, N.J.: Princeton University Press, 2001).

16. Sean Gailmard and Jeffery A. Jenkins, "Minority-Party Power in the Senate and the House of Representatives," in *Why Not Parties? Party Effects in the United States Senate,* ed. Nathan W. Monroe, Jason M. Roberts, and David W. Rohde (Chicago: University of Chicago Press, 2008), 181–97.

17. Frank Newport, "Congress Ends 2011 With Record-Low 11% Approval," Gallup Politics, December 19, 2011, http://www.gallup.com/poll/151628/Congress-Ends-2011-Record-Low-Approval.aspx.

18. Barry C. Burden and Tammy M. Frisbee, "Preferences, Partisanship, and Whip Activity in the U.S. House of Representatives," *Legislative Studies Quarterly* 29 (2004): 569–90.

19. Ralph Huitt, "Democratic Party Leadership in the Senate," *American Political Science Review* 55 (1961): 333–44.

20. E. Scott Adler and John Wilkerson, "Intended Consequences: Jurisdictional Reform and Issue Control in the U.S. House of Representatives," *Legislative Studies Quarterly* 33, no. 1 (2008): 85–112.

21. Richard E. Cohen, "Dems May Repeal Term Limits for House Chairs," *National Journal Online,* December 31, 2008, updated January 2, 2011, http://www.nationaljournal.com/njonline/no_20081231_6355.php; Sara Burrows, "House Term Limits Repealed, Rangel to Retain Committee Chairmanship," CNSNews.com, January 8, 2009, http://cnsnews.com/news/article/house-term-limits-repealed-rangel-retain-committee-chairmanship.

22. Ron Nixon, "House Committee to Examine Recent Performance of S.B.A.," *New York Times*, February 7, 2007, C7.

23. David W. Rohde, "Committee Reform in the House of Representatives and the Subcommittee Bill of Rights," *Annals of the American Academy of Political and Social Science* 411, no. 1 (1974): 39–47.

24. For a list of current caucuses, see Committee on House Administration, "112th Congress Congressional Member Organizations (CMO)," updated April 11, 2012, accessed June 21, 2012, http://cha.house.gov/sites/republicans .cha.house.gov/files/documents/cmo_cso_docs/cmo _112th_congress.pdf.

25. Daily Digest, *Congressional Record D3-D4,* January 5, 2010; Daily Digest, *Congressional Record D1249-D1250,* December 29, 2010, http://thomas.loc.gov.

26. For an extended discussion of the right of recognition and the powers it affords senators, see Floyd Riddick, *Senate Procedure,* ed. Alan Frumin (Washington D.C.: U.S. Government Printing Office, 1992), 1091–99.

27. Sarah A. Binder and Steven S. Smith, *Politics or Principle: Filibustering in the U.S. Senate* (Washington, D.C.: Brookings Institution Press, 1997). For a discussion of the use of the filibuster by retiring senators, see Martin Overby, L. Overby, and Lauren Bell, "Rational Behavior or the Norm of Cooperation? Filibustering among Retiring Senators," *Journal of Politics* 66 (2004): 906–24.

28. David Stout, Carl Hulse, and Sheryl Gay Stolberg, "Senate Backs Disputed Judicial Nomination," *New York Times*, October 27, 2007, A21.

29. Wendy J. Schiller, "Resolved the Filibuster Should Be Abolished—Con," in *Debating Reform*, 2nd ed., ed. Richard J. Ellis and Michael Nelson (Washington, D.C.: CQ Press, 2012).

30. Wendy J. Schiller, "Senators as Political Entrepreneurs: Using Bill Sponsorship to Shape Legislative Agendas," *American Journal of Political Science* 1 (1995): 186–203.

31. Glen Krutz, *Hitching a Ride: Omnibus Legislating in the U.S. Congress* (Columbus: Ohio State University Press, 2001).

32. For a general discussion on committees, see Keith R. Krehbiel, *Information and Legislative Organization* (Ann Arbor: University of Michigan Press, 1991).

33. For a few examples of this work, see Aage Clausen, *How Congressmen Decide* (New York: St. Martin's Press, 1973); John Kingdon, *Congressmen's Voting Decisions* (New York: Harper & Row, 1989); David W. Brady, *Critical Elections and Congressional Policy Making* (Stanford, Calif.: Stanford University Press, 1988); Stanley Bach and Steven S. Smith, *Managing Uncertainty in the U.S. House of Representatives* (Washington, D.C.: Brookings Institution Press, 1989). For examples of the ideological

examination of roll call voting, see Keith T. Poole and Howard Rosenthal, *Ideology and Congress* (New Brunswick, N.J.: Transaction Publishers, 2009).

34. Shawn Zeller, "2010 Vote Studies: Party Unity," *CQ Weekly*, January 30, 2011, 37.

35. C. Lawrence Evans and Walter J. Oleszek, "Message Politics and Senate Procedure," in *The Contentious Senate: Partisanship, Ideology and the Myth of Cool Judgment,* ed. Colton C. Campbell and Nicol C. Rae (Lanham, Md.: Rowman and Littlefield, 2000).

36. Barbara Sinclair, *Unorthodox Lawmaking: New Legislative Processes in the U.S. Congress,* 3rd ed. (Washington, D.C.: CQ Press, 2007).

37. Congressional Budget and Impoundment Control Act of 1974 (Public Law 93-344). For additional background on budget history, see the Senate Budget Committee's website at http://www.budget.senate.gov/democratic /index.cfm/committee-history.

38. Balanced Budget and Emergency Deficit Control Act of 1985 (Public Law 99-177). For historical tables on the U.S. federal budget, see Congressional Budget Office, "The Budget and Economic Outlook Fiscal Years 2012 to 2022," January 31, 2012, accessed June 21, 2012, http://www.cbo.gov/publication/42905. The Fiscal 1985 budget deficit number is taken from Table F-1, http://www .cbo.gov/publication/42911.

39. See Walter J. Oleszek, *Congressional Procedures and the Policy Process,* 6th ed. (Washington, D.C: CQ Press, 2004), especially 63–69. For a more comprehensive look at the history of budget politics and deficits, see Jasmine Farrier, *Passing the Buck: Congress, Budgets, and Deficits* (Lexington: University of Kentucky Press, 2004).

40. Kathleen Hunter, "GOP Readies Procedural Salvo against Reconciliation Play," *CQ Weekly Online,* March 8, 2010, 568.

41. Charles M. Cameron, *Veto Bargaining: Presidents and the Politics of Negative Power* (New York: Cambridge University Press, 2000).

42. Albert D. Cover and Bruce S. Brumberg, "Baby Books and Ballots: The Impact of Congressional Mail on Constituent Opinion," *American Political Science Review* 76 (1982): 347–59.

43. Richard L. Hall, *Participation in Congress* (New Haven, Conn.: Yale University Press, 1998).

44. Tracy Sulkin, *Issue Politics in Congress* (New York: Cambridge University Press, 2005).

45. Daily Digest, *Congressional Record D3-D4,* January 5, 2010; Daily Digest, *Congressional Record D1249-D1250,* December 29, 2010, http://thomas.loc.gov.

46. For a comprehensive look at this congressional activity, see Diana Evans, *Greasing the Wheels: Using Pork*

Barrel Projects to Build Majority Coalitions in Congress (New York: Cambridge University Press, 2004).

47. Jennifer A. Dlouhy, "Alaska 'Bridge to Nowhere' Funding Gets Nowhere; Lawmakers Delete Project after Critics Bestow Derisive Moniker," *San Francisco Chronicle*, November 17, 2005, A7.

48. Citizens Against Taxpayer Waste, "2010 Pig Book Summary," accessed June 21, 2012, http://www.cagw.org/reports/pig-book/2010/.

49. Congressional Management Foundation, "112th Congress Gold Mouse Awards: Best Practices in Online Communications on Capitol Hill," http://congressfoundation.org/projects/gold-mouse-project/112th-congress-gold-mouse-awards; TweetCongress.org, "Members of Congress on Twitter," accessed June 21, 2012, http://tweetcongress.org/members/index/party:D.

50. Richard F. Fenno Jr., *Home Style: House Members in Their Districts* (Boston: Little, Brown, 1978).

51. David R. Mayhew, *Congress: The Electoral Connection* (New Haven, Conn.: Yale University Press, 1974).

52. Center for Responsive Politics, "Historical Elections: Reelection Rates Over the Years," OpenSecrets.org, accessed June 21, 2012, http://www.opensecrets.org/bigpicture/reelect.php.

53. For details on these programs, see the U.S. Department of Health and Human Services, Centers for Medicare and Medicaid Services (CMS), http://www.cms.hhs.gov.

54. Centers for Disease Control and Prevention, "Early Release of Selected Estimates Based on Data from the 2010 National Health Interview Survey," CDC.gov, updated and accessed June 22, 2012, http://www.cdc.gov/nchs/nhis/released201106.htm.

55. Henry J. Kaiser Family Foundation, "Summary of Coverage Provisions in the Patient Protection and Affordable Care Act," *Focus on Health Reform*, updated April 14, 2011, accessed June 21, 2012, http://www.kff.org/healthreform/uplaod/8023-R.pdf.

56. Open Congress, "H.R.3962—Affordable Health Care for America Act," Participatory Politics Foundation and Sunlight Foundation, accessed June 21, 2012, http://www.opencongress.org/bill/111-h3962/text.

57. Open Congress, "S.1796—America's Healthy Future Act of 2009," Participatory Politics Foundation and Sunlight Foundation, accessed June 21, 2012, http://www.opencongress.org/bill/111-s1796/show.

58. Patricia Murphy, "Senate Passes Sweeping Health Care Reform, but Trouble Lies Ahead," *Capitolist*, December 24, 2009, http://www.politicsdaily.com/2009/12/24/health-care-vote-senate-passes-sweeping-reform-but-trouble-lie/.

59. Michael Beckel, "Number of Special Interests Vying to Influence Health Reform Legislation Swelled As Debate Dragged On," *OpenSecretsblog,* Center for Responsive Politics, March 19, 2010, http://www.opensecrets.org/news/2010/03/number-of-special-interest-groups-v.html.

60. Jonathan Weisman, "Under Pressure, Obama Defends Health Care Plan," *Wall Street Journal*, August 12, 2009; John Amick, "Recess Doesn't Slow Health Care Rhetoric," *Washington Post,* August 9, 2009.

61. Cecilia Muñoz, "Health Reform, Preventive Services, and Religious Institutions," *The White House Blog*, February 1, 2012, http://www.whitehouse.gov/blog/2012/02/01/health-reform-preventive-services-and-religious-institutions.

62. Megan Slack, "President Obama Announces New Policy to Improve Access to Birth Control," *The White House Blog,* February 10, 2012, http://www.whitehouse.gov/blog/2012/02/10/president-obama-announces-new-policy-improve-access-contraception; "President Obama Speaks on Contraception and Religious Institutions," The White House, February 20, 2012, accessed June 21, 2012, http://www.whitehouse.gov/photos-and-video/video/2012/02/10/president-obama-speaks-contraception-and-religious-institutions#transcript.

63. "Contraception and Insurance Coverage (Religious Exemption Debate)," Times Topics, *New York Times,* modified May 21, 2012, http://topics.nytimes.com/top/news/health/diseasesconditionsandhealthtopics/health_insurance_and_managed_care/health_care_reform/contraception/index.html.

Chapter 12

1. This story was compiled from Meena Dev, "Alumna Hits Campaign Trail with Kerry," *Sophian* (Smith College), September 30, 2004; "Stephanie Cutter," http://www.smithsophian.com/features/alumna-hits-campaign-trail-with-kerry-1.2265179#.T_lsQY7bDE7; "Stephanie Cutter," WPPolitics, *Washington Post,* http://www.washingtonpost.com/politics/stephanie-cutter/gIQAVJFb9O_topic.html; White House Office of the Press Secretary, "President Obama Names Stephanie Cutter Assistant to the President for Special Projects," The White House, April 22, 2010, accessed June 22, 2012, http://www.whitehouse.gov/the-press-office/president-obama-names-stephanie-cutter-assistant-president-special-projects; Mike Allen, "Stephanie Cutter to Join Obama 2012 Campaign at End of Year," Politico.com, September 26, 2011, http://www.politico.com/news/stories/0911/64483.html; the chapter-opening quotation is from the *Sophian* article.

2. Charles Jones, *The President in a Separated System* (Washington, D.C.: Brookings Institution Press, 2005).

3. Arthur Schlesinger Jr., *The Imperial Presidency* (New York: Mariner Books, 2004; first published 1973).

4. Charles M. Cameron, *Veto Bargaining: Presidents and the Politics of Negative Power* (New York: Cambridge University Press, 2000).

5. Glenn S. Krutz, *Hitching a Ride*: *Omnibus Legislating in the U.S. Congress* (Columbus: Ohio State University Press, 2001). Also see Cameron, *Veto Bargaining*.

6. William W. Lammers and Michael A. Genovese, *The Presidency and Domestic Policy* (Washington, D.C.: CQ Press, 2000), 315–24.

7. Jeff Cummins, "State of the Union Addresses and the President's Legislative Success," *Congress and the Presidency* 37 (2010): 176–99.

8. Douglas O. Linder, "The Andrew Johnson Impeachment Trial, 1868: A Trial Account," Famous American Trials, 1999, accessed June 22, 2012, http://law2.umkc.edu /faculty/projects/ftrials/impeach/impeachmt.htm.

9. Ibid.

10. Douglas O. Linder, "Map Showing Senate Impeachment Vote," Famous American Trials, 1999, accessed June 22, 2012, http://law2.umkc.edu/faculty/projects/ftrials /impeach/imp_vote.html.

11. The chronology that follows is taken from the *Washington Post*'s history of Watergate, available online at http:// www.washingtonpost.com/wp-srv/onpolitics/watergate /chronology.htm.

12. Ibid.

13. Douglas O. Linder, "The Impeachment Trial of President William Clinton, 1999," Famous American Trials, 2005, accessed June 22, 2012, http://law2.umkc.edu/faculty /projects/ftrials/clinton/clintonhome.html.

14. "A Whitewater Chronology: What Really Happened during the Clinton Years," *Wall Street Journal,* May 28, 2003, http://online.wsj.com/article/SB122721127833145225 .html.

15. Ibid.

16. "A Whitewater Chronology: What Really Happened during the Clinton Years," *Wall Street Journal,* May 28, 2003, http://online.wsj.com/article/SB122721127833145225 .html; Linder, "Impeachment Trial of President William Clinton."

17. William G. Howell, *Power without Persuasion: The Politics of Direct Presidential Action* (Princeton, N.J.: Princeton University Press, 2003).

18. Harold C. Relyea, *Presidential Directives: Background and Overview,* CRS Report for Congress, 98-611 (Washington, D.C.: Congressional Research Service, 2007).

19. Kenneth R. Mayer, "Executive Orders and Presidential Power," *Journal of Politics* 61 (1999): 445–66, especially 448.

20. Ibid.

21. "Executive Order 10730, Providing Assistance for the Removal of an Obstruction of Justice within the State of Arkansas," news release, September 24, 1957, Dwight D. Eisenhower Presidential Library & Museum, http://www .eisenhower.archives.gov/research/online_documents /civil_rights_little_rock/Press_Release_EO_10730.pdf.

22. Christopher S. Kelley and Bryan W. Marshall, "The Last Word: Presidential Power and the Role of Signing Statements," *Presidential Studies Quarterly* 38 (2008): 248–67; Michael J. Berry, "Controversially Executing the Law: George W. Bush and the Constitutional Signing Statement," *Congress and the Presidency* 36 (2009): 244–71.

23. The White House, "Memorandum for the Heads of Executive Departments and Agencies: Subject: Presidential Signing Statements," news release, March 9, 2009, http://www.whitehouse.gov/the-press-office /memorandum-presidential-signing-statements.

24. Gerhard Peters, "Executive Orders Washington–Obama," The American Presidency Project, ed. John T. Woolley and Gerhard Peters, updated September 30, 2012, accessed September 30, 2012, http://www.presidency.ucsb.edu /data/orders.php; John T. Woolley, "Presidential Signing Statements, Hoover–Obama," The American Presidency Project, ed. John T. Woolley and Gerhard Peters, updated September 30, 2012, http://www.presidency.ucsb.edu /signingstatements.php?year=2012&Submit=DISPLAY #axzz1uKYKvi91.

25. Joseph A. Pika and John Anthony Maltese, *The Politics of the Presidency,* 8th ed. (Washington, D.C.: CQ Press, 2012), 14–16.

26. "Bully Pulpit," C-SPAN Congressional Glossary, accessed June 22, 2012, http://legacy.c-span.org/guide/congress /glossary/alphalist.htm.

27. George C. Edwards III, *On Deaf Ears: The Limits of the Bully Pulpit* (New Haven, Conn.: Yale University Press, 2006).

28. See Melvin C. Laracey, *Presidents and People: The Partisan Story of Going Public* (College Station, Tex.: Texas A&M University Press, 2002); Reed L. Welch, "Presidential Success in Communicating with the Public through Televised Addresses," *Presidential Studies Quarterly* 33 (2003): 347 –65; Samuel Kernell and Laurie L. Rice, "Cable and the Partisan Polarization of the President's Audience," *Presidency Studies Quarterly* 41, no. 4 (2011): 693–711.

29. Richard E. Neustadt, *Presidential Power and the Modern Presidents* (New York: Free Press, 1990).

30. Jon R. Bond, Richard Fleisher, and B. Dan Wood, "The Marginal and Time Varying Effect of Public Approval on

Presidential Success in Congress," *Journal of Politics* 65 (2003): 92–110.

31. Andrew Barrett and Matthew Eshbaugh-Soha, "Presidential Success on the Substance of Legislation," *Political Research Quarterly* 60 (2007): 100–12.

32. Emily Jane Charnock, James A. McCann, and Kathryn D. Tenpas, "Presidential Travel from Eisenhower to George W. Bush: An Electoral College Strategy," *Political Science Quarterly* 124 (2009): 323–39.

33. Joint Resolution of Congress, House Joint Resolution 1145, August 7, 1964, *Department of State Bulletin,* August 24, 1964, reprinted in Henry Steele Commager and Milton Cantor, eds., *Documents of American History,* 10th ed. (Englewood Cliffs, N.J.: Prentice Hall, 1988), 2:690.

34. Louis Fisher, *Presidential War Power,* 2nd ed. (Lawrence: University Press of Kansas, 2004), 128–33.

35. Ibid., 144–51.

36. For a longer discussion of this struggle for power over the conduct of war, see William G. Howell and Jon C. Pevenhouse, *Congressional Checks on Presidential War Powers* (Princeton, N.J.: Princeton University Press, 2007).

37. For more on presidential decisions to engage in military conflicts, see James Meernick, "Domestic Politics and the Political Use of Military Force by the United States," *Political Research Quarterly* 54 (2001): 889–904.

38. U.S. House of Representatives, House Joint Resolution, 114 Section 3 (a) 1, Library of Congress, http://thomas.loc.gov. The statistics in the caption on page 420 are from Operation Iraqi Freedom (oif) and Operation New Dawn U.S. casualty status fatalities as of June 14, 2012, http://www.defense.gov/news/casualty.pdf.

39. John J. Kruzel, "Afghanistan Troop Level to Eclipse Iraq by Midyear," United States Army, March 25, 2010, http://www.army.mil/article/36297/.

40. This paragraph is based on "Libya–Revolution and Aftermath," *New York Times,* updated June 11, 2012, http://topics.nytimes.com/top/news/international/countriesandterritories/libya/index.html.

41. This section is based on "Syria," *New York Times,* updated June 18, 2012, http://topicsnytimes.com/top/news/internationalcountriesandterritories/syria/index.html.

42. *Hamdi v. Rumsfeld,* 542 U.S. 507 (2004).

43. *Rasul v. Bush*, 542 U.S. 466 (2004).

44. *Hamdan v. Rumsfeld*, 548 U.S. 557 (2006).

45. *Boumediene v. Bush*, 553 U.S. 723 (2008).

46. Exec. Order No. 13,491, 74 Fed. Reg. 4893 (Jan. 22, 2009); 13,492, 74 Fed. Reg. 4897 (Jan. 22, 2009); and 13,493, 74 Fed. Reg. 4901 (Jan. 22, 2009).

47. James P. Pfiffner, *The Modern Presidency,* 6th ed. (Boston: Wadsworth Cengage Learning, 2011), 99; Executive Office of the President, "Fiscal Year 2013 Congressional Budget Submission," EOP-9, accessed June 22, 2012, http://www.whitehouse.gov/sites/default/files/docs/2013-eop-budget1.pdf.

48. Mondale wrote a detailed memorandum to President Carter outlining his views of the office of vice president. For a broader discussion of Mondale's vice presidential tenure, see Richard Moe, "The Making of the Modern Vice Presidency: A Personal Reflection," *Minnesota History* 60 (2006): 88–99.

49. Joel K. Goldstein, "The Rising Power of the Modern Vice Presidency," *Presidential Studies Quarterly* 38, no. 3 (2008): 389.

50. Stephen Skowronek, *The Politics Presidents Make: Leadership from John Adams to Bill Clinton* (Cambridge, Mass.: Harvard University Press, 1997). Also see Stephen Skowronek, *Presidential Leadership in Political Time: Reprise and Reappraisal* (Lawrence: University Press of Kansas, 2008).

51. Aaron Wildavsky, "The Two Presidencies" in *The Presidency,* ed. Aaron Wildavsky (Boston: Little, Brown, 1969), 231–43.

52. For a more recent test of this theory, see Brandes Canes-Wrone, William G. Howell, and David E. Lewis, "Toward a Broader Understanding of Presidential Power: A Reevaluation of the Two Presidencies Thesis," *Journal of Politics* 69 (2007): 1–16.

53. Lammers and Genovese, *Presidency and Domestic Policy.* See also Neustadt, *Presidential Power and the Modern Presidents.*

54. Samuel Kernell, *Going Public: New Strategies of Presidential Leadership,* 4th ed. (Washington, D.C.: CQ Press, 2007), 131.

55. Ibid., 87–88.

56. Lammers and Genovese, *Presidency and Domestic Policy.*

57. Robert A. Caro, *The Years of Lyndon Johnson: The Passage of Power* (New York: Alfred A. Knopf, 2012), 487. Also see Lyndon Johnson's commencement address at Howard University, "To Fulfill These Rights," June 4, 1965, accessed June 22, 2012, http://www.lbjlib.utexas.edu/johnson/archives.hom/speeches.hom/650604.asp.

58. American Rhetoric, "Top 100 Speeches," accessed June 22, 2012, http://www.americanrhetoric.com/newtop100speeches.htm.

59. D. Andrew Austin and Mindy R. Levit, *The Debt Limit: History and Recent Increases*, CRS Report for Congress, RL31967 (Washington, D.C.: Congressional Research Service, January 20, 2011), http://www.fas.org/sgp/crs/misc/RL31967.pdf.

60. The White House, Office of Management and Budget, Historical Tables, Table 1.1—Summary of Receipts, Outlays, and Surpluses or Deficits (–): 1789–2017; The White House, Office of Management and Budget, Historical Tables, Table 7.1—Federal Debt at the End of Year:–2017. Both tables are available at http://www.whitehouse.gov/omb/budget/Historicals/.

61. Hank C. Jenkins-Smith, Carol L. Silva, and Richard W. Waterman, "Micro- and Macro-level Models of the Presidential Expectations Gap," *Journal of Politics* 67 (2005): 690–715.

Chapter 13

1. This story has been compiled from Marilyn Adams, "Pair of Flier Advocates Fight for Airline Passengers' Rights," *USA Today*, May 19, 2008; Joan Lowy, "Government Asking Why Passengers Were Stranded," Associated Press, August 12, 2009, http://www.realclearpolitics.com/news/ap/politics/2009/Aug/12/gov_t_asking_why_airline_passengers_were_stranded.html; Jeff Bailey, "An Air Travel Activist Is Born," *New York Times*, September 20, 2007; Matthew L. Wald, "Stiff Fines Are Set for Long Wait on the Tarmac," *New York Times*, December 21, 2009; Coalition for an Airline Passengers' Bill of Rights, "An Early Christmas Present for the Flying Public," December 23, 2009, http://FlyersRights.org; Bureau of Transportation Statistics, "Airlines Report Seven Tarmac Delays Longer than Three Hours On Domestic Flights, 11 Longer Than Four Hours on International Flights in October," Research and Innovative Technology Administration (RITA), December 12, 2011, accessed June 27, 2012, http://www.bts.gov/press_releases/2011/dot162_11/html/dot162_11.html, and an e-mail interview with Kate Hanni, January 22, 2010, conducted for this textbook, from which the chapter-opening quotation is taken.

2. Max Weber, *Economy and Society*, ed. Guenther Roth and Claus Wittich (Berkeley, Calif.: University of California Press, 1978).

3. The White House, Office of Management and Budget, *Analytical Perspectives, Budget of the U.S. Government FY 2013* (Washington, D.C.: U.S. Government Printing Office, 2012), Table 11-2, Total Federal Employment, p. 120, accessed June 27, 2012, http://www.whitehouse.gov/omb/budget/Analytical_Perspectives; Note that the total number of federal employees cited above does not include active and reserve members of the National Guard.

4. "President Jefferson in the White House," EyeWitness to History, 2006, accessed June 27, 2012, http://www.eyewitnesstohistory.com/jeffersonwhitehouse.htm.

5. The White House, Office of Management and Budget, *Analytical Perspectives, Budget*, Table 11.2; The White House, Office of Management and Budget, *The Budget for Fiscal Year 2013*, U.S. Department of Health and Human Services, p. 115, accessed June 27, 2012, http://www.whitehouse.gov/sites/default/files/omb/budget/fy2013/assets/health.pdf.

6. National Council of State Legislatures, "Children's Health Insurance Program (CHIP)," NCSL.org, accessed June 27, 2012, http://www.ncsl.org/issues-research/health/childrens-health-insurance-program-overview.aspx. The program was originally called SCHIP, the Supplemental Children's Health Insurance Program.

7. U.S. Department of Health and Human Services, "HealthCare.gov," http://www.healthcare.gov.

8. The White House, Office of Management and Budget, *Analytical Perspectives, Budget*, Table 11.2.

9. U.S. Department of Transportation, *Budget Estimates Fiscal Year 2013, Federal Aviation Administration*, Exhibit II-6, accessed June 27, 2012, http://www.dot.gov/budget/2013/faa_%20fy_%202013_budget_estimate.pdf.

10. Federal Aviation Administration, http://www.faa.gov.

11. U.S. Department of Health and Human Services, "About HHS," accessed June 27, 2012, http://www.hhs.gov/about/.

12. James Q. Wilson, *Bureaucracy* (New York: Basic Books, 1989), 91.

13. Donald F. Kettl, *System under Stress: Homeland Security and American Politics*, 2nd ed. (Washington, D.C.: CQ Press, 2007), 37–39.

14. Kettl, *System under Stress*. Also see David E. Lewis, *The Politics of Presidential Appointments: Political Control and Bureaucratic Performance* (Princeton, N.J.: Princeton University Press, 2008), 141–71.

15. Matt Egan, "BP, Oil Plaintiffs Hammer Out Settlement," FOXBusiness, April 18, 2012, http://www.foxbusiness.com/industries/2012/04/18/bp-oil-spill-plaintiffs-hammer-out-settlement/.

16. Ian Urbina, "U.S. Said to Allow Drilling without Needed Permits," *New York Times*, May 13, 2010, http://www.nytimes.com/2010/05/14/us/14agency.html?pagewanted=all.

17. NPR staff, "White House Lifts Ban on Offshore Drilling," NPR, October 12, 2010, http://www.npr.org/templates/story/story.php?storyId=130512541.

18. Egan, "BP, Oil Plaintiffs Hammer Out Settlement."

19. Daniel P. Carpenter, *The Forging of Bureaucratic Autonomy: Reputations, Networks, and Policy Innovation in*

Executive Agencies, 1862–1928 (Princeton, N.J.: Princeton University Press, 2001).

20. United States Postal Service, Office of the Postmaster, *The United States Postal Service: An American History, 1775–2006* (Washington, D.C.: Government Relations, United States Postal Service, 2007), 6–7, http://about.usps.com/publications/pub100.pdf.

21. Lewis, *Politics of Presidential Appointments*, 12–13.

22. Theda Skocpol, *Protecting Soldiers and Mothers* (Cambridge, Mass.: Harvard University Press, 1992).

23. Sean M. Theriault, *The Power of the People* (Columbus: Ohio State University Press, 2005), Chapter 3.

24. Lewis, *Politics of Presidential Appointments*, 19–20, especially Figure 2.1.

25. U.S. Office of Personnel Management, "Federal Employment Statistics: Federal Civilian Employment," September 2010, accessed June 27, 2012, http://www.opm.gov/feddata/html/geoagy10.asp.

26. Bureau of Labor Statistics, *Career Guide to Industries, 2010–11 Edition*, http://www.bls.gov/ooh/about/career-guide-to-industries.htm.

27. U.S. Office of Personnel Management, "Salary Table 2012-GS," January 2012, http://www.opm.gov/oca/12tables/pdf/gs.pdf.

28. For more on political appointees, see Jeff Gill and Richard Waterman, "Solidary and Functional Costs: Explaining the Presidential Appointment Contradiction," *Journal of Public Administration Research and Theory* 14 (2004): 547–69.

29. Lewis, *Politics of Presidential Appointments*, 97; "Head Count: Tracking Obama's Appointments," accessed June 27, 2012, *Washington Post,* http://projects.washingtonpost.com/2009/federal-appointments/by-status/.

30. Ibid., 100, Figure 4.3.

31. U.S. Office of Special Counsel, "Hatch Act," updated October 6, 2011, http://www.osc.gov/hatchact.htm, and "Political Activity and the Federal Employee," http://www.osc.gov/documents/hatchact/haflyer.pdf, both accessed June 27, 2012.

32. For more on the relationship between bureaucrats, members of Congress, and interest groups, see Anthony M. Bertelli and Christian R. Grose, "Secretaries of Pork? A New Theory of Distributive Public Policy," *Journal of Politics* 71 (2009): 926–45; and Sanford C. Gordon and Catherine Hafer, "Corporate Influence and the Regulatory Mandate," *Journal of Politics* 69 (2007): 300–19.

33. For in-depth studies of congressional oversight, see Charles R. Shipan, "Regulatory Regimes, Agency Actions, and the Conditional Nature of Congressional Influence," *American Political Science Review* 9 (2004): 467–80; Keith

W. Smith, "Congressional Use of Authorization and Oversight," *Congress and the Presidency* 37 (2010): 45–63.

34. Lisa Rein and Joe Davidson, "GSA Chief Resigns Amid Reports of Excessive Spending," *Washington Post,* April 2, 2012, http://www.washingtonpost.com/politics/gsa-chief-resigns-amid-reports-of-excessive-spending/2012/04/02/gIQABLNNrS_story.html.

35. Daniel P. Carpenter, "Groups, the Media, Agency Waiting Costs, and FDA Drug Approval," *American Journal of Political Science* 46, no. 3 (2002): 490–505. Also see Susan L. Moffitt, "Promoting Agency Reputation through Public Advice: Advisory Committee Use in the FDA," *Journal of Politics* 72, no. 3 (2010): 1–14. For a longer discussion of the history and effectiveness of the FDA, see Daniel P. Carpenter, *Reputation and Power: Organizational Image and Pharmaceutical Regulation at the FDA* (Princeton, N.J.: Princeton University Press, 2010).

36. Stephen Power and Neal King Jr., "Next Challenge on Stimulus: Spending all that Money," *Wall Street Journal,* February 13, 2009, A1.

37. L. Paige Whitaker, *The Whistleblower Protection Act: An Overview*, CRS Report for Congress, RL33918 (Washington, D.C.: Congressional Research Service, March 12, 2007).

38. Gregory Zuckerman and Kara Scannell, "Madoff Misled SEC in '06, Got Off," *Wall Street Journal,* December 18, 2008, http://online.wsj.com/article/SB122956182184616625.html?KEYWORDS=Madoff+2006+Zuckerman.

39. "Rep. Ackerman on Madoff Fraud," Representative Nancy Pelosi's YouTube Channel, February 4, 2009, accessed June 27, 2012, http://www.youtube.com/watch?v=FOKSkaQoF_I. Ackerman spoke at the House Financial Services Subcommittee on Capital Markets, Insurance, and Government Sponsored Enterprises hearing on the Madoff scandal. He was speaking to members of the Securities and Exchange Commission who were testifying at the hearing.

40. Federal Reserve, "History of the Federal Reserve," FederalReserveEducation.org, accessed June 27, 2012, http://www.federalreserveeducation.org; see also the Board of Governors of the Federal Reserve System's website at http://www.federalreserve.gov.

41. RealtyTrac Staff, "Foreclosure Activity Increases 81 Percent in 2008," January 15, 2009, accessed June 27, 2012, http://www.realtytrac.com/content/press-releases/foreclosure-activity-increases-81-percent-in-2008-4551.

42. Staff, "Case Study: The Collapse of Lehman Brothers," Investopedia, April 2, 2009, accessed June 27, 2012, http://www.investopedia.com/articles/economics/09/lehman-brothers-collapse.asp#axzz1xVC6FmpT.

43. U.S. Department of Treasury, "Financial Crisis Response—in Charts," April 13, 2012, http://www.treasury.gov/resource-center/data-chart-center/Pages/Financial-Crisis-Response-In-Charts.aspx, and http://www.slideshare.net/USTreasuryDept/20120413-financial-crisisresponse, Slide #12, both accessed June 27, 2012.

44. Staff, "Details and Eligibility Requirements of the 'Making Home Affordable' Program," *Boston Globe*, March 4, 2009, http://www.boston.com/news/nation/articles/2009/03/04/details_and_eligibility_requirements_of_the_making_home_affordable_program/.

45. Information from this paragraph came from the Making Home Affordable website, http://www.makinghomeaffordable.gov.

46. Clerk of United States House of Representatives, "Final Vote Results for Roll Call 413," June 30, 2010, accessed June 27, 2012, http://clerk.house.gov/evs/2010/roll413.xml.

47. United States Senate, "U.S. Senate Roll Call Votes 111th Congress—2nd Session," July 15, 2010, accessed June 27, 2012, http://www.senate.gov/legislative/LIS/roll_call_lists/roll_call_vote_cfm.cfm?congress=111&session=2&vote=00208.

48. Rachelle Younglai and Jon Paschal, "Factbox: Winners and Losers in the Senate's Financial Bill," Reuters, May 21, 2010, http://www.reuters.com/article/2010/05/21/us-financial-regulation-senate-factbox-idUSTRE64K0B020100521.

49. Clea Benson and Phil Mattingly, "Dodd-Frank Act Forcing Banks to Slim Down, Reshape Swaps: One Year Later," Bloomberg.com, July 10, 2011, http://www.bloomberg.com/news/2011-07-11/dodd-frank-act-forcing-banks-to-slim-down-reshape-swaps-one-year-later.html.

50. Consumer Financial Protection Bureau, "Learn about the Bureau," accessed June 27, 2012, http://www.consumerfinance.gov/the-bureau/.

51. "Testimony: Governor Daniel K. Tarullo: Dodd-Frank Act Implementation," Board of Governors of the Federal Reserve System, December 6, 2011, accessed June 27, 2012, http://www.federalreserve.gov/newsevents/testimony/tarullo20111206a.htm.

52. Consumer Financial Protection Bureau, "Getting Started," on "Learn about the Bureau," accessed June 27, 2012, http://www.consumerfinance.gov/the-bureau/.

53. Information in this paragraph was obtained from the Consumer Financial Protection Bureau, http://www.consumerfinance.gov.

54. "Testimony," December 6, 2011.

55. John Kemp, "More Cost-Benefit Analysis Will Not Help CFTC," Reuters, February 24, 2012, http://www.reuters.com/article/2012/02/24/column-cftc-rulemaking-idUSL5E8DO74P20120224; Davis Polk, "Dodd-Frank Progress Report," http://www.davispolk.com/dodd-frank-rulemaking-progress-report/, accessed September 10, 2012.

Chapter 14

1. This story was compiled from Greg Stohr, *A Black and White Case* (Princeton, N.J.: Bloomberg Press, 2004). Documents related to the cases are available at http://supreme.lp.findlaw.com/. The chapter-opening quotation is from Jennifer Gratz, "MSU Speech, Part 1," November 14, 2008, http://www.youtube.com/watch?v=fD5kpuNCBZs.

2. Harold J. Spaeth, *Supreme Court Policy Making* (San Francisco: W. H. Freeman and Company, 1979), 38.

3. "Federal Judgeships," Administrative Office of the United States Courts, accessed July 7, 2012, http://www.uscourts.gov/JudgesAndJudgeships/FederalJudgeships.aspx.

4. Samuel Chase—The Samuel Chase Impeachment Trial, Law Library, accessed May 10, 2012, http://law.jrank.org/pages/5151/Chase-Samuel-Chase-Impeachment-Trial.htm.

5. Alexander Hamilton, "*Federalist 78*," in the *Federalist Papers*, U.S. Constitution Online, accessed May 10, 2012, http://www.constitution.org/fed/federa78.htm.

6. *Marbury v. Madison*, 5 U.S. 137, 177 (1803).

7. *McCulloch v. Maryland*, 4 Wheaton 316 (1819); *Gibbons v. Ogden*, 9 Wheaton 1 (1824); and *Cohens v. Virginia*, 6 Wheaton 264 (1821).

8. *Dred Scott v. Sandford*, 60 U.S. 393 (1857).

9. *Slaughterhouse Cases*, 83 U.S. 36 (1873).

10. *United States v. Cruikshank*, 92 U.S. 542 (1876).

11. *Civil Rights Cases*, 109 U.S. 3 (1883).

12. *Plessy v. Ferguson*, 163 U.S. 537 (1896).

13. *Wickard v. Filburn*, 317 U.S. 111 (1942).

14. *National Federation of Independent Business et al. v. Sebelius*, 11–393 (2012).

15. *Brandenburg v. Ohio*, 395 U.S. 444 (1969) (speech rights); *New York Times v. Sullivan*, 376 U.S. 254 (1964) (press rights); *Memoirs v. Massachusetts*, 383 U.S. 413 (1966) (obscenity); and *Engel v. Vitale*, 370 U.S. 421 (1962); *Abington Township School District v. Schempp*, 374 U.S. 203 (1963) (prayer and Bible reading).

16. *Brown v. Board of Education*, 347 U.S. 483 (1954); *Wesberry v. Sanders*, 376 U.S. 1 (1964); *Reynolds v. Sims*, 377 U.S. 533 (1964).

17. *Griswold v. Connecticut*, 381 U.S. 479 (1965) (birth control); *Roe v. Wade*, 410 U.S. 113 (1973).

18. *Mapp v. Ohio*, 367 U.S. 643 (1961); *Miranda v. Arizona*, 384 U.S. 436 (1966).

19. "The Law: The Nixon Radicals," *Time*, June 5, 1972.

20. *Swann v. Charlotte-Mecklenburg Board of Education*, 402 U.S. 1 (1971) (busing); *Roe v. Wade*, 410 U.S. 113 (1973) (abortion); *Furman v. Georgia*, 408 U.S. 238 (1972) (death penalty); *Reed v. Reed*, 404 U.S. 71 (1971) (sex discrimination); and *Regents of the University of California v. Bakke*, 438 U.S. 265 (1978) (affirmative action).

21. *San Antonio Independent School District v. Rodriguez*, 411 U.S. 1 (1973) (school funding); *United States v. Leon*, 468 U.S. 897 (1984) (limiting the exclusionary rule); and *New York v. Quarles*, 467 U.S. 649 (1984) (limiting *Miranda*).

22. *United States v. Nixon,* 418 U.S. 683 (1974).

23. *Lawrence v. Texas,* 539 U.S. 558 (2003).

24. *Planned Parenthood v. Casey*, 505 U.S. 833 (1992); *United States v. Lopez*, 514 U.S. 549 (1995); *Gratz v. Bollinger*, 539 U.S. 244 (2003); and *Grutter v. Bollinger*, 539 U.S. 306 (2003).

25. *Bush v. Gore,* 531 U.S. 98 (2000).

26. Adam Liptak, "Justices Offer Receptive Ear to Business Interests," *New York Times*, December 19, 2010, p. A1.

27. *Wal-mart Stores v. Dukes*, 180 L. Ed. 2d 374 (2011).

28. *Citizens United v. Federal Election Commission,* 175 L. Ed. 2d 753 (2010).

29. *National Federation of Independent Business et al. v. Sebelius*, 11–393 (2012).

30. Jeffrey A. Segal and Harold J. Spaeth, *The Supreme Court and the Attitudinal Model Revisited* (New York: Cambridge University Press, 2002), 179.

31. Lee Epstein and Jeffrey A. Segal, *Advice and Consent: The Politics of Judicial Appointments* (New York: Oxford University Press, 2006).

32. Denis Steven Rutkus and Mitchel A. Sollenberger, *Judicial Nomination Statistics: U.S. District and Circuit Courts, 1977–2003,* CRS Report for Congress, RL31635 (Washington, D.C.: Congressional Research Service, February 23, 2004), Table 2(b), http://www.senate.gov /reference/resources/pdf/RL31635.pdf.

33. Ian Millhiser, "Falling Off a Cliff: Judicial Confirmation Rates Have Nosedived in the Obama Presidency," July 30, 2010, Center for American Progress, Figure 3, http:// www.americanprogress.org/issues/2010/07/judicial _confirmations.html.

34. David W. Rohde and Kenneth A. Shepsle, "Advising and Consenting in the 60-Vote Senate: Strategic Appointments to the Supreme Court," *Journal of Politics* 69 (2007): 664–77.

35. Rutkus and Sollenberger, *Judicial Nomination Statistics.*

36. Bernie Becker and David Herszenhorn, "Democrats Lash Out at Secret Holds," *The Caucus* (blog), *New York Times,* May 6, 2010, http://thecaucus.blogs.nytimes .com/2010/05/06/democrats-lash-out-at-secret-holds/.

37. Information is from Democratic strategy memos obtained and reprinted by the *Wall Street Journal*. See "'He Is Latino': Why Dems Borked Estrada, in Their Own Words," *Wall Street Journal,* November 15, 2003.

38. Gregory Caldeira and Jack Wright, "Lobbying for Justice: Organized Interests, Supreme Court Nominations, and the United States Senate," *American Journal of Political Science* 42 (1998): 499.

39. Jonathan P. Kastellec, Jeffrey R. Lax, and Justin H. Phillips, "Public Opinion and Senate Confirmation of Supreme Court Nominees," *Journal of Politics* 72 (2010): 767–84.

40. Christina Boyd, Lee Epstein, and Andrew D. Martin, "Untangling the Causal Effects of Sex on Judging," *American Journal of Political Science* 54 (2010): 389–411.

41. See, e.g., Karen O'Connor and Jeffrey A. Segal, "Justice Sandra Day O'Connor and the Supreme Court's Reaction to Its First Female Member," *Women and Politics* 10 (1990): 95–104.

42. John J. Szmer, Tammy A. Sarver, and Erin B. Kaheny, "Have We Come a Long Way, Baby? The Influence of Attorney Gender on Supreme Court Decision Making," *Politics and Gender* 6 (2010): 1–36.

43. Federal litigation data can be found at "Judicial Facts and Figures 2010," Administrative Office of the U.S. Courts, accessed July 7, 2012, http://www.uscourts.gov /Statistics/JudicialFactsAndFigures/JudicialFacts AndFigures2010.aspx.

44. Paul M. Collins Jr., "Friends of the Court: Examining the Influence of *Amicus Curiae* Participation in U.S. Supreme Court Litigation," *Law and Society Review* 38 (2004): 807–32.

45. Rebecca Salokar, *The Solicitor General: The Politics of Law* (Philadelphia: Temple University Press, 1992).

46. Lisa Solowiej and Paul Collins Jr., "Counteractive Lobbying in the U.S. Supreme Court," *American Politics Research* 37 (2009): 670–99.

47. *Regents of the University of California v. Bakke,* 438 U.S. 265 (1978).

48. Federal Bureau of Investigation, "Offenses Cleared," *Crime in the United States 2009,* September 2010, accessed July 7, 2012, http://www2.fbi.gov/ucr/cius2009 /offenses/clearances/index.html.

49. United States Sentencing Commission, *2003 Sourcebook of Federal Sentencing Statistics* (Washington, D.C.: Author, 2004), 91.

50. Gregory Caldeira and John R. Wright, "Organized Interests and Agenda Setting in the U.S. Supreme Court," *American Political Science Review* 82 (1988): 1109–28.

51. *Hopwood v. Texas*, 78 F.3d 932 (1996).

52. *National Federation of Independent Business et al. v. Sebelius*, 11–393 (2012).

53. Timothy Johnson, Paul Wahlbeck, and James Spriggs, "The Influence of Oral Arguments on the U.S. Supreme Court," *American Political Science Review* 100 (2006): 99.

54. *United States v. Nixon,* 418 U.S. 683 (1974).

55. *Reynolds v. Sims,* 377 U.S. 533 (1964).

56. *Roe v. Wade,* 410 U.S. 113 (1973).

57. Segal and Spaeth, *Supreme Court and the Attitudinal Model.*

58. Lee Epstein and Jack Knight, *The Choices Justices Make* (Washington, D.C.: CQ Press, 1998); Forrest Maltzman, James F. Spriggs II, and Paul J. Wahlbeck, *Crafting Law on the Supreme Court: The Collegial Game* (New York: Cambridge University Press, 2000).

59. Equal Employment Opportunity Commission, "Executive Order 10925: Establishing The President's Committee on Equal Employment Opportunity," March 6, 1961, accessed June 26, 2012, http://www.eeoc.gov/eeoc/history/35th/thelaw/eo-10925.html.

60. Charles V. Dale, *Federal Affirmative Action Law: A Brief History*, CRS Report for Congress, RS22256 (Washington, D.C.: Congressional Research Service, September 13, 2005), online at the University of North Texas Digital Library, accessed June 30, 2012, http://digital.library.unt.edu/ark:/67531/metacrs7360/.

61. See Lawrence Baum, *The Puzzle of Judicial Behavior* (Ann Arbor: University of Michigan Press, 1997).

62. Harold Spaeth, Lee Epstein, Ted Ruger, Keith Whittington, Jeffrey Segal, and Andrew D. Martin, "Analysis Specifications," The Supreme Court Database, http://scdb.wustl.edu/analysis.php.

63. Jeffrey A. Segal and Robert M. Howard, "How Supreme Court Justices Respond to Litigant Requests to Overturn Precedent," *Judicature* 85 (2001): 148–57.

64. Jeffrey A. Segal and Robert M. Howard, "A Preference for Deference? The Supreme Court and Judicial Review," *Political Research Quarterly* 57 (2004): 131–43. See also Lori Ringhand, "The Changing Face of Judicial Activism: An Empirical Examination of Voting Behavior on the Rehnquist Natural Court," *Constitutional Commentary* 24 (2007): 43.

65. Robert Dahl, "Decision Making in a Democracy: The Supreme Court as a National Policy-Maker," *Journal of Public Law* 6 (1957): 179–295.

66. *West Virginia State Board of Education v. Barnette,* 319 U.S. 624 (1943), 638.

Index

Note: Page numbers followed by an "f" indicate figures. Page numbers followed by a "t" indicate tables.